The Best in Children's Books

Written and edited by
Zena Sutherland

The Best in Children's Books

The University of Chicago
Guide to Children's Literature
1979–1984

The University of Chicago Press
Chicago and London

Zena Sutherland is professor emeritus in the Graduate Library School at the University of Chicago and former editor of the University of Chicago's *Bulletin of the Center for Children's Books.*

Z
/037
AIS93

The University of Chicago Press, Chicago 60637
The University of Chicago Press, Ltd., London
© 1986 by The University of Chicago

All rights reserved. Published 1986
Printed in the United States of America

95 94 93 92 91 90 89 88 87 86   54321

Library of Congress Cataloging-in-Publication Data

Sutherland, Zena.
    The best in children's books.

    "Book reviews . . . previously in the Bulletin of the Center for Children's Books"—T.p. verso.
    Includes indexes.
    1. Bibliography—Best Books—Children's literature.   2. Children's literature—Bibliography.   3. Children's literature—Book reviews.   4. Bibliography—Best books—Young adult literature.   5. Young adult literature—Bibliography.   6. Young adult literature—Book reviews. I. University of Chicago. Center for Children's Books.
II. Title.
Z1037.A1S93 1986   016.81'09'9282   85-31820
[PN1009.A1]

ISBN 0-226-78060-0

Book reviews were previously published in the
Bulletin of the Center for Children's Books,
© 1979, 1980, 1981, 1982, 1983, 1984
by The University of Chicago

Contents

Acknowledgments

The critical evaluations used in this book are based on the judgments of the members of the *Bulletin of the Center for Children's Books* advisory committee who served in the years 1979–1984: Yolanda Federici, Isabel McCaul, Hazel Rochman, Robert Strang, and the editor, Zena Sutherland, who is grateful to the members of the advisory committee and to Frances Henne and Alice Brooks McGuire, who were instrumental in establishing the *Bulletin*, to the Graduate Library School which sponsors it, and to the many members of the university and the laboratory schools who have given advice in specialized subject areas.

Introduction

When the Center for Children's Books was established at the University of Chicago in 1945 one of its goals in setting up a collection of trade books written for children was the evaluation and analysis of books in terms of uses, appeals, and literary quality. The *Bulletin of the Center for Children's Books,* which grew out of a memorandum that circulated within the Graduate School of Education, now is sponsored by the Graduate Library School and has international circulation.

Review copies of all children's trade books are sent to the center by publishers. Once each week, members of the advisory committee meet to examine the books and discuss the reviews prepared by the editor. The committee comprises teachers and librarians in public and private schools and libraries. When the editor or the committee feels that the subject matter of any book should be evaluated by an expert, the resources of the University of Chicago faculty are called upon, with teachers in the university's laboratory schools and in the college and divisions participating.

Books for children and young people of all ages are reviewed, and occasionally an adult book that may be of particular interest to adolescent readers is included. It is clear from the reading level index that some spans are heavily represented. There are many more citations listed for grades 4–6, for example, than for grades 4–7; however, material may also be found for the 7th grade reader in such groups as 5–7, 6–9, or 7–10. The book has not been planned as a balanced list in respect to an individual grade or age, or to subject or genre. The editor's selections have been made primarily on the basis of literary quality, with representation of subjects as a secondary consideration. The goal—a list of the best books published in the years 1979–1984.

Why is it important to select children's books with discrimination? For one thing, the years in which such books are appropriate are fleeting, although some books can gratify readers of any age. There are so many activities and competing interests that fill children's time today that only the most inveterate readers read more than half a dozen books yearly beyond those required by their schools.

Second, studies of the adult reading population show how easy it is to fall into the pattern of reading only superficial material. Children exposed to flimsy mass market books, comics, and pedestrian series books will not necessarily proceed to good literature. It is possible for a child to acquire discrimination, but it isn't likely to happen unless some adult—a parent, a teacher, a librarian—suggests better books, encourages the ownership of books, and discusses good books with enthusiasm and understanding. It is incumbent on adults who are concerned with children's reading to select and counsel wisely, to appreciate the importance of both the content of books and the reading habit itself, and to comprehend what the elements of good children's books are.

In many ways, the literary criteria that apply to adult books and children's books are the same. The best books have that most elusive component, a distinctive literary style. A well-constructed plot; sound characterization with no stereotypes; dialogue that flows naturally and is appropriate to the speaker's age, education, and milieu; and a pervasive theme are equally important in children's and adults' fiction. Authoritative knowledge, logical organization of material, and accuracy are major considerations in informational books for any age.

In books for children, there are additional considerations based on limitations of comprehension and experience. Comparatively few children enjoy a story without action or conflict, however delicate the nuances of style, and most young readers abjure the tedious presentation of information in the guise of conversation. For very young children, it is important that a book not contain so much information as to confuse them. The vocabulary need not be rigidly controlled, but it should not include so many terms that the reader is discouraged. The concepts must be comprehensible—for example, a reader in the primary grades is not spatially sophisticated—and the subject appropriate. Format (type size, distribution of print, placement on page) and illustrations should be consistent with the level of the text, and maps or diagrams should be very carefully placed and labeled.

Because children are forming concepts of themselves and their society and are testing and acquiring ethical values, it is imperative that the books they read foster and nurture opinions and attitudes that are intelligent and flexible. Will the books they read serve to do this? The best ones will. Adults should be wary, however, of their own bias and should evaluate very carefully the author's values and assumptions lest agreement with their own ideas be confused with objectivity.

Each book must be judged on its own merits, and each book should be chosen—whether for an individual child, a library, or a classroom collection—with consideration for its strength even though it may have some weaknesses. This has been a precept in critical evaluation of books for the *Bulletin*. It is often illuminating to compare a book with other books by the same author or with similar books on a subject, but the judgment of each book is made on that book alone. With the spate of publication of children's books, selection is difficult. It is our hope that through this bibliography and its indexes, readers may more easily find the best in children's books.

Suggestions for Using This Book

The reviews included here have been selected by the editor from those already published in the *Bulletin of the Center for Children's Books*. Save for a few titles coded as "Additional" or "Special Reader," all of the books listed here had received a rating of "Recommended." An asterisk is used to denote books of special distinction. The reviews are listed alphabetically by the author's name and are numbered in sequence to facilitate the use of the six indexes at the back of this book.

Of the indexes, only the *title index* does not refer the reader to the number assigned each book but gives the last name of the author.

The *developmental values index* is based on the analysis of each book for those elements that illuminate some aspect of achieving maturity, solving problems, or establishing relationships at any developmental stage in the life of a child or young reader. The developmental values covered range from the young child's acquisition of environmental concepts or adjustment to a new baby in the family, to the adolescent's attitudes toward his or her role in marriage.

The *curricular use index* suggests books for incorporation into the school curriculum, or for supplemental reading in relation to curricular units. Lynda Madaras's *The What's Happening to My Body Book for Boys* (no. 871), for example, is included under "Sex Education" in the curricular use index, whereas it is cited under "Physiology" in the subject index.

The *reading level index* is arranged progressively by grades following the books for preschool children, which are listed by age. Books for independent reading begin with first grade, usually age six. The reading levels are given in a span that is intended to suggest probable use rather than to impose limits. A volume of poetry, for example, may be graded 4–6, indicating widest use in grades 4, 5, and 6; it may, however, be read aloud to younger children, used independently by proficient readers in grade 3 or even grade 2, or be read by older children or adults. The levels of reading difficulty have been determined by the *Bulletin* advisory committee after consideration of the vocabulary, the length and complexity of the writing, subject interest, latent content, organization of material, and the appropriateness of content, difficulty, and format to the maturity of the intended reader.

The *subject index* entries include both fiction and nonfiction. Nonfiction books about Africa, for example, are grouped according to subject matter into various subheadings under the general heading "Africa."

Fictional stories set in that region will be found under the "Africa, stories" subheading.

The *type of literature index* makes it possible for the reader to find citations for all of the books of poetry, all of the mystery stories, and so on, that have been selected to be grouped together. The temptation to break this index down into fine categories has been sternly resisted, lest the book become inordinately massive. It is hoped that the separate indexes give ample access to the material in the volume.

Many of the books listed are from countries in the United Kingdom. The appended list of publishers includes British titles available in the United States. It could be said that this bibliography reflects the best in American children's literature and, to the extent that information about British and American copublished books is available, some of the best in British children's literature.

Reviews of Books

1   **Aardema,** Verna. *Half-A-Ball-Of-Kenki; an Ashanti Tale;* illus. by Diane Stanley Zuromskis. Warne, 1979. 78-16135. ISBN 0-7232-6158-X. 33p. $8.95.

K–2   An adaptation of an Ashanti folktale is illustrated with colorful blocked pictures, some framed, that have bold, full use of space and have decorative details based on Ashanti motifs. Kenki is cornmeal mush, and it is Dokonfa, the half-portion of the title, that comes to the rescue of Fly after his rival Leopard has tied him to a tree. Fly and Leopard had gone looking for girls to marry, and Leopard had resented the way the young maids clustered about Fly but ran from him. This is a double why-story, since it ends with Dokonfa throwing Leopard into a fire, producing his spots, and also explains that flies always sit on leaves in which kenki has been wrapped because they are saying thank you on behalf of their ancestor. Nice to read aloud or use for storytelling, the tale has representations of sounds ("Leopard leaped *harrr* out of the bushes . . . she unwound the creeper kpung, kpung, kpung . . . She was stepping daintily pip, pip, pip . . ."), repetition, and the victory of the weak over the strong as appeals, and it's told with verve and humor.

2   **Aardema,** Verna, tr. *The Riddle of the Drum: A Tale from Tizapan, Mexico;* illus. by Tony Chen. Four Winds, 1979. 78-23791. ISBN 0-590-07489-X. 25p. $7.95.

K–3   A traditional Mexican folktale is illustrated with paintings that alternate color and black and white on sets of facing pages, and that are distinctive for their bright colors and clean lines; the pictures incorporate splendid floral and costume details, although there's an odd mix of contemporary and pre-Columbian clothing. A king of Tizapan sends out a crier with a drum to announce that anyone who can guess what kind of leather the drumhead consists of may marry his lovely daughter Fruela. A handsome prince engages a series of people he encounters with a promise of reward if each will help him win the princess; each person has (as in *Fool of the World and the Flying Ship* and similar European variants) a special, magical talent. They help the prince solve the riddle and perform the two other tasks set by the king. The tale is retold in a brisk conversational style and includes many devices of the oral tradition: magic, the three tasks, verse, cumulation, the quest, and the winning of a princess; it is a good choice for storytelling or for reading aloud.

1

3   **Aaron,** Chester. *Gideon.* Lippincott, 1982. 81-48066. Trade ed. ISBN
0-397-31992-4; Library ed. ISBN 0-397-31993-2. 181p. Trade ed. $10.50;
Library ed. $9.89.

7–10   Based on records and on accounts by survivors of Dachau and other
concentration camps, this first person novel has the ring of truth, and a
bitter, shocking truth it is even for the reader who has become familiar
with the details of the Holocaust. Gideon is a young adolescent who,
like so many Polish Jews, is in the end the only survivor in his family.
Determined to survive, he is able to evade Nazis and pro-Nazis in part
because he looks Aryan and has forged papers, in part because of his
daring and courage. A smuggler who works with a gang of young Polish thugs, he is able to help people in the Warsaw ghetto; when at last
he escapes from the city by swimming through the foul sewers, and
takes refuge in a forest, Gideon decides he must go back to try to find
his sister; he is caught and taken to Treblinka. The story, moving and
dramatic, moves with trenchant inevitability to the rebellion of the Jewish prisoners at Treblinka. Less than half escape, Gideon among them;
he eventually comes to the United States, assuming the identity of a
Danish immigrant. A moving and terrible story, written with craft and
conviction.

24   **Adams,** Laurie. *Alice and the Boa Constrictor;* by Laurie Adams and Al-
lison Coudert; illus. by Emily Arnold McCully. Houghton, 1983.
82-15769. ISBN 0-395-33068-8. 87p. $8.95.

3–4   Since he knows that Alice's allowance would have to be saved for
months before she could afford the boa constrictor she wants, Dad gives
his permission—and Alice (in the fourth grade) begins casting about for
ways to earn money. After some abortive and amusing tries, she earns
enough for the snake and a cage. Already a science buff, Alice is an Instant Success when she presents her pet at the fourth grade science
class Show and Tell session; she also finds her snake useful in combat-
ing bullies and a burglar, and she eventually sells it to an eager friend.
This light-hearted story has some exaggeration, but is on the whole believable and keeps up a brisk pace; Alice manipulates her father in a
way that should delight readers. Nice family relationships and a good
reflection of fourth grade power politics in a sunny story.

5   **Adler,** Carole S. *In Our House Scott Is My Brother.* Macmillan, 1980.
79-20693. ISBN 0-02-700140-7. 139p. $7.95.

6–8   Jodi is thirteen, as is her new stepbrother Scott, and there is a wary
truce between them when Scott and his mother Donna come to live in
their home. Donna, beautiful and restless, dislikes Jodi's dog, wants to
redo the house, and—Jodi suspects—wants to redo Jodi. The story is
told with considerable vigor by Jodi, who copes nicely until she realizes
that Donna is an alcoholic and Scott an inveterate liar and a petty thief.
There are groundswells of conflict when Jodi's dog dies (she's sure that

Donna had him put to sleep by the veterinarian) and when Scott frames Jodi as the culprit for his own theft, but the two children are brought together by their protective love for their parents. The writing style is fluid and the characterization has depth, but the outstanding facet of the book is in that protective love: Jodi tries hard to accept Donna because she knows how happy her father is in his second marriage, and Scott is so devoted and supportive toward his pathetic mother that he wins Jodi's respect despite his other traits. When Donna decides to walk out, Jodi weeps as she reads Scott's farewell note, signed "Your brother Scott." She's learned that people are lovable, and even forgivable, despite their weaknesses.

6   **Adler,** Carole S. *The Magic of the Glits;* illus. by Ati Forberg. Macmillan, 1979. 78-12149. 112p. $7.95.

5–7   Jeremy, twelve, is furious when his mother suggests that he take seven-year-old Lynette under his wing for the summer; Mother is a preoccupied artist, and Jeremy is tied down by a cast on his leg. He feels sorry for Lynette, dumped by her stepfather after her mother's death, but at first finds her a nuisance. Gradually, however, her plight, her affection for him, and her small-girl charm stir Jeremy to concern for her future. He tries to teach her so much that her stepfather will be impressed, at the end of the summer, and want to keep her—but he hasn't realized that Lynette's taken matters into her own hands. The solution is believable, if a bit pat; the writing style is competent if not outstanding; the strength of the story lies in the natural way in which a child's protective instinct and sympathy grow. The print is woefully small, alas. Oh, the title: "glits" are small entities that Jeremy invents for Lynette's amusement, things that bring "fizzy joy," as their friendship does. The illustrations are dramatic paintings, black and white and handsomely composed.

7   **Adler,** Carole S. *The Shell Lady's Daughter.* Coward-McCann, 1983. 82-19801. ISBN 0-698-20580-4. 140p. $10.95.

7–9   Kelly, fourteen, begins her story with some comments on the love and friendship she and her mother share, and with her worries about the fact that, now that she has some friends her own age, Mother is often alone. Kelly's father is a pilot, away more than he's home; she calls him in a panic when her mother begins to act peculiar, but she's totally unprepared for the fact that that behavior was only a signal for a deep, suicidal depression. Packed off to stay with her ramrod grandmother in Florida, Kelly is worried, lonely, and resentful because she is told that she cannot even telephone her mother. Periodically, she remembers one of the "shell lady" stories Mother had told her, and wonders why they were always sad. Gradually, talking to her grandmother and father, and to a sympathetic neighbor, Kelly begins to understand her mother's problem, to feel convinced that love and support are needed; she announces she is not going to boarding school as her father had arranged, but will go home to be with her mother, who needs her. She has come to understand herself better: she is the king of the sea, the rescuer in all her mother's shell lady stories. Trenchant and touching, this is a book written with insight and compassion; the story has a natural flow and tight structure, and the few characters are sharply-etched and psychologically intricate and believable.

8   **Adler, David A.** *Bunny Rabbit Rebus;* illus. by Madelaine Gill Linden. Crowell, 1983. 82-45575. Trade ed. ISBN 0-690-04196-9; Library ed. ISBN 0-690-04197-7. 38p. Trade ed. $7.95; Library ed. $7.89.

1–2   Although this will be enjoyed particularly by independent readers, it can also be used with pre-reading children and should amuse both groups because of its game appeal. Using both pictures of objects to substitute for print (drawings of chairs or tables) and pictures that are to be interpreted by sound (a drawing of an eye for "I") the book has small, bright, clear drawings to help tell the story of a rabbit mother who goes to a series of animal friends to get food for her Little Rabbit. By the time he's had a snack at each house, Little Rabbit isn't hungry— but hard-working Mother Rabbit is. There's a glossary of the rebus signs included, and for those who hit a snag there's a non-rebus version appended. This should encourage both reading and visual perception.

9   **Adler,** David A. *Prices Go Up, Prices Go Down: The Laws of Supply and Demand;* illus. by Tom Huffman. Watts, 1984. 84-2212. ISBN 0-531-04628-1. 32p. illus. $8.60.

2–4   Cartoon-style drawings illustrate but do not augment the information given in a succinctly written continuous text. The simplicity of the writing, the logical presentation of ideas, the large type, and the uncrowded pages make this an appropriate book about a basic economic principle for primary grades readers. Adler explains, using clear examples, how supply and demand work in a free economy (with some exceptions) not only to fix prices but also to help decide what goods will be manufactured or what crops will be grown.

10   **Adoff,** Arnold. *All The Colors of the Race;* illus. by John Steptoe. Lothrop, 1982. 81-11777. Trade ed. ISBN 0-688-00879-8; Library ed. ISBN 0-688-00880-1. 56p. Trade ed. $9.50; Library ed. $8.59.

4–6   Adoff's cycle of poems is written from the viewpoint of a child who has one parent who is black and Protestant, one who is white and Jewish. The poetry is free and flowing, reflecting the facets of the child's feelings: resentment at the censorious, pride in the variety of family background, joy in family love, pensiveness in thinking of problems, optimism in thinking of the future, when we "Stop looking / Start loving." The illustrations, brown and white, are often angular in block print style, speckled and stylized, and they echo the vitality and tenderness of the poems' moods.

11   **Adoff,** Arnold. *Eats;* illus. by Susan Russo. Lothrop, 1979. 79-11300. Trade ed. ISBN 0-668-41901-1; Library ed. ISBN 0-688-51901-6. 48p. Trade ed. $6.95; Library ed. $6.67 net.

4–6   Now it can be told: Arnold Adoff is in love with food. In this collection of paeans to chocolate, apple pie, fresh baked bread, and other delights, he includes some recipe poems, but most of the selections sing the praises of some particular food, and there is in most of the poems a wry humor or an ebullient zest that should engage readers—and, as for most poems, the audience is much broader than the middle grades for which this seems most appropriate. Two nibbles from the feast, with apologies for ignoring the poet's use of line and form, ". . . but in between my smiles and bites / I write a message in the sweet and sour pork / I need a fork," concludes a poem on learning to use chop sticks; or, from "At the End of Summer," a pledge of loyalty: "I pledge my loyalty to apple pie and / I insist on deep done dough as heavy as gold / as golden as sweet sun . . ."

12   **Adoff,** Arnold. *I Am the Running Girl;* illus. by Ronald Himler. Harper, 1979. 78-14083. Trade ed. ISBN 0-06-020094-4; Library ed. ISBN 0-06-020095-2. 40p. Trade ed. $6.95; Library ed. $6.89 net.

3–5   Adoff's poems flow from one to another, evocative and insistent in their rhythm, free in form; Himler's pencil sketches echo the concentration and the elation of the running girl through whom the poet speaks. The girl speaks of her mother, who used to run and who now cycles along on early morning runs, she speaks of her feeling of affinity for all the other girls who are running, of the joy of the long pull of muscles, the hard breaths, and the concentration of that last spurt that wins a race. Potent stuff.

13   **Aesop.** *Aesop's Fables;* illus. by Heidi Holder. Viking, 1981. 80-26265. ISBN 0-670-10643-7. 25p. $12.95.

4–
*   Nine fables, with concluding morals printed in italics on spaciously laid-out pages, have been chosen as a show case for a new, self-taught children's book illustrator. Heidi Holder would strike few as either; her intricately designed and detailed paintings, most of which are full-page and delicately framed, have a striking use of perspective and composition, a restrained and sophisticated use of color, and a grave beauty that is reminiscent in mood and technique of the work of Nancy Burkert. Lovely.

14   **Aesop.** *Once In A Wood; Ten Tales From Aesop;* ad. and illus. by Eve Rice. Greenwillow, 1979. 78-16294. Trade ed. ISBN 0-688-80191-9; Library ed.

ISBN 0-688-84191-0. 64p. (Read-alone Books) Trade ed. $5.95; Library ed. $5.71 net.

1–3   Very nicely adapted for young readers, these ten Aesop stories are simple, direct, and pithy with a good narrative flow and—in most cases—a rhyming conclusion that helps point out the moral. The illustrations are gravely decorative, black and white pictures of flora and fauna, deftly textured and composed and resembling old lithographs in style and mood.

15   **Afanasyev,** Alexander Nikolaevich. *Russian Folk Tales;* illus. by Ivan Bilibin; tr. by Robert Chandler. Shambhala/Random House, 1980. 80-50746. Shambhala ISBN 0-87773-195-0; Random House ISBN 0-394-51353-3. 78p. $14.95.

4–6   Despite an occasional awkwardness in translation, this selection of folktales from the major Russian collector is particularly delightful because of the reproduction of Bilibin's work; the paintings, framed in decorative borders, express both the romantic, florid style of turn-of-the-century art and the Slavic motifs of decorative folk art. The book includes seven classic tales; among the most familiar to English-language readers will be "Vasilisa the Beautiful" and "Ivan Tsarevich, the Grey Wolf, and the Firebird."

16   **Ahlberg,** Janet. *The Baby's Catalogue;* written and illus. by Janet and Allan Ahlberg. Little, 1983. 82-9928. ISBN 0-316-02037-0. 27p. $10.50.

1–3
yrs.   Titles and labels are the only print on the pages of a book that begins with a page headed "Babies" and goes through the objects and activities and people that most babies see on a typical day. There are Moms, Dads, brothers and sisters, toys, high chairs, diapers, meals, books, baths, bedtimes, etc. The softly colored paintings are cheerful and amusing, the format is clean and uncluttered, and the whole should provide happy hours of pointing, identification, and naming.

17   **Aiken,** Joan. *Arabel and Mortimer;* illus. by Quentin Blake. Doubleday, 1981. 79-6577. Trade ed. ISBN 0-385-15642-1; Library ed. ISBN 0-385-15643-X. 143p. Trade ed. $9.95; Library ed. $10.90.

4–6   Back after seven years, the trouble-oriented pet of sweet little Arabel gets into one jam after another in three hilarious stories in which the author successfully attempts to avoid the believable and combines arrant nonsense with a bland delivery. Very effective, this nonsense, and Aiken throws in Arabel's mother, a rival to Mrs. Malaprop, a series of deliberately stereotyped characters, occasionally speaking deliberately stereotyped dialect ("Och, mairrcy," says the ship's engineer Hamish McTavish) and sundry improbable coincidences in three adventures: a frantic cruise, a foiled mass animalnapping at a zoo, and a dig at which Mortimer flies off with what just might be Arthur's true sword.

18   **Aiken,** Joan. *The Kingdom Under The Sea and Other Stories;* illus. by Jan Pienkowski. Jonathan Cape, 1979. ISBN 0-224-61882-2. 104p. $7.95.

5–7   First published in England, eleven folktales from eastern Europe are retold in a graceful, witty style that has a distinctive narrative flow yet preserves the directness of the oral tradition. Save for Berlic-Mazuranic's *Croatian Tales of Long Ago,* the source for three of the stories, no sources are cited. The collection includes two quasi-religious stories, one of which is unexpectedly humorous; most of the tales, however, are the traditional hand-of-princess, or kindness-rewarded, or magical-intervention stories common in all traditional lore. The illustrations are striking; some of the pictures are in silhouette, effectively detailed and often comic, but even more attractive are those pictures in which Pienkowski has used silhouette against backgrounds of colorful marbling. The tales and the pictures are beautifully matched.

19   **Aiken,** Joan. *Mortimer's Cross;* illus. by Quentin Blake. Harper, 1984. 83-49475. Library ed. ISBN 0-06-020033-2; Trade ed. ISBN 0-06-020032-4. 154p. Library ed. $10.89; Trade ed. $11.06.

4–6   Readers who enjoyed the two earlier comic novels about Arabel and her pet raven, Mortimer, will welcome this latest extravaganza, for Aiken has again compounded a series of improbable and hilarious adventures in which everything that can happen does. There are three longish stories that include an iceberg off the coast of Ireland (with a dinosaur frozen in it) and the rescue of a pop singer from an abandoned building and a convenient flood that helps trap a book thief and more. The exaggeration is so broad and so good-humored that it doesn't pall.

20   **Aiken,** Joan. *The Shadow Guests.* Delacorte, 1980. 80-11984. ISBN 0-440-07746-X. 150p. $7.95.

6–8   Cousin Eunice, a mathematics professor at Oxford, makes Cosmo feel welcome when he arrives from Australia, and he adjusts as well as a boy could whose mother and older brother have mysteriously disappeared. He feels at ease in the home which had long been in the family, but not until after Cousin Eunice tells him about the family curse (Eldest sons will die in battle, and their mothers die of grief) does Cosmo find the area is still haunted. In separate fantastic adventures he encounters ghosts who are elder brothers preparing for battle; at the end of the story he learns more about his family's history, and his encounters with the past are accepted by the two friends he's made amongst his classmates. He also learns from his father, who has come to England to stay, that his mother and brother had been found lying on a hillside, dead. Aiken's polished, fluent writing style, her skill at blending fantasy and realism, and her perceptive characterization fuse to good effect in a story with excellent structure and pace.

21   **Aiken,** Joan. *The Stolen Lake.* Delacorte, 1981. 81-5015. ISBN 0-440-08317-6. 291p. $10.95.

5–8   Remember *Nightbirds on Nantucket?* This is just as outrageously flagrant a fanciful romp, as the indomitable Dido Twite, age twelve, is homeward bound to England and never gets there. Her ship is summoned to help the Queen of New Cumbria, in a never-never land and time, for the country is in South America, where the people are descendants of ancient Britons who fled their own country when it was invaded by Saxons. The problem: the queen wants her stolen lake back; King Mabon has taken it because the queen is holding his daughter hostage. The mission is, of course, accomplished, but not before Dido has encountered a series of villains and heroes, is kidnapped, discovers that the evil Queen Ginevra is waiting for her long-lost mate King Arthur (missing for thirteen hundred years) and narrowly escapes a flow of glacial ice. And more. The story is full of half-familiar names, salty characters, saltier dialogue, and amusing magic, all combined in Aiken's yeasty style.

22   **Ainsworth,** Ruth, *The Talking Rock;* illus. by Joanna Stubbs. Andre Deutsch, 1979. ISBN 0-233-97080-0. 154p. $6.95.

4–6   Because he has been exposed to measles, Jakes (who appears to be about eight in the profuse and capable pencil drawings) cannot go with his family when they move to Africa; he stays behind with an elderly couple who are family friends. At first lonely, he creates an imaginary friend in the sand; Sandboy has delicate pink shells for nails, hair of seaweed, and white coral teeth. The talking rock is a real rock, huge and solitary, that—in Jakes' imagination—is the ruler of the world of sea and sand in which he plays. The fantasy adventures of Jakes and Sandboy, their mermaid friend, and the malicious sea-monster Glumper are nicely paced and sustained, but they are really given substance by the realistic facet of the story, the developing affection between Jakes and the childless couple who are so kind, so understanding, and so respectful of a small boy's right to privacy in his imaginary adventures.

23   **Aksakov,** Sergei. *A Russian Schoolboy;* tr. by J. D. Duff; illus. by Kirill Sokolov. Oxford, 1979. 193p. $10.95.

7–   First published in Russia in 1856, these reminiscences of childhood in the country and life at school have a direct, ingenuous quality that belies the oppressive appearance of the pages, solid and heavy with print. Aksakov's story pours out, fond and rueful, as he recalls the heady joys of country life and the security of family love (both he and his mother were given to swooning with emotion) from which he was removed when he went, as a government scholar, to live at school. The book carries Aksakov through his university years, and he writes with as much zest of academic and cultural pursuits as he does of the bucolic charms of his home, Aksakovo, and with as much tenderness and spontaneity of his friends and teachers as he does of his family and the dear, familiar countryside of home. This is both an engaging personal document and a vivid picture of middle-class country life in Russia almost two hundred years ago, since the author was born in 1791.

24   **Alcock,** Vivien. *The Haunting of Cassie Palmer.* Delacorte, 1982. 81-15230. ISBN 0-440-03538-4. 149p. $9.95.

5–8   Seventh child of a seventh child, thirteen-year-old Cassie is expected by her mother, a medium, to have psychic powers. Cassie doesn't have the heart to tell Mum that she abhors the idea, and she's stunned with dismay when, on a dare, she attempts to raise a ghost and is successful. Homely and shabby, Deverill appears, announces his friendship and his gratitude at being brought back from limbo, and proceeds to make Cassie's life miserable. There is a quickening tempo to the relationship and its impact on family affairs; within the parameters of the fantasy's logic, there is a perfectly logical and touching conclusion. This is an impressive first novel from a British writer, with a fusion of realism and fantasy that are remarkably smooth. The characterization adds depth to the story, particularly in the depiction of Cassie's mother, big and blowsy, a psychic past her prime and repeatedly exposed as fraudulent, but a loving and garrulous woman.

25   **Alcock,** Vivien. *The Stonewalkers.* Delacorte. 1983. 82-13956. ISBN 0-440-08321-4. 151p. $12.95.

5–8   Because of her widowed mother's recurrent hospitalization, Poppy feels uncomfortable with her and calls her "Mother Brown" just as she has addressed her many foster mothers. Now her mother has a housekeeping job, and Poppy is with her—but neither knows how to break the barrier of coldness that lies between them. This is the realistic background for a fantasy adventure in which Poppy (via an ancient bracelet) brings a statue to life; the statue uses the device to bring animation to other statues, and the heavy, threatening figures pursue Poppy and her friend Emma across the moor. Caught, imprisoned in what appears to be an old mine, the girls barely escape death and are freed when the statues' efforts to reach them on the high ledge where they've climbed result in a smashing of stone bodies, a collapse of the old walls, and a heap of rubble. This portion of the story has a well-paced aura of impending doom and a solution that is logical within the parameters of the fantasy. The fanciful and the realistic are meshed by the musing of Poppy's anxious mother as she thinks of her dead husband, and weeps for his missing child, "If Jack had lived . . . After he died, it was like I was turned to stone." The story ends on a poignant note when the girls are rescued; Poppy sees her mother and runs to her, joyfully calling "Mom!"

26   **Alcock,** Vivien. *The Sylvia Game: A Novel of the Supernatural.* Delacorte, 1984. 84-3279. ISBN 0-385-29341-0. 186p. $14.95.

6–9   The title is misleading, for the focus in this deftly crafted book is on some very real problems: ethical behavior, class snobbery, friendship values, and the relationship between filial trust and parental (in this case, paternal) obligation. Sounds heavy? Alcock uses these elements to create a fast-paced, intriguing mystery story in which Emily, suspicious of her father's odd behavior, secretly follows him and thereby becomes involved in an attempted art forgery, the bringing together of two adolescent boys who had lost touch, and the exposure of the "Sylvia game" the boys had played, a game based on a dramatic drowning a century before. Strong characters, strong plot.

27   **Alexander,** Lloyd. *The Beggar Queen.* Dutton, 1984. 83-25502. ISBN 0-525-44103-4. 248p. $11.95.

5–8   Third in the trilogy that included *Westmark* and *The Kestrel,* this is just as
*   fine a piece of craftsmanship as the first two books, and just as exciting a story. Alexander is deft at incorporating references to the past, so the book is linked to—and continues from—its predecessors, but it also stands nicely as a literary entity. Here the young queen of Westmark and her advisors learn that their arch enemy Cabbarus is planning to take over the country; he does, and the beggar queen must fight to retrieve it and to decide whether she will wed the commoner Theo (the Kestrel) and give up her throne after victory is won. Theo is the hero of the story, a character who grows and develops, but he is only one of many vivid characters in a story that has pace, polished style, and suspense.

28   **Alexander,** Lloyd. *The Kestrel.* Dutton, 1982. 81-15290. ISBN 0-525-45110-2. 244p. $10.95.

5–8   In a sequel to *Westmark* Alexander moves, as he did in the Prydain cy-
*   cle, to deeper issues and subtler levels. This is no less appealing as an adventure tale with a strong story line and rounded, consistent characterizations, but it also considers the ambivalence its protagonist feels when having to choose between love and loyalty or duty, the compassion one may feel for a foe, the decision between battle and conciliation, and the assuming and sharing of responsibility. The book has the added appeal of familiar characters, as Theo (who in the course of war becomes known as the Kestrel) and Mickle (the waif who proved to be a princess and now is a queen) join with their old friends of *Westmark* to rid their land of traitors from within and enemies from across the border. Another smasher.

29   **Alexander,** Lloyd. *Westmark.* Dutton, 1981. 80-22242. ISBN 0-525-42335-4.184p. $10.25.

5–8   A superb craftsman, Alexander has concocted a marvelous tale of high
*   adventure, replete with a lost princess, an engaging scoundrel, a modest orphan-hero, and an enjoyably hateful villain, and he makes them and their adventures wholly credible. In the land of Westmark, the bereaved king mourns his lost daughter and relies on the maleficent chief

minister Cabbarus, whose oppressive rule is a prelude to his designs on the throne. He is unmasked, finally, hoist by his own petard, for he has had a waif captured who looks like the long-lost princess; his plans to fool the king are foiled when the girl proves indeed to be the long-lost princess. It's a smash ending, the way for which has been artfully paved, in a story that includes some amusing incidents with a con man and his troupe, a love story, some good chase scenes, and some militant action by those who rebel against the regime. Indeed, the political situation in Westmark gives the author scope for some pithy comments on oppressive governance. Lloyd Alexander is a master of writing dialogue, of blending many facets and plot threads into a smooth whole, and above all of conceiving characters with depth and conviction.

30   **Alexander,** Martha. *Marty McGee's Space Lab, No Girls Allowed;* written and illus. by Martha Alexander. Dial, 1981. 81-2479. Trade ed. ISBN 0-8037-5156-7; Library ed. ISBN 0-8037-5157-5. 28p. Trade ed. $7.50; Library ed. $7.44.

K–2   Science fantasy for the read-aloud audience? And feminism, too? Sounds like heavy stuff, but it isn't, not in Alexander's practiced hands. Belligerently ordering his little sister Rachel to stay out of his room, where he's making a space helmet, Marty never thinks of the possibility that baby Jenny will climb out of her playpen, put on the helmet, and fly. But she does. Trying to learn her secret, Marty is forced to accept his sisters, who have united against him, as members of his space team. Realism, piquant if light in weight, is nicely mixed with a touch of fantasy in a blithely told, engagingly illustrated book in which the neat little drawings match a deft little story.

31   **Alexander,** Martha. *Move Over, Twerp;* written and illus. by Martha Alexander. Dial, 1981. 80-21405. Trade ed. ISBN 0-8037-6139-2; Library ed. ISBN 0-8037-6140-6. 28p. Trade ed. $6.95; Library ed. $6.46.

4–6 yrs.   Tones of green and yellow add brightness to the neat, small-scale drawings of children in a heartening little story in which a very small boy outwits a bully. Jeffrey, on his first day of riding the school bus, finds the perfect seat but is ousted by a bigger boy. His father advises refusing to move, his older sister advises a show of strength. Neither tactic works; the same boy who said "Clear out, Twerp," just lifts Jeffrey into another seat. Then Jeffrey himself thinks of a way to cope, using humor and capitalizing on the term "Twerp." He crayons "Supertwerp" on his shirt and so amuses the older children that they go along with the idea: "Boy, I wouldn't tangle with you. We better watch this guy. He means business." Simply, lightly told in monologue or dialogue, a story that should satisfy the youngest set.

32   **Alexander,** Martha. *When The New Baby Comes, I'm Moving Out;* written and illus. by Martha Alexander. Dial, 1979. 79-4275. Trade ed. ISBN

0-8037-9557-2; Library ed. ISBN 0-8037-9558-0. 29p. Trade ed. $5.95; Library ed. $5.47 net.

3–5
yrs.

To readers who know Alexander's *Nobody Asked Me If I Wanted a Baby Sister*, it will be clear that this book comes earlier; here Oliver's mother is pregnant and Oliver is already resentful because his old crib and high chair are being repainted. He needs them, he says, for a launching pad and a wild animal cage. Surly, he threatens to leave; Mother points out how sad and lonely that would make her. Oliver brightens. He decides she needs him, so he had better stay. "You know, Oliver, big brothers get to do lots of very special things." Big smile, as a balloon picture shows Oliver lounging, surrounded by favorite foods, watching the late show. Meanwhile, the balloon picture coming from Mother's head shows Mother lounging and watching a daytime show while Oliver gives the baby a bottle. The story is told entirely in dialogue, and the dialogue is natural and humorous; the dethronement problem is handled lightly but sympathetically, and the clean, small-scale pictures echo the warmth and humor of the story.

33   **Alexander,** Sue. *Nadia the Willful;* illus. by Lloyd Bloom. Pantheon, 1983. 82-12602. Trade ed. ISBN 0-394-85265-6; Library ed. ISBN 0-394-95265-0. 44p. Trade ed. $10.95; Library ed. $10.99.

2–4

A forceful Bedouin child, Nadia is so willful that her father, the sheik Tarik, doesn't know how to handle her; only her eldest brother Hamed can calm Nadia's temper. Sent into the desert to look for a new oasis, Hamed is lost, and Tarik forbids anyone in the tribe to utter his name. Nadia disobeys; she finds that talking to others about her beloved brother helps ease her grief, and eventually she convinces her father that he, too, can better adjust to bereavement if he doesn't try to shut the subject out. Although slight in structure, this is perceptive in handling and universal in application, and the style is direct and simple. The soft black and white illustrations have a strong sense of design and, although some of the pictures have a blurry quality, are particularly effective in their play of light and shadow.

34   **Alexander,** Sue. *Seymour the Prince;* illus. by Lillian Hoban. Pantheon, 1979. 78-31406. Trade ed. ISBN 0-394-84141-7; Library ed. ISBN 0-394-94141-1. 48p. (I Am Reading Books) Trade ed. $3.95; Library ed. $4.99 net.

1–2

When the Maple Street Club decides to put on a performance of "Sleeping Beauty," Seymour balks at being assigned the role of the Prince, since he's sure that the audience will laugh at him when he kisses Sleeping Beauty. He stalls and fumes for days, is told somebody else will take the role, mopes because his friends are all busy with the production, and worries because they threaten to cashier him if he won't cooperate. He is asked to stand in at dress rehearsal and discovers it's a performance, and he is surprised and delighted when his kiss of life is greeted by applause and cheers rather than laughter. The slightly scruffy Hoban children are just right for the story, which—despite the slight overemphasis on Seymour's traumatic reaction to kissing a girl— is amusing, light in tone and easy to read, nicely constructed, and has large print set off by ample white space.

35   **Aliki.** *Digging Up Dinosaurs;* written and illus. by Aliki. Crowell, 1981. 80-2250. Trade ed. ISBN 0-690-04098-9; Library ed. ISBN 0-690- 04099-7. 33p. (Let's-Read-and-Find-Out Books) Trade ed. $8.95; Library ed. $8.79.

2–4   A companion volume to the author's *My Visit to the Dinosaurs* and *Fossils Tell of Long Ago.* Here the text begins with a survey of some dino-saur exhibits in a museum and goes on to describe the ways in which scientists and their colleagues excavate, label, preserve, and pack the fossil remains, and the techniques used by museum staff members to assemble and mount dinosaur skeletons. In all of the drawings (alter-nately black and white or tinted in browns and greens) there are side remarks in comic strip balloons, the comments hand-printed in unfortu-nately small size. The latter is the only weakness of the book, however, which on the whole does a fine job of explaining procedures simply and clearly.

36   **Aliki.** *A Medieval Feast;* written and illus. by Aliki. Crowell, 1983. 82-45923. Trade ed. ISBN 0-690-04245-0; Library ed. ISBN 0-690-04246-9. Trade ed. $9.95; Library ed. $9.89.

2–4   The lord and lady of Camdenton Manor are told that the king and his entourage will spend a few nights there en route to their destination. Aliki describes and pictures the estate, the preparations, and the long, elaborate feast when the party arrives. The focus is on the medieval menu and dining customs, but the book also gives a picture of the way of life of that period, and the illustrations, rich in color and often intri-cately framed, of the architecture and clothing are handsome.

37   **Aliki.** *The Two of Them;* written and illus. by Aliki. Greenwillow, 1979. 79-10161. Trade ed. ISBN 0-688-80225-7; Library ed. ISBN 0-688-84225-9. 32p. Trade ed. $7.95; Library ed. $7.63 net.

K–3
*   Soft pencil and crayon drawings capture the tender tone of a poetic text, sedate but touching, about the love between a child and her grandparent. All through her infancy he makes her things to use and play with, tells her stories and sings to her; when she is a little older he gladly accepts her help with his work, "and every year she loved him even more than the things he made for her." Then her grandfather be-comes bedridden, and she brings him food, and sings to him, and tells him stories just as he did when she was a baby. She knows he will die, but is not aware of how deep her grief will be. When he dies, she sits in the orchard he loves and thinks of how the blossoms come each year

and are followed by the fruit, and, the story ends, "She would be there to watch it grow, and pick the fruit, and to remember." A quiet, poignant book.

38   **Allan,** Mabel Esther. *A Dream of Hunger Moss.* Dodd, 1983. 83-14036. ISBN 0-396-08224-6. 188p. $10.95.

7–9   Because of her mother's hospitalization, Alice (the narrator) and her brother Adam are sent to stay on the farm near Oxford where Mother had spent her childhood holidays. Alice loved the place; Adam, afraid of some animals, was less pleased until he started working and found he enjoyed it. Both were fascinated by Hunger Moss, a dangerously boggy piece of land that held a ruined tower. It was there they met Reuben, and Alice found it mysterious and intriguing that Mother had once had a friend by the same name, whom she'd met secretly in the same place, and who had disappeared. Because England goes to war, local families take in city children, and it is partly through that fact that Alice gets to know Reuben's imperious great-grandmother and solves the mystery of her mother's lost friend. The story is nicely knit, capably written, and structured with good pace and some suspense.

39   **Allard,** Harry. *The Stupids Die;* illus. by James Marshall. Houghton, 1981. 80-27103. ISBN 0-395-30347-8. 31p. $7.95.

K–2   Daft as ever, the four equally dim members of the Stupid family, who breakfast in the shower and mow the rug, decide that they must be dead when there is a power failure. When the lights come on again, the sensible dog and cat having changed a fuse, the Stupids are sure they are in heaven and are delighted by the fact that it's so homey. Grandfather stops in and is welcomed to heaven. "This isn't heaven," he says, "This is Cleveland." Allard's scrawly line, his scruffy characters, and the light, bright tones he uses add to the merry insanity of another silly story that should appeal to all the fans of the confused Stupids; the text is brisk and simple.

40   **Allen,** Anne. *Sports for the Handicapped.* Walker, 1981. 81-50738. Trade ed. ISBN 0-8027-6436-3; Library ed. ISBN 0-8027-6437-1. 80p. illus. with photographs. Trade ed. $9.95; Library ed. $10.85.

6–9   Allen, a journalist, gives good coverage of some of the major sports in which handicapped persons can participate in this briskly written and informative book. The text covers football, horseback riding, skiing, swimming, track and field, and wheelchair basketball; it is partially anecdotal, giving the viewpoints of both the participants and their coaches, it describes the programs and the adapted rules, and it has a rather cheerful and encouraging tone. There is no index, but the table of contents gives broad access, and an appended list of resource and sports organizations serving the handicapped adds to the book's usefulness.

41   **Allen,** Pamela. *Mr. Archimedes' Bath;* written and illus. by Pamela Allen. Lothrop, 1980. 79-13368. Trade ed. ISBN 0-688-41919-4; Library ed. ISBN 0-688-51919-9. 26p. Trade ed. $8.95; Library ed. $8.59.

K–2   An Australian author's version of Archimedes' discovery is illustrated by line drawings (tinted on alternate pages) that are spaciously composed, humorous, and repetitive. Sharing his large, round tub with a kangaroo, a goat, and a wombat, Archimedes is bothered by the fact that the tub always overflows; he tries various combinations of animals and finally concludes that each creature displaces water by its own weight. Allen doesn't go into physical principles, but pares the idea down to a level comprehensible to the read-aloud audience, and she does it with good humor and flair.

42   **Allen,** Pamela. *Who Sank the Boat?;* written and illus. by Pamela Allen. Coward, 1983. 82-19832. ISBN 0-698-20576-6. 28p. $10.95.

K–2   From one of the best Australian picture book artists, this amusing story uses repetition in telling the tale of four animals who climb into a boat for a relaxing row, and capsize. Who caused the accident? Those in the read-aloud audience who notice that the boat is sinking lower and lower in the water will have the answer. A bright, brisk tale, simply told, is illustrated by cheerful, comical pictures.

43   **Ames,** Mildred. *The Silver Link, the Silken Tie.* Scribner, 1984. 83-20337. ISBN 0-684-18065-0. 215p. $12.95.

7–9   Two high school students who are loners meet and help each other gain security as their friendship turns to love. That's a common enough treatment; what makes this story different is the exposition and development of Felice's involvement in a group of idealists who meet under the guidance of a teacher, and of Tim's growing suspicion that the teacher is practicing mind control and manipulating his students. Exposed, the teacher is fired. But he gets a good job, and, in a stark ending, it becomes clear that the direction of the cult group is really under the aegis of the headmaster, who quickly finds another cult member to replace the teacher. The story has suspense and pace, and Ames creates an aura of evil most convincingly.

44   **Andersen,** Hans Christian. *Fairytales;* illus. by Kay Nielsen. Viking/Metropolitan Museum of Art, 1981. 81-43012. ISBN 0-670-30557-X. 155p. $14.95.

4–6   Like the book below, this is a partial collection of Andersen's tales; there are few of the most familiar tales in this volume: eleven stories, the only overlap with the book below being "The Snow Queen." The illustrations are reproduced from a 1924 edition; here the ecru pages have an ornamental border, there are decorations that precede each story, and the full-color paintings, framed and delicately detailed, are not always placed near the textual references, although the phrase or passage each illustrates is repeated on a page that faces the painting. There are, in addition, some single-color drawings (brown, like the print) that combine effectively textured detail with a sense of line and composition that are often reminiscent of the work of Aubrey Beardsley.

45   **Andersen, Hans Christian.** *Michael Hague's Favourite Hans Christian Andersen Fairy Tales;* comp. and illus. by Michael Hague. Holt, 1981. 81-47455. ISBN 0-03-059528-2. 162p. $14.95.

4–6   Nine tales by Andersen, including such favorites as "Thumbelina," "The Ugly Duckling," "The Emperor's New Clothes," "The Snow Queen," and "The Little Match Girl," are illustrated by gravely romantic paintings, traditional in mood and rich in color, with Hague's typical touch of a heavy black outline. The type is close-set but large, the illustrations carefully placed in relation to textual references. A handsome addition to collections of Andersen stories.

46   **Andersen, Hans Christian.** *The Snow Queen;* illus. by Susan Jeffers; ad. by Amy Ehrlich. Dial, 1982. 82-70199. Trade ed. ISBN 0-8037-8011-7; Library ed. ISBN 0-8037-8029-X. 40p. Trade ed. $12.95; Library ed. $12.89.

3–5   A smooth and simplified retelling of Andersen's classic story of the power of love, this is in oversize format that affords the artist an opportunity for stunning paintings, soft and romantic in hues and mood but strong in composition and in the use of imaginative details, often sensuously textured. While the book can be used for reading aloud to younger children, the length of the story and the concept of love's transmuting power indicate the middle grades as prime audience.

47   **Andersen, Karen Born.** *What's the Matter, Sylvie, Can't You Ride?* written and illus. by Karen Born Andersen. Dial, 1981. 80-12514. Trade ed. ISBN 0-8037-9607-2; Library ed. ISBN 0-8037-9621-8. 26p. Trade ed. $8.95; Library ed. $8.44.

K–2   Every child who's ever nervously wobbled through a first try at riding a bicycle can sympathize with Sylvie, who tries and tries and can't make it, while her friends whizz past. She's afraid of falling, and she's embarrassed about being afraid. Then—as readers will know—she finds that she's in control, and as she speeds past a nervous first-time rider she bawls out, as others have to her, "Can't you ride?" Line and wash, the illustrations have good composition and texture but some are confusing: for example, one page, in which there are four overlapping Sylvies, is cut across the middle by a band of white space with two lines of print, so that eight feet but no wheels show. The text is light and amusing, but it may elicit some questions about why neither of Sylvie's parents helps her.

48   **Anderson, David.** *The Piano Makers;* written and illus. with photographs by David Anderson. Pantheon, 1982. 82-6513. Trade ed. ISBN 0-394-

85353-9; Library ed. 0-394-95353-3. 55p. Trade ed. $10.95; Library ed. $10.99.

5–7   A photodocumentary shows, step by step, how the various parts of a grand piano are made and assembled, and the clearly written text explains the reasons for processes in addition to giving a description of each. While the numbered picture that explains key action might have been more useful at an earlier page (it concludes the book) the explanations of processes are adequate, and the book as a whole gives interesting information.

49   **Anderson,** Lydia. *Death.* Watts, 1980. 79-23683. ISBN 0-531-04107-7. 66p. illus. with photographs. $5.90.

4–6   Written in a direct and simple style, comprehensive in coverage and candid in tone, this covers almost every aspect of the topic briefly but adequately. Anderson discusses the cycle of life for all living things, including human beings; the ways in which we mourn and bury (or cremate, or donate to medical research) the dead; the legal definition of death, and what the end to life means medically; beliefs in life after death; and the changes in medical knowledge and hygiene that have made the aged a larger component of our population. A bibliography and an index are appended.

50   **Anderson,** Madelyn Klein. *Counting on You: the United States Census.* Vanguard, 1980. 79-67813. ISBN 0-8149-0824-1. 96p. illus. with photographs. $7.95.

6–9   This may answer more questions about the census than you've ever asked; Anderson writes in an easy, direct style on many aspects of the subject, describing the history of census-taking in the United States and explaining the many ways in which census figures are used: for allocation of federal funds, for determining representation in Congress, for predicting school needs, housing needs, and many other purposes. The text describes the changes in the taking of a census over the years, the methods used to distribute and collect and collaborate today, and the efforts made to protect privacy. All timely, and lucidly explained. A relative index is appended.

51   **Anderson,** Margaret. *The Journey of the Shadow Bairns.* Knopf, 1980. 80-12057. Trade ed. ISBN 0-394-84511-0; Library ed. ISBN 0-394-94511-5. 177p. Trade ed. $7.95; Library ed. $7.63.

4–6   Their parents had been saving money to start a new life in Canada, and the tickets had been purchased, but after Papa was killed in an accident and Mama died of a respiratory illness, Elspeth decided she and young Rob must get to Canada to escape being taken by the authorities and separated. The story begins in 1902, describing the voyage on which

Elspeth and Rob tried to be as inconspicuous as they could (therefore the title) and goes on to relate the problems they have for the next two years: they cannot find their kin, they are separated for a time, Elspeth works at a hotel for a hard taskmistress. The book ends with the brother and sister reunited; Elspeth, now fifteen, is encouraged to dream again because they have found a family who offer them permanence, security, and affection. The story line loses strength as the book progresses, but the book creates a compelling picture of the arduous task of wilderness settlers, and the style and characterization are competent.

52   **Anderson,** Margaret J. *Light in the Mountain.* Knopf, 1982. 81-14266. Trade ed. ISBN 0-394-84791-1; Library ed. ISBN 0-394-94791-6. 177p. Trade ed. $9.95; Library ed. $9.99.

6–9   A dramatic story of the Maori migration to New Zealand is fiction, but it has the sweep and stature of legend despite one time sequence that seems rushed. On their home island the people lived in awe of their god of fire, Atua Ahi, and when his mountains rumbled angrily, it was their custom to sacrifice a maiden. This time the crippled child Rana is chosen to be the volcano's bride; but there are those who do not believe, and they use Rana as a false sign: she is spared and she will be the new leader of the people, Ahi-Rana, the instrument of deliverance. A small group sails to the Land of the Long White Cloud, where Ahi-Rana, intended as a puppet ruler, becomes the true leader of her people and, after her, the new priestess, Ngaio. The story covers the lives of the two women, each with her problems of adjustment to a life of dedication and sacrifice. Ending with Ngaio's decision to lead her people over the mountain to a safer, better life, the book has a compelling flow and strength.

53   **Anderson,** Norman D. *Ferris Wheels;* by Norman D. Anderson and Walter R. Brown. Pantheon, 1983. 83-3959. Trade ed. ISBN 0-394-85460-8; Library ed. ISBN 0-394-95460-2. 53p. illus. with photographs. Library ed. $10.99; Trade ed. $10.95.

5–8   Although almost all wheels that give people rides are referred to as Ferris wheels, similar devices—smaller and hand-powered—were recorded as being in existence as long ago as 1620. Several wheels, hand or steam powered, were operating in the United States by the time George Ferris, an engineer, proposed to the planners of the 1893 Columbian Exposition in Chicago that he build a giant wheel with thirty-six cars, each carrying forty passengers, so that fair-goers could view the grounds from above. A huge success, it was imitated—and continues to be—at small carnivals and giant amusement parks throughout the world. The authors provide interesting details about the structure, the problems, and the success or failure of many wheels, in a text that is profusely illustrated by drawings and photographs and that is written in a brisk, straightforward style.

54 **Anderson,** Norman D. *Halley's Comet;* written by Norman D. Anderson and Walter R. Brown; illus. with photographs and prints. Dodd, 1981. 81-3314. ISBN 0-396-07974-1. 78p. $7.95.

5–9 Written by a former high school science teacher and a professor of science education, this book exemplifies the scientific approach, stressing the difference between fact and theory, emphasizing the fact that Halley's work was built on the body of knowledge to which so many earlier scientists had contributed, and carefully pointing out alternate theories when discussing scientists' conjectures about the formation and composition of comets. The text, well organized and clearly written, describes Halley's research and his prediction of the return of the comet which was named for him; it focuses on the orbits and behavior of comets, and closes with instructions to readers who may want to become comet-watchers. A list of the dates on which Halley's comet has appeared (first recorded appearance: 467 B.C., expected again in 1985) and an index are appended.

55 **Anderson,** Rachel. *The Poacher's Son.* Oxford, 1983. ISBN 0-19-271468-6. 137p. $11.95.

6–9 Set in rural England in the years before World War I, this is a finely-crafted novel that testifies vividly to the rigidity of the class system, and to the acceptance by the poor of the unthinking snobbery of gentry. Arthur, the poacher's son, detests school and cannot understand why his sister Alice loves to learn. Their father is a gamekeeper but has been accused of helping poachers; turned out of their home, Arthur's family takes over a shanty and makes a bare living. After Pa dies, Arthur does become a poacher so that the family can have some food, and he's caught and put in Reform School. Eventually he joins the army and learns to read and write from the regiment's chaplain; the book ends with the family broken up; the war is over, Alice is in household service, her dreams of being a teacher forgotten, and Arthur's future is uncertain. The book is forceful in its depiction of the viciousness and superficial piety of those who have power and status, and of the obstacles for those they disdain: poverty, illness, ignorance, illiteracy, and a meek acceptance of the fact that their place in life is menial and almost impossible to change. Anderson's characters come to life, the setting and the period details are maintained with consistency, and the writing style, serious and fluent, is appropriate in dialogue and attitudes for the period.

56 **Angell,** Judie. *Dear Lola; Or How to Build Your Own Family.* Bradbury, 1980. 80-15111. ISBN 0-87888-170-0. 166p. $7.95.

4–6 Annie is one of the five orphans who leave St. Theresa's Home and School with the sixth and oldest orphan, Lola, to make a new life for themselves as a family. Annie's ten, Lola is eighteen and making an adequate income as a syndicated columnist; all of them want to be together, so they hike until they are far enough away to feel safe, and Lola buys a house. Lola, unbeknownst to his public, is really Arthur Beniker, and all the children take his name; they share the chores, they go to school and make new friends, and they are very happy—until some adults discover that "Grandfather," who's been the putative head of the family, is only eighteen. Taken to court, the younger children are put into Lola's care temporarily and later the decision is made to take the minor children from him—so they all hop in a van and take off again; the final chapter is written a year later, when Annie reports that they've been living in California and are doing very nicely, thank you, no problems. Patient, loving, wise, and compassionate, Lola is one of the nicest father figures in fiction; if the story isn't wholly believable, it's still wholly beguiling: good style, good characters, a fresh plot, and the perennial appeal of a dream come true.

57   **Angell,** Judie. *Suds, A New Daytime Drama.* Bradbury, 1983. 82-22732. ISBN 0-02-705570-1. 167p. $9.95.

6–9   This is a romp from page one, and the author must have had as much fun as her readers will, savoring the blatant spoof of soap operas. Sue Sudley's story begins when her parents, each flying solo (in different directions) collide in midair while Sue descends in her designer para-chute. She leaves her mansion to live with an aunt and uncle in a small town and becomes involved in the pseudo-dramatic, nonsensical, and highly enjoyable complexities of life—including the boy next door, a football hero confined to a wheelchair because he can never walk, who regains the use of his legs when he impulsively propels himself onto the gridiron during a homecoming game. This has everything the soaps have: the trite situations, the cardboard characters, the contrived dia-logue, all presented in bland style with tongue firmly in cheek.

58   **Angell,** Judie. *A Word From Our Sponsor or My Friend Alfred.* Bradbury, 1979. 78-25716. 140p. $6.95.

5–7   Rudy, twelve, tells a story that, despite the yeasty style of writing and the humor of the dialogue, has a painlessly pithy message about harm-ful products, advertising, and consumer protection. Rudy and Gillian help a third friend, Alfred, get public attention focused on a drinking cup (a promotional giveaway) that they've tested and in which they've found a dangerous amount of lead; the fact that Alfred's father is re-sponsible for the sponsor's advertising makes it difficult—but they are successful. There's a bit too much cuteness from a young brother, but it's easily outweighed by the tight structure, the believable achievement, the combination of light tone and serious purpose, and the solid friend-ship and cooperation among the three children.

59   **Anno,** Masaichiro. *Anno's Mysterious Multiplying Jar;* by Masaichiro and Mitsumasa Anno; illus. by Mitsumasa Anno. Philomel, 1983. 82-22413. ISBN 0-399-20951-4. 42p. $10.95.

5–   Like other books for which Mitsumasa Anno has done the illustrations, this is beautiful. It begins with a painting of a handsome blue and white lidded jar, moves into fantasy with pictures of the water in the jar becoming a sea on which an old sailing ship is moving, transfers to an island on the sea, and goes on to describe the rooms in the houses in the kingdoms on the mountains in the countries on the island. Each time the number grows: one island, two countries, three mountains, etc. How many jars, then, were in the boxes that were in the cupboards in the rooms? Answer: 3,628,800. Why? Because in each box "There were 10! jars." The text then explains, and elaborates on the translation of 10! to "10 Factorial." The explanation is in itself clear, and is expanded by other examples of factorials. The weakness of the book is that the first set of pages seems designed, in appearance and concept, for very young children, whereas the final pages are more appropriate for older ones.

60   **Anno,** Mitsumasa, illus. *Anno's Britain.* Philomel, 1982. 81-21058. ISBN 0-399-20861-5. 42p. $10.95.

All
ages
*
Like other Anno travel books, this is an artful mingling of period costume, anachronistic objects, and fictional characters, all of this smoothly incorporated in a larger pattern, in which a tiny blue-clad wayfarer debarks from a small boat to begin his journey through the British Isles. He moves—buying a horse en route—from the countryside through hamlets and towns to London, and reverses the procedure to embark at the shore and row off. There's also a chronological development, although Anno cheerfully disregards reality in placement of details and inclusion of a Robin Hood here or a Pooh there. All of this is great fun; it has a puzzle element for the enjoyment of nonreaders, allure in its details for the addicted Anglophile, and an equal attraction for art lovers, for the paintings are exquisite in details and remarkable in perspective composition. Another stunner.

61   **Anno,** Mitsumasa, illus. *Anno's Counting House.* Philomel, 1982. 82-617. ISBN 0-399-20896-8. 49p. $12.95.

4–7
yrs.
Surely one of the most imaginative and innovative of today's author-illustrators, Anno has constructed a wordless book that can be used to learn mathematical concepts by following the directions in the preface; understanding the directions, however, may require the participation of an older person. Alternate double-page spreads are used, showing the exteriors and interiors of two houses, with cut-out windows in alternate leaves. The alternate pages hide varying numbers of the ten little people who move from house to house. Guided by the shapes of the houses, children can use counters (as suggested in the preface) to answer such questions as "How many people are there?" "How many are girls?" The paintings are precisely and beautifully detailed, and the book has a game element that should appeal to children although the initial interest

may depend on guidance. A note to adults is appended, discussing the fostering of mathematical concepts in the early years.

62   **Anno,** Mitsumasa, illus. *Anno's Italy*. Collins, 1980. 79-17649. Trade ed. ISBN 0-529-05559-7; Library ed. ISBN 0-529-05560-0. 48p. Trade ed. $8.95; Library ed. $8.91 net.

All
ages
*

As he did in *Anno's Journey*, the author begins with paintings of the countryside, moves from village to town, and from town to city. There is no text; none is necessary, for the pictures tell the story, and the profusion of exquisite details of landscape and architecture are story enough. The composition and perspective are impressive and there are bits of quirky humor hidden here and there. For those who have visited some of the Italian cities pictured, the roofs of Siennese brown or the canals or cathedrals will provide the pleasure of recognition, and the pages take the viewer back again to the open countryside and—eventually—the calm blue sea. Young children may not appreciate the significance of every detail, but they can appreciate the beauty.

63   **Anno,** Mitsumasa. *Anno's Magical ABC: An Anamorphic Alphabet*; written and illus. by Mitsumasa Anno; lettering by Masaichiro Anno. Philomel. 1981. 80-26024. ISBN 0-399-20788-0. 59p. $16.95.

All
ages
*

Since the book requires a sheet of mirror paper (bent into a tubular column) to correct the proportions of the paintings and letters on the pages, it may be too frail for library collections—but what a nice gift item! The pages contain two alphabets, one in lower case, illustrated by paintings of animals that look distorted and out of perspective on the page, as do the letters, and the second (and separate) set in upper case letters, with similarly skewed pictures of an angel, a balalaika, a cassette, a doll, et cetera. When the mirror page is placed over a central circle, the pictures, ink and watercolor, are seen in proper proportion. They are quite beautiful. This example of anamorphic art is intriguing, not the best way to learn the alphabet, perhaps—since the letter can't be seen at the same time as the picture when the paper tube is held at the center of the page—but a fine way to enjoy another example of the inventive whimsy of one of Japan's most distinguished illustrators.

64   **Anno,** Mitsumasa. *Anno's Medieval World*; written and illus. by Mitsumasa Anno; ad. from the translation by Ursula Synge. Philomel, 1980. 79-28367. Trade ed. ISBN 0-399-20742-2; Library ed. ISBN 0-399-61153-3. 49p. Trade ed. $9.95; Library ed. $9.99.

4–6
*

The title of this book, first published in Japan, unfortunately does not indicate the fact that the text—and this has far more text than readers of previous Anno books might expect—focuses on the concepts held by medieval people and the theories of medieval astronomers about the functioning of our universe. Expectably handsome paintings, beautifully detailed, and framed with a scrolled floral border, show both the real activities and some of the fanciful concepts of the people; while the text describes some of the beliefs (witches, alchemy) of medieval times, the emphasis is on conflicting theories (and their acceptance or rejection) about the shape of the earth, the paths of solar bodies, etc. Anno does not use names, but in the author's note he is explicit, in referring to statements made in the text, about Copernican and Ptolemaic theories, the burning of Bruno, the rejection and persecution of Galileo; a chronology is included. A nice introduction, a beautiful book.

65   **Anno,** Mitsumasa, illus. *Anno's USA.* Philomel, 1983. 83-13107. ISBN 0-399-20974-3. 47p. $10.95.

All
ages
*

Like other books of Anno's in which he has a traveller who journeys through a country, this begins with rural scenes, takes a traveller into more heavily populated areas, and ends with an embarkation. Anno deliberately mixes costumes, vehicles, and other representations of various periods in the handsome double-page spreads that are beautifully composed; his use of color and perspective are admirable; his command of architectural drawing is impressive. What may appeal most to readers, however, are the small visual jokes that enliven the pages: the lions of the New York Public Library on a parade float, the policeman and ducks from *Make Way for Ducklings,* Tom Sawyer painting the fence. Delicious.

66   **Apfel,** Necia H. *It's All Relative: Einstein's Theory of Relativity;* diagrams by Yukio Kondo; illus. with photographs. Lothrop, 1981. 80-28188. Trade ed. ISBN 0-688-41981-X; Library ed. ISBN 0-688-51981-4. 141p. Trade ed $9.95; Library ed. $9.59.

6–

With his revolutionary statement in 1905 that the velocity of light is constant everywhere and at all times, Albert Einstein refuted a basic assumption upon which much of the science of that time was based. What seems to be a difference, based on individual frames of reference (i.e., two moving objects passing each other, comparing measurements), the "time dilation," is relative. From this, Einstein moved to his theory that a small amount of matter is equal to an enormous amount of energy: $E = mc^2$. He also developed the theory that gravitation and acceleration are the same, the "principle of equivalence," rejecting Newton's theory of gravitation. The discussion of these concepts and of such concepts as the bending of light rays or the curvature of space are explained clearly, with illuminating home experiments that demonstrate how such phenomena function. The language of the text is lucid but the concepts intricate, so that the book requires close attention; given that attention, Einstein's theory become comprehensible. This may be due in large measure to the fact that the author is experienced in lecturing on astronomy to elementary and high school students; her material is logically arranged and sequentially developed. A glossary and an index are provided.

67   **Archer,** Jules. *You Can't Do That to Me! Famous Fights for Human Rights.* Macmillan, 1980. 79-5127. ISBN 0-02-705600-7. 232p. $8.95.

7–10   Not a full history, this account of the long struggle for human rights focuses on individuals or groups who have achieved fame because of their contributions or their situations: Spartacus, the barons whose protest produced the Magna Carta, Bolivar, the Chinese general strike of 1922, and several instances of contemporary leaders and causes. The tone is objective, the coverage in each section adequate and usually including ample background information, and the writing style is a bit heavy but not burdensome and always straightforward. Archer seldom interprets events, but he is a careful and intelligent researcher and reporter; he concludes with a chapter that discusses the protection of human rights and the offenses against them in today's world, making some suggestions for improving the situation now and in the future. A divided bibliography and an index are appended.

68   **Ardley,** Neil, *Computers,* Warwick/Watts, 1983. ISBN 0-531-09219-4. 73p. $9.90.

5–8   Printed in two columns, lavishly and usefully illustrated with photographs, diagrams, and flowcharts, this is a clearly written text with broader scope than most books on the subject written for children. Ardley gives some historical background and discusses the impact of computer technology on our society; he describes the ways in which computers operate and are programmed; he distinguishes between different kinds of computers and computer languages; he notes the many applications of computers in business, medicine, and other fields. A glossary and an index make accessible the considerable amount of material in the book. Ardley has also produced a simpler book that can be used by somewhat younger readers, *Using the Computer,* which suggests activities that show how a computer works.

69   **Arnold,** Caroline. *My Friend from Outer Space;* illus. by Carol Nicklaus. Watts, 1981. 80-22045. Trade ed. ISBN 0-531-02473-3; Library ed. ISBN 0-531-04192-1. 28p. (Easy-Read Books) Trade ed. $3.95; Library ed. $6.90.

2–3   Almost in strip format and style (framed pictures have the illustrations in a top box, with text printed against a yellow background in the bottom box) the casual drawings give the only clue to the other-world appearance of Sherry when she casts off (or so she claims) her Earth-disguise. Her nameless best friend, who tells the story, is not convinced by any of Sherry's plausible answers that she's really from outer space. They go into Sherry's dark garage, crawl into an even darker box, and go "a million miles an hour," says Sherry. When they get there it still looks like Sherry's garage. Sherry explains that, too. She had picked a place on earth that looked like home so she wouldn't get homesick. She disappears briefly, returning in hideous guise and convincing her friend it's true; the guise is shed, they get back into the box. "Now do you believe I come from outer space?" "Yes." A brisk and amusing story, very nicely told in simple dialogue, will have primary-grade readers feeling that they're in on a good scam; this should also appeal to the read-aloud audience.

70   **Arnold,** Caroline, *Pets Without Homes;* photographs by Richard Hewett. Houghton/Clarion, 1983, 83-2106. ISBN 0-89919-191-6. 48p. $10.95.

2–3   Photographs of good quality illustrate a text written with direct simplicity, one that should appeal to the read-aloud audience as well as independent readers. The book focuses on one puppy picked up by a police officer whose job includes work for the city's animal shelter, enforcement of municipal laws about animals, and giving talks at schools. The pictures should appeal to readers, since the animals are engaging, and the text gives, by example and precept, information about how to take good care of pets.

71   **Arnow,** Jan. *Louisville Slugger: The Making of a Baseball Bat;* written and photographed by Jan Arnow. Pantheon, 1984. 84-7049. Library ed. ISBN 0-394-96297-4; Trade ed. ISBN 0-394-86297-X. 39p. Library ed. $11.99; Trade ed. $11.95.

4–6   Photographs are judiciously used to best advantage on spaciously laid-out pages to accompany a text that describes the origins of the bats ("Louisville Sluggers") made by the firm of Hillerich & Bradsby. The book has some interesting comments on the idiosyncratic preferences of some of baseball's great stars, but it focuses on how bats are made, from choosing the right ash tree to mailing the finished and labelled product. Clear and informative, the book should appeal to baseball fans.

72   **Arrick,** Fran. *Chernowitz!* Bradbury, 1981. 81-7712. ISBN 0-87888-190-5. 165p. $8.95.

7–10   Bob Cherno, who tells the story, is fifteen, and he looks back on his whole experience with Emmett Sundback with bitter candor. Sundback is a bully and a bigot, a classmate who advanced from sneering and blustering to a hate campaign that drew other classmates into overt antisemitism that made Bob a bewildered victim. Only when his parents were exposed did Bob tell them the whole story, and the book ends with two scenes: first, a dramatic and open confrontation at a school meeting and, second, a scene alone between Emmett and Bob. It is the latter that is the message of the book, for Emmett is totally unaffected by the concentration camp scenes (film) that have sent other students, weeping or nauseated, from the assembly; in fact, he still taunts and jeers. Bob concludes: "There was nothing I could do to him that would make him change except kill him. And even if I could do that it wouldn't kill his ideas . . . Or any other bigot . . . I know it's all thoughtless and mindless . . . But it hurt so much. It hurt so much I wanted to do something about it." Effective, affective, honest, and perceptive.

73   **Arrick,** Fran. *God's Radar.* Bradbury, 1983. 83-2666. ISBN 0-02-705710-0. 224p. $10.95.

7–10   Roxie Cable and her parents have moved from Syracuse to a small Georgia town; their neighbors, the Pregers, are very friendly and urge the Cables to join the Baptist Church to which they belong, a church headed by a nationally-known conservative evangelist. Pressure is put on Roxie, too, by the new friends she makes—all friends of the Preger's daughter—during the summer. In the fall, just as she has adjusted to the public high school, Roxie is stunned when her parents announce they are sending her to the church school. She is torn: the unswerving faith and the belief in simple virtues of the Baptist group are not unappealing, but the rigidity, the control, and the bias of the church make her uncomfortable. When she has to choose between the new pressure from her parents and the new affection she feels for a boy who's in trouble with the church, Roxie's decision shows what has become the dominating factor in her life. This is a trenchant story, skillfully developed, candid in its assessment of the relationship between the group and the individual, and written with objectivity and sensitivity.

74   **Arrick,** Fran. *Nice Girl from Good Home.* Bradbury, 1984. 84-11002. ISBN 0-02-705840-9. 199p. $11.95.

7–10   A family almost disintegrates when the father of the household loses his job; he turns to alcohol, his neurotic wife slips into a psychotic state, his daughter Dory cuts school and spends her time with some tough companions. Only the son, Jeremy, takes constructive action; not only does he get a job as a house-painter, but it is he who suggests a solution to his father for a way to earn money and keep the family together. Caught in an act of malicious mischief, Dory (spoiled and selfish) repents and mends her ways. As the story ends, all signs are encouraging; even Mom, in an institution where she is getting therapy, is slowly improving. Arrick's story is dark and starkly realistic; the characters are convincing and their problems (and solutions) believable; the one weakness of the book is that Dory's rebellion and her temporarily hostile attitude seem over-reactions.

75   **Arrick,** Fran. *Tunnel Vision.* Bradbury, 1980. 79-25939. ISBN 0-87888-163-8. 167p. $8.95.

7–12   What impels a fifteen-year-old who is a good student, popular, an athlete, apparently happy with his friends and his family, to commit suicide? All of the people who loved him were aware that he had changed, but just before he took his own life he seemed to have changed back to the old Anthony, much to their relief. The story begins with Anthony's death and it is through the probing of memories (and some interpo-lated, italicized flash-back conversations) that the pattern and the moti-vation emerge. Almost everyone feels guilty, and while each person has contributed to the pressures in Anthony's life, there is no single person who is culpable; Arrick draws a convincing and moving picture of the unhappy Anthony's search for a peace he could only envision through surrender, and a perceptive picture of the anguished adjustment of his family and friends. Tragic though the event is, it brings better under-standing to them and, to some of them, a better relationship with each other.

76   **Aruego,** Jose, *We Hide, You Seek*; written and illus. by Jose Aruego and Ariane Dewey, Greenwillow, 1979. 78-13638. Trade ed. ISBN 0-688-80201-X; Library ed. ISBN 0-688-84201-1. 38p. Trade ed. $7.95; Library ed. $7.63 net.

2–5
yrs.
*

There are only three lines of text (and they're all that is needed) in a picture book in which a rhinoceros attempts to find his varied animal friends as they play a game of hide and seek. The pictures have humor and vitality as well as a game element; most of the animals are well-camouflaged by their protective coloration, so that the rhino barges about surrounded by dozens of friends but can't see them. Finally bore-dom sets in and the hunter chases a butterfly; after a tumble, he an-nounces he wants his turn to hide. Last page, a nice visual gag: the rhino is in full sight, but he's in the midst of a herd of rhinos, and the other animals look on, baffled; they know he's there, but which one is he? Aruego and Dewey have outdone themselves visually; endpaper drawings identify the many animals.

77   **Asbjørnsen,** Peter Christen. *The Runaway Pancake*; by P. Chr. Asbjørn-sen and Jørgen Moe; Illus. by Svend Otto S.; tr. by Joan Tate. Larousse, 1980. 80-80439. ISBN 0-8332-137-8. 23p. $7.95.

3–6
yrs.

An oversize book affords the eminent Danish illustrator a splendid op-portunity to show his skill at composition and to give details without cluttering a page, as he interprets a favorite nursery tale. The color is bright, but used with restraint; the line is free; the figures are imbued with vitality and humor. The cumulation, the reiteration, and the ap-peal of the chase, as the runaway pancake is finally outwitted, may be more familiar to some listeners as the story of the gingerbread boy, but this smooth translation should captivate them whether the tale is famil-iar or not.

78   **Asch,** Frank. *Pearl's Promise*; written and illus. by Frank Asch. Dela-corte, 1984. 83-17153. Library ed. ISBN 0-385-29321-6; Trade ed. ISBN 0-385-29325-9. 160p. Library ed. $12.95; Trade ed. $12.95.

2–4

"I'll never forget the day Momma and Poppa were sold," this begins briskly, and it soon is clear that Pearl (the narrator) is a white mouse, that her parents have been sold by the pet store owner, and that she has promised that she will take care of her little brother Tony. Her other brother, Albert, is too preoccupied with his desire to learn to write (they all learned reading from TV) and so it is Pearl who takes charge. When the pet store owner buys his first snake and tosses Tony in the cage, Pearl knows she has to think of a fast solution . . . but she herself is sold. She escapes and has a series of adventures that include a session with a cat who has parapsychological powers. This is a lively, amusing fantasy that is deftly conceived and executed, and it has a surprise ending that should delight readers.

79   **Asch,** Frank, *Sand Cake;* written and illus. by Frank Asch. Parents' Magazine, 1979. 78-11183. Trade ed. ISBN 0-8193-0985-0; Library ed. ISBN 0-8193-0986-9. 28p. Trade ed. $4.95; Library ed. $4.99 net.

3–5 yrs.   Bright, solid colors are used to illustrate a story in which a small bear matches his father's imaginative play. Restless while his parents are sunning at the beach, Baby Bear offers to make a cake if his father will eat it. Yes, he will, if his offspring will use milk, eggs, and flour. No way. Yes, there is, says Papa Bear, and he draws eggs, wheat, and a cow in the sand. Baby Bear looks at the resultant sand cake with no appetite, then draws a picture of himself around it. "Here I am, and I have eaten the cake. See it in my stomach?" Happy to be outwitted, Papa Bear hugs his child, and they both move with alacrity to the real cake that Mama Bear brings out of the picnic basket. The pictures can help the small child understand the joke, and the book has a cozy happy-family feeling.

80   **Ashabranner,** Brent, *Gavriel and Jemal: Two Boys of Jerusalem;* illus. with photographs by Paul Conklin. Dodd, 1984. 84-8135. ISBN 0-396-08455-9. 94p. $10.95.

4–6   Photographs of Jerusalem, where the Arab Jemal and the Jewish Gavriel live, give breadth to a text that also is illustrated by many pictures of the two boys and their families. Living close to each other in the Old City, the two boys have never met, but in many ways their lives are similar. Both are serious about an education, devout in their religious observances, devoted to their loving families. Like every resident of Jerusalem, both are aware of, and troubled by, the hostility and tension that fill their city and all of the Middle East. Ashabranner gives good background information to help readers understand problems, similarities, and differences between Jews and Palestinian Arabs, and he does so with scrupulous objectivity and with clarity. A brief index is included.

81   **Ashabranner,** Brent. *Morning Star, Black Sun: The Northern Cheyenne Indians and American's Energy Crisis;* photographs by Paul Conklin. Dodd, 1982. 81-19501. ISBN 0-396-08045-6. 154p. $10.95.

7–   The author provides a history of the Cheyenne Indians of the North (another group, in an amicable separation, had gone south) and of their confrontation with white settlers and soldiers, as background to a discussion of the contemporary challenge to tribal life. Assigned to a Montana reservation, the Cheyenne have lived in peace if not great prosperity for almost a century. It was discovered that coal lay beneath the reservation land. The Cheyenne experience with the heavy hand of the Bureau of Indian Affairs (originally called the Indian Bureau) had made them justifiably dubious about outside management of tribal concerns; now the threat was that the one thing the Cheyenne held most dear, the land on which they live, might go (via large-tract leases) to the coal mining companies which had not offered equitable royalty revenue to the owners. Particularly vexatious had been the prospect that instead of shipping coal, the companies would set up generating plants and transmit electrical power—a process that would contribute to pollution at the sites. This would also have brought even more workers into the reservation area, inevitably changing the peaceful Cheyenne way of life. In 1973, learning some of the facts behind the offers, the tribal council petitioned the Bureau to cancel all leases. Thus began a long legal battle, into which the Environmental Protection Agency entered, to avert the "black sun" of the title and to annul the leases; this happened in 1980. A final chapter describes the lives of the Cheyenne today, an interesting but poorly placed section of the book. An index gives access to the text, which is a bit dry but competent in style, and is based on research that has resulted in a detailed, informative, and well-organized book.

82   **Asher,** Sandy, *Things are Seldom What They Seem.* Delacorte, 1983. 82-72819. ISBN 0-440-08932-8. 134p. $11.95.

7–9   Debbie, who tells the story, is just starting high school and hopes that it won't affect her the way it has affected her older sister: Maggie now wants to be called Margaret, she is aloof with members of her family, and she is completely devoted to Mr. Carraway, the handsome teacher who is coaching the drama club play. Equally devoted is Debbie's best friend, Karen, who's just been given a role in the play. Debbie's puzzled. Why are the other two so defensive about Mr. Carraway? She's even more puzzled when Karen abruptly quits the cast. Missing Karen, Debbie has become good friends with Murray, despite the fact that they are teased because he's shorter than she; Murray tries to help her find out what's going on. When Karen does confess that the teacher had kissed and caressed her, she makes Debbie promise not to tell. That she knows and won't tell makes Murray angry; her knowledge also leads to a realization that the same thing must have happened to Maggie. With family support, Maggie finally goes to the school principal, and Karen (who does not have parental support) joins them. Eventually Murray learns the truth and admits Debbie did the right thing by keeping Karen's secret. Although the story occasionally lags in pace, it is honest and clear-sighted, and it's written with compassion and humor.

83 **Ashley,** Bernard, *Dodgem.* Watts, 1982. 81-82129. ISBN 0-531-04363-0. 222p. $9.90.

7–10 In a fine story from England, adolescent Simon is worried about his father, disturbed and uncommunicative, and devotes all his time to caring for his Dad, hoping to keep him out of an institution. The authorities do investigate, put Dad into a home, and send Simon to a custodial institution. He is helped to escape by Rose, also remanded, and together they work out a plan for escape; Rose's uncle, who travels about from fair to fair, will rescue Alex, Simon's father, and the four of them will take to the road. It works, and while Simon is helping with carnival rides (hence the title) Alex works as a sign-painter and recovers slowly from his despondency and lethargy. This has depth and perception in the depiction of characters and their relationships, it has pace and suspense, it is given breadth by the changes and developments in Simon and Alex and their relationships with other people, and it has an interesting background. The handling of dialogue and dialect are particularly impressive, part of a strong and controlled writing style.

84 **Ashley,** Bernard. *A Kind of Wild Justice;* illus. by Charles Keeping, Phillips, 1979. 78-10899. 182p. $8.95.

6–9 Ronnie, in this English story, lives in constant fear of violence from the criminals for whom his father does odd jobs; what the malevolent Bradshaw brothers had said was, "One word outta place, Steven, my son, and we break the kid's back, right?" Ronnie, motherless, is a surly child, friendless, unhappy at school, and eager to find someone weaker than he; his victim is a timid Indian girl who shares the time of a special reading teacher. When Ronnie becomes involved in a criminal act, he is pursued with quiet persistence by the police of London's East End, who have long known about the Bradshaws and hope this will be the time to catch them. This is a dramatic adventure story with good pace and suspense, but it is also a vivid picture of a poor, multi-ethnic community and is given depth by the astute characterization and the relationships between characters.

85 **Asimov,** Isaac. *How Did We Find Out About Genes?* Walker, 1983. 83-1211. Trade ed. ISBN 0-8027-6499-1; Library ed. 0-8027-6500-9. 31p. Trade ed. $7.95; Library ed. $8.85.

4–6 In a clear, straightforward account of the work of scientists over the centuries, Asimov begins with a simple explanation of the pioneer work of Gregor Mendel, whose discovery of genetic laws was ignored by his contemporaries and their successors. Several decades later, other scientists realized that their research corroborated Mendelian findings; with the body of known knowledge plus the new instruments that developed, other scientists were able to gain information about the internal structure of chromosomes, linked genes, and dominant strains. The material has been covered in other books for children, but never more succinctly, and Asimov shows how the individual scientist draws on, and contributes to, the pool of knowledge.

86   **Asimov,** Isaac. *How Did We Find Out About the Beginning of Life?* illus. by David Wool. Walker, 1982. 81-71196. Trade ed. ISBN 0-8027-6447-9; Library ed. ISBN 0-8027-6448-7. 54p. Trade ed. $7.95; Library ed. $8.85.

5–7   Asimov's writing is always laudable for the way it shows how a body of scientific knowledge is based on the work of many scientists, both those who succeeded in their experiments and those who did not, and for its illustration of the fact that all findings are subject to re-examination. Here, in a clearly written and logically arranged text, he describes the work of those researchers of earlier centuries who demonstrated the error of the theory of spontaneous generation, compares the work of Lamarck and Darwin, and concludes with the statement that scientists are in agreement that species emerged (and are emerging) from other species. The second half of the text discusses the work of contemporary scientists in examining the ways in which, given a source of energy and the proper chemical constituents, it is possible to create new chemical combinations that resemble those of living things. An index is included; phonetic spelling is parenthetically provided for the more difficult words of names.

87   **Asimov,** Isaac, ed. *Sherlock Holmes Through Time and Space;* ed. by Isaac Asimov, Martin Harry Greenberg, and Charles G. Waugh. Bluejay Books, 1984. 84-18580. ISBN 0-312-94400-4. 355p. $14.95.

7–   Holmes, Watson, and Moriarty are featured in a selection of stories that should especially delight Conan Doyle fans, but that should also appeal to readers who enjoy mystery stories and science fiction. A very impressive group of authors deals in various ways with extensions of the Holmesian omniscience. He appears as an articulate dog in "The Adventure of the Misplaced Hound," or is a talking doll in "Death in the Christmas Hour." There's a sense of relish in the book, as though the authors had enjoyed their embellishments of the Holmesian mythology.

88   **Asimov,** Isaac, ed. *Tomorrow's T.V.;* ed. by Isaac Asimov, Martin Harry Greenberg, and Charles Waugh; illus. by Greg Hargreaves, Raintree, 1982. 81-17737. ISBN 0-8172-1735-5. 48p. $8.95.

5–   A collection of science fiction short stories that have to do with television in the future: all have been published previously, and the contributors are, in addition to Asimov, Jack Haldemann, Ray Bradbury, Robert Bloch, and Ray Nelson. The illustrations are lurid, the stories variable in quality: Asimov's "The Fun They Had," in which children of the future, machine-taught, look back enviously on the days of schools, is the most vivid in envisioning a future society; Bloch's "Crime Machine" is certainly the most amusing. While the quality isn't even, all of the stories have some substance, and the genre and subject should make the book appealing to science fiction buffs.

89   **Asimov, Isaac,** ed. *Young Extraterrestrials;* ed. by Isaac Asimov, Martin Greenberg, and Charles Waugh. Harper, 1984. 83-49489. Library ed. ISBN 0-06-020168-1; Paper ed. ISBN 0-06-020167-3. 240p. Library ed. $10.89; Paper ed. $7.95.

7–   In eleven stories about alien children, the editors have chosen with acumen and discrimination a variety of material of good quality; this anthology will certainly appeal to science fiction fans and it may even create some new ones. One of the stories is about an outer space dentist whose young patient has a tooth twelve feet high (Piers Anthony's "In the Jaws of Danger") and in Murray Leinster's "Keyhole" the tables are turned when men on the moon try to teach a moon-creature how to communicate. Possibly the story with the widest appeal will be Lloyd Biggle's "Who's on First?" in which four young space visitors show remarkable prowess at baseball, which is organized in quite a different way in 1998.

90   **Asimov, Isaac,** ed. *Young Mutants;* ed. by Isaac Asimov, Martin Green berg, and Charles Waugh. Harper, 1984. 83-48444. Library ed. ISBN 0-06-020157-6; Paper ed. ISBN 0-06-020156-8. 224p. Library ed. $10.89; Paper ed. $7.95.

6–   An intriguing collection gets off to a fine start with Ray Bradbury's "Hail and Farewell" and Frederic Brown's "Keep Out," the first as poignant as the second is chilling. This is one of the best in the series of theme-oriented anthologies of science fiction that Asimov, Greenberg, and Waugh have compiled; save for the over-extended "The Children's Room," by Raymond Jones (and it's not bad) the book is notable for the high quality and the variety of the selections.

91   **Aska, Warabe** (Takeshi Masuda). *Who Goes to the Park;* written and illus. by Warabe Aska. Tundra Books, 1984. ISBN 0-88776-162-3. 28p. $17.95.

3–5   Published in honor of Toronto's sesquicentennial celebration and honor-
*   ing its beautiful city park (High Park) this combination of beautiful paintings and a poetic text that describes events and seasonal changes is stunning in concept and execution. The author-illustrator, whose real name is Takeshi Masuda, has a strong sense of design and a subtle appreciation of color; his composition is striking and his realism given pointed contrast by a Chagall-like fancy here and there. A delight.

92   **Association for Childhood Education International.** *And Everywhere, Children!* Greenwillow, 1979. 78-25932. 281p. $8.95.

4–6   An anthology with an international flavor, this has twelve excerpts and a short story from a range of distinguished books. The authors include Bødker, Pearce, O'Dell, Thiele, and Van Iterson; the settings include the U.S.S.R., Africa, Norway, Holland, and Colombia. Some of the material has been adapted or abridged; this has been done with care. Because of the range of material—from Vestly's little heroine Aurora to the adolescent pearl-diver of O'Dell's *The Black Pearl*—and because of the fact that most of the selections are easily available, this seems best suited to a home collection.

93   **Atil**, Esin. *Kalila wa Dimna: Fables from a Fourteenth-Century Arabic Manuscript.* Smithsonian, 1981. 81-607053. Cloth ed. ISBN 0-87474-216-1; Paper ed. ISBN 0-87474-215-3. 95p. illus with photographs. Cloth ed. $17.50; Paper ed. $9.95.

5–   A scholarly preface, a concluding literary essay, and copious notes on the stories (often published as the fables of Bidpai) indicate that the book is intended for an adult audience—but the fables themselves are appropriate for, and should be made available to, young readers. The heavy paper and broad margins, as well as the delicate tones of the illustrations, make the book handsome; the margins also contribute by compensating visually for the solid print of the text. The fables range from brief animal stories and parables to longer tales that explore human weaknesses and relationships, and the sustaining motif is that all creatures are part of a whole, an entity that has a common fate. The book is valuable both because of its literary components and because it is a handsome example of a fourteenth century Arabic manuscript.

94   **Attenborough**, David. *Life on Earth: A Natural History.* Little, 1981. 79-90108. ISBN 0-316-05745-2 319p. illus. with photographs. $22.50.

6–   Based on a BBC television series that has also been seen in the United
*   States, this is written for the general reader; Attenborough explains in his prefatory notes that he has not used scientific names for plants and animals, or cited the work of individual scientists, or used formal time divisions, for the purpose of clarity. Indeed, he has compressed—in lucid prose that has an easy conversational flow—the history of living things, since life evolved, with remarkable success. The book is profusely illustrated with stunning color photographs from the original film; the text is knowledgeable (the author is a zoologist) and authoritative; appended material includes an index that provides scientific names and a simplified chart showing the emergence and duration of species.

95   **Avi.** *The Fighting Ground.* Lippincott, 1984. 82-47719. Library ed. ISBN 0-397-32074-4; Trade ed. ISBN 0-397-32073-6. 157p. Library ed. $11.89; Trade ed. $11.50.

5–7   A small stunner. Thirteen-year-old Jonathan has longed to go to war
*   against the hated British, and one morning, April 3, 1778 at 11:00 a.m., he gets his chance. Joining a small band of American soldiers he skirmishes with Hessians near Rocktown, New Jersey, and is captured: "Jonathan tried to rekindle his hatred, but all he could muster was the desire to stand close to them, to be taken care of." What is superb is the control. The story takes place in one day, detailed minute by minute. There is constant closeness—huddled soldiers, Jonathan hid-

ing—tightly held and suffocated by darkness or fog. Readers hear the Hessians as Jonathan does, only speaking German, frightening and disorienting. All this makes the war personal and immediate: not history or event, but experience; near and within oneself, and horrible.

96   **Avi.** *Shadrach's Crossing.* Pantheon, 1983. 82-19008. Trade ed. ISBN 0-394-85816-6; Library ed. ISBN 0-394-95816-0. 148p. Trade ed. $10.95; Library ed. $10.99.

5–7   Set in the Depression Era, this is the story of a boy of twelve who is determined to end the terrorizing of his island's residents by the men who are smuggling contraband liquor; it's the Prohibition period, and some of the islanders need money so desperately that they participate in the smuggling just to be paid. Shadrach, whose father will not participate, is nevertheless cowed into silence, and the boy is furious at the way his parents have been frightened and insulted. Shadrach confides in a man who purports to be a government meteorologist and spies on a mysterious visitor; he guesses wrong about both men, but when confrontation comes, Shadrach is instrumental in catching the organizer of the smuggling operation. This is a fast-paced story, competently written and sturdily structured; Shadrach's successful efforts are believably portrayed.

97   **Azarian,** Mary, illus. *A Farmer's Alphabet;* illus. by Mary Azarian. Godine, 1981. 80-84938. Hardcover ed. ISBN 0-87923-394-X; Softcover ed. ISBN 0-87923-397-4. 26 leaves. Hardcover ed. $10.95; Softcover ed. $6.95.

4–6   Although this was designed as a learning tool by a former teacher who
yrs.   wanted to preserve for children some aspects of rural life, it is interesting enough as an example of woodcut technique to attract a far wider audience. The oversize pages are fine stock, creamy and sturdy; the handsomely detailed and composed prints are in black and white, with upper and lower case letters (at the top of the page) and the word beginning with that letter (at the bottom of the page) in deep, rich red. All of the prints have farm-related objects (barn, cow, quilt, woodburning stove, maple sugar) although some (neighbor, vegetable, kite) are not exclusively rural. Useful as an alphabet book, this is also a graphic joy.

98   **Bach,** Alice. *Waiting for Johnny Miracle.* Harper, 1980. 79-2813. Trade ed. ISBN 0-06-020348-X; Library ed. ISBN 0-06-020349-8. 240p. Trade ed. $8.95; Library ed. $8.79.

7–10   Bach quotes one of the adolescent patients, in her jacket-flap note, as a prime reason for writing this novel based on her experience as a volunteer working with children who have cancer: "If you write about what it's really like for us, maybe people will treat me the way they did before they heard about my cancer." This is one of the strong themes in the story of Becky, an adolescent who has an operable malignant tumor;

another is the way in which the patients' families are affected. Becky's twin, Theo, is the sounding board for many of Bach's observations in a candid, sophisticated story about the way a cancer patient feels about her illness, about the hospital and other patients, about her future. The writing has vitality and depth as well as inherent drama; it concludes with a successful plan to arrange a night of love for Becky's dying roommate, a fifteen-year-old who has wistfully told Becky that she would like to experience sex before she dies.

99   **Baer,** Edith. *A Frost in the Night.* Pantheon Books, 1980. 79-27774, Trade ed. ISBN 0-394-84364-9; Library ed. ISBN 0-394-94364-3. 208p. Trade ed. $8.95; Library ed. $8.99.

7–9   For Eva Bentheim, living in Thalstadt in 1932, life was secure and comfortable; although she was an only child, her cousins and her grandfather lived in the same building, other members of the family lived nearby, and all of the Bentheim adults were respected, substantial citizens of the town where their ancestors had been respected, substantial citizens. Not like the olden days, Grandfather said, when Jews were persecuted. The rumblings of political upheaval are faint at first, but in this richly detailed story of family life Eva sees the first signs, like the school bully who taunts her—then the worried predictions of American cousins—then the growing strength of the Nazi Party's political victories. Even before the book ends (it closes with Hitler's appointment as chancellor of Germany) the Bentheims sense impending disaster. Nicely understated, this is written with depth and polish.

100   **Baer,** Frank. *Max's Gang;* tr. by Ivanka Roberts. Little, 1983. 82-24918. ISBN 0-316-07517-5. 281p. $15.95.

6–9   Translated from the German, this is the story of a group of displaced children trying to get to Berlin at the end of World War II. First published in 1979 under the title *Die Magermilch-Bande,* this begins with the closing of one of the many German Children's Evacuation Camps, and in the course of their arduous journey, three boys become separated from the others. Max is the leader, Peter a restive follower, Adolf a gentle and compliant child. In the course of their long trek home, they gather other companions, face illness and poverty on the roads clogged with other refugees, encounter enemy troops, steal and scrounge to stay alive, at times have transport but most of the time plod wearily homeward. The story is dramatic and trenchant in its depiction of the desolation of war, vigorous in its characterization, and strong in style and structure.

101   **Baker,** Alan. *Benjamin's Book;* written and illus. by Alan Baker. Lothrop, 1983. 82-4605. Trade ed. ISBN 0-688-01697-9; Library ed. ISBN 0-688-01698-7. 28p. $8.50.

3–5
yrs.   Handsomely textured paintings with restrained use of color in cleanly composed pages illustrate a story with minimal text. Benjamin is a hamster who inadvertently leaves a paw print on a large, clean piece of paper (to children, it may look like a white wall, since the "paper" is the full page of the book) and tries to clean it up; every attempt to clean or cover the original spot makes the paper messier. Finally, a despairing Benjamin tears the page out and throws it away. "I do like to leave things as I find them," he says, going off with relief and never noticing that he's just left a paw print on the new page. First published in Great Britain, this is visually appealing, has a quiet humor, and tells a story that's just right in length, scope, and familiarity for the preschool child.

102   **Baker, Betty.** *And Me, Coyote!* illus. by Maria Horvath. Macmillan, 1982. 82-7134. ISBN 0-02-708280-6. 32p. $8.95.

K–3   Strong stylized linoleum cut illustrations, dramatic in black and white, effectively echo the sturdy quality of a story based on creation myths of the California Indians, although they do not look like Indian art. A major figure in Native American mythology, Coyote is shrewd and arrogant, a braggart who often takes credit for the work of his brother, World Maker. World Maker makes the land and its animals, the sun and the creatures of the original deeps, and he makes people, two of each color of the earth. Nice to read aloud, read alone, or use for storytelling, this is adapted with humor and vitality.

103   **Baker, Betty.** *The Great Desert Race.* Macmillan, 1980. 80-16483. ISBN 0-02-708200-8. 144p. $8.95.

6–8   A lively story, set in 1908, is based on a real race that was run annually for several years between Los Angeles and Phoenix. Baker's addition of two sixteen-year-old girls as the driving team for a steam-powered automobile is fiction, and delightful fiction, as Trudy and Alberta compromise between the expected ladylike behavior of the period and their natural determination and ebullience. There's a stout vein of humor, clear characterization, good period and technical details, and a brisk narrative flow.

104   **Baker, Olaf.** *Where the Buffaloes Begin;* illus. by Stephen Gammell. Warne, 1981. 80-23319. ISBN 0-7232-6195-4. 41p. $8.95.

3–4
*   The illustrations for a story first published in the *St. Nicholas Magazine* in 1915 are an example of the best kind of book art, pictures that extend and complement the story, that are appropriate in mood, and that are distinctive in themselves. Blurred and soft, the spacious black and white scenes have a mystic quality as well as dramatic strength, echoing the mythic mood of the story and its sense of isolation. Stirred by the legend of his tribe, ten-year-old Little Wolf rides to the silvery lake where the buffalo are created, and he sees them rise from the water, mighty and gleaming in the moonlight. Shouting for joy, he is answered by the

roar of the animals as they begin a thundering stampede; Little Wolf joins them, and as they near his village he sees that an enemy is about to attack, leads the buffalo to ride over them, and saves his people.

105   **Balian,** Lorna. *Mother's Mother's Day;* written and illus. by Lorna Balian. Abingdon, 1982. 81-10988. ISBN 0-687-27253-X. 29p. $9.95.

4–6   While an understanding of the relationships among generations, and an
yrs.   understanding of the fact that generations of mice can co-exist while six generations of a human family would be rare, may be beyond the knowledge of young children, it is not beyond their comprehension. In this bright, brisk little story a mouse who brings her mother a gift finds no one at home because Mother has gone to bring her own mother a gift, and so on, unto the last generation, Great-Great-Great Grand- mother. And *she's* gone to see the youngest, so they are all assembled at the end of a slight but engaging story. The illustrations are a bit on the greeting-card-pretty side, but they have mice (appealing) as a sub- ject, clear colors, and graceful floral details, all set off by an ample amount of white space.

106   **Ballard,** Robert D. *Exploring Our Living Planet.* National Geographic, 1983. 83-2336. Trade ed. ISBN 0-87044-459-X; Library ed. ISBN 0-87044-397-6. 366p. illus. with photographs. Trade ed. $19.50; Library ed. $23.95.

7–   An oversize book about the knowledge gleaned from earth sciences is comprehensive, lavishly illustrated with color photographs (many that are stunningly handsome) and diagrams. The massive book describes the beginning of the planet Earth according to current theory, and dis- cusses the changes in the earth's surface (visible or underseas) and the causes for those changes. The text explains not only how such phenom- ena as continental drift and sea floor spreading occur, but also the work of scientists whose theories and research have given us knowledge of how mountains rise, why earthquakes occur and volcanoes erupt, and what goes on under the seemingly solid crust of land. Capably written and comprehensive, the book closes with some conjecture about what may happen in the future and about what questions remain unan- swered as yet. A glossary and an index are appended.

107   **Bang,** Molly. *Dawn;* written and illus. by Molly Bang. Morrow, 1983. 83-886. Trade ed. ISBN 0-688-02400-9; Library ed. ISBN 0-688-02404-1. 32p. Trade ed. $10.00; Library ed. $9.12.

2–4   A widowed shipbuilder tells his daughter Dawn the story of her mother, who died because he had insisted that she weave for a cus- tomer some sails of the same quality as the "Wings of Steel" she'd made for their own boat. Forbidden to enter the room, the man dis- obeyed and found a Canada goose (he had saved the life of one before the woman who became his wife appeared) but lost her when a flock of geese flew in and carried her away. Bang's story is a variant of a traditional folk theme, the animal-mate who resumes his or her original shape; the author has made a touching and effective tale of this, and has illustrated it handsomely with, alternately, delicately detailed framed paintings or soft black and white pictures; each page faces a page of calligraphy. The story ends with young Dawn setting off to find her mother and saying. "We'll be back in the spring, when the geese come north again." The addition of a child to the story, and the open ending, add little dignity to the tale, but it is possible that having a child character may be appealing to young readers.

108   **Bang,** Molly. *Ten, Nine, Eight;* written and illus. by Molly Bang. Greenwillow, 1983. 81-20106. Trade ed. ISBN 0-688-00906-9; Library ed. ISBN 0-688-00907-7. 19p. Trade ed. $10.50; Library ed. $9.55.

2–4   In countdown style, the text of this counting book begins with "10
yrs.   small toes all washed and warm," and ends with "1 big girl all ready for bed." The captions rhyme (albeit with flaws like "warm" and "room") and the pictures—warm, bright paintings—show a black father and child snuggling in a chair, the child yawning, and the child hugging her toy bear after some loving good night kisses. Useful as a counting book, this evokes a cozy feeling of being warm, clean, loved, and sleepy.

109   **Barber,** Richard. *A Companion to World Mythology;* illus. by Pauline Baynes. Delacorte, 1980. 79-16843. ISBN 0-440-00750-X. 312p. $14.95.

5–   Like Uden's *Dictionary of Chivalry,* this is in alphabetical arrangement,
*   the text printed in inner columns and the broad outer margins most beautifully illustrated by Baynes in color and in black and white. The pictures have no captions, and the one weakness of the book is that one cannot always tell what drawing matches what entry, but the entries are full enough to satisfy the reader's needs; they give enough information to enable users to pursue other sources. The intent of the book is the identification of the gods of the major myths of the world, and it is by their names that the text is arranged. Some entries are quite brief, just a few lines, but many give an abbreviated version of a myth, and among the several indexes is a useful one that refers from minor characters to the major ones listed in the text. A handsome book, and as useful as it is handsome.

110   **Bargar,** Gary W. *Life. Is. Not. Fair.* Houghton/Clarion, 1984. 83-15299. ISBN 0-89919-218-1. 174p. $11.95.

6–9   Louis, the narrator, has just entered junior high and he yearns to be one of the "cools," the small in-group that dominates the school socially. It isn't fair that his efforts to pull out, once involved and disillusioned, have no result, nor is it fair that a skit he devises to get revenge on the cools backfires: they think it's just wonderful. But Louis has already learned from DeWitt that life isn't fair; DeWitt is black, perse-

cuted by the cools and ignored by almost all his other classmates. He
has just become Louis' next door neighbor and he's the strongest character in the book: wise, self-contained and self-respecting, a cultured
and sophisticated adolescent. Another strongly drawn character is
Louis' aunt, with whom he lives: she's not a bad woman, but she's stupid and credulous, biased about the black family next door but willing
to be neighborly when there's trouble. Above all, this effective novel
gives a vivid picture of the power hierarchy of the classroom, with consistently good depictions of characters and their relationships.

111   **Bargar,** Gary W. *What Happened to Mr. Forster?* Houghton/Clarion, 1981.
80-28259. ISBN 0-395-31021-0. 171p. $8.95.

5–7   Tired of his babyish nickname, ''Billy Lou,'' Louis Lamb is determined
that things are going to be different now that he's in sixth grade. The
time is 1958, the place is Kansas City, the speaker is Louis, and there is
something new and different in his life: Mr. Forster, the teacher who
helps Louis realize that he can write and who coaches him in softball.
What happens to Mr. Forster is that, instigated by the vindictive
remarks of a woman whose daughter is the only child left out of a party
given by one of the boys in the class, the rumor that he is homosexual
spreads. And, after Mr. Forster has been fired, Louis goes to visit him
and learns that it is true—but he also knows that it has never been a
factor in his relationship with his teacher. Mr. Forster lives with another
man whom he loves, he explains. The writing in this first novel has
style and substance, emerging convincingly from Louis' viewpoint and
establishing—without overstressing—the unhappy situation of a rarely
good teacher who loses his position because of personal aspects of his
life.

112   **Barkin,** Carol. *The Complete Babysitter's Handbook;* by Carol Barkin and
Elizabeth James; illus. by Rita Floden Leydon. Wanderer/Simon &
Schuster, 1981. 80-12350. ISBN 0-671-33067-5. 128p. Spiral bound. $4.95.

6–10   Like other books by Barkin and James, this is a solid and sensible book,
with well-organized text and useful advice; written in a light, conversational style, it has moments of humor as well. There is advice on getting
and keeping babysitting jobs, handling children, indoor and outdoor
activities, appropriate books for children of different ages, and on the
practical matters of food, dress, bath, and bedtime. Sample sheets for
emergency information and for practical information are included, the
latter accommodating facts that may differ in different households, facts
about regular routines for meals, naps, bedtime hours, location of
clothes, rules about play and play equipment, et cetera.

113   **Barrett,** Ron. *Hi-Yo, Fido!;* written and illus. by Ron Barrett. Crown,
1984. 83-15110. ISBN 0-571-55215-9. 29p. $9.95.

2–4   The pinks and blues of the cartoon-style drawings don't seem to fit the
robust nonsense of this tall tale, but most readers will be too busy

snickering to object. Barrett has done a spoof of the Old West tale that takes a poke at all sorts of stereotypes, uses puns and word-play with abandon, and purportedly explains how cattle came to the Western plains. (They'd formerly been house pets, and were offered in exchange for the doggies that had inhabited the area and been stolen by rustlers). The humor is at just the right level for the intended audience.

114   **Barrie,** James Matthew. *Peter Pan;* illus. by Trina Schart Hyman. Scribner, 1980. 80-14510. ISBN 0-684-16611-9. 184p. $14.95.

4–6   In this new edition of a beloved classic, the minor attraction (in addition to the story of the boy who doesn't want to grow up) is the clear, large print and the major attraction the illustrations. Both in the black and white line drawings and in the full-page, full-color paintings, Hyman's elegant line and delicacy of detail are combined in effective compositions that have vitality and humor.

115   **Barth,** Edna, ad. *Balder and the Mistletoe: A Story for the Winter Holidays;* illus. by Richard Cuffari. Seabury, 1979. 78-4523. ISBN 0-8164-3215-5. 64p. $7.95.

4–6   Although the writing style is subdued, it seems not inappropriate for the gravity of this adaptation of a portion of Norse mythology; Barth has eschewed the softer variations and based her version of Balder's death on the Sturluson telling of the Icelandic Edda, and she has done a fine job of clarifying the complexities of the mythic characters. The goddess Frigga asks every living and non-living thing in the world to swear they will not harm her son Balder when he says he has dreamt of his own death—everything but the mistletoe. That information is cunningly drawn from her by the wicked Loki, and he uses it to kill Balder. The story ends with Balder in the underworld, doomed to stay until the final battle between the gods and the frost giants who threaten the world; a brief author's note describes the ways in which Balder was remembered in the rites of Norse, Celtic, and Germanic peoples and the symbolic use of mistletoe. Clean pages and good-sized print, combined with the directness and simplicity of the style, make this an eminently readable version, and it is enhanced by the dramatic and graceful Cuffari drawings, strong compositions of grays and white against an ochre background.

116   **Barton,** Byron. *Airport;* written and illus. by Byron Barton. T. Y. Crowell, 1982. 79-7816. ISBN 0-690-04168-3. 31p. Trade ed. $9.95; Library ed. $9.89.

2–4   Although this doesn't give as many details about flying as do several
yrs.   other books, it is an excellent choice for very young children: the text is minimal, the pictures are big and bold and bright, and it covers the salient points that a young child is likely to notice in the period that begins with arrival at the airport and ends with lift-off. The text shows the

bustle of passengers arriving and then waiting to board, the crews that check and load the airplane, and the preparatory work of control tower and flight crew.

117   **Barton,** Byron. *Building a House;* written and illus. by Byron Barton. Greenwillow, 1981. 80-22674. Trade ed. ISBN 0-688-80291-5; Library ed. ISBN 0-688-84291-7. 31p. Trade ed. $7.95; Library ed. $7.63.

3–6   Like the books by Anne and Harlow Rockwell, this has minimal text
yrs.   (never more than a line per page) and clear, spacious format and illustrations; the latter are spare, also, never cluttered with detail but given interest by strong colors and the use of perspective. Although there are a few double-page spreads, the format is primarily a full-page picture facing a white page with its single sentence: "Builders hammer and saw," or "Carpenters come and make a wooden floor," or "A plumber puts in pipes for water." Simple, clear, informative.

118   **Basile,** Giambattista. *Petrosinella: A Neapolitan Rapunzel;* ad. from the translation by John Edward Taylor; illus. by Diane Stanley. Warne, 1981. 80-25840. ISBN 0-7232-6196-2. 27p. $11.95; $10.95 until 12/31/81.

3–5   Based on the Taylor translation of 1847, this variant of the more familiar "Rapunzel" was first published in a collection of Italian tales compiled by Basile at the start of the seventeenth century. Typical of the source is the fact that the ogress of the story lives next door to the woman who later gives birth to the lovely little Petrosinella. (Pregnant, the woman had an uncontrollable urge to steal the parsley, the petrosinella, that grew in the ogress' garden.) The imprisonment in a tower, the coming of a handsome prince, the use of Petrosinella's long hair as a ladder, and the escape of the lovers are all expectable, but there are some differences in this Mediterranean version of the story, particularly in the lack of a refrain like "Rapunzel, Rapunzel, let down your hair" and in the details of the lovers' escape. This is a useful variant for the storyteller, it can be read aloud to younger children, and it can be enjoyed by readers of any age for the illustrations, strongly composed paintings with rich use of color and great delicacy of detail, softly grave in the true romantic tradition.

119   **Baskin,** Leonard. *Imps-Demons-Hobgoblins-Witches-Fairies & Elves;* written and illus. by Leonard Baskin. Pantheon Books, 1984. 84-2911. Library ed. ISBN 0-394-95963-9; Trade ed. ISBN 0-394-85963-4. 44p. Library ed. $12.99; Trade ed. $12.95.

4–7   The noted artist has let his imagination run riot in this collection of fey creatures, some of which are from literature, some from legend, and some invented. The paintings have great variety and spontaneity, a subtle use of color, and occasional notes of the humorous or the grotesque. Facing each picture is some kind of text: it may be a story (The Three Billy Goats Gruff, The Shoemaker and the Elves) in abbreviated version, or it may be identification and context (Ariel and Caliban) or it may be simply, eerily descriptive (the Witch of Dark Adventures, the Tooth Fairy, or Bloody Bones). If it weren't so clear that the author is having fun, this might be frightening. It's certainly memorable.

120   **Baskin,** Tobias. *Hosie's Aviary;* by Tobias Baskin & others; illus. by Leonard Baskin. Viking, 1979. 78-27027. ISBN 0-670-37965-4. 42p. $10.00.

4–   Twenty-one full page paintings (some, alas, cropped to fit the page) face brief, lyric statements written by the artist's wife and children. The pictures are stunning in their vigor, in the use of color, and in the way the artist has captured the personality of each bird. The layout is handsome and spacious, the text of variable quality: some descriptions have a haiku quality ("The thrush: How peevish! How melancholic!" or "Long hair and pencil bill, does this egret write poems?") while others ("Freedom's eagle") serve only as captions, and still others seem obscure ("Aloo Alix Egiy / The beak of the secretary bird / vents raucous screams") or intricate ("The bald eaglet screaming for food: the condition of growth—caught and revealed.") Younger children can enjoy the beauty of the paintings alone.

121   **Bates,** Betty. *My Mom, the Money Nut.* Holiday House, 1979. 78-24213. ISBN 0-8234-0347-5. 158p. $6.95.

4–6   Fritzi, adjusting to eighth grade in a new school, tells the story of her conflict with her mother, who wants Fritzi to go to business school when she's through high school, to get a part-time job, to forget singing (which is all Fritzi wants to do) and who has a drive to accumulate possessions. Not until she visits her grandfather and learns about the kind of childhood her mother had, does Fritzi understand: Mom's mother had died when she was four, and she had grown up with hard work and poverty, a life she wanted to put behind her forever. It helps a bit when Fritzi gets a solo part, helps even more when she finds a sympathetic teacher; she's then able to say "Poor Mom! All of a sudden I feel achy for her . . . I'm glad I can grow up, even if she can't." The family situation, explored with perceptive understanding, is balanced by Fritzi's experiences with friends and in school, the writing style is competent, and the development in Fritzi's understanding and acceptance is completely believable.

122   **Bauer,** Marion Dane. *Rain of Fire.* Houghton/Clarion, 1983. 83-2065. ISBN 0-89919-190-8. 153p. $10.95.

5–7   Set in the period just after World War II, this is a trenchant story of the ways in which children's attitudes toward war, enemies, heroism, and ethical conduct are shaped by events, by the ideas of adults, and by their own needs to be accepted and feel secure. Steve is twelve, bothered because his older brother has come back from Japan morose and

taciturn. Why won't Matthew talk to him as he once did? Steve's problems mushroom when Celestino, a bully who is older than Steve, calls
Matthew a "Jap-lover," and Steve, to protect his brother, weaves a network of defensive lies. Eventually, expectably, his lying is unmasked
and then Matthew explains for the first time his horror of killing, his
agony over what he has seen in Hiroshima. Steve, in self-created trouble with his few friends and in fear of Celestino, finally faces the fact
that his lies have made matters worse and begins to understand both
his own motivation for lying and his brother's feelings about the "rain
of fire." This is a serious but not a somber story, beautifully laminated
and perceptive in unfolding the intricacy of human relationships and
psychological interaction; it has good pace and momentum within its
tight frame.

123   **Bauer,** Marion Dane. *Tangled Butterfly.* Houghton/Clarion, 1980.
        79-23405. ISBN 0-395-29110-0. 162p. $7.95.

7–10   Remote and withdrawn, seventeen-year-old Michelle makes a scene at
        her beloved brother's wedding; her father suggests a doctor, but Mich-
        elle refuses. Her mother, a self-centered snob, won't hear of therapy,
        and decides to take Michelle on a little vacation. On a ferry en route to
        an island resort, Michelle's attempted suicide is foiled by a man who
        has watched her; Paul is a young Ojibway who has given up teaching
        because of his pain at being unable to help a psychotic student. Refus-
        ing to see what she can't bring herself to admit, Michelle's mother
        leaves the island; Paul and his wife care for Michelle, but it is Paul's
        concern and insight that bring Michelle to disclose the fact that she is
        ruled by another, inner, voice, the "grandmother" who counsels her. A
        second near-tragedy (Michelle kidnaps Paul's baby) brings a crisis and
        makes it clear to Michelle's family that she needs deep therapy; in a
        brief addendum, Michelle herself describes her feelings, her growing
        stability after therapy, and her plan to go back home to finish high
        school. "Butterflies look delicate, but they're really quite strong," she
        comments. Bauer's characterization is powerful, and her depiction of
        the intricacies of human relationships is as trenchant and sensitive as
        her insight into Michelle's troubled psyche.

124   **Baum,** Lyman Frank. *The Wizard of OZ;* illus. by Michael Hague. Holt,
        1982. 82-1109. ISBN 0-03-061661-1. 219p. $18.95.

3–5   A new edition of an old favorite is profusely illustrated with full-color
        paintings, rich in detail, romantic in mood but with touches of comedy,
        and quite attuned in mood and style to the period of publication: Doro-
        thy, for example, looks as though she had been drawn by an artist who
        was the contemporary of the original illustrator, W. W. Denslow. In
        sum, Michael Hague's paintings are handsome, they interpret the story
        beautifully, and they are particularly striking in depicting the setting.

125   **Bawden,** Nina. *Kept in the Dark.* Lothrop, 1982. 81-20765. ISBN 0-688-
        00900-X. 160p. $9.00.

5–7   Bawden at her best, and her best is very good indeed; in this taut story
  *   of a household menaced by a cruel bully, the suspense builds with terri-
       ble inevitability, and the interplay between and among characters is
       masterful. The viewpoint never shifts completely, but it changes in em-
       phasis as each of the three children, who are staying with their grand-
       parents because of parental illness, moves into the foreground almost as
       though they were on stage. An older cousin, swaggering and sadistic,
       foists himself on the household, terrorizes them and only at the point of
       crisis is driven away, more by accident than by the action of the chil-
       dren or the two old people. It is Clara who, when her parents return,
       makes the decision not to tell them what has happened; forever fretting
       about being kept in the dark by adults, Clara now understands why, for
       she realizes that her parents would only be upset if they knew, and that
       they could do nothing. A perceptive book, a good read, and a natural
       for film.

126   **Bawden,** Nina. *The Robbers.* Lothrop, 1979. 79-4152. Trade ed. ISBN 0-
       688-41902-X; Library ed. ISBN 0-688-51902-4. Trade ed. $6.95; Library
       ed. $6.67.

4–6   Solitary and happy, nine-year-old Philip lived with his grandmother in
       an apartment in a seaside castle; his mother was dead, his father a peri-
       patetic television reporter. When his father married an American, Philip
       went to London for what he thought was a visit; it proved to be a long
       stay. Precocious and articulate, Philip made only one friend, Darcy, a
       street-wise boy whose family (an arthritic father, brother Bing who was
       a street peddler, Bing's black wife Addie, a beautiful and sensitive
       woman) made Philip welcome. It is when Bing is sentenced for selling
       stolen goods that the two boys, desperate, plan their robbery of a rich
       neighbor's home. The deed is particularly significant because Philip's
       ethical sense is so strong; it is his sympathy (Bing jailed; Addie preg-
       nant) and loyalty to Darcy that make him break his own code. And it is
       in the disparate reactions of his cold, bullying father and his
       understanding grandmother (who goes to see Addie) that Philip finds
       the answer to the question of his future: he chooses to live with his
       grandmother. The characterization is superb, perceptive and trenchant;
       the writing style is polished, the book beautifully structured.

127   **Beatty,** Patricia. *The Staffordshire Terror.* Morrow, 1979. 79-21787. Trade
       ed. ISBN 0-688-22201-3; Library ed. ISBN 0-688-32201-8. 223p. Trade ed.
       $7.95; Library ed. $7.63 net.

5–7   Beatty has a message, the condemnation of dogfights, an illegal but
       flourishing business, but she doesn't let the message get in the way of
       the story. This hasn't the breezy humor of her Old West historical fic-
       tion, but it has just about everything else that makes a good story: be-
       lievable and well-differentiated characters, a well-structured story line, a
       brisk pace, and a smooth writing style that includes natural dialogue.

The pup that Cissie and her father found after its mother had been killed in a road accident proved to be a purebred Staffordshire terrier, a breed known for its fearlessness and belligerence. Cissie's uncle Cletus is the villain of the book, a coarse and brutal man whose timid daughter has left him; her escape had been engineered by Cissie and her cousin, so Cletus steals the dog—partly for revenge, partly to enter him in fights and make money. Cissie, with the cooperation of her family, tracks her dog down, calls in the police, and breaks up the local group who are sponsoring dogfights.

128   **Beatty,** Patricia. *Turn Homeward, Hannalee.* Morrow, 1984. 84-8960. ISBN 0-688-03871-9. 193p. $10.50.

5–8   More serious than most of Beatty's stories, this solid historical fiction shows how the Civil War affected one segment of the population—the southern mill workers—and is based on fact. Northern soldiers did burn down textile mills and, considering the workers traitors, sent them away from their homes. Here the protagonists are Hannalee and Jem, twelve and ten, who are shipped from their Georgia town (and their recently widowed, pregnant mother) to Indiana, where they are offered as workers to anyone who wants them. Jem is sent to a farm, Hannalee works as housemaid for a mistress so demanding that she runs away; after earning some money, Hannalee (by now disguised, for safety's sake, as a boy) collects her brother and they make their way back to home and mother. This is a very effective story, creating vividly the tragedy and disruption for ordinary people, showing clearly that there were villains and heroes on both sides of the bitter conflict. Structure, characterization, and style are solid; an extensive author's note points out those parts of the story that are factual and gives some background information about the Civil War.

129   **Beckman,** Delores. *My Own Private Sky.* Dutton, 1980. 79-23341. ISBN 0-525-35510-3. 154p. $7.95.

4–6   Arthur, eleven, describes his feelings of inadequacy and apprehension
  *   when he faces a new school and new peers; he's slight, he has prominent buck teeth, and he's terrified by the swimming lessons his mother insists he take. Because his widowed mother works, Arthur has to have supervision, and it is arranged that he stay with elderly Mrs. Kearns. The prospect is not enchanting—but Arthur very quickly succumbs to his new friend's warmth, honesty, and enjoyably eccentric ways. He is therefore stunned when she is in an accident and loses a leg, and he is deeply troubled by the fact that she loses her initiative and refuses to try to walk with an artificial leg. Arthur's facing his own trial at the same time: the test in his swimming class; and he comes to the pool even more shaken because he has just angrily berated Mrs. Kearns for her apathy. The story ends, believably, with each of the two drawing strength from the other's loving concern. Never mawkish, the story is

deeply moving, quietly amusing, always perceptive; while some of the characters are odd, all are strongly drawn, and the writing style is outstanding. An excellent first book.

130   **Belloc,** Joseph Hilaire Pierre. *The Bad Child's Book of Beasts;* illus. by Wallace Tripp. Sparhawk, 1982. 82-5939. ISBN 0-9605776-3-7. 42p. $4.95.

3-6   The rhythmic verses of an old favorite, first published in London in 1897, are newly and delightfully illustrated by the comic line drawings of a contemporary artist. Tripp's stout Victorian gentlemen seem straight out of a political cartoon, his children have an exaggerated air of sweetness or acerbity, and his animal faces have personality; occasionally the witty drawings are extended by balloon captions.

131   **Benjamin,** Carol Lea. *Nobody's Baby Now.* Macmillan, 1984. 83-18714. ISBN 0-02-708850-2. 144p. $10.95.

6-9   Fifteen-year-old Olivia is the narrator in a story that is lively, often funny, and just as often subtly sensitive. Overweight, Livi has a desperate crush on Brian, a schoolmate who regards her as a chum, someone to whom he can talk about the pretty blonde girls he finds attractive. That's one problem; the other is Grandma. First, Livi resents the fact that Grandma's been given Livi's room, then she's appalled by the fact that Grandma never talks or reacts to anything. Ambivalent about whether or not Grandma should or shouldn't be sent to a nursing home, she tries desperately to break through Grandma's wall—and she succeeds, Grandma begins to talk again. Then the question of home versus nursing home becomes even more acute. Both problems are solved realistically: Livi surprises Brian by kissing him (he responds with alacrity) and the book ends on a rosy note; the question of what to do about Grandma is settled when Livi tries to show how independent Grandma can be, almost causes an injury, and admits that Grandma can't live without having help available all the time. A believable handling of two common problems.

132   **Bennett,** Jill, comp. *Days Are Where We Live, and Other Poems;* illus. by Maureen Roffey. Lothrop, 1981. 81-8353. ISBN 0-688-00852-6. 39p. $8.50.

3-6   Slightly rakish pictures, more deft than comic valentines but in that
yrs.   style, are poster-simple, bold and bright, and they match the poems nicely. As she has in earlier mini-anthologies for young children, Bennett—a nursery school teacher—has chosen with discrimination; the poems are of high quality and appealing to children. Light, often funny, consistently seen from the child's viewpoint, the poetry represents the work of many of the best contemporary children's poets.

133   **Bennett,** Jill, comp. *Roger Was a Razor Fish; and Other Poems;* illus. by Maureen Roffey. Lothrop, 1981. 80-17166. Trade ed. ISBN 0-688-41986-0. 40p. Trade ed. $7.95.

1–2   First published in England, a modest selection of poems chosen by a nursery school teacher as appropriate for beginning independent readers; they are suitable, also, for reading aloud to very young children. Bright pastel paintings, discrete in composition and lightly humorous, illustrate a well-chosen group of brief poems; the authors represented are British and American.

134   **Berger,** Melvin. *Why I Cough, Sneeze, Shiver, Hiccup, and Yawn;* illus. by Holly Keller. Crowell, 1983. 82-45587. Trade ed. ISBN 0-690-04253-1; Library ed. ISBN 0-690-04254-X. 34p. Trade ed. $10.95; Library ed. $10.89.

K–3   Line drawings and diagrams illustrate a simple, lucid and accurate explanation of the several reflex actions cited in the title. Berger begins anecdotally: you're well-hidden in a game of hide-and-seek—and then you sneeze and everyone knows where you are. "Why do you sneeze—even when you don't want to?" In addition to the explanations of the reflex actions, the text discusses the familiar knee-jerk reaction, and it suggests trying another reflex test (making toes curl) that children can do for themselves.

135   **Berger,** Terry. *Ben's ABC Day;* illus. with photographs by Alice Kandell. Lothrop, 1982. 81-13754. Trade ed. ISBN 0-688-00881-X; Library ed. ISBN 0-688-00882-8. 26p. Trade ed. $9.50; Library ed. $8.59.

2–5 yrs.   Color photographs of good quality are used for an alphabet book that focuses on action: awakening, brushing, combing, dressing, and so on through the day until washing, x-ing (crossing the day off on the calendar), yawning and "zzzzzzzzz." The capital letter and the word appear, in large print, set off at the bottom of each page. This has, in addition to a clear presentation of letters and their association with words, the appeal of objects and events familiar to most young children as part of their daily routine, and it includes such activities as making cookies with a friend (under adult supervision one hopes, although this is not made specific) and helping with some household chores, as well as taking care of a pet—so it fosters concepts of independence, helpfulness, and cooperative behavior without preaching about them.

136   **Berndt,** Catherine H., ad. *Land of the Rainbow Snake: Aboriginal Children's Stories and Songs from Western Arnhem Land;* ad. and tr. by Catherine H. Berndt; illus. by Djoki Yunupingu. Collins, 1983. ISBN 0-00-184384-2. 96p. $10.95.

4–6   First published in Australia in 1979, this is a collection of tales gathered by the author, an anthropologist, from women Aborigines of western Arnhem Land; both the tales and the fifteen children's songs that are included at the back of the book were told in the Gunwinggu language. The songs (words in Gunwinggu and English) are briefly explained, and each story is followed by an explanation of the message or moral. Many of the tales are "why" stories, others incorporate taboos or cultural mores. The style is simple but rather static, so that the stories may be better used as a source for telling than for reading aloud. The book should be of interest to all students of folklore.

137   **Bess,** Clayton. *Story for a Black Night.* Houghton, 1982. 81-13396. ISBN 0-395-31857-2. 84p. $7.95.

5–8   "Ain't the night is black tonight? You would like to run playing, but the
*   darkness be too great for you. By force of storm, electric current came to fail . . ." And so a Liberian father tells his children a story of his childhood. Locked into their house, widowed Ma, baby sister Meatta, blind Old Ma, the grandmother, and the narrator, Momo, are startled when two women beg to be let in with their baby. Old Ma is opposed to taking them in, but Ma insists; in the morning, the women are gone and the baby clearly has been abandoned because she has smallpox. That is how tragedy comes to Momo's family, for Ma insists on nursing the waif. Meatta sickens and dies, while the other baby lives, and Ma herself contracts the disease and almost dies. The villagers nearby won't come near the house, but they solicitously bring food and medicine. Momo, too, gets smallpox and recovers. When the baby's grandmother turns up, her daughter dead, to claim the child, Ma refuses to give her up: the baby was abandoned, she saved the child, it is now her baby. The story is taut and tender, deftly structured, vivid in its depiction of the village community as well as of the family, but it is most distinctive in the writing style, which captures the lovely cadence of the language in its dialogue and has the warmth and sonority of the best kind of storytelling in its exposition. A stunning first novel.

138   **Betancourt,** Jeanne. *Smile! How to Cope With Braces;* illus. by Mimi Harrison. Knopf, 1982. 81-11800. Library ed. ISBN 0-394-94732-0; Paper ed. ISBN 0-394-84732-6. 84p. Library ed. $8.99; Paper ed. $5.95.

5–9   Betancourt begins with an explanation of dental structure and of the causes and classes of malocclusion, and with a description of the many dental problems that may result from malocclusion. The text discusses choosing an orthodontist, the devices used in orthodontic therapy, and the ways in which children cope, physically and emotionally, with wearing braces. The book concludes with an explanation of the importance of using a positioner or retainer after braces come out, so that teeth are kept straight and the individual's bite stays corrected. A short history of dentistry, an index, and the titles of several other books on orthodontics are provided, one of which (Alvin and Virginia Silverstein's *So You're Getting Braces: A Guide to Orthodontics*) is better illustrated, and covers most of the same material. Like the Silverstein book, this is written in a brisk, informal style and is logically organized and accurate.

139   **Bethancourt,** T. Ernesto. *Doris Fein: Quartz Boyar.* Holiday House, 1980. 80-15920. ISBN 0-8234-0378-5. 187p. $8.95.

6–9   A sequel to *Doris Fein: Superspy* has the same pell-mell ebullience and almost-mocking of the razzle-dazzle formula spy story. What Bethancourt does is keep the action going, but on a small scale. Doris, agreeing to transport what she thinks is a precious botanical sample to France, goes hurtling from Paris to Rome to London because the sample delivery is a cover operation for the tracking down of a Romanov chess piece (the boyar) made by Fabergé, and ultimately tracking down a master criminal who covets the boyar. Doris is in and out of danger; she is wooed by a charming Frenchman who then seems to be a villain and even later proves to be a hero (i.e. on her team); she is, at the end, ready to make more-than-friends. Lots of action, some humor; not a great spy story, but an easily assimilable one that's lots of fun.

140   **Bethancourt,** T. Ernesto. *Doris Fein: Superspy.* Holiday House, 1980. 79-23339. ISBN 0-8234-0408-0. 155p. $7.95.

6–9   A trip to New York is her high school graduation present; since her parents have already left for their vacation, Doris decides to get to New York a day early. After all, if her aunt and uncle aren't home, she can always stay in a hotel for one night. Her aunt isn't home, but her uncle, a UN representative of the small (invented) country of Dakama, is. There's a crisis, plans are changed, and she can't stay in their apartment, he says. At the hotel, she gets a note, purportedly from her aunt, but the handwriting's wrong. And that's how Doris and the attractive police department detective Carl Suzuki get embroiled in an intricate, dangerous, and fast-paced adventure. It's almost believable, save for some stock figures and for the fact that Doris emerges with twenty thousand dollars (her pay as a member of a federal agency, the employment having been a technicality at one point) with which she proposes to go off to Paris. What gives the story some substance—in addition to the pace and suspense—are the candor with which the Jewish protagonist and her Sansei colleague discuss minority groups and bias, and the cheerful honesty about her feelings expressed by Doris, who tells the story.

141   **Bethancourt,** T. Ernesto. *The Tomorrow Connection.* Holiday House, 1984. 84-47836. ISBN 0-8234-0543-5. 134p. $10.95.

6–9   Richie, the narrator, and his friend Matty have a time-travel adventure, going from 1976 to 1906, with a brief and unpleasant stop in 1912. They know that they can return only by passing through a gate to the future, but where is it and how do they get there? Taken under the wing of Houdini, the boys get jobs as assistants to the great magician's relative, Manfred, a not-so-great magician; however, his circuit takes the time travellers to San Francisco, where they think the gate is. In a dramatic climax, they find the gate after the famous earthquake, and then they learn what their futures will be after 1976. Matty will be the first black president of the U.S.A. and Richie a great historian. This has good pace, a brisk style, humor and some serious aspects, especially in the reaction of both Richie and Matty, but especially in the latter, to the way black people were treated in the beginning of the century. The presentation of Houdini isn't very convincing, despite the inclusion of several books about him in an appended bibliography that indicates authorial research, but the story does give interesting information about vaudeville in the period.

142   **Bible.** *A Child Is Born: The Christmas Story;* ad. by Elizabeth Winthrop; illus. by Charles Mikolaycak. Holiday House, 1983. 82-11728. ISBN 0-8234-0472-2. 26p. $14.95.

K–3   A deftly simplified story of the Nativity is based on the Books of St. Luke and St. Matthew, King James version. There are some omissions, but none of import, and Winthrop has kept the beauty of the Biblical language, deleting only for the sake of easy comprehension; for example, "sore" is deleted from the phrase ". . . and they were sore afraid." Mikolaycak's paintings are stunning; they are bold in composition but reverent in mood, colorful, and dramatic.

143   **Bible.** *I Am Joseph;* adapted by Barbara Cohen; illus. by Charles Mikolaycak. Lothrop, 1980. 79-20001. Trade ed. ISBN 0-688-41933-X; Library ed. ISBN 0-688-51933-4. 42p. Trade ed. $9.95; Library ed. $9.55.

3–5   In an adaptation that adheres to the Old Testament story, Joseph describes his brothers' jealousy, his captivity and rise to power in Egypt, and his reunion with his brothers and father. The use of first person adds depth and color to Joseph's story, making him a more rounded character; Cohen omits no part of the Biblical version, and her retelling is simple but trenchant. It is the illustrations that give the book its greatest impact, however: delicately framed against a quiet buff background, the pictures are spaciously composed but intricately detailed, sensuous, richly colored, and effective in the contrast between the softly modeled human forms and the geometric precision of costume or interior details.

144   **Bible.** *Jonah and the Great Fish;* ad. and illus. by Warwick Hutton. Atheneum, 1984. 83-15477. ISBN 0-689-50283-4. 30p. $12.95.

K–3   Hutton's retelling of a favorite Bible story is simple and casual; it is certainly appropriate for the read-aloud audience, but it is the illustrations rather than the text that will probably appeal to them. Hutton's watercolors, full-page or double-page spread, have vitality in their movement and a fine, controlled handling of color, and—above all—great sweep in composition.

145   **Bible.** *The Seven Days of Creation;* ad. and illus. by Leonard Everett Fisher. Holiday House, 1981. 81-2952. ISBN 0-8234-0398-X. 28p. $11.95.

all
ages

Oversize pages are used for the stunning paintings that show the creation of light and darkness, land and sea, of birds and beasts and fish and people, of the sun and moon and stars. Fisher's colors are rich, his composition bold, his adaptation simple without deviating from the spirit of the Biblical version. "Once there was a watery vastness without life or light. Only the spirit of God moved across the darkness," the book begins, the letters printed in electric blue against the black/blue/green stippling of the first page. Very handsome indeed.

146   **Bierhorst, John.** *A Cry From the Earth: Music of the North American Indians.* Four Winds, 1979. 78-21538. 113p. illus. $8.95.

6–

A description of American Indian songs and, to a lesser extent, of the instruments used to accompany singers, is designed both to show the wide variety of songs and to demonstrate the ways in which song is used in daily life as well as for ceremonial occasions. Bierhorst describes the techniques for vocal production, the sound coming from a tight throat and with a pulsing quality; he discusses the origins of American Indian song, and the variations of styles and techniques. Much of the text is devoted to descriptions—with notation—of different kinds of songs: songs for very young children, songs of war or mourning or love, prayer songs, dance songs. A most interesting book, written with simplicity and authority, has useful appended material: a key to musical symbols, another to pronunciation, a list of sources, suggestions for further reading and for listening, and an index to the songs by musical area and tribe.

147   **Bierhorst, John,** ed. *The Hungry Woman: Myths and Legends of the Aztecs;* illus. by Aztec Artists of the Sixteenth Century. Morrow, 1984. 83-25068. ISBN 0-688-02766-0. 148p. $10.50.

4–

Drawing directly from the 16th century Aztec narratives recorded shortly after the Spanish Conquest, Bierhorst's collection combines the stark dramatic stories with scholarship about their sources and meaning. In the traditional sequence the selection begins with the creation myths, including the story of "the hungry woman" with mouths all over her body "biting and moaning;" then come the sad stories of the fall of the great Tula civilization and the flight of the god Quetzalcoatl; fierce legends of the founding of Mexico, with the goddess crying to be fed with human blood; and the final rich legends of the coming of Cortes and Christianity, and the destruction of Mexico. Poetic, immediate, often grim (a creation myth ends, "there will be earthquakes. There will be hunger") these stories will appeal to all ages, for reading and telling. The spacious print is interspersed with black and white reproductions of original 16th century Aztec illustrations: painted under Spanish direction, these miniature pictures combine the more realistic European techniques with the diagram quality and comic-strip style frames of pre-Conquest tradition. In addition there are notes on sources, a pronunciation guide, glossary, and references; a long introduction analyzes the main features of the stories, their relations to Aztec history and belief, and the women figures still alive in popular tradition.

148   **Bierhorst,** John, ed. *The Sacred Path: Spells, Prayers and Power Songs of the American Indians.* Morrow, 1983. 82-14118. ISBN 0-688-01699-5. 191p. $9.50.

5–   Containing both traditional and contemporary material, this is a compilation of American Indian poetry that is arranged by stages of the life cycle, beginning with poems and chants of birth and infancy, and progressing through stages and activities of life to prayers and songs for the dying and the dead. As in his other anthologies, Bierhorst has chosen with discrimination; his preface discusses the ritual objects used on ceremonial occasions and the differences between forms of poetry in the Native American tradition. The tribal source for each selection is printed below the poem; appended are editorial notes, a bibliography of sources, and a glossary of tribes, cultures, and languages.

149   **Bierhorst,** John, tr. *Spirit Child: A Story of the Nativity;* illus. by Barbara Cooney. Morrow, 1984. 84-270. Library ed. ISBN 0-688-02610-9; Trade ed. ISBN 0-688-02609-5. 26p. Library ed. $11.04; Trade ed. $12.00.

3–4   Influenced by late Middle-Ages European tradition, composed in the Aztec language, and performed in Mexico City to the accompaniment of music in the middle of the sixteenth century, this has never before been translated into English. This combination of Biblical text, medieval lore, and Aztec culture is distinctive and colorful, told in a polished and poetic style. The illustrations are equally colorful, handsome in their composition, and faithful in interpretation, with the angel Gabriel carrying a feather fan and wearing his hair in the Aztec top-knot, as does the feather-crowned gold-braceleted Herod.

150   **Billings,** Charlene W. *Microchip: Small Wonder.* Dodd, 1984. 84-10179. ISBN 0-396-08452-4. 48p. illus. with photographs. $7.95.

3–5   Photographs of unimpressive quality illustrate a text that is capably organized, simply written, and spaciously printed. Billings explains how the microchip is made, how it functions, and what an improvement it is in making it possible for computers to do more faster. The text includes an explanation of the binary system and discusses possible advances of the future, such as biochips that will be instructed to "assemble more molecules like themselves." A one-page index is included.

151   **Black,** Hallie. *Animal Cooperation: A Look at Sociobiology;* illus. by photographs. Morrow, 1981. 81-1355. Trade ed. ISBN 0-688-00360-5; Library ed. ISBN 0-688-00361-3. 64p. Trade ed. $7.95; Library ed. $7.63.

6–9   An interesting introduction to a comparatively new scientific field is organized logically, first discussing sociobiology as an emergent science, next looking at recorded variations of social behavior among animals other than human beings, and finally discussing the implications of applied sociobiology to human beings and the controversy it has provoked. Black is scrupulous in distinguishing between fact and theory, lucid in explaining interpretations of human behavior in sociobiological terms, and objective in describing the strengths and weaknesses of sociobiology as a science. As for answers to the conflict among scientists, she points out, there are none at this time. An informative and provocative book concludes with a bibliography and a relative index.

152   **Blake,** Quentin. *Mister Magnolia;* written and illus. by Quentin Blake. Jonathan Cape, 1980. ISBN 0-224-01612-1. 30p. $8.95.

2–5 yrs.   Ebullient and vigorous, Blake's ink and watercolor pictures are in bright pastel colors set off by ample white space; his story is nonsensical, blithe, told in rhyme and—until the end—using innumerable words that rhyme with "boot." It begins "Mr. Magnolia has only one boot/ He has an old trumpet that goes rooty-toot/ And two lovely sisters who play on the flute/ But Mr. Magnolia has only one boot/ In his pond live a frog and a toad and a newt . . ." and so on. At the end, he feverishly unwraps a many-layered package: a boot! It doesn't match the one he has, but it gives him great joy. A merry, appealing book.

153   **Blegvad,** Erik, illus. *The Three Little Pigs.* Atheneum, 1980. 80-10410. ISBN 0-689-50139-0. 32p. $8.95.

3–5 yrs.   The delicate line, soft tints, and harmonious composition of Blegvad's small-scale drawings are nicely placed and appropriate in mood for a long-loved nursery tale. The pigs are amiable and the wolf ferocious in the story of one pig who, after two others have been eaten by the wolf who blows down their houses, not only has chosen the bricks that make his little house strong, but also outwits the wolf several times. Children enjoy the pattern, the suspense, the repetition of phrases, and the just fate that befalls the predator in this read-aloud story.

154   **Blos,** Joan W. *A Gathering of Days; A New England Girl's Journal, 1830–1832.* Scribner, 1979. 79-16898. ISBN 0-684-16340-3. 144p. $7.95.

5–7   Catherine is thirteen in 1830, when her journal begins; since the book is in diary form it has no plot, although it is given continuity by one thread: the mystery of the identity of the fugitive for whom Cath has left food and a blanket, and about whom she has ambivalent feelings. She adjusts to a stepmother, mourns the death of her best friend, and records the small pleasures of New Hampshire life: nutting, berrying, sugaring off, as well as her own small problems—like making a quilt in reparation for having given away the one she'd taken for the fugitive slave. Both in the incident of the slave (was she right to be humane, or was her father right in his attitude about upholding the law?) and in many references to historical events, the author gives a good sense of the period and its concerns, and a sense of the peaceful rural community.

155   **Bluestone,** Naomi. *"So You Want to Be a Doctor?" The Realities of Pursuing Medicine As a Career.* Lothrop, 1981. 81-2545. ISBN 0-688-00739-2. 241p. $12.95.

8–   Tough, practical, at times caustic in her humor, the author of this combination of experience and advice is not of the it's-beautiful-to-help-serve-humanity school. Bluestone had trouble as a Jew and a woman, and she also had her share of the problems all medical students have of adjusting to a heavy schedule and a great deal of information to absorb, of the long program and the burden of responsibility, of the feelings of inadequacy and resentment that becoming a doctor can—and usually do—evoke. There's no nonsense here but a good deal of wit, salting the style and the author's occasionally acidulous but well-expressed attitudes.

156   **Blumberg,** Rhoda. *The First Travel Guide to the Bottom of the Sea;* illus. by Gen Shimada. Lothrop, 1983. 82-17938. ISBN 0-688-01692-8. 74p. $9.50.

4–6   As she did in *The First Travel Guide to the Moon* Blumberg posits a voyage and describes the fictional accommodations, meals, entertainment, etc. This has rather less the format and style of a guidebook, since the passengers are not able to leave the submarine, but it gives a great deal of information about topographical phenomena of the sea bottom and about the creatures of the deep sea. The writing style is competent, casual, and direct; an index and a bibliography are included.

157   **Blumberg,** Rhoda. *The First Travel Guide to the Moon; What to Pack, How to Go, and What to See When You Get There;* illus. by Roy Doty. Four Winds, 1980. 80-66244. ISBN 0-590-07663-9. 83p. $7.95.

4–8   A straight-faced spoof, this covers all of the usual facets of travel literature; planning the trip, packing, advice about the trip itself, facts about hotels, excursions, sports, newspapers, entertainment, etc. Brisk and imaginative, this incorporates many facts about space flight and about the moon, and anticipates lunar tourism in blithe fashion.

158   **Blume,** Judy. *The Pain and the Great One;* illus. by Irene Trivas. Bradbury, 1984. 84-11009. ISBN 0-02-711100-8. 28p. $10.95.

K–3   Ink and watercolor illustrations that have considerable vitality and humor extend a text that is based on part of *Free to Be. . . You and Me*, by Marlo Thomas and others. Blume adds insight and wit in this fresh and wistfully funny adaptation; in separate monologues, a boy of six (The Pain) is described by his sister, two years older (The Great One) and he offers his scathing opinion of her in the other. What emerges is a perfect picture of sibling rivalry and jealousy, and both monologues end with "I think they love her/him better than me." In both cases, this gloomy suspicion is preceded by a hearty "YUCK!" as a climax to the listing of the most grievous sins of the other. Right on target and very amusing.

159   **Blume,** Judy. *Superfudge.* Dutton, 1980. 80-10439. ISBN 0-525-40522-4. 166p. $7.95.

3–5   In a sequel to *Tales of a Fourth Grade Nothing* Peter, now in fifth grade, views with gloom the prospect of spending the next year in another town while Dad takes a leave of absence to write a book. He's not enthralled to learn that his mother is pregnant and even less so at the prospect of having his pesky small brother, Fudge, going to the same school. This is better knit than the first book, since there are several threads that tie the episodic chapters together, but basically it is another series of anecdotes about the redoubtable, precocious Fudge and it's very funny: lightly sophisticated, wry but sunny, with firm characterization and good dialogue.

160   **Blumenthal,** Shirley. *Coming to America; Immigrants from the British Isles;* by Shirley Blumenthal and Jerome S. Ozer. Delacorte, 1980. 80-65841. ISBN 0-440-01071-3. 184p. $9.95.

7–10   In a survey that has both depth and breadth, the authors describe the English, Irish, Welsh, and Scottish immigrants who came to the United States, examining the several reasons that impelled their immigration: political persecution, a desire for religious freedom, or famine being the primary causes. The text discusses some of their experiences en route and on arrival in the United States, and is given variety by the inclusion of excerpts from letters, journals, and contemporary books. The coverage is full, including examples of recent immigrants and of participation in public life by those of British or Irish heritage. Well written and well researched, the book includes a section of notes (divided by chapters and distinguishing between primary and secondary sources), a bibliography, a chronological list of U.S. immigration laws, and a relative index.

161   **Bober,** Natalie S. *Breaking Tradition: The Story of Louise Nevelson.* Atheneum, 1984. 83-15618. ISBN 0-689-31036-6. 192p. $12.95.

7–10   Coming from a Russian shtetl to a New England seacoast town was a big change for the Berliawsky family, but Louise and the other children adjusted fairly happily to their new environment. A sympathetic art teacher helped Louise find her way, and after marriage and a move to New York the new Mrs. Nevelson explored and expanded; she was interested in singing, in dance, in art above all. Most of this biography shows how an individual artist moves toward a form of expression in which she or he feels there is integrity and a personal voice. Now in her eighties and acknowledged as one of the major artists in the United States, Nevelson is portrayed as a dynamic and dramatic figure. The writing style is a bit tedious, but the vibrancy of the subject compensates for this. A list of sources is provided in the chapter notes; also appended is a divided bibliography.

162   **Bodecker,** N. M. *Snowman Sniffles;* written and illus. by N. M. Bodecker. Atheneum, 1983. 82-13927. ISBN 0-689-50263-X. 67p. $8.95.

2–4   Line drawings, very small and very animated, illustrate a cheerful collection of deft and usually brief poems that are just as suitable for reading aloud to younger children as for the independent reader in the primary grades. The poems have wit and humor, and—albeit less often—evocative imagery, and they are all child-oriented, many of them about animals or weather. The book has nice integration of text and illustration on pages with plenty of space to set off the poems.

163   **Bond,** Michael. *Paddington Takes the Test;* illus. by Peggy Fortnum. Houghton, 1980. 80-16972. ISBN 0-395-29519-X. 126p. $6.95.

3–5   Paddington, for the eleventh time, again illustrated by the remarkably economic and rakish line drawings of Fortnum. All of Paddington's fans know exactly what to expect and they get just that, as the small bear stumbles into one catastrophe after another. Every time, of course, Paddington emerges in mild triumph, usually quite unaware that he has left a trail of baffled or frustrated Londoners in his wake. The style is sprightly, as always, in this volume, in which Paddington takes a driving test, poses as a model for an art class, and accidentally locks a disagreeable neighbor into a steam bath.

164   **Bond,** Nancy. *Country of Broken Stone.* Atheneum, 1980. 79-23271. ISBN 0-689-50136-3. 271p. $10.95.

6–9   Fourteen-year-old Penelope acts as a buffer state between her engaging but self-centered father and her rebellious brother; she's adjusted to living with a stepmother, Valerie, whose twin boys are obstreperous and whose small daughter is bereft—for all of them have come to stay in a gloomy old house in the north of England while Valerie works on a dig. Excavating a Roman fort, the archaeological team is aware that they're unwanted by the local residents, that the number of things going wrong at the dig is unprecedented. Penelope becomes involved with a local lad who is clearly torn between admiration for her and resentment because she is one of the interlopers. She begins to understand, through him, why there are currents of hostility, and so—when a fire does so much damage that the archaeological project has to be abandoned—she is able to have a last meeting with her friend and feel no rancor. The story has an interesting setting and solid structure, but it is the writing style, polished and fluent, that dominates the story; Bond's characters are drawn with depth, they are distinct and consistent, and she uses dialogue—and dialect within the dialogue—masterfully, both to develop characterization and to establish mood.

165   **Bond,** Nancy. *A Place to Come Back To.* Atheneum, 1984. 83-48745. ISBN 0-689-50302-4. 204p. $12.95.

6–9   Charlotte, who was twelve years old in *The Best of Enemies* is now an adolescent. She doesn't quite understand why it is so unsatisfying that she is always paired with Andy, and Oliver with Andy's sister Kath; her developing awareness of her love for Oliver is one of the two plot lines of the book—the other is Oliver's painful adjustment to the death of the great-uncle with whom he happily has lived. Oliver inherits the house, and it (as well as the Concord setting) is his "place to come back to," a promise for the future after he goes away with his mother and her new husband, who feel he is too young to stay in Concord on his own. This is more cohesive than the first book, a perceptive story written in polished style.

166   **Bond,** Nancy. *The Voyage Begun.* Atheneum, 1981. 81-3481. ISBN 0-689-50204-4. 319p. $12.95.

6–10   Paul has come to Cape Cod with his parents because the government has sent his stern, rigid father to the Research Station; his mother tries to keep up her social standards in the isolation of their lives; Paul is ignored by the local adolescents (who meet him at school) because he's a "Station kid." For this is the future, a future in which the region is ecologically moribund, a victim of the pollution and greed that have affected the energy resources and the economy of the whole country. This is the setting for what is probably Bond's most gripping story (and the others have been very good indeed) and one that is most pertinent to our lives. The characters, drawn with depth and nuance, are oddly assorted: a tough girl of eleven, her even tougher brother (a young adolescent and already a petty criminal), and two adult friends brought in by Paul, all united in a secret effort to find and recondition an abandoned boat so that one old man can be stirred from his lethargy and moved out of a nursing home. The chapters are usually from either Paul's or Mickey's (the girl's) viewpoint and move together in a smooth fusing that is like the fusing of Mickey's interests and those of the old man, or of Mickey's friendship with Paul, a relationship that begins with suspicion and hostility. Hard to say which is the more impressive, the merging of characters and story line, or the convincingly bleak context for the events.

167   **Bonham,** Frank. *The Forever Formula.* Dutton, 1979. 79-11381. ISBN 0-525-30025-2. 181p. $8.50.

7–10   Science fiction buffs will find the familiar device of revival after cryogenic storage used here as an interesting device for exploration of the problems that might be caused by having longevity as the controlling factor in a brave new world. Evan is thawed and revived in a hospital of the future where a doctor is determined to pull from the young man's brain the secret of eternal life; Evan had heard his father, a research scientist, refer to it before his death. Evan becomes involved in the struggle between the elderly (people over 150) who are in power and the underground network of people who are tired of the heaped garbage, deserted cities, depletion of oxygen, infestation by rodents and insect pests, and other side effects of a civilization in which the majority of inhabitants are sitting about waiting (many of them, feeling bored and useless, hoping) to die. Bonham quite deftly works a love story (Evan and his cloned nurse) into a book with plenty of action and some provocative ideas.

168   **Bonners,** Susan. *A Penguin Year;* written and illus. by Susan Bonners. Delacorte, 1981. 79-53595. Trade ed. ISBN 0-440-00166-8; Library ed. ISBN 0-440-00170-6. 44p. Trade ed. $9.95; Library ed. $9.43.

K–3   Soft watercolor pictures (blue, black, and white) effectively illustrate a simply written text that, while it gives names to a pair of penguin parents, has no anthropomorphism. As the title indicates, the text describes the cycle of the penguin year; it focuses on mating, nesting, and caring for the young. While there are several good books on penguins for the primary and middle grades, including the Todd book on the topic, none is quite so appropriate for the preschool child's introduction to the subject as this concise and handsomely illustrated book.

169   **Bonsall,** Crosby Newell. *The Case of the Double Cross;* written and illus. by Crosby Bonsall. Harper, 1980. 80-7768. Trade ed. ISBN 0-06-020602-0; Library ed. ISBN 0-06-020603-9. 64p. (I Can Read Books) Trade ed. $6.95; Library ed. $7.89.

1–3   Bonsall's bouncy sketches of raffish children add action to an easy to read story about boy-girl relations; although the breezy tale is humorous, it makes a point. Irritated because the boys have a clubhouse sign that says "No Girls," Marigold and her friends execute a plan to baffle the boys. A funny little bearded man gives the youngest boy a coded note; the boys try with frenzied frustration to catch the man (readers will see from the pictures that there are several small, bearded men) and when they discover it's Marigold (and friends) they offer to let the girls join the club. Marigold holds out for removal of the sign, and for a change of name that will indicate the change of heart, and everybody's satisfied. Readers will probably enjoy the fact that the last page ends with, "The Beginning." A bit exaggerated, but it's fun, and it's good reading practice for beginners.

170   **Booss,** Claire, ed. *Scandinavian Folk and Fairy Tales.* Crown, 1984. 84-442. ISBN 0-517-43620-5. 666p. illus. $7.98.

4–6   It is too bad that the print is small and the illustrations somber in this otherwise impressive anthology of traditional folk and literary tales from Norway, Sweden, Denmark, Finland, and Iceland. A long and interesting introduction precedes the tales, but seems addressed to adults rather than to children. Within the material from each country, there are division of different kinds: Swedish tales are divided geographically, for example, Icelandic tales by subject, and Norwegian are not divided. There is no index by titles, unfortunately. Older readers who are studying folklore as a genre should find the book interesting.

171   **Borghese,** Anita. *The Down to Earth Cookbook;* rev. ed.; illus. by Ray Cruz. Scribner, 1980. 80-21483. ISBN 0-684-16618-6. 144p. $8.95.

5–7   The material that precedes the recipes in a well-organized cookbook includes a discussion of American dietary habits, descriptions of some natural foods, definitions of culinary terms and utensils, and some general instructions on reading recipes, assembling materials, and taking safety precautions. Lists of ingredients are given clearly. A temperature conversion chart and index are appended.

172   **Bosse,** Malcolm J. *Ganesh.* T. Y. Crowell, 1981. 80-2453. Trade ed. ISBN 0-690-04102-0; Library ed. ISBN 0-690-04103-9. 185p. Trade ed. $8.95; Library ed. $8.79.

6–9   Jeffrey had lived most of his fourteen years in India, where his nickname was Ganesh. When his father died, the boy came to his only relative, Aunt Betty; as unaccustomed to the climate as he was to the mores and interests of his peer group, Jeffrey has some adjustment problems, but he arouses the interest of classmates when he beats the school record for staying under water, a feat accomplished by the controlled breathing he's learned in studying Yoga. Then they become interested in Hinduism, and Jeffrey begins to make friends. The dramatic action culminates in a group of friends participating in a sit-down to prevent the state from taking over Aunt Betty's home for a highway, a sit-down that concludes with a hunger strike, that wins the approbation of the community, and that is successful. An interesting story of cultural fusion and peer relationships has a quiet dignity that contrasts effectively with the colorful and unusual material about India and its cultural patterns.

173   **Bossom,** Naomi. *A Scale Full of Fish and Other Turnabouts;* written and illus. by Naomi Bossom. Greenwillow, 1979. 78-13293. Trade ed. ISBN 0-688-80203-6; Library ed. ISBN 0-688-84203-8. 24p. Trade ed. $6.95; Library ed. $6.67 net.

4–7
yrs.   Boldly designed color woodcuts illustrate a text that plays with words in a way that should amuse young children and may encourage them to try their own "turnabouts." A few examples of the paired statements on facing pages: "Box in a ring" shows sparring partners, and "Ring in a box" shows a small jewelry box: "Race for a train" shows scurrying passengers, and "Train for a race" shows three runners; "A scale full of fish" shows fish being weighed, while "A fish full of scales" shows a single fish.

174   **Boutet De Monvel,** Maurice. *Joan of Arc;* written and illus. by Maurice Boutet De Monvel; introduction by Gerald Gottlieb. Viking, 1980. 80-5169. ISBN 0-670-40735-6. 55p. $12.95.

4–6   An introduction by Gerald Gottlieb, Curator of Early Children's Books at the Pierpont Morgan Library, which owns a copy of the 1896 edition from which this was adapted, gives background about both the subject and the artist. The biography has dramatic and historical appeal, and the stunning paintings, intricately detailed but never cluttered, filled with action, and authentic in costume, architecture, and military equipment, add to the value of the book.

175   **Boutis,** Victoria. *Katy Did It;* illus. by Gail Owens. Greenwillow, 1982. 81-1034. Trade ed. ISBN 0-688-00688-4; Library ed. ISBN 0-688-00689-2. 88p. Trade ed. $9.50; Library ed. $8.59.

2–4   Eight-year-old Katy, although she didn't enjoy hiking as much as the rest of her family did, couldn't resist the offer from Daddy to go off alone with him on a three-day hike in the Adirondacks, with their dog Toby as a companion. This has no moments of high drama, but is a realistic account (buttressed by the realism of soft pencil drawings in tones of gray) of some of the pleasures and some of the hardships of backpacking. Katy does not enjoy the chill rain, the night noises, or the weight of her pack, but there are minor pleasures and, at the close of the book, the major pleasure of having accomplished her goal, reaching the top of the mountain. There's a warm father-daughter relationship, the satisfaction of achievement, and authentic details of hiking to give breadth to a smoothly written story.

176   **Bowe,** Frank. *Comeback: Six Remarkable People Who Triumphed Over Disability.* Harper, 1981. 80-8195. ISBN 0-06-010489-9. 172p. $12.50.

8–   Bowe, who has himself adjusted to the handicap of deafness, describes six men and women who have not only adjusted to their disabilities, but who have also been signally successful in their chosen careers. Although Bowe describes events from his subjects' viewpoints and frequently cites their comments, this is descriptive narrative rather than edited interviews; the writing style is forthright, the tone candid. The profiles give well-balanced accounts of the personal and professional lives, the obstacles and the triumphs, of a poet, a physicist, a restaurant worker, a neurochemist, a social activist, and a sex counselor who works with the handicapped. Sources of additional information are cited, and a bibliography that includes background information as well as works by some of the six subjects of the book is provided.

177   **Boynton,** Sandra. *A is for Angry;* written and illus. By Sandra Boynton. Workman, 1983. 83-40038. ISBN 0-89480-453-7. 37p. $9.95.

4–6   The idea of combining an alphabet book with a series of adjectives
yrs.   probably shouldn't work, but it does—con brio! First, this fulfills the

primary requirements of an alphabet book: the letters are large and
clear, the word-association is provided, and readers can see upper and
lower case letters. The pages are spacious, the concept handled with
humor, and the animal characters that illustrate the adjectives are well-
drawn, appropriately angry (anteater) or bashful (bear). Slightly car-
toonish, the drawings are brisk, bright, and funny. A winner.

178   **Brancato,** Robin F. *Sweet Bells Jangled Out of Tune.* Knopf, 1982. 81-
14283.Trade ed. ISBN 0-394-84809-8; Library ed. ISBN 0-394-94809-2.
200p. Trade ed. $9.95; Library ed. $9.99.

6–9   Ellen, fifteen, lives in a small town with her widowed mother; her maternal grandparents live nearby, and so does Eva, her father's mother—
but she is forbidden to see Grandma Eva, who has become increasingly
eccentric and senile and lives alone in a dilapidated mansion at the edge
of town. Eva, once the wealthy and beautiful town belle, is tolerated by
everybody, even when she steals, but she is also an outcast, and Ellen—who remembers Eva's love and kindness in the past—is miserably
aware that only she cares for the old woman. She secretly visits her and
realizes that she must get help although she fears that intervention will
lead to Eva's being put into an institution. Ellen's dilemma about Eva is
deftly meshed with her relationships with her other grandparents and
her mother, and with a growing affection for a sympathetic boy who
knows about Eva and helps Ellen long before she capitulates, tells her
mother, and gets professional help. Brancato's insight and perception
make Ellen's ambivalence clear and also make the attitudes of others
understandable in a smoothly written story that has suspense and
pace—and just a bittersweet trace of pathos.

179   **Brandenberg,** Franz. *Aunt Nina's Visit;* illus. by Aliki. Greenwillow,
1984. 83-16531. Library ed. ISBN 0-688-01766-5; Trade ed. ISBN
0-688-01764-9. 29p. Library ed. $10.51; Trade ed. $11.50.

4–7
yrs.   Aliki's animated and colorful pictures, line and wash, are exactly right
for the cheerful tone and busy scenes of a lively story about pets and
play. Moping about on a rainy day, Alex and Alexandra are delighted
by visits from two sets of cousins. Just as they face the awful truth—if
everybody's in the puppet show there won't be an audience—Aunt
Nina shows up to serve that function and to distribute six kittens. The
kittens disrupt the puppet show, lunch time, and a communal rest period, but everybody enjoys every minute. Nicely written and illustrated,
this should have universal appeal.

180   **Brandenberg,** Franz. *Leo and Emily;* illus. by Aliki, Greenwillow, 1981.
80-19657. Trade ed. ISBN 0-688-80292-3; Library ed. ISBN 0-688-84292-5.
55p. Trade ed. $5.95; Library ed. $5.71.

1–2   In three chapters, this book for beginning independent readers incorporates humor, friendship values, enterprise, and some excellent familial

relationships. Next door neighbors, Leo and Emily are given to dawn meetings that necessitate dressing in the dark, thereby permitting parents to sleep but producing some odd results in appearance; they trade precious possessions for a day (Emily's grandmother's wig and Leo's family's rabbit) and they put on a magic show. Every adult—even wigless Grandma—is tolerant about small lapses and appreciative about small accomplishments. Aliki's people are small, brisk, and amusing; a nice integration—both in mood and in page layout—of drawings and text.

181   **Branley,** Franklyn Mansfield. *Comets;* illus. by Giulio Maestro. Crowell, 1984. 83-46161. Library ed. ISBN 0-690-00415-1; Trade ed. ISBN 0-690-04414-3. 30p. (Let's-Read-And-Find-Out Science Books). Library ed. $10.89; Trade ed. $11.50.

K–3   Former chairman of the Hayden Planetarium and a prolific author of children's astronomy books, Branley writes with authority, simplicity, and clarity, in a carefully illustrated book on comets. He explains their development, their orbits, and their composition and focuses on what is known about Halley's comet, which will be visible in 1986. Maestro uses a black night sky as the background for most of his pictures, a very effective way of showing planets, comets, dust clouds, and other phenomena that are bright against the darkness. Like most of Branley's books, impeccable.

182   **Branley,** Franklyn Mansfield. *Feast or Famine? The Energy Future.* T. Y. Crowell, 1980. 79-7817. Trade ed. ISBN 0-690-04040-7; Library ed. ISBN 0-690-04041-5. 87p. Trade ed. $7.95; Library ed. $7.89.

6–9   Branley, always explicit and lucid in his science writing for children and young people, discusses in a well-organized text some of the specific problems and solutions of the energy crisis. He addresses first the problem of providing alternate sources, other than forms of fossil fuels, for cars, houses, and transportation; he then moves to various ways of eliminating or reducing waste, and goes on to describe the production of electrical energy, including nuclear, solar, tidal, and geothermal energy as well as wind power, the processing of organic wastes, and photosynthesis. A well-rounded survey, the book makes it clear that although supplies of gas and oil are not yet depleted, they will be—and that the time to conserve what we have and to plan for alternative sources is now. A list of books for further reading is included.

183   **Branley,** Franklyn Mansfield. *Is There Life in Outer Space?;* illus. by Don Madden. Crowell, 1984. 83-45057. Library ed. ISBN 0-690-04375-9; Trade ed. ISBN 0-690-04374-0. 29p. (Let's-Read-And-Find-Out Science Book.) Library ed. $10.89; Trade ed. $11.50.

2–3   This should be as intriguing and, when read aloud, as comprehensible to the preschool child as it is to the independent reader. It is written

simply, but with no condescension, it has lively and imaginative illustrations, and it is both succinct and lucid in describing what investigations have shown about the moon and Mars, what is known about
other planets in the solar system that makes it unlikely that they sustain
life, and what probably exists of life on planets in other galaxies. Good
scientist that he is, Branley makes it clear that his opinions on the last
topic are conjectural.

184   **Branley,** Franklyn Mansfield. *Mysteries of the Universe;* illus. with diagrams by Sally J. Bensusen. Lodestar, 1984. 83-25302. ISBN
0-525-66914-0. 71p. $10.95.

6–   A distinguished astronomer who has been a prolific author of excellent
science books for children and young people, Branley here again exemplifies good scientific principles. There are clear distinctions drawn between facts and theories, the information is authoritative and is logically
arranged, and the text moves always from the more to the less familiar.
Giving background information to help readers understand the nature
of the questions he poses (What are supernovas? How and when did
galaxies form? Why do pulsars pulse?) and answers. A bibliography and
a carefully compiled index are appended.

185   **Branley,** Franklyn Mansfield. *Shivers and Goose Bumps: How We Keep
Warm;* illus. by True Kelley. Crowell, 1984. 82-45921. Library ed. ISBN
0-690-04335-X; Trade ed. ISBN 0-690-04334-1. 95p. Library ed. $10.89;
Trade ed. $11.50.

5–8   Clearly written, authoritative, and comprehensive, this is an excellent
discussion of the ways in which the human body loses heat and copes
with that heat loss. There are descriptions of the ways animals keep
warm, and the range of solutions for people extends from such involun-
tary mechanisms as shivers and goose bumps to kinds of clothing,
houses, and building insulation. A brief bibliography and a fairly extensive index are provided.

186   **Braymer,** Marjorie. *Atlantis: The Biography of a Legend.* Atheneum, 1983.
82-16727. ISBN 0-689-50264-8. 215p. $12.95.

7–   This is a fine example both of objective and comprehensive reporting
and of painstaking research; in a smooth-flowing account, Braymer
discusses all of the theories, archeological discoveries, arguments and
counter-arguments, and writings about the legend of the rich land lost
beneath the sea—or was it buried by a combination of flood and volcanic debris? Painstakingly, the text traces every discovery that led
explorers to claim they had found the legendary land; it concludes
with the research of Angelos Galanopoulos, in 1956, that led to his announcement of an error in the Platonic account that had included the
measurements of Atlantis as well as the date on which it had been described by Solon (on whom Plato drew) as the time when Atlantis sank

into the sea, and goes on to describe the excavations at Thera (now called Santorini), an island that fits the physical description by Plato, that has ruins shown by carbon dating to be of the correct period, and that has a highly complex, planned city of sophisticated architecture and artifacts buried and damaged by volcanic action. A bibliography and an index are added to a text that combines historical interest and the appeal of a mystery story.

187   **Bridgers,** Sue Ellen. *All Together Now.* Knopf, 1979. 78-12244. 238p. Trade ed. $7.95; Library ed. $7.99 net.

5–7
*

Twelve-year-old Casey (K.C.) spends a summer with her grandparents and has more joy—and sorrow—than the boredom she'd expected, primarily because Dwayne Pickens becomes her friend. A retarded man of thirty, Dwayne assumes that Casey is a boy, his new baseball buddy, and she cannot bear to disillusion him. She also acts as a catalyst in the reunion of a middle-aged couple who had quarreled and separated on their honeymoon. Casey's sorrow is due to a court case, Dwayne's embarrassed brother having tried to have Dwayne committed to an institution, a move that is prevented when all Dwayne's friends rally to testify on his behalf. Bridgers achieves a difficult task, making her story child-focused despite the fact that Casey is the only child in it, an achievement due in part to the perspicacity of her interpretation of Casey's feelings, and in part to the fact that the viewpoint is always that of the narrator or of Casey herself. A mature story, nicely knit and paced, and giving an affective picture of a small southern community as well as of a sensitive child.

188   **Briggs,** Raymond. *When the Wind Blows;* written and illus. by Raymond Briggs. Schocken Books, 1982. 82-5780. ISBN 0-8052-3829-8. 38p. $10.95.

8–

From England, a shocker. Briggs tells a story in cartoon strips, using only two characters: an elderly husband and wife who don't understand what is happening, and whose dialogue is full of baffled ignorance and malapropisms. They hear that an atomic bomb has been launched, try to follow the confusing directions for safety measures, fuss about inconvenience, remember the last war with nostalgia, emerge from their ineffectual shelter before they are supposed to, and find that the utilities don't work and the garden is scorched. The book ends with their doleful prayers after they have begun to show symptoms of radiation sickness which they don't recognize. Three times the pattern of the format is broken by a dark, foreboding double-page spread: a space missile is launched, a malevolent black shape looms in the ocean, and the shadows of bombers move across a cold gray sky. For all its sardonic humor, the book is tough and grim, focused on its message and effective in conveying that message despite the details that slow the pace but ramify the concept that many—if not most—of us are uninformed and unprepared in the event of nuclear war.

189   **Brooks,** Jerome. *Make Me a Hero.* Dutton, 1980. 79-20269. ISBN 0-525-34475-6. 152p. $8.95.

6–9   A story set in a heterogeneous Chicago neighborhood during World War II is impressive both because of its vivid evocation of a time and a place, and because of the depth and insight with which Brooks develops his protagonist, Jake Ackerman. Jake is twelve, the youngest of four, and aware that his parents' emotional concerns are focused on the three older boys, all in the service. He desperately wants to make his mark, make his parents proud of him; he gets a job with elderly Mr. Gold, who takes a fancy to him, but that doesn't seem enough. Jake's had no religious education, and he decides to join another boy, Harry Katz, and study for his Bar Mitzvah. Jake looks up to Harry, and is amazed when Harry is just as afraid as he is of the bigoted bullies who periodically have taunted and attacked him. It is old Mr. Gold, rather than Jake's parents, who helps the boy understand human frailty and the need to compromise, who helps Jake gain tolerance and accept responsibility. A touching and trenchant story, strong in characterization, is firmly structured and cohesive.

190   **Brooks,** Polly Schoyer. *Queen Eleanor: Independent Spirit of the Medieval World.* Lippincott, 1983. 82-48776. Trade ed. ISBN 0-397-31994-0; Library ed. ISBN 0-397-31995-9. 160p. Trade ed. $9.95; Library ed. $9.89.

7–   This is a full, candid, and vivacious biography of Eleanor of Aquitaine, first Queen of France and then Queen of England, that forceful and reputedly beautiful woman who rode with her husband on a Crusade to fight for Jerusalem, who was a patroness of the performing arts, who raised a king's ransom for her imprisoned son, Richard the Lion Heart. It is also a vivid picture of the twelfth century and especially of the intrigue and counter-intrigue among the royalty and the nobility of England and France. Well-researched, this is as colorful as it is informative. A chronological chart, a bibliography, and an index are provided.

191   **Brown,** Marc. *Arthur Goes to Camp;* written and illus. by Marc Brown. Little, 1982. 81-15588. ISBN 0-316-11218-6. 31p. $9.95.

2–3   All of the characters in this camp story are animals, and the theme is that in union there is strength. Arthur, who hadn't wanted to go to camp, finds the boys' counselor tough, the girl campers who tease and trick the boys a menace, and the food uninspiring. He writes pathetic letters to his parents. Like his fellow-campers, he dreads the scavenger hunt in which his camp will compete with the children at another camp. However, the boys and the girls work together and, thanks to Arthur's accidentally turning up with a flashlight, win the event. Last page, a letter from Arthur: "The scavenger hunt was great. Camp is great. I want to come back next year." This is an amusing variant on the adjustment-to-camp story, it's told in a direct, simple style, and most of the humor lies in the situation and in the illustrations, which are colorful, lively, and peopled by slightly grotesque animal figures.

192   **Brown,** Marc Tolon. *Arthur's Christmas;* written and illus. by Marc Brown. Little, 1984. 84-4373. ISBN 0-316-11180-5. 31p. $12.95.

2–3   Trying to decide on a gift to Santa, Arthur notes that everywhere he goes, Santa seems to be eating. (Readers will enjoy feeling superior as *they* note that all the Santas are different.) Arthur mixes up some dreadful food combinations, and his crafty sister gets rid of the food and leaves a letter (ostensibly from Santa) to thank Arthur. It ends, "P.S. Aren't you lucky to have such a nice little sister?" Young readers or the lap audience for which this is also appropriate will enjoy, as they have with earlier Arthur books, the animal characters, the scruffy paintings of everyday objects, and the light style that unerringly reflects children's attitudes.

193   **Brown,** Marc Tolon. *The Bionic Bunny Show;* by Marc Brown and Laurene Krasny Brown; illus. by Marc Brown. Little, 1984. 83-22211. ISBN 0-316-11120-1. 32p. $13.95.

K–2   The read-aloud audience should be enchanted by this story within a story, as a perfectly ordinary rabbit dons costume and makeup to become Bionic Bunny, star of a television series. One episode of the series is filmed during the course of the story, and this permits the authors and illustrator to give a good deal of information about how a show is filmed and how special effects are achieved. This is fast, funny and meaty.

194   **Brown,** Marcia Joan. *Listen To A Shape;* written and illus. with photographs by Marcia Joan Brown. Watts, 1979. 78-31616. Trade ed. ISBN 0-531-02383-4; Library ed. ISBN 0-531-02930-1. 32p. Trade ed. $4.95; Library ed. $7.90 net.

2–4   Already distinguished for her versatility, Brown adds a new medium to her repertory in this concept book, illustrated with handsome full-color photographs accompanying a poetic text. The pictures are all of natural objects: the spikes of iris buds in spring, the circle made by dandelion petals, the curved shadow of a straight tree limb, the wind-made ripples on sand or water. "What shape is a cloud? . . . What shape is a flame?" the captions ask, or comment "A miracle: Young things have inside them the plan for the shape they will become. So do you!" This can stir a child's imagination, teach observation, and encourage aesthetic appreciation.

195   **Brown,** Marcia Joan. *Touch Will Tell;* written and illus. with photographs by Marcia Brown. Watts, 1979. 78-27260. Trade ed. ISBN 0-531-02384-2; Library ed. ISBN 0-531-02931-X. 32p. Trade ed. $4.95; Library ed. $7.90 net.

Brown, Marcia Joan. *Walk with Your Eyes;* written and illus. with photographs by Marcia Brown. Watts, 1979. 78-27688. Trade ed. ISBN

0-531-02385-0; Library ed. ISBN 0-531-02925-5. 32p. Trade ed. $4.95; Library ed. $7.90 net.

2–4   Like *Listen to a Shape* these books comprise a poetic and provocative text and handsome color photographs of plants, animals, and landscapes in the changing seasons. The texts and pictures are beautifully combined, a pleasure to read and see, an encouragement to sharpen the reader's powers of observation and appreciation of beauty in nature. In *Touch Will Tell*, Brown focuses on texture: the velvety petals of pansies, the way air can vary from a caressing breeze to a bracing wind, the sharpness of icicles or cactus, and the ways in which creatures touch to express love or seek security. In *Walk with Your Eyes*, the emphasis is on seeing small things, seeing imaginatively, being curious about and open to the world around us. Some readers may wish the objects in the photographs were identified.

196   **Brown,** Tricia. *Someone Special, Just Like You*; illus. with photographs by Fran Ortiz. Holt, 1984. 83-18377. ISBN 0-03-069706-9. 64p. $11.95.

K–2   Upbeat black-and-white photographs with a simple large-type text show preschool disabled children actively playing and learning, alone, with their teachers, and with their peers. The emphasis is on the pleasures they share with all children: eating ice-cream, swimming, finger-painting, going on school trips to the dolphin in the aquarium. Wheelchairs, hearing-aids, and leg-braces are depicted as a natural part of the everyday activities. All children will be fascinated by the disabled's special skills (reading with their fingers, speaking with their hands) and will identify with the visually impaired boy's rubbing his cheek on a pet rabbit's fur, and with the pride of the girl walking the balance beam. In dispelling the fear of the unknown and showing our common needs for physical affection, community, skills, and independence, this book should do much to help the disabled gain acceptance from other children. The annotated bibliography includes references for adults and books (divided by type of handicap) for preschool through age eight.

197   **de Brunhoff,** Jean. *Babar's Anniversary Album: 6 Favorite Stories*; written and illus. by Jean and Laurent de Brunhoff. Random House, 1981. 81-5182. Trade ed. ISBN 0-394-84813-6; Library ed. ISBN 0-394-94813-0. 144p. Trade ed. $12.95; Library ed. $13.99.

K–2   In a promisingly plump oversize book are collected a half-dozen loved and familiar Babar stories, three by Jean de Brunhoff, three by his son Laurent. They are preceded by a long, loving, and perceptive introduction by Maurice Sendak and, sharing the pages of that introduction, a "picture" story by Laurent de Brunhoff, with photographs, sketches, and reproductions of paintings that—with their lengthy captions—pay tribute to his father as a father and as an artist. After fifty years of individually pleasing books, a bonanza.

198   Bulla, Clyde Robert. *The Cardboard Crown;* illus. by Michele Chessare. Crowell, 1984. 83-45049. Library ed. ISBN 0-690-04361-9; Trade ed. ISBN 0-690-04360-0. 79p. Library ed. $10.89; Trade ed. $10.95.

3–5   Adam, eleven, is much impressed when Olivia appears at their door one night, wearing a cardboard crown, claiming that she is a princess, and asking that Adam and his father give her lodging. Adam's dour father, a widower, thinks Olivia is a silly girl with an overactive imagination, an opinion shared by their neighbor, the aunt with whom Olivia is staying. This is a gentle story, close to static, in which only two things happen—but they are important things: Olivia runs away and returns, and Adam sells his beloved calf to fund the runaway. Written in a direct and simple style, this quiet book may appeal primarily to readers who feel sympathy for Adam's sacrificial gesture.

199   Bunting, Eve. *Clancy's Coat;* illus. by Lorinda Bryan Cauley. Warne, 1984. 83-6575. ISBN 0-7232-6252-7. 43p. $11.95.

K–3   Double-page spreads are alternately illustrated in black and white and in color, both media having a soft technique and a humorous quality. The story is told in a direct style that is an effective contrast to the sly humor of the situation, in which two old friends cautiously make up after a quarrel. Clancy brings his shabby old coat to Tippitt (a tailor) who promises to fix it very quickly; there are, however, so many delays that several visits are necessary, by which time the two men have come back to a friendly relationship.

200   Bunting, Eve. *The Cloverdale Switch.* Lippincott, 1979. 79-2404. Trade ed. ISBN 0-397-31866-9; Library ed. ISBN 0-397-31867-7. 119p. Trade ed. $7.95; Library ed. $7.89. net.

7–10   The first time it happened, John was in the woods with Cindy, and suddenly all the colors around him changed, as though the scene were a photographic negative—and after that Cindy seemed different: cold, and watchful. That was the start of a series of strange blackouts in Cloverdale, events that made John and his grandfather wary of everyone around them, suspicious that there were alien presences who were taking over the bodies of people they knew. Even John's mother. In a science fantasy that is a smooth blend of fantasy and realism, Bunting has structured a convincing, fast-paced story that has logic within the parameters she has set for her characters.

201   Bunting, Eve. *Someone is Hiding on Alcatraz Island.* Houghton/Clarion, 1984. 84-5019. ISBN 0-89919-219-X. 136p. $10.95.

6–9   The narrator, Danny, is fourteen, short and slight and understandably afraid of the four tough bullies who call themselves the Outlaws and who are pursuing him along the San Francisco waterfront. Danny leaps on to the deck of a tourist ferry bound for Alcatraz to evade them—but it doesn't last long. The Outlaws show up on the next boat and the nightmare begins, as Danny and Biddy, a ranger, are trapped and taunted through the night in the deserted prison. This is a taut and tough story, and it maintains suspense impressively, incorporating strong characterization and dialogue, both of which are deliberately un-pleasant.

202   **Bunting,** Eve. *Surrogate Sister*. Lippincott, 1984. 83-49483. Library ed. ISBN 0-397-32099-X; Trade ed. ISBN 0-397-32098-1. 213p. Library ed. $11.89; Trade ed. $12.50.

7–10   There is something new under the sun, at least new in books for young adults, for Bunting, in a nicely structured and thoughtfully written novel, explores the feelings of a sixteen-year-old-girl whose widowed mother has become pregnant (by artificial insemination) in response to a desperate appeal from a childless couple whom she never meets. For her daughter, the decision seems an outrage. What will her friends say? (They say some very nasty things, some of them; others think Cassie's mother is wonderful). Cassie fears that her mother is accepting the money for this childbearing to help her, but learns that Mom plans to use it for a long-dreamed-of nursing course. Cassie's also disturbed by falling in love with a college student who's about to go off for a year of study abroad. The book has strong characters, good pace, balanced treatment, and a very good handling of the issues of surrogate mother-hood, incorporating them smoothly into the narrative so that this is not a fictionalized case history but a compelling story.

203   **Burch,** Robert. *Christmas with Ida Early*. Viking, 1983. 83-5792. ISBN 0-670-22131-7. 168p. $10.95.

4–6   In a sequel to *Ida Early Comes Over the Mountain* in which the tall, irre-pressible Ida brought comfort to a family of children who had recently lost their mother, the antics and tall tales of Ida are equalled by her warmth and wisdom. The book does have plot threads (the relationship between Ida and the new minister; the burden of crusty Aunt Earnest-ine, whose illness prolongs her visit) and it culminates in an animated Christmas program that is very funny. A blithe and comic tale.

204   **Burch,** Robert. *Ida Early Comes over the Mountain*. Viking, 1980. 79-20532. ISBN 0-670-39169-7. 145p. $8.95.

4–6   The place is rural Georgia, the time is the Depression Era, and the pro-tagonist is a tall, awkward, merry woman who shows up at the Sutton home looking for a job. Since the mother of the four Sutton children has died recently, Mr. Sutton takes Ida Early on as a housekeeper. Ida Early is casual about chores and tells tall tales about her past, but her humor and understanding endear her to the children. Burch has created a memorable character, but she's more than entertaining: through their embarrassment when Ida Early appears at school, is jeered at for her appearance (haysstack hair, overalls, and clodhoppers) and not defended by the two older Sutton children, the latter learn the shame of denying a friend. The lesson is gently taught, with a poignant tenderness, and Ida Early's sudden departure (and subsequent return) gives structure to an otherwise episodic story, written with a light, sure touch.

205   **Burningham,** John. *Avocado Baby*. Crowell, 1982. 81-43844. Trade ed. ISBN 0-690-04243-4; Library ed. ISBN 0-690-04244-2. 24p. illus. Trade ed. $8.95; Library ed. $8.89.

2–5
yrs.
Clean, spacious illustrations with economical use of line and with subdued but strong colors add to the humor of a nursery tall tale blandly told. None of the four members of the Hargreaves family is very strong, and they worry when the new baby (never called he or she) is puny and dislikes all food. The older children suggest giving the baby an avocado that has mysteriously appeared in a bowl of fruit. The avocado is accepted with relish and others are administered daily; the baby becomes incredibly strong, lifting pianos, pushing the car when it won't start, and—in the final episode—tossing two large bullies in the lake when they persecute its much-older siblings. Palatable nonsense creates an infant hero figure with whom small listeners can identify.

206   **Burningham,** John. *Read One;* written and illus. by John Burningham. Viking, 1983. 82-051281. ISBN 0-670-58986-1. 6p. $4.95.

3–5
yrs.
One of a series of six small books designed to help young children become familiar with elementary mathematical concepts. Each book is in leporello form, with a flap that folds over each section; Burningham uses the device to full advantage, to extend concepts and/or add humor. This is the best kind of toy book: it's ingenious, sturdy, attractive, and useful, with Burningham's pictures maintaining a high standard of visual art. In this book the number signs and words are linked; in other books, concepts such as addition (*Pigs Plus*), subtraction (*Ride Off*), numbers as signs (*Five Down*), sets (*Count Up*), and groups (*Just Cats*) are presented.

207   **Burningham.** John. *The Shopping Basket;* written and illus. by John Burningham. T. Y. Crowell, 1980. 80-7987. Trade ed. ISBN 0-690-04082-2; Library ed. ISBN 0-690-04083-0. 30p. Trade ed. $9.95; Library ed. $9.79.

4–7
yrs.
A mild foray into mathematical concepts is incorporated into a blithe story that introduces into its modest, realistic story line one repeated note of fantasy. Sent to the store to buy six eggs, five bananas, four apples, three oranges, two doughnuts, and a package of crisps, Steven remembers everything. Unfortunately, he's waylaid on the way home by a series of beasts; for example, a bear demands the eggs, and Steven bets that the bear is so slow he couldn't catch an egg if Steven threw it up in the air. Next picture: bear with egg on its face. In each case, a

page that shows the items in inverse pyramid has one egg or banana or apple missing. Steven gets home, his mother wants to know what took him so long, and Steven just stands there looking hapless and innocent. A brisk, fresh story with just enough nonsense to keep it entertaining rather than silly, this is illustrated with nicely composed line and wash drawings that have an understated humor.

208   **Busnar,** Gene. *Careers in Music.* Messner, 1982. 82-2290. ISBN 0-671-42410-6. 255p. illus. with photographs. $9.29.

8–12   A useful book for adolescents considering a career in either a supportive role or as a performer, this covers popular and classical music; music teaching; working as a music journalist, or in radio, either as critic or promoter; and doing such technical jobs as instrument repair or acoustics expert, and it even suggests areas of part-time employment, such as a record store or as a music copyist. Although the index does not give full access to contents (neither "composer" nor "conductor" is cited separately, although they are included under classical music) the comprehensive coverage, sensible advice, candor about financial returns in a highly competitive field, sources listed at the ends of chapters and "Fact Guides" within chapters, make this an excellent book for vocational guidance. A glossary and a bibliography are included in this useful book, written with authority in a direct, clear style.

209   **Butterworth,** Emma Macalik. *As the Waltz Was Ending.* Four Winds, 1983. 82-70402. ISBN 0-590-07835-6. 187p. $9.95.

7–   In this autobiographical account, Emmy is eight when she begins the study of ballet, a promising pupil who expects to devote her life to dancing. She's aware that her father despises Hitler and argues with his brother about the Nazi movement, but it doesn't impinge on her life until the Germans come to Austria. Suddenly all her classmates are joining the Bund Deutscher Mädel, and Emmy is an outsider. At first things look better: her father, who had lost his job during the depression, is given a post; Emmy is excused from BDM participation because she is in the national ballet school; they have enough ration coupons. But coupons can't buy shoes or food if they are not sold. Father is conscripted. Jewish friends are persecuted. The war is being lost, and when the Russians enter Vienna, Emmy is raped. The city is bombed. The book ends with the arrival of American troops, and an epilogue describes the fates of the people in the story, including the author, now an American citizen. At times grim, always vivid, the book gives a touching picture of the contrast between the schlag-und-kultur elegance of prewar Vienna and the bitter suffering of wartime.

210   **Butterworth,** William E. *LeRoy and the Old Man.* Four Winds, 1980. 79-6553. ISBN 0-590-07638-8. 154p. $7.95.

7–9   LeRoy, a black adolescent who has witnessed a mugging, is sent to Mississippi to stay with the paternal grandfather he's never met; his mother has insisted he leave Chicago, fearing for his safety. LeRoy tends to be superior about his grandfather and his grandfather's lifestyle; he doesn't want to help run a shrimp business, he doesn't like living in the country, and he looks with a dubious eye on the white men who seem to respect the old man. When LeRoy is called home to testify, his grandfather insists that he must go, that it is his duty. At this point LeRoy's father turns up (he had deserted his wife years ago) and offers his son the easy way out: come to New York and be a numbers runner. Easy money, working for his father, and no chance that the Chicago gang will seek vengeance. But LeRoy has learned more than shrimping from the old man, he's learned what truth and duty are, and the story ends with the old man seeing LeRoy off to board a plane to Chicago, proud that his boy is doing the right thing. Butterworth has created a strong and sympathetic character whose ethical concepts are absorbed by, rather than thrust upon, the protagonist and the reader; the plot is nicely knit, and the development of the change in LeRoy's attitude toward old age and toward rural life is gradual and believable.

211   **Butterworth,** William E. *A Member of the Family.* Four Winds, 1982. 82-70403. ISBN 0-590-07828-3. 172p. $9.95.

7–9   Adolescent Tom, the only one of the three Lockwood children still at home, bears the brunt of the family's problems with their large sheepdog, Precious. A loving animal, Precious becomes ferocious when he is frightened or when he thinks one of his family is in danger. The trouble is that the dog seems to have no judgment about the reality of such danger—and Tom is told by a veterinarian that the dog is schizoid. The Lockwoods try therapeutic surgery, but Precious isn't cured, and in the end, Tom and his father have the dog given a fatal drug after almost every member of the family has been bitten. Written with casual fluency and a sympathy that never becomes maudlin, this is a moving animal story based in part on a similar situation in the author's family.

212   **Byars,** Betsy. *The Animal, the Vegetable, and John D Jones;* illus. by Ruth Sanderson. Delacorte, 1982. 81-69665. Trade ed. ISBN 0-440-00122-6; Library ed. ISBN 0-440-00131-5. 150p. Trade ed. $9.95; Library ed. $9.89.

5–8
*   Although the whole story is told by the author, alternate chapters are from the viewpoint of John D or from the viewpoint of Deanie and Clara, the daughters of a divorced man who has his children with him for a fortnight's beach vacation. To their horror, Dad has arranged for John D's mother to share the beach house. Deanie and Clara bicker a great deal, but they are united in their contempt for John D, an emotion he cordially returns. Only when Clara comes close to drowning do her sister and John D see beyond the pettiness of their hostility; Deanie even softens toward John D's mother, toward whom she had felt resentment. This doesn't have as strong a story line as some of Byars' stories, but it has the same perceptive exposition of the intricacy of ambiv-

alent relationships. The use of shifting viewpoints works well, partly because of the smoothness of the writing style, partly because the characters and relationships are so quickly and definitely established.

213   **Byars,** Betsy C. *The Cybil War;* illus. by Gail Owens. Viking, 1981. 80-26912. ISBN 0-670-25248-4. 126p. $8.95.

3–5   A joy. Simon is deeply smitten by Cybil, a fourth-grade classmate, and
  *   just as deeply angered by his once-closest friend Tony, a blithely inventive liar who persists in telling fibs to and about Cybil to strengthen his cause: Tony is also smitten by Cybil. The writing seems deceptively simple, but it has a polished fluency and spontaneity. The children, separately and together, are vividly characterized; the relationship between Simon and his mother has a particular warmth, and the story is permeated by an affectionate humor, especially in the dialogue.

214   **Byars,** Betsy C. *The Night Swimmers;* illus. by Troy Howell. Delacorte, 1980. 79-53597. Trade ed. ISBN 0-440-06261-6; Library ed. ISBN 0-440-06262-4. 144p. Trade ed. $7.95; Library ed. $7.45 net.

5–7   A poignant and perceptive story about the relationships among three
  *   children in a family in which the mother is dead and the father a small-time but ambitious country-western singer-composer. Because Dad is gone at night, Retta (the oldest) is able to take her younger brothers, of whom she is in complete charge, to stealthily swim in a neighbor's pool, and it is when the pool's owner discovers the children and calls their father that the change comes into their lives; good-natured, affectionate Brendelle, their father's girlfriend, makes it clear that she's moving in. Retta is the protagonist and, although the feelings of her brothers are expressed, it is from her viewpoint that the story is written. What Byars achieves is a remarkably touching picture of a girl who has almost given up childhood; her mother gone, her father well-meaning but more concerned with his career than his children, Retta has been giving all her love and attention to her brothers. She is in despair and anger when the older of the two boys finds a friend of his own, and when the younger boy turns to his brother as a leader. *She's* always been the leader; she's always been the person to whom they turn for comfort and leadership, and suddenly she has learned that she needs the boys more than they need her. The final incident at the pool takes place when both boys have slipped away without her and she has angrily followed them, and it is a sweet relief, beautifully understated, when she can relinquish the role of mother and become a child. The story, deftly constructed and smoothly told and developed, ends with Brendelle making supper for Dad, while Retta half-listens from her bed, "And in the comfortable silence that followed, Retta fell asleep."

215   **Bykov,** Vasil. *Pack of Wolves;* tr. from the Russian by Lynn Solotaroff. T. Y. Crowell, 1981. 80-2456. Trade ed. ISBN 0-690-04114-4; Library ed. ISBN 0-690-04115-2. 181p. Trade ed. $10.50; Library ed. $9.89.

7–   A story within a story, this capably-translated Russian tale of a post-war
search is both stirring and poignant. Save for the infant whose rescue is
described in the inner story, there are no child characters, yet the pace,
suspense, and setting should appeal to adolescent readers. Levchuk, an
elderly man, has made a long trip to see someone in another town,
someone who doesn't expect him and clearly won't know him: Victor,
whose father Levchuk had known thirty years before. Nodding in the
sunshine as he waits for Victor to come home, Levchuk remembers . . .
and the things he remembers include hiding from the Germans and
their dogs when he was a soldier, rescuing the newly-born infant son of
Klava, the group's radio operator, fleeing through a swamp with the
infant after Klava was killed, shouting that the child's name was Victor
as he handed him over. And then, back to the present, as Levchuk prepares to walk in to see the man who can't possibly remember him and
who may not even know he owes his life to his visitor. Well-paced and
dramatic, a story written with a good sense of theater.

216   **Byrd,** Elizabeth. *I'll Get By.* Viking, 1981. 80-29471. ISBN 0-670-39134-4.
204p. $9.95.

7–10   In her first novel for young adults, Byrd bases her story on her own
experiences in Manhattan in the year that preceded the stock market
crash. Julie, fifteen, is the narrator. She attends a progressive school,
she's socially sophisticated and sexually naive, and she mopes romanti-
cally because her handsome, beloved father is never in town. Her
mother, prim and practical, is a snob and can't tolerate Julie's growing
love for Rick because he's from an Italian-American family. Dad's mine
finally brings in money, lots of money, and he comes back to New
York; they move to an expensive apartment, and Julie's mother at last
has the security she's longed for; Dad even approves of Rick. That's the
way the book ends—in October, 1929. The hit song of the time is "I'll
Get By," but astute readers will understand the irony of the timing,
with the crash and the depression looming. Perceptive in its delineation
of characters, motivations, and relationships, the story is smoothly written, often acid and just as often amusing.

217   **Caines,** Jeanette Franklin. *Just Us Women;* illus. by Pat Cummings.
Harper, 1982. 81-48655. Trade ed. ISBN 0-06-020941-0; Library ed. ISBN
0-06-020942-0. 32p. Trade ed. $9.50; Library ed. $9.89.

K–3   In soft two-color illustrations, the joys of a leisurely motor trip with the
narrator's aunt are depicted. This has only incidental action, as the
small black girl who tells the story of what they'll do on their trip to
North Carolina anticipates the freedom and companionship they'll enjoy. Nobody to hurry them, time to stop at roadside stands and have
picnics, or to go to fancy restaurants, or even just stop to walk in the
rain. The text has a warm, happy tone; it's written in a free, casual style
and concludes with the response to the North Carolina relatives who

might ask, "What took you so long?" "We'll just tell them we had a lot of girl talk to do between the two of us. No boys and no men—just us women."

218   Callen, Larry. *The Muskrat War.* Atlantic-Little, Brown, 1980. 80-36700. ISBN 0-316-12498-2. 132p. $8.95.

5–7   Another story is, like *Pinch, The Deadly Mandrake,* and *Sorrow's Song,* set in the small town of Four Corners, Louisiana. It's Pinch who tells the story of Mr. Short and Mrs. Long, two artful swindlers who find the credulous folk of Four Corners easy dupes. Although the duplicity is discovered, the culprits escape—teaching Pinch and his neighbors to be less gullible. The title refers to the muskrat hides with which the swindlers escape, and to the quarrel between Pinch's father and a neighbor over territorial trapping rights. The book has the appeal of familiar characters, it has humor and an entertaining story line; like many of Callen's other books, however, it depends for comic effect on the acceptance of the fact that the denizens of Four Corners are all naive and stupid.

219   Callen, Larry. *Sorrow's Song;* illus. by Marvin Friedman. Atlantic-Little, Brown, 1979. 78-31789. ISBN 0-316-124974. 150p. $7.95.

5–7   In a third story about the inhabitants of Four Corners, Pinch describes the tribulations he and his mute friend Sorrow have when they discover a small, disabled whooping crane. Unfortunately, others discover the bird as well; the Zoo Man wants the bird for his collection, and the renegade John Barrow wants her so that he can sell her, and the Sweet brothers want her for food. Readers who are birdlovers or conservationists will be happy with the outcome, but Callen puts more depth into the story than just girl-saves-bird, for he introduces—through Pinch— the more substantive issues of friendship values and ethical behavior. Callen's art is that these issues emerge naturally in a story that has folksy humor without corn, and sweetness without sentimentality.

220   Calvert, Patricia. *The Hour of the Wolf.* Scribner, 1983. 85-14184. ISBN 0-684-17961-X. 147p. $11.95.

7–9   Jake had been sent to Alaska by his macho father after the teenager had attempted suicide; living with his father's old friend Doc Smalley, Jake has begun to feel more self-confidence. In part that is why, when his friend Danny Yumiat dies, Jake decides he will take Danny's place in the Last Great Race, the dog-sled run from Anchorage to Nome, over a thousand miles. During the race, Jake becomes friendly with Danny's sister, who is also running the race for Danny. Although there's a bit too much sugar in the ending (Dad, understanding at last, makes amends) the book is, in the main, solidly plotted; it has characters that are believable if not drawn in great depth, and it has strength in the pace and setting.

221   Calvino, Italo, comp. *Italian Folktales;* comp. and ad. by Italo Calvino; tr. by George Martin. Harcourt, 1980. 80-11879. ISBN 0-15-145770-0. 763p. $25.00.

5–
*   Although the erudite introduction, the scholarly bibliography, and the extensive section of appended notes indicate that the book's primary audience is the student of folklore, this fine anthology should also be available to children, for it provides a rich source for the reader as well as for the storyteller. While some of the tales are easily identifiable variants (for example "Bellinda and the Monster" is a variant of "Beauty and the Beast") many will be unfamiliar to English language readers. The stories have, among them, all the standard folklore themes and devices, but they have also a fresh, robust, and often humorous style that is engaging. To both teller and translator, bravo!

222   Cameron, Ann. *The Stories Julian Tells;* illus. by Ann Strugnell. Pantheon, 1981. 80-18023. ISBN 0-394-94301-5. 71p. $7.95.

2–3   Julian is the narrator for five short, easy-to-read stories illustrated with softly detailed black and white drawings that are realistic in approach but that include some of the imaginative details of the stories Julian tells about his little brother Huey and himself. The tone is quiet, the small adventures believable: Julian makes a new friend; Julian and Huey suffer the logical consequences of eating a pudding their father has made as a surprise for their mother; Julian loses a tooth; Huey is convinced (by Julian) that you can order cats from a catalog, et cetera. Pleasant, low-keyed, not very exciting but comfortably familiar in the kinds of events and family relationships it describes, the book depicts with mild humor some everyday happenings in the life of a black family.

223   Cameron, Eleanor. *Julia's Magic;* illus. by Gail Owens. Dutton, 1984. 84-8118. ISBN 0-525-44114-X. 148p. $9.95.

3–5   Another story about Julia; this one is set just before and leading into *That Julia Redfern* and has the same structure: a nicely flowing narrative into which linked episodes are woven. Julia's undiscovered misdeed precipitates a crisis in her uncle's household, and Julia makes amends; Julia's parents are told by a waspish landlady that she's sold their house (true) and that they'll have to move (untrue) and Julia begins to differentiate between reality and the magic of her imagination.

224   Cameron, Eleanor. *That Julia Redfern.* Dutton, 1982. 82-2405. ISBN 0-525-44015. 144p. $9.95.

3–5   In each book about Julia, the author moves back to an earlier part of her childhood; here she is younger than in *Julia and the Hand of God* and her father has not yet gone off to war as the story starts. Most of the book is anecdotal, as feisty Julia gets into a series of scrapes, but there are some threads that bind the episodes together: one is the use of Julia's imagination (she gives up an imaginary companion but becomes confirmed in her desire to be a writer) and the other is the writing her father has been doing, for after his death they find and publish the best writing he has ever done. This has more substance than most of the many stage-of-childhood books for children, since it has depth and consistency of characterization, strong dialogue and exposition, and a credible change and growth in the protagonist.

225   **Carlson,** Dale Bick. *Boys Have Feelings Too; Growing Up Male for Boys;* illus. by Carol Nicklaus. Atheneum, 1980. 80-12895. ISBN 0-689-30770-5. 167p. $8.95.

6–9   Carlson points out the many ways in which society (parents, teachers, the media, peers) pressures boys and men to conform to cultural stereotypes; she points out that although boys still have more freedom of choice than girls, they also have less freedom to choose behavior patterns or careers or life styles that are different. She counsels on specific subjects: relationships with girls, expressing emotion, admitting emotional needs, choosing careers; and she is consistently candid and sensible. Carlson has the ability to deal with a serious subject in a conversational tone, in direct prose, without being heavy-handed; it would be simplistic to say her text boils down to "be yourself," but she does— very deftly—show all the reasons for the conformity to the image that exists, offers convincing evidence that such conformity brings little happiness, and suggests the ways in which boys can indeed be themselves, selves that can be content to be imperfect or to differ from the popular image of the macho overachiever.

226   **Carlson,** Natalie Savage. *A Grandmother for the Orphelines;* illus. by David White. Harper, 1980. 80-7769. Trade ed. ISBN 0-06-020993-3; Library ed. ISBN 0-06-020994-1. 91p. Trade ed. $8.95; Library ed. $8.79.

3–5   Another book about the orphans who live, lovingly cared for by Madame Flattot and Genevieve, in an old castle in the forest of Fontainebleau. Here the twin themes are the children's adjustment to losing their beloved Genevieve, who marries a young farmer, and their determination to acquire a grandmother. Prime mover in the campaign is the youngest orphan, Josine, who even locks one candidate in the castle dungeon, promising to let her out if she will be the orphanage grandmother. When a pair of elderly travellers turns up in the barn, it is clear they were destined to become grandmother and grandfather; in fact, since Madame needs help with her work, they are hired, to their and everybody's delight. This sequel has the same ingenuous sweetness and ebullience as the earlier books; the writing ripples on in engaging fashion, there are no villains, and it is a world in which children are lovable and loved.

227   **Carlson,** Natalie Savage. *King of the Cats and Other Tales;* illus. by David Frampton. Doubleday, 1980. 79-7861. Trade ed. ISBN 0-385-15427-5; Library ed. ISBN 0-385-15428-3. 72p. Trade ed. $7.95; Library ed. $8.90.

3–5   Carlson uses the legendary creatures of Brittany in eight stories told to a small girl by her godmother (incorrectly designated as Yvette's grandmother on the jacket copy) and each tale begins, "In another time when strange things happened. . . ." Each tale closes with a framing device, as the godmother, Mam Marig, points out the crux or moral of the tale to Yvette. The illustrations are woodcuts, harsh and vigorous. There are the little people, the korrigans, demons and ghosts and giants, a sea siren and a magical horse that race through the night, the cobwebby Houper and the cat of the title story. All of the tales have to do with simple folk and their encounters with magical beings; there are no "why" stories, no courtly romances, no creation tales. The writing style is smooth and colloquial, and the book can serve as a source for storytellers as well as for independent reading. No sources or notes are provided.

228   **Carlson,** Natalie Savage. *Surprise in the Mountains;* illus. by Elise Primavera. Harper, 1983. 82-47716. Trade ed. ISBN 0-06-021008-7; Library ed. ISBN 0-06-021009-5. 26p. Trade ed. $9.95; Library ed. $9.89.

2–4   Illustrations that are somewhat reminiscent of Galdone's work in their technique and humor (a craggy, grizzled miner, a pop-eyed burro) are in greys and tawny tones; they echo the simplicity and humor of the story. Old Quill, the prospector, is not greedy; all he wants is enough gold to feed himself and his beloved burro. Whatever little he has, Old Quill shares with the wild creatures that are near the abandoned cabin in which he's taken refuge for the cold mountain winter. The surprise that lies under a tiny tree is a nugget of gold, left by a pack rat. Not much, but enough to buy food at the trading post and know it will last through the winter. The writing never becomes saccharine, but has a fresh, breezy quality, controlled structure, and considerable humor as the old man talks to his only companion and interprets each flick of the ears or pawing of the ground as a response. "Knew you'd understand," says Old Quill, or "Knew you'd have somethin' to say about that."

229   **Carrick,** Donald. *Harald and the Giant Knight;* written and illus. by Donald Carrick. Houghton, 1982. 81-10243. ISBN 0-89919-060-X. 29p. $10.95.

2–4   Earth-tone tints are used in framed line drawings that reflect the dramatic actions of a story set in the Middle Ages. Although the story is simply told, it makes some aspects of feudal life and the caste system clear, adding depth to a plot that is stripped but that shows how a child can change when he sees through a facade. Harald is the only son of a poor farmer who supplements his income by making objects of woven reeds. Infatuated by the glamor of knightly jousts and tournaments, young Harald sees a different aspect of knighthood when the knights camp on his father's land to practice. They ruin the crops, hack at fruit trees, eat the poultry and pigs. Disillusioned, Harald comes up with an idea for getting rid of the knights; the chief object in his plan is a huge woven figure of a knight. The ploy is intriguing and successful, a satisfying ending to a satisfying story.

230   **Carrick,** Malcolm. *Mr. Tod's Trap;* written and illus. by Malcolm Carrick. Harper, 1980. 79-2012. Trade ed. ISBN 0-06-021113-X; Library ed. ISBN 0-06-021114-8. 64p. (I Can Read Books). Trade ed. $5.95; Library ed. $6.89.

1–2   A Mr. Micawber among foxes, Mr. Tod is full of ideas; his wife and children, duly impressed by his eloquent statements and ingenious plans for catching rabbits, are disappointed repeatedly when his plans go awry. They are also hungry. Finally Mrs. Tod suggests that, since the children love having their father home to tell stories and tuck them in at bedtime, she will forage for food and Mr. Tod can stay at home and make the cubs happy. Naturally, Mr. Tod soon thinks it was his own fine idea. The softly colored line drawings have humorous details, sometimes hard to see on those pages that are crowded. The story has humor, a reversal of stock sex roles, and a feeling of family affection; the brisk text has a nice balance of exposition and dialogue, the latter dominant.

231   **Carrier,** Roch. *The Hockey Sweater;* tr. by Sheila Fischman; illus. by Sheldon Cohen. Tundra Books, 1984. ISBN 0-88776-169-0. 22p. $14.95.

3–5   First published five years ago (in French and English) as an unillustrated short story, this became very popular in Canada and was used as the script for an animated film which has won many prizes. Here the animator has condensed the images from the film version to create a picture book for the middle grades. Readers who are not committed hockey fans or players may not share the protagonist's feelings, but children anywhere can appreciate the sort of dedication to a sports hero felt by the author when, as a boy, he shared with other French Canadian boys a conviction that Montreal had the best team in the world and that the best player was Maurice Richard. In fact, every boy Roch played with had a sweater with Richard's number. A Canadiens' sweater, of course. What a dilemma faces Roch when the sweater his mother's ordered through a catalog turns out to be a Toronto Maple Leaf sweater—and he has to wear it. In public. An amusing story, nicely told.

232   **Carter,** Peter. *Children of the Book.* Oxford/Merrimack, 1984. ISBN 0-19-271456-2. 271p. $13.95.

8–   In an engrossing account of the Siege of Vienna in 1683, Carter puts together a wonderfully coherent and cohesive collage, focusing on individuals who played major roles in the conflict (kings and counselors and military leaders) and on individuals who are the little people of history. The leaders are real, the little people (like a Viennese baker's family, a Polish lout, a young recruit in the Turkish army) are fictional, and the story knits their lives together smoothly, deftly, in a polished style and with gathering momentum. The text has been carelessly edited ("It's incredible. Simple incredible," or ". . . the fords. . . was defended . . .") but the errors are minor when weighed against the sweep of the story, the wit of the writing, and the breadth of historical information.

233   **Cassedy,** Sylvia. *Behind the Attic Wall.* Crowell, 1983. 82-45922. Trade ed. ISBN 0-690-04336-8; Library ed. ISBN 0-690-04337-6. 311p. Trade ed. $11.95; Library ed. $11.89.

5–7   A deftly-crafted fantasy has a twelve-year-old protagonist who is an incorrigible rebel; Maggie, an orphan, had been ejected from every boarding school she'd attended. Now she is sent to stay with two elderly great-aunts; like other guardians, they are horrified by the behavior of the thin, pale, hostile child who comes to live with them and who throws away the doll ("Dolls are dumb.") they have bought her. That is the realistic matrix for a fantasy world behind the attic wall, where Maggie finds two dolls who are articulate and who draw her into their world so that she becomes engaged and protective. The story is framed by episodes that show that Maggie has at last found a happy home (presumably as a foster child) after the rigid great-aunts have sent her away. What Cassedy achieves is the creation of a situation in which the stark characters are believable, in which the fantasy segment is both touching and comic, and in which the conversion of Maggie from a suspicious cynic to a concerned participant is made credible. A memorable story.

234   **Cazet,** Denys. *You Make the Angels Cry;* written and illus. by Denys Cazet. Bradbury, 1983. 82-9581. ISBN 0-02-717830-7. 26p. $12.95.

3–5 yrs.   An amusing and ingenuous story has warmth and gentle humor, qualities reflected in the watercolor pictures of a small rabbit and his mother. Finding her child with a broken cookie jar, Mom is exasperated. "You make the angels cry." Albert plods through the rain to a hilltop, earnestly explains to the angels that a window blew open and knocked the jar over, and comes home when the rain stops to explain where he's been. Mom hugs him and says, "You make the sun shine." "I know," says Albert.

235   **Cendrars,** Blaise. *Shadow;* tr. and illus. by Marcia Brown. Scribner, 1982. 81-9424. ISBN 0-684-17226-7. 36p. $12.95.

all ages *   Although the poem by Cendrars is polished and dramatic, many-layered in its imagery and percipience, it is the beautiful illustrations, collage and paint, that are the more impressive. Brown, twice a Caldecott Medal winner, and outstanding for the variety of techniques she has used in adapting media to match the moods of texts, is also noted for the power and beauty of her work. Here the lore of African stories and storytellers that inspired Cendrars is conveyed by strong use of pure color, by eerie wisps of superimposed images, and by strong silhouettes, all in handsome double-page spreads that are remarkable in their composition.

236   **Ceserani,** Gian Paolo. *Grand Constructions;* illus. by Piero Ventura. Putnam, 1983. 82-12212. ISBN 0-399-20942-5. 104p. $12.95.

6–
*   An oversize book offers good scope for Ventura's impressively detailed and colorful examples of architectural landmarks and some examples of famous sites (rather than buildings) like the gardens at Versailles or typical architectural structures like the imperial hall of the episcopal palace at Würzburg. Ventura does not give the sort of diagrammed details that David Macaulay provides; his paintings have the combined design and sweep of Anno's architectural drawings, especially in their use of perspective. Each page, or double-page picture, has an accompanying text that provides background information as well as some facts about the structure that is illustrated. This should also appeal, visually, to readers for whom the text may be too difficult.

237   **Ceserani,** Gian Paolo. *Marco Polo;* illus. by Piero Ventura. Putnam, 1982. 81-15685. ISBN 0-339-20843-7. 32p. $9.95.

3–6   First published in Italy under the title *Il Viaggio di Marco Polo,* this oversize book affords the artist an opportunity to do splendid large-scale scenes with meticulously detailed minutiae. Ventura's paintings have the same use of color, the same sense of movement as Peter Spier's large canvases, and they also include some excellent botanical drawings. The text is lucid, forthright, and informative, giving the background for Marco Polo's long stay in China, with his father and uncle, at the courts of Kublai Khan; it concludes with an account of Polo's return to Venice, his imprisonment, and his publication of an account of his travels.

238   **Chaback,** Elaine. *The Official Kids' Survival Kit: How to Do Things on Your Own;* written by Elaine Chaback and Pat Fortunato; illus. by Bill Ogden. Little, Brown, 1981. 81-11743. Hardcover ed. ISBN 0-316-13532-1. Paper ed. ISBN 0-316-13531-3. 223p. Hardcover ed. $13.95; Paper ed. $8.95.

5–8   Although this has a preface to parents, and a place at the end of each section for added parental notes, it is a good choice for a library collection as well as for home use. The book is alphabetically arranged by such topics as accident prevention, arguments, entertaining children, nutrition, safety and security, and working parents. There is commonsense advice on preventing problems and on solving them; the coverage is broad, the tone is brisk and the approach candid, and the material is cross-referenced. Within each section of this useful compendium, there is separate treatment of many subjects; under "Safety and Security," for example, the authors discuss aspects of safety at home and while traveling, with explicit tips on what to do if you detect an attempted break-

in, or are being followed, or see someone in an elevator cage who
makes you feel uncomfortable; there's also a section on how to cope
with sexual advances, and all of these things may be mentioned in
other sections as well, as when there's advice on handling people who
come to the door when you are home alone, under the heading of "De-
liveries."

239   **Chaikin,** Miriam. *Make Noise, Make Merry: The Story and Meaning of
Purim;* illus. by Demi. Clarion, 1983. 82-12926. ISBN 0-89919-140-1. 90p.
$10.95.

4–6   Providing a first section on the historical background for the period in
which the Persian king Ahasweros (Xerxes) reigned, Chaikin then
tells—in a smooth fictionalization—the story of his queen, Esther, who
saved the lives of her people, the Persian Jews. The last sections of the
book focus on how the holiday grew in importance and on how it is
celebrated. An index, a glossary, and a brief bibliography are included.
The format is handsome, with wide margins and with deep purple illustrations, delicate in detail and strong in composition, often incorporating traditional designs or motifs of Mid-Eastern art. Although the material contains some repetitions (it is explained in the story that the
wicked Haman, who plotted to kill all the Jews and whose plot Esther
foiled, was an Amalekite, and in the section on how the holiday is celebrated the text states "We are told in the Esther story that Haman was
an Amalekite.") the book is on the whole capably written, carefully organized, and informative; it should be especially useful in religious education programs.

240   **Chalmers,** Mary. *Come to the Doctor, Harry;* written and illus. by Mary
Chalmers. Harper, 1981. 80-7910. Trade ed. ISBN 0-06-021178-4; Library
ed. ISBN 0-06-021179-2. 32p. Trade ed. $5.95; Library ed. $5.89.

2–5
yrs.
It's been a long time between Harry stories, and in this little book with
its small-scale, tidy, engaging drawings, it's clear that Chalmer's touch
is still deft in story as in pictures. Harry is not anxious to visit the doctor when his tail gets caught in a door, but his mother insists. He
doesn't like doctors, he says. ("Why?" "Because.") The waiting room
proves to be full of interesting patients, and the confrontation with the
doctor painless. Harry emerges filled with his own importance and articulate about his bravery; he even consoles three waiting kittens and
tells them there's nothing to seeing a doctor. Ah, he's still beguiling,
that Harry.

241   **Chapman,** Carol. *The Tale of Meshka the Kvetch;* illus. by Arnold Lobel.
Dutton, 1980. 80-11225. ISBN 0-525-40745-6. 29p. $8.95.

K–3   Lobel's sturdy peasant characters and clean compositions are just right
for a tale in the folk tradition; written in a direct, simple style, the story
has good structure and humor. "Kvetch" is the Yiddish word for a com-

plainer, and Meshka is the kvetch par excellence of her village. Her feet are as swollen as melons, her son does nothing but read, sitting around the house like a bump on a pickle, her husband should have built a bigger house, and so on, and so on. One morning Meshka wakes with an itching tongue and suffers a series of disasters: her feet DO turn into melons, a huge pickle lies on her son's bed, etc. The rabbi tells her she has the Kvetch's Itch, and the only way to cure it is to praise the good in her life—so Meshka does, and like magic, her feet are back, so is her son, and her house (which had seized her in its grip) becomes a comfortable home.

242   **Cheney,** Glenn Alan. *Mohandas Gandhi.* Watts, 1983. 82-24848. ISBN 0-531-04600-1. 114p. $8.90.

7–   In a biography of Gandhi that gives much the same information as is in the many other biographies about him, Cheney gives good coverage to the various periods in the Mahatma's life, using familiar incidents. Although this is explicit in describing Gandhi's philosophy, and is adequately written, it focuses on events rather than personality, lacking the warmth (and style) of Betty Schecter's shorter biography in *The Peaceable Revolution.* The latter describes the lives and thoughts of Thoreau, Gandhi, and King; Cheney refers briefly to the influence of Thoreau and Tolstoy on Gandhi, and devotes several pages to Martin Luther King at the close of the book. A brief bibliography and an index are provided.

243   **Cherry,** Mike. *Steel Beams & Iron Men.* Four Winds, 1980. 80-66246. ISBN 0-590-07591-8. 87p. illus. with photographs. $9.95.

6–12   A former schoolteacher seeking more exciting work, Cherry became an ironworker after finding a mill job boring (The mill work was driving me bananas with its monotony . . .") and feels that construction work is just "hazardous enough to keep the adrenalin flowing." His descriptions of the many kinds of work that ironworkers do is enlivened by anecdotes; the writing style is colorful, conversational, rough, and vivid. The photographs are not always informative, but they are always dramatic.

244   **Chevalier,** Christa. *Spence and the Sleepytime Monster;* written and illus. by Christa Chevalier. Whitman, 1984. 83-25988. ISBN 0-8075-7574-7. 29p. $9.25.

4–6   Spence assures his concerned mother that it is not imaginary, that he
yrs.   really has seen a monster in his room. Mother leaves the door open, leaves a light in the hall, and promises to come with a big stick if. . .Soon a big shadow appears on Spence's wall and a hairy form jumps on his bed; he traps it in the bedclothes, calls his mother frantically, and reveals the family cat. Shadows do make things look bigger, his mother explains, and does a little dance to show how her shadow looks. Light, but reassuring, a nice handling of night fears.

245   *Children's Dictionary.* Houghton, 1979. 78-27636. ISBN 0-395-27512-1.
       816p. illus. $10.95.

3–6   In a single-column format, wide margins carry illustrations, some of
       which seem poorly chosen since the object being illustrated is dim or is
       in the background of a photograph. The entries include phonetic pro-
       nunciation, part of speech, other forms of the word (plural forms of
       nouns, tenses of verbs), definitions, and—usually—examples. All forms
       of the entry word are in boldface; examples are printed in italics. A pro-
       nunciation key is repeated at the bottom of each verso column. Deriva-
       tions are not included; variant meanings and explanations of idiomatic
       use are. All in all, a middle-grades dictionary that is easy on the eyes,
       easy to use, and quite extensive, with over 30,000 entries.

246   **Childress,** Alice. *Rainbow Jordan.* Coward, 1981. 81-596. ISBN 0-698-
       20531-6. 142p. $8.95.

6–9   "I never really had a *mama* and a *daddy*. I got a Kathie and a Leroy,"
       says fourteen-year-old Rainbow, whose mother is only twenty-nine,
       flighty, self-centered, occasionally abusive. And occasionally not there;
       at such times Rainbow stays with Josephine, a foster mother who dotes
       on Rainbow. Josephine is middle-aged, clinging to a much younger hus-
       band (who walks out during the course of the story) and resentful of
       the fact that Rainbow accepts her love so casually, while adoring frivo-
       lous Kathie. Each of the three women speaks in turn, so that the intri-
       cate meshing of motivation, action, and reaction becomes a vivid pat-
       tern. Unlike *A Hero Ain't Nothin But a Sandwich,* in which the several
       narrators were used to intensify the picture of the protagonist, this
       shows both the pattern of the generations and the individuality of each
       speaker; there is also a fourth, minor figure, a friend and neighbor who
       is almost eighty, Miss Rachel, but she is really not an integral part of the
       story. Miss Rachel is white, the others are black. While Rainbow is con-
       cerned with her particular problem, a delinquent mother, she is also
       beset by other, typical adolescent concerns—how to hold a boy without
       becoming his lover, how to accept the faults in a friend. Three distinct
       voices, like spotlights, move and cross; crossing, they illuminate.

247   **Christian,** Mary Blount. *April Fool;* illus. by Diane Dawson. Macmillan,
       1981. 81-3782. ISBN 0-02-718280-0. 48p. (Ready To Read). $7.95.

1–3   In the folklore of almost every country, there is a town that has a repu-
       tation of being the home of fools—Chelm, for example, or Gotham. Al-
       though the town in this story is given no name, the tale is based on the
       legend of how the April Fool tradition began in England in the town of
       Gotham. Aware that there will be trouble if the King adheres to his de-
       cision to build a house so that he can hunt and fish, the townspeople
       are dismayed; they know that the paths he travels become public roads,
       they know he is an ill-tempered man, and they can predict the loss of
       peace and plenty. They plan to fight King John, but a better plan is pre-

sented by the young man they've always taunted with being an idler: Seth the Dreamer. Seth uses his wits, the whole town cooperates (on the first of April) to impress on King John the fact that they are noodleheads, and the town is saved. The style is a bit choppy, but the story is fun, it's easy to read, and it's a useful source for storytelling.

248   Christopher, John. *Fireball.* Dutton, 1981. 80-22094. ISBN 0-525-29738-3. 148p. $10.25.

7–10   Neither Simon nor his American cousin Brad expected to enjoy the closeness that was being forced on them, since each had had other plans for the summer. They adjusted to friendship; what they hadn't expected was to be separated, not in London, but in another time and place. The transfer device is the fireball of the title, and the time is that period in which the early Christians were battling for power while Rome ruled Britain. The story has pace, suspense, adventure, and some humor in dialogue; it is crafted with skill and avoids a stereotyped ending, for Brad and Simon do not return to the contemporary London they've left, but sail in a small boat to the southeast coast of North America.

249   Christopher, John. *New Found Land.* Dutton, 1983. 82-18354. ISBN 0-525-44049-6. 135p. $9.95.

7–10   This is a sequel to *Fireball* in which Simon and his American cousin Brad have been shifted to a parallel world where the two boys are in America with two Roman soldiers. Aware of the hostility of Algonquian neighbors, suffering from the cold winter, they decide to build a raft and hope that the ocean current will carry them south. They capsize, are rescued by Vikings who mean them no good; warned by a Viking girl who is smitten by Brad and who runs away with them, they move on to find an Aztec civilization and realize that in this alternate world the culture has become a dominant one. After diverse adventures, the two reach the West Coast and find a Chinese pagoda in the wilderness. This has a fresh concept, good pace and style, effective dialogue and characterization, and a lively plot that begs for a sequel.

250   Clapp, Patricia. *Witches' Children: A Story of Salem.* Lothrop, 1982. 81-13678. ISBN 0-688-00890-9. 160p. $9.00.

6–9   As she did in *Constance,* Clapp uses a first-person account to give immediacy to events in colonial New England. This time the tale is told by Mary Warren, a young girl who is bound to service in a Salem household. Like the other restless adolescent girls who are her friends, Mary is at first only curious about Tituba's fortune-telling, aware that it is sly Abigail Williams who is pushing the slave to further titillation. There is nothing new in the story of the mass hysteria and witch-hunting in Salem; what Clapp does is make the role of the participants more comprehensible in a vivid and convincing narrative.

251   **Cleary,** Beverly. *Dear Mr. Henshaw;* illus. by Paul O. Zelinsky, Morrow, 1983. 83-5372. Trade ed. ISBN 0-688-02405-X; Library ed. ISBN 0-688-02406-8. 134p. Trade ed. $8.50; Library ed. $7.63.

4–6   In a story told through a series of letters and journal entries, Cleary astutely and convincingly takes her protagonist from second grade ("My teacher read your book about the dog to our class. It was funny. We licked it. You freind, Leigh Botts.") to sixth grade. He has begun the journal at the suggestion of Mr. Henshaw, recipient of all Leigh's letters, and the last entries show the ways in which Leigh has matured, adjusting to his parents' separation and accepting the fact that Dad does love him even though he's left home. This is touching, often funny, adroitly structured and written with craft and compassion.

252   **Cleary,** Beverly. *Ralph S. Mouse;* illus. by Paul O. Zelinsky. Morrow, 1982. 82-3516. Trade ed. ISBN 0-688-01452-6; Library ed. ISBN 0-688-01455-0. 160p. Trade ed. $8.50; Library ed. $7.63.

3–5   In a sequel worthy of *The Mouse and the Motorcycle* and *Runaway Ralph,* the dauntless mouse Ralph goes to school. He has ridden his toy motorcycle through puddles in the hotel lobby and decides he will go to school with his friend Ryan because the maintenance man at the hotel has been threatened with dismissal—and Ralph knows that the muddy floor is his fault. The scenes in the fifth grade classroom are most diverting; Cleary captures the essence of classroom bickering and the warm relationship between a good teacher and her students. Ralph, introduced to the class as Ryan's pet mouse, gets flattering attention, a damning newspaper article on mice in the school, and a solution in which he is doubly benefited: he gets a model car to drive after one of the boys has inadvertently smashed his beloved motorcycle, and he discovers when he gets back to the hotel that he's picked up some effective techniques from the teacher and can now handle the unruly mob of cousins who used to pester him for rides. The story is a deft blend of realism and fantasy, quietly and consistently funny, and occasionally touching without being the least saccharine. Again. bravo.

253   **Cleary,** Beverly. *Ramona Forever;* illus. by Alan Tiegreen. Morrow, 1984. 84-704. Library ed. ISBN 0-688-03786-0; Trade ed. ISBN 0-688-03785-2. 182p. Library ed. $9.36; Trade ed. $9.95.

3–5   A gentle comedy, a warm and realistic family story, and a perceptive study of a child: *Ramona Forever* is all three, a sequel as beguiling as its predecessors. The title refers to Ramona's glimpse of eternity as she sees herself in the endlessly reflecting mirrors of a bridal shop. She and Beezus are to be attendants at an aunt's wedding, and the ceremony is the final episode of a story that focuses on family relationships with a keen eye and a light touch.

254   **Cleary,** Beverly. *Ramona Quimby, Age 8;* illus. by Alan Tiegreen. Morrow, 1981. 80-28425. Trade ed. ISBN 0-688-00477-6; Library ed. ISBN 0-688-00478-4. 182p. Trade ed. $6.95; Library ed. $6.67.

2–4
*   A fifth book about Ramona has all the warmth, spontaneity, and humor of its predecessors, in another realistic and engaging story about the redoubtable child and her small adventures at home and at school. The classroom scenes are hilarious, the family scenes touching, as Ramona battles her way through each challenging day, adjusting to a new school and a new teacher, to having Daddy back in college, and to putting up with a spoiled four-year-old each afternoon because only if Ramona stays with a sitter can Daddy go to school and Mother work. The style is bubbly and fluent; the characters and dialogue ring true.

255   **Cleaver,** Vera. *Sugar Blue.* Lothrop, 1984. 83-19910. ISBN 0-688-02720-2. 128p. $12.00.

4–6   Cleaver has created here not one but two memorable child characters: eleven-year-old Amy, the crusty little protagonist who tries to harden her heart against the love and innocence of a four-year-old niece (Ella is almost too charming and good to be true, but she's fetching). That's really the story, as Amy reacts to being loved in a situation in which she's getting little show of affection from anyone else; all relationships improve in the course of the story, and almost all the improvement emanates, in a ripple effect, from the little child who leads them. While some of the writing seems precious, some of it is powerful. In other words, Cleaver at her almost best.

256   **Clifton,** Lucille. *Everett Anderson's Goodbye;* illus. by Ann Grifalconi. Holt, 1983. 82-23426. ISBN 0-03-063518-7. 16p. $9.70.

K–3   Grifalconi's pencil drawings, soft in style and tender in mood, are (although some are disappointingly cropped) both attractive and appropriate for the simple, poignant verses about a child's adjustment to his father's death. The poetry is preceded by a listing of the five stages of grief (denial, anger, bargaining, depression, and acceptance) and illustrates them as Everett struggles with bereavement; the writing is honed to simplicity, written from the child's viewpoint and easily comprehensible to other children.

257   **Clifton,** Lucille. *My Friend Jacob;* illus. by Thomas Digrazia. Dutton, 1980. 79-19168. ISBN 0-525-35487-5. 26p. $7.95.

K–2   Subtly textured black and white drawings echo the gentle tone of a story in which a black child speaks with affection and patience of his friendship with a white adolescent neighbor (Jacob is seventeen, Sam eight) who is retarded. Jacob is Sam's "very very best friend" and all of his best qualities are appreciated by Sam, just as all of his limitations are accepted. This isn't structured, it has no story line and little action, but it is strong in the simplicity and warmth with which a handicapped person is loved rather than pitied, enjoyed rather than tolerated.

258   **Clymer,** Eleanor. *Horse in the Attic;* illus. by Ted Lewin. Bradbury, 1983. 83-6377. ISBN 0-02-719040-4. 70p. $9.95.

4–6   Although the narrator, Caroline, loves horses and is taking riding lessons, there is not literally a horse in the attic, but a splendid painting of a race horse. Having become enamored of the small town where they have spent a vacation, Caroline's family has bought a house there; the painting is found by Caroline, the twelve-year-old narrator, and it's she who does the research that spurs the sale of the painting and gains some much-needed cash. The writing is direct and controlled, with good pace and adequate characterization; the mystery of the painter's identity adds suspense; what is most effective, however, is the convincing delineation of relationships within a family in which the members are mutually supportive, cooperating and compromising for the general good. The realistic black and white pictures are strong in draughtsmanship and effective in the play of light and shadow.

259   **Clymer,** Eleanor Lowenton. *My Mother Is the Smartest Woman in the World;* illus. by Nancy Kincade. Atheneum, 1982. 82-1685. ISBN 0-689-30916-3. 86p. $8.95.

4–6   Kathleen, fourteen, describes the events that led to her suggesting to her mother that as an intelligent woman interested and active in community affairs, she should run for mayor. There's nothing surprising in the story of the campaign and the election, which Kathleen's mother wins, but this is an appealing story because of the brisk pace and style, it gives a good picture of small-town politics and the roles family and friends can play, and it has warm, supportive familial relationships.

260   **Cobb,** Vicki. *Bet You Can't! Science Impossibilities to Fool You;* by Vicki Cobb and Kathy Darling; illus. by Martha Weston. Lothrop, 1980. 79-9254. Trade ed. ISBN 0-688-41905-4; Library ed. ISBN 0-688-51905-9. 128p. Trade ed. $6.95; Library ed. $6.67.

4–7   Cobb and Darling have compiled a series of impossible tasks, suggest-
[4]   ing to the reader that it will be fun to stump their families and friends by betting they can't perform them. The demonstrations are simple (trying to pick something up when one's feet are together, heels against the wall; trying to make a candle flame pass through a metal strainer) and the results guaranteed: the tricks can't be done. All of this is fun, and should appeal to children; what gives the book added value is the fact that the authors explain why the tricks can't be done in terms of physical principles; the tricks are grouped by such principles, with a section based on the law of gravity, another on fluids, another on mathematics, and so on. Brisk line drawings clarify the instruction; an index is appended.

261   **Cobb,** Vicki. *How to Really Fool Yourself: Illusions for All Your Senses;* illus. by Leslie Morrill. Lippincott, 1981. 79-9620. Library ed. ISBN 0-397-31907-X; Trade ed. ISBN 0-397-31906-1; Paper ed. ISBN 0-397-31908-8. 145p. Library ed. $8.79; Trade ed. $9.30; Paper ed. $4.95.

6–9   There are many books that demonstrate, through experiments and home demonstrations, how to observe or create phenomena that are illusory; Cobb goes a step beyond that and explains why a liquid may feel cold to one hand but warm to another, why you see spots before your eyes, how it is possible to make water taste sweet with no additives. She shows how all of the sensory responses can be manipulated, closing the text with a chapter on "Great Misconceptions," that takes a brisk look at such mistaken beliefs of ancient times as the flatness of the earth and the earth's central position in the universe. The material is intriguing, the experiments clearly described, the book informative and stimulating.

262   **Cobb,** Vicki. *The Monsters Who Died;* illus. by Greg Wenzel. Coward-McCann, 1983. 82-14252. ISBN 0-698-20571-5. 63p. $9.95.

3–5   Cobb takes a fresh approach to the subject of dinosaurs; although there are many good books about them, this is a fine addition. Drawings that are carefully labelled and are placed in juxtaposition to textual references are used to give clues to readers: one curved claw on the front foot, a thigh bone as tall as a man, a small skull with very weak teeth, etc. "Behold the Brontosaurus!" and an explanation—of how the clues were deciphered, the fossil remains compared with those of other species, and conclusions reached—follows. The text covers most of the better known species. It begins with a clear explanation of how paleontologists made deductions about the first fossils found, and of how the store of knowledge about dinosaurs has grown since that time, two hundred years ago. The final chapter describes some of the theories about what caused the dinosaurs to become extinct. An index gives access to a carefully organized text that is smoothly written and authoritative.

263   **Cobb,** Vicki. *Truth On Trial; The Story of Galileo Galilei;* illus. by George Ulrich. Coward, 1979. 79-237. ISBN 0-698-30709-7. 63p. $5.49.

4–5   While Cobb introduces invented dialogue, most of her text is authoritative in a biography that focuses on Galileo's ideas rather than his personal life. She makes the question of conflicting theories the center of the book, explaining lucidly the differences between Ptolemaic and Copernican theories of the structure of the universe; equally vivid is her presentation of Galileo's persecution by the Church of Rome, with his capitulation to the demands of the court of the Inquisition that he renounce his support of the Copernican theory that the sun was the center of the system, a fact that Galileo had corroborated through the use of the telescope he had perfected. The text ends without sentimentality, but there is an inherent poignancy in its picture of the aging Galileo, forced to deny the truth he believed in, living out the rest of his life engaged in creative research but burdened by the fact that he had denied his beliefs to save his life. A brief bibliography is appended.

264   **Cober,** Alan E. *Cober's Choice;* written and illus. by Alan E. Cober. Dutton, 1979. 79-11882. ISBN 0-525-28065-0. 48p. $9.95.

3–
*   Since this oversize book is important for the art rather than the text, it should be of interest also to children too young to find the minimal captioning of interest. Cober uses the space (single pages or double-page spreads, a few of which are marred by tight binding) admirably; at times his black and white drawings are set against lavish white space, at times they fill the page. And at all times they are marvelously textured, even when they have an unfinished look (as some do), and marvelous in their juxtaposition of sweeping line and tiny detail, in the contrast of solidity of body and lightness of fur or feathers. Cober's twenty-three animal drawings are accompanied by brief, patternless captions, some of which indicate whether he drew from life or used a stuffed animal, some of which give facts about species or simply comment on a personal reaction; there are also some scrawled personal notes in cursive writing, few of which are easily legible or particularly pertinent.

265   **Coerr,** Eleanor. *Gigi; A Baby Whale Borrowed for Science and Returned to the Sea;* by Eleanor Coerr and William E. Evans. Putnam, 1980. 80-10346. ISBN 0-399-20558-6. 128p. illus. with photographs. $8.95.

6–9   Photographs of variable quality illustrate Coerr's detailed account of the capturing and observation of a bady gray whale. The text, which begins with some background information about the habits and the migratory patterns of gray whales, documents the whale's ability to learn, and the ways in which it communicated with trainers and with the dolphin that became its companion. The scientists who planned the experiment were successful in their hopes of learning more about the gray whale, and they were delighted when Gigi, as planned, was returned to the sea and adapted to freedom. The writing style is direct and matter-of-fact; the book concludes with a glossary, an index, a bibliography, and a list of sources from which readers may obtain further information.

266   **Cohen,** Barbara. *Fat Jack.* Atheneum, 1980. 80-12510. ISBN 0-689-30772-1. 182p. $8.95.

8–10   Judy, who tells the story, frames the memories of her high school experiences at a meeting with an old classmate, Jack. Jack had been the class fat boy, the butt of so many wounding quips that Judy had felt sorry for him. She'd been convinced that he would make a superb Falstaff in the class production of *Henry IV, Part One;* the only other person who thought so was the school librarian, Jack's only friend. It is not his appearance but his talent that makes Jack a fine Falstaff. Once the play is a hit, Jack gains popularity and Judy loses him; in the concluding dialogue the older Jack and Judy reveal that each had been bitter in feeling the other had been disloyal. The details of the theatrical production are nicely blended with the theme of the developing friendship between Jack and Judy, and the changes in their friendship that come as a reaction to changes in their situation (especially the acceptance of Jack by others) are seen with insight and described with compassionate acuity.

267   **Cohen,** Barbara, *The Innkeeper's Daughter.* Lothrop, 1979. 79-2421. Trade ed. ISBN 0-688-41906-2; Library ed. ISBN 0-688-51906-7. 160p. Trade ed. $6.95; Library ed. $6.67 net.

6–9   Rachel Gold is the oldest of three children whose mother runs a small hotel; while she is not friendless, the inn is the focus of her life: the staff are friends, as are some of the loyal guests. She is especially fond of young Jeff Dulac, but he moves on to another town; her few ventures into social life with peers have been unsatisfactory. Although the story proceeds with little drama until the end of the book, it accelerates then, as a fire destroys the inn. The one thing the firemen proudly save is a large portrait Rachel has always disliked as much as her mother likes it; it is Rachel who, remembering the interest of a guest at the inn who was an art dealer, investigates the signature and discovers that the painting is worth many thousands. Her mother is considering marrying another guest, Mr. Jensen, and is surprised when her children (all of whom she had thought wanted a "normal" home life) want her to use the money to rebuild the inn, whether she marries Jensen or not. The characters are convincing, and the writing style has an easy, smooth narrative flow and natural dialogue.

268   **Cohen,** Barbara. *Molly's Pilgrim;* illus. by Michael J. Deraney. Lothrop, 1983. 83-797. Trade ed. ISBN 0-688-02103-4; Library ed. ISBN 0-688-02104-2. 32p. Trade ed. $9.50; Library ed. $8.59.

2–3   Molly, whose family had come from Europe the year before, was unhappy at being teased about her accent and appearance by her classmates. When she was asked, as part of a class project, to bring a doll dressed like a woman Pilgrim, Molly turned up with a clothespin doll her mother had carefully dressed in her own image. It looked Russian or Polish, a classmate scoffed; what did that have to do with the Pilgrims? The Pilgrims had taken the idea of Thanksgiving, the teacher said, from the Jewish celebration of the Harvest that they'd read about in the Bible. Molly's mother was right, she added. "Pilgrims are still coming to America." It was just as Mama said: like the first settlers, they had come to escape, to worship in their own way, to live in peace and freedom. Molly tells the story with poignant simplicity; the black and white illustrations have strength despite the awkward handling of figure drawing. The story could serve well as a focus for discussion of prejudice.

269   **Cohen,** Barbara. *Seven Daughters and Seven Sons;* by Barbara Cohen and
       Bahija Lovejoy. Atheneum, 1982. 81-8092. ISBN 0-689-30875-2. 216p.
       $10.95.

6–8   "I am Buran," the story begins, "daughter of Malik and the fourth of
       the seven female children born to him . . ." and the lively protagonist
       goes on to explain, in a tale set in ancient Baghdad, that her father has
       educated her as though she were a son, taught her chess, talked to her
       of important things. Wrathful because her uncle will accept none of her
       sisters as brides for his seven sons (he's rich, Buran's family is poor)
       Buran decides to go out into the world, posing as a man, and become a
       success. The story is told in three parts: the second is narrated by
       Prince Mahmud of Tyre, whose admiring friendship for the wealthy
       young merchant Nasir turns to suspicion that Nasir is really a woman,
       the third is told again by Buran (Nasir) after she has fled Tyre and re-
       turned to Baghdad, pining for love of Mahmud. It will surprise few
       readers that he pursues her, woos her, and wins her. What is surpris-
       ing, since this is basically a meets-loses-gets love story, is that it runs at
       such a lively pace, contains so much feminist philosophy, and is so con-
       vincing in its creation of a time past.

270   **Cohen,** Daniel. *How to Buy a Car;* illus. with photographs by Maureen
       McNicholas. Watts, 1982. 82-6899. ISBN 0-531-04494-7. 87p. $8.40.

7–   In a sensible, practical compendium of advice to the adolescent reader,
       Cohen addresses a range of problems and decisions in direct, informally
       written style. He suggests that one consider whether or not one really
       needs a car, discusses whether to buy a new or used car and what is
       entailed financially; and describes what to look for, how to guard
       against chicanery, and what legal measures and papers are required. An
       index gives access to the text.

271   **Cohen,** Miriam. *Born to Dance Samba;* illus. by Gioia Fiammenghi.
       Harper, 1984. 83-47690. Library ed. ISBN 0-06-021359-0; Trade ed. ISBN
       0-06-021358-2. 149p. Library ed. $10.89; Trade ed. $10.95.

4–6   Maria Antonia, eleven, describes her happy life in the shanty commu-
       nity on the hills of Rio de Janeiro and her consuming desire to be the
       soloist when the children of the Hill dance at the annual carnival.
       Cohen, who lived in Brazil for two years, has made the setting and the
       shared passion for Carnival and samba dancing vivid and believable.
       While Maria Antonia's obsession and her jealousy of another girl (who
       does get chosen as soloist) seem over-emphasized, there are enough
       incidents to give contrast. Above all, the story shows colorfully and
       convincingly the warm family life, the sense of community, the pride
       and joy of slum children, and the fact that they make the best of their
       situation and share the dreams and needs of children everywhere.

272   Cohen, Miriam. *First Grade Takes a Test;* illus. by Lillian Hoban. Greenwillow, 1980. 80-10316. Trade ed. ISBN 0-688-80265-6; Library ed. ISBN 0-688-84265-8. 29p. Trade ed. $7.95; Library ed. $7.63.

1-2   The affable children of *The New Teacher* and *No Good in Art* take their
  *   first multiple choice test, as a result of which one child is moved to a class for the gifted. Jealous, the hitherto peaceful group begins squabbling and has to be reassured by their wise teacher. Anna Maria, the child who had left, returns after a week by her own request, because she'd missed her friends, so the group is back together again. Hoban's endearing small children are a multiethnic group, the story has good structure and gives a warm picture of the relationship between children and their teacher; the book also reflects the group dynamics of the classroom and introduces the test in a humorous way: presented with alternate choices for "What do firemen do?" (make bread, sing, put out fires) Sammy worries because none of the boxes provide an opportunity to say that firemen pull your head out when it's stuck, which had happened to his uncle.

273   Cohen, Miriam. *See You Tomorrow, Charles;* illus. by Lillian Hoban. Greenwillow, 1983. 82-11834. Trade ed. ISBN 0-688-01804-1; Library ed. ISBN 0-688-01805-X. 26p. Trade ed. $10.00; Library ed. $9.55.

K-2   There's an addition to the first-grade class that Cohen has described in earlier books for beginning independent readers as well as for the read-aloud audience. Like the other books, this has a simple, mildly humorous text that is tuned in to the language and behavior of young children and is appropriate in subject and concept for that group. Here Charles, a new boy who is blind, adjusts to a group of sighted children, and they to him, as they learn that there are many things Charles can do well, that he may have limitations of performance but none of imagination and intelligence, and that there are times when he can fend for himself as well as times he can use help.

274   Cole, Brock. *No More Baths;* written and illus. by Brock Cole. Doubleday, 1980. 78-22790. Trade ed. ISBN 0-385-14714-7; Library ed. ISBN 0-385-14715-5. 40p. Trade ed. $7.95; Library ed. $8.90.

K-2   Annoyed because her parents and her older brother tease her about being dirty, and more annoyed because her mother says she has to take a bath in the middle of the day, Jessie decides to decamp. She runs into a chicken who tells her to try life chicken-style, and shows her how to frazzle, which entails nestling down into some sand and then shaking your feathers. Jessie tries it; she can't get sand out of her hair, and she itches all over. Then she tries grooming herself like a cat, at the cat's suggestion; then she wallows with the pig. None of it works, so Jessie goes home and has a bath. Wrapped in a towel and cuddled on her mother's lap, Jessie is hugged. "There now," her mother says, "There are worse things than taking a bath, aren't there?" And Jessie answers,

"Nope." Children should enjoy that ending as well as the situation, and readers-aloud should enjoy the lightness and humor of the writing; for example, when Jessie makes her poor try at frazzling, Mrs. Chicken says, "Not just anybody can be a chicken. Why, frazzling is child's play compared to laying eggs." The illustrations, watercolors that have a light touch and intriguing detail that is reminiscent of Peter Spier's style, are engaging in detail and attractive in composition.

275   Cole, Joanna, comp. *Best-Loved Folktales of the World;* comp. by Joanna Cole; illus. by Jill Karla Schwarz. Doubleday, 1982. 81-43288. ISBN 0-385-18520-0. 792p. $15.95.

4–6   A collection of two hundred folktales is divided by large geographical areas (West Europe, Middle East, Pacific, North America, etc.) and indexed by category of tale: humorous tales, men and boys, fools and noodleheads and so on. Although the print is small and the list of sources long enough to make finding them a bit of a chore (the selection gives the country of origin; the list of acknowledgements is alphabetical by compiler or adapter) the variety, number, and quality of the tales selected makes this a useful book for independent reading, reading aloud, and storytelling.

276   Cole, Joanna. *A Bird's Body;* illus. with photographs by Jerome Wexler. Morrow, 1982. 82-6446. Trade ed. ISBN 0-688-01470-4; Library ed. ISBN 0-688-01471-2. 48p. Trade ed. $8.50; Library ed. $7.59.

3–5   A continuous text is written in a straightforward style and is illustrated by photographs of excellent quality, many magnified, and by clear, simple diagrams. Using a parakeet and a cockatiel as examples, the author shows how their anatomical features (feathers, shape, hollow bones, air sacs, rapid heartbeat) all contribute to flight, and briefly describes diet, nesting, and hatching patterns. A good introduction to the study of birds, this can also be used for reading aloud to younger children.

277   Cole, Joanna. *Bony-Legs;* illus. by Dirk Zimmer, Four Winds, 1983. 82-7424. ISBN 0-590-07882-8. 44p. $8.95.

1–3   Bright pictures with a strong sense of design illustrate a simplified retelling of one of the Baba Yaga stories. Sent to borrow needle and thread from a neighbor, little Sasha wanders into the home of Bony-Legs (Baba Yaga, the Russian witch whose house stands on chicken legs) and is saved from being the witch's dinner when the dog, cat, and gate repay Sasha's kindness and help her escape. Although this is intended (and nicely gauged) for the beginning independent reader, it's also a good choice for reading aloud to younger children.

278   Cole, Joanna. *Cars and How They Go;* illus. by Gail Gibbons. Crowell, 1983. 82-45575. Trade ed. ISBN 0-690-04261-2; Library ed. ISBN 0-690-04262-0. 30p. Trade ed. $9.95; Library ed. $9.89.

2–4   In clear language and in logical sequence, Cole explains that wheels make cars go, and describes the several procedures that turn the wheels and the moving or stationary parts that are involved. A useful book, this is profusely illustrated with clear diagrams and some drawings, all of which are carefully placed in relation to textual references and all of which (save for one page that shows two horse-drawn vehicles with no attachment between the vehicle and the horse) are explicit and adequately labelled.

279   Cole, Joanna. *How You Were Born.* Morrow, 1984. 83-17314. Library ed. ISBN 0-688-1709-6; Trade ed. ISBN 0-688-1710-X. 48p. Library ed. $9.55; Trade ed. $10.25.

3–6   Photographs and diagrams illustrate a book on gestation and birth (it
yrs.   does not discuss conception) that is written simply, clearly, candidly. The text is in second person, which tends to make listeners feel involved. A preface directed to parents describes the aims of the book and the ways it may be used with children of different ages. Cole describes changes in utero and in infancy, ending on a note that is warm and positive: just as babies have learned new skills, so will the listener continue to grow and change and become a unique person.

280   Cole, Joanna. *An Insect's Body;* illus. with photographs by Jerome Wexler and Raymond A. Mendez. Morrow, 1984. 83-22027. Library ed. ISBN 0-688-02772-5; Trade ed. ISBN 0-688-02771-7. 48p. Library ed. $8.59; Trade ed. $9.50.

2–4   With the lucid, spaciously laid out text and clear diagrams that distinguish other books in this anatomical series, and with stunning photographs by Wexler and by Mendez, Cole uses the common house cricket as her example of how an insect's body helps it to survive. She moves smoothly from the evolution (probably from a prehistoric worm) through the anatomy (the mouthparts "form a kind of Swiss army knife"), presenting detailed factual material in a lively style suitable for reading aloud to younger children. The circulation works "almost like stirring;" the blood "sloshes about." The nervous system has "assistant brains" called ganglia: that is why a headless cricket can chirp, and a headless praying mantis can mate. The excellent discussion of reproduction focuses on the cricket, with dramatic photographs (stills and action shots) of the mating, egg-laying, and hatching.

281   Cole, Joanna, comp. *A New Treasury of Children's Poetry: Old Favorites and New Discoveries;* illus. by Judith Gwyn Brown. Doubleday, 1984. 83-20821. ISBN 0-385-18539-1. 224p. $12.95.

K–6   Animated line drawings, some soberly representational but most comical and/or grotesque, illustrate a book in which the selections are arranged so that they progress from simple poems for very young children and, with increasing complexity, move on to poems for older readers. Most of the poems were originally written for children, and most of the poets are contemporary. There's little unusual here, but it's an anthology of solid worth.

282   **Cole,** William, comp. *Poem Stew;* illus. by Karen Ann Weinhaus. Lippincott, 1981. 81-47106. Trade ed. ISBN 0-397-31963-0; Library ed. ISBN 0-397-31964-9. 84p. Trade ed. $10.50; Library ed. $7.89.

3-6   Illustrated by line and wash drawings, greytoned and comic, this mini-anthology of humorous poetry focuses on food. There's nothing serious or deep here, but most of the selections are good of their kind, whether they are by such well-known writers of children's poetry as Myra Cohn Livingston or Cole himself, poets who write for a broader audience, like Ogden Nash or John Updike, or writers who are less familiar.

283   **Collier,** James Lincoln. *Jump Ship to Freedom;* written by James Lincoln and Christopher Collier. Delacorte, 1981. 81-65492. ISBN 0-440-04205-4. 198p. $9.95.

6-10   A story set in 1787 is told by young Dan Arabus, whose father had fought in the patriots' army and had become a free man, while Dan and his mother still belonged to Captain Ivers. In an adventurous tale of danger and pursuit, Dan runs away after a frightening sea voyage and is taken under the wing of an elderly Quaker who is en route to the Constitutional Convention in Philadelphia. It is Dan who carries to the convention the proposal that becomes known as the fugitive slave law, a compromise measure. The notes that follow the story draw a careful distinction between fact and fiction, and explain the authors' decision to shape the dialogue and terminology to preserve accuracy and convey a period flavor. The dramatic story is solidly constructed, well-paced save for a rather lengthy description of a storm at sea, and sensitive to the changes in Dan as he begins to understand that a man can be proud, intelligent, and compassionate whether he is rich or poor, black or white; it is, however, inconsistent in the use of plural and singular in "plain talk," the Quaker speech patterns.

284   **Collier,** James Lincoln. *War Comes to Willy Freeman;* by James Lincoln Collier and Christopher Collier. Delacorte, 1983. 82-70317. ISBN 0-440-09642-1. 178p. $12.95.

7-9   Willy is thirteen when she begins her story, which takes place during the last two years of the Revolutionary War; her father, a free man, has been killed fighting against the British, her mother has disappeared. Willy makes her danger-fraught way to Fraunces Tavern in New York, her uncle, Jack Arabus, having told her that Mr. Fraunces may be able to help her. She works at the tavern until the war is over, goes to the Arabus home to find her mother dying, and participates in the trial (historically accurate save for the fictional addition of Willy) in which her uncle sues for his freedom and wins, testing the law that stipulated that a black man had to be set free if he joined the military. An author's note explains that the language Willy uses and the ideas she expresses are those that seem proper for her time and station, but the poor grammar in dialogue and the use of terms that may seem offensive to contemporary readers are obtrusive; the historical details are interesting, the pace variable.

285   **Collins,** Jean E. *She Was There; Stories of Pioneering Women Journalists;* illus. with photographs. Messner, 1980. 80-36769. ISBN 0-671-33082-9. 191p. $8.79.

7–10   Although the emphasis is on professional experiences in this collective biography of women journalists, there is some personal material; the book is based on interviews, with an editorial note about the subject preceding each first-person account. The book has variety, drama, the multiple appeals of the worlds of the press, theater, public life, military adventure, and the success stories of fifteen women who have found gratification in exciting careers, many of them overcoming prejudice in reaching their goals.

286   **Collodi,** Carlo. *The Adventures of Pinocchio;* tr. by M. L. Rosenthal; illus. by Troy Howell. Lothrop, 1983. 83-801. ISBN 0-688-02267-7. 254p. $17.50.

4–6   Profusely and beautifully illustrated with some striking paintings and line drawings, this new edition of a children's classic is a translation authorized by the Collodi Foundation to commemorate the hundredth anniversary of the book's existence. The text here has a more contemporary language pattern, and the translator has anglicized some words: Mastro Cherry is now Mr. Cherry; Geppetto's nickname, Polendina, is now Old Corny, etc. Basically, the story is unchanged, the tale of a puppet who becomes a boy because of his kindness to his creator-father; the mischief and magic are still there to appeal to readers, and some of them may find this edition more readable. All of them will find it, surely, more appealing visually.

287   **Conford,** Ellen. *Lenny Kandell, Smart Aleck;* illus. by Walter Gaffney-Kessell. Little, 1983. 83-989. ISBN 0-316-15313-3. 108p. $9.50.

3–5   Two threads bind this episodic and very funny story: Lenny's desire to be a comedian, and his relationships with his classmates, particularly the lovely Georgina and the bully Mousie (Maurice) who seeks vengeance because Lenny tripped him in the theater. Backing up the action is a series of family scenes, and they lead to a poignant note at the end of the story, when Lenny admits he's always known that his father had died falling down a troop ship gangway rather than in a military engagement of World War II.

288   **Conford,** Ellen. *Seven Days to a Brand-New Me.* Little, 1981. 80-25994. ISBN 0-316-153117. 136p. $7.95.

6–9   As Maddy describes herself, she's dull and shy, adequate in face and figure but no more, drab in dress; her only good quality is a quick wit—and she is so smitten by the handsome new boy, Adam, who has the locker next to hers that she can't talk to him. Spurred by a book on self-improvement and encouraged by her four best friends, Maddy buys new clothes, tries subtle makeup, and finally brings herself to say more than "Hi" to her hero. There are a few ups and downs, logical and amusing rather than dramatic, but in the end Maddy discovers that Adam is indeed attracted to her and that he's so shy he's been getting therapeutic counseling so that he could nerve himself to the point of making overtures. Basically, this is a girl-meets-boy story, but it's balanced by the warmth of the relationships between Maddy and her friends and the less frequent but equally affectionate exchanges between Maddy and her mother. Above all, it's the lively style, especially in the dialogue, that makes the book enjoyable.

289   Cook, Fred J. *The Crimes of Watergate.* Watts, 1981. 81-10497. ISBN 0-531-04353-3. 183p. illus. with photographs. $8.90.

8–   At the time the news of the Watergate break-in was making headlines, and in the months that followed, the accusations, revelations, allegations and denials, and eventually the televised hearings gave the American public a confused view of events, confused because many of them were revealed out of sequence. Cook, assembling facts and testimony, explains and illuminates the course of events that led to the first resignation of a United States President so that the pattern and motivation were clear. Sordid and criminal, the true story can hardly be viewed objectively, but the text achieves a measure of objectivity through its calm tone; it excels in the organization of material and clarity of development, and it has, still, all the terrible drama that the scandal had at the time the Nixon government came to its abrupt end. A relative index and a selective bibliography are appended.

290   Cook, Fred J. *The Ku Klux Klan; America's Recurring Nightmare;* illus. Messner, 1980. 80-19325. ISBN 0-671-34055-7. 159p. $8.29.

7–12   It began innocently enough, a social group for Southern men who were dispirited veterans during the reconstruction period; as "pranksters" they rode at night but soon saw that they could take advantage of the reaction of fear. Officially disbanded, the Klan was reconstituted at the end of World War I by William Simmons, a defrocked itinerant preacher, and the modern Klan emerged, an organization of terror, secrecy, violence, and hate. The major part of the book is devoted to a carefully researched account of some of the documented excesses and crimes committed by Klan groups and individuals, a chilling record. Well organized and competently written, the book has an objective tone despite the author's opinion of the Ku Klux Klan (as indicated by the title) and is lucid and informative; a bibliography and an index are appended.

291   **Cookson,** Catherine. *Mrs. Flannagan's Trumpet.* **Lothrop, 1980.** 79-26352.
Trade ed. ISBN 0-688-41940-2; Library ed. ISBN 0-688-51940-7. 192p.
Trade ed. $7.95; Library ed. $7.63.

6–8   Because their widowed mother needs a long stay in a nursing home,
Eddie and his younger sister must go to stay with their maternal grandparents, the Flannagans. Eddie has always detested his grandmother
because she had refused to admit his father to her home, feeling that
her daughter had married beneath her. And he detested the way she
used her ear trumpet, the way she barked at him. Only at the end of a
long, dramatic adventure in which his sister and the Flannagan maid
(his sweetheart) were kidnapped by, and rescued from, white slavers,
did Eddie come to appreciate his grandmother's heroic nature, and to
understand that her gruffness hid love and pride. In the end, when all
the family is safe and reunited, Eddie also realizes that he loves his
Gran, trumpet and all. The setting is Victorian, an English coastal village, and the writing style has vitality and color; characterization and
dialogue are strong, and the plot, although on the melodramatic side
and touched with one fanciful element (a ghostly figure appears in Eddie's dreams and leads to a real-life rescue), is deftly structured.

292   **Cooney,** Barbara. *Miss Rumphius;* written and illus. by Barbara Cooney.
Viking, 1982. 82-2837. ISBN 0-670-47958-6. 32p. $12.95.

2–4   Although young children may not understand all the words in this
 *   beautiful picture book, they are an appropriate audience for the story in
addition to the audience of independent readers. It is the life story of a
woman who, as a child, loved to paint in her grandfather's workshop,
where he painted and also carved figureheads for ships. One thing she
must do, grandfather told her, was something to make the world more
beautiful. The story is given variety, in text and pictures, by the travels
of Miss Alice Rumphius; when she returns to her home by the sea she
enjoys looking at the blue and rose and purple lupines visible from her
window, and she decides that her gift of beauty to the world will be to
plant more and more lupines for everyone to enjoy. The story ends
with a very old woman telling her great-niece that the one thing she
must do is something to make the world more beautiful, and the child
agreeing that she will—but she's not sure, yet, what that is. The idea of
offering beauty as one's heritage is appealing, the story is nicely told,
and the illustrations are quite lovely, especially the closing scenes of a
hill covered with flowers being gathered by children.

293   **Cooper,** Margaret C. *Solution: Escape;* illus. by Rod Burke. Walker, 1980.
80-50496. Trade ed. ISBN 0-8027-6404-5; Library ed. ISBN 0-8029-6405-3.
94p. $8.95.

6–8   A science fiction story is set in an unnamed Slavic country, in the
twenty-first century, where Stefan is a thirteen-year-old student at a
top-secret research center. One day, having stolen into another build-

ing, Stefan sees a boy that is his double, and as he does he is seized by a guard. He learns from his sympathetic teacher (who is sent away) that he and the other boy have been cloned, that they are being separately trained by the evil, power-hungry Dr. Zorak to be his puppets in a scheme to control the government. Stefan meets his clone-twin, Evonn, and with the help of the ousted teacher and Stefan's precocious knowledge of biochemistry, the boys work out an escape plan. When they succeed, in a nice final twist of the story, a mysterious third boy (a clone-triplet they don't know exists) happily watches them on a screen and punches out "All Clear" rather than the alarm signal. An ingenious plot is structured with suspense and good pace, the writing style is competent if not distinguished, and the characterization adequate. While this ends as though there might be another, following book, it stands alone as an adventure story.

294   **Cooper,** Susan. *Seaward.* Atheneum, 1983. 83-7055. ISBN 0-689-50275-3. 177p. $10.95.

6–9   As is true in other fantasies by Cooper, the story is imbued with the eternal battle between good and evil, and here they are personified by the evil and beautiful Taranis, bringer of death, and the protector of life, Lugan. The two young people who have separately crossed the border of time and place are Westerly and Calliope, each seeking a way to the sea and a solution to a private quest. Their way is beset with danger and adventure, and their stories are smoothly fused into a book with depth and momentum; the characters are convincing, the writing is polished, and the ending is both logical and poignant.

295   **Cooper,** Susan, ad. *The Silver Cow: A Welsh Tale;* illus. by Warwick Hutton. Atheneum. 1983. ISBN 0-7011-2672-8. 28p. $11.95.

K–3   Cooper has added one character, the son, in her fluent retelling of a folk tale that explains why white water lilies float on a lake in the Welsh mountains. Stern and greedy, Gwilym refuses to let his son Huw go to school as do the other boys, although it is through Huw that he has become wealthy. The magic people of the lake had sent Huw a silver cow in return for his skill as a harper, and the cow and her silver progeny gave milk so rich that they had brought riches to their owner. When the silver cow grew old and Gwilym arranged to have her slaughtered, a voice from the lake called all the silver cows—and where they had returned to their watery home, a water lily grew, one for each silver cow. The story is poignant and firmly structured; the watercolor paintings are distinctive for their use of light and shadow as well as for the softness of their colors, especially in the outdoor scenes.

296   **Corcoran,** Barbara. *Child of the Morning.* Atheneum, 1982. 81-8057. ISBN 0-689-30876-0. 112p. $9.95.

6–9   The family doctor said it was nothing to worry about, but Susan and her parents were baffled by the fact that she had had brief spells of un-

consciousness ever since she'd had a head injury during a school vol-
leyball game. Sometimes, when this happened, she'd fall. Nobody in
her small town would give her a summer job but she did get one, part
time, as odd-job girl for a summer theater group; later she was asked to
dance in one production. Her performance was fine, although it ended
in a blackout. But this time there was a new doctor in town, and he recognized her seizures as epileptic. After a worrisome series of drugs produced only adverse side effects, the right drug for Susan was isolated,
and the book ends with Susan at last feeling that her condition can be
controlled, and that the future can hold a career in dance for her. Although the parental apathy and medical inertia strain credulity a bit, the
story is otherwise nicely crafted, with strong minor characters, good
pace, and the theatrical milieu that adds appeal.

297   **Corcoran,** Barbara. *Strike!* Atheneum, 1983. 82-13759. ISBN 0-689-30952-
X. 144p. $10.95.

7–10   At first, when the teachers in his high school went on strike to protest
the censorious campaign by the town's Committee for a Balanced Curriculum, which involved removing books (and even one attempt to burn
books) Barry was sympathetic but uninvolved. He doted on one pretty
teacher who was an activist, and he also tended to react negatively to
the conservatism of his bullying father. However, participation forced
him to think seriously about the issues, and soon Barry found that he
felt strongly about the right to read. The story builds to a logical climax,
and Barry is deeply pleased when both of his parents rally to join the
cause in which he has come to believe. This has a message, but it's not
a book in which the message gets in the way of the story, for Corcoran
so carefully integrates her characters and their beliefs with their actions
and reactions that the plot flows naturally. A thoughtful approach to a
current problem blends smoothly with a perceptive study of an adolescent and his problems.

298   **Corcoran,** Barbara. *The Woman in Your Life.* Atheneum, 1984. 84-2942.
ISBN 0-689-31044-7. 159p. $10.95.

8–10   So deeply in love with Aaron that she'd dropped out of college and
gone with him to Mexico, Monty doesn't understand that he's exposing
her to trouble when he insists she drive back over the border in a borrowed truck with mescaline packed into the spare tire. Aaron is never
caught, Monty is jailed. Most of the book is based on Monty's experiences in a woman's prison; part is told by the author, and the italicized
sections are by Monty. The two formats work together, giving a blend
of immediacy and detachment. The time in prison is a period of growth
for Monty, who learns to judge individuals more clearly, to establish
priorities for the future, and above all to understand that the important
woman in her life is the decision-maker and judge, herself. Serious,
perceptive, and written with craft.

299   **Coren, Alan.** *Arthur and the Great Detective;* illus. by John Astrop. Little, 1980. 79-23511. ISBN 0-316-15736-8. 74p. $6.95.

4–6   En route to England, the fearless, peerless hero of Coren's spoofs of frontier life encounters that other great detective, Sherlock Holmes. There's a red herring subplot about a stolen ruby, but the real mystery is: who has purloined the score and libretto for a new theatrical venture by Gilbert and Sullivan? They, like Holmes and Watson, are broadly caricatured in a breezy shipboard story in which Arthur outdetects Holmes to find the missing papers and the culprit, a member of the ship's crew who yearns to be a singer and has perpetrated the theft so that he can memorize the part (he does), perform for Gilbert and Sullivan (he does), and hope that they will hire him (they do). An intentionally nonsensical plot and a light style with seriocomic dialogue should appeal to established Arthur fans and potential new ones.

300   **Coren, Alan.** *Arthur and the Purple Panic;* illus. by John Astrop. Parkwest Publications, 1984. 83-61281. ISBN 0-88186-001-8. 64p. $6.50.

4–6   First published in Great Britain in 1981, this is another zany adventure of the prodigy Arthur, Boy Expert at Everything, and an old favorite of American as well as British readers. This is a bit more slapdash, even within the bounds of deliberate exaggeration, than many of the earlier books, but it's still very funny. Watson is apoplectic and stupid, Sherlock Holmes is brilliant and intuitive, but it is young Arthur, with his keen deductive mind and intrepid nature, who solves the mystery of who has been painting the tops of London's monuments purple and how they got up there. Nonsense, but palatable nonsense.

301   **Cormier, Robert.** *After the First Death.* Pantheon, 1979. 78-11770. 239p. Trade ed. $7.95; Library ed. $7.99 net.

7–10   As he did in *I Am the Cheese,* Cormier uses different voices to tell a story; at times it is adolescent Ben Marchand, at times the voice of the narrator, and at times Ben's father, a man engaged in a secret government project that is threatened by the main action of the book, the hijacking of a bus full of children by terrorists—and at times, one of the terrorists, or of the girl who is the bus driver. What's achieved resembles a series of overlays, so that not until the end does the reader see all of the pattern and discern the fate of all the characters. Although the tale is filled with drama and action and suspense, and despite the craftsmanship of the writing, there are long and often introspective passages that may challenge all but the most sophisticated readers. Again, as he did in *I Am the Cheese,* Cormier explores the concept of the individual who is sacrificed by the group; again, he insists on truth however bitter or violent that truth is.

302   **Cormier, Robert.** *The Bumblebee Flies Anyway.* Pantheon, 1983. 83-2458. Trade ed. ISBN 0-394-86120-5; Library ed. ISBN 0-394-96120-X. 211p. Trade ed. $10.95; Library ed. $10.99.

7–10   In a story that is as trenchant as it is poignant, Cormier shows the courage and desperation of adolescents who know that their deaths are imminent. Barney, sixteen, is the only patient who is in the experimental
hospital who is not in the group of the doomed but is there as a control; all of them are there voluntarily, some to contribute to research
and some, like Mazzo, hoping for a quick death. In love with Mazzo's
twin sister, Cassie, who turns to Barney for help because her brother
refuses to see anyone in his family, Barney thinks of a plan that will
give Mazzo the quick, daring death he wants; secretly he reconstructs a
life-size model of a car from the dump next door, pulls the plug on
Mazzo's life-support system, and helps him to the roof where the car
waits to be pushed off for one last glorious flight. The story, which has
an element of twin telepathy, involves questions of medical ethics and
freedom of choice, and ends with Barney, who in the course of his
treatments and his conversation with his doctor, has learned that he too
is going to die, remembering with persistent joy, despite his gray fog of
pain, the beauty of the flight, his last achievement. This is, although it
is tragic, a stunning book: Cormier creates convincingly the hospital
world of the terminally ill, the pathos of Barney's love for Cassie and
his struggles with the hallucinations induced by the treatments that are
designed to block his knowledge and help him forget his true condition.
It moves, with relentless inevitability, like an ancient Greek tragedy,
with the compassion of the staff a contrapuntal note, to the requiem of
hopeless despair that, for each patient, still holds some passion for an
affirmative act of life.

303   **Cormier,** Robert. *Eight Plus One; Stories.* Pantheon Books, 1980.
80-13512. Trade ed. ISBN 0-394-84595-1; Library ed. ISBN 0-394-94595-6.
172p. Trade ed. $7.95; Library ed. $7.99.

8–   Each of Cormier's nine stories is preceded by his explanation of how it
came to be written, the explanation occasionally including comments on
literary aspects of the story. While the book should interest many
young adult Cormier fans, it seems even more suitable for an adult audience, not because of the difficulty or sophistication of the writing but
because of the subject matter; most of the stories are written from an
adult's viewpoint. Many have autobiographical overtones, and while
they are not as trenchant or exciting as the author's *The Chocolate War*
and *I Am the Cheese,* they are adroitly crafted, perceptive, and often poignant vignettes about the complexities of human relationships.

304   **Corrin,** Sara, ed. *The Faber Book of Modern Fairy Tales;* ed. by Sara and
Stephen Corrin; illus. by Ann Strugnell. Faber, 1982. ISBN
0-571-11768-6. 312p. $15.50.

4–6   A collection of fifteen original stories in the fairy tale tradition is illustrated with black and white drawings, notable for their chiaroscuro and
line, romantic in mood. The tales have been written over the past cen-

tury, and the anthology includes such authors as A. A. Milne, Eleanor Farjeon, Laurence Housman, James Thurber, and Philippa Pearce. Here and there a strong pedantic strain appears (F. Anstey's "The Good Little Girl") but most of the tales incorporate the standard motifs and literary devices of the genre. Although there is variation, the calibre of the whole is high; possibly the most engaging tale is E. Nesbit's "The Charmed Life."

305   **Corrin,** Sara, ed. *Once Upon a Rhyme;* ed. by Sara and Stephen Corrin; illus. by Jill Bennett. Faber, 1982. ISBN 0-571-11913-1. 157p. $9.95.

2–4   Line drawings that are deft, animated, and carefully integrated with the poems on the page illustrate a poetry anthology intended for the primary grades but also useful for reading aloud to preschool children. Most of the selections are light and humorous, and they have been chosen with an awareness of both the qualities that appeal to children and the criteria for poetic excellence.

306   **Corrin,** Sara, comp. *A Time to Laugh; Thirty Stories for Young Children;* comp. by Sara and Stephen Corrin; illus. by Gerald Rose. Faber, 1980. ISBN 0-571-09950-5. 205p. $6.95.

3–5   First published in England, a book that can be used for reading aloud to younger children as well as for independent reading by children in the middle grades is illustrated with comic-grotesque line drawings. While most of the material is easily available elsewhere, the short stories and excerpts from books are durable stuff with time-tested appeal: an assortment of folktales from varied sources, appearances by familiar characters like Pooh, Mrs. Pepperpot, or Brer Rabbit, and stories by such popular authors as Edith Nesbit, Eleanor Farjeon, and Ruth Ainsworth. The introduction discusses the types of humor that appeal to children, and the stories in this anthology reflect the diversity of readers' opinions about what is funny.

307   **Costello,** Elaine. *Signing: How to Speak with Your Hands;* illus. by Lois A. Lehman. Bantam, 1983. 82-45947. ISBN 0-553-01458-7. 248p. $9.95.

6–   A long introduction explains how American Sign Language originated, how it differs from other ways of communicating with the deaf, how it varies regionally, and how the author chose the twelve thousand basic signs pictured in the text. The material is divided into such chapters as "Numbers, Money, and Math," or "Descriptions," or "Health and Survival," with each chapter subdivided into appropriate topics and starting with linguistic principles. Save for some minor weaknesses in arrangement (references to the "5" hand or the "v" hand before those terms are explained) and the inherent problem of describing movement rather than showing it, the book serves admirably as a guide to those who would like to learn this broadly used method of communication.

308   **Counsel,** June. *But Martin!;* illus. by Carolyn Dinan. Faber, 1984. ISBN 0-571-13349-5. 31p. $7.95.

K–2   Here's the pattern: "Lee's face was smooth and golden, Lloyd's face was round and brown, Billy's face was square and red, and Angela's face was long and white, but Martin's face was (turn of the page) GREEN!" Martin is an extraterrestrial child who comes to visit a multi-ethnic classroom. Martin knows how to do everything, but he doesn't irritate anyone because he gladly shares his knowledge. At the end of the day, each of the other children gets home by a different method (walking, biking, riding in a car) but "Martin went home in his SAU-CER!" A very palatable mix of fantasy and story and message, with good layout and adequate line and wash drawings of the variously-tinted children and head-to-toe green Martin.

309   **Cowen,** Ida. *A Spy for Freedom: The Story of Sarah Aaronsohn;* by Ida Cowen and Irene Gunther. Lodestar, 1984. 84-10193. ISBN 0-525-67150-1. 158p. illus. with photographs. $14.95.

7–10   This is not a full biography but a highly fictionalized account of the adolescence and young womanhood of Sarah Aaronsohn, who lived in Turkish-owned Palestine in the days before World War I, and who left her husband during the war to serve in the Jewish intelligence network that reported Turkish activities to the British military. Based on interviews and on original sources that include recently declassified documents, this is adequately written, a bit heavy in style, a bit inclined to ignore Aaronsohn's mistakes and focus on the courage and loyalty which she indeed displayed. For most readers, this will introduce an unfamiliar aspect of the first world war and a dedicated freedom fighter who killed herself rather than chance her own weakness under torture when she was caught.

310   **Cowley,** Joy. *The Silent One;* illus. by Hermann Greissle. Knopf, 1981. 80-21853. Trade ed. ISBN 0-384-84761-X; Library ed. ISBN 0-384-94761-4. 136p. Trade ed. $8.95; Library ed. $8.99.

4–6   A story set in the South Pacific by a New Zealand author has a haunting quality that is due in part to the grave simplicity of the writing style, and in part to the touching picture of the plight of a deaf-mute in a rather primitive island society. Jonasi, the hero, doesn't understand his own condition; he only knows that the others of his island community move their mouths. In his silent world, he cannot comprehend the superstitious fear with which the people of his village regard him; he knows that they want to get the albino turtle that has become his pet as they swim together, but not that his neighbors think the creature is magical and evil. The few people who love him are taking him to a school for the deaf in another community when, with the tragic inevitability of mythic events, the boy jumps from the boat to save his turtle—and is never seen again.

311   **Crane,** Walter. *An Alphabet of Old Friends and the Absurd A B C;* written and illus. by Walter Crane. Metropolitan Museum of Art/Thames and

Hudson, 1981. 81-9449. MM ISBN 0-87099-272-4; T and H ISBN 0-500-01260-1. 28p. $10.95.

all
ages

The strong use of line and color, the vigor, and the humor that made Crane one of the first great illustrators of children's books are reproduced here in the reprinting of two alphabet books first published in 1874. In the first set, familiar nursery rhymes are faced by a page of pictures (with one double-page spread) in which large black letters are shown in gold circles. Here the only association between verse and letter is that the first letter of the verse ("A carrion . . . Ba,ba . . . Cock . . . Dickery . . ." etc.) is related. In the second, "absurd" ABC, the relationship is stated: "A for the apple . . . B is the baby . . . C for the cat that played on the fiddle, When cows jumped higher than 'Heigh Diddle Diddle'!" The last (C) is an example of the rhyme that's been based on a nursery rhyme, but is shorter, funnier, easier to remember, and better as an associative device for children learning the alphabet. However, it's the pictures that appeal, with their vigor and humor. Although this is graded here for the usual age for alphabet books, it will also be of great interest to students of children's literature, particularly because of the informative preface by Bryan Holme, who has written excellent art books for children.

312   **Cresswell, Helen.** *Bagthorpes V. The World; Being the Fourth Part of The Bagthorpe Saga.* Macmillan, 1979. 79-13260. ISBN 0-02-725420-8. 193p. $6.95.

5–7
*

In the fourth volume about the eccentric, engaging Bagthorpe family, a crisis is precipitated when Mr. Bagthorpe (an extremely excitable and often irascible man) sees his bank statement, which indicates he is overdrawn by millions. Although it is clearly a computer error, the hysterical man decides the family must completely alter its way of life: no more store-bought vegetables, no more household help, no use of electricity, and the acquisition of some food-producing livestock. Given the various degrees of inspired lunacy of the individual Bagthorpes, the ebullience of Cresswell's writing style, and sophisticated humor, this is as expectably entertaining as were the first three books.

313   **Cresswell, Helen.** *Dear Shrink.* Macmillan, 1982. 81-7728. ISBN 0-02-725560-3. 204p. $9.95.

5–8

Oliver, the narrator, is thirteen. William and Lucy, his brother and sister, are fifteen and seven; they are all intelligent and articulate and horrified at the prospect of being separated when their parents, both botanists, go off on a six-month visit to the Amazon. Their mother has obligingly tracked down an older woman who had looked after her when she was a child, Mrs. Bartle. Unfortunately, Mrs. Bartle, shortly after arriving, has a fatal heart attack, and the children are indeed separated, sent to foster homes, and reunited after the first placement doesn't work out. They run off to the family's summer cottage, unable to bear the idea of being in the foster home for Christmas. After a series of near-disasters, there's a happy solution when Mum and Dad (also unable to bear the separation) turn up. This story by a British author of note should have universal appeal, in part because of the warmth of the family ties, in part because of the humor and compassion of the putative author, and in part because of the wit and humor of the vigorous style of writing. Creswell is skilled at structure and pacing, but it is in the vivid, perceptive characterization and dialogue that her greatest strength lies. Part of the story is told by Oliver's journal, written as letters to Carl Jung, "because you are someone I think I will be able to tell my inmost thoughts to, and also because you were the first name that came into my head," and the formal "Dear Mr. Jung" turns into "Dear Shrink," hence the title.

314   **Cresswell,** Helen. *The Secret World of Polly Flint;* illus. by Shirley Felts. Macmillan, 1984. 83-24861. ISBN 0-02-725400-3. 176p. $10.95.

5–7   There are those who are trapped in time, and a few who can slip its
  *   net. When Polly's beloved father, Tom, English coalminer and poet, is injured in a pit accident and confined to bed, she must move to her rigid Aunt Em's while her mother accompanies Tom to a distant hospital. Polly believes Old Mazy, the strange outcast, when he tells her the legend of the whole village of Grimstone that disappeared to live secretly underground forever; she sees the Grimstone children slip back to dance around the ancient maypole at dawn. Deep in the woods she meets the Porter family, Time Gypsies from Grimstone, who have accidentally become trapped in the modern world. She helps them through the time tunnel, even daring to go down with them to Grimstone, and returns to find her father recovered from *his* accident and her family able to go home. The story is exquisitely told in lucid, rhythmic prose and dramatic dialogue. The characterization is sharp and complex; ragged Granny Porter, "dismal and fraught," is as ill-tempered a nag as Aunt Em, and there are other strange parallels between the lonely and displaced of both worlds. The exciting adventure will grab readers; its subtlety and depth will stay with them a long time.

315   **Crews,** Donald. *Carousel;* written and illus. by Donald Crews. Greenwillow, 1982. 82-3062. Trade ed. ISBN 0-688-00908-5; Library ed. ISBN 0-688-00909-3. 32p. Trade ed. $9.50; Library ed. $8.59.

K–2   Crews uses both color photography of words and paintings in Art Deco style of the carousel; a brief text describes the ride, from the horses waiting, silent and still, to the end of a whirling ride. The speeded, blurred pictures of the carousel in motion and of the words (boom, toot) that signify the calliope sounds are very effective. Despite the lack of story line, this should appeal to children because of the brilliant color, the impression of speed, and the carousel itself.

316   **Crews,** Donald. *Parade;* written and illus. by Donald Crews. Greenwillow, 1983. 82-20927. Trade ed. ISBN 0-688-01995-1; Library ed. ISBN 0-688-01996-X. 30p. Trade ed. $9.00; Library ed. $8.59.

4–7
yrs.

The bright frieze of pictures shows the vendors, the gathering crowd, and then the parade: marching band, baton twirlers, floats, antique cars and bicycles, and a fire engine. The crowd disperses, and the book ends as it began, with a truck from the Sanitation Department cleaning the parade route. Most children enjoy the color and action and music of a parade, and this is a vivid depiction that should have instant appeal.

317   **Crews,** Donald. *Truck;* illus. by Donald Crews. Greenwillow, 1980. 79-19031. Trade ed. ISBN 0-688-80244-3; Library ed. ISBN 0-688-84244-5. 32p. Trade ed. $7.95; Library ed. $7.63 net.

2–5
yrs.

In the same illustrative style as the author's *Freight Train,* this picture book without text has the bold, clean use of space and the solid blocks of color that make posters effective. Here the pictures follow a large truck from its loading station to its destination, and Crews introduces road signs and many highway scenes that show other trucks, a truck stop, and the intricate road system on which the big red truck travels. Easy to follow, informative, and handsome.

318   **Cross,** Gillian. *Born of the Sun.* Holiday House, 1984. 84-3740. ISBN 0-8234-0528-1. 229p. $11.95.

7–10

Paula has always adored her father, an exuberant man who was a famous explorer; when he asked her to go along on a journey to find a lost city of the Incas, she was thrilled. On the slow, tortuous trail through jungle and mountains, it became clear that something was deeply wrong with her father, Karel, and that her stoical mother knew what it was and couldn't talk about it. The author has done a superlative job of establishing the setting, defining characters, and knitting together the three strands of the story: the hunt for the fabulous city, the illness that is cured by an Indian healer, and the quest that is paralleled by an inner journey that changes and matures each member of the small band, particularly Paula.

319   **Cross,** Gillian. *The Demon Headmaster;* illus. by Gary Rees. Oxford, 1983. 0-19-271460-0. 174p. $6.95.

4–6

This is not to be believed, but it is certainly to be enjoyed; a fast-paced story that posits an unbelievable situation in which a small group of children is pitted against the cold cunning of a schoolmaster who has every other child in school under rigid hypnotic control. Dinah, who has just become a foster sister to Lloyd and Harvey, is the catalyst in the plot to learn what the evil headmaster is doing, how he's doing it, and what his ultimate goal is. Cross uses a realistic setting, writes capably, relieves the tension by humorous dialogue, and concludes with a happy if slam-bang ending.

320   **Cross,** Gillian. *Revolt at Ratcliffe's Rags.* Oxford, 1980. ISBN 0-19-271439-2. 144p. $10.95.

5–7   In an English story about a strike, three children are the catalyst for the revolt at Ratcliffe's small clothing factory; their investigation begins as a school project. Abby is the volatile leader, shy Susan the reluctant participant, and Christopher the grudging and ambivalent onlooker—at first. For Chris, one problem is that his mother works at the factory and refuses to join the strikers; another problem for him is that the two girls seem to him wealthy and snobbish. He is not aware that Abby's parents, socially conscious liberals, are pushing their daughter, or that Susan's conservative parents are outraged by her activism. Although the book focuses on the issues of working conditions and on conflicting views of labor and management, it captures the mounting tension of the protest, it gives (although sympathetic to the strikers) some idea of the managerial viewpoint, and it never loses sight of the three children, all of whom change their behavior realistically in response to social pressure and parental attitudes as well as their economic situations.

321   **Cross,** Helen Reeder. *The Real Tom Thumb;* illus. by Stephen Gammell. Four Winds, 1980. 80-11447. ISBN 0-590-07606-X. 92p. $8.95.

4–6   A biography of Charles Stratton, the midget who was given the stage name of "Tom Thumb" by his mentor and friend, Phineas Barnum. While this is just a bit on the gushy side, it is a carefully researched book, revealing the fact that the midget was actually not quite five when he began his public appearances (Barnum's publicity announced that Tom Thumb was eleven) and did not make public announcement of his real age until he was nineteen. The biography includes information about Tom Thumb's romance and marriage, his wealth, his generosity and charm, and his loyalty to Barnum, but it focuses primarily on his career and on such highlights as his command audience with Queen Victoria. Some of the interest in the book may rest on the fact that Tom Thumb was both a curiosity and a legend in his time; some of the appeal is in the glamor of show business.

322   **Crouch,** Marcus. *The Whole World Storybook;* illus. by William Stobbs. Oxford, 1983. 0-19-278103-0. 168p. $12.95.

4–6   Twenty-six folktales, each from a different country, are included in a book illustrated with distinctive line and wash drawings. The stories are retold in an animated and casual style that makes them effective to read aloud or to use for storytelling, as well as for independent reading. While there are a few tales that have been frequently anthologized, most are less familiar; among them are some fascinating variants on familiar tales, such as "Piglet and the Cow," a fairly sunny version of the Cinderella story from Korea, and "Prince of Nettles," a Hungarian tale in which a fox plays the same role as Puss in Boots. No sources are cited.

323   **Cumming,** Robert. *Just Look . . . A Book about Paintings.* Scribner, 1980. 79-9315. ISBN 0-684-16339-X. 61p. illus. $9.95.

4–6   First published in England, a book by a former Tate Gallery staff member who designed art education projects is meant to help children understand the components of painting so that they may better appreciate it. Although the question technique ("In which of them has the artist used lines that meet together?" "How has Titian used light?" "Are all the blue shapes the same, or do they differ in color or size?") often seems simplistic, it is used in combination with explanations that teach readers how to look for perspective and emphasis, to see the elements of composition, to judge the effects of color and light. The discussion of color is preceded by some descriptive material about primary and complementary colors and by charts that show how adding black, white, or grey affects the spectrum.

324   **Cummings,** E. E. *Hist Whist and Other Poems for Children;* ed. by George James Firmage; illus. by David Calsada. Liveright, 1983. ISBN 0-87140-640-3. 40p. $10.95.

3–6   Finely detailed drawings, black and white, have a range of effectiveness in composition; on almost every page of this tall book, an illustration faces one of twenty children's poems, sixteen of which were privately printed in 1962. Like other works of this poet, these selections convey a strong relish for word-play, word-turning; subjects are child-oriented, and the added appeal for many children will be the humor of the concepts.

325   **Curry,** Jane Louise. *Ghost Lane.* Atheneum, 1979. 78-73399. ISBN 0-689-50129-3. 158p. $7.95.

5–7   An excellent mystery-adventure story gives evidence of Curry's maturity as a writer, for here she combines strong characters, good dialogue, an intriguing setting, and a well-constructed story-line. Richard is eleven, delighted to be away from the strict aunt with whom he's been living since his mother's death, and equally delighted to be with his father, an opera singer who has taken a cottage near Glyndebourne for the season. Becoming friendly with elderly, cherubic Mr. Drew, whose home is filled with valuable antiques, Richard cannot believe that it is Mr. Drew who is back of a ring of art thefts, although evidence seems to point to the fact that he is guilty. Everything works out logically in a solution that is not too pat, and the story moves at a brisk, but not relentless, pace.

326   **Curtis,** Patricia. *Cindy: A Hearing Ear Dog;* illus. with photographs by David Cupp. Dutton, 1981. 80-24487. ISBN 0-525-27950-4. 55p. $10.25.

3–5   It never lessens a book's appeal to have photographs of a beguiling small animal, and the pictures of the energetic and affectionate Cindy being trained as a hearing ear dog add that appeal here. A comparatively new program (less than a decade old) to aid the hearing-impaired, this training of dog and owner is described in a brisk, straightforward text, the description being followed by a discussion of such training programs, a list of organizations that have training programs, and a relative index.

327   **Cusack,** Isabel Langis. *Mr. Wheatfield's Loft;* illus. by Richard Egielski. Holt, 1981. 79-984. ISBN 0-03-049581-4. 143p. $9.95.

6–8   Since he was three and saw his father killed by lightning, Ellis has been dumb, communicating through notes and gestures. Interested in homing pigeons, he goes to Mr. Wheatfield, a former pigeon-racer, for information and is offered the use of a loft as well as advice. When Ellis buys a pigeon, he is fooled by an unscrupulous seller: his new pet is a pigeon, but not a homing pigeon; doting on the bird, Ellis refuses to believe it won't fly home. The crisis in the story is the disappearance and eventual return of the bird, a return that moves Ellis to speak at last. This is tied to several minor plots: the gap between Ellis and his stepfather, the friendship between Ellis and a Cuban migrant—Jaime—who is staying at Mr. Wheatfield's along with his sister Rosalia, the sacrifice Rosalia makes (prostitution) to help her adored brother, and, lastly, the romantic relationship between Rosalia and a young policeman, who knows what she has done and why, and wants to marry her. All these are smoothly put together, but there's just a bit too much going on. Characters and dialogue are smoothly handled, the former with some depth and the latter with vigor; it's just the plot development that seems overburdened.

328   **Dabcovich,** Lydia. *Sleepy Bear;* written and illus. by Lydia Dabcovich. Dutton, 1982. 81-9729. ISBN 0-525-39465-6. 26p. $9.50.

3–5   A big, brown, amicable bear almost fills some of the pages in a gentle
yrs.   story about hibernation; the text is minimal and printed in enormously large type; "It's getting cold. Leaves are falling. Birds are leaving," and so on, each sentence on a double-page spread. The bear gets sleepy, snuggles into a cozy cave, sleeps through the winter, and rouses in the spring when the sun is strong and the birds come back and the sound of bees remind him that there is honey to be had. The scale, simplicity, and tone make this an exemplary book for very young children.

329   **Dahl,** Roald. *Boy: Tales of Childhood.* Farrar, 1984. 84-48462. ISBN 374-37374-4. 160p. illus. $10.95.

5–8   This should be of particular interest to Dahl's fans, but it should also appeal to anyone who likes writing that is direct, candid, and freeflowing. In these reminiscences of his boyhood, Dahl draws a vivid picture of a large Norwegian-English family and particularly a vivid and not flattering picture of the British public school system as it was when Dahl was a homesick little boarder, terrified by the masters and prefects, cowed by Matron, resentful of the punishment so harshly meted out for so little reason. Many young adults and adults will probably enjoy this as much as do readers in the upper elementary grades.

330   **Dallas-Smith,** Peter. *Trouble for Trumpets;* illus. by Peter Cross. Random House, 1984. 83-43115. Library ed. ISBN 0-394-96513-2; Trade ed. ISBN 0-394-86513-8. 30p. Library ed. $9.99; Trade ed. $9.95.

2–4   First published in England, this oversize book gives little sign that the
*   story was written after the illustrations were completed. This is an animal fantasy, a parable of the seasons, something of a nature book, with the added appeals of a game element (hidden faces) and humor (plugging in crocus bulbs). The story is told by Podd, one of the Trumpets who live in a land of sunshine, whose adventures lead him into participation in the defensive war against the Grumpets, the hostile warriors of a dark and frozen land. The story is capably told, the plot's cohesive, but the book's charm is in its illustrations, some in navy and white, some in color. Both kinds of pictures are infinitely detailed, but it is in the paintings that Cross excels, with the sort of natural abundance that is in some Burkert backgrounds (less delicate, more dramatic here) and combining real and fanciful objects to which there is identification access through tiny numbers that correspond to a chart. A tour de force, visually.

331   **Dallinger,** Jane. *Swallowtail Butterflies;* by Jane Dallinger and Cynthia Overbeck; from the original by Nobotu Motofuji; tr. by Kay Kushino. Lerner. 1983. 82-15294. ISBN 0-8225-1465-6. 48p. $8.95.

3–5   First published in Japan, the text is based on Kushino's translation of Motofuji's original text, and is continuous, clear, and explicit. The fine color photographs (from the original publication) are carefully placed in relation to textual references; they and the diagrams are adequately labelled. The book describes the anatomy, habits, and life cycle of the swallowtail, focusing particularly on the four stages of that cycle: egg, larva (or caterpillar), pupa, and adult butterfly.

332   **Danziger,** Paula. *The Divorce Express.* Delacorte, 1982. 82-70318. ISBN 0-440-02035-2. 144p. $10.95.

6–8   Fourteen, Phoebe (who tells the story) has become adjusted to shuttling back and forth between her father's home in Woodstock and her mother's apartment in Manhattan via the bus she calls "The Divorce Express" because there are so many children like her who ride it. She has *not* become adjusted to the man her mother is planning to marry, and feels more and more at home in Woodstock, especially when she makes a new friend, Rosie, whose parents (one black, one white and Jewish) are also divorced. The story ends with Phoebe and Rosie accepting with some pleasure the fact that Phoebe's father and Rosie's mother have formed an alliance, and with Phoebe's realization that she'll be able to cope with her new stepfather. This isn't structurally strong or innovative in concept, but it's written with great vitality and humor, and it remarks with perception on the ambivalence of a child's divided loyalties and her adaptability.

333   **Danziger,** Paula. *There's a Bat in Bunk Five.* Delacorte, 1980. 80-15581. Trade ed. ISBN 0-440-08605-1; Library ed. ISBN 0-440-08600-X. 150p. Trade ed. $7.95; Library ed. $7.45.

6–8   A sequel to *The Cat Ate My Gym Suit* in which Marcy's favorite teacher, Ms. Finney, was fired, is set two years later. Marcy, now almost fifteen, has been invited by Ms. Finney, now married, to be a junior counselor at the camp she and her husband run. In some ways this is the usual camping story of pranks, bunkmates, adjustment to separation from parents etc. This doesn't, however, follow a formula plot; it has depth in the relationships and characterizations; and it's written with vigor and humor. Marcy learns not to expect too much from others, not to assume that all problems will—or can—be solved; she also learns not to expect too much from herself.

334   **Davies,** Andrew, *Conrad's War.* Crown, 1980. 79-2-8289. ISBN 0-517-54007-X. 128p. $7.95.

5–7   Winner of the 1978 Guardian Award, this amusing borderline fantasy depicts the sustained imaginative play of a boy who is infatuated with war games, a young English Walter Mitty. Davies makes fun of war novels and war movies in the spoofs of stereotyped German officers, heroic deeds of the cool, indomitable Conrad, and the ineptness of his father (known as The Great Writer) who humbly participates as a bungling disciple; in depicting the father, Davies pokes fun at himself as absent-minded, inept, bald, and corpulent. The heavy emphasis on war sequences may weigh on some readers, as Conrad imagines himself taking part in World War II in his homemade tank, but taken with a grain of salt this is a very funny book.

335   **Davis,** Edward E. *Into The Dark; A Beginner's Guide to Developing and Printing Black and White Negatives.* Atheneum, 1979. 78-11284. ISBN 0-689-30676-8. 210p. illus. $9.95.

6–   Despite the author's claim, in his introduction, that "It avoids the fault of trying to teach the beginner too much," this text does seem to contain an enormous amount of advice and information. However, the material is logically organized and the advice specific; the writing style is clear and not too formal, and instructions are given in a careful step-by-step form at those points where explanations of a procedure are needed. Davis gives suggestions for what to buy (and not to buy) in the way of cameras, film, light meters, lenses, and all of the equipment needed for developing and printing film, and includes suggestions for buying some pieces of equipment secondhand. Sources of information are given, although the list is not extensive, in an appended note; a bibliography and an index are appended.

336   **Dean,** Anabel. *Up, Up, and Away! The Story of Ballooning.* Westminster, 1980. 79-23427. ISBN 0-664-32658-7. 192p. illus. with photographs. $11.95.

6–8   Lightened by occasional fictionalized passages or bits of dialogue, this is a comprehensive and well-organized history of ballooning that begins with the experiments of the Montgolfier brothers in 1782 after they had seen, and been intrigued by, some Japanese floating lanterns. From a fad and a sport, ballooning became a serious venture, used for transportation, for military purposes, and for research. The test is chronological, with deviations from the chronology because of such topical chapters as "Balloons in War," and it is quite profusely illustrated with photographs, drawings, and diagrams. The explanation, in the first chapter, of the physical principles of balloon flight, is brief but clear. A glossary, bibliography, and index are appended.

337   **De Clements.** Barthe. *Seventeen and In-Between.* Viking, 1984. 84-5282. ISBN 0-670-63615-0. 162p. $11.95.

6–9   It takes a long time to become secure when you've had as bad a childhood as Elsie had: so fat (in *Nothing's Fair in Fifth Grade*) that her cold, strict mother had put her on so stringent a diet that Elsie stole from her classmates; so unsure of herself (in *How Do You Lose Those Ninth Grade Blues?*) that she couldn't believe that Craddoc, a handsome upperclassman, really loved her. Now Elsie is seventeen. Craddoc, when he's back from college, wants sexual consummation; Elsie's reluctant. Her mother wants to improve their relationship; Elsie balks. In fact, Elsie's feelings of suspension and ambivalence move into positive paths in several ways, as she realizes that she's grown past Craddoc, becomes aware of moral commitments, concedes that her mother is really trying to make amends, and acknowledges to herself that she has been afraid to grow and change, but that she must do so. The author, who has worked as a school counselor, has developed with perception the character of an adolescent whose developmental patterns are complex, and she has used Elsie skillfully as narrator to give immediacy to the story.

338   **Degens,** T. *The Visit;* Viking, 1982. 82-2600. ISBN 0-670-74712-2. 150p. $10.95.

7–9   Kate begins her story by quoting Aunt Sylvia: "Hitler did a lot of wonderful things," and Kate comments "Not long ago I loved and admired Aunt Sylvia." Sylvia is visiting her brother in Berlin, and she is not aware of the fact that Kate has been reading the diary of another Kate, Sylvia's younger sister. The text moves between a narration of the present and the diary entries, giving both a perceptive development of the younger Kate's changing attitude toward Sylvia, and an acute, at times bitter, picture of the roles of the sisters when they were at a Nazi girls' camp. Inexorably the story moves from Sylvia's domineering flamboyance as a camp leader and Kate's subservience to the growing resentment and perspective that made Kate see how her sister used other people (masking her selfishness and cruelty with patriotic zeal) and, eventually, to Kate's efforts to help some prisoners of war and her resultant death.

339   **Delton,** Judy. *Near Occasion of Sin.* Harcourt, 1984. 84-4597. ISBN 0-15-256738-0. 152p. $12.95.

7–10   An only child, a docile Catholic, always fearful and guilty about the sins for which the nuns had told her she would go to purgatory or hell, Tess looked to marriage as the perfect solution to her yearnings, the only right way of life. When she fell in love with Duane, it was hard to resist his sinful if pleasurable caresses, and Tess agreed to a quick marriage. Taught that a husband was to be venerated however he behaved, Tess put up with machismo, bullying, irrational anger, deception, and the growing awareness that she had married a neurotic ne'er-do-well until—just before her baby was due—she simply walked out and went home to her parents. In a chilling ending, the baby is baptized and the whole pattern, it is implied, will start again. This is Delton's most powerful book, a vivid if depressing picture of Catholic education.

340   **Demuth,** Jack. *City Horse;* by Jack and Patricia Demuth; photographs by Jack Demuth. Dodd, 1979. 78-23651. 80p. $6.95.

4–6   Profusely illustrated with photographs, the text describes all aspects of the life of a New York City policeman's horse. One of a group of twenty Tennessee Walkers, the horse, Hannon, has had to get accustomed to the hard pavements, the heavy traffic and noise, and the strange objects (he was frightened by vendors' umbrellas, for example) of city streets. Some of the text describes the work of Hannon's rider, but most of it is devoted to descriptions of Hannon's training, his accommodations, the work of the blacksmith, the attention he gets from children, and the hazards police work in the city present for horse and rider. The writing style is casual and includes many comments by Hannon's rider, Officer Mike Sicignano, whose affection for his horse adds warmth to the book.

341   **Demuth,** Patricia. *Joel: Growing Up a Farm Man;* illus. with photographs by Jack Demuth. Dodd, 1982. 81-43218. ISBN 0-396-07997-0. 144p. $12.95.

4–7   A photodocumentary gives a great deal of information about the way of life on an Illinois livestock farm and focuses on the youngest child. Joel, thirteen, is a good student, and he has time for extracurricular activities, but most of his time after school and on days when there is no school is devoted to doing a full share of the farm work. Demuth describes in great detail each procedure and some of the problems in caring for the hogs that are solely Joel's responsibility; among his other tasks are field work, cleaning, caring for machinery, and harvesting the feed crop. Photographs of good quality make processes and equipment more comprehensible to readers with no experience of farm life. The text is capably written, carefully detailed, and informative, making it clear that farm life may be difficult but that it can also be satisfying and lucrative.

342   **De Paola,** Thomas Anthony. *The Knight and the Dragon;* written and illus. by Tomie de Paola. Putnam, 1980. 79-18131. Hardcover ed. ISBN 0-399-20707-4; Paper ed. ISBN 0-399-20708-2. 27p. Hardcover ed. $8.95; Paper ed. $3.95.

K–3   A knight who's never fought a dragon reads a how-to book and makes his own armor and weapons; a dragon who's never fought a knight reads a how-to book and practices looking fierce and swishing his lethal tail. They meet once and rush right past each other; on the second charge the dragon lands in a pond and the knight in a tree. The castle librarian, going by in her bookmobile (a horse-drawn cart) gives them books: *The Outdoor Cook Book* and *How to Build a Bar-B-Q,* and a partnership is born, the K & D Bar-B-Q Stand. The ineptness of the two protagonists should amuse small children, the suggested power of the book should amuse their elders, and the amicably silly tale should appeal to both; the pictures are typical of de Paola's work, and if they are much like the pictures in other books they are still deft and agreeable.

343   **De Paola,** Thomas Anthony. *Now One Foot, Now the Other;* written and illus. by Tomie de Paola. Putnam, 1981. 80-22239. Hardcover ed. ISBN 0-399-20774-0; Paper ed. ISBN 0-399-20775-9. 43p. Hardcover ed. $7.95; Paper ed. $3.95.

K–2   Like de Paola's *Nana Upstairs and Nana Downstairs,* this is a loving testament to the special bond that can exist between a child and a grandparent. Here it's the love between Bobby and the grandfather, Bob, for whom he was named. Bob had helped his grandson learn to walk (see title) and little Bobby loved to hear the story over and over again. When Bob has a stroke, Bobby is unhappy and frightened; when his grandfather is brought home from the hospital, Bobby is disturbed because his grandfather can't walk or talk and doesn't seem to know him. But Bobby tries to communicate and is encouraged when Bob responds. Little by little his grandfather improves, and soon Bobby is helping his grandfather walk ("Now one foot . . .") just as the old man had helped him. Brown and blue tones are used for the illustrations, a bit simpler and more subdued than de Paola's usual work; the writing style is direct and pleasing. While the book may lead children to think that all those who suffer a stroke improve, and while it's not quite believable that no other person gives therapeutic assistance to the old man, it's still a satisfying story of one kind of family love.

344   **De Pauw,** Linda Grant. *Seafaring Women.* Houghton, 1982. 82-9254. ISBN 0-395-32434-3. 246p. $10.95.

7–   The author has gathered an amazing amount of material for this interesting account of women who were pirates, whalers, privateers, traders, or fighters at sea. Because this covers a longer chronological period than does dePauw's *Founding Mothers: Women of America in the Revolutionary Era,* and a broader area (the world) it is more diffuse, with a wider range of material but not as much treatment in depth. Some of the stories become a bit repetitive, but most are dramatic, replete with danger and with examples of courage and cunning. Good, brisk pace and a straightforward writing style make the information both accessible and enjoyable; the index is fairly extensive, and the bibliography of suggested readings is divided by chapters.

345   **De Regniers,** Beatrice Schenk, ad. *Everyone Is Good for Something;* illus. by Margot Tomes. Houghton/Clarion, 1980. 79-12223. ISBN 0-395-28967-X. 27p. $8.95.

K–3   A Slavic folktale is retold with zest and humor, and is illustrated with pictures that share both qualities; Tomes uses repetition to advantage, as the boy tries approaching some of his potential employers a second time, with identical small-print captions. De Regniers begins with brio, in good folktale style, "There was this boy. His mother said he was good for nothing. And so the boy, too, thought he was good for nothing." As in so many folktales, the boy (no name is used) is rewarded for his kindness to other creatures, there's a touch of magic to implement this (a talking cat), and the ending is cozy and secure, as the cat is proved right; everyone is good for something. Nice to read alone or aloud, or to use for storytelling.

346   **De Roo,** Anne. *Scrub Fire.* Atheneum, 1980. 80-12267. ISBN 0-68-380775-6. 106p. $7.95.

4–6   Michelle, fourteen, is the oldest of the three Seton children who are taken into the New Zealand wilderness by an aunt and uncle who are delighted by the idea of camping; Andrew and Jason, twelve and nine, are thrilled, but Michelle goes with sullen reluctance. A brush fire set off by inept Uncle Don sends Michelle running off on her own; later reunited with her brothers, she hopes that the two adults are safe. The Setons are not, they are quite lost. The rest (and major) part of the story has a Robinson Crusoe appeal, as the three children learn to cope with the wilderness; Michelle is resourceful, but it is Andrew's camping experiences and knowledge of survival techniques that carries them through the ordeal and back to safety. The setting, the danger, the self-reliance mustered by the children, are all appealing aspects of a story that is well enough written to sustain pace and interest despite the narrow scope.

347   **Dewey,** Ariane, ad. *Pecos Bill;* ad. and illus. by Ariane Dewey. Greenwillow, 1983. 82-9229. Trade ed. ISBN 0-688-01410-0; Library ed. ISBN
0-688-01412-7. 56p. Trade ed. $9.50; Library ed. $8.59.

2–3   The large print, short sentences, simple vocabulary, and clean, bare
tinted line drawings indicate that the primary audience for this book is
the young independent reader, but the action and humor make it a
good choice, also, for reading aloud to the very young child. It's a good
introduction to the tall tale hero who rides a lion, uses a snake for a
lasso, and rescues his bride after she has bounced for three days on her
bustle. The ending is a bit abrupt, but the adaptation is otherwise competent, an appropriate selection of the many tales of Pecos Bill for the
primary grades reader.

348   **De Wit,** Dorothy, ed. *The Talking Stone; An Anthology of Native American
Tales and Legends;* illus. by Donald Crews. Greenwillow, 1979. 79-13798.
Trade. ed. ISBN 0-688-80204-4; Library ed. ISBN 0-688-84204-6. 213p.
Trade ed. $8.95; Library ed. $8.59 net.

5–7   The stories are grouped by region, with tribal sources ascribed, in a
nicely varied selection that includes pourquoi stories, creation myths,
humorous tales, and stories of tribal heroes. Some background material
is provided, as is a section of notes and sources.

349   **Dickinson,** Emily. *Acts of Light;* introduction by Jane Langton; illus. by
Nancy Ekholm Burkert. Little/New York Graphic, 1980. 80-19848. Trade
ed. ISBN 0-8212-1098-X; Deluxe ed. ISBN 0-8212-1118-8. 166p. Trade ed.
$24.95; Deluxe ed. $75.00.

7–
 *   Kudos to all concerned: to Emily Dickinson, of course, to the artist, to
the editor and art director, and to Jane Langton for her sensitive "appreciation," an introduction that is both a biography and a critical commentary on the poet's work. The book includes eighty poems, indexed
by first lines; notes, sources, and a bibliography of works about the
poet are included. The introduction is illustrated by delicate line drawings, the poems by full-page paintings; these are not the intricately detailed work with which Burkert has illustrated several books for children, but evocative interpretations of Dickinson's person and her
poems: a scribbled poem tucked into the pocket of a primly-printed
apron, a doorway through which lush flowers spill, an old-fashioned
circus wagon, and—the frontispiece—one huge white chrysanthemum,
its intricately curled petals curved about a blue-shadowed center. The
format is spacious and dignified. A beautiful book.

350   **Dickinson,** Peter. *The Seventh Raven.* Dutton, 1981. 81-3213. ISBN
0-525-39150-9. 192p. $11.50.

7–9   The seventh raven is Juan O'Grady, added to the cast of an original children's opera put on each year in an English church. There were to have
been six ravens; Juan has been added at the request of Doll's father

(Doll, seventeen, is the narrator) who wants Juan in as a political favor, since the boy is the son of the ambassador of a country (fictional) that may be an ally. The story is moving gently along, amusing as a back-stage melange of humor, theatrical politics, and personal commentary by Doll, when a group of revolutionaries from Juan's country burst in to take the whole cast and staff hostage. Their goal: to kidnap Juan, who is immediately hidden and protected by the others. There is a trial of sorts, during which Doll's mother is shot in the hand (she's a concert-calibre cellist) but Juan is kept safe and the terrorists are caught. This has a diverting setting, good writing style and characterization, and a quiet and very British humor, and although the dramatic development is slow to start, it has enjoyable suspense and convincing structure once it does start.

351   **D'Ignazio,** Fred. *Electronic Games.* Watts, 1982. 82-1962. ISBN 0-531-04396-7. 64p. illus. with photographs. $7.90.

6–9   Beginning with a discussion of how electronic games were invented and a description of how they work, the author goes on to describe different kinds of popular games and rules for play, gives advice on play strategy, and envisions electronic games of the future. A divided list of game manufacturers, a bibliography, and an index are appended to a text that is clearly written and should have wide appeal.

352   **D'Ignazio,** Fred. *The New Astronomy: Probing the Secrets of Space.* Watts, 1982. 81-21817. ISBN 0-531-04386-X. 72p. illus. with photographs. $7.90.

7–   A good overview of contemporary research and discovery in astronomy, this describes the findings and consistently indicates the way in which the work of today's astronomers is based on earlier knowledge but ac-celerated and augmented by today's scientific tools. It also distinguishes between the fact and theory, especially important in those sections in which D'Ignazio speculates about future research equipment and future astronomical developments in our violent universe. The text is as sim-ply written as is consistent with the use of scientific terminology and complex concepts. A glossary, a bibliography, and an index are appended.

353   **Dillon,** Barbara. *The Beast in the Bed;* illus. by Chris Conover. Morrow, 1981. 80-15069. Trade ed. ISBN 0-688-22254-4; Library ed. ISBN 0-688-32254-9. 24p. Trade ed. $7.95; Library ed. $7.63.

K–2   Tiny, spiny, and plump, the little beast slips into Marcia's bedroom and makes himself at home; at first Marcia's frightened, but the agreeable little creature soon becomes her best friend. He's sad when Marcia starts school, because then he has to leave. And then, one day, he spots a small, lonely looking boy watching the school bus, for which he is too young, pulling away. He offers to walk the boy home, then says he's tired and needs to be carried. Thus, cuddled in the arms of his new boy, the little creature whose mission it is to become the companion of lonely children is happy again. There are so many stories about children's imaginary companions, it's nice to have one told from the viewpoint of the companion, and told with a gentle, cheerful tone that is echoed by the tidy little black and white drawings (some in silhouette) in which the only color is the green of the little beast.

354   **Dolan,** Edward F. *Child Abuse.* Watts, 1980. 79-26266. ISBN 0-531-02864-X. 115p. $6.90.

8–   The abused are young children and adolescents, they are in all socioeconomic strata, and their numbers are increasing. Whether the increase is due to more child abuse or more reported cases, a government survey showed that by 1976, reported cases (in a year) totalled over a half-million. Dolan discusses the history of child abuse and the legislation that has dealt with it, especially recent steps that have given children more protection; he describes the various forms of child abuse, the causes of abuse, and the ways in which one can get help for abused children—including therapy programs for abusive adults. The writing is serious but not heavy, the tone objective, the coverage broad. A reading list and an index are appended.

355   **Dolan,** Edward F. *Gun Control: A Decision for Americans.* Rev. ed. Watts, 1982. 78-5576. ISBN 0-531-02202-1. 115p. $7.90.

7–   As topical and controversial as it was at the time the original edition was published, gun control is a topic that concerns all citizens of all ages. The information on statistics, traditions, organizations involved on both sides of the controversy, and legislation has been brought up to date, with the focus still on the arguments for and against gun control. The text is detailed, informative, and clearly written; the tone is objective; perhaps the one weakness of the book is that in the analysis of public opinion, Dolan uses figures from a 1975 poll on banning handguns, but mentions later polls that are less specific about the cause of crime. A divided reading list and an index are appended.

356   **Domanska,** Janina. *King Krakus and the Dragon;* written and illus. by Janina Domanska. Greenwillow, 1979. 78-12934. Trade ed. ISBN 0-688-80189-7; Library ed. ISBN 0-688-84189-9. 34p. Trade ed. $8.95; Library ed. $8.59 net.

K–3   Domanska's combination of stylized, geometric treatment and lavish use
  *   of color and design have never been more effective than they are in illustrating a traditional Polish tale about a humble shoemaker's apprentice who found a way to slay the dragon who was ravaging the land in the long-ago days of King Krakus. Dratevka, the orphaned shoemaker's apprentice, filled a ram's skin with tar and sulphur; the awful dragon ate it and died, and Dratevka was appointed court shoemaker. An ornamented frieze runs across the tops and bottoms of the pages; opposite

each full-page painting, the text is handsomely set in ample space, with first-letter ornamentation adding to the medieval look. Beautiful.

357   **Donnelly,** Elfie. *Offbeat Friends;* tr. from the German by Anthea Bell. Crown, 1982. 82-7995. ISBN 0-517-54617-5. 128p. $8.95.

4-6   Eleven-year-old Mari meets an eccentric old woman, Mrs. Panacek, sitting on a park bench and is later baffled by the hostility her parents show when she tells them about her new friend. Mrs. Panacek is dowdy, confused, and often irrational in her conversation, but Mari finds her touching and lovable. When the old woman runs away from the mental institution where she lives, convinced that her son-in-law wants to kill her, Mari sneaks Mrs. Panacek into her bedroom. Naturally, this is discovered, but the woman's plight touches Mari's parents also, and they kindly, gently take charge. A competent, smooth translation brings out the distinctive writing style and the sensitivity in the author's portrayal of the offbeat friends. This deftly structured story was first published in Germany under the title *Der Rote Strumpf.*

358   **Donnelly,** Elfie. *So Long, Grandpa;* tr. from the German by Anthea Bell. Crown, 1981. 81-3241. ISBN 0-517-54423-7. 92p. $7.95.

4-6   Translated from the German, a candid and touching story of a child's first experience with the death of a beloved family member is told convincingly by ten-year-old Michael. He has a deep love for his grandfather, who lives with them, and is taken aback when his father tells him that Grandpa has cancer. Grandpa is impatient with euphemisms, and tells Michael he dislikes such evasions as "passing on," he wants no pretense. Grandpa's pain increases, he loses weight, and then he dies. Michael mourns, but Grandpa himself has helped Michael prepare for death, has made it easier to accept the fact that he had had a happy life and recognized the simple inevitability of death. This is a purposive book, but the author is honest about the purpose and perceptive in describing the adjustment made by the dying and by those around them.

359   **Dowden,** Anne Ophelia Todd. *From Flower to Fruit;* written and illus. by Anne Ophelia Dowden. Crowell, 1984. 83-46163. Library ed. ISBN 0-690-04403-8; Trade ed. ISBN 0-690-04402-X. 56p. Library ed. $12.89; Trade ed. $13.50.

6-   Beautiful color paintings and line drawings, both meticulously detailed, illustrate a book that is almost as distinctive for its text as for its pictures, although Dowden is known primarily as a botanical artist. Here she describes flowers, seeds, and patterns of reproduction, fertilization, and distribution of seeds that result in many kinds of fruits, both fleshy and dry. The book has both a subject index and a plant index; in the latter, entries are common names, with scientific names following.

360   **Drucker,** Malka. *Series TV: How a Television Show is Made;* by Malka Drucker and Elizabeth James. Houghton/Clarion, 1983. 83-2119. ISBN 0-89919-142-8. 110p. illus. with photographs. $11.95.

5–9   In a comprehensive and detailed survey of how episodes for filmed or taped television series are made, the authors begin with a story idea and story conference, and discuss every aspect of rehearsing, planning, sets (in the studio or on location or backlots), filming or taping, performing, editing, and rating. The text, written in a crisp and lucid style, includes explanations of the work of the production crew, also of costumers, makeup experts, nurse, caterers, and all of the ancillary performers, like extras or stunt people. An index gives access to a text that should be intriguing and informative for television viewers.

361   **Duncan,** Lois. *Stranger with My Face.* Little, Brown, 1981. 81-8299. ISBN 0-316-19551-0. 250p. $8.95.

7–10   Laurie, who tells the story, is seventeen. Oldest of three children, she lives a happy and uneventful life on an island off the New England coast, attending school on the mainland, enjoying her friends and her artistic and pleasantly off-beat parents. At first Laurie is puzzled when people say they've seen her in places she hasn't been. Then she sees her doppelgänger—and the book smoothly moves into the occult plane as Laurie learns that the "stranger with her face" is a twin sister who has learned astral projection and can be visible to others as well as to Laurie. Lia, her name is, and she is evil—as Laurie gradually learns when a jealous Lia hurts one person after another so that she can have her twin to herself. One must, of course, suspend disbelief to accept the story, but Duncan makes it possible and palatable by a deft twining of fantasy and reality, by giving depth to characters and relationships, and by writing with perception and vitality about other, universal aspects of adolescent life as well as the more dramatic core of the story, a core that includes Laurie's discovery that she is adopted—a fact she stumbles on as she tries to learn about her malevolent twin.

362   **Duncan,** Lois. *The Third Eye.* Little, 1984. 83-26777. ISBN 0-316-19553-7. 220p. $12.95.

6–10   Duncan's forte is the suspenseful page-turner, and here she has done well. When a little boy she is babysitting disappears, Karen finds she is able to "see" where he is. This ability comes in handy when Karen is abducted while all the babies in the daycare center where she works are kidnapped. Karen's extra-sensory perceptions are convincing and well-described—eerie, elusive, and exhausting. Some ideas are toyed with rather than explored, and while this story rarely stops for reflection, readers will find they won't want to stop, either.

363   **Dunlop,** Eileen. *Fox Farm.* Holt, 1979. 78-14091. ISBN 0-03-049051-0. 149p. $7.95.

5–7   Adam had come as a foster child to the Darke family; despite the fact
that he was the same age as Richard Darke, the two boys had never
become friends, nor had Richard's parents been able to gain Adam's
affection. What they didn't know was that he had a secret hope that his
father, remarried and living in Australia, would send for him, and that
he was hoarding his little money in anticipation of that day. What
brings the boys together is "Foxy," the baby animal they discover after
Mr. Darke has shot a fox that had been after his poultry. They hide
Foxy, care for him, use their pocket money (even Adam's hoard) to feed
him. It is a bitter blow to Adam when he receives a scathing letter from
his stepmother, dismissing impatiently his suggestion that he come to
Australia. Adam, once he has adjusted to the blow, can fully accept his
foster family's affection, and he is comforted by the fact that Foxy
proves to be a dog and he can now keep the pet he adores. The story
line has good structure and is intense in focus, but it is the perceptively
drawn characters and their relationships, and the combination of craftsmanship and narrative sense in the writing style that give the book impact and substance.

364   **Dunn,** Marylois. *The Absolutely Perfect Horse;* by Marylois Dunn and
Ardath Mayhar. Harper, 1983. 82-47726. Trade ed. ISBN 0-06-21773-1;
Library ed. ISBN 0-06-021774-X. 186p. Trade ed. $9.95; Library ed.
$9.89.

5–7   How nice to find a horse story that isn't formula fiction. Annie is fifteen, has been saving her money to buy the perfect horse; and instead
buys a very old one to save it from being sold to the knackers. Petey,
her younger brother and the narrator, is scornful, but Annie loves old
Chief even if her snobbish friends make fun of him. The family has just
moved to a Texas farm and has just adopted a Vietnamese boy to
whom Annie is merely civil; the others feel he is a member of the family. In a dramatic but not melodramatic climax, Petey and the horse
come to the rescue of the baby of the family, attacked by a pack of feral
dogs; they and Annie, who also tries to help, are injured, but it is Taro
Chan who shoots the attacking pack and saves their lives. When the
story ends, Annie is adjusting to the fact that her beloved Chief, exhausted, has died, and she calls Taro Chan her brother for the first
time. This has depth and consistency of characterization, warm familial
relationships, and a plot that has good pace and balance; the writing
style is smooth, the ethical concepts sturdy.

365   **Earle,** Sylvia A. *Exploring the Deep Frontier; The Adventure of Man in the
Sea;* by Sylvia A. Earle and Al Giddings. National Geographic, 1980.
80-7567. ISBN 0-87044-343-7. 296p. illus. $14.95.

7–
*   Written by a marine botanist and an underwater photographer, this
oversize book is profusely illustrated by diagrams and photographs,
many of the latter in full color and quite beautiful; the writing style is

graceful, occasionally striking in its imagery, and the information is authoritative and lucidly presented. The book is oversize, with a single column and a broad margin on each pale blue page. The text covers such subjects as the history of underwater exploration, treasures and treasure hunting, marine life, seafloor mining, and marine farming. There are many instances of the authors' personal observations included; a bibliography, a chronology of the highlights of diving history, and an extensive index are appended.

366   **Ecke,** Wolfgang. *The Stolen Paintings;* tr. from the German by Stella and Vernon Humphries; illus. by Rolf Rettich. Prentice-Hall, 1981. 81-8644. ISBN 0-13-84685-6. 140p. $7.95.

6–10   Seventeen brief mystery stories, graded for three levels of intricacy, are presented for the reader to solve; answers are given at the back of the book. The stories are told at a brisk pace, the settings vary, and the solutions are plausible; this isn't great fiction, but it is great fun for puzzle fans.

367   **Ellis,** Anne Leo. *Dabble Duck;* illus. by Sue Truedell. Harper, 1984. 83-47692. Library ed. ISBN 0-06-021818-5; Trade ed. ISBN 0-06-021817-7. 30p. Library ed. $10.89; Trade ed. $11.50.

K–2   Bright, breezy humorous illustrations reflect the sunny mood of a story that deviates from the usual odd-pet book. Dabble's been raised from ducklinghood in a city apartment, and she's used to it but is lonesome when her boy Jason is at school. His mother has accepted Dabble's messiness but is worried about the duck being unhappy and investigates the possibility of a nice home in the country. That's the usual pattern, giving up a pet for its own good; here everyone is indeed thinking of Dabble's good, but a different solution is found: a stray dog, bedraggled and injured, follows Jason and Dabble in the park; Jason brings the dog home, where it is clear that he's the answer to the duck's loneliness. Jason's parents are models of kindness and tolerance, the animals (and the family's love for them) are appealing, and it's nice to have a story in which a city apartment is the right place for pets.

368   **El-Shamy,** Hasan M. *Folktales of Egypt.* University of Chicago Press, 1980. 79-9316. ISBN 0-226-20624-6. 347p. $25.00.

6–   All folk literature reflects the culture from which it emanates, but seldom can so many changes over so many centuries be as evident as they are in this collection. The tales are grouped by genre: fantasy tales, religious tales, trickster tales, etc. and include some (especially in the final section, "Humorous Narratives and Jokes") that are contemporary variants. As is true of earlier books in this excellent series, this is useful as independent reading or reading aloud, as a source for storytelling, and as a reference book for serious students or teachers of folklore. It has an erudite but lively foreword by the series editor, Richard Dorson, and an informative introduction by the editor-translator, who himself collected the materials in the book; it includes extensive notes on the tales (in very small print) that identify the contents according to the Aarne-Thompson Type index and relate the tales to their cross-cultural matrices; it includes an index of motifs, a lengthy bibliography, and a relative index.

369   **Engdahl,** Sylvia Louise. *Tool For Tomorrow: New Knowledge About Genes;* by Sylivia Engdahl and Rick Roberson. Atheneum, 1979. 78-13777. ISBN 0-689-30679-2. 94p. illus. $5.95.

8–   This is not the usual discussion of Mendelian characteristics and DNA; Engdahl and Roberson explore some of the present achievements and future possibilities of genetic engineering, from agricultural gene banks to therapeutic eugenics, from experiments designed to improve global food supply to the recombinant technology that has emerged within the study of molecular genetics. While the authors are fairly positive about research in the field, they recognize the fact that social and ethical implications have made some scientists as well as some of the public dubious. Since the book does not give information about the structure of DNA and RNA, and since it assumes some general knowledge on the part of the reader, it is perhaps best suited for older readers who are more likely to bring such background to their reading. A final chapter, "Some Ideas for the Distant Future," discusses cloning, implanting fertilized ova, and extending life span as some of the possible areas of future genetic research; an index is provided.

370   **Englander,** Roger. *Opera: What's All the Screaming About?* Walker, 1983. 82-23742. ISBN 0-8027-6491-6. 192p. $10.95.

7–
*   An opera stage director, Englander writes with authority and wit about the creators, interpreters, and appreciators (audience and critics) of opera. His lively text begins with a brief history of the art, including—instead of the lengthy plot descriptions of some books on opera—an amusing set of caption-descriptions of fifty popular operas in newspaper headline style: "Captured Maidens Rescued from Turkish Harem" for *The Abduction from the Seraglio,* and "Philandering Husband Lands in Slammer Duped by Wife and Maid" for *Die Fledermaus.* What Englander gives, in a text with vitality and flow, is a great deal of information about people, performances, standards, techniques, trends, and stagecraft. Appended material includes lists of leading composers, leading librettists, leading opera companies (divided by country and, in the United States, by states), a glossary, and an index.

371   **Englebardt,** Leland S. *You Have a Right; A Guide for Minors.* Lothrop, 1979. 79-4678. Trade ed. ISBN 0-688-41893-7; Library ed. ISBN 0-688-51893-1. 128p. Trade ed. $6.95; Library ed. $6.67 net.

7–12   A lawyer explains the ways in which the laws protect minors in such areas as employment obligations, property rental, signing contracts, and making major purchases, as well as those rights and benefits that accrue in more personal matters such as child abuse, marriage, or having access and privacy in various medical matters. Englebardt's text is logically organized, his explanations lucid and made more explicit by the use of fictional examples. Sources of help in getting legal aid precede the index.

372   **English,** Betty Lou. *You Can't Be Timid with a Trumpet; Notes from the Orchestra;* written and illus. with photographs by Betty Lou English; with drawings by Stan Skardinski. Lothrop, 1980. 80-13348. Trade ed. ISBN 0-688-41963-1; Library ed. ISBN 0-688-51963-6. 80p. Trade ed. $7.95; Library ed. $7.63.

5-7   Arranged by major instrumental groups (strings, woodwinds, brass, percussion, harp, and keyboard instruments) and with a preface in each section that describes the instruments and explains how they evolved and how they are constructed, the text consists primarily of interviews with musicians in several major orchestras. Each speaks of how he or she became interested in becoming a musician, of their training and their careers, and of some of the pleasures (and occasionally problems) of the musician's life. The book concludes with a comparable statement by a symphony conductor and a glossary of musical terms. This has variety in the interviews, yet they have a sense of dedication and an enthusiasm that are common to all. The book is informative, and should be useful for the general reader, but should appeal especially to those children who are music lovers and/or music students.

373   **Epstein,** Samuel. *Kids in Court: The ACLU Defends Their Rights;* by Sam and Beryl Epstein. Four Winds, 1982. 81-69515. ISBN 0-590-07669-8. 233p. $9.95.

8-   Beginning with a history of the American Civil Liberties Union and an explanation of its role, the Epsteins describe eleven cases in which the ACLU acted on behalf of adolescents who have brought suit in defense of their rights as minor citizens. The cases involve such principles as the right of free speech, the right to be secure against unreasonable search (a strip-search in a school drug hunt), sexual discrimination, and invasion of privacy. The writing is primarily descriptive, dry and matter-of-fact, given variety by the inclusion of cited comments and court transcripts. An index is appended.

374   **Epstein,** Samuel. *Secret in a Sealed Bottle: Lazzaro Spallanzani's Work with Microbes;* by Sam and Beryl Epstein; illus. by Jane Sterrett. Coward, 1979. 78-1494. 63p. $5.49.

4-6   It says much about Lazzaro Spallanzani that, having finished his studies in natural history, he was able to continue them and support himself by taking a post as a professor of Latin, Greek, and mathematics. One of the great scientists of the 18th century, Spallanzani was the first to prove, by his research, that the microbes known to the scientific world since the invention of the microscope did not appear through spontaneous generation. The authors give a dramatic account of his repeated tests, improvised and repeatedly improved procedures, and his elation when he could finally announce to fellow scientists that the "little beasties" came from their own kind, not—as one group held—from nowhere but borne by air. The book covers other research done by Spallanzani, focusing on his scientific achievements rather than his personal life; it is written with vitality in a narrative but not unduly fictionalized style, and it shows clearly how scientists build a body of knowledge by trial, error, exchange of opinions, and objective evaluation of their own research findings. A brief bibliography, a glossary, and an annotated list of "Some People to Know About" (other scientists of the 17th and 18th centuries) are included.

375   **Epstein,** Samuel. *She Never Looked Back; Margaret Mead in Samoa;* by Sam and Beryl Epstein; illus. by Victor Juhasz. Coward, 1980. 78-31821. ISBN 0-698-30715-1. 64p. $5.99.

4–6   Although this focuses on Mead's life and work in Samoa, gathering material for *The Coming of Age in Samoa,* it also gives biographical information that covers the whole span of her life and her distinguished career. This covers an interesting period in Mead's life, and although the writing is rather dry, the book has good balance and reflects the scientific attitudes and the research methods used by anthropologists in the field. The illustrations are adequate, more decorative than informative and, in two instances, seem in conflict with the text about a minor detail of dress.

376   **Erdoes,** Richard. *The Native Americans: Navajos;* written and illus. with photographs by Richard Erdoes. Sterling, 1979. 78-57885. 84p. Trade ed. $12.95; Library ed. $11.69 net.

4–6   An oversize book, profusely illustrated with color photographs, gives the history of the Navajos, describes the beauty and the harshness of the land in which they live, the "Four Corners," and devotes separate chapters to discussions of traditional and modern ways of life—living patterns which are at times in conflict. Erdoes, who has written many books about native Americans, is knowledgeable, sympathetic, and lucid. The one weakness of the book is that occasionally the text is broken by a double-page spread of captioned photographs, interrupting its flow. The photograph-and-caption pages are used effectively (as with pictures of the natural beauty of the reservation) instead of text, in some page sequences. The author is candid about Navajo problems, respectful toward Navajo traditions, and objective in assessing the dignity and resilience with which the Navajos are coping—as they have in the past—with change. An index is appended.

377   **Erlanger,** Ellen. *Jane Fonda: More than a Movie Star.* Lerner, 1984. 83-27542. ISBN 0-8225-0485-5. 56p. illus. with photographs. $6.95.

5–9   Although this biography is appreciative of the status gained by Jane
Fonda for her acting ability, it is fortunately without the hyperbole of
the gushing and laudatory puff piece. Rather soberly, it reviews Fonda's
relationship with her father, her professional and personal life, her political activism (and the fact that many people criticize it) and her newest success as a writer of books on physical fitness. The writing style is
not impressive, but it's adequately straightforward and fairly objective.

378   **Estes,** Eleanor. *The Moffat Museum;* written and illus. by Eleanor Estes.
Harcourt, 1983. 83-8427. ISBN 0-15-255086-0. 160p. $10.95.

3–5   After a long, long lapse, a sequel to the beloved Moffat stories appears,
and although they are older (Sylvie marries in the course of the story,
and Joey turns sixteen, quits school, and gets a job) they are little
changed. Ingenuous, loving, and ingenious, the Moffat children go
through life with zest and good humor. Most of the incidents in the
book center on Rufus and Jane, and many of their ploys have to do
with the do-it-yourself museum they set up in the unused barn back of
their little house. The writing has a deceptively bland quality, the humor is gentle, the characterization consistent; like the other Moffat
books, this is a warm family story and it's nice to read aloud to younger
children.

379   **Evans,** Mari. *Jim Flying High;* illus. by Ashley Bryan. Doubleday, 1979.
78-22628. Trade ed. ISBN 0-385-14129-7; Library ed. ISBN 0-385-14130-0.
32p. Trade ed. $7.95; Library ed. $8.90 net.

3–4   Bryan uses strong but muted colors in paintings that are intricate and
stylized to illustrate a story in black idiom by Evans, and there's a
matching in text and pictures of cheerfulness and humor. The commentator is one of the boys who sees Jim, a flying fish, get stuck in a tree.
Jim gasps as he dries out, but he refuses to acknowledge that he needs
help, even when his parents swim up ("Boy, you better get down outa
that tree," his mother says) and even when Olukun, Ruler-of-the-Wa-
ter, urges him to come down. He isn't tired, says Jim, he likes it. When
everybody takes pity on the stubborn fish and tosses water at him, Jim
recuperates, takes off, and executes some fancy flying before returning
to the water. The writing is poetic and also has a fine storytelling quality, and the story is a good choice for reading aloud to younger children
as well as being appropriate for the independent reader.

380   **Evslin,** Bernard. *Hercules;* illus. by Jos. A. Smith. Morrow, 1984. 83-
23834. ISBN 0-688-02748-2. 144p. $9.50.

5–8   Wonderful for reading aloud, with a smooth integration of the epic and
the colloquial, Evslin's re-telling of the Hercules story takes place in a
"terrible magical world" that is also "like ours in some ways." The dramatic full-page drawings show Hercules in violent combat with hideous

terrifying monsters, and Evslin powerfully describes those heroic struggles which push Hercules to the very limits of his strength, wit and en-
durance. The colloquial elements are usually comic (as in the words of
jealous Hera, "I'll get rid of that overgrown brat if it's the last thing I
do"); they can also intensify the terror (the Nemean lion comes on like
"pure yellow murder".) There is no madness, no rage; Hercules is as
gentle as he is strong and brave, and even ecologically minded. But
though the monsters appear to be all outside, Evslin is also concerned
with the "terrible inner war," with the hero's perilous journey as a met-
aphor for personal growth; from the innocent baby's discovery of evil
with the monster-snakes in the cradle, to Hercules' sad words to Atlas
holding up the sky; "I, too, have burdens which I can't pass on to anyone else."

381   **Faber,** Doris. *Love & Rivalry;* illus. with photographs. Viking, 1983.
       83-6566. ISBN 0-670-44221-6. 200p. $13.95.

7–   In three interesting biographical sketches, carefully researched and ca-
       pably written, Faber explores the relationships between three famous
       women of the nineteenth century and their less well known sisters. The
       three pairs are Catharine Beecher and Harriet Beecher Stowe, Charlotte
       Cushman and Susan Cushman Muspratt, and Emily and Lavinia Dick-
       inson. The author is perceptive in her analysis of the relationships be-
       tween the sisters, explicit in distinguishing between fact and conjecture,
       and scrupulous in attributing no dialogue that has not been verified in
       primary source materials. A bibliography of sources, with notes, and an
       index are provided.

382   **Facklam,** Margery. *The Brain: Magnificent Mind Machine;* by Margery and
       Howard Facklam; illus. by Paul Facklam. Harcourt, 1982. 81-47529. ISBN
       0-15-211388-6. 118p. $12.95.

7–   An excellent text, authoritative and comprehensive, has a logical ar-
       rangement of material, describing the structure and function of the
       brain before moving on to the major portion of the text. After a survey
       of the brain research of the past, the Facklams discuss current research,
       describing the new techniques and tools that make such research possi-
       ble; they also describe some of the resulting diagnostic and therapeutic
       advances in medicine. A glossary, a bibliography, and an index are pro-
       vided.

383   **Farber,** Norma. *Mercy Short.* Dutton, 1982. 82-5013. ISBN 0-525-44014-3.
       139p. $11.95.

7–10   Mercy's diary covers the period of December 1691 to March 1692; she is
       seventeen, she had been captured by Indians, borne an infant son who
       died, marched to Quebec and been recently ransomed by the Boston
       church for which Cotton Mather is the minister. Arduously he prays
       with Mercy to rescue her from the witches and specters that torment

her. The diary is written for his benefit, so that he may better understand what demons he must exorcise. Mercy believes in her demons (as
did most colonists in this period of frenzied witch-hunting) but what
emerges from her diary is an ambivalence about her experiences that is
pictured with profound insight: anguish about her murdered parents
and the child of her Indian lover, but appreciation of the Indian way of
life, with its kindness to children, it closeness to nature, and its freedom to celebrate with joy. While this is internalized and at times somber in its contents, it gives a remarkably vivid picture of the dour and
vigorous religion of the Massachusetts colony and particularly of the
fervent Mather, with his penchant for redeeming young girls. The diary
ends with a long and happy entry by Mercy, cured of her torments and
looking forward to a happy marriage, and with a postscript by Mather,
written several years later, noting that Mercy has been excommunicated
for the sin of adultery. As is usually true of the best kind of historical
fiction, there is evidence of careful research, but the evidence does not
get in the way of the narrative.

384   **Feder,** Paula Kurzband. *Where Does the Teacher Live?* illus. by Lillian
Hoban. Dutton, 1979. 78-13157. ISBN 0-525-42586-1. 48p. $5.95.

1–2   Three enterprising members of Class 2–3, arguing about where Mrs.
Greengrass, their teacher, lives, decide to play detective and watch her.
One day she walks, another she takes a bus, once she hails a cab, one
day a friend picks her up. They are baffled, and ask her; she tells them
she lives on the West Side and gives the three a ride home in her uncle's ice cream truck. Each lives in a different kind of building, but none
of them sees Mrs. Greengrass reach home. Last picture: Mrs. Greengrass reading contentedly on the deck of her houseboat. Hoban's pictures have their usual casual air, the text is simple and well-paced, the
type is large and spaciously set, and the ending should delight beginning independent readers.

385   **Feeney,** Stephanie. *A Is for Aloha;* illus. with photographs by Hella
Hammid. University Press of Hawaii, 1980. 80-5462. ISBN 0-8248-0722-7.
58p. $7.95.

3–5   This is both an alphabet book and an introduction to the Hawaiian set-
yrs.   ting; two pages are devoted to each letter, upper and lower case, and
the word or words beginning with the letter are in a bright green, easily
legible box that contrasts with the double-page photograph. The words
are simple and most are familiar; those that are not can be found in a
glossary at the back of the book, with small-scale pictures matched with
explanatory captions. This can also be used to introduce facts about Ha-
waiian culture to the post-alphabet group.

386   **Felix,** Monique. illus. *The Story of a Little Mouse Trapped in a Book.* Green
Tiger, 1983. ISBN 0-914676-52-0. 26p. $6.95.

3–5   In a wordless picture book, the first few pages show an attractive
yrs.   mouse looking increasingly worried as it tries various directions, look-
       ing for an escape route. Finally the mouse begins nibbling along the
       edge of a page, peeking at the scene disclosed; encouraged, it completes
       the nibbling, pulls back the square of paper and discloses a sunny rural
       landscape. Laboriously the small creature folds the paper until it has a
       paper airplane; it rides downward into the countryside and (last picture)
       is soon happily nibbling at some grain. The pictures are deft and divert-
       ing; the story is clearly told; the concept, ingenious and fresh, should
       appeal to young children as much as the subject.

387   **Filson,** Brent. *Exploring with Lasers;* illus. by Brigita Fuhrmann. Messner,
       1984. 84-14731. ISBN 0-671-50573-4. 95p. $8.79.

7–10   Filson's explanations of the nature of light and the conditions that must
       obtain in order to create a laser beam are lucid although not simplified.
       After descriptions of laser construction and types of lasers, the text dis-
       cusses, in separate chapters, such subjects as medical use of lasers, la-
       sers in industry, holograms, etc. and concludes with the topic of possi-
       ble future uses of lasers. The stimulating topic compensates for the
       occasional heaviness of the writing style. A glossary, a bibliography,
       and an index are appended.

388   **Fine,** Anne. *The Summer-House Loon.* T. Y. Crowell, 1979. 78-19515. ISBN
       0-690-03933-6. 127p. $6.95.

6–9   First published in England, this is a story that encompasses only
       twenty-four hours, but it creates considerable change in the attitudes of
       adolescent Ione, only child of a widowed father who is blind and is a
       professor of history. The "loon" of the title is one of the professor's stu-
       dents, Ned Hump, amiably nonconformist and hopelessly in love with
       Caroline, the secretary who transcribes the professor's Braille notes.
       When Ned happens on a gloomy Ione brooding in the summer-house,
       neither has any idea how much each will affect the other, for Ned's in-
       stantly so dear to Ione that she becomes more tender and thoughtful
       toward everyone, and it is in part due to her intercession that Ned
       passes his final exam and wins an academic post. The characters are
       distinctive, the plot and writing style sophisticated, and the many affec-
       tionate digs at the foibles of academic life are one of the several amus-
       ing aspects of the story.

389   **Fisher,** Aileen Lucia. *Out in the Dark and Daylight;* illus. by Gail Owens.
       Harper, 1980. 78-22492. Trade ed. ISBN 0-06-021902-5; Library ed. ISBN
       0-06-021903-3. 151p. Trade ed. $8.95; Library ed. $8.79.

3–5   Soft, grainy pencil drawings, realistically detailed and deft in their evo-
       cation of light and shadow, illustrate a collection of poems, many of
       which were originally published in magazines. Although the poems are
       not grouped, the arrangement of selections follows the cycle of the year;

some are as specific as "Summer Stars," or "Early Snow," while others ("Mother Cat," or "All That Sky") are more general. Most of the poems are about some aspect of nature; less frequent are those that speak of a child's emotion or attitude, as do "Going Calling" and "Birthday Present." The poems are brief, fresh, deft, and often illuminating, and they are pleasant to read alone or aloud; the book could be used for reading aloud to pre-readers as well as by the independent reader.

390   **Fisher,** Aileen. *Rabbits, Rabbits;* illus. by Gail Niemann. Harper, 1983. 82-48849. Trade ed. ISBN 0-06-021896-7; Library ed. ISBN 0-06-021899-1. 27p. Trade ed. $9.95; Library ed. $9.89.

K–3   Small, neat, and appealingly verdant, the light, bright paintings are nicely appropriate for an assortment of equally bright, brisk poems. All of the selections are brief and lilting, and they range from agreeable to memorable, with Fisher's usual unobtrusive control of rhythm, rhyme, and meter. Sample, "Spring Fever": "When green tints the meadows/and gold shines the tree/and Winter is over/and rivers run free/do you feel all leapy/and hoppy . . . like *me*/Rabbit?"

391   **Fisher,** Leonard Everett. *Boxes! Boxes!;* written and illus. by Leonard Everett Fisher. Viking, 1984. 83-14761. ISBN 0-670-18334-2. 27p. $9.95.

K–2   Children will enjoy the variety of boxes shown, and they may infer concepts of size and shape, but the chief attraction of the book will surely be the beauty of the innovative selection of objects Fisher has chosen. The text is minimal and rhyming: "A box can be small. A box can be tall. Narrow and slim/Or filled to the rim." The illustrations, acrylic paintings, for these four are two small boxes, a case in which there's a toy soldier, a case of colored pencils, and a delectable box of chocolates. The bright, clean colors and the deft use of shadows add to the effectiveness of the artist's compositions.

392   **Fisher,** Leonard Everett. *The Newspapers;* written and illus. by Leonard Everett Fisher. Holiday House, 1981. 80-8812. ISBN 0-8234-0387-4. 62p. (Nineteenth Century America) $7.95.

5–7   Like other books in this series, the material here is not merely descriptive, but also relates sociologically to the society in which it existed. Fisher points out, for example, that because local news traveled quickly and published news was late, the earliest newspapers focused on political events of national or international interest, and that because subscriptions were expensive and few people could afford them (or even read them) the slant was toward the interests of the educated, the wealthy, and the owners of businesses rather than toward the concerns of the private citizen. The text describes the changes (universal education, machines that set type, improved gathering of news) that made the newspapers available and popular; it discusses freedom of the press and the obligations (not always observed, early on) to tell the truth.

Fisher describes the growth of some of the great newspapers and chains in a serious, information-packed, and intelligent overview of the newspaper industry, an account enlivened by some of the dramatic events in which its representatives were involved. Indexed, the book is illustrated by Fisher's distinctive, dramatic scratchboard pictures.

393   **Fisher,** Leonard Everett. *The Olympians: Great Gods and Goddesses of Ancient Greece;* written and illus. by Leonard Everett Fisher. Holiday House, 1984. 84-516. ISBN 0-8234-0522-2. 28p. $14.95.

4–6   In an oversize book, Fisher describes and pictures the twelve gods and goddesses who dwelt on Mount Olympus. Each portrait has a massive, almost sculptured look despite the fact that the paintings are in full color; facing each portrait is a page that gives the Greek and Roman names of the Olympian, his or her parentage, symbols, (fire for Hestia, and the owl, shield, or olive branch for Athena) and their titles (Hades is both God of the Lower World and God of Wealth). On each page a paragraph (sometimes hard to read because of the colored background) describes the god or goddess. This is a handsome book, and it's an excellent introduction to the Greek/Roman pantheon.

394   **Fisher,** Leonard Everett. *The Schools;* written and illus. by Leonard Everett Fisher. Holiday House, 1983. 82-18710. ISBN 0-8234-0477-3. 60p. (Nineteenth Century America) $10.95.

5–7   The author provides an excellent background for his description of nineteenth century education by describing first the political, religious, and cultural forces that brought about the first system of free public education in the world, that produced in the United States the first coeducational and women's colleges, that subsidized public education by taxing citizens. The text examines the various kinds of reforms and improvements brought about through the efforts of educators and reformers, and discusses land-grant colleges, private as well as public education, and the connection between free and required elementary school education and the benefits accruing to the society because of an educated citizenry. An index is provided; dramatic scratchboard illustrations are informative as well as handsome.

395   **Fisher,** Leonard Everett. *The Unions;* written and illus. by Leonard Everett Fisher. Holiday House, 1982. 81-6632. ISBN 0-8234-0434-X. 62p. $9.95.

5–7   Strong and effective scratchboard illustrations (a medium in which Fisher has no peer) extend a text that focuses, as do others in the author's excellent series of books about the United States in the nineteenth century, on the period under examination but that gives some background of labor disputes and organizations in colonial times. One of the crucial decisions that shaped the movement and public opinion was the 1806 court decision that a society of shoemakers was a criminal conspiracy: their crime was organizing themselves into a union, trying to force their employers into giving them pay raises. The text, well-organized and thoroughly researched, describes the many groups and legislative measures of the century, culminating in the founding of the Knights of Labor, the American Federation of Labor, labor-backed political action, and the series of famous strikes that included Homestead and Pullman. The book ends with an account of the establishment of Labor Day as a national holiday and, in 1898, of the Erdman Act, which established the policy of government mediation. An index is included.

396   **Fisk,** Nicholas. *A Rag, A Bone and a Hank of Hair.* Crown, 1982. 81-22192. ISBN 0-517-54635-3. 123p. $8.95.

5–7   Brin is one of the élite, in this science fantasy set in the twenty-first century; because he is young, and in a society in which people can rarely have children, the young are deferred to. He is chosen to make a trip back to a simulated 1940, in a project designed to monitor three "Reborns," chemically created humans, who are capable of reproduction. Brin's problem, as he comes to know the Reborns, is that he feels sympathy for them and their lifestyle, and the authorities warn him that he is thereby interfering with the experiment. Both he and they are in danger of elimination, but Brin is warned that he is the most expendable. The ending is tragic but logical, in a story that is imaginative and thoughtful, a well-told adventure story that is also a provocative reminder that the conflict between individual initiative and compassion and a controlled society is timeless.

397   **Fleischman,** Albert Sidney. *McBroom's Almanac;* illus. by Walter Lorraine. Atlantic-Little, Brown, 1984. 83-9043. Trade ed. ISBN 0-316-26009-6; Paper ed. ISBN 0-316-26011-8. 88p. Trade ed. $12.95; Paper ed. $5.95.

3–6   Deft, comic line drawings illustrate a compendium of pseudo-advice and humor that is often hilarious. As in other McBroom books, there are tales that depend, in tall-tale style, on exaggeration for their humor; there is word-play ("Freeze & thaw & sunshine fickle—Mercury rides a Pogo stickle" is the October motto) and there are ridiculous farming tips, proverbs ("Birds of a feather that flock together make a good target") and assorted bits of nonsensical nature hints and household lore. It's all great fun, and the fact that there are many short bits indicate a potential usefulness for slow or reluctant readers who will find the humor as appealing as do their more proficient peers.

398   **Fleischman,** Paul. *Finzel the Farsighted;* illus. by Marcia Sewall. Dutton, 1983. 83-1416. ISBN 0-525-44057-7. 48p. $9.95.

3–5   In the best noodlehead tradition, this tale in folk style is a joy to read
*   aloud or alone, and it's a natural for storytellers. Although very near-sighted, Finzel was famed in his village (Chelm, Gotham, any town of

fools) for his ability to read the past or the future in produce grown by an individual. Because of his myopia, Finzel mixes up some lemons, nuts, etc. and convinces the strapping Pavel that he hasn't long to live; this gives honest Pavel's villainous brother an idea for a way to rob Finzel. He does, but the trickster is outwitted. A satisfying conclusion to a story written with grace and humor and illustrated with soft pencil drawings that are spare and comic.

399   **Fleischman,** Paul. *Graven Images;* illus. by Andrew Glass. Harper, 1982. 81-48649. Trade ed. ISBN 0-06-021906-8; Library ed. ISBN 0-06-021907-6. 85p. Trade ed. $9.95; Library ed. $9.89.

8–   Three short stories are linked because each focuses on a chiseled figure. "The Binnacle Boy" is a statue taken from a ship on which all had perished, and it is the repository of whispered secrets—but one secret is never found out, and the crew's poisoner lives grimly on. In "St. Crispin's Follower," an awkward apprentice finally gets the attention of a girl with whom he's been hopelessly smitten, and in "The Man of Influence" a sculptor is commissioned by a ghost to carve his likeness. The macabre tone is deftly maintained in the tales, which themselves have the combination of strength, mass, structure, and delicacy in portraying details that are the characteristics of graven images.

400   **Fodor,** Ronald V. *Nickels, Dimes, and Dollars; How Currency Works;* illus. Morrow, 1980. 79-22539. Trade ed. ISBN 0-688-22220-X; Library ed. ISBN 0-688-32220-4. 94p. Trade ed. $6.95; Library ed. $6.67.

4–6   Fodor, after describing the kinds of material that were used for exchange historically, discusses today's currency and what it stands for as a medium of exchange. In a clear, straightforward style, he explains how money is used, nationally and internationally, and how the market works, from the policies set by the Federal Reserve and the protective manipulation of the federal government to the intricacies of the stock market and international exchange. Fodor also discusses inflation, depression, and personal management of money. Lucid, useful, and well-organized. An index is included.

401   **Forman,** James D. *Call Back Yesterday.* Scribner, 1981. 81-14416. ISBN 0-684-17168-6. 163p. $10.95.

7–10   Cindy wakes to find herself in a hospital, unable to remember what has happened, and upset because the doctor will tell her nothing but persists in questioning her. In retrospect, the text leads through events to the tragic climax, and readers learn that the year is 1988, that Cindy had joined her parents at the United States embassy in Saudi Arabia where her father was ambassador. There is, as always, political ferment, and this is exacerbated at the embassy by the jealously of a young Arab who admires Cindy and resents an American admirer. There is a revolution and the embassy residents are taken hostage. Settlement seems close, but one personal catastrophe—in a startling dramatic ending—precipitates a third world war. Taut, vivid, sadly believable, this compelling story reaffirms the interest in the plight of young people caught in political problems and the hatred of war that are evident in so many of Forman's earlier books.

402   **Foster,** John. comp. *A Fourth Poetry Book;* illus. by Peter Benton, Noel Connor, Allan Curless, Arthur Robins, and Martin White. Oxford, 1983. Trade ed. ISBN 0-19-918152-7; Paper ed. ISBN 0-19-918151-9. 127p. Trade ed. $9.95; Paper ed. $4.95.

A Third Poetry Book; illus. by Allan Curless, Michael McManus, and John Raynes. Oxford, 1983. Trade ed. ISBN 0-19-918140-3; Paper ed. ISBN 0-19-918139-X. 122p. Trade ed. $9.95; Paper ed. $4.95.

4–7   Although the fact that neither book has any announced divisions on the pages or in the tables of contents makes the poems less accessible, the material chosen for readers in the upper elementary grades is of such high caliber and offers such variety that it compensates for that weakness. Both books are illustrated by a range of artists, with pictures in many moods, and the use of different techniques. Although there are no section headings, the poems are grouped loosely by theme or topic; a number of animal poems may be arranged sequentially, as may seasonal poems or monster poems. Most of the poems are brief; many are humorous; many poets, both those well-known and those less familiar, are represented. A first-line index is provided in each book.

403   **Fox,** Mary Virginia. *Women Astronauts: Aboard the Shuttle.* Messner, 1984. 84-1126. ISBN 0-671-53105-0. 159p. illus with photographs. $9.79.

6–9   In three selections, this text is written in a brisk and informative style, its tone marred somewhat by a frequent note of adulation. It is profusely illustrated with photographs, all officially issued by NASA; it describes the launch and flight of the *Challenger,* gives brief biographies of Sally Ride and seven other women astronauts, and devotes several chapters to such subjects as clothing, flight simulation, and survival training. Despite the occasional gushing, this should be appealing to readers, in part because there is as yet so little available on the subject, and in part because the text gives interesting details about life aboard a shuttle. A brief bibliography and an index are appended.

404   **Fox,** Paula. *One-Eyed Cat.* Bradbury, 1984. 84-10964. ISBN 0-02-735540-3. 192p. $11.95.

5–7   Few contemporary writers create their characters with the depth, nu-
 *   ance, and compassion that Paula Fox does, and if her story unfolds slowly, it is worth the patience and concentration it takes to follow the many-layered development of the characters, especially of the eleven-year-old protagonist, Ned. Told by his father that he's too young for the

air rifle an uncle gives him as a birthday present, Ned sneaks the gun out one night and takes a shot at a shadowy creature. He is subsequently smitten with guilt when he sees a one-eyed feral cat, and the knowledge that he may have been responsible as well as disobeying his father colors all his days. Tautly structured, perceptive, compelling.

405   **Fox,** Paula. *A Place Apart.* Farrar, 1980. 80-36717. ISBN 0-374-35985-7. 192p. $9.95.

7–   Victoria is thirteen when she begins her story; her father has recently died, she and her mother have moved to a small town, and she is quickly enthralled by Hugh, several years older than she. Oddly self-contained, Hugh dominates her thoughts if not her time, and Victoria admires him although her one other friend, Elizabeth, and her mother think he is a poseur. Hugh drops her for a new classmate, and then Victoria learns that Hugh is just as quick to drop Tom; finally, she sees that Hugh has no real affection for anyone, and what she misses is not Hugh himself but the way he had made her feel. When the breach comes (Hugh's family moves, and Victoria's mother is about to remarry and move also) Victoria is over her pain. This is almost an adult novel, subtle and percipient in its relationships, mature in its bittersweetness; the characters are firmly drawn and the style is grave and polished.

406   **Francis,** Anna B. *Pleasant Dreams;* written and illus. by Anna B. Francis. Holt, 1983. 83-6171. ISBN 0-03-060574-1. 28p. $11.95.

K–2   Curls and a hair-ribbon are the only things visible in the first pages that show a child sleeping in a dim, quiet room; a door creaks, and—bit by bit—a scaly, fanged green monster appears. It comes closer, looms larger, and then, from another door another monster emerges. "Don't wake the child," the first says, as they approach the bed. The child wakes and sits up . . . and it's a baby monster, just as green and scaly. "Pleasant dreams," says mother monster, and "Goodnight, Mom and Dad," the story ends. Most children gravitate toward monster stories, and this one is an amusing variant in which the pictures (a bit busy with detail but nicely conceived and composed) tell most of the story and make the few words used all the more effective.

407   **Franco,** Marjorie. *Love in a Different Key.* Houghton, 1983. 83-10653. ISBN 0-395-34827-7. 154p. $9.95.

7–9   The double threads in the structure of a serious story are Neenah's love for Michael and her despair when he has an emotional breakdown, and her dedication to her career as a pianist. When Michael is sent to a mental hospital, Neenah performs badly at a recital where she and another student play a two-piano composition; she decides she will give up playing, but as time passes and Michael improves, she changes her mind. The book ends on a positive note with Michael's recovery and Neenah's performing at a school concert. Franco is perceptive in depicting characters and their relationships, and her writing has both candor and fluency.

408   **Freedman,** Russell. *Farm Babies.* Holiday House, 1981. 81-2898. ISBN 0-8234-0426-9. 40p. illus. with photographs. $8.95.

K–2   Although the engaging pictures of animal young may appeal to very young children, the amount and the level of the facts given in this text make it more appropriate for the child in kindergarten or primary grades. The fact that the publishers use phonetic spellings for species indicate an expected use by the independent reader. The text, which includes barn owls and barn swallows in addition to the usual farm animals, describes what each animal is like at birth, what it can do, and how the young are taken care of by their mothers. An index is appended.

409   **Freedman,** Russell. *Killer Fish.* Holiday House, 1982. 81-85089. ISBN 0-8234-0449-8. 40p. illus. with photographs. $8.95.

2–4   Large, usually clear photographs illustrate a text that is topically arranged and is written in a clear, straightforward style. Freedman describes some varieties of sharks, stingrays and jellyfish, barracudas and piranhas, the electric rays and eels, and species of octopuses, all creatures whose bite, sting, shock, or stranglehold are dangerous and at times fatal. The text describes the ways in which these deadly creatures attack, sometimes in defense, sometimes offensively. An index is appended.

410   **Freedman,** Russell. *They Lived with the Dinosaurs.* Holiday House, 1980. 80-15851. ISBN 0-8234-0424-2. 40p. illus. with photographs. $7.95.

3–4   Photographs of fossils and of those creatures that have survived as a species since the age of the dinosaurs appear on almost every page of a book that describes such species, from the less common tuatara and coelocanth to the more familiar cockroach, hermit crab, and dragonfly. The type-face is large and clear, the pages have ample white space, and the writing is direct and simple; Freedman discusses some of the differences between contemporary creatures and their remote ancestors, often pointing out those anatomical features that have helped species survive. An index to the continuous text is provided.

411   **Freeman,** Gaail. *Alien Thunder.* Bradbury, 1982. 82-9578. ISBN 0-87888-206-5 201p. $10.95.

7–10   Seventeen-year-old Walker Lennon is the narrator of a science fantasy set in a future time, and his story begins with the near-drowning of his mother when she goes for a night swim. He can't understand it, since his mother is an excellent swimmer. Could it have anything to do with the strange thunder he and his little brother Danny heard at the time? Hospitalized briefly, his mother recovers enough to go back to teaching, but she's become a strange teacher who plays a circle game with her students, over and over. The game, it appears, is "learning to travel without your body," and Walker's mother is training the children to leave the earth, for she is now a dual personality since the "drowning," her corpus shared by someone from outer space who has come to rescue children from a dying planet. The story has a good narrative flow, although the pace is uneven and at times slowed by minor plots that are not necessary for the main plot line; it has action, drama, and an effectively shocking ending.

412   **Freschet,** Bernice. *Bernard and the Catnip Caper;* illus. by Gina Freschet. Scribner, 1981. 81-5322. ISBN 0-684-17157-0 37p. $9.95.

K–3   Bernard, the Beacon Hill mouse, is living a peaceful life after his adventures (*Bernard of Scotland Yard*) when a rock crashes through his window, the attached note informing him that his friend Catnip, the house cat, has been catnapped. Our hero musters the help of his siblings and of the outdoor cat, Tiger II, and they go with the ransom (clams) to rescue Catnip. Turns out that the house cat, bored, had sent the note himself. However, since other cats had joined the party and turned it into a fight, Catnip was glad to go back to being bored. This has lively pencil illustrations, humorous if not polished. The story has good structure in the sense of conflict/resolution but has a less impressive story line; the writing style is light and flowing.

413   **Freschet,** Berniece. *Raccoon Baby;* illus. by Jim Arnosky. Putnam, 1984. 83-4634. ISBN 0-399-61149-5. 48p. $6.99.

1–2   Soft, realistic pencil drawings, with alternate double-page spreads having earth colors added, illustrate a very simply written text that is appropriate in length, vocabulary difficulty, and concepts for the beginning independent reader. The material is well-organized, the print large, the pages uncluttered; the text, lightly fictionalized, describes the progress of three raccoon cubs from their birth in the spring to the start of their first winter hibernation.

414   **Friedman,** Ina R. *How My Parents Learned to Eat;* illus. by Allen Say. Houghton, 1984. 83-18553. ISBN 0-395-35379-3. 30p. $12.95.

K–3   In a simple but appealing story, a small girl describes the courtship of her parents, and how they learned to adjust to two styles of eating. Father was an American sailor stationed in Yokohama, and Mother a pretty Japanese girl who responded to his admiration. Each hoped to please the other, both learned, and that's why, the story concludes, "at our house some days we eat with chopsticks and some days we eat with knives and forks." The illustrations have precise use of line and soft colors, and the composition is economical. A warm and gentle story of an interracial family.

415   **Fritz,** Jean. *The Double Life of Pocahontas;* illus. by Ed Young. Putnam, 1983. 83-9662. ISBN 0-399-21016-4. 96p. $9.95.

4–6   Expectably, Fritz bases her work on careful research; expectably, the research does not obtrude on the biographical/historical narrative. This is almost as much a description of the Jamestown colony and its relations with Powhatan (father of Pocahontas) as it is about the Indian princess who loved her adoptive brother, John Smith, as a child, later marrying John Rolfe and coming to live in England with him. It's a colorful story and Fritz tells it with polished simplicity, stressing the dichotomy at which the title hints: the divided loyalties of the young, proud girl who loved both her tribe and the English friends with whom that tribe was in conflict. A section of notes, a bibliography, and an index are included.

416   **Fritz,** Jean. *The Good Giants and the Bad Pukwudgies;* illus. by Tomie de Paola. Putnam, 1982. 81-17921. Hardcover ed. ISBN 0-399-20870-4; Paper ed. ISBN 0-399-20871-2. 38p. $10.95.

K–3   An eminent author retells a legend of the Wampanoag Indians of Massachusetts, combining several tales to form a "why" story that explains how Buzzard's Bay, Nantucket, and Martha's Vineyard as well as some smaller islands were formed. The people of the Narrow Land (Cape Cod) were plagued by the small, malicious Pukwudgies who could turn themselves into stinging mosquitos or shoot their tiny arrows; only the good giant Maushop could control them, which he lazily did when the First People complained. In developing the story, which is told with flair and humor, Fritz includes other facets of Algonquin legend, like the Sea Woman who lures Maushop into forgetting his family, but the focus is on the giant, whose restless sleep digs out a bay, whose flinging of sand from a moccasin creates an island. There's some crowding of plot, but it's compensated for by the style, the humor (especially in the terse New England speech pattern in dialogues between Maushop and his wife) and in the illustrations, which are, like all de Paola's work, stylized and rather stiff, but excellent in color and composition.

417   **Fritz,** Jean. *Homesick: My Own Story;* illus. by Margot Tomes. Putnam, 1982. 82-7646. ISBN 0-399-20933-6. 176p. $9.95.

6–   Jean Fritz describes, in a partial autobiography, the end of her child-
*   hood in China, when the turbulence of political transition made it imperative that the "white devils" leave. The book covers a two-year span and concludes with a happy child getting to know the grandparents and the family farm she had so longed to see; the author explains, in her preface, that she has compressed time and included some of her memories of earlier years. No seams are visible; the story flows smoothly, richly, intimately. The descriptions of places and the times are vivid in a book that brings to the reader, with sharp clarity and candor, the yearnings and fears and ambivalent loyalties of a young girl.

418   **Fritz,** Jean. *Stonewall;* illus. by Stephen Gammell. Putnam, 1979. 79-12506. Trade ed. ISBN 0-399-20698-1; Paper ed. ISBN 0-399-20699-X. 157p. Trade ed. $7.95; Paper ed. $3.95.

6–9   There is no adulatory writing, no overdramatization in this biography of the rigid, zealous, in some instances fanatical Jackson; Jean Fritz focuses on Jackson's prowess as a military leader, and most of the book is concerned with the years of the Civil War, but the early portion of the text so skillfully establishes Jackson's probity, eccentricity, and toughness that the later portion serves to amplify the personal portrait as well as to give a vivid picture of the war years. An extensive bibliography corroborates the evidence of careful research that permeates a well-written and carefull structured text.

419   **Fritz,** Jean. *Where Do You Think You're Going, Christopher Columbus?* illus. by Margot Tomes. Putnam, 1980. 80-11377. Hardcover ed. ISBN 0-399-20723-6; Paper ed. ISBN 0-399-20734-1. 80p. Hardcover ed. $7.95; Paper ed. $3.95.

3–5   As always, based on thorough research; as always, written in a smooth, informal style that is leavened with humor. As in her previous books about historical figures, Jean Fritz evokes more than just the facts: her Columbus is an excellent seaman but a man blinded by his own convictions and hampered by the geographic ignorance of his time, a man who is courageous, determined, mercenary, querulous, and self-assured. The text gives interesting details about the four voyages to the New World, which Columbus insisted must be the Indies, and describes his last years, wealthy and avaricious, unaware that the American continents existed. "The last thing that he had wanted to do," the book ends, "was to discover a New World." An index and a section of notes are appended.

420   **Galdone,** Paul, ad. *The Teeny-Tiny Woman: A Ghost Story;* retold and illus. by Paul Galdone. Houghton/Clarion, 1984. 84-4311. ISBN 0-89919-270-X. 30p. $11.95.

K–3   Although the repetition and accumulating tension in this ghostly tale from English folklore are at their most effective when the story is told, it reads well here. The teeny-tiny woman who takes a teeny-tiny bone from a teeny-tiny grave and puts it into her teeny-tiny cupboard is kept awake by a voice that gets louder each time it demands "Give me my bone!" Only when she says "Take it!" is there quiet. Galdone illustrates all this with relish as the pop-eyed teeny-tiny woman copes with the eerie voice.

421   **Galdone,** Paul. *What's in Fox's Sack?* ad. and illus. by Paul Galdone. Houghton, 1982. 81-10251. ISBN 0-89919-062-6. 29p. $9.95.

K–2   It's partly the marvelously expressive faces (animal and human) that Galdone gives his characters, partly the vitality of his drawing, and partly the exuberant humor of the illustrative details that make this version of an English folktale so engaging. This is the story of a trickster who is tricked, a sly fox who leaves his sack at a series of homes, each time warning the occupant not to peek; each time she does, and he takes better booty for his sack. From a bumblebee to a rooster to a pig to a boy (with improving prospects for the fox's dinner) until the last woman, suspicious, substitutes a large ferocious dog for the boy. The fox runs for his life, the released boy and the large dog share a treat of gingerbread fresh out of the oven. There's a restrained use of repetition and a pattern within the story, nicely told and as appropriate for story-telling as for reading aloud.

422   **Gallant,** Roy A. *Memory; How It Works and How to Improve It.* Four Winds, 1980. 79-6342. ISBN 0-590-07613-2. 108p. $8.95.

7–10   Serious, thorough in coverage, and explicit, this useful text describes how the brain works to store information and what the stages of memo-rization are, explaining the importance of "rehearsal," or practice, in both short term and long term memorization. Gallant points out that the ability to memorize improves with use, that distraction (music to study by) is an obstacle to memorizing, and that a facility for memoriza-tion does not equate with high intelligence. There is a section on com-puter memory, and another on "How to Improve Your Memory." An index is appended.

423   **Gardam,** Jane. *Bridget and William;* illus. by Janet Rawlins. Watts, 1981. 80-83006. ISBN 0-531-04280-4. 46p. $5.95.

2–4   Brisk, small pen sketches illustrate an English story that is not unusual in plot (a pet unwanted by parents does something useful and is then accepted) but is delightful because of the deceptive simplicity and the flavor of the style, the vivid evocation of setting, and the satisfying warmth of family relationships. This has little of the humor that has dis-tinguished Gardam's books for older readers, but it is written in a style far more appropriate for the primary grades audience for which animal stories and those about achievement (and this is both) appeal. For American readers some terms may be puzzling, but in most cases the context makes words clear enough. The story: Bridget's father is not pleased when an aunt sends her money for a pony; on the high land of their new farm, horses are only a nuisance, he feels. But it is the pony, William, that gets Bridget down to the village in a severe snowstorm and thus gets the doctor in time to deliver a baby brother.

424   **Gardam,** Jane. *The Hollow Land;* illus. by Janet Rawlins. Greenwillow, 1981. 81-6620. ISBN 0-688-00873-9. 152p. $9.50.

5–7   This is not at all like Jane Gardam's other books, but it is just as pol-
*   ished and entertaining. The people are warm and real, but it is the sense of the land and the rural community that plays the stronger part. Bell begins his story when he's eight, and he introduces the London family whose "little lad," Harry, becomes his friend. The setting is the Cumbrian Fells, that part of England where the rivers run below

ground, the "Hollow Land" of the title. This is a series of stories, but they are so closely linked that there is no sense of separation; the writing style is smooth and flowing, with a judicious use of local dialect. The characters are strongly developed, and the shifting viewpoint (sometimes first person, sometimes third) gives a good coverage of the several generations who participate in Bell's and Harry's lifelong friendship. Because of the structure, this is an excellent book for reading aloud in installments to a group.

425   **Garden,** Nancy. *Annie on My Mind.* Farrar, 1982. 82-9189. ISBN 0-374-30366-5. 234p. $10.95.

8–10   Liza, the narrator, struck up an acquaintance with Annie in the Metropolitan Museum of Art, and their friendship grew into so intense a relationship that Liza herself found it hard to understand, at first. Gradually she became aware that what she felt was love, painfully she recognized that she was a lesbian, and joyfully she acknowledged her love when she knew that Annie felt the same way. Nervous about physical expression of her love, Liza gave in to her longing only when she and Annie were alone together in the home of a teacher (away on vacation) for whom Liza was doing some chores. When another teacher and a classmate unexpectedly came to the house, the relationship became known; not only did Liza suffer, knowing how much unhappiness she was causing, but the teacher in whose home the confrontation took place was dismissed, since it became clear that she and the woman who shared the house had a long-standing lesbian relationship. The story is written in retrospect: Liza is at M.I.T. and Annie at Berkeley at the end of the book, and they have had little contact for a long time; at the close of the story, Liza telephones to ask Annie if they can meet during Christmas vacation, and the two reaffirm their love. This is candid, dignified, perceptive, and touching; although the crux of the story line is the encounter that makes a physical relationship clear, it is the romantic element that dominates the book, with its strong characters and its tender love story.

426   **Garfield,** Leon. *Footsteps.* Delacorte, 1980. 80-65834. ISBN 0-440-02634-2. 192p. $8.95.

5–8   With his usual Dickensian panache, Garfield describes an eighteenth century London adventure that is rich in the idiom of the period, and—since the story is told by the protagonist, twelve-year-old William Jones—fraught with the emotions that a child would feel but that might be excessive if told from the authorial viewpoint. Just before his death, William's father (creator of the pacing footsteps that haunt the boy) had told him that he had once robbed his business partner, Alfred Diamond. William runs off to London to find either Diamond or his son and purge his conscience on his father's behalf, and not until he has several encounters with a man named Robinson does he realize that

"Robinson" is Diamond's son and is bent on destroying the Jones family. The delightfully lurid tale ends with young William rescuing Diamond from the Jones house where he is trapped in the blaze he vengefully started. Colorful, fast-paced, and written with craftsmanship.

427   **Garfield,** Leon. *The Night of the Comet; A Comedy of Courtship Featuring Bostock and Harris.* Delacorte, 1979. 79-50670. Trade ed. ISBN 0-440-06656-5; Library ed. ISBN 0-440-06657-3. 149p. Trade ed. $7.95; Library ed. $7.45 net.

6–8   The path of true love, or even of reasonable facsimiles thereof, runs far from smoothly in Garfield's romping and egregiously ridiculous tale of three tangled love affairs. Cassidy, a travelling roofer and thatcher, hunts throughout England for Mary Flatley from Dublin. A garrulous rogue with an eye for the ladies, Cassidy is so unfortunate as to have his Mary spot him in Brighton while he's flattering another woman. The other woman has an off-on relationship with her music teacher; the third hapless lover is a lad whose friend's young sister spurns him— and no wonder, since the friend's advice on affairs of the heart is consistently unfortunate. All of these matters are embroidered, elaborated upon, and exaggerated in Garfield's usually ebullient style, and they all come to a head on the night when a long-heralded comet arrives. It's fun, although this seems a bit more labored than most of Garfield's stories, and the characterization is sacrificed to the style.

428   **Garner,** Alan. *The Aimer Gate,* illus. by Michael Foreman. Collins/World, 1979. 78-20964. 79p. $6.95.

4–6   One of the quartet of books (*The Stone Book, Granny Reardun, Tom
*   Fobble's Day*) that link the generations of a rural Cheshire family but that stand alone, each a small gem. Here the protagonist is Robert, grandchild of Mary in *The Stone Book,* and one of the high points of the story is Robert's discovery, when he climbs to touch the capstone of the church steeple, that it is carved with his own name, carved by the earlier Robert who was Mary's father. "He knew it wouldn't be seen, but he did it as good as any," he says, wondering. That pride in one's craft is a theme that carries through the books, and it is Robert's indecision about his own choice of craft that is the crux of the story. He thinks he wants to be a soldier like his uncle, who counsels him and who himself looks forward to going through "the aimer gate," giving up the army for his chosen craft. The writing is wonderfully, deceptively simple yet colored by the local idiom, and it is permeated by the warmth and solidarity of family ties and by the intricate cohesion of the rural community.

429   **Garner,** Alan. *Tom Fobble's Day;* illus. by Michael Foreman. Collins, 1979. 78-26927. 72p. $6.95.

3–5   Continuing the story of a rural family in England that began with the
 *   short novels *The Stone Book* and *Granny Reardun*, this focuses on a day in
      the life of William, grandson of the lad who, in *Granny Reardun*, so joy-
      fully became an apprentice smith. Now he is old Joseph, William's Gran-
      dad, and the time is World War II; despite the sirens and enemy
      planes, William and his friends delight in sledging down a steep hill.
      Grandad makes the boy a new sledge when his old one shatters, and
      William watches the skill and love with which his sledge is fastened,
      feeling the strength of the family lineage as Grandad talks about the
      past. Garner has always been adept at infusing his stories with local
      color, using local idiom in dialogue, and suggesting more than he tells;
      in this, as in the two earlier books, he adds a sweetness that makes it a
      memorable cameo.

430   **Geibel,** James. *The Blond Brother.* Putnam, 1979. 78-16330. 201p. $7.95.

7–10 Rich Gaskins had been a basketball star in his first high school and is a
      natural for the Marchmont team when he transfers. But Marchmont is a
      school with few white students, so Rich has a double handicap: he's
      white, and he's expected to be the coach's pet. All Rich wants is to
      play. His life is complicated by the fact that he begins dating a black
      girl, Glen, and creates further resentment. Some of the other boys on
      the team learn that Rich is not only friendly but more anxious for team
      success than for personal success, and they accept him—it's the white
      boys who beat him up. Glen breaks up their relationship; the team
      (with a crippled Rich playing) loses the tournament; what heartens
      Rich, in the end, is that some of his team come to see him as a demon-
      stration of the fact that he's still their blond brother. Geibel handles the
      racial conflict with honesty in a story that has good style and pace;
      there are good game sequences, but not too many, and the book es-
      chews the usual sports story formulae.

431   **Gemming,** Elizabeth. *Lost City in the Clouds; The Discovery of Machu
      Picchu;* illus. by Mike Eagle. Coward, 1980. 78-31877. ISBN 0-698-
      30698-8. 75p. $5.99.

6–8   It was while he was at a meeting in Cuzco in 1909 that the young
      American history professor Hiram Bingham first heard the legend of the
      Peruvian "lost city in the clouds." Two years later he came back to Peru
      as head of an expedition to hunt for the lost city, and found the mas-
      sive, well-preserved remains of the huge mountain complex that he
      named Machu Picchu; after another two years he directed another expe-
      dition to the site, and the city was cleared and mapped, with all its
      streets, homes, temples, and fountains. He found human remains, but
      who lived in Machu Picchu, why the massive complex was abandoned
      is still not known, although some of the theories about it are explained
      in Gemming's final chapter. It's fascinating material, adequately
      although rather densely told; the dialogue (which lightens the style to

an extent) is invented but is based on Bingham's accounts of his several journeys. A glossary, a chronology, and a selected bibliography are appended.

432   **George,** Jean Craighead. *The Cry of the Crow.* Harper, 1980. 79-2016. Trade ed. ISBN 0-06-021956-4; Lib. ed. ISBN 0-06-021957-2. 160p. Trade ed. $7.95; Library ed. $7.89 net.

5-7   In a story set in the Florida Everglades, George combines her authoritative knowledge of animal life and her craft as a writer to create a touching tale of a child's love for, and protection of, a pet crow. Her father and older brothers detest crows, and Mandy knows they will shoot her pet, Nina, if they see her. Imprinted as a nestling, the crow has learned to imitate human speech and so Mandy can, to a limited extent, communicate with Nina. The story is concerned with Mandy's efforts to train and protect Nina, and it has more focus, more structured conflict-and-resolution than George's recent fiction; it is smooth and well-paced, with a strong and poignant ending, a twist that is a welcome change from the heavyhearted release of a pet so that it may join its kind—although that enters the story. Undoubtedly, however, the greatest appeal of the book is the lore of crows that the author has so smoothly integrated into a story with good characterization and dialogue.

433   **George,** Jean (Craighead). *One Day in the Desert;* illus. by Fred Brenner. Crowell, 1983. 82-45924. Trade ed. ISBN 0-690-04340-6; Library ed. ISBN 0-690-04341-4. 48p. Library ed. $9.89; Trade ed. $9.95.

4-6   Meticulously drawn black and white illustrations, given a soft effect by the use of parallel lines rather than strong outlines, add to the effectiveness of a text that is clear, direct, authoritative, and informative. George describes the way a particularly stressful day of intense heat followed by a cloudburst affects the creatures of the Sonora Desert. Her text has cohesion and focus in part because she makes two Papago Indians (mother and child) and a wounded mountain lion the main characters, in part because the dramatic quality of the setting and the natural events bind the people and animals together.

434   **George,** Jean (Craighead). *The Talking Earth.* Harper, 1983. 82-48850. Trade ed. ISBN 0-06-021975-0; Library ed. ISBN 0-06-021976-9. 160p. Trade ed. $9.95; Library ed. $9.89.

6-9   Rebuked for her lack of faith in the legends of her Seminole tribe, thirteen-year-old Billie Wind chooses her own punishment: she will go alone into the Everglades and "stay until I hear the animals talk, see the serpent and meet the little people who live underground." This is the story of her lonely adventure, a story that is imbued with Seminole lore, is appealing because of the pitting of one human being against the elements, and is—if occasionally slow-moving—convincing in its plot development and impressive in its descriptions of natural phenomena.

435   **George,** Jean Craighead. *The Wild, Wild Cookbook;* illus. by Walter Kessell. Crowell, 1982. 82-45187. Trade ed. ISBN 0-690-04314-7; Library ed. ISBN 0-690-04315-5; Paper ed. ISBN 0-690-04319-8. 182p. Trade ed. $10.50; Library ed. $10.89; Paper ed. $4.95.

6–   In a wild-food cookbook, the material is organized by seasons, beginning with spring, and the plants used include both such widely-found species as dandelions, ferns, plantain, purslane, and acorns as well as more localized species like manzanita and prickly pear. George warns that mushrooms should be avoided, since there are some that are poisonous, and adjures readers not to use any plant unless sure of its identity. A drawing of each plant precedes the recipe or recipes given for its use, as does a note on distinguishing features and habitat. Cooking time and a list of utensils are given for each recipe in addition to ingredients, and the step-by-step directions are clear and concise. Plants in each section are listed alphabetically; an index is provided.

436   **Gerrard,** Roy. *Sir Cedric;* written and illus. by Roy Gerrard. Farrar, 1984. 84-6111. ISBN 374-36959-3. 30p. $11.95.

K–3   A bouncy narrative poem has the appeal of a brave and gentle hero, lilting rhythm and rhyme, and the triumph of good over evil—but the illustrations are the most attractive part of the book. Gerrard's squat little people move in a fairytale landscape of daisy-starred grass, romantic castles, impossibly imposing horses with long legs and gorgeous trappings. The paintings are deft in technique and composition, humorous in effect, and often beautifully detailed and ornamented. The story: little Sir Cedric the Good defeats the very bad Black Ned in a battle that is so clearly a victory that the war stops for tea.

437   **Gerstein,** Mordicai. *Arnold of the Ducks;* written and illus. by Mordicai Gerstein. Harper, 1983. 82-47735. Trade ed. ISBN 0-06-022002-3; Library ed. ISBN 0-06-022003-1. 54p. Trade ed. $10.50; Library ed. $10.89.

K–2   Tinted in soft colors, animated and humorous line drawings illustrate a fantasy in which the bland style and the whimsical plot are foils for each other. Snatched as an infant by a pelican, Arnold is dropped from the bird's beak into a nest of ducklings, and adopted by Mrs. Leda Duck as one of her own. An odd duckling, but she loves him. With mud and marsh slime, the others paste feathers over Arnold so that he won't look so odd, and that's how Arnold is able to fly. Alas, investigating a kite one day (although his "mother" has told him to stay away from it) Arnold's caught. He falls, is rescued by a huge dog, taken to a house, and cleaned up by the people who live there and who recognize him as their own boy. Nicely told, with a wistful ending that rounds out the concept of the fantasy.

438   **Gibbons,** Gail. *Department Store;* written and illus. by Gail Gibbons. Crowell, 1984. 83-45053. Library ed. ISBN 0-690-04367-8; Trade ed. ISBN 0-690-04366-X. 30p. Library ed. $9.89; Trade ed. $9.95.

K–3   Illustrations with clean lines, almost garish colors, and tidy composition show the many departments, the store layout, and some of the special services of a department store. The text is direct and simple; some of the pictures use balloon captions to give additional information. For most children, the variety and bustle of a large store is interesting; this will give them some background to help them understand the complexity and diversity of a department store.

439   **Gibbons,** Gail. *Tunnels;* written and illus. by Gail Gibbons. Holiday House, 1984. 83-18589. ISBN 0-8234-0507-9. 32p. $12.95.

K–2   Gibbons points out that many animals build and live in tunnels, that children dig tunnels for fun, and that some tunnels are major engineering projects, serving various industrial or vehicular purposes. She describes the different kinds of tunnels and illustrates their structures in cutaway diagrams. Most children find the subject appealing, and this introduces it very simply. The flat colors in some pictures combined with a stylized treatment of mass add a static note.

440   **Giblin,** James Cross. *Chimney Sweeps: Yesterday and Today;* illus. by Margot Tomes. Crowell, 1982. 81-43878. Trade ed. ISBN 0-690-04192-6; Library ed. ISBN 0-690-04193-4. 56p. Trade ed. $10.50; Library ed. $10.89.

4–8   Beginning in the twelfth century, when chimneys were first built, the trade of the chimney sweep was established, waning with the substitution of furnaces for fireplaces, waxing again today as more people use wood stoves and fireplaces to conserve energy. Giblin writes in a smooth, straightforward style of the use of young children, especially in England, and of the long struggle of reformers to alleviate the harsh treatment such children received; he discusses briefly the status of sweeps in several countries, and some of the superstitions about sweeps; he describes chimney-sweeping in America from colonial times on, and discusses the sweeps of today. An index and a bibliography add to the usefulness of a nicely compiled book on an unusual topic.

441   **Giblin,** James Cross. *The Skyscraper Book;* illus. by Anthony Kramer; photographs by David Anderson. T. Y. Crowell, 1981. 81-43038. Trade ed. ISBN 0-690-04154-3; Library ed. ISBN 0-690-04155-1. 86p. Trade ed. $9.50; Library ed. $8.89.

5–9   An excellent survey of the development and proliferation of an architectural phenomenon is illustrated with well-placed photographs of good quality. This does not focus on the way in which a skyscraper is constructed, although the author includes descriptions of structural innovations as they occurred historically and as they influenced design; the book emphasizes the major skyscrapers in the United States as it gives a history of skyscrapers and their architects. A smooth and straightforward fusion of highlights in the history of tall office buildings, this concludes with a list of "fabulous facts," a glossary of some architectural terms, a bibliography, and an index.

442   **Giblin,** James Cross. *Walls: Defenses Throughout History;* illus. with drawings by Anthony Kramer and with photographs. Little Brown, 1984. 84-15444. ISBN 0-316-30954-0. 113p. $13.95.

4–9   Well-placed and adequately labelled drawings and photographs extend and complement the text of a book that is carefully organized, capably written, and nicely varied. Giblin focuses on actual structures: the walls of Jericho, Hadrian's Wall, the Great Wall of China, etc. (concluding with the Maginot Line) and uses each example to give information both about the specific structure or, when applicable, the type it represents. He is careful to point out the reasons for the walls being constructed and for structural details. A glossary, a bibliography, and an index are provided.

443   **Giff,** Patricia Reilly. *The Almost Awful Play;* illus. by Susanna Natti. Viking, 1984. 83-17101. ISBN 0-670-11458-8. 28p. $9.95.

2–4   Ronald is the narrator in this brief, humorous story about the planning of a class play and the near-disaster of the performance. The princess carps at everything, the prince forgets his lines, the wooden cage (witch's dungeon) Ronald and the prince have made collapses on stage. It is Ronald who steps in when the prince freezes, whips off his cat mask, and announces that he is another prince, come to save the princess. So Ronald saves the day and the play. Simply told, the story should appeal to primary grades readers because of the action, the almost-disaster humor, and the realism of the children's behavior.

444   **Gilbert,** Sara. *How to Live with a Single Parent.* Lothrop, 1982. 81-12413. Library ed. ISBN 0-668-00633-7; Paper ed. ISBN 0-688-00587-X. 128p. Library ed. $9.55; Paper ed. $6.50.

6–9   Gilbert doesn't talk down to her readers, nor does she promise them a rose garden; her discussion of some of the problems that exist in relationships within a one-parent home is sensible and moderate, and it includes a variety of situations, using specific cases to illustrate the points she is making and give variety to the text. There is a slight tendency to make flat statements about what should be done or said in a given situation, but it *is* slight, and the advice usually strikes a good balance between being sympathetic and being firm about the needs and rights of others. A final chapter is addressed to parents. Appended are lists of fiction and nonfiction books that may help readers, another list for parents, organizations for parents and for progeny, and an index.

445   **Gilbert,** Sara. *What Happens in Therapy.* Lothrop, 1982. 82-15233. Library ed. ISBN 0-688-01458-5; Paper ed. ISBN 0-688-01459. 144p. Library ed. $8.63; Paper ed. $6.50.

7–12   Matter-of-fact in tone, sensible in approach, full in coverage, and written in a crisp, informal style, this is a useful and perceptive introduction to the therapeutic process. It is addressed particularly to adolescents and their needs and problems. Gilbert describes various therapeutic methods, discusses the practitioners and their qualifications and differences, and uses several cases as examples of a range of problems that are treated by a range of techniques. The book discusses costs, suggests ways in which individuals can judge and select therapists, lists danger signals, reminds readers to have a physician check on physical symptoms, and discusses candidly the pitfalls and satisfactions of the client-therapist relationship. A glossary, an index, and a useful series of lists of sources of information (advice on legal rights, advice on therapists' credentials, advice on mental health treatment, fiction and nonfiction bibliographies) is included.

446   **Gillham,** Bill. *Let's Look for Opposites;* by Bill Gillham and Susan Hulme; illus. with photographs by Jan Siegieda. Coward, 1984. 83-24065. ISBN 0-698-20614-2.
Let's Look for Colors; 83-24047. ISBN 0-698-20612-6. *Let's Look for Numbers;* 83-24066. ISBN 0-698-20613-4. *Let's Look for Shapes;* 83-25177. ISBN 0-698-20615-0. All books in the series have 22p. and are $4.95.

2–4   First published in England, this set of four concept books is excellent in
yrs.   every way: the size is right for small hands, the print is large to encourage pre-readers, the text is limited in length and simply written, the color photographs are of good quality, and—in each book—a second page reinforces the concept. In the color book, for example, a field of yellow flowers faces a yellow rubber duck in a baby's bath; in the numbers book, a picture of a horse's ears faces a picture of a child trying on two red shoes, and so on. This has been done before, but not better.

447   **Ginsburg,** Mirra, ad. *The Magic Stove;* illus. by Linda Heller. Coward-McCann, 1983. 82-12523. ISBN 0-698-20566-9. 28p. $10.95.

K–2   In a competent adaptation of a Russian folktale, a poor man's kindness is rewarded, a magic device is used, and justice triumphs over greed. All these traditional themes are combined in the story of a rooster who produces a magic stove (it makes any kind of pie one requests) and then retrieves it from the avaricious king who has stolen it from the peasant couple who had kindly shared their home and their bounty. The illustrations, pastel-tinted, have a spacious quality, a brisk use of line, and ornamental costume details; they are often naive in perspective or figure-drawing, but vigorous.

448   **Ginsburg,** Mirra, comp. and ad. *The Twelve Clever Brothers and Other Fools;* illus. by Charles Mikolaycak. Lippincott, 1979. 79-2409. Trade ed. ISBN 0-397-31822-7; Library ed. ISBN 0-397-31862-6. 96p. Trade ed. $8.95; Library ed. $8.89 net.

3–5   A frieze that looks like a band of red and white embroidery is a handsome contrast to the black and white of the print and the boldly designed but subtly executed pictures that introduce each story. Sources are identified: Russian, Latvian, Assyrian, Moldavian, etc. Many of the tales are variants of noodlehead stories from other cultures; the twelve clever brothers, for example, return to their own village by mistake, just as do the fools of Chelm, and the old familiar counting donkeys device is the base of another story. A very pleasant collection, adapted in sprightly style, and nice for reading aloud or alone, as well as for storytelling.

449   **Girard,** Linda Walvoord. *My Body is Private;* illus. by Rodney Pate. Whitman, 1984. 84-17220. ISBN 0-8075-5320-4. 25p. $9.25.

2–3   Julie discusses the fact that some things should be private, and includes certain parts of the body (an odd mix of external and internal parts) and how she feels about her right to say "stop" even to a brother who is innocently tickling her. She and her mother talk about what someone (stranger, friend, or family member) might try to do; Julie's mother points out that it isn't likely this will happen, but that one should know what to do if it does, just as one learns what to do if a fire erupts. The stress is on one's right to privacy and on the importance of telling a parent or some other responsible adult. The tone is a bit preachy, but the book does a better job than many of striking a nice balance between a calm attitude about the likelihood of harassment and a serious attitude about what to do if it occurs.

450   **Girard,** Linda Walvoord. *You Were Born on Your Very First Birthday;* illus. by Christa Kieffer. Whitman, 1983. 82-13700. ISBN 0-8075-9455-5. 29p. $8.25.

K–3   A gentle introduction to gestation and birth begins with the infant in embryo, and describes the period of gestation from the child's viewpoint, informing the audience that an unborn child can, once it has reached a certain size, hear and feel. And, as pregnant mothers know, kick and hiccup. "And then—you felt a squeeze like a hug . . . One hug after another, bigger and bigger." The text and the soft pictures and diagrams, some in color, are mutually extensive in showing the love and joy of mother and father, both before and after birth.

451   **Girion,** Barbara. *A Handful of Stars.* Scribner, 1981. 81-14476. ISBN 0-684-17167-8. 179p. $10.95.

7–9   Because Julie, just starting high school, tells her own story, this has an immediacy that makes her worries and fears about her physical condition the more vivid and poignant. Happy in her friendships and her family life, excited about being in school theatricals, Julie is upset because—periodically—she does something strange, she's told, and can't remember it. Like getting up during a meal and walking around the table. What can be wrong? Epilepsy. And so Julie, and Julie's family, have to adjust to her physical limitations, to the need for controlling medication, and—worst of all—the bias she encounters when her condition becomes known. Told in retrospect on the night of high school graduation, this is a moving and perceptive story that is candid in dealing with the resentment, despair, and anger that Julie must overcome if she is to adjust (as she does) and take a positive attitude toward her liability and her future.

452   **Girion,** Barbara. *A Tangle of Roots.* Scribner, 1979. 78-27243. ISBN 0-684-16074-9. 154p. $7.95.

7–10   Sixteen-year-old Beth is stunned, when she's called into the school office only a few hours after leaving her mother, to learn that Mom has had a cerebral hemorrhage and died instantly. In addition to her anguish, Beth is troubled by feelings of responsibility for her father, by the rift that develops between her and her boyfriend because she gives so much time to her father, by her irritation with her nagging, pitiful grandmother who lives in the same building, and by her resentment against the women who gravitate toward Daddy. Not all Beth's problems are happily solved, but she adjusts to those problems in a realistic way. Girion handles both the reactions to bereavement and to the resultant difficulties with honesty and sensitivity, and the story is so convincingly told by Beth that the perceptive characterization (even the tart picture of Grandma) seems to flow naturally from her rather than from the author.

453   **Gitanjali.** *Poems of Gitanjali.* Oriel Press/Routledge & Kegan Paul, 1983. Trade ed. ISBN 0-85362-195-0; Paper ed. ISBN 0-85362-202-7. 155p. Trade ed. $12.95; Paper ed. $8.95.

8–   A posthumous publication, this is a collection of poems gathered by her mother after Gitanjali's death at the age of sixteen. A cancer victim, Gitanjali wrote of her deep love for her family, her grief at their suffering, her own burdens of pain and sorrow, and—permeating all the poems— her faith in God's mercy. Some of the poetry is technically flawed, but the sincerity and passion of the writing more than compensate for this. Deeply poignant, deeply moving.

454   **Glass,** Andrew. *My Brother Tries to Make Me Laugh;* written and illus. by Andrew Glass. Lothrop, 1984. 83-14989. Library ed. ISBN 0-688-02259-6; Trade ed. ISBN 0-688-02257-X. 30p. Library ed. $10.51; Trade ed. $11.50.

3–6   Sprightly crayon drawings of the narrator and her brother, purple crea-
yrs.   tures with long snouts and eyes on stalks, add to the fun of a text in which there is conjecture about the creatures called Earthlings and then a confrontation. Odeon tries, all through the long space voyage, to make his sister laugh with no success, although she apparently enjoys fun at the expense of their lazy robot and their easy-to-tease computer.

As they prepare to land, Mother warns the children to be friendly to the Earthlings, not to comment on their odd appearance (such tiny noses!) or make fun of them; the meeting is wholly amicable and, when the robot plays a little joke, there's laughter all around. How could this miss? Monsters, space flight, role reversal, humor, and a text that has a casual, conversational tone.

455   **Glazer,** Tom. *Music for Ones and Twos: Songs and Games for the Very Young Child*; illus. by Karen Ann Weinhaus. Doubleday, 1983. 82-45199. ISBN 0-385-14252-8. 96p. $7.95.

1–5 yrs.   Brisk little line drawings illustrate an excellent collection of songs, many of which serve also as games, finger plays, or learning devices. Glazer explains, in his preface, that he has chosen the material in the book to reflect a young child's interests, vocabulary, and speech patterns. Also addressed to adults is a section on "Using This Material," which explains that a few nonmusical games are included. The songs have been astutely chosen and are grouped under such headings as "A Child's Day," "The Playground," and "Favorite Fingerplays," making it easier to locate material for specific purposes or occasions. It is unfortunate that the book, because it does not lie flat, cannot be used at the piano.

456   **Glenn,** Mel. *Class Dismissed: High School Poems.* Houghton, 1982. 81-38441. ISBN 0-89919-075-8. 96p. $10.95.

7–10   For each poem in this collection, the title is the name of an adolescent student; photographs of teen-age boys and girls illustrate the book. Many of the poems are related to school: peers, teachers, hopes for college, or to events that took place in a school setting (ripping off a girl's gold chain in the hallway, pulling a prank in Spanish class) but most are about the worries, interests, and experiences that are common in the adolescent years. Each poem is in first person, free verse that is direct and concise, candid in tone and varied in subject and attitude. Not great poetry but good poetry written with perception and sympathy.

457   **Glubok,** Shirley. *The Art of Egypt under the Pharoahs*; designed by Gerard Nook. Macmillan, 1980. 79-23336. ISBN 0-02-736470-4. 44p. illus. $9.95.

4–6   Photographs, black and white, show the statues, reliefs, jewelry, tombs, and temples; the pages are handsomely laid out in this book, an addition to a series in the same format. This volume has a bit more history and a bit less representation and description of art objects of the eighteenth dynasty. Although the writing style is dry, it is clear and direct, and the book—like others in the series—smoothly blends information about art and about the culture it reflected.

458   **Goble,** Paul. *Buffalo Woman*; written and illus. by Paul Goble. Bradbury, 1984. 83-15704. ISBN 0-02-737720-2. 28p. $12.95.

4–6   "Mitakuye oyasin—We are all related" is the theme of an animal-bride story in which the loving husband, Straight-up-Person, follows his buffalo wife and son when the members of his family send her away. Carefully structured and told, this legend of the Buffalo People is illustrated by handsomely designed, stylized paintings notable for their use of color and for the bright blocks of solid tones.

459   **Goble,** Paul, ad. *Star Boy;* ad. and illus. by Paul Goble. Bradbury, 1983. 82-20599. ISBN 0-02-722660-3. 27p. $12.95.

2–4   The strong sense of design, the restrained and effective use of color, and the stylized use of Native American motifs in bold composition contribute to the distinctive work that won Goble the Caldecott Medal. Here they are used, with the addition on many pages of a running frieze of large dots, based on Blackfeet tipi designs, to illustrate a gravely-told version of a Blackfeet Indian legend. The scarred grandchild of the Sun, to win his bride, goes to the Sky World to plead with his Grandfather, who grants his wish and removes the scar and who tells Star Boy that if the people build a lodge in his honor each summer he will restore their sick people to health. And that is why, each summer, the people build a Sun Dance lodge, round as the earth and sky, and there they dance and pray to their Creator.

460   **Godden,** Rumer. *The Dragon of Og;* illus. by Pauline Baynes. Viking, 1981. 81-2620. ISBN 0-670-28168-9 60p. $9.95.

4–7
*   Illustrated with both richly colored paintings and lively, effective black and white line drawings, this is a happy union between a distinguished illustrator and an equally distinguished writer. Godden's whimsy never becomes cloying, her writing style is fluent and deft, her people—and dragons—are fully-fleshed. Young, shy, and gentle, the Dragon lived in the waters of the estate that Angus Og inherited; the beast responded with love to the kindness of Og's wife Matilda, and she grew fond of him. When Angus learned that the dragon fed on an occasional bullock, he was so angry he hired a courtly knight to kill the beast. However, due to Angus' own stinginess and stubborness, one thing led to another (with Matilda's help) and by the end of the story the dragon was brought back from death, Angus was resigned to the creature's having a bullock now and then, and everyone went on firmly believing that their dragon was the good luck of the castle and its folk. This is a perfect soufflé of a book: light, melting, tasty, and substantial withal.

461   **Goffstein,** M. B. *Natural History;* written and illus. by M. B. Goffstein. Farrar, 1979. 79-7318. ISBN 0-374-35498-7. 30p. $6.95.

3–6
yrs.   Goffstein's familiar line, simple and uncluttered, is for the first time combined with watercolor, giving more richness to pictures that are in harmony with her theme of earth's natural abundance, and our obligation to use resources with care and to cherish other people and all life

with peaceful love. The writing is gentle and direct, a quiet flow of tender concern: "Every living creature is our brother and our sister, dearer than the jewels at the center of the earth. So let us be like tiny grains of sand, and protect all life from fear and suffering! Then, when the stars shine, we can sleep in peace, with the moon as our quiet night-light."

462   **Golden,** Frederic. *The Trembling Earth: Probing & Predicting Quakes.* Scribner, 1983. 83-3262. ISBN 0-684-17884-2. 175p. $13.95.

8–   The science editor of *Time* magazine competently addresses not only the aspects of earthquake activity indicated by the title, but also related phenomena that are pertinent to the subject, such as the research that contributed to present understanding of plate tectonics or studies of abnormal animal behavior that indicate imminent earthquake activity. Much of the material in the text has been covered in other books for young people, but none of them does a better job of synthesizing theory, research, proven facts, and the history of seismology. Carefully organized and written with authority, this excellent overview concludes with a bibliography and an index.

463   **Goldner,** Kathryn Allen. *Why Mount St. Helens Blew Its Top;* written by Kathryn Allen Goldner and Carole Garbuny Vogel; illus. by Roberta Aggarwal and by photographs. Dillon, 1981. 81-12482. ISBN 0-87518-219-4. 88p. $8.95.

4–7   The authors describe the tragedy and drama of the volcanic eruption of 1980, giving details of some dramatic incidents in which hikers or residents or campers were able to escape—or were not. The text discusses the ways in which volcanoes are formed and erupt, describes the changes caused on or near St. Helens by the fire, mud, and ash, and also mentions briefly some of the other volcanic disasters of history. The text is written with brisk capability, the photographs and diagrams are informative and well-placed; a bibliography, a glossary, and an index are appended.

464   **Goldreich,** Gloria. *A Treasury of Jewish Literature from Biblical Times to Today.* Holt, 1982. 81-6967. ISBN 0-03-053831-9. 243p. $13.50.

7–   Goldreich, who is known chiefly for her career biographies of women, written for children, and for several adult novels and short stories, has compiled an impressive anthology of religious and secular materials, all focused on the Jewish experience, history, and religion. Each section (the Apocrypha, the Talmud, American Jewish literature, for example) is prefaced by an introductory explanation about the work or genre. A glossary, bibliography, and index extend the usefulness of the book, which includes excerpts from the work of such writers as Bernard Malamud, Philip Roth, Sholom Aleichem, and Arthur Miller.

465   **Goldston,** Robert C. *Sinister Touches: The Secret War Against Hitler.* Dial, 1982. 81-65853. ISBN 0-8037-7903-8. 192p. $11.95.

7–   One of Goldston's best, this is a lively, detailed, and well-documented
*   report of the covert operations—chiefly British—that affected many of
      the battle plans, the strategic shifts, and the personal activities of men
      and women who participated in the secret war that was waged while
      the open warfare of World War II was raging. The author lets the hero-
      ism of such men and women speak for itself; he wisely does not laud,
      he informs. Much of the information in the book remained secret for
      decades after the war was over; the text deftly combines information
      about the work of secret agents in diverse operations into a smooth ac-
      count that is buttressed by a "War Diary," or chronology, that precedes
      each chapter and that is augmented by an index and a bibliography.

466   **Goldston,** Robert C. *The Sword of the Prophet; A History of the Arab World
      from the Time of Mohammed to the Present Day.* Dial, 1979. 78-72200. ISBN
      0-8037-8372-8. 246p. $8.95.

8–   Goldston surveys the history of the Arab world objectively and seri-
      ously, in a chronological arrangement that covers much of the same ma-
      terial as *Arabs and the Islamic World* by Ross but does not explore the arts
      and sciences as does the Ross book. It is more up-to-date, including the
      revolution in Iran, however, and while it is heavier in writing style, is
      rather more penetrating, and has a more extensive and scholarly bibli-
      ography of sources; this is followed by a brief list of suggestions for fur-
      ther reading and an index. Ross examines all aspects of Arab cultures
      while Goldston's approach is primarily political; both books are excel-
      lent.

467   **Goodall,** John S. *Above and Below Stairs;* written and illus. by John S.
      Goodall. Atheneum, 1983. 82-48528. ISBN 0-689-50238-9. 60p. $9.95.

4–   Using the device of his earlier books, (half-pages that alternate with full
      pages to shift scenes), Goodall provides a brief pictorial resume of
      changing life-styles, costumes, and architecture from the Middle Ages
      to today. Each double-page spread has a label, usually the name of an
      English monarch with dates of his or her reign, or of a period (Middle
      Ages, Restoration). Most of the scene shifts are in the upstairs-down-
      stairs tradition, but there are exceptions: children playing, children at
      their lessons; actors on stage, actors in their dressing room. The paint-
      ings are full of animation and color, giving an interesting view of social
      history.

468   **Goor,** Ron. *In the Driver's Seat;* by Ron and Nancy Goor. Crowell, 1982.
      81-43885. Trade ed. ISBN 0-690-04176-4; Library ed. ISBN 0-690-04177-2.
      88p. illus. with photographs. Trade ed. $10.50; Library ed. $10.89.

2–4   Large print and ample spacing facilitate reading ease in a book that de-
      scribes, each within a slight narrative framework ("You are the pilot of
      a Concorde . . . Today you are flying 100 passengers 3,423 miles . . .")
      what the pilot or driver does when handling all sorts of vehicles, from

an 18-wheel truck or a combine to a jet plane or a train. The subject and the photographs should interest many primary grades readers, the writing style is clear and direct, and the vocabulary is as simple as is consistent with accuracy.

469   **Goor,** Ron. *Shadows: Here, There, and Everywhere;* written and illus. by Ron and Nancy Goor. T. Y. Crowell, 1981. 81-43036. Trade ed. ISBN 0-690-04132-2; Library ed. ISBN 0-690-04133-0. 47p. Trade ed. $8.25; Library ed. $7.89.

K–3   A direct, simple text encourages viewers to understand how shadows are formed, and how variations in light sources cause similar variations in the size, shape, and direction of shadows. The pictures are excellent, both as art objects and as illustrations of the author's explanations. Not just a nice book about shadows, this can also be a spur to thoughtful observations in general.

470   **Gormley,** Beatrice. *Mail-Order Wings;* illus. by Emily Arnold McCully. Dutton, 1981. 81-3283. ISBN 0-525-34450-0. 164p. $10.25.

4–6   Andrea didn't know exactly what to expect when she sent off an order for an easy-to-assemble Wonda-Wings kit, but she didn't really believe the Aero-Joy Juice that came with the kit would make it possible for her to fly—but fly she did. Awkward at first, Andrea soon learned the joy of riding a soaring current, dipping and swooping through the night sky. Her flights were secret; she tried to explain to her older brother, but he brushed her off. What made things difficult was that she couldn't get the wings off; what could she do? Answering another ad, Andrea met the evil scientist who wanted her to become a bird, to give up her humanity. She was saved by a hasty gulp of the scientist's brew called "Pteroterminate," and by the sudden appearance of her brother on a rescue mission, and not a whit too soon. Although this sags a bit in the center of the story, it's adequately structured, competently written, and ingeniously conceived; it has a good integration of the realistic and the fanciful, and there are moments of humor to give contrast.

471   **Gould,** Joan. *Otherborn.* Coward, 1980. 79-26735. ISBN 0-698-20497-2. 160p. $8.95.

6–9   Because of a storm at sea, Mark and his sister Leggy (Allegra) are cast ashore on a tropical island, where they find one boy, who seems about their age, who speaks English fluently. The others are friendly but seldom communicative. Mark and Leggy can't quite understand their captors; are they willing to let them go or are they keeping them prisoners? Are they shielding some secret when they refuse to let Mark go up to the mountain village? Why are the villagers so jubilant when they find a very old person? Up to this point, the book seems a good but not unusual adventure story, but with the answers to the children's questions comes the fantastic element: birth is different in the Land of Light, where those who appear very old (born in caves, or "otherborn") are the beloved infants, and those who look like children are the tribal elders. An intriguing concept is convincing within the framework of the fantasy, which has good pace and suspense. Through her island characters, Gould also gives an interesting viewpoint of the comparative advantages and disadvantages of primitive life and the technological advances of today's civilization. In all, an exciting story.

472   **Graham,** Ada. *Careers in Conservation;* by Ada and Frank Graham; illus. by Drake Jordan. Sierra Club/Scribner, 1980. 79-20793. ISBN 0-684-16472-8. 166p. $9.95.

6–10   In a book as useful for those interested in a career in wildlife or wilderness conservation as it is appealing to conservationists in general, the Grahams describe the roles of thirteen men and women who are actively engaged in such work. The accounts, based largely on interviews and in part on observation, cover a wide range of jobs: an industrial ecologist, a lobbyist, a park administrator, a deputy director of the National Park Service, a biologist working for the National Audubon Society, etc. The writing is serious but not dry, covering both preparation for jobs and descriptions of the work each person does; it is enlivened by personal experiences in cited comments and by occasional anecdotes. A brief final section, "Beginning Your Career," includes sources of information and precedes an index.

473   **Graham,** Ada. *The Changing Desert;* by Ada and Frank Graham; illus. by Robert Shetterly. Sierra Club/Scribner, 1981. 81-8961. ISBN 0-684-17146-5. 90p. $11.95.

5–8   Creamy paper is a soft and effective setting for finely-detailed line drawings that are both realistic and elegant, with identifying captions for the desert plants and animals they show; the illustrations are not, however, always placed well. A picture of a jackrabbit, for example, is in a section devoted to Mexican gray wolves. The book describes the desert ecology and the ways in which human incursion is affecting it through carelessness (motorcycle damage) or accident (the introduction of the dominating burro that crowds out indigenous animals) or design (thieves who steal cactus). The authors point out ways in which such factors, as well as grazing and irrigation, have adversely affected the ecological balance of much of the wilderness of the American Southwest in a book that is all the more an effective plea for conservation because of its moderate tone and direct, capable writing style.

474   **Grahame,** Kenneth. *The Wind in the Willows;* illus. by John Burningham. Viking, 1983. 82-16022. ISBN 0-670-77120-1. 240p. $15.75.

5–7   The Burningham illustrations for a new edition of a British classic are much more like the original Shepard pictures than are those by Michael Hague. There are several full-color, full-page pictures here, and they are both attractive and appropriate for the tone of the story; the many black and white drawings are, like Shepard's, small in scale, delicate and deft in use of line, and gently humorous. The one disappointment of this edition is that some of the pictures are poorly placed; in the chapter "The Open Road," for example, it does detract from the impact of the last sentence (Toad's purchase of a large, expensive motor-car) when a plate showing Toad and his new car precedes the end of the chapter by several pages.

475   **Grahame,** Kenneth. *The Wind in the Willows;* illus. by Michael Hague. Ariel/Holt, 1980. 80-12509. ISBN 0-03-056294-5. 205p. $16.95.

5–7
 *   A new edition of a much-loved classic is illustrated by beautifully detailed paintings in full color, the pictures at times humorous but more often romantic in conventional representational style; the composition and use of color are impressive, as is the felicity with which Hague echoes the varying moods of the story. For those fortunate enough to have a first reading of the story as a new experience, it is about the diverting adventures of Toad, Mole, Badger, and Water Rat, and it's one of the most durable animal fantasies.

476   **Grant,** Susan. *Beauty and the Beast: The Coevolution of Plants and Animals;* illus. by Laszlo Kubinyi. Scribner, 1984. 84-10609. ISBN 0-684-18186-X. 215p. $14.95.

8–   The title has not been chosen capriciously, for Grant compares the plants and animals she discusses to the fairytale characters, noting that study reveals in nature, as it does in fiction, the true qualities of the protagonists, whether the relationship is mutually beneficial or mutually hostile in coevolutionary patterns. A biologist, Grant writes with grace and animation, adding for readers the enjoyment of style and wit to the authoritative array of fascinating information about how plants and animals change and adapt in accommodation to the defensive and offensive behavior of each other. The bibliography is extensive and is divided by chapters; the index is equally extensive and is carefully compiled.

477   **Greenberg,** Jan. *The Iceberg and Its Shadow.* Farrar, 1980. 80-20060. ISBN 0-374-33624-5. 119p. $8.95.

4–6   "Mindy was the first friend I ever had who scared me." Anabeth, the narrator, was in sixth grade; she was popular and happy, secure in the friendship of quiet Rachel. When Mindy joined the class, Anabeth wasn't frightened at all: bold, tough, lively Mindy fascinated her even though it was clear that Rachel was being squeezed out. In time, Anabeth felt uneasy about Mindy's domineering harshness and protested—and that's when she became afraid; Mindy contrived to make Anabeth the class pariah. This is not a new theme in children's literature but it is very well handled: Anabeth's change of feeling is believably gradual, her family is warm and supportive when they learn about her problems, and the ending is realistic, with no convenient reversal, no contrived revenge. Anabeth adjusts to being an outsider, recovers from her humiliation enough to make overtures to some classmates, and—when vacation begins—successfully renews her friendship with Rachel. Good writing style, good pace.

478   **Greenberg,** Jan. *The Pig-Out Blues.* Farrar, 1982. 82-2552. ISBN 0-374-35937-7. 150p. $9.95.

7–9   Jodie and her mother, Vanessa, had a hostile relationship in which screaming arguments were followed by days of sullen silence. Most of the time the fights were about Jodie's compulsive eating and her result-ant pudginess; when she went on a strenuous diet, Vanessa happily cooperated—but the fasting had been undertaken so that Jodie might get the part of Juliet in a school play, and when she fainted during an audition, she lost that chance. In her despair, Jodie began stuffing her-self again. Only after her mother returned from a trip taken to forget the rift between her and the man she loved, did she and Jodie make the first tentative steps toward mutual tolerance. Jodie has been helped, during Vanessa's absence, by the kindness of her best friend Heather and Heather's warm, loving family. This is a well-paced and perceptive story written with restraint and with a clear indication of the fact that in the complexity of human relationships there is no black and white, no saints or sinners.

479   **Greenberg,** Jan W. *Theater Careers: A Comprehensive Guide to Non-Acting Careers in the Theater.* Holt, 1983. 83-4386. ISBN 0-03-061568-2. 206p. $13.95.

8–   A theatrical press agent, Greenberg writes with articulate knowledge-ability about the range and diversity of non-acting jobs in both commer-cial and not-for-profit theater. She is explicit in warning readers that employment may be erratic, that financial rewards are far from lavish, and that union membership will usually be required. After the introduc-tory chapter, each chapter focuses on one kind of job (producer, man-ager) or group of jobs (costume, set, sound, or lighting design) and in-cludes interviews with people working on those jobs. An appended list of sources for further information includes theatrical organizations and institutions, unions, schools, and publications; an index follows. This will interest any theater buff, and should be useful for vocational guid-ance.

480   **Greene,** Bette. *Get On Out of Here, Philip Hall.* Dial, 1981. 80-22775. Trade ed. ISBN 0-8037-2871-9; Library ed. ISBN 0-8037-2872-7. 150p. Trade ed. $9.95; Library ed. $9.43.

4–6   In a sequel to *Philip Hall Likes Me. I Reckon Maybe,* perky Beth Lambert continues the saga of her rivalry with Philip for the leadership crown of Pocahontas, Arkansas. The trouble is that Beth really dotes on Philip.

The further trouble is that there are others who covet Beth's niche in the town, her reputation as a leader and catalyst. Boastful and overly confident, Beth is so embarrassed by a series of defeats that she goes to stay with her grandmother for some months; she tries to become a follower, but initiative and ebullience will out, and soon Beth has organized so splendid a town festival that many of her friends as well as her family drive over to attend. And so does Philip, with whom Beth has a most satisfactory reunion. This is just as much fun as the first book, Beth is just as attractive a character, and Bette Greene's fans will no doubt relish this sequel; it will probably seem to them a minor weakness that, save for Philip, none of Beth's friends seems to have any loyalty or compassion.

481   **Greene,** Constance C. *Al(exandra) the Great.* Viking, 1982. 81-16058. ISBN 0-670-11197-X. 133p. $9.95.

5–7
 *
In the fourth book about an enduring friendship, the story is again told by Al's never-named friend, who is loving and perceptive, a good foil for Al's more volatile personality. In this sequel, the problem is that Al, looking forward to a visit with her father and his second family, excited about the prospect of seeing a boy friend she'd made on her last visit and of being the guest of honor at a barn dance, is in a dilemma. Her mother is in the hospital. Should she cancel or postpone her visit to stay with her mother during convalescence? She decides to stay, and her father and stepmother send her a sweatshirt with the words of the book's title printed thereon. The narrator, too, knows that *her* parents are proud of her for the support she's given Al during this trying time. What Greene has done, in this story, is to blend the warmth of friendship and of family love with the engagingly sophisticated dialogue of two bright, attractive protagonists and with a Manhattan background that is colorful as it's seen through the shrewd, perceptive authorial vision.

482   **Greene,** Constance C. *Dotty's Suitcase.* Viking, 1980. 80-10949. ISBN 0-670-28050-X. 147p. $8.95.

5–7
An imaginative, articulate twelve-year-old, Dotty dreams of having a suitcase; she thinks of it as her passport to adventure and romance, an escape from the burdens of the Depression Era and from the home where, as the youngest of three motherless girls, she does chores because her sisters work. Dotty finds a suitcase while trudging along the road with a neighbor, Jud (age eight), and it proves to be the case tossed out of a car by bank robbers who are being pursued. That's how the adventure begins; the children are picked up by a mercenary adolescent from whom they escape, then by an older man who helps them reach the town to which Dotty's best friend has moved, and from which they eventually return home. This is as vivid as *Bonnie and Clyde* in evoking the period, it is adroitly structured and paced, and it's writ-

ten with practiced smoothness. The characterization has depth and perception, with astute depiction of relationships both in exposition and in the excellent dialogue.

483   **Greene,** Constance C. *Isabelle Shows Her Stuff*. Viking, 1984. 84-40255. ISBN 0-670-41103-5. 138p. $11.95.

3–5   Feisty and funny, Isabelle is always in trouble, and she volunteers to help her new neighbor, Guy, find a way to get in trouble also. Guy is eight, two years younger than Isabelle; he's sweet and shy and tired of his reputation as "goody-goody-Guy." Guy finally achieves his goal in a believably dramatic way, in a story that has brisk pace, humor, an easy flow, and some acutely observed and occasionally touching relationships: Guy and his grandmother, Isabelle and her teacher, and the sociopolitical structure of a fifth grade class.

484   **Greenfeld,** Howard. *Rosh Hashanah and Yom Kippur;* illus. by Elaine Grove. Holt, 1979. 79-4818. ISBN 0-03-044756-9. 31p. $5.95.

5–7   Framed pictures of Biblical scenes, stylized and with a medieval quality, illustrate a serious and dignified text that describes the meaning, the importance, and the details of the religious observances of two major Jewish holidays. Greenfeld treats his subject with reverence, stressing the spiritual quality of the celebration of Rosh Hashanah and Yom Kippur.

485   **Greenfield,** Eloise. *Daydreamers;* illus. by Tom Feelings. Dial, 1981. 80-26092. Trade ed. ISBN 0-8037-2137-4; Library ed. ISBN 0-8037-2134-X. 26p. Trade ed. $9.95; Library ed. $9.43.

3–5   A tender poem about the child who daydreams, and who is changed by the introspective quiet of that dreaming, is spaced over pages profusely illustrated by pictures (some full length, most portraits) of children. Black and beautiful, the serene or wistful faces are in a broad range; the sensitive interpretation of the faces is in tones of grays and browns. This is a mood piece, lovely to look at, with text and illustration nicely matched. It may be too quiet, too monochrome for some readers, but it should appeal to the poetry lovers and dreamers.

486   **Greenwald,** Sheila. *Blissful Joy and the SATs: A Multiple-Choice Romance*. Atlantic-Little, Brown, 1982. 81-23692. ISBN 0-316-32673-9. 128p. $9.95.

7–10   Both of sixteen-year-old Blissful's divorced parents are actors, and while she loves them, she feels that she is the only practical and sensible person in the family. A bit of a prig, Bliss is shaken by the change in her self-image when she gets a low grade on her first SAT try. Why is she so bad at it when her school grades are so good? It isn't until her old friend Jenny and her newest friend Colin point out to her that she's romantic and imaginative (qualities she'd sneered at in her parents) that Bliss understands herself. The romance is treated lightly but perceptively, the relationship between Bliss and her parents is handled with sensitivity and warmth, and the sophisticated humor of the writing is in both dialogue and exposition of a smoothly flowing story.

487   **Greenwald,** Sheila. *Give Us a Great Big Smile, Rosy Cole;* written and illus. by Sheila Greenwald. Atlantic-Little, Brown, 1981. 80-24319. ISBN 0-316-32672-0. 76p. $7.95.

3–5   Rosy, who tells the story with wry humor, has just turned ten; as she has feared, her Uncle Ralph wants to put her in a book as he had done with her two sisters as each of them turned ten. The trouble was that Anitra could dance and Pippa ride horseback, so Uncle Ralph had something to take photographs of, while Rosy couldn't do anything. Well, she took violin lessons, but she hated them and knew she played badly. In this story of the fall and rise of a potential if reluctant star, it's the humor that carries the plot; the latter is adequate but not substantial, while the former extracts a great deal of fun out of mocking the Krementz series as a concept. Rosy manages to extricate herself from the threat of being exposed to the world and pushed into a limelight she doesn't deserve. There's a tinge of exaggeration in the writing, but it's just enough to spice the fun.

488   **Greenwald,** Sheila. *It All Began with Jane Eyre; Or, the Secret Life of Franny Dillman;* written and illus. by Sheila Greenwald. Atlantic-Little, Brown, 1980. 79-26901. ISBN 0-316-32671-2. 117p. $7.95.

5–8   Franny is thirteen. A voracious reader, she "doesn't just read," her mother says, "She hurtles herself into books and glues herself to the pages." Worried because Franny identifies with Jane Eyre's passions and problems, Mrs. Dillman brings home some contemporary fiction. Amazed by the drama of divorce, handicaps, and abortion, Franny decides to keep a journal. Now identifying with her new heroines, the imaginative Franny convinces herself that her brother is in love with a girl, that the girl is pregnant, that her (Franny's) father is the father of the baby. Franny's subsequent detective work leads her sister to think Franny's pregnant, and her parents are horrified when they learn that the journal has been turned in to Franny's teacher. The web of errors is untangled, and no real harm done; in the process of telling this very funny, witty story Greenwald takes some sly pokes at contemporary realistic fiction (one of the books is *Lord, Can I Call You Collect?*) but the strength of the book is in the characterization and dialogue, both of which ring true.

489   **Griffith,** Helen V. *Alex and the Cat;* illus. by Joseph Low. Greenwillow, 1982. 81-11608. Trade ed. ISBN 0-688-00420-2; Library ed. ISBN 0-688-00421-0. 63p. (Read-alone Books). Trade ed. $6.50; Library ed. $5.71.

1–2   Three short stories about an earnest and amicable dog, Alex, and his small adventures, are told partly through his dialogue with the family's other pet, a rather languid and sophisticated cat. The stories are appropriate in length, vocabulary difficulty, and concept for the beginning reader, the illustrations are amusing, almost aqueous wash and line, and the book can also be used for reading aloud to the preschool child. Alex learns to tell the difference between a young chicken and a robin, he decides a cat's life is enviable but changes his mind after imitating the cat's indolence, and he definitely decides not to be a night hunter after one expedition with the cat. What makes the book a joy to read aloud or alone is the terse humor of the talks between Alex and his blasé companion.

490   **Griffiths,** Helen. *Rafa's Dog.* Holiday House, 1983. 83-4384. ISBN 0-8234-0492-7. 107p. $9.95.

4–6   Set in contemporary Spain, this is a boy-dog story that has more depth than most animal tales. Rafa, sent with his younger sister to stay with an aunt and uncle in a small town, worries about Mama back in Madrid, because he knows her heart condition makes her imminent delivery of a third child dangerous. Papa assuages him; Rafa relaxes, and the focus of his life becomes the stray dog, Moro, who attaches himself to the boy. In a sadly poignant climax, Mama dies. Rafa goes back to Madrid, misses his dog, and finally simply takes some money, goes to the village, and claims Moro. The adults agree and so Rafa has some consolation. Save for a few instances of dialogue that are jarringly British (a reference to "babies messing their nappies" and Rafa's little sister saying "Cor!"), the writing style is competent; the characterization is not deep but it is convincing, and the story line—while it moves at an uneven pace—is sturdy.

491   **Grimm,** Jakob Ludwig Karl. *The Devil with the Three Golden Hairs;* ad. and illus. by Nonny Hogrogian. Knopf, 1983. 82-12735. Trade ed. ISBN 0-394-85560-4; Library ed. ISBN 0-394-95560-9. 27p. Trade ed. $10.95; Library ed. $10.99.

K–2   The oversize pages of this picture book version of a traditional tale give
*   the artist the opportunity for pictures that are soft in texture and tone, the brilliant red of the devil's cloak a vibrant note against the surrounding soft pastel hues. The distinctive marbling of the endpapers is a small bonus, in this direct retelling of the story of the peasant boy who pitted his wits against the machinations of a greedy king, outwitted the devil, and won a princess and a kingdom.

492   **Grimm,** Jakob Ludwig Karl. *The Fisherman and His Wife; A Tale from the Brothers Grimm;* tr. by Randall Jarrell; illus, by Margot Zemach. Farrar, 1980. 79-3248. ISBN 0-374-32340-2. 28p. $10.95.

K–3   The hilarious tale of greed and retribution is handsomely illustrated in
*   an oversize format that is used to full advantage by Zemach, whose paintings are imaginative, comic, and effective in composition and color.

Jarrell's translation of the story is flowing and colloquial, as nice to use for storytelling as it is to read aloud. The humble fisherman who has let a talking fish return to the sea is repeatedly sent back to ask this clearly magical and powerful creature for higher status; from a hut to a cottage to a palace, from a fisherman's wife to king, emperor, and pope—and only when the ambitious woman insists that her husband ask the fish to make her "like the good Lord," so that she can control the sun and moon, does the fish rebel—and the story ends as it began, the circle neatly closed, with the fisherman and his wife back in their tiny shanty, back in their ragged clothing. Lovely.

493   **Grimm,** Jakob Ludwig Karl. *Hansel and Gretel;* tr. from the German by Elizabeth D. Crawford; illus. by Lisbeth Zwerger. Morrow, 1980. 79-989. Trade ed. ISBN 0-688-22198-X; Library ed. ISBN 0-688-32198-4. 26p. Trade ed. $7.95; Library ed. $7.63 net.

K–3   In a picture book format, a new translation of a familiar story adheres closely to the original but is smoothly and discriminatingly simplified. The illustrations, by an eminent Austrian illustrator, are in ink and wash; save for an occasional background detail, the backgrounds are in blended earth tones. The figures are strongly defined, but delicately tinted and detailed, and they are prominent in full-color pages with effectively simple composition.

494   **Grimm,** Jakob Ludwig Karl. *Little Red Riding Hood;* ad. and illus. by Trina Schart Hyman. Holiday House, 1983. 82-7700. ISBN 0-8234-0470-6. 28p. $13.95.

2–4   A smooth retelling of the familiar folktale is handsomely illustrated by framed pictures, the ornamental borders combining small paintings and geometric print designs, the paintings within beautifully detailed and composed. Hyman's blending of sturdy shapes, misty flora, cozy interiors, and strong figure drawing in unified by her varied and expert handling of light and shadow.

495   **Grimm,** Jakob Ludwig Karl. *Rare Treasures from Grimm: Fifteen Little-Known Tales;* comp. and tr. by Ralph Manheim; illus. with paintings by Erik Blegvad. Doubleday, 1981. 80-2350. Trade ed. ISBN 0-385-14548-9; Prebound ed. ISBN 0-385-14549-7. 99p. Trade ed. $12.95; Prebound ed. $13.90.

4–6   Although recommended by the publisher for children up to age eight, this seems more appropriate for readers in the middle grades who can cope with the closely-printed pages and the vocabulary of Manheim's fluid, direct translation. There is one full-page, full-color painting by Blegvad for each of the fifteen tales, and their clear colors and precise details demonstrate again that he is discriminating in adapting mood and technique to the varying moods of the texts he is illustrating. While some of the stories are, indeed, often omitted from collections, some of the tales, despite the title, will be familiar to many readers: "King Thrushbeard," for example, or "Clever Gretel."

496   **Grinnell,** George Bird, comp. *The Whistling Skeleton: American Indian Tales of the Supernatural;* comp. by George Bird Grinnell; ed. by John Bierhorst; illus. by Robert Andrew Parker. Four Winds, 1982. 81-69517. ISBN 0-590-07801-1. 110p. $12.95.

5–7   Dramatic, wavery black and white drawings echo the eerie notes of nine tales from three sources: Blackfeet, Cheyenne, and Pawnee. The editorial preface is lengthy and informative, giving good background information about the Plains Indians, including information on the tellers whose stories Grinnell collected in the late nineteenth century. The stories are told in a rather flat, straightforward style; each incorporates some aspect of the supernatural; in the title story a man is pursued by an angry skeleton, while in many of the stories the fanciful element is in the depiction of an animal. These are perhaps of less interest to the storyteller than to the student of Native American culture.

497   **Gross,** Ruth Belov, ad. *The Girl Who Wouldn't Get Married;* illus. by Jack Kent. Four Winds, 1983. 83-1458. ISBN 0-590-07908-5. 30p. $9.95.

1–3   Based on the Norwegian story "The Squire's Bride," in the collection by Asbjornsen and Moe, this has bright, brisk illustrations in cartoon style; dialogue (in small print) is included with the drawings. The story, simply retold, describes the obdurate, wealthy farmer who was determined to wed his neighbor's daughter; the plan developed to deceive her went awry when the girl out-tricked the trickster and sent a horse to be clad in wedding finery and take her place.

498   **Gutman,** Bill. *Women Who Work with Animals.* Dodd, 1982. 81-22125, ISBN 0-396-08035-9. illus. with photographs. 160p. $7.95.

4–6   Of the six women whose careers are described, one is a veterinarian, one a horse trainer, one a trainer and handler of dogs, two work in zoo programs, and the last trains dolphins and sea lions for public performance. The text has a good balance of exposition and commentary by the subjects, all of whom are forthright about the difficulties they have had as women in careers that were traditionally male-dominated. The writing style is direct, the subjects interesting, and the book should be useful for slow older readers as well as for the grade range indicated. The block letters of the typeface and the ample spacing may contribute toward that end but have the look of an office handout.

499   **Guy,** Rosa. *The Disappearance.* Delacorte, 1979. 79-50672. ISBN 0-440-01189-2, 246p. $8.95.

7–10   At the instigation of Mrs. Aimsley, the family takes into custody adolescent Imamu Jones, acquitted of a serious crime and remanded from the care of his mother, an alcoholic. The older daughter in the family, Gail, is cool toward him, but when Imamu is suspected of having done something to her small sister, who disappears, it is Gail who is sympathetic, who cannot believe the young man would have harmed little Perk. Imamu knows he must find the criminal if he is to be cleared— and he does, in a taut, sometimes bitter but always sensitive story with a tragic ending.

500   **Haber,** Louis. *Women Pioneers of Science.* Harcourt, 1979. 79-87517. ISBN 0-15-299202-2. 171p. illus. with photographs. $7.95.

7–10   Most of the dozen women scientists whose lives and professional contributions are described live or lived in the United States; the distinguished roster includes several physicians, chemists and physicists, a marine biologist, biochemists, a crystallographer, and a psychologist. Each section gives some personal data, but focuses on the scientist's career, her distinctive contributions to her field, the problems she may have had as a woman in that field, and the honors she won. The first chapter, which makes it clear that many women have, throughout recorded history, made significant scientific contributions, also serves as a position paper for the author, a confirmed and eloquent feminist. The final section is a listing of professional women's groups, and is followed by a bibliography and an index, the latter in very small type. The writing style is dry, but that is compensated for by the interesting and well-researched material.

501   **Haddad,** Helen R. *Potato Printing;* written and illus. by Helen R. Haddad. T. Y. Crowell, 1981. 80-2458. Trade ed. ISBN 0-690-04088-1; Library ed. ISBN 0-690-04089-X. 64p. Trade ed. $9.13; Library ed. $8.89.

3–6   This is an exemplary how-to book. The material is arranged in order of increasing complexity, with the text always built on earlier procedures. The explanations are crisp and direct, including step-by-step instructions and safety warnings. The materials are inexpensive, the suggested projects are attractive, the author encourages creativity, and the index gives access to procedures, materials, and subjects.

502   **Haley,** Gail E. *Birdsong;* written and illus. by Gail E. Haley. Crown, 1984. 83-14372. ISBN 0-517-55051-2. 27p. $10.95.

K–3   Birdsong, an orphan girl, is lured home by old Jorinella the Birdcatcher with promises of food and shelter. Birdsong does not realize that the old woman plans to use her ability to trap unwary birds, for the young girl plays with such understanding that the birds flock to her pipes. When Birdsong sets all the birds free after Jorinella has trapped them, she is in danger—but it is the birds that drive the old woman off, rescue Birdsong, and fly her to a wonderful secret country where she and other musicians play in a garden that is a shelter for birds. The message is nicely incorporated into a story that has a folk-like quality; the paintings are intricately detailed, deft in color and composition.

503   **Haley,** Gail E. *The Green Man;* written and illus. by Gail E. Haley. Scribner, 1980. 79-20490. ISBN 0-684-16338-1. 29p. $9.95.

3–5   A traditional figure in old world legendry, the Green Man was revered for his magical abilities, his courage, but above all for his tender care of the forest and all growing things. Haley has given a nice twist to the legend, suggesting that there were a succession of Green Men; in her version an arrogant youth is lost in the forest and his clothes stolen while he's having a swim. He shelters in a cave, ashamed to be seen naked when he hears the horns of the men sent out to find him. Staying in the forest, he learns (in Crusoe style) to plant and reap, to care for wild creatures; he becomes kindly and generous, even leaving behind some of the food left out for the Green Man by nearby villagers, a custom at which he once scoffed. One day he spies a man swimming; he takes the man's clothes and horse, leaving the stranger in the same plight he'd been in, and goes home. Presumably the stranger will become the next Green Man. There seems to be one inconsistency in the story: why, if the hero could walk to the village, did he not borrow a horse to ride home? Still, it's a pleasant, vernal story and it's illustrated with handsome pictures, in strong but not harsh colors, that have interesting details of medieval clothing and architecture.

504   **Hall,** Donald. *The Man Who Lived Alone;* illus. by Mary Azarian. Godine, 1984. 84-47655. ISBN 0-87923-538-1. 30p. $11.95.

2–4   Profusely illustrated by Azarian's handsome woodcuts, this is a quiet prose poem about the life of one man, never given a name. After a childhood in which he had some unhappy years, the man who lived alone had returned to his independence, but not to isolation; he visited and helped succeeding generations of the family of cousins who had provided his happiest boyhood years; he was self-sufficient as repairman, peddler, gardener, cook, and carpenter. And when he grew old, the story ends, "He kept his beard winter and summer now, because it was easier/and as he got older and older, it grew so long that it covered the darns on his shirt." For many children this may seem too static to be appealing; it paints a vivid word picture, but has little narrative flow.

505   **Hall,** Donald. *Ox-Cart Man;* illus. by Barbara Cooney. Viking, 1979. 79-14466. ISBN 0-670-53328-9. 40p. $8.95.

K–3   In October the ox-cart man packed all the things his family had grown or made during the year, trudged the long miles to a harbor town, and sold everything—even the ox and cart. With a few purchases, and coins in his pocket, he plodded back home . . . and the cycle begins again, with carving, planting, whittling, shearing, embroidering, and so on. The text has the lulling quality of a bucolic idyll, and the picture it draws of a self-sufficient farm family of the early nineteenth century in New England is made specific by the lovely Cooney paintings: melting sunset colors, misty hills, a froth of pink and white blossoms in a springtime orchard, and several interiors that are distinctive for their play of light and shadow. In all of the illustrations, the figures have a slightly stiff simplicity that is reminiscent of the art of the period.

506   Hall, Lynn. *The Boy in the Off-White Hat*. Scribner, 1984. 84-13982. ISBN 0-684-18224-6. 87p. $11.95.

5–7   The story is told by Skeeter, whose summer job is taking care of nine-year-old Shane, thin and insecure and homely and lovable. Skeeter becomes fond of Shane quickly, and admires his mother, Maxine, who runs a horse ranch and also has a part-time job. Maxine doesn't demonstrate her love for her son, and so when a friendly man, Burge, comes along, the boy delightedly adopts him as surrogate father. Maxine admits to Skeeter that she would like to marry Burge, but Skeeter—although she can't say why—feels uneasy about the man. Her fears are justified, for a terrorized Shane, victim of Burge's sexual abuse, becomes (curably) psychotic, presenting a new personality, John, to replace the Shane who has done bad things. This has no tinge of a fictionalized case history, but it has the ring of truth. The characters are drawn with depth and perception, the observations and understanding are believably those of a thirteen-year-old, and the reactions Shane has are equally convincing. A fine book (one of Hall's best) in its presentation of a potentially tragic situation.

507   Hall, Lynn. *Danza!* Scribner, 1981. 81-8992. ISBN 0-684-17158-9. 186p. $10.95.

5–7   More substantial in story line and structure than most of Hall's animal stories, this describes the protective love of a Puerto Rican boy, Paulo, for one of his grandfather's horses; Danza is a Paso Fino, a breed that Grandfather thinks is unappreciated. Macho, parochial, and dictatorial, Grandfather sneers at Paulo, who adores and fears the tough old man. The boy goes with Danza to the Louisiana horse farm, taken on loan (slightly contrived circumstance) by Major Kessler (just a touch of patronage here?) who is wonderfully kind to both Danza and Paulo. The horse is very ill; Kessler's very patient; Paulo's very insecure at the beginning of the visit and gains in self-confidence as the horse improves and the ways of the Americans become more familiar. The book ends with Grandfather coming to Louisiana and Danza winning first place in a show. A bit pat in the finish, but this is a horse story with variety and pace.

508   Halsey, William D., ed. *Macmillan Dictionary for Students*. Macmillan, 1984. 84-3880. ISBN 0-02-761560-X, 1190p. $16.95.

4–   Given the number of pages, the thin paper, and the small (but readable) type, it's not surprising that the chief disadvantage of this new dictionary (90,000 entry words and 120,000 definitions) is its weight. It should be a welcome addition to the family of dictionaries, since the prefatory and explanatory material is clear and full, the entries succinct but not terse, and the various appended materials useful, including a handbook of style, a glossary of computer terms, and a brief history of the English language. Above all, the book is recommended because the entries are adequate in their treatment of derivation, word forms, alternate meanings, and examples.

509   **Hamill,** Dorothy. *Dorothy Hamill On and Off the Ice;* by Dorothy Hamill and Elva Clairmont. Knopf, 1983. 83-6170. Trade ed. ISBN 0-394-85610-4; Library ed. ISBN 0-394-95610-9. 181p. Trade ed. $10.95; Library ed. $10.99.

6–9   Like many sports biographies, this emphasizes the long years of dedicated practice, the need to give up many of the leisure time pursuits of most children and adolescents, the move from the first, nervous public appearance to the intense focus of the seasoned (if still nervous) performer. The authors have a winning combination of dramatic sense, capable style, and the acuteness of observation achieved by a participant—plus the glamor of an internationally famous and popular skating star, and of other stellar figures in the world of figure skating.

510   **Hamilton,** Alan. *Queen Elizabeth II;* illus. by Karen Heywood. Hamish Hamilton, 1983. ISBN 0-241-10850-0. 64p. $7.95.

3–5   A biography of the Queen of England is candid, balanced in treatment, and simply written, with a tone of respect rather than adulation, and with good background to explain decisions and changes that have shaped the Queen's reign. The author is direct: "King George was not a clever man, but clever men do not always make the best kings," or, "After a few years, when the excitement of the Coronation had worn off, some people began to criticize the monarchy and the way it worked." For American readers this may answer some questions that British children have no need to ask, such as "What does the Queen do?" Black and white illustrations are almost photographic in style.

511   **Hamilton,** Virginia. *Dustland.* Greenwillow, 1980. 79-19003. Trade ed. ISBN 0-688-80228-1; Library ed. ISBN 0-688-84228-3. 192p. Trade ed. $8.95; Library ed. $8.59 net.

7–   In a sequel to *Justice and Her Brothers,* in which eleven-year-old Justice discovered that she had supersensory powers and found that her friend Dorian and her twin brothers, Thomas and Levi, also had them, the story moves to another time and place. The four children, whose combined power is called "the unit," are psychically in a land of dust inhabited by strange creatures, several of which communicate telepathically with them. This does not begin, as the first book did, with a realistic base; the children come back to Earth at the close of the book. Their bodies have been sitting, it is then disclosed, under a tree, hands linked, while they were in Dustland. While there are encounters with

Dustland creatures, most of the true action/conflict is in the power struggle between Justice and Thomas, the brother and sister who have never had an amicable or easy relationship. Thomas, for example, breaks away from the others and weakens the power of the unit, even endangering the life of his twin in order to resist the superior powers of Justice, "the Watcher." This isn't easy to read; it calls for total immersion by the reader and for no small degree of comprehension of concept and appreciation of style, but the style is outstanding and the fantasy wholly conceived—and fiction of such depth, for children or adults, never is easy to read.

512   **Hamilton,** Virginia. *The Gathering.* Greenwillow, 1981. 80-12512. Trade ed. ISBN 0-688-80269-9; Library ed. ISBN 0-688-84269-0. 192p. Trade ed. $8.95; Library ed. $8.59.

7–10   In the last book of a science fiction trilogy (*Justice and Her Brothers, Dustland*) the four time travellers whose parapsychological powers have carried them into the strangeness of another culture unite to fight their final battle, combining their psychic force to defeat the dark Mal. Rescuing others, they have come to the domed land from which power emanates and learn that Dustland is the future of their own time; they return home to family love and security but know that they still have power, that their knowledge of the future is not in vain. This volume, as beautifully written and as intricate as its predecessor, is a bit slow in starting; for those who have not read *Dustland* the proliferation of strange creatures, strange names, and odd speech patterns may be cumbersome at first. The story gathers momentum, however, and comes to a sharp focus and strong action. What is perhaps most impressive about Hamilton's writing is her superb ability to fuse the mystical and the dramatic; like a skilled musician, she is in control of both the music and the instrument.

513   **Hamilton,** Virginia. *Jahdu;* illus. by Jerry Pinkney. Greenwillow, 1980. 79-16039. Trade ed. ISBN 0-688-80246-X; Library ed. ISBN 0-688-84246-1. 55p. (Read-Alone Books) Trade ed. $5.95; Library ed. $5.71.

1–3   Curiously carved and lucent beads on a storyteller's chain, anecdotes about the great Jahdu (*The Time-Ago Tales of Jahdu*) are linked to form a story for beginning readers. Although more simply written, the prose has the same lyric quality as Hamilton's first Jahdu tales. Here Jahdu is taunted as he meets other creatures, is told that he has lost his power, and is upset because he has lost his shadow. Being Jahdu, he solves the situation and regains his power, in an ending that should satisfy readers; what may appeal to some readers even more, however, is the imagery Hamilton uses and the playfulness with which she invents words: "Don't get so pooft and pahft," Shadow says, and repeatedly Jahdu says, in moments of stress, "Woogily!"

514   **Hamilton,** Virginia. *A Little Love.* Philomel, 1984. 84-1753. ISBN 0-399-21046-6. 207p. $10.95.

7–10   "How can you miss what you ain't never had?" But Sheema, when Forrest asks that, knows she does long for the father who had walked out when she was born and her mother died. Her yearning makes her prevail on Forrest to go south with her to hunt for her father, an abortive attempt to establish a relationship that sends Sheema back to the grandparents who have brought her up, aware of the importance of their love and Forrest's. Although Sheema and Forrest are lovers, it is the romantic element in their relationship that is stressed in all its tenderness and devotion. The same steadfast love, in fact, that has endured in the marriage of Granmon and Granpop. Hamilton uses black dialect like poetry, and she has created a strong, touching character in Sheema, a teenager who is short and overweight, filled with doubt, aware of her own limited ability as a scholar, equally aware that she is talented as a food service student at a vocational school, not understanding Forrest's unmasked adoration but accepting the fact that he brings warmth and security. Structurally deft, a trenchant and affective story.

514   **Hamilton,** Virginia. *The Magical Adventures of Pretty Pearl.* Harper, 1983. 82-48629. Trade ed. ISBN 0-06-022186-0; Library ed. ISBN 0-06-022187-9. 306p. Trade ed. $11.50; Library ed. $11.89.

5–9
*
A rich blend of fantasy, African and American folklore, history, and marvelous invention, this is the story of a young god, Pretty Pearl, who comes from Mount Highness, in Africa, with her older brother John de Conquer, to America. They rest in the soil for many years, and Pretty Pearl frets, wanting to try her power; John creates for her the John de Conquer root, which she wears around her neck and uses to wield magic. She emerges during the Reconstruction Era and finds a hidden community, Promise Land, where a group of black people live in secrecy and are helped by some Cherokees. Pearl by now has become two gods, herself and the grandmotherly Mother Pearl, and both live with the "inside people" until their paradise is threatened by the advent of bird hunters and railway builders. They are again helped by their Cherokee friends and by John Henry, but Pretty Pearl is frightened. And then John de Conquer appears, rebuking Pearl for having broken the rules he laid down when he gave her the root and the power, but he forgives her, sets everyone straight, and disappears. They walk, gods and humans, for days, then John de Conquer reappears and takes Mother Pearl with him; they cross the Jordan and come to Ohio. And they take the name of Perry, and when Pearl tells everyone of herself and the other gods of Mount Highness, they laugh with pleasure and it becomes part of their legend. The author has used a bit of family (Perry) history in addition to the other real and mythic and imaginary aspects of this intricate panoply that testifies to the human spirit and the black experience.

516   **Hamilton,** Virginia. *Sweet Whispers, Brother Rush.* Philomel, 1982. 81-22745. ISBN 0-399-20894-1. 224p. $10.95.

6–8   Although this has a fantasy element, it is the realistic matrix that is
  *   most touching and most trenchant. Tree (Teresa) lives with, loves, and
       protects her brother Dab, who is a gentle, retarded seventeen, two
       years older than Tree. Their mother, Vy, supports them but must live
       away from them in order to do so; their father has long ago decamped.
       Tree repeatedly sees visions of Brother Rush, her mother's brother, and
       in those visions she sees the past, so that gradually she pieces together
       the tragic family history; the tragedy culminates, for Tree, in the death
       of her brother after Vy (a practical nurse) has recognized the symptoms
       of a hereditary disease, porphyria. Heartbroken, Tree decides to run
       away, but the counsel and love she gets from Vy, Vy's gentle and com-
       passionate friend Silversmith, and the elderly woman Vy invites to stay
       with Tree make her realize that Dab's death was inevitable, that Vy—
       despite her faults—is doing the best she can, and that not having to
       take care of Dab means that she can have some of the freedom and
       friendship that she has had to live without. Hamilton's writing style is
       always distinctive, never easy reading; here the start has an element of
       obscurity, but it serves almost as does the obscurity in detective fiction,
       to lure rather than to discourage. The characters and their relationships
       are drawn with strength and sensitivity, fusing and interacting with in-
       evitability in a positive affirmation of the power of love, an affirmation
       for which Tree's visions serve as a contrapuntal theme.

517   **Hamilton,** Virginia. *Willie Bea and the Time the Martians Landed.* Green-
       willow, 1983. 83-1659. ISBN 0-688-02390-8. 208p. $11.50.

5–8   The focal point of an absorbing family story is its reaction to the now-
  *   famous Orson Welles broadcast that frightened so many people
       throughout the United States. Willie Bea is as credulous and convinced
       as are other members of her family, even though she hasn't heard the
       broadcast, because it's an adult (glamorous Aunt Leah, always drama-
       tic) who brings the news that the Martians have landed in New Jersey.
       Hamilton uses the material with great skill, but—exciting as it is—the
       most impressive facet of the book is the vibrant, loving picture it draws
       of an extended black family. The story takes place in 1938 on Hallow-
       een, and most of the children and grandchildren of an Ohio farm family
       are gathered together for dinner, a time of cousins squabbling, sisters
       gossiping, grandmother calmly organizing, all the small events of a re-
       union under and through which are the sustaining love and security of
       family life. Willie Bea is a touching heroine, volatile and imaginative,
       protective toward her younger siblings, candid and intelligent. Like the
       book, she's a winner.

518   **Haney,** Lynn. *I Am a Dancer;* illus. with photographs by Bruce Curtis.
       Putnam, 1981. 80-26285. Hardcover ed. ISBN 0-399-20724-4; Paper ed.
       ISBN 0-399-20792-9. 64p. Hardcover ed. $8.95; paper ed. $4.95.

5–8   An informative photographic essay that focuses on three young dancers
       is especially interesting because two of the three—unlike the children

about whom most ballet books are written—are boys. Michael and Stephen Austin are brothers, twelve and fourteen; their classmate Danielle is thirteen; all have performed as well as studied, all are students at the Neubert Ballet Institute. The book gives a good picture of the demands made upon young dancers, the satisfaction and joy they get from their art, and the way in which ballet training helps improve their performance in other fields (many sports, for example). The pictures are of fine quality, the text competently written.

519   **Haney,** Lynn. *Skaters: Profile of a Pair;* photographs by Bruce Curtis. Putnam, 1983. 83-13655. ISBN 0-399-21013-X. 64p. $10.95.

5–   Television has made pairs figure skating a popular spectator sport, although its devotees think of it (and ice dancing) as more an art form than an athletic event. In this documentary, the authors examine the careers of Amy Grossman and Robert Davenport, entrants in the Junior World Championship Figure Skating competition. Save for a little gushiness (". . . they give the crowd a thriller, the death spiral . . . The audience gasps . . ." In fact, the death spiral is performed by almost every skating pair and is less dangerous than many of the jumps and lifts) the text is adequately written. Like other photodocumentaries about young performing artists, this describes their training, their dedication, the way their careers impinge on other areas of their lives, the necessity of parental involvement and support. A glossary of skating terms is provided.

520   **Hanlon,** Emily. *Love Is No Excuse.* Bradbury, 1982. 82-9580. ISBN 0-87888-204-9. 227p. $10.95.

7–10   Ethical concepts and parental image are an intrinsic part of a perceptive story about the way in which an adolescent becomes aware of her father's dishonesty and the way in which, under the guise of love, he attempts to control and direct her behavior. A popular math teacher, Julia's father is so anxious to have his daughter in his advanced math class that he uses unethical means to help her achieve that goal. Julia knows she doesn't have the requisite ability, and she finally rebels; part of her declaration of independence is an insistence that she be treated as a young adult in other aspects of their relationship, but primarily Julia feels she must make it clear (and she does) that her father must see, as she sees, that the status he wanted Julia to have was for his own pride, not for hers. The characterization is strong, the relationships are seen with sensitivity, and the writing style is polished, with natural-sounding dialogue.

521   **Hansen,** Joyce. *The Gift-Giver.* Houghton/Clarion, 1980. 80-12969. ISBN 0-395-29433-9. 118p. $7.95.

4–5   Fifth-grader Doris tells the story of Amir, the new boy who has just joined her class. Amir is slight, quiet, and mature; he doesn't join the boys' games, yet—Doris can't understand why—he is accepted; he doesn't feel a need to conform, yet he belongs. This is in Black English, sometimes with discrepant usages, and believably an account by a ten-year-old. It conveys effectively the atmosphere (the Bronx) and has strong characters, particularly Amir, who helps a lonely old woman, helps Doris when she has to take on new responsibilities at home, and is more understanding than any of the other children when one of their classmates runs away from a foster home. This hasn't a strong story line, but it has well-developed plot threads that are nicely knit, a memorable depiction of a person whose understanding and compassion are gifts to his friends, and a poignantly realistic ending: Amir, whose own experience of foster homes has given him his compassionate understanding, is sent to another place yet again, leaving Doris and his other friends sadly aware of the loss they have suffered. A substantial first novel.

522   **Hardendorff,** Jeanne B. *Libraries and How to Use Them;* illus. with photographs. Watts. 1979. 78-12992. ISBN 0-531-02259-5. 61p. $5.45.

4–6   A former librarian and teacher of library science provides an explicit and well-organized text for the child who needs information on organization and use of library materials; the book should also be useful for older readers for whom English is a second language. First giving some historical background, Hardendorff devotes separate chapters to lucid explanations of the Decimal Classification System and the Library of Congress Classification System, including enough about the rationale of classification to make comprehension easier; she describes the catalog in some detail, gives a brief explanation of borrowing procedures, and concludes with an overview of type of reference books. A useful book, written with crisp authority, this includes an index comprising terms printed in bold face in the text.

523   **Harris,** Christie. *The Trouble with Princesses;* illus. by Douglas Tait. Atheneum, 1980. 79-22129. ISBN 0-689-30744-6. 167p. $8.95.

5–   Each of the seven stories about the New World princesses of the northwest coast is prefaced by an introduction that draws a parallel between the heroic Native American princess and her counterparts in the fairy-tale literature of the Old World. Each introduction begins, "The trouble with princesses was that . . ." and the theme is introduced. The familiar figures of Mouse Woman and Raven appear in the stories, which are long magical tales with doughty heroines, retold with polished zest. Notes on the sources (Kwakiutl, Haida, Tlingit, and others) are appended.

524   **Harris,** Geraldine. *Prince of the Godborn.* Greenwillow, 1983. ISBN 0-688-01792-4. 192p. $9.00.

7–9   In the first of a fantasy-adventure quartet, the Emperor of the land of Galkis selects his third-born and best-loved son, Kerish-lo-Taan, for a crucial mission. As one of the ruling clan, the Godborn, Kerish must search for the seven keys of seven sorcerers to rescue "The Savior." Too young to go alone, Kerish is accompanied by his older half-brother Forollkin to the seven citadels of the sorcerers (if he can find where they are) and thus save Galkis from the enemies within and beyond its borders. The writing is filled with action, colored by strange names and intricate relationships, richly conceived; in this first volume are the first two adventures of Kerish, who wins two of the seven keys he seeks.

525   **Harris,** Geraldine. *The Seventh Gate.* Greenwillow, 1984. 83-14084. ISBN 0-688-01759-2. 243p. $9.50.

7–9   The last of a series of four books, "Seven Citadels," first published in England and strong in the tradition of high fantasy and a selfless quest. To save his country, Prince Kerish has been arduously collecting the keys of sorcerers—and now must find the seventh and last. Imprisoned, Kerish and his companions escape to aid in the war that Galkis (his homeland) is waging against a coalition led by O-grak. Kerish journeys to a jungle in search of the seventh sorcerer, who proves to be a woman, the enchantress Tebreega. He gains the seventh key and faces his last mission: using the keys to free the imprisoned "savior of Galkis." Kerish is stunned to see his own reflection. He must choose between withdrawal and peace, and the pain of reincarnation and service as the last Emperor of Galkis. . .and he chooses the latter. Like most high fantasy, this is intricate in structure and crowded with characters—but Harris has compensated for this by writing with pace and momentum, providing action and variety, and—above all—creating characters with depth and distinction.

526   **Harris,** Janet. *The Woman Who Created Frankenstein; A Portrait of Mary Shelley.* Harper, 1979. 78-19481. Trade ed. ISBN 0-06-022228-X; Library ed. ISBN 0-06-022229-8. 216p. Trade ed. $7.95; Library ed. $7.89 net.

8–   Daughter of two famous social thinkers and reformers, Mary Godwin disgraced herself in the prim world of 1814 by running off with the poet Shelley, a married man, when she was sixteen, and bearing his child. Although they later married, the two were never accepted by society, never forgiven by Mary's father. She wrote *Frankenstein* when she was nineteen, and much of this biography is devoted to the book as a pioneer volume of science fiction, as an incorporation of many of Mary Shelley's ideas and personal experiences, and as the catalyst for almost thirty films. As a biography this is candid and comprehensive, well-written save for the author's occasional digression into background information, as in the sixth chapter, in which Harris goes back to ancient times to begin an assessment of social, political, theological, and scientific attitudes as they changed and led to the period in which Mary Shelley lived. An index, a divided bibliography, a chronology, and an annotated list of films are appended.

527   **Harris,** Mark Jonathan. *The Last Run.* Lothrop, 1981. 81-5110. Trade ed.
ISBN 0-688-00634-5; Library ed. ISBN 0-688-00635-3. 160p. Trade ed.
$8.95; Library ed. $8.59.

5–8   Lyle, a loner in eighth grade and convinced that his parents favored a
younger brother, invested most of his feelings of love and security in
his grandfather, once a notable mustang-catcher among his cowboy colleagues. It's due to that influence that Lyle yearns passionately to participate in catching a wild horse. This isn't the usual patterned horse
story; it has much more depth in relationships, in the subtle effects of
events on people and in the resultant changes in people's (Lyle's, particularly) behavior. When their companion, an old friend of grandfather's and a non-stereotyped Native American, is killed by a stampede
of wild horses, Lyle is determined to catch the stallion. He's jubilant
when, on the last run, he does, but he decides to let the weary, bedraggled animal go. Save for the fact that Lyle seems much older than an
eighth-grader, this is a good read: solid in structure, varied in pace,
spare and pointed in characterization.

528   **Harris,** Rosemary. *Zed.* Faber, 1984. ISBN 0-571-11947-6. 185p. $12.95.

7–9   A trenchant novel, percipient and sophisticated, is told by Thomas
Zachary, called Zed; he writes the account of being held hostage as a
small boy with some reluctance, responding to a teacher's request that
it be done for the school magazine's Centenary Number. Caught with
his father and uncle in the group of men held hostage in an office building in London by Arab terrorists (Zed is part Arab) the boy learns a
great deal about cowardice (his father) and courage (his uncle) and compassion (his own). An unusual setting adds appeal to a story with
depth and insight and momentum.

529   **Harrison,** Michael, ed. *The Oxford Book of Christmas Poems;* ed. by Michael Harrison and Christopher Stuart-Clark. Oxford/Merrimack, 1984.
ISBN 0-19-276051-3. 160p. illus. $12.95.

4–   A very good anthology is illustrated (both in color and in black and
white) by a number of artists; many of the pictures are distinctive
enough stylistically to be recognizable, but only minimal identification is
provided. The first group of poems celebrates the coming of winter and
Advent, the last focuses on the coming of the new year. Poets' names
are provided at the close of each selection in a book that is broad in
range and as discriminating in quality as it is handsome; many of the
poems are appropriate, also, for reading aloud to younger children.

530   **Hart,** Jane, comp. *Singing Bee!* illus. by Anita Lobel. Lothrop, 1982.
82-15296. ISBN 0-688-41975-5. 160p. $16.50.

K–3   A fine collection of songs for young children, arranged primarily by ori-
*   gin (English traditional) but partly by form (rounds) or by season
(Christmas, Hanukkah) or by function (singing games). Subject and title

indexes give access to the selections, and both simple guitar chords and simple piano accompaniments are provided. Anita Lobel's illustrations (double-page spreads alternate, full color, with black and white) are imaginatively adapted to the songs, sprightly, and inventively detailed. The use of illustrations on the pages is refreshingly varied.

531   **Hartman,** Evert. *War Without Friends;* tr. by Patricia Crampton. Crown, 1982. 82-10093. ISBN 0-517-54754-6. 218p. $10.95.

7–10   The time is World War II. The setting is Holland, then under German occupation. The protagonist is fifteen-year-old Arnold Westervoort, whose father is a zealous member of the NSB, the Dutch National Socialist Movement. Fanatically loyal to Hitler and to the Dutch Nazi leader Mussert, Westervoort is an irascible bully to his family and a toady to his superiors; he forces his family to go along with his beliefs. At first credulous and supportive, Arnold becomes increasingly resistant as he is mocked at school, avoided by the girl he likes, accused of being a spy and an informer by his classmates. His slow growth toward change and independence are convincingly depicted in a trenchant story, smoothly translated, that has strong characterization, a dramatic and carefully paced plot, and a powerful ending. This look at Nazi philosophy from the inside is as lucid an exposé as nonfiction analysis, and yet there is no trace of the tract in the book, which is an exciting and perceptive story.

532   **Haseley,** Dennis. *The Scared One;* illus. by Deborah Howland. Warne, 1983. 82-20109. ISBN 0-7232-6185-7. 26p. $10.95.

4–6   All of the other boys in the Indian village called him "The Scared One," and he was indeed timid, fearful of being alone, too shy to do anything but smile when he was taunted. Sent to catch the family's goat, which had wandered off, the boy who is the narrator is caught in a thunderstorm; stunned, he sleeps and wakes to see a large injured bird that cannot fly. He takes the bird to Old Wolf, but when he sees all the stuffed animal heads the old man has, he runs off with the bird. *"Kinan Po!* Fly now," he cries, *"Ake Akisne!* You must grow strong while you fly!" This is really a prose poem about a quest and the rites of passage; it is gravely told, and touching; its one weakness is that a bird that is able to fly (as this one does) is not likely to have come close to the boy and so meekly accepted being caught and carried. The illustrations, which show contemporary Native Americans, are softly executed pencil drawings, effective in black and white.

533   **Haskins,** James S. *Black Theatre in America;* illus. with photographs. Crowell, 1982. 81-43874. Trade ed. ISBN 0-690-04128-4; Library ed. ISBN 0-690-04129-2. 160p. Trade ed. $9.50; Library ed. $9.89.

8–   Comprehensive and well-organized, this history of black entertainers, comic or serious, is a useful compendium of information, although the occasional errors (a show that opened in 1908 had a star who fell ill "during its run" and "died in 1907") and the occasional imposition of authorial viewpoint or conjecture ("If he were alive today, DuBois would be amazed . . .") weaken it somewhat. One of the book's stronger points is the consistency with which Haskins makes connections between what was happening in black theatre to what was happening in the changing status of blacks and to the economic influences on theatre in general.

534   **Haskins**, James S. *Lena Horne*. Coward, 1983. 83-15411. ISBN 0-698-20586-3. 160p. illus. with photographs. $10.95.

7–   Spectacular as Lena Horne's career has been, it is rivalled in drama by her personal life; torn from her grandparents' home with its stability and culture to traipse about the country with her mother (an unsuccessful actress) and badgered by her Cuban stepfather, she had an unhappy first marriage that ended with her husband keeping one of their two children. Always a political activist, she was on the *Red Channels* list of banned artists; her marriage to a white man (a marriage that was a long and happy one) brought further problems. Horne struggled throughout her career to improve the image of blacks in the roles she played, and her story is one of battles and triumphs. This has a more even quality in the writing style than some of Haskins' recent biographies, and he writes with a candor that is, like his appreciation of the beautiful Lena Horne, controlled.

535   **Haskins**, James S. *The Quiet Revolution; The Struggle for the Rights of Disabled Americans;* by James Haskins with J. M. Stifle. T. Y. Crowell, 1979. 77-27664. Trade ed. ISBN 0-690-03981-6; Library ed. ISBN 0-690-03982-4. 147p. illus. with photographs. Trade ed. $7.95; Library ed. $7.89 net.

7–   This may be considered a companion volume to Haskins' *Who Are the Handicapped?* Here the emphasis is not on who the handicapped or disabled citizens are but on what is, or can be, done to solve or alleviate their problems in living in a world in which they encounter not only discrimination but also physical barriers that make it difficult—in some cases, impossible—to live normal lives or take advantage of those rights to which they are entitled. The writing is forceful without being melodramatic, strong in pleading for means to give the disabled human and civil rights, the book a weapon in the quiet revolution that is going on today. The index is prefaced by an extensive divided bibliography.

536   **Haskins**, James S. *Space Challenger: The Story of Guion Bluford;* by Jim Haskins and Kathleen Benson. Carolrhoda, 1984. 84-4251. ISBN 0-87614-259-5. 64p. illus. with photographs. $8.95.

4–6   A glossary and an index are provided for a simply written biography that gives a dignified picture of the first black astronaut. The text covers adequately the facts of Bluford's life; without becoming laudatory, it affirms the subject's calm dedication to his goal of becoming an aerospace engineer and a pilot, his self-confidence and modesty. There is enough information about the flight of the *Challenger* to satisfy readers.

537   **Hassler,** Jon. *Jemmy.* Atheneum, 1980. 79-23091. ISBN 0-689-50130-7. 180p. $7.95.

7–9   Jemmy's mother, a Chippewa, is dead; her father, white, is a lazy alcoholic who decides that Jemmy should quit school so that she can take care of her younger siblings. A grave, quiet girl of seventeen, Jemmy accepts this stoically. It isn't until Jemmy gets to know the Chapmans (an artist and his wife) and they encourage her artistic ability that she begins to see that she may be able to escape her dull life. This isn't the typical story of Indian-white conflict, since Jemmy accepts her lot tranquilly, but it is strong in that tranquility: Jemmy is like a rock, a person with innate strength and dignity; the story also gives a convincing picture of a rural Minnesota community.

538   **Haugaard,** Erik Christian. *Chase Me, Catch Nobody!.* Houghton, 1980. 80-371. ISBN 0-395-29208-5. 209p. $7.95.

6–9   Erik, who tells the story in retrospect, was fourteen in 1937; part of a school group taking a holiday outing in Germany, Erik is politically naive but soon becomes sharply aware of the visible outrages perpetrated by the Nazi regime. On the ferry from Denmark to Germany, he had been given a package by an innocuous-looking man; he had instructions for delivery if the man failed to retrieve the package. Since the man was marched off the ferry by the Gestapo, Erik knew that he must make the delivery when he got to Hamburg. His other adventure was rescuing a Jewish girl who had been hidden in an attic for a year; he was helped by his one friend in his school group, and the three of them were pursued by the evil Freiherr von Klein, reaching safety by crossing into Danish waters in a leaky punt. This is a good adventure story, but it's much more than that; it's an indictment of a cruel regime, and it is also a perceptive, smooth development of a growing political awareness on Erik's part, an awareness that stirs a sense of justice, an anger at injustice, a willingness to become involved, and that results in an impressive (and credible) display of courage and initiative. The story is strengthened by vivid characterization and relieved by some very funny dialogue and pranks among the group of boys.

539   **Haugaard,** Erik Christian. *Leif the Unlucky.* Houghton, 1982. 82-1053. ISBN 0-395-32156-5. 206p. $9.95.

7–9   Haugaard writes commandingly of the last remnants of the Greenland colony in the early fifteenth century, a group of farmers whose lives were being strangled by the increasingly bitter cold winters, whose dreams of returning to Norway were thwarted because they had neither ships nor wood to build them. Leif, aware that the older members of the community have lost all initiative, gathers a group of young people to battle another such group led by the power-hungry Egil. It is a struggle that can end only in tragedy—as indeed happens. This primitive world is brought to vivid life in a story that is as effective in picturing the bleak desolation of the moribund colony as it is in creating strongly individual characters. There is a sense of doom and inevitability about the story, yet it has high drama and action; this has some of the major attributes of good historical fiction: vivid details of time and place, association with historical characters, and focus on fictional characters whose lives engage the reader.

540   **Haugaard,** Erik Christian. *The Samurai's Tale.* Houghton, 1984. 83-22746. ISBN 0-395-34559-6. 234p. $12.95.

7–10   Taro's growth to manhood is largely determined by the power struggles of the feudal warlords of 16th century Japan, from the massacre that leaves him an orphan at age four, to the final ferocious slaughter of his lord's soldiers and household. Looking back as an old man, Taro remembers his rise under the great Lord Akiyama's protection, from servant's servant and stable-boy to trusted aide, secret messenger and samurai. Though he yearns for heroism in battle, Taro is never brutalized: various father figures teach him to read and to care; he falls in love with a nobleman's daughter and woos her with poetry; with a close friend, Yoshitoki he enjoys a brief golden adolescence, even as Yoshitoki foresees his own early death. Against a mountainous Japanese landscape Haugaard vividly describes the turbulent sweep of events, with characters of all ranks in the strictly hierarchical society, and the beliefs and pressures which molded them. Yet even as he shows the individual caught up in history, Haugaard dramatizes the personal, and the ambition of the powerful to rule Japan is mirrored in Taro's drive to become a glorious samurai warrior. Readers will welcome the sequel that seems promised, the "attempt to avenge my master."

541   **Haugen,** Tormod. *The Night Birds;* tr. from the Norwegian by Sheila La Farge. Delacorte, 1982. 82-70311. Trade ed. ISBN 0-440-06451-1; Library ed. ISBN 0-440-06452-X. 160p. Trade ed. $9.95; Library ed. $9.89.

3–5   Translated with a fluent appreciation of the author's style, which is
  *   reminiscent of the ingenuous directness of Maria Gripe's writing, this (first published in Norway as *Nattfuglene*) is a touching, gentle story that treats a painful situation with honesty and sympathy. Jake is in second grade, worried because his father has emotional problems, because his mother comes home tired each day after working at a job she dislikes but must keep to make ends meet, because he is convinced that there are ferocious birds of prey locked in the closet of his bedroom. It soon becomes clear that Jake's night fears wax and wane in accord with his father's ups and downs. There is an encouraging note at the end of the

story, but—fortunately—no improbably neat happy ending. What comes through the whole story is love, love of each member of the family for the other two. Jake matures a bit, getting over some of his fears when he learns that the girl who enjoys frightening him is inventing grim stories. His father comes a little closer to understanding his own fears, and his mother to maintaining family stability. The writing style is distinctive, direct and consistent in identifying with Jake's viewpoint.

542   **Hautzig,** Deborah. *The Handsomest Father;* illus. by Muriel Batherman. Greenwillow, 1979. 78-21277. Trade ed. ISBN 0-688-80214-1; Library ed. ISBN 0-688-84214-3. 47p. (Read-Alone Books) Trade ed. $5.95; Library ed. $5.71.

K–2   Marsha began having qualms the day before Fathers' Visiting Day. What if he did something awful? What if everyone laughed? Worst of all, what if he looked different? It didn't help a bit when Marsha's friend Kathryn announced that *her* father was the handsomest in the world. Marsha lost her appetite, she tried to pretend she was ill, she assured her father that he didn't really have to come. Came the Big Day. Nervous at first, Marsha soon realized that there was nothing different about her father and nothing that people would laugh at, so she relaxed and enjoyed the visit. "I'm sure glad you came," she said at the end of the school day. "And you know what else? . . . You're the handsomest father here." The illustrations are simple, subdued and lightly colored line drawings with just a touch of Gluyas Williams style; the story is direct, ingenuous without being too cute, and lightly amusing in the way it expresses a reaction many children share.

543   **Hautzig,** Deborah. *Second Star to the Right.* Greenwillow, 1981. 81-1589. Trade ed. ISBN 0-688-00498-9; Library ed. ISBN 0-688-00499-7. 151p. Trade ed. $7.95; Library ed. $7.63.

7–10   Leslie has loving parents, a comfortable home, a good friend, and she's a bit heavier than she wants to be; after losing a few pounds during an illness, she decides to diet. That's the beginning of her trouble, anorexia nervosa, and she cannot herself understand the compulsion she feels to lose still more weight. Even when she knows she's thin, she doesn't feel thin enough. Eventually she is hospitalized and, through therapy sessions, begins to understand the motives for her self-starvation, motives she has buried because it is so painful to admit the resentment she feels against a mother she loves deeply. The story is told by Leslie, giving it an immediacy and depth that make her compulsion pathetically comprehensible and revealing with articulate insight the complexities of a mother-daughter relationship; psychologically sound, dramatically constructed, the story is lightened by a wry humor in dialogue and warmed by compassion.

544   **Haynes,** Mary. *Pot Belly Tales;* illus. by Michael J. Deraney. Lothrop, 1982. 81-12325. Trade ed. ISBN 0-688-00892-5; Library ed. ISBN 0-688-00893-3. 77p. Trade ed. $9.50; Library ed. $8.59.

3–5   Perhaps because she doesn't force the historical details that create a flavor of the several periods (presented in vignettes) that span almost a century, Haynes creates a good narrative flow in telling about the series of owners of one artifact, a pot belly stove. The account begins with the casting, seen from the viewpoint of the manufacturer's little daughter in 1888; it continues to describe separate incidents as the stove changed hands, eleven incidents in all. The soft, almost blurred black and white drawings have depth and vigor in their realistic portrayal of the many and varied events in the story.

545   **Haynes,** Mary. *Wordchanger;* illus. by Eric Nones. Lothrop, 1983. 83-773. ISBN 0-688-02273-1. 254p. $9.50.

6–8   William is twelve. Suspicious of his stepfather, aware that Bruno's fatherly friendliness is a veneer for hostility, William is surprised and pleased when his mother suddenly announces that they are leaving, instantly and with no traces. When she and William pool their knowledge, they discover that Bruno has built on the research done by William's dead father, that Bruno has no affection for his wife or stepchild, and that Bruno has invented a machine that really does change words, a machine with infinite possibilities. Periodically the story shifts to Lily, another child, and eventually they meet and share adventures. As the three drive toward San Francisco, they fear that Bruno has picked up their trail. In a final dramatic confrontation (unfortunately followed by an all-but-the-bad-guys cast party, a weak ending) Lily and William, with the unexpected help of several adults, expose the villain and save the wordchanger from being used as a means to gain personal power. The story has good pace and suspense, adequate characterization and dialogue, a fresh and sturdy plot, and action galore.

546   **Haywood,** Carolyn. *The King's Monster;* illus. by Victor Ambrus. Morrow, 1980. 79-18134. Trade ed. ISBN 0-688-22214-5; Library ed. ISBN 0-688-32214-X. 30p. Trade ed. $7.95; Library ed. $7.63.

K–2   The king is amused by his subjects' complaints about his monster and all the ways it troubles them: its fetid breath that pollutes the atmosphere, its roaring in the night. Only a man who can overcome the monster, the king decrees, can win the hand of his beautiful daughter; frightened by the awesome reputation of the monster, all but one suitor decamp, despite the beauty and charm of the princess. The one aspirant, who has loved and been loved by the princess since childhood, goes with the princess to the palace dungeon and discovers that there is no monster and never has been. It's a myth. So, in addition to the wedding-bells ending, the story of the monster is used thereafter by mothers to rebuke children who bring home terrible, exaggerated tales. The illustrations are rich in color and humor, nicely detailed but spacious in composition; the story is adequately told although the vocabulary seems sophisticated for the picture book audience for whom this original tale in the fairy tale tradition is told: "It was a day of revels and much buffoonery," or, "He was always the victor, always unseating his opponent." Haywood's hints that the monster is imaginary are plentiful, and therefore the discovery of the empty dungeon seems rather anticlimatic.

547   **Hazen,** Barbara Shook. *Even If I Did Something Awful;* illus. by Nancy Kincade. Atheneum, 1981. 81-1907. ISBN 0-689-30843-4. 27p. $9.95.

K–2   Can there be a child anywhere who won't recognize the careful testing process by which the child in this story leads up to her confession of guilt? The story is told completely in dialogue, the child asking one test question after another ("Would you still love me if I got orange crayon on the carpet?") and being told that of course she'd still be loved—but there would be logical consequences: "I'd love you even if you crayoned the whole house. But I'd make you clean it up." Finally, the truth comes out: the child played ball (having been told not to) in the living room and broke the vase Daddy had given Mommy for her birthday. She really has done something awful (she thinks) and Mommy, after a few home truths, makes it clear that she may not like what her child does, but it doesn't change her love. This has no tone of didacticism, but is more a clearing of the air. The line drawings, pink-tinted, add another dimension, incorporating the child's imaginative play (she was in a football game when disaster struck) and reflecting the affection between mother and child.

548   **Heide,** Florence Parry. *The Problem with Pulcifer;* illus. by Judy Glasser. Lippincott, 1982. 81-48606. Trade ed. ISBN 0-397-32001-9; Library ed. ISBN 0-397-32002-7. 54p. Trade ed. $8.95; Library ed. $8.89.

3–5   Heide pokes fun at television addicts, conformity, and certain adult-child relations in a very funny book that is written with acidulated exaggeration but that has a strong unstated message. Everybody worries about Pulcifer, who refuses to watch television as all normal people do; instead he reads b--ks. Shameful! Frustrating to the teachers, to his parents, to a psychiatrist who points out that he read as a child and understands, but *he* broke the habit. Even the school librarian worries when Pulcifer checks out books instead of the AV equipment that dominates the shelves. *Everybody* watches television but Pulcifer. He's not motivated, the psychiatrist explains; Pulcifer's parents tell him the fact that everyone else watches should be motivation enough. Not a good reason, Pulcifer says. Sadly his parents tell him they love him anyway; they go off to watch television and Pulcifer settles happily into an armchair with his stack of new library books. Heide makes her point with humor, deriding not television but television addiction in a clever story illustrated with cartoon style drawings, angular, stiff, and spare.

549   **Heide,** Florence Parry. *Time Flies;* illus. by Marylin Hafner. Holiday House, 1984. 84-47833. ISBN 0-8234-0542-7. 97p. $10.95.

4–6   There's a bit of off-beat Treehorn-type humor in this amusing story told
       by Noah, who's busy evading chores set by his time-expert father, who
       adjusts to the burden of a noisy new sibling, who gains confidence as
       one after another of his ideas (deliberately or accidentally) proves fruit-
       ful. Heide's at her best when she writes with a light, wry touch, and in
       this book that's maintained throughout. The scribbly line drawings pick
       up the note of casual, cheerful muddle very nicely.

550   **Heide,** Florence Parry. *Treehorn's Treasure;* illus. by Edward Gorey. Holi-
       day House, 1981. 81-4043. ISBN 0-8234-0425-0. 60p. $7.95.

3–6   Macabre and elegant, Gorey's sophisticated line drawings are perfectly
       suited to the dry wit of the story, a pointed commentary on the mani-
       fold imperfections of human communication, particularly on those
       adults who hear children but don't really listen. It's true that in the
       course of the story there is one fanciful fact that listeners dismiss when-
       ever Treehorn tries to tell them that the leaves on a tree in his yard are
       turning into dollar bills, but that's the crux of the story. This is Heide at
       her best.

551   **Hentoff,** Nat. *The Day They Came to Arrest the Book.* Delacorte, 1982.
       82-71100. ISBN 0-440-02039-5. 160p. $10.95.

7–10   A censorship crisis is precipitated when an angry parent attacks the use
       of Mark Twain's *Huckleberry Finn* as required reading for a history class.
       Soon both the town and the high school are in a state of conflict; par-
       ents are divided, as are students and teachers. The case goes to a re-
       view committee, and then to the school board and it gets national me-
       dia coverage. The censors lose; the book stays. Much of the credit for
       the victory goes to the school librarian. These are the bones of the
       story, with Hentoff using all the arguments that have been used on
       both sides in real life. Only the fact that Hentoff is a capable writer
       keeps this from being a case history, but he has done a fine job of
       bringing both the characters and the issues to life.

552   **Hentoff,** Nat. *Does This School Have Capital Punishment?* Delacorte, 1981.
       80-68733. ISBN 0-440-02051-4. 170p. $8.95.

6–9   In a sequel to *This School is Driving Me Crazy* Sam Davidson, whose fa-
       ther is headmaster in a private school, is now enrolled at another
       school; he gets off to a bad start when he uses a friend's expired sub-
       way pass, is caught, and has to go to court. On probationary status,
       Sam is warned by his new headmaster that his record must be impecca-
       ble—and then Sam and another boy are framed, accused of smoking
       pot by the classmate who had actually been the culprit. This plot line
       then merges with another, Sam's new friendship with an elderly black
       jazz musician, Kelley, who is the real hero of the story. Kelley goes to a
       great deal of trouble and expense to prove Sam's innocence and to help
       the boy who got Sam in trouble; both boys have become enchanted by

their introduction, via Kelley, to jazz. The merging of the plots is smooth and enables Hentoff to focus on two of his long-expressed interests: jazz and education. As with the first book, there is some exaggeration of character (the director of the high school, a man whose philosophy is contrasted with that of the head-master) to make the author's point about teaching and teachers' attitudes, but the characterization on the whole is vivid and credible; the dialogue is witty, with humor inherent in situations rather than in action. Like the first book, this is a better-than-average school story, both in the sense of being provocative and being an enjoyable read.

553   **Herbst,** Judith. *Sky Above and Worlds Beyond;* illus. by Richard Rosenblum; sky charts by George Lovi. Atheneum, 1983. 82-13749. ISBN 0-689-30974-0. 219p. $14.95.

6–   An enthusiastic and informed amateur star-lover, Herbst writes in a vigorous, informal style about early civilizations and their knowledge of astronomy, about the solar system and all of its planets, moons, stars, black holes, and supernovas, about other galaxies, about space exploration and what it may bring in the future. Occasionally the text deviates from its informational role to include (for example) an imaginary tour group visiting the moon under NASA sponsorship. Despite this sort of interpolation, usually a bit on the cute side, the book could, because of its coverage and its enthusiasm, serve well to interest readers enough to encourage further reading. A bibliography, seasonal star maps, and an index are appended.

554   **Herda.** D. J. *Vegetables in a Pot;* illus. by Kathy Fritz McBride and with photographs. Messner, 1979. 78-23936. ISBN 0-671-32929-4. 94p. $7.29.

4–7   While there are many books that tell young readers how to grow vegetables in containers, indoors or out, there's always room for another that is clear and explicit, as this is. Herda covers all aspects save for plant diseases (to which there is only a passing reference) and describes every step in plant care from preparing the soil and cleaning pots to fertilizing the growing plant, and he writes for the beginner, explaining how to water, for example, and how much to water, and how to test the soil to see if watering is needed. A section that describes some appropriate varieties of different kinds of vegetables includes space and depth needed, and germination-to-maturity time; a list of seed companies and an index are appended.

555   **Herman,** Charlotte. *My Mother Didn't Kiss Me Goodnight;* illus. by Bruce Degen. Dutton, 1980. 80-190. ISBN 0-525-35495-6. 27p. $7.95.

4–6 yrs.   Why, Leon wonders, hadn't his mother kissed him goodnight the way she usually did? Was it because he'd let a pet snake loose and it had crawled into a visitor's shoe? Because he'd answered a telephone caller and said his mother had cramps? (And so on and so on) Miffed, Leon decides he doesn't really care—but when his mother comes in to say good-night and explains that she can't kiss him because she has a cold, Leon is relieved. The pictures are rather cluttered but mildly amusing; the text sags a bit in the middle, when Leon is examining his sins-of-the-day, but the approach is appropriately childlike, the situation one with which most children can identify, and the ending both logical and satisfying.

556   **Hermes,** Patricia. *Who Will Take Care of Me?* Harcourt, 1983. 82-48757. ISBN 0-15-296265-4. 99p. $10.95.

4–6   Orphaned, twelve-year-old Mark and his younger brother Pete live with their grandmother, and Mark is as fearful as he is bereaved when she dies. It isn't just worry about who will take care of him, because he knows Aunt Agnes will, but what will happen to Pete? Pete is ten, has the mental development of a child of five, and depends completely on his older brother. Overhearing Aunt Agnes talk about sending Pete to a special school, Mark takes his brother secretly to their summer cottage. Terrified when Pete wanders off, Mark realizes that he does need help; he agrees to visit the special school and then he finds, when Pete has attended it for a week, that his little brother has new friends, new interests, and new independence. And that he, Mark, has a new freedom. This is a tender story, written with insight, that has good pace and structure and a believable solution to a child's problems.

557   **Herzig.** Alison Cragin. *Oh, Boy! Babies!* by Alison Cragin Herzig and Jane Lawrence Mali; illus. with photographs by Katrina Thomas. Little, 1980. 80-16575. Hardcover ed. ISBN 0-316-35896-7; Paper ed. ISBN 0-316-35897-5. 106p. Hardcover ed. $9.95; Paper ed. $5.95.

4–6   A photodocumentary about an elective course in a boys' school, this
*   includes many pictures of the boys attacking with relish their assignments of feeding, diapering, soothing, bathing, and playing with babies. Baby pictures are always beguiling, but here the boys' faces, expressing delight, tenderness, shock, or absorption, are even more attractive. The text is partly descriptive, partly based on the students' comments and questions; a lively bunch, the boys are zealous and intelligent as they (and their readers) learn how to care for babies of assorted ages and what to do when they take care of babies on their own: safety precautions, questions to ask parents, etc. In the last week's class, the boys proudly collect their certificates; a note from the authors states that the course, then being given for the first time, became one of the most popular electives, one original class member stealthily enrolling so that he could have the fun of being with babies again. Useful, amusing, and engaging, a charming book.

558   **Herzig.** Alison Cragin. *Thaddeus;* by Alison Cragin Herzig and Jane Lawrence Mali; illus. by Stephen Gammel. Little, 1984. 84-5725. ISBN 0-316-35899-1. 85p. $14.95.

K–3
*
Whether in black and white or in color, the illustrations here are clever in design, handsome to look at, and in perfect accord with the text, which manages to be restrainedly whimsical without ever being cloying. It describes the first seven Christmas birthdays of little Thaddeus, each celebrated in the company of a wonderfully eccentric and inventive great-great uncle. It is told both directly (by the authors) and indirectly, in a book written by Great-Great-Uncle Thaddeus (now in his nineties) for little Tad. A loving story, and an ingenious one, nice for Christmas and birthdays and all the days between.

559   **Hess,** Lilo. *A Cat's Nine Lives;* written and illus. with photographs by Lilo Hess. Scribner, 1984. 83-20236. ISBN 0-684-18073-1. 48p. $11.95.

3–5
Although this text, profusely illustrated with photographs of fine quality, is primarily about the various stages in the life of Misty, a young Persian cat, it also gives a considerable amount of information about breeds and show cats. Implicit throughout the text is a concern for the care and welfare of animals. Misty is at one point abandoned as she passes through the hands of a series of owners, another time returned to an animal shelter, at one point injured. As the book ends, she is the new and dearly loved pet of a child who has been withdrawn and for whom Misty opens new avenues of interest and achievement. Very nice balance here.

560   **Hewett,** Joan. *Watching Them Grow; Inside a Zoo Nursery;* illus. with photographs by Richard Hewett. Little, 1979. 79-13345. ISBN 0-316-35968-8. 64p. $7.95.

4–6
Based on the records kept by a nursery attendant at the San Diego zoo, this account of typical days runs from November to March; it consists of descriptions rather than of entries, and is liberally illustrated with photographs of the several baby animals cared for by Loretta Owens, the night attendant. The photographs are a bit repetitious but are predictably beguiling; the text, save for an implication that all nursery attendants are female ("That's the first thing that every woman who's trained as a nursery attendant learns.") is direct and informative, and makes amply clear the affection and care given to a zoo's animal babies.

561   **Hewett,** Joan. *When You Fight the Tiger;* illus. with photographs by Richard Hewett. Little, Brown, 1984. 84-10067. ISBN 0-316-35956-4. 90p. $12.95.

5–9
A text that should appeal to animal lovers, because the description it gives of life at an animal-training ranch is based on the "Affection Training" credo of its owners, this is illustrated with many photographs of the animals at Gentle Jungle. Here wild animals are tamed and trained for work in television and movies; the writing is informal and anecdotal, the material fascinating.

562   **Hewitt,** Kathryn. *Two by Two: The Untold Story;* written and illus. by Kathryn Hewitt. Harcourt, 1984. 84-4579. ISBN 0-15-291801-9. 29p. $12.95.

K–3   In an amusing adaptation of the Biblical version, so light-hearted it would be hard for even the most devout to take offense, Hewitt postulates a different kind of voyage for Noah and his arkful. To entice the reluctant animals aboard, he has advertised the voyage as a pleasure cruise; the rain spoils the planned fun, but eventually the sun comes out, the land dries up, and the dove returns with a (stuffed) olive branch. The paintings are not polished but they have an exuberant vitality and some comic touches (God's messenger is a bellboy, the giraffe gets stuck in a doorway, a pig shows a sunburn line when her sunsuit strap slips) and the text has the same kind of humor: the animals, gloating over their invitations, say, "On a deluxe vessel, too! Well, when it rains, it pours!" Uninhibited fun.

563   **Hickman,** Martha Whitmore. *Last Week My Brother Anthony Died;* illus. by Randie Julien. Abingdon, 1984. 84-2891. ISBN 0-687-21128-X. 26p. $10.95.

K–2   Among the many books that have been published to help children understand and adjust to bereavement, there are few that deal with infant death. Here, told in first person by a little girl, is the story of a child's questions and feelings about the death of a four-week-old brother with a heart defect. "It's funny how you can miss a person you didn't even used to know," Julie says, remembering how Anthony had kicked when he was in the womb and they didn't even know it was Anthony. This is simple, direct, and gentle, a perceptive story. The illustrations are of poor quality.

564   **Highwater,** Jamake. *Legend Days.* Harper, 1984. 82-48852. Library ed. ISBN 0-06-022304-9; Trade ed. ISBN 0-06-022303-0. 147p. Library ed. $10.89; Trade ed. $10.95.

8–   "You must take this vision we give you and draw it into your heart, where it must remain like the storm that fills the cloud with lightning." Gifted by the fox, Amana has in her heart the power of a warrior. She is different, challenging the role of women in her society, challenging the forces, both of the white settlers and of nature, which threaten her entire people. The tragedy, cruelty, and violence contained in this novel are relentless yet never gratuitous—they starkly present the destruction of Native American society, and add a mythic dimension to Amana's struggle. Says the maddened Yellow Bird Woman, beaten and mutilated because she ran off from her husband, "Within you, Amana, the spirit of our people lives, and through the legends of your life all of us will be remembered." A strong heroine, in a story notable for its compelling narrative power.

565   **Hinton,** S. E. *Tex.* Delacorte, 1979. 78-50448. ISBN 0-440-08641-8. 191p. $8.95.

7–10   "Love ought to be a real simple thing," Tex says as he concludes his story, ". . . with humans it gets so mixed up it's hard to know what you feel, much less how to say it." There are other facets to Tex's story, and other kinds of love, but it is primarily a story of the love between brothers. Tex and his older brother Mason are often alone for months while their father follows the rodeo circuit; what will Tex do when Mason goes to college? He's always been aware that Mason was Pop's favorite—but it comes as a terrible shock to learn that Pop isn't his father, that he had been born when Pop was in jail. Rash in despair and anger, Tex loses his temper while with some thugs; he's shot. While recovering, he does some thinking—and that's when he thinks about his brother, how he's hated Mason's bossing him, and how much he loves him. Hinton balances this with some of Tex's relationships with friends, with his tendresse for a girl, and with one dramatic and convincing episode in which Mason and Tex, having picked up a hitch-hiker, are in serious danger. The facets of the story are smoothly meshed, the dialogue has a natural flow, and the first-person narration works beautifully.

566   **Hlibok,** Bruce. *Silent Dancer;* illus. with photographs by Liz Glasgow. Messner, 1981. 81-14011. ISBN 0-671-43260-5. 64p. $8.29.

3–5   While most photodocumentaries about children who are studying ballet focus on either the techniques or the student's devotion and perseverance, this describes the way in which ten-year-old Nancy and her classmates, all deaf, learn ballet. They are in a special class at the Joffrey Ballet School, and they are students at the Lexington School for the Deaf. The book is illustrated with the customary photographs of floor work, barre exercises, and delighted children who are costumed for a public performance. This doesn't tell you as much about ballet as the other books, but it tells a great deal about the resilience and potential of handicapped children, and it's written without sugar icing.

567   **Hoban,** Lillian. *Arthur's Halloween Costume;* written and illus. by Lillian Hoban. Harper, 1984. 83-49465. Library ed. ISBN 0-06-022391-X; Trade ed. ISBN 0-06-022387-1. 64p. (I Can Read Books). Library ed. $8.89; Trade ed. $8.95.

1–2   Disappointed because other children are going to a school party dressed as ghosts just as he is, Arthur feels he will neither win a prize for originality nor will he frighten anyone. By the time Arthur has spilled ketchup on his sheet, acquired a wig from the trash can and a few other accessories, it is clear that he has a costume that is unique. He doesn't know what it is, but an admiring older student announces that Arthur is the Spirit of Halloween. Arthur, as those addicted to earlier books about him know, is a chimpanzee. This hasn't the same kind of humor as the earlier books; here it's more slapstick/disaster than invested in personalities and relationships, but the humor is right for the beginning independent reader, and the Halloween setting has appeal.

568   **Hoban,** Lillian. *The Laziest Robot in Zone One;* by Lillian and Phoebe Hoban; illus. by Lillian Hoban. Harper, 1983. 82-48613. Trade ed. ISBN

0-06-022349-9; Library ed. ISBN 0-06-022352-9. 64p. Trade ed. $7.95; Library ed. $8.89.

2–3   A sequel to *Ready, Set, Robot!* in which Sol-1 is a tubby little robot who uses his "brains," this is a story in which Sol-1, ordered by his mother to do his chores, helps his robot friends and is in turn helped by them. This has rather more substance than the first book, and primary grades readers will probably delight in the technological references. This is a good story to read aloud to younger children, too.

569   **Hoban,** Russell. *The Flight of Bembel Rudzuk;* illus. by Colin McNaughton. Philomel, 1982. 81-21056. Trade ed. ISBN 0-399-20888-7; Library ed. ISBN 0-399-61198-3. 24p. Trade ed. $6.99.

2–4   The three lively boys who enjoyed an imaginative play session in *They Came From Aargh!* are at it again. This time two of them make a wet mess as they crawl about under a piece of cloth, their flippered feet protuding as they attack the princess (mother) in her high tower (footstool). They go hunting for their brother, and the three make inroads on a newly-made cake; mother comes back from an errand, sees the cake, wonders pointedly if mice have been at it. "Squeak!" say Bembel Rudzuk and his brothers. The illustrations are fresh, funny, and vigorous, and the story is ebullient and original. Like the other book, this can be enjoyed as a read-aloud book for younger children, but the nuances of the humor and the words used within illustrations indicate a primary grades audience.

570   **Hoban,** Russell C. *They Came From Aargh!* illus. by Colin McNaughton. Philomel, 1981. 81-5020. Trade ed. ISBN 0-399-20817-8; Library ed. ISBN 0-399-61182-7. 24p. Trade ed. $6.95; Library ed. $6.99.

2–4   This small book looks like a read-aloud picture book and it can indeed be used for reading aloud, but it will probably be most appreciated by the primary grades readers who recognize the spoofing of space flight talk ("Plovsnat at thirty-seven zeems and holding vummitch") and appreciate the humor of the mother-children encounter. Three boys who have concocted an amazing vehicle out of chairs, kitchen utensils, an odd wheel, an umbrella, etc. are interrupted in their examination of the strange planet by meeting a mummosaurus who offers them food after they have determined that her presence indicates intelligent life on Plovsnat. (She calls it "Earth.") Bright, sunny, funny paintings use balloon captions to repeat some of the dialogue in a brisk, bright story about imaginative play.

571   **Hoban,** Tana, illus. *I Read Signs;* illus. with photographs by Tana Hoban. Greenwillow, 1983. 83-1482. Trade ed. ISBN 0-688-02317-7; Library ed. ISBN 0-688-02318-5. 30p. Trade ed. $10.50; Library ed. $9.55. *I Read Symbols;* illus. with photographs by Tana Hoban. Greenwillow,

1983. 83-1481. Trade ed. ISBN 0-688-02331-2; Library ed. ISBN 0-688-02332-0. 29p. Trade ed. $10.50; Library ed. $9.55.

3–6
yrs.

Both books consist of excellent color photographs and no text—and none needed. *I Read Signs* has some pictures in which the signs also carry symbols, but most have none; many will be familiar to young children and can serve as an incentive to reading. In *I Read Symbols*, again, most of the photographs can be easily identified: signs for a bend in the road, directional arrows, children on a seesaw, a bar across a burning cigarette. In this book, a double-page spread of reduced pictures repeats the symbols and includes captions. Both books are attractive; both encourage observation and have some of the appeal of a game.

572   **Hoban,** Tana, photographer. *Round and Round and Round.* Greenwillow, 1983. 82-11984. Trade ed. ISBN 0-688-01813-0; Library ed. ISBN 0-688-01814-9. 28p. Trade ed. $9.50; Library ed. $8.59.

2–4
yrs.
*

A wordless picture book consists of a series of color photographs of excellent quality and considerable diversity; each full-page picture has at least one round object, and almost all are familiar and child-oriented. This is a good choice for encouragement of a child's powers of observation as well as to emphasize a concept of shape, and the pictures of a scoop of ice cream, a raccoon peering out of a hole in a tree, bright balloons, irridescent soap bubbles, and a seal balancing a ball should appeal to young children.

573   **Hoban,** Tana. *Take Another Look;* illus. with photographs by Tana Hoban. Greenwillow, 1981. 80-21342. Trade ed. ISBN 0-688-80298-2; Library ed. ISBN 0-688-84298-4. 18p. Trade ed. $7.95; Library ed. $7.63.

3–5
yrs.

This is not the first book to use the idea of a cut-out page that shows part of an object, inviting identification; however, it is a nice example of the type. The photographs—some enlarged—are clear, the objects familiar, and the format more than adequate for identification and for showing comparative size, so that no captions are necessary. Three pages are allotted to each object: first, the page with a circle cut out, through which a part of a photograph can be seen; second, the photograph itself, occupying the full-page space; third, a photograph that shows the object in relation to something or someone else. The objects are as familiar as a daisy, a cat, an umbrella, et cetera, with only one perhaps less familiar object, a lizard. A nice concept book, this has a guessing game appeal.

574   **Hoberman,** Mary Ann. *The Cozy Book;* illus. by Tony Chen. Viking, 1982. 80-10916. ISBN 0-670-24447-3. 45p. $12.95.

K–2

Softly detailed, brightly colored paintings that are reminiscent of the work of the Provensens illustrate a long, rhyming text that celebrates all kinds of cozy, happy things. There are cozy words, cozy foods, cozy sounds and smells, cozy things to do on a day when ". . . you wake up bright and early/In your roasty toasty bed . . ." And, at the end of the day, back to bed: "Droopy/Drifty/Drowsy/Dozy/Dream of everything that's cozy." Every child may not like every food or activity in the book, but all children will find some joys they share, and everyone can appreciate the lilt of the rhymes, the relish for words, and the pictures, busy but never cluttered.

575   **Hoberman,** Mary Ann. *Yellow Butter, Purple Jelly, Red Jam, Black Bread;* illus. by Chaya Burstein. Viking, 1981. 80-26555. ISBN 0-670-79382-5. 60p. $6.95.

3–5
yrs.
A tall, narrow book, illustrated with soft brown line drawings that are nicely incorporated into the page layouts, has bouncy, cheery poems about children and animals. The subjects, the rhyme, the rhythm and word play will appeal to the lap audience and some of the literary devices (alliteration, repetition) may unobtrusively strengthen pre-reading skills. There are brisk nonsense poems about zoo animals, poems about play, and some (fewer) quiet and thoughtful poems about emotions. In sum, a very nice new selection for young children, deftly written by a practiced hand.

576   **Hodges,** Margaret. *The Avenger.* Scribner, 1982. 82-10246. ISBN 0-684-17636-X. 178p. $11.95.

7–10
An absorbing historical novel is well-researched and smoothly written; set in ancient Greece, it covers two years, 492 B.C. to 490 B.C. The protagonist, Alexis, is a young adolescent who burns to avenge his family's honor against the king of a neighboring city, especially after the king's son, Glaukon, defeats Alexis' brother in a boxing match at the Olympic games. Glaukon becomes an ally, if not a friend, when he and Alexis are captured by pirates and sold as slaves in Athens. Both are given their freedom in exchange for military service at Marathon, the great battle with which the story ends and during which Alexis saves Glaukon's life. What Alexis has found as he matures is that there are better ways than combat and vengeance to heal a breach. The story moves at a good pace, with a strong plot as well as historical interest; Hodges is meticulous but unobtrusive in providing background details.

577   **Hodges,** Margaret, ad. *If You Had a Horse: Steeds of Myth and Legend;* illus. by D. Benjamin van Steenburgh. Scribner, 1984. 84-14024. ISBN 0-684-18220-3. 131p. $12.95.

4–6
A black and white drawing precedes each of the stories about horses from folk literature, and notes on the stories are appended. An experienced author and anthologist, Hodges has done an excellent job of providing variety of style and tone within the subject parameters here, with classic tales (Norse, Irish, Persian, etc.) from many countries retold in smooth narrative style.

578   **Hodges,** Margaret, ad. *Saint George and the Dragon;* adapted from
Edmund Spenser's *Faerie Queene;* illus. by Trina Schart Hyman. Little,
1984. 83-19980. ISBN 0-316-36789-3. 32p. $13.95.

4–6   At her romantic best, Hyman illustrates this classic tale, adapted from
*   Edmund Spenser's *Faerie Queene,* with paintings of a marvelously fierce
dragon, an impeccably heroic knight, a dazzlingly lovely Princess Una.
Notable for their color and composition, the illustrations are framed by
borders that often have a Tiffany look. The adaptation by Hodges is capable, simplifying Spenserian language but not abandoning it altogether
as she retells the dramatic story of the gallant Red Cross Knight who
fought the dragon, won a princess, and became the patron saint of England.

579   **Hodgman,** Ann. *Skystars: The History of Women in Aviation;* written by
Ann Hodgman and Rudy Djabbaroff. Atheneum, 1981. 81-5075. ISBN
0-689-30870-1. 186p. illus. with photographs. $11.95.

7–   A history of women flyers begins with those intrepid Frenchwomen
who were, despite censure as being unladylike, participants in early balloon flights at the end of the eighteenth century. The authors include all
major women in aviation, and many minor figures as well, women who
were—one by one—setting new records, trying new stunts, breaking
into fields dominated by men. This gives international coverage in text
and pictures, includes the contributions of women aviators to military
and scientific projects, and closes with a chapter on women who are
candidates in the United States for space shuttle pilots or astronauts.
Interesting material, carefully researched and compiled, is presented in
a solid but not heavy text. A bibliography of adult and juvenile titles
and an index are appended.

580   **Hoffman,** E. T. A. *Nutcracker;* tr. by Ralph Manheim; illus by Maurice
Sendak. Crown, 1984. 83-25266. ISBN 0-517-55285-X. 99p. $19.95.

8–   To those familiar with the usual ballet version of Hoffman's story, there
*   will be elements missing here, and unexpected additions. Manheim has
translated the original story of 1816, and Sendak has illustrated it, with
a sense of fidelity to the original but with an imaginative interpretation
rather than a literal one. The book includes the story of the Princess
Pirlipat and the Hard Nut, and there are passages that seem extended
or repetitive, but the tale is so beautifully bound together by profuse
and stunning illustrations that it is a joy simply to leaf through the
book; children may become restive at the lag in pace, but scholars
should be fascinated by the variations between this version and the
1983 publication, also based on the original rather than the ballet, translated by Anthea Bell and illustrated by Lisbeth Zwerger. This is more
for adults than for children, but there will be many children who will
enjoy it.

581   Hoffman, E. T. A. *The Nutcracker;* ad. by Janet Schulman; illus. by Kay Chorao. Dutton, 1979. 79-11223. ISBN 0-525-36245-2. 64p. $6.95.

3–5   Schulman has gone to Hoffman's original story, *The Nutcracker and the King of Mice,* published in Germany in 1816, rather than to the more familiar ballet version on which most adaptations for children are based; her one addition from the ballet is the Sugar Plum Fairy. The adaptation is smoothly told and lively in pace; the illustrations, pencil drawings that tend to be overcrowded but that capture the story's combination of the romantic and the grotesque, are nicely matched with the text.

582   **Holbrook,** Sabra. *Canada's Kids.* Atheneum. 1983. 83-6355. ISBN 0-689-31002-1. 161p. illus. with photographs and maps. $11.95.

6–8   A most useful book about the variety of ethnic groups and life styles in Canada also gives a great deal of information about political, educational, and industrial facets of Canadian life. Although the author uses the sort of authoritative detail that comes from living with families, as she did, this never gains the personal touch that made the Gidal series so popular. However, it is even more useful as supplementary material for a social studies unit, and it is candid about conflicts and problems between groups and within them. A bibliography and an index are appended.

583   **Holland,** Isabelle. *The Empty House.* Lippincott, 1983. 83-48464. Trade ed. ISBN 0-397-32005-1; Library ed. ISBN 0-397-32006-X. 128p. Trade ed. $10.50; Library ed. $10.89.

7–9   Betsy, the narrator, is fifteen; her mother is in Europe on a new assignment, so Betsy and her younger brother Roddy have come to stay with Aunt Marian at her house on the Jersey shore, their divorced father jailed on a charge of having attempted to defraud the government. Passionately convinced of his innocence, Betsy finds support from an elderly recluse, but Ted, the boy she's in love with, is also a help. The mystery element is nicely balanced by the love interest and by Betsy's concerns about her brother, afraid that his new friends will learn that he is subject to epileptic seizures. The structure and style of the story give solidity to a book that has good pace, convincing characters, and a logically developed plot.

584   **Holman,** Felice. *The Wild Children.* Scribner, 1983. 83-8974. ISBN 0-684-17970-9. 152p. $11.95.

6–9   In the early 1920's, bands of homeless children roamed the streets of Russian towns and cities, desperate for food and clothing, robbing and begging to keep alive. This is the story of one such band; they take Alex in when he is bereft on the Moscow streets, having come to find an uncle who's been taken by the police as have the members of Alex's family. Like the children of Virginia Hamilton's *The Planet of Junior Brown,* these boys (and later one small girl) share what they can beg or steal, help each other, follow the orders of their leader. They leave their cellar to jump a train, hoping things will be better in the south; eventually, through a contact Alex provides, they are secretly taken to Finland, the first stop on the journey to America. This is both grim and dramatic, a touching story that has momentum and conviction; the characters are solidly drawn, the setting vividly evoked, the message of youth's resilience and courage all the more effective for being shown rather than stated.

585   **Holme,** Bryan. *Creatures of Paradise; Pictures to Grow Up With.* Oxford, 1980. 80-10867. ISBN 0-19-520205-8. 96p. $12.95.

3–6   Holme uses the appeal of animals to children to introduce the latter to works of art; beginning with some scenes of the animals of Eden, he moves to pictures of individual animals (some pages of elephants, some of lions, horses, cats, birds, et cetera) and concludes with a brief section on mythical beasts. The book is not divided formally; the text consists of comments on the pictures, including descriptive, interpretative, and critical commentary; the tone is light. Most of the reproductions are in black and white, and there is no effort to impose chronological order on the pictures. While the combination of subject matter and vocabulary difficulty indicate middle grades readers as a primary audience, this should—like any art book—appeal to both younger and older browsers as well.

586   **Holz,** Loretta. *The Christmas Spider: A Puppet Play from Poland & Other Traditional Games, Crafts, and Activities;* illus. by Charles Mikolaycak. Philomel, 1980. 79-24770. ISBN 0-399-20754-X; Library ed. ISBN 0-399-61164-9. 26p. Trade ed. $5.95; Library ed. $5.99.

4–6   In addition to the puppet play, with instructions for making the scenery and the puppets, other projects that are related to the cut-paper folk art of Poland are tree decorations, Easter Eggs, and the lovely designs of wycinanki, the cut-paper designs that vary according to regions within Poland. There are also directions for playing some Polish games; all the projects are illustrated by the bright, nicely detailed collage pictures; the instructions are clear and not too complicated.

587   **Hooks,** William H. *Circle of Fire.* Atheneum, 1982. 82-3982. ISBN 0-689-50241-9. 144p. $9.95.

5–8   The time is 1936, the place is the tidewater country of North Carolina, and the narrator is eleven-year-old Harrison, who is white and who feels uncomfortable when anyone suggests that he ought to make some white friends, since he's perfectly happy with Kitty and Scrap, a black brother and sister. When a group of Irish tinkers who have escaped Klan vengeance in South Carolina camp on Harrison's family's land, the local Klansmen mobilize. Kitty and Scrap are frightened and so is Harrison, who isn't sure whether his father is a member of the KKK or not;

despite his fear, Harrison sneaks out at night to warn the tinkers, and his horror at the behavior of the Klan ends only when the sheriff and his men (called by Harrison's father) arrive on the scene. Despite the slightly contrived ending—a baby is born in the barn where a young tinker couple has taken refuge on Christmas Eve—this is a story with good pace and structure, and it gives a vivid and convincing picture of the cruelty and prejudice of the KKK.

588   **Hoover,** H. M. *The Shepherd Moon.* Viking, 1984. 83-16784. ISBN 0-670-63977-X. 149p. $11.95.

6–9   Merry is alone on the family's country estate when she meets the strange and beautiful young man who has come from an artificial moon, the shepherd moon, to dominate the earth. Mikel has superhuman powers, immense arrogance, and a childlike disposition; he is amoral, and eventually he is outwitted and defeated by Merry's grandfather. The novel is set in the 48th century and has a good balance of realism and fantasy, posing thoughtful problems about the direction of man's progress. The characterization is competent, the writing style smooth, the pace of the story brisk.

589   **Hoover,** H. M. *This Time of Darkness.* Viking, 1980. 80-15923. ISBN 0-670-50026-7. 161p. $9.95.

6–8   A science fiction novel is set in a future time in the huge, domed city that is, the inhabitants are told, the only safe place to live. Outside, the air is too polluted to sustain life. Still, when eleven-year-old Amy becomes bored by the regimented, guarded quality of her life, she is ready to believe Axel's story that Outside is safe. He had lived there, been captured, and is going to try to escape; he is willing to take Amy with him. It is a dangerous venture, but the children eventually escape to Outside and a family-structured, free society that welcomes Amy. The vast halls and corridors of the City, the atmosphere of rigid supervision, and the stultifying quality of City life are vividly captured; the details of the children's flight are imbued with action and suspense.

590   **Hopf,** Alice L. *Biography of a Snowy Owl;* illus. by Fran Stiles. Putnam, 1979. 78-16533. 63p. $5.49.

3–5   Hopf, in following the life cycle of a male snowy owl, includes facts about nesting and brooding, care of young, feeding and predators, migration and adaptability, and the adult owl's role in courting and mating. Concise and accurate, the book is consistent in relating the snowy owl's behavior to its ecological milieu. Black and white line drawings are realistically detailed if a bit hazy in technique.

591   **Hopkins,** Lee Bennett, comp. *A Song in Stone: City Poems;* photographs by Anna Held Audette. Crowell, 1983. 82-45589. Trade ed. ISBN

0-690-04269-8; Library ed. ISBN 0-690-04270-1. 39p. Trade ed. $9.95.; Library ed. $9.89.

2–4   A nicely chosen selection of urban poems, each section faced by a full-page photograph, includes the work of most of today's major children's poets. Hopkins, an indefatigable and knowledgeable anthologist, has chosen poems that are brief and positive, all of fine quality.

592   **Horwitz,** Elinor Lander. *On the Land; American Agriculture from Past to Present;* illus. with photographs. Atheneum, 1980. 79-3545. ISBN 0-689-50165-X. 132p. $8.95.

8–   A fine text considers the complex answer to a question posed in the author's preface: "How did a nation of small landholders become a country in which over one hundred thousand farm families are forced each year to abandon the land?" Does expanding productivity equate with successful progress? The changes in agricultural practices that have accompanied technological and agrarian improvement, the effects of economic and social pressures, and the urbanization that makes incursions on available farm land have all tended to decimate the small family farm and militate toward the large corporate farm. Horwitz gives ample historical background for understanding the changes and the problems; in a text that is carefully organized and lucid, she concludes with a chapter entitled "Can We Save the Family Farm?" that considers federal legislation and programs that affect agriculture, state extension programs, changes in estate tax laws, the encouragement of cooperative programs, help to minority farmers, and the establishment of marketing projects like the Greenmarket in New York or Quincy Market in Boston. Suggestions for further reading are included.

593   **Horwitz,** Elinor Lander. *Sometimes It Happens;* illus. by Susan Jeschke. Harper, 1981. 79-2687. Trade ed. ISBN 0-06-022596-3; Library ed. ISBN 0-06-022597-1. 30p. Trade ed. $7.89; Library ed. $8.25.

2–4   The deft pencil drawings of homely, slightly pop-eyed children and adults add a comic note to a gently humorous text about an unquenchable dreamer. Victor imagines himself the hero of one rescue plot after another, and candidly admits he wants to be a hero when he grows up. That's not a career, he's told, but there's no way to stop Victor's lively imagination, even by making fun of him. His mother soothes him with the down-to-earth thought that it's possible to be a hero on a small scale. Like saving some birds, he asks his mother? (He's just saved a bird's nest from being poked off its branch.) Exactly, she says—but a minute later Victor, who can't stop dreaming, envisions an act of supernatural strength; it *can* sometimes happen, he says, when there's a hero around. Nice style, nice concept, and a nice development.

594   **Horwitz,** Joshua. *Doll Hospital;* written and photographed by Joshua Horwitz. Pantheon, 1983. 82-14508. Trade ed. ISBN 0-394-85332-6; Library ed. ISBN 0-394-95332-0. 52p. $10.95.

3–5   A photodocumentary describes the work done by Irving Chais, propri-
etor of the New York Doll Hospital. A family business since 1900, the
establishment specializes in doll repair and restoration, and the text and
pictures together explain some of the ways in which dolls are mended,
spare parts are stocked, or new wigs or clothes provided. The writing is
matter-of-fact, the text informative, the dedication to craftsmanship
made evident.

595   **Houghton,** Eric. *Steps Out of Time.* Lothrop, 1980. Trade ed. ISBN
0-688-41970-4; Library ed. ISBN 0-688-51970-9. Trade ed. $6.95; Library
ed. $6.67.

6–8   Jonathan has just moved with his widowed father to a town where his
new classmates, who feel Jonathan is a show-off Londoner, are
unfriendly. Lonely, he is baffled by the fact that the dense local fogs
seem to precipitate another period of time: it's his house he's in, but it
looks different, and he is himself, only the girl who seems to be his sister calls him "Peter." With each step out of time, Jonathan learns more
about Peter, and about the sister who admires Peter's ability as an artist; indeed, he gains a confidence in drawing that carries over into his
real life. The mystery is in the relationship between Jonathan and Peter,
and science fiction buffs should enjoy the twist the solution provides.
Nicely crafted and structured, the story is weakened a bit by the ending
(rather sudden admiration and acceptance from one classmate) but is
sturdy enough to compensate for this, and is strengthened by the warm
father-son relationship.

596   **Houston,** James. *Long Claw: An Arctic Adventure;* written and illus. by
James Houston. Atheneum, 1981. 81-3478. ISBN 0-689-50206-0. 32p.
$8.95.

4–6   As always, Houston vividly evokes, in pictures and story, the icy desolation and danger of the Arctic scene. Here, in a dramatic survival
story, an Eskimo brother and sister go off on a trek, hoping to find the
caribou that their grandfather had buried when hunting. Their father is
dead, grandfather is not strong enough to carry the meat alone, and the
family is near starvation. Pitohok and Upik escape from a grizzly, cope
with an ice fog, resourcefully find a way to get the meat home although
they have lost the use of their sled. Taut with suspense, this is an exciting adventure story.

597   **Houston,** James. *River Runners; A Tale of Hardship And Bravery;* written
and illus. by James Houston. Atheneum, 1979. 79-14337. ISBN 0-689-
50151-X. 142p. $7.95.

7–9   Andrew, fifteen and big for his age, has come to an Alaskan trading
post as clerk-apprentice to the manager. The post is on the Hudson
Strait, in Naskapi territory, and Andrew is fortunate enough to be befriended by a Naskapi his own age, Pashak. It is from Pashak that An-

drew learns many of the skills that enable him to survive the trek to a fur-trading outpost in a bitter winter. This is primarily an adventure story, written with practiced smoothness and many dramatic incidents. What gives it substance is the author's familiarity with the region and its people; Houston does not introduce cultural details, they are simply there, permeating the book, as is an obvious respect for the Naskapi people and their way of life.

598   Howard, Ellen. *Circle of Giving.* Atheneum, 1984. 83-15631. ISBN 0-689-31027-7. 99p. $9.95.

5–7   Jeannie is the narrator, but it is her older sister Marguerite who is the moving spirit in a story that just avoids bogging down in sentimentality, especially at the ending. It's Marguerite who decides that everybody is wrong about their neighbor Francie, that a child with cerebral palsy can learn to read and write. With infinite patience, Francie is taught, and her achievement is unveiled at a party of neighbors when Jeannie's parents decide everybody in the new housing development is just as homesick for a big family Christmas as they are. Adequately written, adequately structured, this has some interesting characters as well as some with stereotypical traits; it is appealing chiefly because of the interest the sisters take in Francie and the prowess Francie shows.

599   Howe, Deborah. *Bunnicula: A Rabbit-Tale of Mystery;* by Deborah and James Howe; illus. by Alan Daniel. Atheneum, 1979. 78-11472. 98p. $7.95.

4–6   Bunnicula is a rabbit discovered by the Monroe family when they went to see the film *Dracula,* and he's kept as a pet; the other Monroe pets are Chester, a literate and suspicious cat, and the dog Harold, who tells the story. Harold simply can't agree with Chester's opinion that Bunnicula is a vampire; he does admit that it's odd that during the night a succession of vegetables turn white, presumably drained of their color by some agency. Chester, who has read that vampires fear garlic, takes to spending his nights outside Bunnicula's garlic-surrounded cage, and there's some corroboration of the cat's suspicion when the rabbit weakens from starvation. A veterinarian puts Bunnicula on a liquid diet—and that ends the problem; Chester, whose peculiar behavior has worried the Monroes, is given therapy and immediately becomes passionately interested in self-help therapy. The vampire issue is never clarified, which may disappoint some readers, but the plot is less important in the story than the style: blithe, sophisticated, and distinguished for the wit and humor of the dialogue. If readers like shaggy dog stories at all, they'd have to search hard for a funnier one.

600   Howe, Deborah. *Teddy Bear's Scrapbook;* by Deborah and James Howe; illus. by David S. Rose. Atheneum, 1980. 79-22794. ISBN 0-689-30746-2. 73p. $7.95.

2–4   Just right for the primary grades readers, and the episodic structure of
*   this blithe story makes it just right for reading aloud to younger chil-
        dren—especially since the remembered adventures are told by a teddy
        bear to his owner. The seven tales are part dialogue between the two,
        part recounting by Teddy; they are framed by a conversation that sets
        the stage and are concluded by a charming bit of dialogue between
        Teddy and the little girl, an affirmation of their deep affection. The light
        tone, the humor, the yeastiness and wit of the writing style and the ad-
        ventures themselves (Teddy as a cowboy, an ace reporter, the discov-
        erer of the abominable snowman, etc.) have vitality, pace, and some
        unexpected twists—for example, the abominable snowman proves to be
        an oversize teddy bear named Clive Neville-Phillips who is a secret con-
        tributor to a major literary magazine.

601   **Howe,** James. *The Hospital Book;* illus. with photographs by Mal War-
        shaw. Crown, 1981. 80-27747. Hardcover ed. ISBN 0-517-54168-8; Paper
        ed. ISBN 0-517-54235-8. 95p. Hardcover ed. $10.95; Paper ed. $4.95.

2–4   Clear photographs on almost every page extend the text of an excellent
*   introduction to hospital procedures; this is simply enough written to be
        read, also, to younger children. Howe is candid and comprehensive in
        his descriptions of procedures, equipment, and personnel and equally
        candid about pain, differentiating between treatment that is painless
        (X-ray), uncomfortable but not painful (CAT scan) or painful if brief
        (drawing blood from a vein). The whole book is permeated by a sense
        that children are rational people, that telling them exactly what hurts or
        what's going to happen will evoke their cooperation and tolerance—and
        when the author addresses the question of stress and reaction, he never
        implies that children are any more or any less frightened or angry than
        adults. The text is in second person, and always clear.

602   **Howe,** James. *A Night Without Stars.* Atheneum, 1983. 82-16278. ISBN
        0-689-30957-0. 178p. $10.95.

5–7   The meaning of the title is the deep sleep of anesthesia, as eleven-year-
        old Maria learns from another hospital patient, Donald, so badly burn-
        scarred that other young patients call him "Monster Man." Maria is
        frightened about having open-heart surgery, in part because she doesn't
        understand what's being done to her. Gradually, she learns what's en-
        tailed, makes friends with other patients, and in particular learns to
        know Donald and enjoy his friendship. Reclusive, Donald responds
        warmly to Maria, the first child to accept him despite his appearance,
        and when the story ends it is clear that the friendship will continue af-
        ter the hospital experience is over. The plot is of less importance in this
        story than the perceptive handling of relationships, not only the friend-
        ship between Maria and Donald, but the supportive family relationships
        and the easy familiarity among the girls who are patients. The details of
        hospital routines and medical procedures are accurate and smoothly ab-
        sorbed into the narrative.

603   **Huddy,** Delia. *The Humboldt Effect.* Greenwillow, 1982. 82-9212. ISBN 0-688-01526-3. 157p. $9.50.

7–10
*
A sequel to *Time Piper* in which a time machine explained a twelfth-century legend about a Pied Piper and Luke, the protagonist of both stories, had worked on Tom Humboldt's time machine. Now Humboldt has a more advanced theory about time travel, and Luke heads the crew that carries out the research while on a submarine in the Mediterranean Sea. This is fine science fiction, deftly crafted in structure and style; it's also an effective story of love and friendship and the assumption of responsibility; it has drama and pace and one surprising twist that explains, within the fantasy framework, the genesis of a biblical legend. Super.

604   **Huddy,** Delia. *Time Piper.* Greenwillow, 1979. 78-24339. Trade ed. ISBN 0-688-80212-5; Library ed. ISBN 0-688-84212-7. 247p. Trade ed. $7.95; Library ed. $7.63 net.

7–9
In a particularly deft meshing of fantasy and realism, Huddy brings a medieval legend into the story of a strange and isolated girl and the young man who feels a protective love for her. This story, first published in England, is not a love story, however, but a science fantasy; it is written with depth and perception, at once tender in mood and gravid with suspense. Luke had known the girl, who called herself "Hare," in their village, where she was regarded with dislike and suspicion. Aloof, withdrawn, and independent, Hare turned up in London, where Luke had a temporary job on a project directed by a brilliant young scientist, Tom Humboldt. Humboldt had received funding for building a time machine. Is there something about him that draws Hare and others like her—for Luke discovers there are others like her—to him? Why have they massed, silently, to follow him? Does it have something to do with the children of twelfth-century Hamelin? Was there really a Pied Piper, or were these children drawn out of their time by Humboldt's machine? By the time of the stunning and satisfying conclusion, Luke knows he loves Hare and begins to feel that there may be hope for her response in the future. And all through the book, the details of the project, the relationships Luke has with the staff, the way in which a puzzled Luke keeps a secret watch on Hare build and knit toward the conclusion.

605   **Hughes,** Monica. *The Guardian of Isis.* Atheneum, 1982. 81-10837. ISBN 0-689-30902-2. 140p. $8.95.

7–10
In a sequel to *Keeper of the Isis Light,* the story begins several generations later with a protagonist who is the grandson and namesake of Jody N'Komo, who was a small boy and a minor character in the first book. The year, Earth time, is 2136; the community on the planet Isis is backward, primitive, and superstitious; and Jody is repeatedly in trouble because of a shrewd, questing mind that cannot accept the harsh dicta of

President Mark London. Those who have read the first book will recognize the fact that under Mark's reign, the regression to a primitive society has been deliberate and they will guess why. However, this second book stands on its own, and although new readers of the series may not enjoy the nuances, they will learn at the end of the book, when Jody ventures into the mountains and meets both the Guardian (a robot who has become deified) and the Keeper (who has become a symbol of ugliness and death) what the links are between the history of Isis and its mythology. This has a strong protagonist, good structure and pace, and a smooth, disciplined style.

606   **Hughes,** Monica. *Hunter in the Dark.* Atheneum, 1983. 82-13807. ISBN 0-689-30959-7. 131p. $9.95.

6–9   Mike's story begins as he drives through the pre-dawn darkness to an isolated camp site where he hopes to shoot a white-tail buck, to gain the antlered head that will mark both prowess and rite of passage. As he drives, settles into the camp site, and explores the wilderness, there are flashbacks, smoothly incorporated, that disclose his situation. Protected by his parents from the facts about the mysterious illness that has interrupted his adolescent years, Mike has discovered that he has leukemia. The flashback sequences are candid and perceptive in their depiction of the shattering effect on Mike and his parents, of his fear of death, and of his deep need to know and face the truth. It is his supportive friend Doug who has made it possible for Mike to collect his gear, borrow a truck, and fulfill his long-felt need to become a hunter. In the end, Mike finds he cannot pull the trigger and end the life of a beautiful animal, and with this comes his resignation and acceptance of his own death. A sad but not grim story, this speaks to the courage of youth with compassion and conviction.

607   **Hughes,** Monica. *The Keeper of the Isis Light.* Atheneum, 1981. 81-1340. ISBN 0-689-30847-7. 136p. $8.95.

7–10   In all the sixteen years since her parents had died, Olwen has never seen another human being on Isis, the planet where she lived quite happily with Guardian, a robot who was her friend and teacher. When a ship arrived from Earth, she introduced herself as the Keeper and welcomed them. Guardian insisted that she always must wear protective clothing and a mask, but Olwen didn't understand until Mark, the young man with whom she had a budding love affair, saw her—by chance—without those garments, and then she learned that she didn't look human, that Guardian had adapted her for survival in the harsh atmosphere of Isis. Mark's horror and her grief are a shocking and dramatic climax to an exciting and tautly-structured science fantasy, written with polish and developed with good momentum. The story ends with Olwen adjusted to her fate and aware for the first time, sympathetically, that her dear Guardian will be alone with the settlers when she dies. The theme of the story is inherent in Olwen's remark to the spaceship captain, who plans to return to Earth for another load of settlers: "What a pity that the prejudices cannot be left behind when you go into star-drive."

608   **Hughes,** Shirley. *Alfie Gets in First;* written and illus. by Shirley Hughes. Lothrop, 1982. 81-8427. Trade ed. ISBN 0-688-00848-8; Library ed. ISBN 0-688-00849-6. 29p. Trade ed. $8.50; Library ed. $7.63.

3–5
yrs.   The bow-windowed row houses of a typically British street are the background for Hughes' deftly realistic ink and wash drawings in a simple story that is firm in structure and smooth in writing style. Alfie, racing ahead of his mother and his baby sister as they return from grocery shopping, reaches the front door first; after Mom has unlocked the door and gone down the steps to get the baby, Alfie dashes into the hall shouting "I've won!" Unfortunately, he slams the door. Unfortunately, Mom's key is inside with Alfie. Crisis! Just as the milkman brings a ladder for the window cleaner to use in getting to an upstairs window, the door opens: a beaming Alfie has thought of a way the solve the problem. This should be very gratifying for young children who can share Alfie's pride in resourcefulness.

609   **Hughes,** Shirley. *Alfie Gives a Hand;* written and illus. by Shirley Hughes. Lothrop, 1984. 83-14883. Library ed. ISBN 0-688-02387-8; Trade ed. ISBN 0-688-02386-X. 30p. Library ed. $7.63; Trade ed. $8.50.

3–5
yrs.   A third story about a small English boy is as nice as the first two. Softly colored, the realistic pictures show some engagingly scruffy children of various ethnic backgrounds at a backyard birthday party at which the birthday boy, Bernard, is tiresomely obstreperous and aggressive. His mother copes as best she can, and the other children adjust to Bernard's behavior. Alfie is complimented on his behavior; a bit timid at his first party, Alfie clings to his security blanket until he has to choose between it and giving a comforting hand to another child. So what Alfie learns is that maybe, next time, he can manage without the blanket. Very nicely done: an appealing subject and protagonist add to the substance of a well-told story about a familiar situation.

610   **Hull,** Eleanor (Means). *The Summer People.* Atheneum, 1984. 83-15580. ISBN 0-689-31037-4. 217p. $11.95.

7–9   Periodically, as she rides the train from Denver to Baltimore, Genevieve looks back at her adolescent years in the small Colorado town where she has spent her summers. Primarily this is the story of a friendship and of Jenny's realization that the fact that she is Jewish will always mean, to her friend, that she is different. Hull gives a good picture of the ambivalent feelings of the summer people, and a touching, vivid picture of the social intricacies and loyalties of the colony as it affects Jenny.

611   **Hunt,** Patricia. *Koalas;* illus. with photographs. Dodd, 1980. 80-13717. ISBN 0-396-07849-4. 45p. $4.95.

2-4   Nature editor of *Life* magazine for many years as well as an elementary school teacher, Hunt writes direct and simple prose; the tone is quietly authoritative and the style casual but dignified. A continuous text is broken by topic headings, lightened by the use of photographs, and made accessible by an index. The text describes the koala and other marsupials, group and individual behavior, and the patterns of feeding, courtship, mating, breeding, and so on. Hunt also discusses predators, including people, and the experiences zoos have had with koalas.

612   **Hunt,** Roderick. *The Oxford Christmas Book for Children.* Oxford/Merrimack, 1983. ISBN 0-19-278104-9. 158p. $11.95.

4-6   A potpourri of Christmas material, this contains stories, poems, a play, information about Christmas customs, cartoons, projects, songs, etc. Illustrations are both diverse and profuse: photographs in black and white and in color, paintings and line drawings, and diagrams. There's even a crossword puzzle. Clearly the book, first published in England in 1981, has something for everybody and its range is broader than the focal group (grades 4–6) cited above. In a sense, therefore, it is diffuse, but the quality of most of the material is high; this should be useful in both home and institutional collections.

613   **Hunter,** Mollie. *Hold On to Love.* Harper, 1984. 83-47695. Trade ed. ISBN 0-06-022687-0; Library ed. ISBN 0-06-022688-9. 288p. Library ed. $11.89; Trade ed. $11.50.

7-10   A sequel to *A Sound of Chariots* is probably destined to be more popular with readers, both because of the love interest and because it is less concerned with bereavement. Bridie, now working in her grandfather's flower shop in Edinburgh, is taking night classes to help in her goal of becoming a writer. She is unconscionably rude to Peter, a classmate, because of a disappointment over a teacher; it's a year before she sees him again. Peter is "nice" enough to win even her very conservative grandparents' approbation, but his possessiveness irritates Bridie, and there's a rupture in the relationship. The advent of World War II and Peter's enlistment make Bridie remember her grandmother's advice about holding on to love, so she makes the overture; Peter responds joyfully, and the story ends with a marriage when Peter comes home on Survivor's Leave after his ship goes down at Dunkirk. This is a strong love story, not too sweet, and it evokes a vivid picture of the Scottish conservative, that stratum of urban merchants who had all the answers, and against whom Bridie could so easily have rebelled—save for the fact that she loved her kinfolk. This is also the story of a struggling young writer and as such it should appeal to all those readers who, secretly or openly, share Bridie's dreams.

614　　**Hunter,** Mollie. *The Knight of the Golden Plain;* illus. by Marc Simont. Harper, 1983. 82-48747. Trade ed. ISBN 0-06-022685-4; Library ed. ISBN 0-06-022686-2. 48p. Trade ed. $10.95; Library ed. $10.89.

3–5　　Young and handsome Sir Dauntless, dragon slayer supreme, is thwarted in his quest for a tiny golden bird by the evil Arriman, the demon magician. Arriman had stolen the voice of the lovely Princess Dorabella, and the dashing Sir Dauntless (who had of course immediately fallen in love with the mute beauty) had vowed to retrieve her voice, changed to a bird by Arriman's magic. His mission completed, Sir Dauntless rode toward his love but he remembered that he might be late for tea, and that "his lady mother would be extremely angry with him." This can be read as a gentle spoof or as the product of a child's imagination, and it's delightful either way. The style is fluent (nice to read aloud) and the structure tight. The story has a quiet humor that is echoed in the illustrations, which have the same combination of deliberate romantic cliché and just enough tongue-in-cheek to add spice.

615　　**Hunter,** Mollie. *The Third Eye.* Harper, 1979. 78-22159. 251p. Trade ed. $7.95; Library ed. $7.89 net.

6–9　　Dextrously constructed and smoothly written, a story set in contempo-
　*　　rary Scotland begins with an attention-getting incident, as fourteen-year-old Jinty (Janet) responds to a notice that she must come to the Office of the Procurator Fiscal to give evidence. Most of the story is told in flashbacks, as Jinty remembers her long-standing fear of the old earl whose death is being investigated, her growing awareness that he was—despite his reputation—a kind man, but one beset by fear. What he feared was the family curse, which stipulated that no eldest son would live to inherit the title. The earl has one son, and on his twenty-first birthday the earl dies. Jinty is one of the few who knows that his suicide is a father's sacrifice, and she is determined not to let the Procurator Fiscal discover this. There is a balance of other plot-threads: Jinty's discovery of her mother's past, her friendship with a blind child, and her concern about an older sister who has alienated their mother by marrying against her wishes. Hunter does a superb job of weaving the plot-threads into a rich whole, giving vivid impressions both of the well-defined characters and of the cohesive intricacy and continuity of village life.

616　　**Hunter,** Mollie. *You Never Knew Her As I Did!* Harper, 1981. 81-47114. Trade ed. ISBN 0-06-022678-1; Library ed. ISBN 0-06-022679-X. 216p. Trade ed. $10.50; Library ed. $9.89.

7–10　　The story of a period of time in the life of Mary, Queen of Scots, is told by Will Douglas, a sixteen-year-old by-blow of Sir William Douglas, who had been assigned the task of keeping Mary prisoner on an island. This is set at the time when Bothwell is in disgrace, suspected of the slaying of Darnley; Mary is the victim of the Earl of Moray's lust for power, and she is forced to abdicate so that Moray can act as regent. Young Will feels a loyalty to the Queen that changes to a devoted love as he comes to know her and helps to plan her escape. The story is adroitly fictionalized; Hunter uses facts when they are known and bases imagined incidents or dialogue on what is known of the persons who played parts in her tragic life story. This is written with skill, polish, and a high narrative sense; it brings history to life.

617   **Hurd,** Michael. *The Oxford Junior Companion to Music.* Second ed. Oxford, 1980. ISBN 0-19-314302-X. 353p. illus. $25.00.

6–   Hurd's revision is based on the original version by Percy Scholes; it has been brought up to date, simplified, and given a new format: double columns with space enough between them for pictures of musicians, some use of color in the illustrations, insets that spread across the two columns, and cross-referencing through bold type and arrows. Some of the older material about minor figures or developments has been dropped, and an effort has been made to give the book wider geographical scope. Since no single-volume book can include everything, there may be users who feel bereft because of omissions (Beatles, yes; Presley, no) but on the whole this is—as it was in the first edition—a fine reference source. The alphabetized entries are preceded by material on musical notation. The one weakness of the book is that the use of boxed insets at times interrupts the text; the entry for "programme music," for example, is broken by a full page of boxed articles on "Printing and engraving music" and "Puccini" and continues on the page after that.

618   **Hurd,** Thacher. *Mama Don't Allow;* written and illus. by Thacher Hurd. Harper, 1984. 83-47703. Library ed. ISBN 0-06-022690-0; Trade ed. ISBN 0-06-022689-7. 37p. Library ed. $11.89; Trade ed. $11.95.

K–2   In an engaging and nonsensical romp, a young possum whose uncle has sent him a saxophone for his birthday annoys his parents and local residents by his loud practicing; when Miles Possum forms a combo with three other animals, they are not appreciated save by the alligators. The combo is invited to play for an alligators' party aboard a riverboat. They're a success, but they find they are also destined to be the meal—they ingeniously save their lives by playing a lullaby so softly and sweetly that the alligators all fall asleep and the musicians can escape. Ebullient, fast-paced, and funny, the book includes the musical notation for the title song.

619   **Hurd,** Thacher. *Mystery on the Docks;* written and illus. by Thacher Hurd. Harper, 1983. 82-48261. Trade ed. ISBN 0-06-022701-X; Library ed. ISBN 0-06-022702-8. 29p. Trade ed. $9.95; Library ed. $9.89.

K–2   Bright, vigorous watercolor pictures illustrate a brisk little adventure story in which a humble restaurant cook, Ralph, is instrumental in rescuing his favorite opera star, Eduardo, from the dastardly rats who have kidnapped him. The two heroes, who jump into the fray when the police arrive on board, are mice, as are the police. The story takes place in the dockside diner where Ralph works and on the large ship on which he and Eduardo are held; Ralph uses flares in the crow's nest to attract police and Eduardo uses his powerful voice. There's plenty of action, a triumphant ending, and a sturdy story line, and the writing style is direct and nicely gauged for the read-aloud audience.

620   **Hurmence,** Belinda. *Tancy.* Houghton/Clarion, 1984. 83-19035. ISBN 0-89919-228-9. 203p. $11.95.

8–10   Born into slavery and working since childhood as personal attendant to her mistress, sixteen-year-old Tancy has grown up knowing only the small North Carolina plantation and its suppression, though she has been taught to read and write. When Emancipation comes, it takes her a while to leave "home," but the drive to find her mother (sold when Tancy was barely two) impels her into the wider world, where she finds love, work, and independence. Tancy's final integration of all the parts of her life is slightly contrived, but her striving for personal emancipation is movingly depicted against the turmoil of the period; her interaction with a wide range of interesting characters (black and white) dramatizes the suffering of slavery and the hopes and broken promises of freedom.

621   **Hurmence,** Belinda. *Tough Tiffany.* Doubleday, 1980. 79-6979. Trade ed. ISBN 0-385-15082-2; Library ed. ISBN 0-385-15083-0. 139p. Trade ed. $7.95; Library ed. $8.90 net.

5–7   Tiffany is eleven, a sensitive, curious child who likes to think she's tough; she is tough in the sense of having courage and stamina, but she's also charitable and loving. Youngest child of a large family, she is fascinated by the stories her grandmother tells of slave ancestors and local lore; she's worried about her mother's extravagance and eternal indebtedness; she's upset because an older sister is pregnant. Hurmence uses enough dialet to flavor the dialogue without burdening it; her characterizations are sharply drawn, and she has—in a fine first novel—used every situation in the book to develop and extend her characters, particularly the redoubtable Tiffany.

622   **Hurwitz,** Johanna. *Baseball Fever;* illus. by Ray Cruz. Morrow, 1981. 81-5633. Trade ed. ISBN 0-688-00701-4; Library ed. ISBN 0-688-00711-2. 128p. Trade ed. $7.95; Library ed. $7.63.

3–5   Ezra, ten, is a devoted baseball fan, a fact that is neither understood or condoned by his father, a European-born academician. There's frequent friction between the two, as Dad tries to get Ezra to read good books or to play chess; he buys Ezra a computerized chess game for his tenth birthday and agrees that he'll go to a ball game if Ezra can beat him in a chess game. That does happen, and it's the closing episode of the story, but the turning point in improved father-son relations comes when an influential colleague of Dad's discovers Ezra's knowledge, discloses his own love of baseball, and convinces Dad that Ezra's concentrated interest and apt memorization of baseball data indicate a high intelligence that will some day turn to other fields. A brisk, breezy story about a believable family is told with warmth and humor.

623   **Hurwitz,** Johanna. *Rip-Roaring Russell;* illus. by Lillian Hoban. Morrow, 1983. 83-1019. Trade ed. ISBN 0-688-02347-9; Library ed. ISBN 0-688-02348-7. 80p. Trade ed. $8.50; Library ed. $7.63.

4–6 yrs.   Six episodic chapters about the activities and problems of a preschool child who attends nursery school, envies his baby sister, and plays with neighborhood children. The action is low-keyed: Russell makes a friend at school, tries to watch a late television program but can't stay awake, learns that it's no fun to be treated as a baby, etc. This is both realistic and sunny, with good adult-child relationships, the appeal of everyday life experiences, and a light, humorous treatment.

624   **Hutchins,** Pat. *The Mona Lisa Mystery;* illus. by Laurence Hutchins. Greenwillow, 1981. 79-20263. Trade ed. ISBN 0-688-80243-5; Library ed. ISBN 0-688-84243-7. 184p. Trade ed. $8.95; Library ed. $8.59.

2–4   The lively third grade class that had an exciting, if improbable, adventure the year before (in *Follow That Bus!*) now takes off by bus and ferry for Paris and another, equally nonsensical swashing and buckling romp. There are mysterious bearded men, a theft of the *Mona Lisa*, a patently fake French teacher, much chasing about, the discovery that the school's head mistress is imprisoned in a Paris cellar, and of course, a triumphant conclusion, complete with recovery of the painting, television coverage, and the award of the Legion of Honor to the class. Absolutely nothing is meant to be taken seriously, so that all of the exaggeration, coincidence, contrivance, and stereotyped characterization become part of the fun.

625   **Hutchins,** Pat. *1 Hunter;* written and illus. by Pat Hutchins. Greenwillow, 1982. 81-6352. Trade ed. ISBN 0-688-00614-0; Library ed. ISBN 0-688-00615-9. 22p. Trade ed. $9.50; Library ed. $8.59.

2–5 yrs.   Many counting books move from one to ten, as this does; some of them recapitulate, as this does. But few of them tell a story that has a gentle message and is amusing, *and* is illustrated with the sort of originality and craftsmanship that has won the Kate Greenway Medal for its creator (*The Wind Blew*, 1974). Here an elderly hunter, bespectacled and grim, stalks past two elephants, three giraffes, four ostriches, and so on—and never sees any of them. The visual joke, easy for small children to spot, is that each group of animals is seen twice: first in part (as when the hunter marches between the tall legs of the giraffes or strides across the green stepping stones (crocodiles) of a pond, and second in fully identifiable view after the hunter has passed. As decorative as it is useful.

626   **Hutchins,** Pat. *The Tale of Thomas Mead;* written and illus. by Pat Hutchins. Greenwillow, 1980. 79-6398. Trade ed. ISBN 0-688-80282-6; Library ed. ISBN 0-688-84282-8. 31p. (Read-alone Books) Trade ed. $5.95; Library ed. $5.71.

1–2   Hutchins's humorous and colorful drawings add to the fun of a rhyming, mock-didactic text for beginning independent readers. The poetic refrain provides repetition, the vocabulary is simple but not stultified, and the rhyme and scansion are tidy. This is a tallish tale, and a funny one, as Thomas, who adamantly refuses to learn to read, has a series of disasters that culminate in his causing a multi-vehicle pile-up. (He couldn't read the "Don't Cross" sign). Jailed for jaywalking, Thomas receives a parental edict: he stays there until he learns to read. He's taught by two hulking cellmates, and learns rather easily; now he reads all the time. But his answer, when told to put his book away, is the same one he had given when he was coaxed to learn to read: "Why should I?"

627   **Huynh Quang Nhuong.** *The Land I Lost: Adventures of a Boy in Vietnam;* illus. by Vo-Dinh Mai. Harper, 1982. 80-8437. Trade ed. ISBN 0-06-024592-1; Library ed. ISBN 0-06-024593-X. 115p. Trade ed. $10.50; Library ed. $9.89.

5–7   Each chapter, in this book of reminiscence about the author's boyhood in a hamlet in the Vietnamese highlands, is a separate episode, although the same characters appear in many of the episodes. Some of the chapters are about members of the author's family, several are about family pets or work-animals, and several about encounters with some of the dangerous creatures of the area. The writing has an ingenuous quality that adds to the appeal of the strong sense of familial and communal ties that pervades the story; although some of the chapters are so detailed in describing animal encounters as to verge on the tedious, they are the exceptions; most of the text is direct and some of it is dramatic.

628   **Hyde,** Margaret Oldroyd. *Cry Softly! The Story of Child Abuse.* Westminister, 1980. 80-16465. ISBN 0-664-32666-8. 96p. $8.95.

6–9   Hyde discusses the physical, emotional, and sexual abuse of children by adults, primarily by parents, and cites the statistics of known cases as evidence of the fact that child abuse is growing in the United States; she also gives historical material about child abuse, with separate chapters on abusive practices in England and the United States. While the material is not as carefully organized as in most of Hyde's books, the text gives a great deal of information, not only about child abuse practices, but also about how to recognize cases of it, what the reader can do to report such cases, what kinds of help can be given battered children and abusive parents, what organizations (including hotlines) can provide such help. The author is careful to point out that other situations can cause similar symptoms, and that therefore professional opinion should be sought before action is taken. Sources of further information are listed, as is an index.

629   **Hyde,** Margaret Oldroyd. *Energy: the New Look.* McGraw-Hill, 1981. 80-21376. ISBN 0-07-031552-3. 138p. $7.95.

6–9   Always a dependably lucid and accurate writer, Hyde examines the problems of the dwindling sources of natural fuels, and investigates the ways in which people the world over are finding alternative sources of energy: solar power, windmills, synthetic fuels, fuels from waste, geothermal energy, fusion techniques, and many other methods—some old, some new—that can fill the needs of our society. Pollution and conservation are also discussed, as are the needs for large-scale cooperation in a global fuel emergency. The material is well organized, the coverage broad. Appended are a list of sources of information, a bibliography, a list of energy hotlines, and an index.

630   **Hyde,** Margaret O. *Foster Care and Adoption.* Watts, 1982. 81-21971. ISBN 0-531-04403-3. 90p. $8.90.

6–9   With her usual objectivity and clarity, Hyde surveys many aspects of foster care: the rights of children and of parents, the strengths and weaknesses of placement practices, the possibility that preventive or early therapeutic care for families could improve situations that, if allowed to continue, could or would develop a need for acute or sustained or unsuccessful action, for which the state pays a financial toll and—more important—the individuals may pay a tragic toll. The topic of adoption is less fully covered, but the coverage is adequate; access to the information provided in the book is given through an index; also appended are a bibliography and a list of sources for further information.

631   **Hyde,** Margaret O. *The Rights of the Victim.* Watts, 1983. 82-17610. ISBN 0-531-04596-X. 117p. $9.90.

7–   Because the American system of justice is oriented toward the rights of the accused, government has traditionally taken little recognition of the welfare of the victim, and little responsibility for victims. Statistics from the Bureau of Justice show that murder occurs in our country at the rate of one every 24 minutes; rape, one every 7 minutes; home burglary every 10 seconds, etc. There are, therefore, thousands of victims; the processes of litigation and imprisonment cost taxpayers millions. Who helps the victim? Can those victimized help themselves? Is there anything one can do to avert victimization? Hyde discusses the historical relationship of the criminal to victims, gives some answers to the questions posed here, and describes some of the growing number of programs that have been instituted on behalf of victims of crimes. The crisp and informative text should be useful because of the facts it gives about what help is available and what precautions one can take in specific circumstances. A bibliography, a glossary, and an index are included, as well as lists of state offices that deal with redress for crime victims and of sources of further information.

632   **Hyde,** Margaret Oldroyd. *Sexual Abuse: Let's Talk About It.* Westminster, 1984. 83-27346. ISBN 0-664-32713-3. 93p. $8.95.

7–   Although this book seems to be primarily addressed to adults, it may also be of interest to young adults who are baby-sitters, have younger siblings, or still suffer from the effects of sexual abuse when they were younger. Although she mentions fleetingly that there are female offenders, Hyde describes a male abuser of children in every example she cites. Save for that minor flaw, the book is very good: it is forthright and lucid, it gives good advice on helping children cope with advances without frightening them, and it gives information about sources of help (hot lines, publications, and agencies of various kinds) both within the text and in two lists that precede the index.

633   **Ireson,** Barbara, ed. and comp. *Tales Out of Time.* Philomel, 1981. 80-25362. ISBN 0-399-20786-4. 247p. $9.95.

7–10   A fine collection of tales, some from such established masters of science fiction as Ray Bradbury and John Wyndham, others from writers who usually work in another genre, such as Walter de la Mare and John Rowe Townsend. The unifying theme, as the title indicates, is time-shift, and it is handled in an interesting variety of ways in this anthology.

634   **Irwin,** Hadley. *What About Grandma?* by Lee Hadley and Ann Irwin. Atheneum, 1982. 81-10809. ISBN 0-689-50224-9. 165p. $8.95.

6–9   Wyn, the Grandma of the title, is in a nursing home when the story starts, recovering from a broken hip; she has told her son that she doesn't think she can manage alone in a big house, so her daughter and grandchild, sixteen-year-old Rhys, arrive to clean the house and prepare it for sale. Wyn, however, changes her mind, signs herself out, and comes home. When her mother decides to stay for the summer, Rhys is delighted, because by then she's become smitten with the young golf instructor she sees often, on and off the links. As the summer passes, all three generations of the family grow closer, know each other better, love with more compassion; the story ends with Grandma's death. There are no dramatic events in the story, but it moves with a strong flow, perceptive in its characterization and particularly acute in exploring the many facets of the relationship of Wyn and her daughter; the authors (Lee Hadley and Ann Irwin) focus on the sadness of an old woman's final days, but they provide contrast by having other characters who look back on other times and other loves.

635   **Isadora,** Rachel. *Ben's Trumpet;* written and illus. by Rachel Isadora. Greenwillow, 1979. 78-12885. 30p. $6.95.

K–3   Isadora uses a variety of techniques in black and white illustrations that are startling in their effectiveness, very much in the mood of the twenties and art deco. Sophisticated and often abstract, the pictures may appeal more to adults than to children, particularly in the movement and rhythm of the musicians. Ben is a small black boy who, listening to music that reaches his fire escape perch from the nearby Zig Zag Jazz Club, plays an imaginary trumpet; on his way home from school each day, he stops to watch the practice sessions. Other children tease him, but Ben's moment of glory comes when the trumpeter comes out for a break, sees the child, and takes him to the Club. He hands Ben a trumpet and, the story ends, ". . . we'll see what we can do." The story is slight, the appeal and strength of the book being in the evocative art.

636   **Isadora,** Rachel. *City Seen from A to Z;* written and illus. by Rachel Isadora. Greenwillow, 1983. 82-11966. Trade ed. ISBN 0-688-01802-5; Library ed. ISBN 0-688-01803-3. 28p. Trade ed. $8.00; Library ed. $7.63.

3–6 yrs.   While the activities or objects or concepts in this urban alphabet book are not always restricted to the city scene (friend, hat, music, night) the illustrations show the city background most of the time. They reflect the multiethnic composition of a city, and they seldom include words that are not easily comprehensible. The first letter of each word (sometimes two words, like "Roller skate") is in brown, the rest of the word in black, adequately distinguished from, but blending with the soft, soft illustrations that are highly textured, often stippled, dramatic in composition.

637   **Isadora,** Rachel. *Opening Night;* written and illus. by Rachel Isadora. Greenwillow, 1984. 83-20791. Library ed. ISBN 0-688-02727-X; Trade ed. ISBN 0-688-02726-1. 30p. Library ed. $9.55; Trade ed. $10.25.

K–2   The versatile Isadora uses watercolor in soft-edged paintings that capture the backstage atmosphere, the beauty of the costumes, and the fluidity of the dancers in a story that is more setting than plot. Heather and Libby are bugs in the faerie world of "Midsummer Night's Dream" and Heather is nervous about her brief solo on opening night. The text does not give the name of the ballet or explain who Bottom is; there's simply a reference, "There's Bottom. He's so funny," as a male dancer sits with ass-head in place but otherwise uncostumed. This may have to be explained to some children, but most of the activity and dancers' roles are made clear, and the excitement and triumph (roses for both children!) are vividly conveyed.

638   **Isele,** Elizabeth, *Pooks;* illus. by Chris L. Demarest. Lippincott, 1983.
82-48462. Trade ed. ISBN 0-397-32044-2; Library ed. ISBN 0-397-32045-0.
25p. Trade ed. $8.95; Library ed. $8.89.

5–7   Jaunty, flyaway line drawings, with touches of red to give variety, show
yrs.   the affection between the busy conductor-cellist, Mstislav Rostropovich,
and the tiny dog Pooks, his constant companion. Pooks should delight
children: she's always there, strapped into her own airplane seat (with
the Maestro in the middle and his cello on its own seat), dozing next to
the podium, or winding her leash about her master's legs. The ending
is the only nonsensical note, as Pooks dashes onstage where a singer is
receiving applause, bangs on the piano keys, and is given a rose by the
soloist. A bright, brisk little story.

639   **Isenbart,** Hans-Heinrich. *A Duckling Is Born;* tr. by Catherine Edwards
Sadler; illus. with photographs by Othmar Baumli. Putnam, 1981.
81-5205. ISBN 0-399-20778-3. 36p. $9.95.

2–4   Color photography of good quality includes enlargements and action
*   shots; the pictures are smoothly integrated with the text, which is direct, clear, and informative and is not written down to young readers—
i.e., Isenbart uses correct terms like "retina" and "embryo" but uses no
difficult words unnecessarily. A handsome book and an informative
one.

640   **Jacobs,** Francine. *Supersaurus;* illus. by D. D. Tyler. Putnam, 1982.
81-7375. ISBN 0-399-61150-9. 48p. (A See and Read Book). $6.99.

1–3   Simply written but not written down for beginning readers, this
describes the discovery, in 1972, of an enormous dinosaur bone. Found
and identified by a scientist, the fossil proved to be the hip bone of a
dinosaur larger than any yet known. The subject is appealing, the narrative framework restrained, the text useful in establishing the ways in
which scientists compare and classify materials.

641   **Jacobs,** Joseph. *King of the Cats;* ad. and illus. by Paul Galdone.
Houghton/Clarion, 1980. 79-16659. ISBN 0-395-29030-9. 32p. $8.95.

K–3   Galdone follows closely, in his adaptation, the version by Joseph Jacobs
*   on which this tale is based (from *More English Fairy Tales*) but has simplified the exposition and removed the dialect from the dialogue. A
smooth retelling, the story is handsomely illustrated by large-scale pictures that fill, but do not crowd, the pages; Galdone's draughtsmanship
is at its best here, with effective composition and use of color to create
the eerie graveyard scenes and the staring, frightened eyes of the old
gravedigger and his wife as he tells the tale of the burial service for the
King of Cats. The style isn't quite as flavorful as that of Jacobs, but the
simplified language makes this version a good choice for telling to
young children or for reading aloud.

642   **Jacobs,** Joseph. *The Three Sillies;* ad. and illus. by Paul Galdone. Houghton/Clarion, 1981. 80-22197. ISBN 0-395-30172-6. 38p. $9.95.

K–3   Galdone's wild-eyed, active people and animals, drawn with comic flair and livened with just enough color, add a slighty manic dimension to a traditional noodlehead story from English folklore. The bonny (but daft) fiancee of a stalwart youth is overcome by how awful it would be if she married and if her husband were to go to the cellar and if an ax fell on his head—and she sobs bitterly. Each of her equally silly parents sobs sympathetically at the terrible thought. The bridegroom goes off saying that if he ever finds three sillier people he'll come back to be wed. He does find them, he decides his three sillies are not so bad, and he comes home to marry his own dear silly. An amusing tale, as nice for telling as for reading, is adapted and illustrated in equally blithe spirits.

643   **Jacobs,** William Jay. *Mother, Aunt Susan and Me; The First Fight For Women's Rights.* Coward, 1979. 78-25715. ISBN 0-698-20480-8. 61p. illus. with photographs. $7.50.

5–7   The story of the long battle for women's rights is told from the viewpoint of Harriot Stanton, whose life spanned the early struggles of her mother, Elizabeth Cady Stanton, and her "aunt," Susan B. Anthony, to obtain the vote for women, and the beginning of the battle to pass an Equal Rights Amendment, a cause in which she herself was active in the 1930s. Although the contributions of Anthony and Stanton are recorded in many books for young readers, this has—due to the first-person format—an intimacy and immediacy that make the details of the fight for equality vivid. Liberally illustrated with photographs, the book is well researched, capably written, and prudent in its balance of dramatic events and personal observations by the putative "author," Harriot.

644   **Jagendorf,** Moritz Adolf. *The Magic Boat and Other Chinese Folk Stories;* by M. A. Jagendorf and Virginia Weng; illus. by Wan-Go Weng. Vanguard, 1980. 79-67814. ISBN 0-8149-0823-3. 236p. $9.95.

4–7   The focus of this anthology is on the diverse peoples within China; the tales have been chosen in part to represent this diversity, grouping the selections by source and including substantial background information in the "Notes About the Ethnic Groups" that precedes the bibliography. There are stories of folk heroes, why stories, beast tales, tales of filial or marital devotion, and—among the few stories with humor—some trickster tales. Competently told, the stories include many of the themes and motifs that are in folk material everywhere: the magic talisman, kindness rewarded, justice (or revenge) deserved, the setting of tasks, or the quest. A fine anthology for reading alone, reading aloud, or storytelling.

645   **James,** Elizabeth. *How to Write a Great School Report;* by Elizabeth James and Carol Barkin. Lothrop, 1983. 83-764. Library ed. ISBN 0-688-02283-9; Paper ed. ISBN 0-688-02278-2. 76p. Library ed. $7.63; Paper ed. $5.50.

4–6   The authors give sensible advice very clearly in a crisp and logically organized text, with good examples to help clarify the procedures they advocate for gathering and collating material as well as for the actual writing of a school report. Included in the book are suggestions for finding sources of information, using library catalogs and reference books, assembling material in a chart, choosing material from notes, and the form of the paper.

646   **Janeczko,** Paul B. *Don't Forget To Fly: A Cycle of Modern Poems;* ed. by Paul B. Janeczko. Bradbury, 1981. 81-10220. ISBN 0-87888-187-5. 144p. $9.95.

7–   A splendid selection of modern poetry has been chosen with discrimina-
*   tion and arranged in an innovatory and sensible pattern, for Janeczko has grouped the poems so that they flow from one subject to another. Almost every major contemporary poet is represented, and most of the poems are brief, lyric, quiet, and strong. A lovely book to read alone or aloud.

647   **Janeczko,** Paul B. *Loads of Codes and Secret Ciphers.* Macmillan, 1984. 84-5791. ISBN 0-02-747810-6. 108p. illus. with diagrams. $10.95.

5–   There are many excellent books about codes, and most of them, after describing codes and ciphers, give some examples for the readers to try; here, the emphasis shifts, and the focus is on how-to-do-it. Janeczko gives suggestions for setting up one's own code, for decoding, for assembling a cipher wheel or building a telegraph key. An index gives access to the contents, which include historical material and are clear in giving instructions for compiling and cracking the various systems it describes.

648   **Janeczko,** Paul B. *Postcard Poems; A Collection of Poetry for Sharing.* Bradbury, 1979. 79-14192. ISBN 0-87888-155-7. 105p. $8.95.

5–   A very pleasant, very personal choice of poems short enough to be used on a postcard, this; the compiler, a high school English teacher, takes as his theme the lines from the first selection, Judith Hemsche-meyer's "Gift," "Let me wrap a poem around you . . . a poor shawl for your perfect throat." The introduction suggests that the poems be shared by passing them on, that "Good poetry is an endangered species. It needs to be protected from extinction." Most of Janeczko's choices are the work of contemporary writers: Shapiro, Nemerov, Swenson, Brautigan, Hughes, Sandburg, Giovanni, Graves . . . a knowledgeable skimming of brief delights.

649   **Jaquith,** Priscilla. *Bo Rabbit Smart for True: Folktales from the Gullah;* illus. by Ed Young. Philomel, 1981. 80-13275. Trade ed. ISBN 0-399-20793-7; Library ed. ISBN 0-399-61179-7. 55p. Trade ed. $9.95; Library ed. $9.99.

K–3   Scholarly notes about the theories of Gullah origin precede the retelling
*   of four tales, and notes on those tales follow them, as does a bibliography. The craftiness of Bo Rabbit will be familiar and appealing to most children; indeed the tales themselves will be familiar, since they appear in several cultures as variants. Here the illustrations add to the humor of the stories, flavorful in their restrained use of the distinctive Gullah speech, with deft, soft pencil drawings that are arranged in strips of frames (like a reel of film) down the outside edges of each page. Text and pictures are beautifully integrated, the stories are timeless and universal in appeal, and the telling has a vitality that makes this an excellent choice for reading alone or aloud, as well as for storytelling.

650   **Jaspersohn,** William. *The Ballpark;* written and illus. with photographs by William Jaspersohn. Little, 1980. 79-22835. Hardcover ed. ISBN 0-316-45812-0; Paper ed. ISBN 0-316-45811-2. 120p. Hardcover ed. $8.95; Paper ed. $4.95.

4–7   Profusely illustrated with photographs, the text describes in great detail all of the myriad activities that go on in a major league ballpark on the day of a home game. The place is Fenway Park, the game is played between the Red Sox and the Kansas City Royals, and there are many pictures of the players on both teams; the focus is not on the game, however, but on other aspects of the day, and baseball fans should enjoy the behind-the-scenes view of preparations in the commissary, the offices, the press box, the locker rooms, the scoreboard, and on the field. Bits of odd information include such items as the fact that an array of toiletries is provided for visiting teams, or the fact that the home plate umpire spends time before the game rubbing a special kind of mud on sixty baseballs. The writing is crisp and rather dry, but there's inherent appeal in the subject, and the material is nicely organized and informative.

651   **Jaspersohn,** William. *A Day in the Life of a Television News Reporter;* written and illus. with photographs by William Jaspersohn. Little, Brown, 1981. 80-26203. ISBN 0-316-45813-9. 96p. $9.95.

4–6   Clear photographs, carefully placed so that no captions are needed, illustrate a text printed on pages that have a clean, spacious appearance. As he has done in *One Day in the Life of a Veterinarian,* Jaspersohn gives as much information about techniques, career preparation, milieu, etc. as he does about his subject. The news reporter whose day is covered is Dan Rea, on the staff of WBZ-TV in Boston; the text not only describes Rea's day but also the equipment used on location and in the studio, the work of the other members of the station, and the way in which a script is prepared and processed. The material should be of interest to readers, it's given clearly, and the information is nicely spaced and paced in a continuous text.

652   **Jennings,** Coleman A., ed. *Plays Children Love: A Treasury of Contemporary and Classic Plays for Children;* ed. by Coleman A. Jennings and Aurand Harris; illus. by Susan Swan. Doubleday, 1981. 80-2412. ISBN 0-385-17096-3. 678p. $15.95.

4–   In this useful collection of favorite plays, seven are for adult performers and the other seven meant for children to perform. Those in the first group are longer, and each is preceded by information on where to get scripts and pay royalties, information also provided for the second set of plays. Production notes are provided. The second portion of the book begins with a long introduction to an improvisational approach to staging, which more or less serves as a substitute for individual production notes; the plays in the second group tend to be both shorter and simpler than those in the first. Among the plays are "The Sleeping Beauty," "Tom Sawyer," "Punch and Judy," "Winnie-the-Pooh," "Jack and the Beanstalk," and "Androcles and the Lion."

653   **Jeschke,** Susan. *Perfect the Pig;* written and illus. by Susan Jeschke. Holt, 1981. 80-39998. ISBN 0-03-058622-4. 36p. $9.95.

K–2   Strong lines and soft textures are combined in Jeschke's pencil drawings, spare and occasionally humorous in details. They illustrate a love-lost-and-found story that has a nice contrast between the fantasy of the events and the blandness of the style. The writing is direct and simple, the plot equally modest: spurned by the other pigs because he has wings (awarded by a fairy pigmother for his good deed) a piglet flies to the city and is lucky enough to meet an artist who dotes on him, uses him as a model, and feeds him tasty foods. One day, exercising, Perfect is lost in a fog, picked up by an exploitive showman, and forced to fly in costume for his captor, who feeds the pig on garbage. Fortunately, the artist sees a poster, comes to the show, claims her pig, and they live happily if not forever after in a new little house in the country.

654   **Jesperson,** James. *Rams, Roms, & Robots;* written by James Jesperson and Jane Fitz-Randolph; illus. with diagrams by Bruce Hiscock and with photographs. Atheneum, 1984. 84-3001. ISBN 0-689-31063-3. 149p. $13.95.

7–10   There have been many books published that describe the history, operation, usefulness, and potential of the computer. Few of them are as clear and precise as is this book, which also has easily readable albeit not too simplified writing. The text draws a clear distinction between the analog and digital computer, giving adequate historical background; as the title suggests, computer memory and robots are discussed, and so are many other facets of computer function: encoding, storage of information by laser beams, and artificial intelligence. A glossary and a relative index are included.

655   **Jessel,** Camilla. *Life at the Royal Ballet School;* written and illus. with photographs by Camilla Jessel. Methuen, 1979. 79-12162. ISBN 0-416-30191-6. 144p. $10.95.

6–   Unlike most books about ballet, this is designed neither to present ballet history, attempt to teach the art, or introduce contemporary dancers and choreographers. It is a most successful effort to show the slow, arduous, dedicated work that goes into becoming a ballet dancer; the focus is not on examples of perfection but on improvement. Jessel's excellent photographs show individual children and class groups as they progress through degrees of proficiency, and the pictures—like the text—emphasize both the exercises that strengthen the dancer's body and the individual movements to which they contribute grace and control. The text also describes the ways in which students are evaluated, schooled in other subjects, and guided to either a career in the Royal Ballet, or, if they must, for any reason, be dropped from the school's program, to an alternate career. Informative, clearly written, and crisp in attitude.

656   **Jonas,** Ann. *Round Trip;* written and illus. by Ann Jonas. Greenwillow, 1983. 82-12026. Trade ed. ISBN 0-688-01772-X; Library ed. ISBN 0-688-01781-9. 30p. Trade ed. $8.50; Library ed. $7.63.

K–4   Black and white drawings, dramatic and effective, are used to illustrate a trip from a small town to the city and—turning the book upside down so that the pictures are reversed—back again. The text consists of one descriptive line on each page of a double-page spread; whichever way the book is held, the single line is on the verso page. Occasionally some of the details that will form part of the reversed picture are obvious (the upside-down words that will form part of a sign, the black rectangles that will be chimneys) but the treat-to-come is never wholly identifiable before it's seen right-side-up. Ingenious and attractive, this should encourage children to enjoy being observant.

657   **Jonas,** Ann. *When You Were a Baby;* written and illus. by Ann Jonas. Greenwillow, 1982. 81-12800. Trade ed. ISBN 0-688-00863-1; Library ed. ISBN 0-688-00864-X. 24p. Trade ed. $9.00; Library ed. $8.59.

2–4   Although this has more ornamental detail it is in the same style as the yrs.   paintings of Harlow Rockwell: simply composed, uncluttered, using large blocks of color. This shows, at the beginning, a baby's plump, brown feet waving in the air above its crib (and looking a bit out of scale) and, at the end, two sturdy legs in socks and shoes planted firmly, independently on the floor. In between, there's a list of all the things you couldn't do when you were a baby: build blocks, make sand molds, eat with a spoon, sail boats in a bathtub, etc. "But now you can!" the text ends. Not a wholly new idea, but nicely executed, probably a morale builder to a small child who doesn't always realize how much she or he has already learned.

658   **Jones,** Adrienne. *A Matter of Spunk.* Harper, 1983. 82-47710. Trade ed.
ISBN 0-06-023053-3. Library ed. ISBN 0-06-023054-1. 320p. Trade ed.
$12.95; Library ed. $12.89.

6–9   In a sequel to *Whistle Down a Dark Lane* Margery continues her reminiscences about her childhood in the 1920's. Deserted (albeit politely) by
her husband, Margery's mother has taken her two daughters to California, to a Theosophical colony where they meet a movie star, a hermit,
and a hypochondriac who's foisted on them as a houseguest. Eventually the three adjust to separation and divorce, to being homesick for
Atlanta, to independence and—in 1929—to the depression. All through
these years, the two girls grow and change and react to their changing
circumstances, the inflections and nuances of their lives pictured with
insight and described in a story with a controlled but sustained narrative flow.

659   **Jones,** Adrienne. *Whistle Down a Dark Lane.* Harper, 1982. 81-48661.
Trade ed. ISBN 0-06-023063-0; Library ed. ISBN 0-06-023064-9. 288p.
Trade ed. $12.95; Library ed. $12.89.

6–9   The story Margery tells as an adult looks back to the years just after
World War I, when she was seven and her sister Blainey ten. Although
this is primarily the story of the children's reaction (and their mother's)
to Daddy's decision to leave them, it is also a good period story that
includes some trenchant and sensitive observations on black-white relationships, and on the suffragette movement. Jones is astute in describing the intricacies of relationships in the summer colony in the Blue
Ridge Mountains where most of the action occurs, and equally perceptive in depicting the ways in which her major characters adapt to
change; one of the most dramatic episodes of the book concerns the Ku
Klux Klan. A strong story, smoothly structured and written.

660   **Jones,** Diana Wynne. *Archer's Goon.* Greenwillow, 1983. 83-17199. ISBN
0-688-02582-X. 241p. $10.50.

7–10   Howard is an adolescent, his sister Anthea (always called Awful) is a
  *   belligerent eight, and both of them are surprised, when they come
home from school one day, to find the Goon sitting in their kitchen.
Very tall, strong, and taciturn, the Goon announces that he's come to
collect the two thousand their father owes Archer. It isn't money, it develops, but two thousand words he owes Archer. That's the realistic
beginning of a highly original fantasy in which seven wizard siblings
have taken over control of an English town. One of them is using the
words that Howard's father writes every month to consolidate his
power—but which one? Persecuted by all of them, Howard's family
leads a beleaguered life until the last surprising discovery of the identity
of the seventh wizard. The story is a smooth integration of realism and
fantasy; the writing has flow and wit; the characters are strongly defined, the structure intricate but so deftly developed that it is not confusing. A most intriguing book.

661   Jones, Diana Wynne. *Fire and Hemlock.* Greenwillow, 1984. 84-4084. ISBN 0-688-02963-9. 341p. $13.00

6–9   An intricately woven, highly original fantasy is firmly meshed in its realistic matrix to provide a long and satisfying read that also has a subtle but powerful love interest. The story begins with Polly, packing for her first year at college, musing over her childhood and trying to piece together some wispy memories that don't quite fit, some associations that are elusive. As the past events emerge, it becomes increasingly clear that occult forces have played a part in her childhood friendship with a young musician who has befriended her—but why are there some people who seem bent on thwarting the friendship and who even threaten her welfare? The characters, the dialogue, and the style are impressive.

662   Jones, Diana Wynne. *The Magicians of Caprona.* Greenwillow, 1980. 79-26272. Trade ed. ISBN 0-688-80283-4; Library ed. ISBN 0-688-84283-6. 223p. Trade ed. $7.95; Library ed. $7.63.

5–7   In the parallel world of Chrestomanci (*Charmed Life*) the great enchanter appears again, this time playing a brief but vital role in the story of two fueding Italian families. The mythical town is Caprona, the families are the Petrocchis and the Montanas, and the cause of their great enmity is as little remembered as their burning rivalry is little forgotten. For the two are rivals in the creation of spells, and no business, in Caprona, can be transacted without the protection of spells. When Tonino Montana disappears, his kin are sure it is the Petrocchis (the Petrocchis are sure that the Montanas have taken their little Angelica) and it takes the combined powers of Chrestomanci, the Montana's telepathic cat, and the spell-casting ability of the two children to detect the dark enchanter who is fomenting trouble between the families and plunging Caprona into war. Tonino and Angelica, thrown together and magically reduced to a small Punch and a small Judy, have each felt inadequate because they were less gifted than others in their families; they discover that together they have a potent magic, and through them (and Chrestomanci) the family feud ends, the Romeo-and-Juliet secret love of Rosa Montana and Marco Petrocchi is bared. Best of all, Tonino and Angelica, by pooling their magic, find the true words of the guardian Angel of Caprona, a golden figure that takes flight when the true words of the Capronese hymn are sung. As is always true of the best fantasy, this is firmly based in—and adroitly meshed with—realism; the setting, the characters, and the dialogue are vivid, and the writing style is polished. What adds a special patina to the story are the ingenuity of the whole concept and the zest and pace of its development.

663   Jones, Diana Wynne. *Witch Week.* Greenwillow, 1982. 82-6074. ISBN 0-688-01534-4. 211p. $9.50.

5–7   Why would a teacher in an English school be so disturbed when he
*   finds an anonymous note saying that somebody in the class is a witch?

Because, in this outstandingly crafted fantasy, witchcraft is the ultimate evil in the society, and several of the resident pupils are suspected of being witches—as indeed they are, although their witchery is not evil. Charles knows that he is a witch, but all he wants to do is get away from the school and its bullies; most of the class he's in suspect Nan, who doesn't even realize she's a witch until a broom she's been teased to fly actually takes off. They and three other children get into a fearful tangle and are saved by the urbane and omniscient Chrestomanci, the magician who has appeared in the author's earlier stories. This is a remarkably adroit blending of vivid fantasy, a funny and perceptive school story, and a thoughtful commentary on how thin the line is that separates what is from what might be.

664   **Jones,** Rebecca C. *Angie and Me.* Macmillan, 1981. 81-4367. ISBN 0-02-747980-3. 113p. $7.95.

4–6   "Who ever heard of someone dying of swollen knees," Jenna thinks, as she waits for the family doctor to tell her what's wrong. She's quite unprepared for the diagnosis: juvenile rheumatoid arthritis. Arthritis? At age eleven? But Jenna is sent to a hospital and finds she's scheduled for a long program of therapy and medication. She also finds Angie, her roommate. Angie is honest, tough, friendly and more courageous than Jenna knows until she finally learns how ill Angie is; she dies just before Jenna is ready to be discharged, and it's a painful adjustment. The first-person approach is convincingly that of a pre-teenager, the hospital atmosphere and medical facts are smoothly incorporated into the writing, and the story—although it has no strong story line—holds interest both because of the setting and because it so vividly conveys the change in attitude and viewpoint of one who has had a serious illness that may prove a permanent handicap.

665   **Jones,** Terry. *Fairy Tales;* illus. by Michael Foreman. Schocken, 1983. 81-23227. ISBN 0-8052-3807-7. 127p. $14.95.

3–5   First published in England, this oversize book is based on stories Jones invented for his daughter, and the illustrations—whether small black and white sketches or rich, imaginative full-color-pages—are beautifully attuned to the combined strains of the romantic and of the comic/grotesque that are in the writing. Not all the thirty stories are of high calibre, but many of them have touches that are reminiscent of Andersen when he is humorous or of Thurber when he is satirical. All of the stories are short, are fitting by their style and pace to read aloud, and are humorous; the one weakness of the book is that occasionally Jones works too hard at being funny.

666   **Jones,** Toeckey. *Go Well, Stay Well.* Harper, 1980. 79-3603. Trade ed. ISBN 0-06-023061-4; Library ed. ISBN 0-06-023062-2. 202p. Trade ed. $7.95; Library ed. $7.89.

7–10   The story of an interracial friendship in South Africa is told from the viewpoint of fifteen-year-old Candy, a member of the English community. She first meets Becky, a Zulu, when they are shopping in Johannesburg; Candy hurts her ankle and Becky helps her. It is hard for the girls to overcome both their own prejudice and their fear of the reactions of others. Where can they meet without censure or even hostility? Candy's parents have always been liberal, but they show their disapproval of Becky's visits to their home, the only safe place for the two girls to meet. Jones examines a range of attitudes on apartheid, including the differences between those of the British community and those of the Afrikaans; she doesn't minimize the harshness and persecution of apartheid or posit any easy solution for Becky and Candy: they have acknowledged difficulties in accepting each other. What she does say is that with time, patience, and candor, friendship is possible. The characters and their relationships are depicted clearly and with some depth, and the setting should be of particular interest to readers, since so little material about contemporary South Africa is available for children and young adults.

667   **Judy,** Susan. *Putting on a Play;* by Susan and Stephen Judy. Scribner, 1982. 82-3179. ISBN 0-684-17452-9. 150p. illus. $12.95.

5–9   The authors, English professors who have had experience in conducting theater workshops, address their readers in a casual, conversational style. Their general approach is to give advice on preparation, publicity, and performance but to leave the specifics of execution to the readers, i.e., to inform and encourage rather than to direct. Since they give a great deal of sensible advice about every aspect of putting on a play, the approach should be successful in stimulating creative expression. The text includes discussions about warming up, role playing, tips on acting and using one's voice, and making costume, props, and scenery as well as the many kinds of plays one can put on (reader's theater, puppet plays, improvisations, radio plays, etc.) and it also gives suggestions for writing a play. This is comprehensive, practical, and often imaginative. An index and a glossary of stage terms are provided.

668   **Jukes,** Mavis. *Like Jake and Me;* illus. by Lloyd Bloom. Knopf, 1984. 83-8380. Library ed. ISBN 0-394-95608-7; Trade ed. ISBN 0-394-85608-2. 28p. Library ed. $11.99; Trade ed. $11.95.

2–4   Soft pastel paintings capture the glow of day's end to accompany a gentle story with a quiet note of humor and an unusually affective depiction of the relationship between a boy and his stepfather. Young Alex's offers to help Jake as he splits wood and brings a load into the house are turned down; Jake's not unkind, but he's intent on what he's doing. However, an unexpected bond is created when Alex spots a spider on Jake's clothes, learns that the big ex-cowboy is afraid of spiders, and conducts a strip search. It's a fragment, but a warm and touching one that ends in bonhomie, and it has an ingenuous, direct style that is appealing.

669   **Jukes,** Mavis. *No One is Going to Nashville;* illus. by Lloyd Bloom. Knopf, 1983. 82-18901. Trade ed. ISBN 0-394-85609-0; Library ed. ISBN 0-394-95609-5. 42p. Trade ed. $8.95; Library ed. $8.99.

2–4   Grey and white pictures, so softly painted as to seem blurred, illustrate an amusing and effective story in which girl meets dog. Sonia, who spends weekends with her father and stepmother, finds a dog just outside the house and names him Max. Her father says no dog; her mother, when she is telephoned, says that no dogs are allowed in their apartment building. Sonia reluctantly agrees to an advertisement, but when somebody comes to get Max, it's her stepmother who balks at giving the dog away. She puts Max in Sonia's arms, saying, ". . . from your Wicked Stepmother and from your father, with love. Discussion closed." Nothing sugary here, but there's a sweetness and warmth in the story, and the writing style is light and witty.

670   **Kamen,** Gloria. *Fiorello: His Honor, the Little Flower;* written and illus. by Gloria Kamen. Atheneum 1981. 81-2282. ISBN 0-689-30869-8. 60p. $8.95.

3–5   Perky, often humorous line and wash drawings illustrate a biography that gives all the salient facts in a light writing style. Kamen describes La Guardia's boyhood, the beginning of his political career, and his tenure as mayor in an admiring rather than an adulatory style, and she succeeds in conveying some of the integrity and tenacity that made the "Little Flower" a nationally known figure as well as New York's beloved mayor.

671   **Kamien,** Janet. *What If You Couldn't? A Book About Special Needs;* illus. by Signe Hanson. Scribner, 1979. 78-26659. 83p. $7.95.

5–7   Like *Who Are the Handicapped?* the book by Haskins for older readers, this deals with particular kinds of handicaps in separate chapters and explains some of the causes; it is more simply written, however, and more direct, much of the time addressing the reader: "If you were retarded, you could still learn . . ." or "If you couldn't hear as well as everyone else . . ." With directness and candor, Kamien describes the problems associated with each handicap, the devices or procedures that help handicapped persons adjust, the ways in which they receive special education, and their need for the same kinds of emotional and social satisfactions desired by those who are not handicapped. The author makes it clear that handicapped people don't want pity, and there is no note of pity in her text, but a crisp and sensible attitude that recognizes the fact that understanding and communication can alleviate the uncomfortable distance normal children often feel between themselves and the handicapped.

672   **Karl,** Jean E. *But We Are Not of Earth.* Dutton, 1981. 80-21849. ISBN 0-525-27342-5. 170p. $10.25.

7–10   In a science fiction story told by Romula Linders, she goes on an adventurous mission with her three best friends at the School/Home for Discoverers' Children. It's an assignment that challenges the wits and the training of the four adolescents, who are sent on a space exploration program with a teacher who is supposed to help but not direct them. There's a great deal of vitality and humor in the dialogue, an unexpected element of danger as well as the expected adventure, and the added appeals of space flight and of a mission accomplished. This will surely appeal to SF buffs, but it may also attract the general reader to the genre.

673   **Katz,** Jane B., ed. *This Song Remembers; Self-Portraits of Native Americans in the Arts.* Houghton, 1980. 80-20593. ISBN 0-395-29522-X. 207p. illus. with photographs. $8.95.

7–   Although the text is largely based on interviews with twenty Native American artists, it is given added depth and coherence by the knowledgeable and sympathetic background notes that precede each section of the book. The material is divided into sections on the performing arts, literature, and—by far the longest part—visual arts, and it is illustrated with photographs of many of the artists and their work. Material is grouped by region in the section on visual arts, and Katz is meticulous in identifying tribal sources. As does any anthology based on personal interviews, this has variety of viewpoint and expression, yet there are strong similarities among the many statements by individual artists: an awareness of the importance of preserving tradition, a pride in that tradition, and a reflection of the close and intricate relationship between art and the culture from which it emanates, particularly in the spiritual beliefs of that culture. Another sort of variety is also evident in the spectrum of individual artistic expressions, via technique, form, medium, etc. The diversity and the sociological implications may be of equal interest to readers, but it is as an introduction to the work of contemporary Native American artists that the book seems most valuable.

674   **Kaufman,** Charles. *The Frog and the Beanpole.* Lothrop, 1980. 79-21377. Trade ed. ISBN 0-688-41938-0; Library ed. ISBN 0-688-51938-5. 192p. Trade ed. $7.95; Library ed. $7.63 net.

4–6   Wesley is a laboratory frog, but not just your garden variety of frog; he's invisible. He's also literate and articulate, and he runs away from the malevolent scientist (bit of type-casting here) to escape whatever horrible fate Professor Snodgrass had planned. Wesley becomes the friend and comforter of ten-year-old Marveline, about to be moved out of a relative's home, and not happy about the prospect. So Marveline, who decides to call herself Holly, runs away with Wesley and they join a circus, since he can perform marvelous leaps, visible because of his costumes. He talks, but only to Holly. They are, of course, pursued by Snodgrass, but they're protected by their circus family and eventually

Wesley goes back to his home in Central America and Holly is retrieved by a welcoming aunt and uncle. The plot is fantastic but the approach is bland, the writing style polished and humorous. Kaufman achieves the goal of all fantasy writers; he makes his characters and their adventures plausible within the parameters of the fantasy—and they are sympathetic and entertaining characters.

675   **Kaufmann,** John. *Flying Giants of Long Ago;* written and illus. by John Kaufmann. Crowell, 1984. 81-43881. Library ed. ISBN 0-690-04220-5; Trade ed. ISBN 0-690-04219-1. 32p. Library ed. $9.89; Trade ed. $9.95.

K-3   In another valuable book in the Let's-Read-and-Find-Out Science series, Kaufmann deals with the largest prehistoric animals which flew. Starting with the time when the only flying creatures were insects, he describes giant dragonflies; then birds, including the scavenging teratorns; then flying reptiles, including the largest flying creature of all, Quetzalcoatlus, whose wings spread forty feet; he concludes with today's largest flying creatures. The drawings, some in color, are especially concerned with scale; many show animals in flight. Kaufmann's approach is carefully scientific: "as far as we know" the Meganeura dragonfly is the largest insect that ever lived. The creatures' full scientific names are used with a clear pronunciation guide: for example, "Argentavis magnificens (Are-jen-TA-vis mag-NIF-i-cens)." A pleasure for the many young readers with an intense interest in prehistoric animals, and an unpatronizing method of stimulating reading.

676   **Kavaler,** Lucy. *Green Magic: Algae Rediscovered;* illus. with photographs and drawings by Jean Helmer. Crowell, 1983. 81-43872. Trade ed. ISBN 0-690-0422 -3; Library ed. ISBN 0-690-04222-1. 120p. Trade ed. $10.95; Library e . $10.89.

6-9   Kavaler is adept at organizing scientific material, giving clear and sequential explanations, and doing the research that brings in new discoveries and current experiments. Here she describes the structure and variety of algae, the fossil findings, established phenomena, old and new uses of algae for food, fertilizer, and sewage purification, and discusses some of the ways in which algae may be used to alleviate food shortages in the future or serve myriad purposes on space flights. An extensive index gives good access to a useful and well-written book on a topic that already has many ramifications and may, in the future, have many more.

677   **Kavaler,** Lucy. *A Matter of Degree: Heat, Life, and Death.* Harper, 1981. 80-8789. ISBN 0-06-014854-3. 226p. $15.55.

7-   Solid pages of small print may discourage readers, but for those who persist, there's a small mine of information in this wide-ranging book. Kavaler is nothing if not thorough; she investigates every imaginable facet of heat: plant and animal adaptation to heat; heat as it affects the human body in illness and in health and in such processes as birth or aging; sociological ties, such as heat and violence; sexual connotations, arson, volcanoes, cookery, tropical diseases, the dangers of over-exposure to the sun, food spoilage. . . . Based on careful research, the text is well-organized and written with vitality; a glossary, an extensive bibliography, and an index are included.

678   Keller, Beverly. *The Bee Sneeze;* illus. by Diane Paterson. Coward, 1982. 81-19509. ISBN 0-698-30740-2. 48p. $6.99.

2–4   Fiona, self-elected saver of bees, is at it again. This time it's a soggy, sugared bee that had been rescued from Fiona's glass of lemonade; bending solicitously over the bee, Fiona hears it sneeze. This starts a chain of events that ends (agreeably, if not altogether logically) in an impromptu neighborhood pot-luck party, and the bee dropping into some berry juice and flying off, pleasantly sticky, and unaware that he's been a catalyst. ". . . but then, bees don't expect much from people," the story ends. Line drawings suit but do not extend the text, save for showing that Fiona's friend Howard is black; the writing has an easy flow, and the affably silly story is just, but just, within the bounds of amused credibility.

679   Keller, Beverly. *My Awful Cousin Norbert;* illus. by Bobby Lewis. Lothrop, 1982. 81-6068. Trade ed. ISBN 0-688-00742-2; Library ed. ISBN 0-688-00743-0. 61p. Trade ed. $8.50; Library ed. $7.63.

2–4   Bad enough to have to get dressed up for dinner but eat in the kitchen with detestable Norbert to keep him company, bad enough to have to tolerate Norbert's nasty remarks about Phil's parents, but when Norbert spoils the special pie Father has made for Mother's visiting boss and blames Phil, it's the bitter end. Or is it? In a humorous, lightly and deftly told story, justice prevails. The boss is delighted with the hastily substituted fruit and cheese dessert, she thinks Phil is a nice boy because her dog licks his shoes (which is where Norbert spilled the pie) and—best of all—Father overhears a remark that makes him aware that the culprit was not Phil, as he'd assumed, but Norbert. Just enough exaggeration adds a fillip to a scratchily illustrated but nicely concocted tale.

680   Kellogg, Steven, ad. *Paul Bunyan;* retold and illus. by Steven Kellogg. Morrow, 1984. 83-26684. Library ed. ISBN 0-688-03850-6; Trade ed. ISBN 0-688-03849-2. 39p. Library ed. $12.88; Trade ed. $13.00.

K–3   Kellogg uses oversize pages for busy, detail-crowded illustrations that have vitality and humor, echoing the exaggeration and ebullience of the story, a compression of some of the tall tales about the legendary Paul Bunyan and his blue ox Babe. Some of the geographical details will make little impact on the read-aloud audience, but there's enough that will be familiar to make this an enjoyable romp for young children.

681   Kellogg, Steven. *Ralph's Secret Weapon;* written and illus. by Steven Kellogg. Dial, 1983. 82-22115. Trade ed. ISBN 0-8037-7086-3; Library ed. ISBN 0-8037-7087-1. 21p. Trade ed. $10.95; Library ed. $10.89.

K–2   It's the ebullience and extravagance of the text as well as of the pictures that should appeal to readers, as Kellogg presents the summertime adventures of Ralph, who has just completed third grade. Sent to stay with his wealthy, domineering Aunt Georgiana, Ralph discovers A—the cake she made to welcome him makes a mouse ill, B—she has arranged for him to have bassoon lessons, and C—at his first lesson, the teacher is horrified and worms come out of apples at Ralph's cacophony. Auntie, nothing daunted, enters Ralph in a snake-charming contest. Sure enough, just like the worms, the snakes are charmed, and Ralph wins the contest. Auntie volunteers Ralph's services for dealing with a sea serpent that's annoying the Navy. Armed with bassoon, Ralph goes aboard. The final adventure is hilarious, Auntie is exhausted, and Ralph spends the rest of the summer in peace, resting up for fourth grade. An example of the integration of text and illustration in this spirited story: the text says, "The sea serpent became angry with Ralph," and the picture shows a hapless Ralph in the coils of the serpent's huge tongue.

682   Kemp, Gene. *Charlie Lewis Plays for Time.* Faber, 1984. 83-25297. ISBN 0-571-13248-0. 132p. $11.95.

6–9   Charlie, an English schoolboy, is the protagonist and narrator of another lively school story by the author of the Carnegie Award book, *The Turbulent Term of Tyke Tiler.* Charlie is the son of a famous concert pianist, Marian Forrest; he's horrified when a teacher he detests begins to court his mother and fawn on him—for Charlie, like all his mates, has conducted a vigorous running battle with the rigid, sexist, and at times vindictive Mr. Carter. The story ends with an animated description of a school program and with a visit from Charlie's Dad (his parents have been separated for years) so that the plot is nicely rounded off without having all ends too neatly tied. Part of the book's appeal is the vigorous, humorous writing style; part of its value is the solid characterization and natural dialogue. Pithy, and very entertaining.

683   Kemp, Gene. *Dog Days and Cat Naps;* illus. by Carolyn Dinan. Faber, 1981. ISBN 0-571-11595-0. 110p. $11.95.

4–6   Most of the short stories in this collection have to do with animals and their owners, some with children only, and all ten are piquant, pointed, and amusing. Some are told in first person, and some characters appear in several stories. Recurrent themes are children's friendship and the love of pets by owners who see their faults with no abating of affection. The resilience and candor of Kemp's style are nowhere more evident than in "Mi3 and the Nine Days' Wonder," a hilarious account of an obstreperous group of classmates and their wise, patient teacher.

684   **Kemp,** Gene. *The Turbulent Term of Tyke Tiler;* illus. by Carolyn Dimas. Faber, 1980. ISBN 0-571-10966-7. 118p. $10.95.

4–6
  *
It is rare indeed for a book to win the prestigious Carnegie Medal and also the Other Award given by the Children's Rights Workshop, but this English story has done that, and it's easy to see why. Tyke, who tells the story, is a lively, active, and articulate girl who gets into as many scrapes because of her compassion for her friend Danny (handicapped by a speech impediment) as she does because of her curiosity and daring. There are delightfully funny classroom scenes, sharp and quick character depictions of classmates and teachers, and dialogue that captures the quality of children's speech. It's a happy, pithy story; the flavor is British but the concerns and humor are universal.

685   **Kennedy,** Richard. *Inside My Feet; The Story of a Giant;* illus. by Ronald Himler. Harper, 1979. 78-19479. Trade ed. ISBN 0-06-023118-1; Library ed. ISBN 0-06-03119-X. 71p. Trade ed. $7.95; Library ed. $7.89 net.

4–6
A first-person narrative, tightly constructed and told with compact urgency, is notable both for its fusion of realistic and fanciful elements and for its pace and suspense. Answering a midnight ringing of the doorbell, the boy and his parents find only a pair of giant boots; they bring the boots in and go back to bed, then they hear steps. The father goes down, and then he and the boots disappear. The same thing happens to the boy's mother, and he is determined it won't happen to him. He will outwit the boots, he will find his parents—and he does, after an encounter with an old, sad giant, a confrontation that is both dramatic and moving. The giant is ruthless and powerful, yet he weeps for the child he once was, the child who was gentle and loving. For the astute reader, this adds another dimension to a story that is absorbing even at surface value.

686   **Kennemore,** Tim. *Changing Times.* Faber, 1984. ISBN 0-571-13285-5. 149p. $14.95.

7–10
Victoria is fifteen, in this story of a London schoolgirl who is pretty, does fairly well at school, has boy and girl friends—and is miserable. Her parents quarrel constantly, and there is clearly a major rift the nature of which Victoria doesn't understand. Into this contemporary problem novel, perceptive and often biting, the author inserts a time-travel element with surprising success. It's the old clock she got for her birthday, Victoria discovers, that propels her backward in time for one day; a frightening experience the first time, but one she later experiments with, including one horrendous trip into the future (she's married to a domineering sexist) that helps Victoria understand herself just as the trips backward in time have helped her understand the rancor between her parents that has engendered her bitterness toward them. Kennemore doesn't use the time-travels for effect, she uses them with dramatic efficiency to forward her candid, powerful story.

687   **Kennemore,** Tim. *Wall of Words.* Faber, 1983. ISBN 0-571-11856-9. 173p. $10.95.

5–7   Oldest of the four Tate girls, thirteen-year-old Kim is most loyal to the father who had left them over a year ago, presumably to write a book. Clever, impulsive, with a quick temper, Kim is usually at war with her youngest sister Anna, a precocious moppet who schemes and calculates her way toward being Everybody's Dimpled Darling. It's Kerry who worries Kim. A year older than Anna, Kerry so hates school that she becomes ill—and no psychologist has been able to help her. It is one of Kim's teachers who diagnoses dyslexia (she is herself dyslexic) in Kerry and gives everyone in the family new hope, especially Kerry, who had begun to fear she was retarded. There are other shifts in family affairs to balance the theme of the title, there's believable change and growth in the major characters, there's a great deal of wit and humor in the writing, especially in the dialogue. A nice mix of a serious problem happily resolved, sisterly squabbles that are not resolved and often funny, and all written in a yeasty style.

688   **Kent,** Jack. *The Once-Upon-a-Time Dragon;* written and illus. by Jack Kent. Harcourt, 1982. 82-2983. ISBN 0-15-257885-4. 32p. $10.95.

2–7 yrs.   Blithe, bright cartoon-style drawings illustrate a light, fanciful tale about an amicable dragon who dotes on bedtime stories and notes that often the dragons in stories are men under enchantment. Maybe he could be a man, too? If not a handsome prince as in the stories, maybe a president or a rock star? When he sees an ad for a body-building course that says, "Be the man you want to become," he sends for the course, decides he wants to be Mr. Johnson (a plump man who feeds the park pigeons on warm afternoons) and practices and, indeed, becomes Mr. Johnson. The two-Johnson dilemma is happily resolved in an entertaining tale in which the bland style is an effective foil for the fantastic things that happen.

689   **Kerr,** M. E. *Him She Loves?* Harper, 1984. 83-48818. Trade ed. ISBN 0-06-023238-2; Library ed. ISBN 0-06-023239-0. 244p. Library ed. $10.89; Trade ed. $10.50..

7–10   Henry Schiller is sixteen, the narrator of a very funny, sometimes touching, always vibrant love story. He's deeply in love with Valerie Kissenwiser, whose father is a comedian known as Al Kiss. Al Kiss is furious when he finds his darling child in Henry's embrace, not least because the Kissenwisers are Jewish and Henry (Al calls him Heinrich) is of German stock. What Al Kiss does is to use Henry as his butt in television shows, making fun of him and disparaging the love affair, always concluding with "*Him* she loves?" The outcome of this contretemps is surprising but not illogical, as Kiss becomes friendly and Valerie loses interest. As is usually true of Kerr's novels, this has a lively and fluent style, strong characterization and dialogue, an innovative story line, and zesty humor.

690   **Kerr,** M. E. *Little Little.* Harper, 1981. 80-8454. Trade ed. ISBN 0-06-023184-X; Library ed. ISBN 0-06-023185-8. 160p. Trade ed. $8.95; Library ed. $8.79.

7–10   In a very funny and very witty story, Kerr takes some caustic pokes at some of the aspects of our society, including snobbery, parent-child relations, show business and promotion, evangelistic entrepreneurs, and the treatment of those who differ from the majority. This is also a love story, and it is told in alternate chapters by Little Little (an attractive and wealthy midget) and by Sydney Cinnamon (an orphaned dwarf who has become famous for his television commercials) as they struggle against the former's parents' desire that their little girl marry the diminutive evangelist Little Lion. Kerr's characters are strong and independent, her plot is novel, and her writing style vigorous, especially notable for dialogue. Hilarious yet provocative, the book elicits laughter, but the reader never laughs at the diminutive people—one laughs with them at the foibles of others.

691   **Kessler,** Leonard P. *Old Turtle's Baseball Stories;* written and illus. by Leonard P. Kessler. Greenwillow, 1982. 81-6390. Trade ed. ISBN 0-688-00723-6; Library ed. ISBN 0-688-00724-4. 55p. (Read-alone Books). Trade ed. $6.50; Library ed. $5.71.

1–2   It's hard to beat the combination of baseball, animals, and humor, and
  *   Kessler provides all three in a simply written book for beginning readers. Scheherezade meets her match in Old Turtle, who sits with other animals around a pot-bellied stove and reminisces about such great stars as Melvin Moose, the great hitter who hit a double with his antlers, or Carla Kangaroo, the great outfielder who tripped while going for a long ball that would have meant a home run for the opponents—but whose Joey jumped out of her pocket to make the catch and save the day. What puts the icing on this tasty cake is the approximation of a storyteller's style: Old Turtle ends each anecdote with "Every word of it," when asked if it's a true story, and begins another with "Let me tell you about . . ."

692   **Kessler,** Leonard. *Old Turtle's Winter Games;* written and illus. by Leonard Kessler, Greenwillow, 1983. 83-1435. Trade ed ISBN 0-688-02309-6; Library ed. ISBN 0-688-02310-X. 47p. (Read-alone Books). Trade ed. $7.50; Library ed. $6.67.

1–2   Old Turtle encourages all his animal friends to learn and enjoy skating, skiing, sledding, and playing ice hockey. There are some tumbles, but everyone takes them in good stride, and the book ends with a grand winter games event in which each participant wins a prize for something—even Old Turtle. The line and wash drawings aren't elegant, but they have vitality and humor; the text has the appeals of animals, play, successful achievement, and good sportsmanship; the vocabulary is very simple, the print large. In fact, a fine book for the beginning independent reader.

693   **Kesteven,** G. R. *The Awakening Water.* Hastings House, 1979. 78-27186.
       160p. $6.95.

6–9   A science fiction novel is set, as are so many, in a future time after man
       has destroyed his own civilization by violence. The concept of a people
       kept submissive is a familiar one, but Kesteven presents it with dra-
       matic conviction by having his protagonist, John (all the children of his
       age have names beginning with J) as dull and apathetic, as are the oth-
       ers in his House; only by accident does he meet one of the "Lost Ones"
       and learn that he and his mates are given tranquilizers in their water.
       The Lost Ones prove to be runaways, and John becomes one of them, a
       small band who garden by night and live in peace, although fearful
       they will be captured by a patrol. The story of John's awakening to real-
       ity, the dangers he and his group face, and the solution of their ulti-
       mate destiny make a taut narrative. Characterization is variable, the pic-
       ture of a rigid society convincing, and the plot doubly appealing
       because of the concepts of man against nature and of the triumph of
       right over might.

694   **Kettelkamp,** Larry. *Lasers; The Miracle Light;* illus. Morrow, 1979. 79-
       17486. Trade ed. ISBN 0-688-22207-2; Library ed. ISBN 0-688-32207-7.
       126p. Trade ed. $6.95; Library ed. $6.67 net.

7–   Like Bova's *The Amazing Laser* and Stambler's *Revolution in Light,* this
       covers the subject of holography in addition to explanations of the na-
       ture of light, the discovery and operation of the laser, the kinds of la-
       sers, and the many uses to which lasers are put. It is as clearly written
       as the other two books, albeit not as well indexed, and since the Bova
       and Stambler books were both published in 1972, contains more exam-
       ples of medical, industrial, and other uses that have been found in re-
       cent years.

695   **Kevles,** Bettyann. *Thinking Gorillas; Testing and Teaching the Greatest Ape;*
       illus. with photographs. Dutton, 1980. 79-12782. ISBN 0-525-41074-0.
       167p. $10.95.

7–9   Kevles describes, in extensive detail, some of the gorillas that have been
       captured or born in zoos and that have been observed, tested, or
       trained by scientists. The accounts are full and fascinating; the com-
       ments by Kevles range from perceptive interpretation to an occasional
       naive remark, but there is comparatively little commentary, most of the
       text being devoted to descriptions based on the writings of scientists or
       on the author's interviews with them. A long, divided bibliography of
       source materials and an index are included.

696   **Kherdian,** David. *The Road from Home; The Story of an Armenian Girl.*
       Greenwillow, 1979. 78-72511. Trade ed. ISBN 0-688-80205-2; Library ed.
       ISBN 0-688-84205-4. 238p. Trade ed. $8.95; Library ed. $8.59 net.

7–   This is not a full biography, but an account of those terrible and dramatic years in the life of Veron Dumehjian (the author's mother) when she, with the rest of her family, was deported from Turkey and, with other Armenians, went on the long march during which so many died of fatigue, disease, malnutrition, and despair. The story is told by Veron, effectively contrasting the comfort and security of her childhood with the abrupt deportation, the fear of the unknown, the bitterness of separation. All of her immediate family died, and she eventually escaped and lived with an aunt in Greece, coming to the United States as a bride in an arranged marriage when she was sixteen. There are some points at which the narrative lags, but it does not often lose momentum, and it is written convincingly from Veron's viewpoint; as a document of tragedy, courage, and hope it is touching.

697   **Kidd,** Ronald. *Sizzle and Splat.* Lodestar, 1983. 83-9022. ISBN 0-525-66917-5. 122p. $10.95.

6–9   Sizzle is the narrator, and she's critical about everything to do with Splat except the way he plays the tuba; she's trumpet soloist in the Pirelli Youth Orchestra. When Pirelli takes her along to plead with composer Hans Kleiman that he write a piece for them so that the orchestra can stay alive financially, Kleiman takes a liking to Sizzle, writes a piece with a trumpet solo, and also provides a cryptogram and a prize for the audience member who can solve it. Kleiman dies, and there are notes threatening disaster if his piece is performed; Kleiman's nephew is kidnapped, Sizzle and Splat are shot at, the score is stolen, etc. Self-elected detectives, the two young people cannot convince the police that their clues are valuable. Needless to say, they encounter danger and solve the mystery—and the orchestra gets a bequest of a million dollars it would have lost had not Sizzle and Splat (Prudence and Arthur, actually) solved the mystery as fast as they had. The plot is not convincing, nor is the obduracy of the policeman they try to persuade, but the book has some strong assets: the dialogue is very funny, there's lots of action and some suspense, and the story is imbued both with musical lore and a comparatively rare depiction of adolescents who are knowledgeable and enthusiastic about classical music.

698   **Kiefer,** Irene. *Nuclear Energy at the Crossroads;* illus. with photographs and with diagrams by Judith Fast. Atheneum, 1982. 82-1681. ISBN 0-689-30926-0. 154p. $10.95.

8–
 *   Kiefer, a science writer with a degree in chemistry, takes a long, hard, and objective look at nuclear energy, discussing the problems, the potential, the alternatives, and the record to date. She gives a lucid explanation of how a nuclear generator works and spells out the dangers of radiation, including the dangers in nuclear waste disposal. There are descriptions of what happened at Three Mile Island and, more briefly, other plants; Kiefer says of waste disposal, "It may be the Achilles' heel

that will determine the future of nuclear power." Arguments pro and con are cited, leaving it to readers to make their own judgments; the book suggests only that decisions should be based on the opinions of Americans of all ages, that "The people must lead the leaders." This timely and informative book is well organized and well written; a glossary and a relative index make the text more comprehensible and accessible.

699   **Kiefer,** Irene. *Poisoned Land: The Problem of Hazardous Waste.* Atheneum, 1981. 80-22120. ISBN 0-689-30837-X. 90p. illus. with photographs. $8.95.

6–9   With a background in chemistry and scientific journalism, Kiefer is well-qualified to discuss the problems posed by the burgeoning chemical industry and the wastes (many dangerous, some lethal) that must be disposed of. In the past, the text points out, lack of laws or enforcement of safety codes led to careless dumping of pollutants into water or land; since the establishment of the Resource Conservation and Recovery Act of 1976, there has been a careful watch kept on hazardous wastes. The author describes the methods that can be used in handling wastes so that dangers are reduced or eliminated, and she discusses ways to avoid problems in the future. A straightforward style, authoritative handling, and a well-organized text give good information on a timely topic; a glossary and index are included.

700   **King,** Clive. *Me and My Million.* T. Y. Crowell, 1979. 78-22501. Trade ed. ISBN 0-690-03971-9; Library ed. ISBN 0-690-03972-7. 180p. Trade ed. $7.95; Library ed. $7.89 net.

4–6
*   Ringo is a tough, street-wise London waif who has a learning disability; his difficulty in reading numbers as well as letters propels him into a series of wild and hilarious adventures. It begins when his brother, a petty criminal, gives Ringo instructions for passing on a stolen picture and Ringo boards a bus that's numbered 14 rather than 41, which he'd been told to take to the end of the line. Ringo, who tells the story, gets mixed up with one peculiar group after another, including a gang of criminals and an artist who's painted a copy of the very picture that London police, the gang, the gallery from which the picture had been stolen, and Ringo's angry brother are seeking. It's wild, but as Ringo tells it, it's believable; what pulls the story together and gives it color and humor is Ringo's viewpoint and language, for King has made him consistently a scruffy street urchin with just enough heart-of-gold to make him a sympathetic character. The dialogue is delicious, the story a romp.

701   **King,** Clive. *The Night the Water Came.* T. Y. Crowell, 1982. 81-43318. Trade ed. ISBN 0-690-04162-4; Library ed. ISBN 0-690-04163-2. 151p. Trade ed. $9.50; Library ed. $8.89.

5–7   Apu, already orphaned by an earlier storm, is an eleven-year-old who tells his story through a series of tapes, and he begins with the night of the cyclone, a night that left him stranded alone in the destruction of his small island in the Indian Ocean. Picked up by some soldiers after a helicopter had dropped some boxes Apu was afraid to open, the boy was taken to an airplane carrier; later he was turned over to a boatload of islanders who took him to land. But the islanders were really pirates; they took all of Apu's possessions and left him stranded. Rescued again, Apu was flown to a city and sent to school, but he ran away with his friend Khoka, trying to get back to his home island. He found his uncle's family in a refugee camp, and when the story ends Apu has happily misled the strangers who come and want to improve his dear island, and when asked if he wants to stay, he says, "Well, I've got to get the place fixed up for the next cyclone." The book is partially based on the author's experiences as a member of a relief expedition in India when over a million people were drowned by a cyclonic wave. This, however, is ingenious in the way it shows the viewpoint of the survivor; the story is vivid, funny, action-filled, and written with consistency and flow.

702   **King,** Clive. *Ninny's Boat;* map by Ian Newsham. Macmillan, 1981. 81-8121. ISBN 0-02-750680-0. 245p. $9.95.

5–8   Using an ingenious first-person approach, King depicts fifth century Britain from the viewpoint of Ninny, who can remember nothing of his early years save a nonsense rhyme. A little-valued slave, Ninny is laughed at when he blurts out the suggestion that his captors, threatened by flood, build a big enough boat to carry everybody to the Isles of Ocean. The situation has dramatic tension and is developed with good pace as the clues grow by which the reader becomes oriented—as does Ninny—to the place and time. While Ninny learns something of himself (the "nonsense" rhyme was a counting rhyme in the language of his people) and gains confidence as he adventures and solves problems, the theme is a timeless one: there are situations in which anyone may be a persecuted minority. And there's a timeless message about brotherhood, suggested by Ninny (who discovers his origins and the fact that his name is Ninian) in a story that has action, humor, lively characters, and an informally fluent style of writing.

703   **King-Smith,** Dick. *Magnus Power-Mouse;* illus. by Mary Rayner. Harper, 1984. 83-48435. Library ed. ISBN 0-06-023232-3; Trade ed. ISBN 0-06-023231-5. 120p. Library ed. $10.89; Trade ed. $10.95.

4–6   Deft line drawings illustrate an appealing fantasy about Magnus, the one mouse of the litter to survive. Unfortunately, the large and greedy Magnus denied his siblings their share of sustenance and soon grew so large that his erudite, loquacious father (an intellectual Micawber) was daunted and his chirpy little mother spent all her time hunting food for her giant son. It is through the offices of an animal-loving human that Magnus, his parents, and their friend the rabbit find love and security.

King-Smith shares with readers his own relish for the contrast between polysyllabic Marcus Aurelius (father mouse) and his language-mangling but sensible spouse.

704   **King-Smith,** Dick. *The Mouse Butcher;* illus. by Margot Apple. Viking, 1982. 81-70656. ISBN 0-670-49145-4. 132p. $10.95.

4-6   Like *Pigs Might Fly* this is an entertaining, witty, and smoothly written animal fantasy; although the style is as yeasty here the plot is less substantial than that of the first book. Still, this is a cut above most comic fantasy. All the characters here are cats, and they live on an island that has been abandoned by people. Tom Plug, the butcher's cat, is a tough and resourceful hunter who arranges with the snobbish head of the Bampton-Bush family (very high-class cats) to do their hunting for them; in the course of this relationship he wins the heart and paw of the lovely young Diana Bampton-Bush, and he bests the fierce and feral Mog, "the Monster of the lime pit."

705   **King-Smith,** Dick. *Pigs Might Fly;* illus. by Mary Rayner. Viking, 1982. 81-11525. ISBN 0-670-55506-1. 158p. $10.95.

4-6   Not since Wilbur has there been so engaging a porcine protagonist as
*   Daggie, the runt of the litter who rises to heroic stature in this touching and comic fantasy, first published in England under the title *Daggie Dogfoot.* Although embarrassed about her child's peculiar deformity (his forefeet were rounded like a puppy's) Mrs. Barleylove, Daggie's mother, was firmly determined that this runt would not be taken away from her. She never dreamed that he would learn to swim (under the tutelage of a clever duck and an avuncular otter) or that his ability to swim would make it possible for Daggie to come to the rescue of all the other pigs during a flash flood. Written with wit and controlled ebullience, this has excellent characterization, pithy dialogue, good pace, and admirable line drawings.

706   **Kitchen,** Bert, illus. *Animal Alphabet.* Dial, 1984. 83-23929. ISBN 0-8037-0117-9. 32p. $11.95.

3-6   The paintings on the oversize pages of a handsome alphabet book are
*   reminiscent, in their fidelity of detail and sense of texture, of the paintings of Bruno Munari. Here the pages are (effectively) even more stark: lots of white space, one huge upper case letter, one animal leaning on, perched on, climbing up, or peering through the letter. Identification is provided at the back of the book. The visual appeal extends far beyond the range of the usual audience for alphabet books.

707   **Klaveness,** Jan O'Donnell. *The Griffin Legacy.* Macmillan, 1983. 83-9353. ISBN 0-02-750760-2. 184p. $9.95.

5-8   A family secret is revealed and the ghosts of an unhappy colonial ancestress and her husband are appeased when Amy and her friends deduce from clues and sightings what the tragedy of the Griffin legacy is. Amy, thirteen, has come to stay with Grandma and Great-aunt Matilda in the old homestead in a Massachusetts village, and Amy is baffled when a minister (ghost) chides her and is hard to convince that she is not her ancestress, Lucy, whom she strongly resembles. Her friends Ben and Betsy are convinced when they, like Amy, see Lucy's ghost; with the help of clairvoyant Aunt Matilda and her two friends, Amy pieces out the odd conversations she has overheard between ghosts or with them, and solves the puzzle. This is a deft blend of fantasy and realism, it has good pace and structure, a controlled narrative flow, and considerable historical interest in the unfolding of the lives of Amy's ancestors during the time of the American Revolution.

708   **Klein,** David. *How Do You Know It's True?;* written by David Klein and Marymae E. Klein. Scribner, 1984. 84-14023. ISBN 0-684-18225-4. 168p. $12.95.

8–10   In a text designed to help readers acquire and maintain an objective and critical viewpoint in analyzing information, the Kleins point out the need for such critical thinking in a world in which hyperbole and statistics (as well as warped or incorrect statements) can color or obscure truth. They discuss the influence of preconception, the range of veracity from lie to truth, the skewing of statistics to serve a purpose, and the methods by which facts have been garnered. The text urges that methods and instruments of fact-finding must be looked at critically, and that individuals should warily ask questions about who is providing information, who or what group stands to gain, when the data were collected, how comprehensive the information package is. Not easy reading, but a valuable guide to the concept and practice of taking a long, careful look at what is presented as the truth. A relative index is appended.

709   **Klein,** Norma. *Snapshots.* Dial, 1984. 84-7115. ISBN 0-8037-0129-2. 167p. $12.95.

7–9   In a story in which Sean Abrahms is the thirteen-year-old narrator, he and his friend Marc get into trouble through a perfectly innocent incident. Marc can't convince his parents that his pretty sister (age eight) would make a successful model, so he takes pictures of her to convince them. It's hot, she happens to be wearing a bikini, somebody who sees the prints suspects commercial pornography. The boys are exonerated, but it proves to be an ordeal; Sean's excitable and critical father is proud of the way Sean handles it and says so when he speaks at Sean's bar mitzvah. The chief plot thread is interesting although it's handled rather heavily; otherwise the writing is very good: smooth, well-paced, convincing as the voice of a bright young adolescent. The book is given color by minor plot threads, including Sean's first substantial relationship with a girl and his militant sister's successful campaign to have the bar mitzvah conducted by a female rabbi.

710   **Klein,** Norma. *Visiting Pamela;* illus. by Kay Chorao. Dial, 1979. 78-72203. Trade ed. ISBN 0-8037-9307-3; Library ed. ISBN 0-8037-9308-1. 30p. Trade ed. $6.95; Library ed. $6.46 net.

3–6
yrs.

Carrie, who tells the story, says that when she turned five, Mommy issued an ultimatum: if Carrie wouldn't visit friends, she couldn't have friends visit her. Reluctantly Carrie accepts an invitation from Pamela, and at first she's unhappy because the baby is smelly and the dog frightens her and they have fruit instead of cookies and she has to play with whatever Pamela tells her. By the time Mommy, hastily summoned, shows up, Carrie's begun to have fun—and also some cookies Pamela snitched, so she decides it wasn't so bad. "I don't think I mind visiting people anymore," she says, and Mommy agrees that the first time is the worst. The black and white illustrations show two frowsty girls against interiors that have good textural contrasts: clothing patterns, hatching, etc. The writing style is simple, with good dialogue, and the book gives a strong, if brief, picture of the shy child that may well appeal to those children who share Carrie's trepidation.

711   **Klein,** Robin. *Thing;* illus. by Alison Lester. Oxford, 1983. ISBN 0-19-554330-0. 30p. $7.95.

2–4

Although Klein uses a familiar device (the pet under threat of banishment foils a burglary and is accepted) her engaging fantasy is so deftly written that it has, despite some British spelling or terms that may puzzle our young readers, great appeal. The smooth rock Robin finds (settling for a pet rock because the landlady will not allow pets) proves to be a little stegosaurus; Emily calls him "Thing," and enjoys his tractable, friendly personality. When the landlady discovers Thing, she issues an ultimatum: one more day—but in that day, Thing prevents two burglars from getting away, and Emily comes home from school to find Thing being fed a lavish meal by the landlady, who suggests that she might take him for a run in the park each day. What makes the story particularly enjoyable is the blandness with which others accept the stegosaurus; the police who come to get the burglars, for example, say "But would you kindly ask your dinosaur to step out of the way?" This is a good choice, too, for reading aloud to younger children.

712   **Knight,** David C. *Robotics: Past, Present, and Future;* illus. with photographs. Morrow, 1983. 82-22918. ISBN 0-688-01490-9. 122p. $8.50.

6–9

Knight defines his terms, gives the history of robots, distinguishes between robots and automatons, and discusses, in separate chapters, robots in industry, medicine, and the home. He describes the differences between playback robots and sequence robots, and between open and closed loop control. The text concludes with a chapter on robotics in the future, predicting increasingly sophisticated sensory devices, unmanned assembly lines, and an increasing use of robots in the home, in medical and space research, and possibly (in all fields) to replace human labor at tedious jobs. The text is logically arranged and clearly written; an index gives access to the contents of a book on a subject that is alluring to many readers.

713   **Knight,** David C. *Viruses: Life's Smallest Enemies;* illus. with photographs; diagrams by Christine Kettner. Morrow, 1981. 81-9554. Trade ed. ISBN 0-688-00712-0; Library ed. ISBN 0-688-00713-9. 127p. Trade ed. $6.95; Library ed. $6.67.

5–8   In a well-organized and crisply written text, Knight describes what is known about viruses and what research resulted in that knowledge. He discusses the several kinds of viruses, explaining clearly how they infect their hosts and by what mechanisms they spread, reproduce, and destroy the tissues of the living plants, animals, or bacteria they infest; he cites some of the viral diseases, pointing out that there is increasing evidence of the link between viruses and cancer. A final chapter discusses current research in the field, including vaccines and interferon as well as studies that contribute to scientists' knowledge of immunology. A list of important events in the development of a body of knowledge in the field, a glossary, and an index are appended.

714   **Knight,** Hilary, illus. *The Twelve Days of Christmas;* illus. by Hilary Knight. Macmillan, 1981. 81-2599. ISBN 0-02-750870-6. 28p. $8.95.

K–4   Soft-toned paintings of engaging animal characters sustain a blithe mood as Knight gives a new interpretation of the words of the familiar holiday song. Each day Benjamin (name on mailbox) trots down the road from his little cabin to the large house where Bedelia (again, mailbox) lives. Busy at her household tasks, Bedelia shows no reaction to her gifts, nor do they seem to clutter the house. Only at the end, when Bedelia displays a poster for a Christmas Fair, and the last (double) page unfolds, can the reader see the full spectacle of the accumulated gifts: the swans in a water ballet, the geese on a ferris wheel, the dancers up in the bandshell. It's a dazzling spectacle, all the more effective for the suspense about where the true love's presents were put. There are some running gags, like the raccoon (a masked bandit) who struggles through picture after picture, trying to open the garbage can, and some amusing conceits, such as the fact that the twelve lords who are a-leaping are frogs.

715   **Knowles,** Anne. *The Halcyon Island.* Harper, 1981. 80-7909. Trade ed. ISBN 0-06-023203-X; Library ed. ISBN 0-06-023204-8. 120p. Trade ed. $8.95; Library ed. $8.79.

5–7   Ken is twelve, a great disappointment to his domineering father, who
 *   cannot understand that a boating accident when Ken was three has left the boy terrified by the idea of being in the water. Vacationing on a river front property, Ken's parents are called away and he is left with a housekeeper; that's when he meets Giles, another boy, who patiently,

gently helps Ken get over his fear to the extent that he can enjoy boating and swimming. Just as Ken's parents return, Giles is gone, his island home abandoned. The story is told with consummate craft, both the dialogue and the characters have a high degree of credibility and vitality; the evocation of long, still summer days is remarkable. What gives the book added strength is the recurrent hint that Giles is a ghost; while all his actions are natural, and Ken never questions his identity, the author carefully structures the story so that nobody else ever talks to Giles, even in scenes where the boys are on the river together, and just before the story ends someone tells Ken about a boy who died trying to rescue his drowning father and brothers. The only previous reference has been Giles' comment, when Ken finds that Giles' family is never home, that "father's not here. He and James and Philip have gone on. I'll join them later." A fine story, set in England and universal in appeal.

716   **Knowles,** Anne. *Under the Shadow.* Harper, 1983. 82-48857. Trade ed. ISBN 0-06-023221-8; Library ed. ISBN 0-06-023222-6. 128p. Trade ed. $9.95; Library ed. $9.89.

6–9   Cathy, whose parents have inherited a country house, Beamsters, becomes fascinated by all of the information about the old place that she gleans from the boy next door, Mark, who tells her that it was originally the beemaster's house. Mark has muscular dystrophy, and Cathy works out an elaborate scheme to help him ride, after she learns how much he has enjoyed his one experience on horseback. Both Mark and Cathy are intrigued by the idea of bringing bees back to Beamsters, and at the close of the book Cathy is thrilled when a swarm settles in the garden. Despite a weak ending, this story from England has appeal and strength in its solid base of good narrative flow, strong characters drawn with insight, and a compassionate but not sentimental view of those who are handicapped and how they like to be treated.

717   **Knox-Wagner,** Elaine. *My Grandpa Retired Today;* illus. by Charles Robinson. Whitman, 1982. 82-1935. ISBN 0-8075-5334-4. 29p. $7.50.

2–3   Margery comes to the farewell party at the barbershop where her grandfather has worked for so many years. The only child there, she eats too much cake and spends some of her time doing the familiar, useful things she's done before. She's wistful about missing the shop as they walk home, but later, when she sees that Grandpa is depressed, she cheers him up; they both look forward to a busy tomorrow when they'll have time to do all the things for which Grandpa had been too busy before. Margery is the narrator of a direct text that has subtle overtones of the loving friendship between the man and the child and of the combined relief and regret that retirement can bring. This is a quiet book, illustrated with blue and brown wash drawings that have vitality and a matching quiet humor.

718   **Koenig,** Alma Johanna. *Gudrun;* tr. from the German by Anthea Bell. Lothrop, 1979. 79-917. Trade ed. ISBN 0-688-41899-6; Library ed. ISBN 0-688-51899-0. 187p. Trade ed. $7.95; Library ed. $7.63 net.

7–9   Smoothly translated from the prose version (published by Koenig half a century ago) that is based on the original Middle High German poetry, this is a dark, heroic romance of the thirteenth century that is thought by some authorities to be a companion to the *Nibelungenlied.* Gudrun, beautiful daughter of a Danish king, is kidnapped as her mother had been; betrothed to the ruler of Zealand, Gudrun and her retinue are kidnapped by a Norman prince. Years pass before she is rescued, years in which she serves the haughty mother of the prince, in which she resists his wooing, and in which battles are fought bitterly. In the end, reunion with her betrothed, and Gudrun's pardon to her captor. The story should appeal to students of medieval history or literature; it is, perhaps, too stately, too turgid in essence if not in style, to appeal to a wide audience.

719   **Kohn,** Bernice. *Echoes;* illus. by Dan Connor. Dandelion, 1979. 78-72139. Trade ed. ISBN 0-89799-102-8; Paper ed. ISBN 0-89799-037-4. 32p. Trade ed. $3.50; Paper ed. $1.50.

2–4   In a direct and simple explanation of a phenomenon that intrigues most children, Kohn explains how sound waves travel to create echoes. She describes some of the ways in which various animals use echolocation (the bat to guide its flight, the fish to locate prey) and how people use echoes in prospecting, in detecting underwater obstacles, or in medical examinations, and how—in addition to such mechanical uses—blind people often become sensitive to echoes as well as to direct sound. The illustrations are not all useful, some being merely decorative, but they are adequate; the text is nicely geared to the primary grades readers, using correct terminology but no unnecessary terms or ancillary information.

720   **Konigsburg,** E. L. *Journey To An 800 Number.* Atheneum, 1982. 81-10829. ISBN 0-689-30901-5. 138p. $9.95.

5–9   Two centuries ago, this might have carried such a subtitle as "The Hu-
*   manization of a Snobbish Boy, as He Meets a Variety of People on His Travels and Learns to Appreciate Them." The story is told by Maximilian, whose mother, remarried, has gone on her honeymoon and sent Max to stay with his father. Insistent on wearing the wool blazer with his private school's crest in the sweltering heat of the Southwest, Max feels superior to his father, his father's way of life (Woody travels with a camel from fair to convention to shopping centers, offering rides) and his father's trailer, to say nothing of his father's odd friends. However, prig though he is (and this is revealed by Max, who is the narrator) Max is also very bright and perceptive. By the time he's ready to go home, he's learned a lot about making allowances for other people, a

lot about loving Woody, and perhaps most of all about himself. The title refers to Max's eagerness to keep in touch with a girl he's met (he's a young adolescent, she's a pre-teen, and they are an enchanting pair) whose mother works for catalog firms at a toll-free number. Konigsburg has a remarkable flair for including off-beat characters who are eccentric but believable, and the story has her usual combination of originality of conception, felicity of style, and suffusion of wit.

721   **Konigsburg,** E. L. *Throwing Shadows.* Atheneum, 1979. 79-10422. ISBN 0-689-30714-4. 151p. $8.95.

6–9   Once again Konigsburg demonstrates that her versatility in approach and concept is equalled by her consistency in polished writing and depth of perception. Each of the five stories in this collection is told by a young person, and in each the protagonist gains insight into his or her own character, although such knowledge emerges in different ways. Each throws a shadow, and the shadows are distinct and unique. Ned, in "On Shark's Tooth Beach," finds that he cannot find satisfaction in outwitting a greedy collector, a pathetic old man; in the end he gives his avid rival a prize specimen and knows for the first time his own capacity for compassion. In Avery's story, "The Catchee," a natural victim of circumstance comes to a recognition of the fact that his experiences of being a shy and quiet victim have had an annealing effect. There's enough action to provide narrative flow, but the strength of the collection is in the provocative depth of the stories.

722   **Kooiker,** Leonie. *Legacy of Magic;* tr. from the Dutch by Patricia Crampton; illus. by Carl Hollander. Morrow, 1981. 81-11013. Trade ed. ISBN 0-688-00721-X; Library ed. ISBN 0-688-00722-8. 224p. Trade ed. $7.95; Library ed. $7.63.

3–5   A sequel to *The Magic Stone,* this pliant translation reflects the author's style and humor admirably, blending the direct, ingenuous tone and sophisticated wit nicely. Here the protagonist of the first book, Chris, is spending the summer with the crabby witch to whom he is apprenticed; the other major figure of the book is Alec, his friend. Alec, spending the summer with his grandfather, has no idea that Chris has supernatural powers, although he knows that Chris is deeply interested in the book of magic that Alec's grandfather has. There's magic and buried treasure to appeal to readers, two likeable boys heading a cast of diverse and believable characters, humor in dialogue, and a tight story line that develops at a good pace.

723   **Korschunow,** Irina. *A Night in Distant Motion;* tr. by Leigh Hafrey. Godine, 1983. 81-47325. ISBN 0-87923-399-0. 151p. $10.95.

7–10   Smoothly translated from the German original, published under the title *Er Hiess Jan,* this is the dramatic story of seventeen-year-old Regine, who had been a loyal Nazi until she met and fell in love with a Polish prisoner, Jan. Shorn and prisoned when her affair was discovered, Regine was saved by an air raid, escaping from captivity to hide in a farm family's garret. She tells her story in retrospect, shifting smoothly from the present to her affair with Jan and, going farther back, to her life before she met Jan. As her circumstances change and as she talks to Jan and others, Regine's opinions of the Nazis and of the war, change in a convincing way. This is written with depth and skill, a strong and touching story of an awakened ethical conscience.

724   **Krasnoff,** Barbara. *Robots: Reel to Real.* Arco, 1982. 81-3514. ISBN 0-688-05139-6. 154p. illus. with photographs. $12.95.

6–   More comprehensive than Jonathan Rutland's *The World of Robots* or *Robots A2Z* by Thomas Metos, this is for a somewhat older group of readers but probably will, because of the appeal of the subject, attract readers in the middle grades as well. Krasnoff gives good coverage to the robots of the entertainment world but points out that present and future robots are unlikely to have the human traits of robots or androids of stories or films. She describes the ways in which robots of varying complexity function, from the simple machines to modular robots or the still more intricate teleoperators and their uses. An interesting survey, written in a fairly informal and eminently readable style, this is made more useful by lists of sources (periodicals, organizations, how-to books, etc.) that precede the index.

725   **Krementz,** Jill. *How It Feels to Be Adopted.* Knopf, 1982. 82-48011. ISBN 0-394-52851-4. 107p. illus. with photographs. $11.95.

4–7   Nineteen children, ranging in age from eight to sixteen, discuss, in separate interviews, their feelings about being adopted; the book is illustrated by fine photographs of the children and their families and the text is preceded by a thoughtful introduction. The monologues are candid and direct, describing the ways each of the adopted children feels about his or her natural parents, whether it makes a difference to have other adopted children in the family, how and when they were told they were adopted, whether or not they want to meet (or have met) their birthparents. Touching and trenchant, this gives a strong picture of the closeness of family relationships between children and their adoptive families, and a clear indication of the wisdom of candor between adoptive parents and their children.

726   **Krementz,** Jill. *How It Feels When a Parent Dies.* Knopf, 1981. 80-8808. ISBN 0-394-51911-6 112p. illus. with photographs. $9.95.

5–8   The author has used the same combination of taped interviews and handsome photographs (although fewer of them) as she did in her series on young performers. Eighteen children between the ages of seven to sixteen speak with candor about their experiences and emotions when a father or mother died (some by accident, some by their own hand, some because of an illness) and on their reactions to various aspects of bereavement: how they wish people had treated them, or how their feelings have changed with the passage of time. This is a sad book, but it is too honest, as the children speak, to be morbid, and it may well prove both consoling to readers who have also lost a parent and clarifying to all readers who feel ambivalence or confusion or guilt about their reactions to death.

727   **Krementz,** Jill. *A Very Young Circus Flyer;* written and illus. with photographs by Jill Krementz. Knopf, 1979. 78-20546. 104p. $9.95.

4–6   Like other Krementz books about young participants in sports or the performing arts, this is based on interviews and told in first person, and is profusely illustrated with excellent photographs, some of which are action shots and some in full color. Nine-year-old Tato Farfan, youngest of a family of aerial performers, prattles on about circus life, the way he trains and rehearses, and the family's performance. This has more material about other aspects of the milieu than do earlier books, so that it's a bit more diffuse, but it has the same casual ease in delivery, and the glamour of the setting should appeal to an even wider audience than do the other books.

728   **Krensky,** Stephen. *Conqueror and Hero: The Search for Alexander;* illus. by Alexander Farquharson. Little, Brown, 1981. 81-3791. Hardcover ed. ISBN 0-316-50373-8; Paperback ed. ISBN 0-316-50374-6. 67p. illus. with photographs. Hardcover ed. $8.95; Paperback ed. $4.95.

5–9   Photographs of objects from the exhibit, "The Search for Alexander," awkward figures in line drawings, and a map of the Greek world at the time of Alexander are used to amplify a text that focuses on the thirteen years during which Alexander the Great built his empire. Krensky provides adequate background information and a brief description of the events that followed Alexander's death. The writing style is casual, almost conversational at times, but never diffuse; the text—being shorter than most Alexandrian biographies—may appeal to reluctant readers.

729   **Krensky,** Stephen. *A Ghostly Business.* Atheneum, 1984. 84-2971. ISBN 0-689-31048-X. 144p. $10.95.

4–6   The five Wynd children come to Boston to visit their Aunt Celia, and they're disturbed to find that she is distraught and that odd things are happening in the house. Both, it develops, are caused by a ghost, the former butler of the household, and a gentle, unhappy creature suffering from a curse. He's also being bullied by some other ghosts who are working for a slick realtor who hopes that Aunt Celia will sell him the house if the ghost really perturbs her. Since the children share with Aunt Celia an ability to do magic, a power struggle begins as they try to help their aunt and their ghost against the machinations of others. This light fantasy is consistent within its illogical parameters, and the light style, the humor, the magic, and the triumph of good over evil provide an entertaining reading experience.

730   **Krensky,** Stephen. *A Troll in Passing.* Atheneum, 1980. 79-22283. ISBN 0-689-30747-0. 144p. $7.95.

4–6   Morgan was a nonconformist. All the other trolls accepted their apprenticeships, doted properly on treasure, and firmly believed that sunlight would turn them to stone. Not Morgan, who kept his eyes and his mind open; that's why it was he who found a way to outwit the army of giant trolls who were bent on evicting Morgan's tribe from their cozy mountain caves. Krensky's writing style, fluent and sophisticated, is not bland, easy reading, but it's well worth pursuing in a nicely crafted story that has pace, humor, and momentum.

731   **Kronenwetter,** Michael. *Are You a Liberal? Are You a Conservative?* Watts, 1984. 83-27417. ISBN 0-531-04751-2. 104p. illus. $8.90.

7–10   An introduction to Western mainstream political thought, this study begins with the advent of liberalism during the Enlightenment. Kronenwetter examines two similar 18th century documents—America's Constitution and the French Declaration of the Rights of Man—to show the differences between (and common goals of) liberal and conservative thought, and how these beliefs have changed and developed to the present day in the United States. His explanation is clear, with interesting detail: the terms "left" and "right" derive from where the nobles and the bourgeoisie sat at a meeting of Louis XVI's Estates-General. Occasionally this is too simple, characterizing liberals as "optimists" and conservatives as "pessimists," but its strength is in conveying the common vision of freedom held by both sides. An index (which should be more detailed) and an annotated bibliography are appended.

732   **Kuklin,** Susan. *Mine for a Year;* written and illus. with photographs by Susan Kuklin. Coward, 1984. 83-23916. ISBN 0-698-20603-7. 77p. $10.95.

4–6   Told from the viewpoint of George, who for one year is responsible for the care and training of a puppy destined to become a guide dog for the blind, this has a subtle poignancy because George fears he himself is going blind (he has poor vision, but learns in the course of the book that it won't get worse) and because he is one of the many foster-sons of a warm, motherly single woman. The photographs, which are of good quality, corroborate the love George expresses for his dog and make more graphic the details of the training the puppy gets. Readers may be interested in the training program, conducted under the auspices of the 4-H Club, as well as impressed by the candor and directness of the text.

733   **Kullman,** Harry. *The Battle Horse;* tr. from the Swedish by George Blecher and Lone Thygesen-Blecher. Bradbury, 1981. 81-2192. ISBN 0-87888-175-1. 183p. $8.95.

6–8   A vivid picture of social strata in Stockholm fifty years ago is told by Roland, one of the public school boys who look up to and envy the "preppies," their opposite numbers in the higher level of the caste system. In fact, in the recurrent game the neighborhood boys play, feudal jousting, Roland and his friends serve—and feel honored to serve—as horses. The action focuses on the identity of the masked Black Knight who defeats all foes until, finally defeated by Roland's hero, Henning, she is revealed—a girl. It is also a girl who serves as Henning's "horse," a girl who first awakens in Roland a realization of the inequities of the gulf between the horses and their riders, a girl who dies as a result of the battle in which she has carried Henning to victory. The story moves slowly at the start but gathers momentum and power as it draws to a trenchant conclusion. Original, provocative, this is a moving novel from an eminent Swedish writer, runner-up in 1980 for the Hans Christian Andersen Medal.

734   **Kumin,** Maxine W. *The Microscope;* illus. by Arnold Lobel. Harper, 1984. 82-47728. Library ed. ISBN 0-06-023524-1; Trade ed. ISBN 0-06-023523-3. 28p. Library ed. $9.89; Trade ed. $9.95.

K–3   Both factual and merry, this brief and deft poem first appeared as one of the selections in *The Wonderful Babies of 1809 (And Other Years)* in 1968. It points out that Anton van Leeuwenhoek neglected his business to pursue investigation of the new worlds visible through the first crude microscopes. This isn't quite accurate, since it ends "That's how we got the microscope." Still, the combined talents of a Pulitzer Prize poet and a Caldecott Medal artist have created a small gem, Lobel's pseudograve pictures having the hatched, incised look of old lithographs.

735   **Kushner,** Donn. *The Violin-Maker's Gift;* illus. by Doug Panton. Farrar, 1982. 81-19406. ISBN 0-374-38155-0. 74p. $8.95.

5–6   Winner of the 1981 Canadian Library Association Book of the Year for Children Award, this is a gentle fantasy in the folk tradition, illustrated by heavily hatched black and white drawings. The setting is the French Pyrenees, where Gaspard the violin-maker lived in contented isolation with his patient donkey, leaving his hut only to take his instruments to market in the town nearby. It was there that he rescued a young bird trapped in the church belfry, later giving the bird to the keeper of the toll gate, Matthias, as a tip for his services. Gaspard began to hear rumors that the bird could not only talk but also predict the future; when he saw the bird, which had grown large and beautiful (looking, in the illustrations, like a lyrebird) and realized that Matthias was exploiting the creature he stole it and set it free. Before it left, the bird told Gaspard a great secret, so that from that time on the violin-maker's instruments sang as though they had a soul. This may not appeal to readers who crave action and excitement, but it has a mellow, almost nostalgic quality and a quiet humor that, combined with the twin appeals of magic and justice, may be enjoyed by readers who can appreciate the nuance of the writing.

736   **Kuskin,** Karla. *Herbert Hated Being Small;* written and illus. by Karla Kuskin. Houghton, 1979. 77-25029. ISBN 0-395-26462-6. 32p. $6.95.

K–3   Bright line and watercolor pictures illustrate a book that presents a concept of comparative size, identifies a problem which many children have, tells a satisfying story, and is written in free, fluent rhyme. Herbert, dismayed because everything and everybody around him is too big (Who likes to be called "shrimp"?) runs off with his bear and some candy to find people his size. Philomel, who lives in another place where she towers over everything and everybody, packs some candy and her bear and runs off to find people as big as she is. (She was tired of hearing "How's the air up there?") They meet, find they are the same size, realize that big or small depends on what size other objects or people are, and are comforted.

737   **Kuskin,** Karla. *The Philharmonic Gets Dressed;* by Marc Simont. Harper, 1982. 81-48658. Trade ed. ISBN 0-06-023622-1; Library ed. ISBN 0-06-023623-X. 42p. Trade ed. $10.50; Library ed. $10.89.

K–2   The vigor and humor of Simont's illustrations add vitality to a direct, simple text that describes the evening's preparation by the conductor and the musicians of the New York Philharmonic Orchestra. Most of the book is devoted to the bathing, shaving, and dressing that goes on in the homes of the thirteen women and ninety-two men. The humor should carry the book for those children who are not familiar with a live performance of symphonic music, since there is little broad action; for children who have been taken to a concert or watched a performance on television it should be even more appealing to think of the producers of music as people who struggle into their garments before going to work.

738   **Laiken,** Deidre S. *Listen to Me, I'm Angry;* by Deidre S. Laiken and Alan J. Schneider; illus. by Bernice Myers. Lothrop, 1980. 79-23406. Trade ed. ISBN 0-688-41943-7; Library ed. ISBN 0-688-51943-1. 125p. Trade ed. $6.95; Library ed. $6.67.

7–10   Laiken and Schneider neither preach nor condemn; in a text that is written in a straightforward style and an equally direct tone, they examine the various causes of anger and the ways in which anger is manifested, and they suggest ways in which people can recognize and deal with their anger. The text is addressed to the adolescent and uses many anecdotes and examples to illustrate the ways in which anger is expressed, or translated into physical illness, or used to manipulate a relationship. The authors make it clear that it is normal to feel angry, and that it can be controlled or directed. A sensible book, this can help adolescents understand their own and other people's anger and—to some extent—to deal with it. A closing chapter gives brisk advice on coping in specific circumstances (bereavement, divorce, physical handicaps, etc.) and suggests the various levels of professional help that are available. A bibliography and an index are appended.

739   **Lampton,** Christopher. *Space Sciences;* illus. by Anne Canevari Green. Watts, 1983. 82-16108. ISBN 0-531-04539-0. 93p. $8.90.

5–   Illustrated with photographs and diagrams that are adequately placed and labelled, this is an alphabetical series of entries about astronomical bodies and phenomena, the space program, astronauts, and astronomers and other scientists whose work is relevant to space science. The entries are crisply written, clear and authoritative, with cross references to aid the reader. Save for the small print, a useful and informative quick reference source.

740   **Landau,** Elaine. *Child Abuse: An American Epidemic.* Messner, 1984. 84-996. ISBN 0-671-47988-1. 117p. $9.97.

7–10   In a text that covers physical, psychological, and sexual abuse of children and adolescents, Landau focuses on abuse by parents or "caretakers." This is, therefore, not comprehensive, but it does a good job of explaining in a candid if dry style some of the causes of the tragic results. Certainly one useful aspect of the book is the amount of information it gives about preventive and palliative measures, and about social services and legal resources that work with parents as well as those individual agencies and networks that help, protect, or defend the victims of child abuse. A bibliography and an index are provided.

741   **Landau,** Elaine. *Why Are They Starving Themselves? Understanding Anorexia Nervosa and Bulimia.* Messner, 1983. 82-24913. ISBN 0-671-45582-6. 110p. $9.29.

7–   Using case histories in anecdotal format, with many statements by girls and women who are victims of the two eating disorders, anorexia and bulimia, Landau explores the emotional and physiological factors that lead people into the pattern of self-starvation of the anorectic adolescent or the binge-purge cycle of bulimia, a pattern that sometimes is associated with anorexia nervosa but is also a discrete illness. The text describes the situations that are typical matrices for these disorders and discusses their progress, symptoms, and treatment. The coverage is full, the tone objective, the facts—dramatic and desperate—provided with calm authority. A bibliography and a relative index are provided.

742   **Lang,** Andrew, ad. *Aladdin and the Wonderful Lamp;* illus. by Errol Le Cain. Viking, 1981. 81-4861. ISBN 0-670-11146-5. 32p. $10.95.

3–5   The rich colors and baroque swirls of ornamentation in the artist's interpretation of the story are in the tradition of Persian painting, with a romantic mood and a high sense of design. Le Cain's interpretation is wonderfully appropriate for the extravagant fantasy of the story of the poor boy whose life was changed when he met the wish-fulfilling genie of the lamp; in the best fairytale tradition, Aladdin outwits the evil magician, wins the hand of a princess, and succeeds to the throne of her father, the sultan.

743   **Lang,** Andrew, comp. *Pink Fairy Book;* ed. by Brian Alderson; illus. by Colin McNaughton. Viking, 1982. 81-70403. ISBN 0-670-55536-3. 332p. $14.95.

4–6   In this new edition of a classic anthology, Alderson has cut some stories, has edited or translated others, and has provided notes that explain his changes or give background information. The black and white illustrations are distinctive for their wit, dramatic sense, and texture. Alderson has succeeded admirably in his goal of making the tales more palatable for a contemporary audience rather than for the Victorian readers who were Lang's audience, and he has done so without oversimplifying the language or sacrificing the narrative flow.

744   **Langner,** Nola. *Freddy My Grandfather;* written and illus. by Nola Langner. Four Winds, 1979. 79-9926. ISBN 0-590-07577-2. 32p. $6.95.

2–3   The author-artist's pencil and wash drawings have a slight touch of the grotesque in the figures, and a chunky, rumpled quality that seems, at times, to over-fill the pages. The text consists of a small girl's thoughts about the grandfather who lives with her and her parents. At times she comments on a habit that irritates her (he stays in her room too long when her friends are visiting) or her mother (he won't say when he'll be home) but for the most part the commentary is on where Freddy came from (Hungary) and what he did (tailoring) and what his room is like, or on the ways in which he comforts her, protects her, and loves her—and she concludes with the best thing about her grandfather: she loves him. There's a warmth in the tone of the writing, and a clear picture of a real person and a real relationship, but the text may well prove too static to appeal to some children.

745   **Langone,** John. *Like, Love, Lust; A View of Sex and Sexuality.* Little, 1980. 79-26428. ISBN 0-316-51429-2. 175p. $7.95.

8–   This is addressed to somewhat older readers than the Comfort book on this topic, and although there is overlap in the discussions about some aspects of sexuality (homosexuality, for example, or pornography) it does not address itself to providing facts about anatomy or sexual intercourse. Langone is concerned with the sexual aspects of human relationships, with the ranges of attitudes about sexual behavior, and with personal adjustments to social institutions, both those that are sanctioned by society (like marriage) and those that are not sanctioned (like prostitution). His exploration of values, concepts, emotions, and psychological influences on their formation is astute and clear-eyed; his writing style is direct and objective. Like the Comforts, Langone is concerned about the individual's responsibility in sexual relationships, including the responsibilities of partners in a marital relationship. A section of notes precedes the index.

746   **Langone,** John. *Violence: Our Fastest-Growing Public Health Problem.* Little, 1984. 84-5674. ISBN 0-316-51431-4. 208p. $12.95.

7–   In a text that has a logical structure and gives good coverage, Langone discusses the causes of both individual violence and of mob behavior, spontaneous or planned. Separate chapters deal with such subjects as violence in sports, violence in prison, domestic violence, rape, and assassination. Throughout the book there are references to violence throughout history and in all parts of the world, making it clear that— although the weapons of today may be more sophisticated—violence is not a new phenomenon nor one restricted to any race, creed, class, or nationality. A final chapter makes some suggestions for dealing with violence; chapter notes precede a fairly extensive index.

747   **Langton,** Jane. *The Fledgling.* Harper, 1980. 79-2008. Trade ed. ISBN 0-06-023678-7; Library ed. ISBN 0-06-023679-5. 182p. Trade ed. $7.95; Library ed. $7.89.

5–7   Walden Pond is the setting for a story that deftly blends realism and fantasy, and that has some of Langton's best writing yet; this has all the imaginative conception of Langton's earlier stories about Eleanor and Eddy (*The Diamond in the Window, The Swing in the Summerhouse*) but it has more passages, also, that are at the same time as delicate and as bold as a frost-etched window. Here Eleanor and Eddy are the bystanders, organized as the Georgie Protection Society to help their odd, shy little cousin from doing crazy things. It is crazy to fly, and Georgie flies. There is a loving rapport between Georgie and an old, solitary Canada goose who teaches her to fly. Her mother worries about Georgie's night adventures, but it is their neighbor, Mr. Preek, who ends Georgie's joyous soaring forever; she has bade goodbye to her goose, and is horrified when Preek shoots him. Her Goose Prince has left a gift for Georgie, a magical gift to comfort her. The ending is poignant, but not sad, in this memorable story.

748   **Langton,** Jane. *The Fragile Flag.* Harper, 1984. 83-49471. Library ed. ISBN 0-06-023699-X; Trade ed. ISBN 0-06-023698-1. 275p. Library ed. $11.89; Trade ed. $11.95.

5–7   Georgie, one of the children of a Concord family that has been promi-
*   nent in earlier fantasies by Langton, is determined that the (fictional) President get her letter about what the flag of the United States stands for. With no other way to get to Washington, Georgie decides to walk, carrying an old flag that has been in the family attic. The flag has magical powers, inducing visions of what war might bring, but it doesn't

have any magical effect upon the action. Georgie's cousins march with her, so do a few friends, including one girl who pushes a baby brother in his carriage. (The willingness of all parents to let their children march through state after state along a major highway requires suspension of disbelief). By the time Georgie and her fragile flag reach the District of Columbia there are thirteen thousand children from all parts of the country who are marching for peace. The President bows to their numbers and calls off the launching of a nuclear missile. This is a message book; it is anti-missile, anti-war; it assumes a militant and reactionary leader and a public and a press who are opposed to his views. There may be differences of opinion about the political-military implications of the story; there can be little disagreement about its effectiveness as a piece of dramatic and polished writing. The book has good pace, momentum, strong characters, and a sturdy story line.

749   **Larrick,** Nancy, comp. *When the Dark Comes Dancing;* illus. by John Wallner. Philomel, 1983. 81-428. ISBN 0-399-20807-0. 79p. $15.95.

2–5   A fine anthology of poems and lullabies for young children is illustrated
yrs.   by double-page spreads, alternately in color and in black and white. The pictures have soft textures, subdued colors, and imaginative details. The poems and lullaby lyrics have been chosen with discriminating care; among the contributors are Eleanor Farjeon, Aileen Fisher, Arthur Guiterman, Karla Kuskin, Myra Cohn Livingston, Eve Merriam, Christina Rossetti, and Robert Louis Stevenson.

750   **Lasker,** Joe. *The Do-Something Day.* Viking, 1982. 81-2508. ISBN 0-670-27503-4. 30p. illus. $12.95.

K–2   Since his parents and his brother reject his help because they're too busy to be interrupted, Bernie feels unwanted and decides to run away. As he stops to say goodby to people working in the neighborhood, each asks his help and each gives him a gift; Lasker uses this for the sort of cumulation children enjoy ("So Bernie walked on with his great big folded road map, his nice salami and sour pickle, his warm rye bread and cookies . . ."). On his last stop, Bernie's given a stray pup that's wandered into a pet shop. He decides to go home, finds his family waiting anxiously and appreciative of the useful goodies he's brought back; his mother hugs him and says, "We need help from one another, Bernie. But we really need you to love." Nicely composed pictures in muted colors show a heterogeneous urban neighborhood; the story should appeal to the read-aloud audience: the feeling of being left out that young children often experience, the pride in being a participant or contributor, and the assurance that one is loved for oneself alone. The writing style is succinct but smooth, the plot stretched a bit but still credible.

751   **Lasker,** Joe. *Nick Joins In;* written and illus. by Joe Lasker. Whitman, 1980. 79-29637. ISBN 0-8075-5612-2. $6.50.

2–3   Nick, who wears braces to help him stand and uses a wheelchair, is very nervous about going to public school; he's been used to having a teacher come to his house. The school installs a ramp, and Nick is self-conscious when he comes into class the first day. His teacher introduces him, gives the class time to ask him questions (his lameness is explained by "Because my legs don't grow right," a congenital condition) and satisfy their curiosity. Nick is accepted and quite happy, but is happiest of all the day he thinks of a way to get a basketball down from a high gutter (the school's window pole) and feels he's really made a contribution. Lasker handles Nick's apprehension and his parent's calm treatment of it, in matter-of-fact fashion; the line and wash drawings are realistic, the writing style is a bit choppy but not obtrusively so; the story focuses on the mainstreaming of exceptional children.

752   **Lasky,** Kathryn. *Beyond the Divide.* Macmillan, 1983. 82-33867. ISBN 0-02-751670-9. 253p. $11.95.

7–10   One of a large Amish family, Meribah decides to leave and go west with her father, who has been shunned by the rest of his family for breaking the strict Amish code. This is the story of that journey; it is preceded by a brief entry dated January, 1850, when Meribah, alone and starving in the Sierra wilderness, fights off two vultures so that she can eat some of the doe on which they had been feeding. The text moves back nine mouths, to describe Meribah's decision and the long, detailed journey in which she suffers the slow privations of the trek, is horrified by the rape and ensuing suicide of the one friend she's made, is bereaved when her father dies of a wound infection, is finally left alone and stranded. Rescued by a group of Yahi Indians, Meribah learns to love them and their way of life; by this time it is June of 1850 and she has decided she will go back, alone, to a fertile valley she had loved when the wagon train had halted there. An afterword explains that soon thereafter, the Yana (of which the Yahi were a tribe) had been exterminated by whites, and that in 1900 the last Yahi was found: Ishi, the last of his tribe. Lasky writes a vivid and stirring tale that takes the pseudo-romance out of westward migration; while the painstaking delineations of minor characters are interesting, they shift the focus from the protagonist, who is going through more than the physical trials of the journey, for she is learning to understand a range of people whose life-styles and interests conflict with Amish mores. Despite the pace, an interesting story.

753   **Lasky,** Kathryn. *Dollmaker: The Eyelight and the Shadow;* illus. with photographs by Christopher G. Knight. Scribner, 1981. 81-9262. ISBN 0-684-17170-8. 64p. $10.95.

6–   Excellent photographs expand and amplify the text, showing each step of the process of Carole Bowling's construction of an amazingly life-like doll modelled on her small son. The pictures are fascinating, as is the text, written in a flowing, direct, informal prose, and together they provide a vivid introduction to the intricate, painstaking artistry that creates a hand-crafted doll.

754   **Lasky,** Kathryn. *My Island Grandma;* illus. by Emily McCully. Warne, 1979. 78-12489. 27p. $7.95.

4–7 yrs.   Abbey describes the joys of her island summer in a book that has no story line but depends on the charm of setting and incidents to appeal to the read-aloud audience. Through Abbey, Lasky gives a vivid picture of the island, the long days of summer, and the relationship between Abbey and her grandmother as they observe nature, take a lazy sail, have a swimming lesson, and enjoy cozy cookie-bakes. Abbey's parents (in a cabin near Grandma's) are conspicuously absent, and astute young listeners will detect a few hints about behavior, but the whole is a sunny, bracing entity, with ink and wash drawings that have vitality expressed through scratchy line and soft bright colors.

755   **Lasky,** Kathryn. *The Night Journey;* illus. by Trina Schart Hyman. Warne, 1981. 81-2225. ISBN 0-7232-6201-2. 150p. $8.95.

4–6   Like Leonard Fisher's *A Russian Farewell* this describes the escape of a Jewish family from the persecutions and pogroms of Tsarist Russia. The story is illustrated with black and white drawings, strong in line and composition, realistic in approach, but romantic in feeling; it is told as a story-within-a-story, as thirteen-year-old Rachel learns, bit by bit, what her greatgrandmother went through as a child. The two parts of the story are deftly woven together, with the contemporary scenes having enough humor and characterization to give them substance but not so much that they detract from the drama of Nana Sashie's exciting tale.

756   **Lasky,** Kathryn. *Sugaring Time;* photographs by Christopher G. Knight. Macmillan, 1983. 82-23928. ISBN 0-02-751680-6. 58p. $10.95.

3–5   Illustrated with photographs of excellent quality, this describes the way in which a Vermont family gathers, converts, and uses the sap of their own small stand of maple trees, their "sugarbush." Lasky's frame for the account, which has a narrative quality but is not fictionalized, is poetic but not prolix; it evokes both a sense of the changing seasons and a sense of the Lacey family's anticipation and—for all the hard work—pleasure. The children help their parents put out sap buckets and gather them, help with the slow procedures by which the sap is converted to syrup, and help with unflinching avidity in tasting, over and over, at every step. This is informative and attractive, less formal and more anecdotal than the equally fine book for the same reading range, Elizabeth's Gemming's *Maple Harvest: The Story of Maple Sugaring.*

757   **Lauber,** Patricia. *Journey to the Planets.* Crown, 1982. 82-1426. ISBN 0-517-54477-6. 90p. illus. with photographs. $11.95.

5–   In an exciting text that incorporates findings from recent space probes,
*   Lauber describes the planets, moons, and rings of our solar system, discussing their formation, composition, and behavior. Photographs are carefully placed and captioned, and an index (with phonetic spellings for difficult words) gives access to the contents. The material is dramatic and Lauber's writing style, straightforward and sequential, is a good foil for that drama; what is most impressive is the clarity with which a mass of technical material is presented. The book is also a fine example of scientific writing, distinguishing between fact and theory, and making the reader aware of the guarded acceptance of evidence by the scientific community.

758   **Lauber,** Patricia. *Seeds; Pop, Stick, Glide;* illus. with photographs by Jerome Wexler. Crown, 1980. 80-14553. ISBN 0-517-54165-3. 57p. $9.95.

2–4   Superbly clear photographs, some magnified, are on every page of a handsome and informative book that introduces readers to the varieties of seeds; individual plants and their seeds are each allotted from one to three pages, and the minimal, clear text includes facts about how the seeds travel. Some are light and float in the air, some have barbs, some are eaten by animals and dropped, some travel by water. A final section gives a brief botanical description of seeds as parts of the parent plants, and discusses how they are formed and how they function.

759   **Lauber,** Patricia. *What's Hatching Out of That Egg?* Crown, 1979. 79-12054. ISBN 0-517-53724-9. 60p. illus. with photographs. $7.95.

2–4   Text and photographs work together very nicely in a book that encourages the reader to be observant and to use deduction. There's a game element in the way the text and pictures are arranged; both give information about the birth of some form of animal life; starting with the nest and the egg, a number of clues are given and, after several pages the reader comes to "These birds are . . ." or "It is a . . ." and, with the turn of the page comes the answer. A few may be difficult for young readers to guess (the platypus, for example) but most of the creatures are likely to be known to readers. A nice concept, nicely executed; the text is crisp and clear, the pictures are, with few exceptions, distinct.

760   **Lauré,** Jason. *South Africa; Coming of Age under Apartheid;* by Jason Lauré and Ettagale Lauré; illus. with photographs by Jason Lauré. Farrar, 1980. 79-23109. ISBN 0-374-37146-6. 180p. $13.95.

7–10   As in their earlier books (*Joi Bangla: The Children of Bangladesh* and *Jovem Portugal: After the Revolution*) the Laurés reflect, through their photojournalistic studies of young people in complex and changing societies, a broad picture of political and sociological facets of each society. Here they report on interviews with eight young South Africans, each of a different ethnic, tribal, or social group. Quoted comments by the subjects and excellent photographs add quick appeal to the depressing yet interesting picture of the imbalances and intricacies of apartheid and the ways in which it affects and limits young people. The picture is not without hope: many of those interviewed are (usually through education) seeing improvement—or hope of improvement—in their own lives; nevertheless, the Laurés conclude this important and eminently readable study by suggesting that major changes are unlikely to occur for many years. A glossary is provided.

761   **Lavine,** Sigmund A. *Wonders of Draft Horses;* by Sigmund A. Lavine and Brigid Casey; illus. with photographs and old prints. Dodd, 1983. 82-46002. ISBN 0-396-08138-X. 79p. $9.95.

5–7   Although the authors state that they have not attempted to be comprehensive, their book gives a great deal of information about the history of heavy horses, the development and improvement of major breeds, the intricacy and functions of the pieces of harness equipment, and the many ways in which draft horses are used today. Most of the text is written with an objective tone; the last chapter, which discusses the resurgent popularity of draft horses in recent years, has an emotional tinge in commenting on the horse (versus mechanized vehicles) as a self-propagating source of energy that does not pollute the atmosphere, contributes fertilizer, needs no repairs, and is enjoyably communicative. An index is included, as are many carefully captioned photographs.

762   **Lavine,** Sigmund A. *Wonders of Mice;* illus. Dodd, 1980. 80-1018. ISBN 0-396-07891-5. 80p. $6.95.

4–6   Like *Mice, All about Them* by Alvin and Virginia Silverstein this covers the topics of laboratory mice, mice in lore and legend, mice as laboratory animals, and the fact that there are mice whose behavior is beneficial to people as well as those (the majority) that are responsible for crop and property damage and the spread of disease. Lavine does not discuss mice as pets, as the Silversteins do, but does also focus on the varieties of species, the adaptability of the mouse, and the physical characteristics that have made the mouse so successful a mammal. Authoritative, clearly written, not quite as extensive in coverage as the Silverstein book but a fine introduction to the topic; an index is appended.

763   **Lawrence,** Louise. *Calling B for Butterfly.* Harper, 1982. 81-48648. Trade ed. ISBN 0-06-023749-X; Library ed. ISBN 0-06-023750-3. 224p. Trade ed. $11.90; Library ed. $11.89.

6–9   In a science fantasy that has pace and suspense, four young people and two small children are the only survivors when a space ship is hit by a catastrophe. None of the four has technical knowledge; sealed into the one section of the ship that has remained intact, they try repeatedly to get in touch with someone at their base, and when they finally succeed, they and the people who are trying to help them become aware that there is a mysterious and perhaps malevolent life force on the ship. The ending is unexpected and dramatic, a strong climax to a story in which the characters are vividly drawn and the situation convincingly desperate as the six people and their ghostly companion cope with tragedy, fear, love and hate, and hope.

764   **Lawrence,** Louise. *The Dram Road.* Harper, 1983. 83-47601. Trade ed. ISBN 0-06-023747-3; Library ed. ISBN 0-06-023748-1. 222p. Trade ed. $10.50; Library ed. $10.89.

6–10   Stuart hadn't meant to hit the man so hard when he and two of his mates were attempting robbery, but when he saw the still and bleeding body, he knew he was a murderer—and he ran. A series of aimless bus rides brought him to a small village, ill after his exposure to the cold, frightened and guilty. Sixteen, Stuart was used to the curses of an alcoholic mother, to being poor and fatherless; intending to rob an old man, Stuart found himself being nursed and protected by the old man he came to call "Grandad," and being given help by others in the village. Although this is in part a love story, in very small part a ghost story (the ghosts of Grandad's wife and son appear on the Dram Road and encourage Stuart to stay and help the old man), it is primarily a story of the change and maturity that come to an English adolescent. Love, trust, and kindness turn the delinquent Stuart into a young man who assumes responsibility, acquires ethical concepts, and learns to give as well as receive affection. The book ends with Stuart's decision, even though he knows by then his victim did not die, to turn himself in to the police, trusting that he will be able to return some day to the village. Smoothly written, tender and dramatic, this is both a credible story of human relationships and a vivid picture of family life.

765   **Lawson,** Annetta. *The Lucky Yak;* illus. by Allen Say. Parnassus/Houghton, 1980. 80-15083. ISBN 0-395-29523-8. 30p. $6.95.

K–3   Meticulous use of stippling, hatching, and parallel lines gives marvelous variety to Say's black and white drawings, clean in line and beautifully, often comically, detailed. Lawson uses the device that is so familiar in folk literature: if you're not content with your lot, try something else (*There's Always Room for One More, Meshka the Kvetch*) and you'll be grateful to go back to what you had. Here it's Edward Yak, who had emigrated with his parents from Tibet when he was very young, received a good education, made a great deal of money as a businessman, and had retired to early boredom. On consulting a psychologist, Edward is told he can take care of the doctor's little girl Muffin for a few days while the doctor goes away to think. An atrocious brat, Muffin soon wears poor Edward to a frazzle, and he is absolutely delighted to go back to the peace and quiet of the existence he had earlier found boring. There's humor and flavor in the writing style, and a nicely matched mood in the illustrations.

766   **Lawson,** Don. *FDR's New Deal;* illus. with photographs. T. Y. Crowell, 1979. 78-4775. ISBN 0-690-03953-0. 152p. $7.95.

7–10   As background for his analysis of the New Deal and the Roosevelt years in office, Lawson discusses the depression that followed the boom period that followed World War I, a series of events that called for emergency measures and was answered by the "new deal" program conceived by Roosevelt when he took office in 1933. His life up to that point is described in a chapter as crisp, lucid, and well-organized as is the rest of the book, which examines major figures, programs, and legislation of the Roosevelt years. An objective, balanced treatment that might well serve to engage older readers with reading or language problems. A section of photographs (the Roosevelt family, some leading political figures, some pictures related to the depression or to such programs as the C.C.C.) is bound in, a bibliography is included, and a lengthy relative index gives good access to the text.

767   **Lawson,** Don. *The War in Vietnam.* Watts, 1981. 81-3064. ISBN 0-531-04331-2. 83p. illus. with photographs. $7.40.

7–10   Lawson begins his survey by giving the historical background of the Indochinese peninsula, with the vacuum left after the French defeat being filled in part by the American "advisors" who were sent by Presidents Eisenhower and Kennedy before we were officially at war with North Vietnam. The text goes on to describe the Gulf of Tonkin resolution which brought the U.S. into open conflict, and the long and tragic struggle that led to "Peace Without Honor," the final chapter of a well-balanced, serious, and objective account of the longest war in United States history, a war the aftermath of which had political repercussions that extended to Watergate. This isn't extensively detailed, but it's a fine resumé; an index and a bibliography are appended.

768   **Leakey,** Richard E. *Human Origins.* Dutton, 1982. 81-23687. ISBN 0-525-66784-9. 87p. illus. $14.95.

7–   An oversize book, printed in two columns and profusely illustrated, this is a comprehensive and authoritative survey of the scientific evidence of the primitive ancestors of human beings, of the sites where that evidence was found, and of the ways in which fossil remains are identified, classified, and dated. Leakey, son of archeologists Louis and Mary Leakey, gives some background information about evolution and natural selection, and about the work of archeologists, and proceeds to a detailed chronological account of the emergence of homo sapiens from the first hominids. The writing style is serious but not dry, and the book concludes with the changes in living styles after (circa twenty thousand years ago) the physical evolution of human beings was complete. A bibliography, a glossary, and a relative index are included.

769   **Lear,** Edward. *An Edward Lear Alphabet;* illus. by Carol Newsom. Lothrop, 1983. 82-10037. Trade ed. ISBN 0-688-00964-6; Library ed. ISBN 0-688-00965-4. 27p. Trade ed. $10.00; Library ed. $9.12.

4–7   Lear's nonsense rhymes, lilting and humorous, are as palatable today as
yrs.   an aid to learning the alphabet as they were when first written, over a
century ago. Here the illustrator uses animal characters in large-scale watercolor paintings, richly detailed and textured, set off by ample white space, for a letter and verse per page. Upper and lower case letters precede each verse and are repeated, larger and in varied, stylized forms elsewhere on the page. The rhyme, rhythm, and fun of "C was once a little cake/Caky/Baky/Maky/Caky/Taky Caky/Little cake!" isn't hurt a bit by a picture of a very small mouse laboriously frosting a very large cake.

770   **Lear,** Edward. *How Pleasant to Know Mr. Lear!* with an introduction and notes by Myra Cohn Livingston. Holiday House, 1982. 82-80822. ISBN 0-8234-0462-5. 123p. illus. $10.95.

6–   Providing biographical information in the introduction, Livingston uses quotations from Lear for each group of poems; for example, his phrase "One of the Singers" heads a section of poems and limericks about performers and instruments, and poems about travel are gathered under the heading, "The Days of His Pilgrimage." Each section begins with a note by the compiler, and notes on sources, as well as a combined title/first line index are appended. While the poetry is easily available elsewhere, it is useful to have the combination of poetry by Lear and information about him, each reinforcing the other.

771   **Lee,** Mildred. *The People Therein.* Houghton/Clarion, 1980. 80-12968. ISBN 0-395-29434-7. 269p. $10.95.

7–10   In a story set in the Smoky Mountains at the turn of the century, crippled Lanthy falls deeply in love with a stranger from far-off Boston, Drew. Although the mountain folk can't understand a man who just wanders around looking at plants, they accept Drew. They don't realize that he is in retreat, trying to conquer alcoholism; Lanthy's father (a strict temperance man) does discover it and is slow to forgive Drew. Drew and Lanthy become lovers; he is called back to Boston (his sister is dying) and doesn't know that Lanthy is pregnant. By the time he comes back to Appalachia, the child is born and the fact that he is the father is known to everyone in Dewfall Gap. Drew and Lanthy marry, the happy ending to a fairly conventional romance—but this is more than that, for Lee's perceptive interpretation of cultural patterns in Southern Appalachia, her fine characterization and her sensitivity to the complexities of human relationships give the book depth and color.

772   **Leech,** Jay. *Bright Fawn and Me;* by Jay Leech and Zane Spencer; illus. by Glo Coalson. T. Y. Crowell, 1979. 78-19215. Trade ed. ISBN

0-690-039737-9; Library ed. ISBN 0-690-03938-7. 30p. Trade ed. $6.95;
Library ed. $6.89 net.

K–2   Set a century ago, the story is told by a Cheyenne child whose family is
participating in an inter-tribal fair, and whose pleasure is dimmed by
the fact that she is in charge of her small sister, Bright Fawn. Bright
Fawn, plump and cheerful, draws fond comments from passersby, but
her sister is not enchanted by the repeated remark, "You have a fine
little sister," while she's coping with a clinging little hand, a dirty and
sticky face that Bright Fawn refuses to have cleaned, and the slow,
stumbling walk that's all Bright Fawn can manage. Still, when another
girl echoes her comment that her little sister is a pest, she becomes irritated, and offers a protective, loving hand. Told with a sweet simplicity,
the story shows the eternal and universal qualities of a sibling relationship, and it's enhanced by the illustrations, in soft earth colors, of two
attractive children in varied scenes of the cheerful bustle of the fair.

773   **LeGuin,** Ursula K. *The Beginning Place.* Harper, 1980. 79-2653. ISBN 0-
06-012573-X. 183p. $8.95.

7–   Hugh lives with a nagging, demanding mother who insists he be at
home every night whether she is there or not; one day he finds that his
woodland ramble has a threshold to a world where time (real time)
stops. Irene, escaping from an unhappy domestic situation, has long
known this threshold, the "beginning place" where she enters another
world. She is loved by the people there, and she resents Hugh's coming, resents even more the fact that the residents of this world of per-
petual twilight, Tembreabrezi, seem to regard Hugh as their hero. For
both young people, Tembreabrezi is a haven until they are presented
with a formidable task: to save the country by going alone into the
mountains to slay the loathsome creature that is preying on the land.
The journey brings the two closer together, first as companions and
then as lovers; coming back to their own world, Hugh and Irene plan
their future together, each strengthened by the other's love. LeGuin is
an articulate spellbinder, weaving realism and fantasy together so that
each augments the other; her characters are developed in depth, her
plot constructed with skill, pace, and suspense.

774   **LeGuin,** Ursula K. *Leese Webster;* illus. by James Brunsman. Atheneum,
1980. 79-10424. ISBN 0-689-30715-2. 30p. $7.95.

K–3   One of many spiders living in a deserted palace, Leese wondered why
her webs, beautiful and practical though they were, must be the same
every time; she began experimenting, and the other spiders looked at
her work with more curiosity than approbation. Leese herself, although
she loved the intricate patterns and pictures she wove, was frustrated
when she looked at the grey uniformity and remembered the flashing
colors of the jewels that had once decorated the throne. When the
building was opened as a museum, Leese's beautiful webs were put

under glass. Leese was put outdoors; when she wove a web to catch a meal and then saw the dew on her web catching the sunlight, she thought it was the most beautiful web she'd made. Save for the slightly grotesque human figures, the illustrations have a spacious fragility that corresponds neatly to the poetic concept and style of the text of this quiet story.

775   **Lehrman,** Robert. *Juggling.* Harper, 1982. 81-48654. Trade ed. ISBN 0-06-023818-6; Library ed. ISBN 0-06-023819-4. 256p. Trade ed. $11.50; Library ed. $11.89.

7–10   Howie Berger, the narrator, is baffled. His father had taught him to play soccer and cheered his prowess on the high school team. Now (1960) Howie wants to go to the one college that highlights soccer, and his father insists that he go to a better school than St. Louis University. That's the background for the immediate action of the book, Howie's participation in an all-Jewish team that consists mostly of older players, most of whom ignore or belittle him. The story ends with Howie's more realistic appraisal of his own game, his understanding of why the older members of the team have not accepted him, and his father's agreement that Howie may go to St. Louis. There's also a love interest (a first affair that ends with the girl going back to a former lover) to balance the emphasis on the father-son relationship and on the soccer team; these are smoothly fused, perceptively explored, and given contrast by the descriptions of game sequences.

776   **Lerner,** Carol. *A Biblical Garden;* written and illus. by Carol Lerner; quotations from the Hebrew Bible tr. by Ralph Lerner. Morrow, 1982. 81-16886. ISBN 0-688-01071-7. 47p. $10.50.

5–
*   Handsome botanical drawings are detailed with scrupulous accuracy and are lovely in their shading, grace of line, and—on some pages—subtlety of color; some of the drawings are black and white. Lerner gives a few facts about each plant, usually including information about how it was known, grown, or used in Biblical times and how it may be used today. Each page of text (almost always two brief paragraphs) is preceded by common and scientific names and a Biblical quotation in which the plant is mentioned; each such page faces a full-page painting or drawing. Attractive, with limited reference use.

777   **Lerner,** Carol. *Flowers Of A Woodland Spring;* written and illus. by Carol Lerner. Morrow, 1979. 78-32154. Trade ed. ISBN 0-668-22190-4; Library ed. ISBN 0-688-32190-9. 27p. Trade ed. $7.95; Library ed. $7.63 net.

3–5
*   The delicacy and fidelity of Lerner's exquisite paintings and drawings (some in color, some in black and white) are set off by spacious and dignified page layout. The text describes the ephemeral flowering plants of early springtime, plants like spring beauty or trout lilies, those early bloomers that disappear as soon as the trees above them come into leaf

and block the sunlight. Lerner shows, in clear diagrams and equally clear text, how the storage systems of such plants (through rhizomes, corms, bulbs, and tubers) carry through the long months between their short blooming seasons. A good book for budding botanists, and a pleasure to look at.

778   **Lerner,** Carol. *Seasons of the Tallgrass Prairie;* written and illus. by Carol Lerner. Morrow, 1980. 80-13078. Trade ed. ISBN 0-688-22245-5; Library ed. ISBN 0-688-32245-X. 48p. Trade ed. $7.95; Library ed. $7.63.

5–
*   Meticulously detailed fine-line drawings, carefully labelled, illustrate a text that describes the grasses and flowering plants in each of the seasons on the tall-grass prairie. Lerner's distinctive work cries for color, but her drawings are so exact that even the black and white pictures can be used for identifying plants. The text goes beyond mere description, however, since it discusses the ways in which prairie plants, deep-rooted, hold the soil and contribute to its richness, and the seasonal changes that bring new blooms and new colors. A list of plants mentioned or illustrated in the book is appended, arranged by common names but with scientific names provided.

779   **LeShan,** Eda. *Grandparents: A Special Kind of Love;* illus. by Tricia Taggart. Macmillan, 1984. 84-5673. ISBN 0-02-756380-4. 119p. $9.95.

4–6   An expert on inter- and intra-family relationships, LeShan discusses almost every conceivable situation, attitude, problem, behavior pattern, and danger (as well as pleasure) in grandparent-child relationships. Her tone is casual and intimate and straightforward, and her suggestions for understanding why grandparents have divergent or fluctuating behavior, for bringing problems into the open or, if one feels too uncomfortable talking about a problem with a grandparent, confiding in a parent or other adults, are sensible, practical, and constructive. Although there may be all kinds of problems in different families, the reiterated emphasis is on grandparental love, and the special feeling that often exists between grandparent and child.

780   **Levoy,** Myron. *A Shadow Like a Leopard.* Harper, 1981. 79-2812. Trade ed. ISBN 0-06-023816-X; Library ed. ISBN 0-06-023817-8. 184p. Trade ed. $8.95; Library ed. $8.79.

7–10   Ramon Santiago, fourteen, is one of a gang, a tough kid who participates in crime, who—with a father in jail for political activity and a mother hospitalized because of a nervous breakdown—is on his own. But Ramon has a tender heart, a gift for the poetic phrase, a deep yearning to be a writer. This is the story of his friendship with an elderly painter. Arnold Glasser, a friendship that springs, curiously, out of Ramon's attempt to rob the wheelchair-bound Glasser. The boy becomes the painter's advocate and manages (credibly) to get him a gallery showing. The story ends with Ramon's father coming home on parole and Ramon having, for the first time, the courage to be himself rather than to conform to his father's concept of what a macho adolescent ought to be. Tough, candid, and perceptive, this is an unusual story, unusually well told.

781   **Levoy,** Myron. *Three Friends.* Harper, 1984. 83-47713. Library ed. ISBN 0-06-023827-5; Trade ed. ISBN 0-06-023826-7. 187p. Library ed. $11.89; Trade ed. $11.50.

7–10   A novel with depth and compassion, the story of the friends is far from the usual triangle. Joshua is a loner who's never had a girl friend and seldom a boy as a friend; he's addicted to high-level tournament chess. Karen and Lori are best friends, Lori shy and sensitive and Karen a forthright, cheerful feminist. What happens when Joshua and Karen begin dating is that Lori, who cares for both of them but thinks she may have a lesbian love for Karen, withdraws and attempts suicide. Both of the others love her and have tried to include her in their plans, but Lori cannot accept the status quo until—during her recovery— Joshua presses her and gets her to admit her jealousy and her injured pride that her two dear friends ever want to do things without her. These are three interesting and well-defined characters, and Levoy has made them and their relationships believable and vivid. There may be a bit too much chess for some readers, but the book is otherwise as well-structured as it is well-written.

782   **Levy,** Elizabeth. *Come Out Smiling.* Delacorte, 1981. 80-68734. ISBN 0-440-01378-X. 192p. $8.95.

7–9   This is not at all the usual story of a summer camp, with patterned adjustment to camp life, for fourteen-year-old Jenny, who tells the story, is spending her final summer at a camp she's loved for many years; she's delighted to be seeing her old friends, to be horseback riding again, to be coached by the counselor on whom she's always had a crush, Peggy. It is a shock to Jenny when she sees Peggy kissing Ann, another counselor. Are they lesbians? Is she herself a lesbian? Upset, confused, and resentful, Jenny is furious when her sarcastic father, while visiting camp, casually comments that Peggy and Ann seem to him to be dykes. She never talks to the two women about her feelings, but she does come to realize that whatever their sexual preferences, they are still people she cares for; she isn't yet sexually responsive, but Jenny seems clearly heterosexual. Part of the story—and it's nicely woven in—has to do with Jenny's feelings about her father and his biting sarcasm, her resentment at being his target, and her realization, after talking to Ann about him, that there are reasons why people are sarcastic. The title refers to the practice Jenny's parents had of sending her to her room when she was angry, telling her not to come out until she could emerge smiling. That's the gist of this story, fine in style and characterization: Jenny is angry—very angry—for several reasons, and her last wish, in the final camp ceremony, is "Give me courage to come out smiling."

783   **Levy,** Elizabeth. *Something Queer on Vacation; A Mystery;* illus. by Mordicai Gerstein. Delacorte, 1980. 78-72858. Trade ed. ISBN 0-440-08346-X; Library ed. ISBN 0-440-08347-8. 42p. Trade ed. $6.95; Library ed. $6.46.

2–4   Jill and Gwen, vacationing on Fire Island, tell Gwen's little sister to keep away from their sand castle; they've never won the Sunday sand-castle contest and are determined to make one that is elaborate and impressive. Twice their project is wrecked, and they doggedly try to find out who wears flippers that have a shark trademark on the sole. Eventually they spot the culprit; they win the big Fourth of July contest, and little sister is banished to her room during the fireworks display. The scrawly, lively drawings have vigor and humor, and the plot is adequately constructed; the writing style is casual and the setting effective. This doesn't display as much detective power as Levy's other "Something Queer . . ." books, but it will probably be just as welcome to mystery-hungry readers in the primary grades.

784   **Lewin,** Hugh. *Jafta and the Wedding;* illus. by Lisa Kopper. Carolrhoda, 1983. 82-12836. ISBN 0-87614-210-2. 22p. $7.95.

K–2   This has more narrative appeal than the first book, since Jafta describes his sister's wedding, a process that gives facts about customs, has action sequences, and incorporates some humor. The illustrations show the beauty of the bride, again in spacious brown and white pictures, and the two together communicate the joy and excitement of a festive occasion. The other two books about Jafta are *Jafta's Mother* and *Jafta's Father,* neither of which has a story line but both of which express a loving parent-child relationship and inform readers about the roles of males and females in the rural society.

785   **Lewin,** Hugh. *Jafta—The Town;* illus. by Lisa Kopper. Carolrhoda, 1984. 84-4950. ISBN 0-87614-266-8. 22p. $7.95.

K–2   Brown-tinted line drawings, bold and usually uncrowded, illustrate a fifth story about a small African child, black and beautiful, in a series first published in England. The text is as simple and direct as the pictures, describing the visit Jafta and his mother make to the city where his father lives and works. Lewin does not dwell on the sadness of a loving family separated for financial survival, but it is mentioned, and it permeates the book.

786   **Lewis,** Marjorie. *Ernie and the Mile-Long Muffler;* illus. by Margot Apple. Coward, 1982. 82-1458. ISBN 0-698-20557-X. 38p. $9.95.

2–4   When his sailor uncle tells Ernie that one of his three favorite leisure time occupations is knitting, Ernie—who is in the bored state of convalescence after a bout with chicken pox—decides that he will not only learn to knit but get into the record books for knitting the longest muffler ever. He brings his project to school and is teased by the other boys; briefly discomforted, Ernie soon rallies. He talks about his uncle and his project, stimulates the class into wool-gathering (literally) and gives knitting lessons. He finally decides he's spending too much time knitting, that his muffler is impressive enough (314 feet long) and he goes back to a more diverse existence than he could have when he was knitting all the time. Ink and wash illustrations are a quiet and amusing foil for the story, which is written in an easy, direct style, is restrainedly non-sexist, and sturdily structured.

787   **Lewis,** Marjorie. *Wrongway Applebaum;* illus. by Margot Apple. Coward, 1984. 84-3242. ISBN 0-698-20610-X. 63p. $9.95.

3–5   Awkward at sports, uncomfortable with his classmates, aware that he's a disappointment to his baseball-loving father, Stanley Applebaum yearns for prowess and popularity. Well, acceptance, at least. When his grandmother becomes coach of a newly-formed fifth grade team, Applebaum has his chance. He never does improve as a ballplayer, but he's a great runner, so that the one time he does make contact (hard contact) with a ball, he has time to respond to his screaming teammates and run the bases the right way after having sped around them backwards. Fans of *Ernie and the Mile-Long Muffler* will recognize and enjoy the lively group of children who here, in the same light vein, amicably squabble, work, and play together.

788   **Lexau,** Joan M. *The Spider Makes a Web;* illus. by Arabelle Wheatley. Hastings House, 1979. 78-75103. ISBN 0-8038-6766-2. 40p. $5.95.

2–3   Illustrated with carefully detailed, realistic tinted drawings that are nicely integrated with the text, this is an accurate but simplified description of the life cycle of one variety of spider, the Shamrock spider. Lexau begins with the new-born spider spinning her silk, floating with the breeze until she lands, and spinning her first web. She describes the way in which the spider catches and feeds on her prey, the way in which she responds to a male spider drumming a mating signal on her web, and (omitting any mention of the mating process) how, at the end of her brief life span, the spider lays her eggs and wraps them in silk to protect them. The text concludes with the emergence of the baby spiders from their silk cradle on a warm, breezy spring day. A very nice first book on the subject, direct and clear.

789   **Lifton,** Betty Jean. *I'm Still Me.* Knopf, 1981. 80-24372. Trade ed. ISBN 0-394-84783-0; Library ed. ISBN 0-394-94783-5. 243p. Trade ed. $8.95; Library ed. $8.99.

7–10   There have been several stories for young adults about an adopted child seeking to learn about, or make contact with, natural parents. This story treats the subject with far more depth and sensitivity than the others;

Ms. Lifton has already written, for an adult audience, *Memoirs of an Adopted Daughter* and *Lost and Found: The Adoption Experience*. The story is told by Lori, a high school junior, and is nicely balanced by material about a younger brother (also adopted) and peer relationships, but it focuses on Lori's efforts to track down her mother, her feelings of guilt about keeping this effort from her loved adoptive parents, and her ambivalence when she does meet her mother. This has good structure, a smoothly flowing writing style, perceptive handling of characters and relationships, and a strong story line with suspense and dramatic contrasts.

790   **Lim,** Sing. *West Coast Chinese Boy;* written and illus. by Sing Lim. Tundra Books, 1979. 79-67110. ISBN 0-88776-121-6. 64p. $12.95.

4–7   Illustrated with brisk line drawings in pen and with monotype paintings, this is one of a series of Tundra books designed to bring children autobiographical accounts by members of Canada's ethnic minorities. Lim's childhood was spent in the Chinese section of Vancouver; although the concluding pages bring the book up to date, most of the text is devoted to the author's childhood, as he writes about his family, his attendance at Chinese school, summer work on a farm, and the many holidays, feasts, customs, local characters, and cultural events of the community. He speaks candidly of the prejudice from which Chinese suffered, but he speaks of it with stoicism rather than bitterness, and he concludes by saying that, when asked recently how he had survived the treatment of Chinese Canadians, "By laughing. It is the sense of humor of the Chinese that help us to live through the unlivable." That humor is evident in his lively story.

791   **Lindbergh,** Anne. *Nobody's Orphan.* Harcourt, 1983. 83-8494. ISBN 0-15-257468-9. 160p. $12.95.

3–5   The narrator is Martha, age ten, who has managed to convince herself that she is adopted; she loves her parents, and most of the time she loves her little brother Kermit, but how can she believe that all her baby pictures were in a suitcase that was lost in Europe? Martha's father is in the Foreign Service, and the family is now in Washington, where Martha makes, loses, and regains a best friend, acquires a dog, struggles with math, and decides (on slim evidence) that the elderly couple she's met, the Ables, are her real grandparents. Much of the humor of the story emanates from the depiction (mostly via dialogue) of the crusty, bossy Mr. Able and his misquoting. He's a bit overdrawn, but not enough so to mar an amusing story that has good style, good characterization on the whole, and warm family relationships.

792   **Lindbergh,** Anne. *The People in Pineapple Place.* Harcourt, 1982. 82-47935. ISBN 0-15-260517-7. 156p. $10.95.

4–6   In a fantasy that merges nicely with its realistic matrix, a lonely child finds a group of friends from another time, and when they move on they leave him the best possible gift, a new and permanent friend his own age. August had just moved to Georgetown with his mother, recently divorced and busy with her new career; he disliked Washington; he disliked the one neighbor his own age, Peter; he dreaded the start of the school year. Then he discovered Pineapple Place, a peripatetic community of six families who had been on the move (from city to city) for over forty years and who were usually invisible to others, but August could see them all, visit them, go with them on expeditions that were startling (like roller-skating in the National Gallery) because nobody could see anyone but August. Most of the time. Occasionally one of the Pineapple Place children would be visible to someone, as Meggie was to August's mother, who finally believed his story. The book is deftly structured, written with a good narrative flow, and satisfying in its ending, for as a parting gift April, August's favorite Pineapple Place friend, brings August and Peter together.

793   **Lindgren,** Astrid (Ericsson). *I Want a Brother or Sister;* illus. by Ilon Wikland; tr. by Barbara Lucas. Harcourt, 1981. ISBN 0-15-239387-0. 29p. $7.95.

4–6   Lindgren's story of Dethronement Blues was first published in Sweden
yrs.   in 1978 under the title *Jag Vill Ocksa Ha Ett Syskon.* Smoothly translated, illustrated with realistic drawings that are weakened occasionally by over-ambitious use of perspective, and written in a guilefully simple style, this is the story of a small boy who discovers that the baby sister he'd wanted isn't all that much fun. Besides, Mama and Papa seem to love Lena more than they love him. Then Mama explains that all babies are lovable and troublesome; and that she needs his help. Having a vested interest proves satisfying; later, there is a third child, and both Peter and Lena see that it's easy to coo at a cuddly infant. Mama is busy, but, that is all right, since Peter and Lena can have uninterrupted pillow fights. No pretense about this one; it's a brisk little tale meant to assuage the pangs of jealousy, and it's very nicely done.

794   **Lindgren,** Barbro. *Sam's Ball;* illus. by Eva Eriksson. Morrow, 1983. 83-722. ISBN 0-688-02359-2. 24p. $5.50.

Sam's Bath; illus. by Eva Eriksson. Morrow, 1983. 83-724. ISBN 0-688-02353-2. 24p. $5.50.

Sam's Lamp; illus. by Eva Eriksson. Morrow, 1983. 83-743. ISBN 0-688-02356-8. 24p. $5.50.

1–3   Three small books, each a delightful vignette of a young child's behav-
yrs.   ior, should entertain readers-aloud as well as their audience, and should also serve as good prereading experiences, since the texts have few and simple words, short sentences, repetition that isn't cloying, and humor. In *Sam's Ball,* Sam finds it's fun to share his toy with a kitten; in *Sam's Bath,* the tub is crowded with an assortment of toys, a

cookie, and a reluctant dog, in *Sam's Lamp,* a climb results in a bump that's alleviated by a bandage. Sample of style: "Sam climbs up on the stool. Sam climbs up on the chair. Sam climbs up on the table. Sam falls down." The illustrations are light and humorous in tone, deft in their comic simplicity.

795   **Lindgren,** Barbro. *The Wild Baby Goes to Sea;* tr. by Jack Prelutsky; illus. by Eva Eriksson. Greenwillow, 1983. 82-15623. Trade ed. ISBN 0-688-01960-9; Library ed. ISBN 0-688-01961-7. 22p. Trade ed. $9.00; Library ed. $8.59.

3–5 yrs.   In a sequel to *The Wild Baby* the happily obstreperous toddler builds a boat and goes to sea with three stuffed animal companions and a large supply of buns. With navigational flair and great sangfroid he pilots his crate through dangers and a storm, and even rescues a chicken before sailing home. Since Mama has relinquished her apron to serve as a sail, and since the journey starts on a rumpled (wavelike) blue rug, the journey is clearly an imaginative one. Why, then, Mama wonders, does her wild baby have a real chicken perching on his chair after they come back? The pictures, deft and animated, have the same cheerful humor as the text, which Prelutsky has translated with good attention to rhyme and scansion.

796   **Lingard,** Joan. *The File on Fraulein Berg.* Elsevier/Nelson, 1980. 80-10447. ISBN 0-525-66684-2. 153p. $7.95.

6–9   Set in Belfast during World War II, a story told by Katie is in retrospect, years later, when she meets Sally. They and Harriet, classmates at a private school, had decided the new teacher (Fraulein Berg's title is used without the usual umlaut) must be a German spy. She'd come over the border from neutral Eire, they were convinced, and so they followed her everywhere they could; inevitably the sad and lonely woman recognized their persecution. Only after she had left did the girls learn that poor Fraulein Berg was a Jewish refugee, the only member of her family still alive. The setting and the period details are vividly created, the characterization has depth and consistency, and the writing has good pace and structure.

797   **Lingard,** Joan. *Strangers in the House.* Dutton, 1983. 83-1714. ISBN 0-525-66912-4. 131p. $10.95.

6–9   In a story set in Scotland, fourteen-year-old Calum resents having to leave the coastal town he loves, is irritated by having to move to Edinburgh when his mother remarries, and is especially hostile toward his new stepsister, Stella. The same age, and equally hostile, Stella resents Calum, his mother, and Calum's small sister Betsy, with whom she has to share a room. Other things happen in the lives of both adolescents (love, friendship, death of a pet, family problems) but the focus is on their acceptance of the new family situation and, in particular, of each other; Lingard makes this progression believably gradual and enlists the reader's understanding on behalf of both Calum and Stella. The characterization is strong, the dialogue and exposition handled with equal skill, and the story line maintained at good pace and in good style.

798   **Lipp,** Frederick J. *Some Lose Their Way*. Atheneum, 1980. 80-13510. ISBN 0-689-50178-1. 118p. $7.95.

6-8   Eighth-grader Vanessa is shy and solitary, close only to the grandmother with whom she lives and their neighbor Charlotte; when Gram goes to help her sick daughter, Vanessa (white) stays with Charlotte (black). Vanessa has been bullied by a classmate, David, and he's the last person in the world she might have expected to become a friend; they are drawn together by an interest in bird life in a nearby marsh, and their relationship grows to the point where Vanessa is terrified when David, caught in the marsh mud, is hospitalized. The story ends with David recovered and delighted by a visit from Vanessa at his new home on Cape Cod. Slow-paced and often introspective, the story has believable characters and perceptive development of changes in relationships; it has conflict and resolution, but the one dramatic event—David's accident—occurs a good bit before the end of the story, so that the last two chapters and the epilogue seem somewhat overextended.

799   **Lipson,** Shelley. *It's Basic: The ABC's of Computer Programming*; illus. by Janice Stapleton. Holt, 1982. 81-20027. ISBN 0-03-061592-5. 47p. $8.95.

4-6   Unlike most children's books about computers, this neither gives a history of how today's computers evolved nor explains how a computer functions. In clear language supplemented by carefully-placed diagrams and examples, it shows the reader the way in which—using BASIC—a computer is programmed. Next to hands-on demonstrations, this is probably as helpful as a lesson can be. It's sequentially arranged, uses technical terminology only when necessary, and is written in a light but lucid style. A glossary and an index are included.

800   **Lipsyte,** Robert. *Summer Rules*. Harper, 1981. 79-2816. Trade ed. ISBN 0-06-023897-6; Library ed. ISBN 0-06-023898-4. 150p. Trade ed. $8.95; Library ed. $8.79.

7-10   The slogan of the Happy Valley Bungalow Colony was "More in 'Fifty-four!" but sixteen-year-old Bobby wanted less of the Happy Valley Day Camp. The protagonist of *One Fat Summer* tells the story; he had other plans for the summer, but his father had insisted on this job as a camp counselor because he didn't want Bobby spending the summer with the rough, tough Rumsons of the first book. Bobby's toughest job was trying to cope with the spoiled, hostile Harley, age nine, motherless child of one of the family that runs the camp. Much of the book is concerned with Bobby's romance with Harley's cousin Sheila, a romance that

quickly loses its appeal, and throughout the story Lipsyte paints an acidly candid picture of camp life, but the climax of the story is serious
and dramatic: Bobby knows that a fire at the camp was started by
Harley, rather than Willie Rumson, released from an institution, confused by shock treatments, and a natural suspect because of his previous record. Shall Bobby let Willie go to jail—which might benefit society—or tell what he knows and have Harley take the merited blame—
which might do further damage to his already-disturbed personality?
Although not difficult reading, this is a sophisticated story, provocative
and perceptive.

801   **Lively,** Penelope. *The Revenge of Samuel Stokes.* Dutton, 1981. 81-3094.
ISBN 0-525-38205-4. 122p. $10.25.

5-7   In an originally conceived and entertaining fantasy that is smoothly
fused with reality, Lively creates not only the ghost of Samuel Stokes
but of the whole estate he had so beautifully landscaped centuries before. The setting is contemporary, a housing development that stands
on the extensive grounds once occupied by a great house and its gardens and outbuildings; the residents of the development are baffled by
such strange events as brick walls that persistently push up through the
ground, or smells of cooking from a washing machine, or a disruption
of a television program by a sputtering, angry man—Stokes. It is one of
the children who first realizes that Stokes is furious because of what is
happening to the grounds he had landscaped. Tim, his friend Jane, and
his eccentric grandfather are the only people who understand what is
going on and who make an effort to get in touch with Stokes and distract him by diverting his attention to another project. The writing has
warmth and vitality, strong characters and dialogue, and an intriguing
situation that is deftly developed.

802   **Lively,** Penelope. *The Voyage of QV 66;* illus. by Harold Jones. Dutton,
1979. 78-12098. 172p. $7.95.

4-6   There have been many stories about a future time in which a major catastrophe has stripped the earth of people, but few of them are told by
a dog. Or told so well. A versatile British author has conceived a world
in which animals are the only inhabitants after a massive flood. A small
assortment of creatures goes on a search for London; most of them are
domestic beasts, but the catalyst in their party is Stanley, whose creative mind and ability to read make him a natural leader, but whose
conceit and selfishness make him the object of exasperation as well as
affection. But what is Stanley? None of them has ever seen a creature
like him, not until they see a zoo poster. (He's a monkey.) There are
many adventures en route to the London Zoo, where Stanley hopes to
find others of his kind—and there's a surprise ending when the small,
intrepid band reaches the zoo. The adventures provide action, but the
joy of this deftly written tale is in the humor of its dialogue, its sly sati-

rizing of human beings, and its warmth and consistency of characterization.

803   Livingston, Myra Cohn. *A Circle of Seasons;* illus. by Leonard Everett Fisher. Holiday House, 1982. 81-20305. ISBN 0-8234-0452-8. 26p. $12.95.

all
ages
*

It's saying a great deal to say that neither the poet nor the painter has ever done better—although each has done equally distinctive work— than in this lovely book. Livingston's poems move through the year, each quatrain followed by a brief three lines that are as evocative as the imagery they follow. For example, after a poem about spring, "O seed / And root / Send forth a tiny shoot!" Or, after an autumn poem, "O earth / Rest well / Under the autumn spell!" The form as well as the subject links the poems, printed in handsome format on a double-page spread in which the poem and the painting are set off by ample white space. The paintings are stunning, bold and stylized but with delicate details; there is variety in the brushwork and use of color, uniformity in the excellent use of space and shape to achieve effective compositions. Nice to read alone or aloud, nice to look at.

804   Livingston, Myra Cohn. *Monkey Puzzle and Other Poems;* illus. with woodcuts by Antonio Frasconi. Atheneum, 1984. 84-3050. ISBN 0-689-50310-5. 54p. $10.95.

5–

A small book of poems about trees is illustrated by handsome black and white woodcuts. Some of the poems are descriptive, with the tree's individual qualities seen by the viewer's eye; some speak as the voice of the tree itself. This is a more serious collection, with less variety than most of Livingston's books. Its limiting parameters may mean a limiting of the audience, but for the nature lover or the poetry lover, this book should appeal.

805   Livingston, Myra Cohn. *Sky Songs;* illus. by Leonard Everett Fisher. Holiday House, 1984. 83-12955. ISBN 0-8234-0502-8. 32p. $14.95.

All
Ages
*

As they did in *A Circle of Seasons,* author and artist combine their talents to create a book that is a pleasure to see and to read. Livingston's poems (planets, moon, and stars; times of day; meteorological phenomena) are honed and sensitive, while Fisher's paintings combine, in doublepage spreads, vibrant colors, an effective use of space, and wonderful variation of mood in handsomely composed paintings.

806   Livingston, Myra Cohn, ed. *Why Am I Grown So Cold? Poems of the Unknowable.* Atheneum, 1982. 82-6646. ISBN 0-689-52042-7. 269p. $12.95.

5–9

In an anthology of poems about the supernatural, Livingston has grouped the selections under such headings as "Devils, Fiends, Giants, Ogres and Wizards" and "Metamorphoses, Transformations and Disguises." There are excerpts from Shakespearian drama, narrative poems, lyric poems and some that are humorous. The poems have been chosen from many languages and several centuries, a pleasantly shivery and varied collection. Author, translator, title, and first line indexes are provided.

807   **Lobel,** Anita, ad. *The Straw Maid,* ad. and illus. by Anita Lobel. Green-willow, 1983. 81-6325. Trade ed. ISBN 0-688-00344-3; Library ed. ISBN 0-688-00330-3. 56p. Trade ed. $9.00; Library ed. $8.59.

1–2   The paintings, a little bit romantic and a little bit comic, deft in composition and intricate in decorative details, are just right for the simplified retelling of a familiar folktale. The daughter of a poor peasant couple is caught by robbers when she goes off to sell the family cow so that they can have food; locked in the robbers' house each day and forced to work for them, the girl coerces them one day to leave the window open. She makes a straw doll just her size, dresses it in her clothes, and escapes through the window, having covered herself with honey and feathers so that she looks like a bird. The robbers see, but do not recognize her, go home, beat the straw maid when it won't speak to them, and then get into a fight with each other. The girl washes in a brook, finds the cow, comes home to her jubilant parents, and they live very well on the gold and the jewels the girl has brought home. Children enjoy the justice of the robbers robbed, and while this is not the best version for reading aloud, it's nicely gauged for the beginning independent reader.

808   **Lobel,** Arnold. *The Book of Pigericks;* written and illus. by Arnold Lobel. Harper, 1983. 82-47730. Trade ed. ISBN 0-06-023982-4; Library ed. ISBN 0-06-023983-2. 48p. Trade ed. $9.95; Library ed. $9.89.

K–3   Neatly framed and softly tinted in pastel hues, Lobel's pigs indulge in extravagant and nonsensical didoes as described in a series of limericks about pigs. Sample: "There was a smart pig who was able / To make use of his three-legged table / He accomplished this trick / Standing still as a stick / To be leg number four of that table." These verses are lightly funny, variable in quality, sometimes bland, sometimes witty.

809   **Lobel,** Arnold. *Days With Frog And Toad;* written and illus. by Arnold Lobel. Harper, 1979. 78-21786. Trade ed. ISBN 0-06-023963-8; Library ed. ISBN 0-06-023964-6. 64p. (I Can Read Books) Trade ed. $5.95; Library ed. $6.89 net.

1–2   Again, five short stories about a friendship distinctive for its tolerance and stability; again, illustrations that echo, in soft tones of brown and green, the affectionate humor of the writing; again, as thousands cheer, Frog and Toad are together. In this distinctive series of books for the beginning independent reader, Lobel eschews didacticism and offers vignettes that, with artful simplicity, describe such small adventures as flying a kite or getting a birthday hat that doesn't fit; the dynamics of the relationship (Frog is sensible, Toad a reed in the wind) can easily involve the reader, as the popularity of earlier Frog and Toad books can attest.

810   **Lobel.** Arnold. *Fables;* written and illus. by Arnold Lobel. Harper, 1980. 79-2004. Trade ed. ISBN 0-06-023973-5; Library ed. ISBN 0-06-023974-3. 41p. Trade ed. $8.95; Library ed. $8.79.

3–5   Move over, Aesop. In an oversize format, Lobel faces each page of text
 *   with a framed illustration that is spaciously composed, rich with soft color and amusing details, and altogether handsome. The texts of the original fables are short, silly but pithy, and smoothly told; all are about animals, and each has—inscribed below in italics—a moral that is not always what one would expect. Very, very, nice.

811   **Lobel,** Arnold. *On Market Street;* illus. by Anita Lobel. Greenwillow, 1981. 80-21418. Trade ed. ISBN 0-688-80309-1; Library ed. ISBN 0-688-84309-3. 34p. Trade ed. $8.95; Library ed. $8.59.

K–3   A framing verse by the Market Street shopper encloses an alphabetical
 *   series of visual triumphs, as Anita Lobel brilliantly concocts (in the style of her 1977 Book Week poster) figures made out of apples, books, clocks, doughnuts, et cetera. Each full-page picture is an ingenious figure and a beautiful one, clever in the use of detail (the instruments that form bent arms and legs in "musical instruments") and particularly striking in the elaborate but controlled details and colors. A smasher.

812   **Lobel,** Arnold. *The Rose in My Garden;* illus. by Anita Lobel. Greenwillow, 1984. 83-14097. Trade ed. ISBN 0-688-02586-2; Library ed. ISBN 0-688-02587-0. 34p. Library ed. $10.51; Trade ed. $11.50.

K–2   A charming diversion, this combination of cumulative verse and rich— also cumulative—paintings of flowers in a profusion of improbably simultaneous bloom. Anita Lobel begins with a luxuriant red rose, adding other flowers and echoing Arnold Lobel's verse story of near-carnage (cat and fieldmouse) in the flower-beds. Lovely to look at, and enjoyable for reading aloud.

813   **Locker,** Thomas. *Where the River Begins;* written and illus. by Thomas Locker. Dutton, 1984. 84-1709. Trade ed. ISBN 0-8037-0089-X; Library ed. ISBN 0-8037-0090-3. 27p. Library ed. $14.89; Trade ed. $15.00.

4–6   Although the two small boys and their grandfather, who trace a small river to its source, are adequately pictured, it is in the painting of the landscapes that Locker excels, in trees and changing skies and the light reflected by the river at different times of day. The story is simple and serene, yet it communicates the feeling that both generations of hikers have about the beauty of the countryside and the flow of "their" river.

814   **Loeper,** John J. *Going to School in 1876;* illus. with old prints. Atheneum, 1984. 83-15669. ISBN 0-689-31015-3. 85p. $9.95.

4–6   In a companion volume to his *Going to School in 1776*, Loeper shows not only the state of education in the United States but also what changes had taken place in the first hundred years of a new country. The idea of tax-supported universal education did not appeal to everyone, and the schools were as diversified as the range of opinion on free and mandatory education. Using an anecdotal approach, Loeper describes the schoolhouses, books, lessons, teachers, and pastimes in schools of all kinds. Reproductions of old prints add to the appeal of a book that is capably written and has both nostalgic and informational value.

815   **Loescher.** Gil. *The World's Refugees: A Test of Humanity;* illus. with photographs. Harcourt, 1982. 82-47936. ISBN 0-15-299650-8. 145p. $13.95.

7–   Beginning with an overview of the many refugee movements in the twentieth century, the authors describe the numbers of refugees today, their locations, and the causes for their displacement; the text is given variety (and pathos) by the inclusion of first-person testimony and accounts of harrowing incidents. Succeeding chapters discuss the journeys, the camps, the resettlement projects, the prejudice or violence that some refugees encounter; the final chapters describe the history of migration to the United States and the history of international organizations that deal with refugees. A sober, candid, comprehensive, and depressing account that is nevertheless interesting, certainly touching, and carefully researched. A bibliography, a relative index, a list of sources of information about refugees, and a directory of organizations are appended.

816   **Longfellow,** Henry Wadsworth. *Hiawatha;* illus. by Susan Jeffers, Dial, 1983. 83-7225. Trade ed. ISBN 0-8037-0013-X; Library ed. ISBN 0-8037-0014-8. 22p. Trade ed. $11.95; Library ed. $11.89.

K–3   Jeffers has chosen part of Longfellow's poem to illustrate, and the oversize pages offer a splendid opportunity for beautifully detailed paintings of the small boy and his grandmother, Nokomis. The technique, which includes minute hatchings and parallel lines, soft colors, misty reflections, and richly vernal scenes, is well suited to the romantic quality of the poetry.

817   **Lord,** Athena V. *A Spirit to Ride the Whirlwind.* Macmillan, 1981. 81-3775. ISBN 0-02-761410-7. 205p. $10.95.

6–9   A story of women workers and their efforts to organize a union is set in the booming mill town of Lowell, Massachusetts (in 1836), where Binnie's widowed mother runs a company boarding house. Anxious to improve the family finances, twelve-year-old Binnie coaxes her mother to let her go to work in the mill and that's how she learns about the oppressive working conditions that cause her to join the protest movement among the factory girls. Although there is, realistically, no resolution of the labor problems, the book has good historical details, gives a convincing picture of one part of the history of the labor movement, and has a sympathetic heroine whose role in the protest is credible and whose reaction is, in part, to plan on an education so that she can have a better future than mill work.

818   **Lord,** Bette Bao. *In the Year of the Boar and Jackie Robinson;* illus. by Marc Simont. Harper, 1984. 83-48440. Library ed. ISBN 0-06-024004-0; Trade ed. ISBN 0-06-024003-2. 169p. Library ed. $9.89; Trade ed. $9.95.

3–5   In a story based in part on the author's experience as an immigrant, Shirley Temple Wong (a name she chose as her American name) arrives in Brooklyn and spends her first year in public school. Feeling an outsider at first; coping with a new language and new mores, and becoming a baseball fan; making new friends and earning money as a babysitter for obstreperous boy triplets, Shirley becomes integrated into her new life without ever forgetting her love of home and her pride in being Chinese. The book has one weakness; it occasionally is too cute in dealing with Shirley's mistakes in English, but the positive qualities outweigh the weakness in a story that has cultural dignity, a warm family relationship, some pathos and some humor, and an affirmation of the resilience of childhood.

819   **Lord,** Harvey G. *Car Care for Kids and Former Kids;* illus. with photographs by Kathryn J. Lord. Atheneum, 1983. 82-13778. ISBN 0-689-30975-9. 90p. $14.95.

6–   Although the quality of some of the photographs makes it difficult to see some of the parts referred to in pictorial captions, this is on the whole a most useful book, explicit and detailed, that makes it possible for a reader to learn new skills and save (perhaps even earn) money by doing repairs (replacing cracked hoses) or routine upkeep jobs (replacing air filters) on a car. As with a cookbook recipe, each section is prefaced by a list of tools and parts needed, and each is given a difficulty rating. There are repeated safety warnings (motor off, parking on level ground, cool engine, etc.) and suggestions that, for some jobs, it is best to have adult supervision, but the text is written in so straightforward a style that adult readers should find the book acceptable for their own use.

820   **Lorimer,** Lawrence T. *Secrets.* Holt, 1981. 81-5025. ISBN 0-03-059049-3. 192p. $10.95.

7–10   In an unusual and trenchant novel, Lorimer explores the character of a weak and charming man as he's seen by the adolescent daughter who moves from innocence to a troubled realization of her father's nature. Told in retrospect (and convincingly) by sixteen-year-old Maggie, the pattern of Harrison Thompson's personality emerges as she sees him first; the charming, beloved pastor of an active congregation who baffles her when she realizes he is telling a lie. Then there's another lie. Maggie resists the knowledge that the lies are masking his affair with a parishioner until the evidence is inescapable. Even when she learns from her unhappy but still protective mother that it's not the first time, Maggie is ready to help defend her father against the formal charges brought by an angry husband. But it's too late: with the irrevocable impetus of a classic tragedy, Hap Thompson has engineered his own destruction and chooses suicide rather than public disgrace. A moving and powerful story, this explores with percipience the divided loyalty of the daughter who detests the deceit but loves the deceiver, who agrees with her mother that the matter is in God's hands. "That's about the only place I can leave it," the book ends, "I only hope that He treats my father kindly."

821   **Louie,** Ai-Ling. *Yeh-Shen: A Cinderella Story from China;* illus. by Ed Young. Philomel, 1982. 80-11745. ISBN 0-399-20900-X. 30p. $10.95.

3–6
*

Probably older than the several European versions that are more familiar to English-speaking children, this Cinderella story has some basic similarities: the orphaned slavey whose stepmother refuses to let her participate in a festival, the magically-produced clothes, the hunt for a girl whose foot fits a slipper. Here the magic comes from the bones of a fish that Yeh-Shen has loved and her stepmother has killed, and here it is not at the festival that the king falls in love; a villager finds the lost slipper and sells it to a merchant who gives it to the king, who then decides he must find the woman who'd worn the tiny, precious slipper. The story is interesting as a folklore variant, but it's also smoothly and simply retold, and the illustrations are stunning: the artist's use of space and mass in composition is restrained and effective, the lines are soft, the colors melting, often trailing off across the page with faintly-seen details of design that echo the stronger use of design at the focus of the painting.

822   **Low,** Joseph. *Mice Twice;* written and illus. by Joseph Low. Atheneum, 1980. 79-23274. ISBN 0-689-50157-9. 28p. $9.95.

K–2

Softly washed in bright, light colors, Low's ink drawings have a casual effect with their broken lines and the vigor of his animals' facial expressions. This is the sort of turnabout story that appeals to children's sense of justice, for the fat cat that expects to eat the mouse and its friend she's invited for dinner finds that Mouse's friend is not another mouse (mice twice had sounded even better to the hungry cat) but a large dog, and that starts a chain of one-upping until a ferocious lion is bested by a wasp. That leaves, and who can fail to enjoy it, the wasp and the mouse to enjoy the feast that the calculating cat had laid out for the lion. Breezy action in a brief story.

823   **Lowry,** Lois. *Anastasia Again!* illus. by Diane DeGroat. Houghton, 1981. 81-6466. ISBN 0-395-31147-0. 145p. $7.95.

4-6   Undoubtedly this will be greeted with joy by those who became instant
*   Anastasia fans with the publication of *Anastasia Krupnik* and who appre-
        ciated the wit and warmth of her creative academic family. This time
        Anastasia's immoderate zest, pro or con, presages the turbulence of the
        teen years ahead. Twelve, precocious, delightful, and acute, Anastasia
        is horrified to learn her parents have decided to move to a suburb, and
        confronts them accusingly with every trite urban prejudice about outer
        suburbia. When she falls in love with an old, rambling house that actu-
        ally has the tower room of which she's dreamed, Anastasia is equally
        fervid. Added to this story of adaptability and adjustment are a running
        theme of the protagonist's diary entries and the recurrent material about
        a precocious—but not cloying—baby brother. Lowry is adept at turning
        such characters to humorous use without in the least making fun of
        them, and she does it in part by particularly deft dialogue.

824   **Lowry,** Lois. *Anastasia, Ask Your Analyst.* Houghton, 1984. 83-26687.
        ISBN 0-395-36011-0. 119p. $9.95.

4-6   In this sequel to earlier books about Anastasia, the redoubtable heroine
        is now thirteen, and the accumulation of adolescent woes (her hor-
        mones, her relationship with her parents, who have suddenly devel-
        oped awful faults, and her feelings about her younger brother) con-
        vinces her she needs therapy. Her problems are perfectly normal for her
        age, her father says, and refuses. Anastasia buys a bust of Freud and
        talks to it, often answering her own questions quite rationally. "I don't
        hate you and Dad anymore," Anastasia tells her mother at the close of
        the book, "I think my hormones are gone." This is up-beat, funny, and
        sophisticatedly witty, like Lowry's other Anastasia stories; the charac-
        ters are solidly conceived, the writing style and dialogue both polished
        and effervescent.

825   **Lowry,** Lois. *Anastasia at Your Service;* illus. by Diane de Groat. Hough-
        ton, 1982. 82-9231. ISBN 0-395-32865-9. 149p. $9.95.

4-6   Anastasia addicts will welcome this third discerning romp about the en-
        terprising daughter of a faculty family that is warm, supportive, and
        very funny. Anastasia always has problems (she's twelve) and this sum-
        mer it's a combination of boredom, depression (the only friend she's
        made since they moved to town has gone to camp) and penury. She
        advertises herself as a Lady's Companion and is taken aback to find the
        job she gets is that of a maid. Resentful, our heroine and her employ-
        er's granddaughter hatch a plot to be revenged. It backfires. The other
        plot line concerns Anastasia's precocious two-year-old brother, who
        doughtily survives a skull fracture. This is just as amusing as the earlier
        books, it's written with the same wit and polish; it isn't quite as sub-
        stantial structurally.

826   **Lowry,** Lois. *Anastasia Krupnik.* Houghton, 1979. 79-18625. ISBN
        0-395-28629-8. 114p. illus. $6.95.

4–6   Anastasia is ten, articulate, precocious, and the only child of a painter
 *   and a professor of literature who grieve her by their announcement that
       she is going to have (tests have shown) a baby brother. Bitterly, she an-
       nounces her departure, but is convinced not to be precipitate; she adds
       'Babies'' to the hate column of the running list she keeps of "Things I
       Love" and "Things I Hate," a device that's used at the end of each
       chapter. Items change columns frequently as Anastasia changes her
       mind about almost everything. There are poignant moments like a holi-
       day visit from a senile grandmother who can't remember Anastasia's
       name or recognize her, hilarious ones like a visit to her father's poetry
       class or a vigorous argument with her mother about changing her name
       because it's so long she can't get it on a tee shirt without having some
       letters under her armpits. The writing is lively, funny, and above all,
       intelligent. The relationship between Anastasia and her parents is su-
       perbly drawn, and the dialogue is a delight. In fact, the whole book is a
       delight.

827   **Lowry,** Lois. *Autumn Street.* Houghton, 1980. 80-376. ISBN 0-395-
       27812-0. 188p. $6.95.

5–7   Elizabeth remembers. It was because of the war that Daddy went away,
 *   and she and Mama had gone to live at Grandfather's; there she learned
       to love Tatie, "bulky and brown and beautiful," and Tatie's illegitimate
       grandson Charles. Grandmother didn't like Elizabeth or her sister, and
       she would certainly not want to see Elizabeth playing with Charles out
       in front of the house where the neighbors could see him. The two small
       children (they're six) play in back of the Autumn Street house, some-
       times with the twins next door, one of whom is placid, the other—
       Noah—a sadistic bully, and they feel tremendous guilt when Noah dies
       after they've been sitting with him, ignoring his crying. They know
       they should stay out of the woods at the end of Autumn Street, but
       Charles wants to look for caves, and Elizabeth goes along and then
       leaves him because she's feeling ill; while she is home and ill, she
       learns that Charles has been murdered by a known eccentric who had
       always been thought harmless. It is Tatie who comforts her, who makes
       Elizabeth understand that her cold, proud grandmother's coming to a
       black church to attend the service for Charles is an act of the deep love
       she cannot bring herself to show. Lowry has most adroitly woven these
       and other familial relationships into a story that has nuance, depth, poi-
       gnancy, and insight; through Elizabeth's memories, she gives a child's
       candid, painful view of fear and love. A memorable book.

828   **Lowry,** Lois. *Taking Care of Terrific.* Houghton, 1983. 82-23331. ISBN
       0-395-34070-5. 157p. $8.95.

6–9   Fourteen-year-old Enid is bright, sophisticated, and articulate, a typical
       Lowry child; she's lacking in self-esteem and bored by the prospect of a
       Boston summer. That's before she begins taking care of a precocious

and lovable four-year-old, Joshua Warwick Cameron IV, who prefers to be called Tom Terrific, before she meets the friendly black musician in the Public Garden, or the bag ladies, before she discovers that that pest of a classmate, Seth, is really a very nice boy. And it all comes together in a story that is touching, inventive, believable, and hilarious, as all of the characters conspire to take a stealthy midnight ride on the Public Garden swan boats and are caught by the police. Great fun, with a solid base of sharp characterization and some pithy commentary on our society.

829   **Lowry,** Lois. *Us and Uncle Fraud.* Houghton, 1984. 84-12783. ISBN 0-395-36833-X. 148p. $10.95.

4–6   Uncle Claude is, according to Father, a cadger and a layabout; according to Mother, her brother Claude is a sweet, gentle dreamer. According to Louise, the narrator, and her brother Marcus, Uncle Claude is fun, an exciting visitor who goes off abruptly leaving them the promise of a treasure hidden in the house—Faberge eggs, they have been led to believe. But they find no treasure, suspect that Claude's a fraud and—even worse—that he's a thief. They know (but can't tell) that Claude knew where there was a hidden key to a house where a robbery had been committed. The story has Lowry's usual wit, humor, and polish; it also has more drama than some of her other books, because of the combination of the excitement of a flood, suspense about the robbery, and tension about an older brother who is swept away in the flood and is for a long time in a coma before he recovers.

830   **Ludel,** Jacqueline. *Margaret Mead.* Watts, 1983. 82-17325. ISBN 0-531-04590-0. 118p. $8.90.

8–   Like Edward Rice's biography of Mead this begins with a description of her sojourn in Samoa and then moves to her childhood for a chronological account of her life and work. The text in both books consists of substantially the same material, although Rice gives more attention to Mead's personal life than does Ludel, while Ludel gives more attention to Mead's theories about the comparative influences of heredity and environment. Both books are well written, but the typeface and solidity of print on the page make the Ludel biography less attractive visually. A partial list of Mead's writings and an index (in unfortunately small type) are appended.

831   **Luenn,** Nancy. *The Dragon Kite;* illus. by Michael Hague. Harcourt, 1982. 81-11709. ISBN 0-15-224196-5. 28p. $12.95.

K–4
*   Although the protagonist, Ishikawa, was a real character (approximately three centuries ago) this is a deftly turned fictional explanation for a robbery he committed. Luenn's fluent but simple style is an appropriate and enjoyable channel for the story of Ishikawa's long years of dedication as an apprentice kite-maker; his mercenary motive is discounted

when balanced against his artistry, for the beautiful dragon kite he has used to steal the gold ornaments from a rooftop later comes to his rescue in magical style. Both the magic and the action should appeal to the read-aloud audience, while both they and those who read to them can enjoy the handsome details and melting colors of the paintings, dramatic in composition, Oriental in mood, strongly framed and delicately bordered.

832   **Lund,** Doris Herold. *Patchwork Clan: How the Sweeney Family Grew.* Little, 1982. 81-19301. ISBN 0-316-53657-1. 238p. illus. with photographs. $12.95.

7–   A lively and perceptive account of a true story that has all the tenderness and drama a reader could ask, and even a bit of suspense, as some of the adoptive children of Ann and John Sweeney resist adjustment. Most of the book focuses on Chuong, the oldest of three children who escaped from Saigon but lost their parents; suspicious and independent, Chuong is slowest (of the boys and girls of assorted colors and nationalities) to accept his new family. The book has the same candor that made the author's *Eric* as strong a book as it was touching; here, too, Lund is direct and detailed, letting the poignant truth dominate the book.

833   **Lurie,** Alison, ad. *Clever Gretchen and Other Forgotten Folktales;* illus. by Margot Tomes. T. Y. Crowell, 1980. 78-22512. ISBN 0-690-03944-1. 113p. Trade ed. $7.95; Library ed. $7.89 net.

4–6   Although the tales chosen, and fluently retold, by Lurie are not all "forgotten," since several are in such collections as Minard's *Womenfolk and Fairy Tales,* or in such standard collections as those by Afanasiev, Grimm, or Asbjörsen and Moe, they are all worthy of inclusion in another anthology. Illustrated with deftly composed and detailed line drawings, the stories stress the valor and ingenuity of their female protagonists, and the styles of the retellings are nicely moderated to suit their individual moods.

834   **Lurie,** Alison, ad. *The Heavenly Zoo; Legends and Tales of the Stars;* illus. by Monika Beisner. Farrar, 1980. 79-21263. ISBN 0-374-32910-9. 61p. $9.95.

4–6   Lurie's retellings of legends about animal constellations are brief and smoothly written and nicely varied in sources if not in style. Each retelling ends with an explanation of how or why the creature is in the sky— most often as a memorial; each tale has one handsome color painting with the creature shown in the firmament, stars superimposed. A nice collection, this should be useful as an adjunct to curricular units on mythology or astronomy as well as standing on its own for individual reading or reading aloud; its one minor drawback is that some of the constellations are not as well known (the Dove, the Whale) as the others (the Crab, the Great Bear) and for those, particularly, it would be useful to have alternate names that might be more familiar.

835   **Luzzatto,** Paola Caboara, ad. *Long Ago When the Earth Was Flat; Three Tales from Africa;* illus. by Aimone Sambuy. Collins, 1980. 79-14426. Trade ed. ISBN 0-529-05541-4; Library ed. ISBN 0-529-05542-2. 44p. Trade ed. $8.95; Library ed. $8.91 net.

K–2   Folktales from three African sources are retold with bland simplicity. From Tanzania, "How the Mountains Came to Be," from Nigeria, "How the Sun Got Into the Sky," and from Zaire, "How People Got Fire." They can be told, as adapted, to very young children, but could use some drama or embellishment as "why" stories told to older children; an author's note explains that African storytellers often introduced the tales with a patterned opening, and that singing, dancing, dramatization, and audience participation enlivened them. The illustrations, framed on oversize pages, are nicely used as part of the page design; although the pictures for the first tale are rather ineffectual pastel and include one snow scene that seems out of place, those for the second and third tales are handsome in their strong colors and composition.

836   **Lyle,** Katie Letcher. *Finders Weepers.* Coward, 1982. 82-1469. ISBN 0-698-20556-1. 203p. $11.95.

7–9   Lee, the narrator, has been voted the "Most Sensible" in her eighth grade class; now she's visiting her grandmother and uncle, and she can't understand why, every summer, so many treasure seekers come to hunt for the storied Beale Treasure. By sheer chance, Lee finds the trove, but feels it brings her only trouble and is relieved when a mudslide buries the site. This aspect of the book should appeal to readers, but many will enjoy equally the perception and candor of Lyle's depictions of Lee's relationships with her dour father, her elderly bachelor uncle (the brother her father sneers at) who is her dear friend, her loved and loving grandmother and other members of the Virginia mountain community that is her summer home.

837   **Lyttle,** Richard B. *Computers in the Home.* Watts, 1984. 84-7357. ISBN 0-531-04845-4. 90p. illus. with photographs. $9.90.

7–9   After discussing the future possibilities for computerized homes, Lyttle describes various kinds of computerized services that may affect people's living and working habits if predicted technological and electronic advances occur. Separate chapters discuss security systems in the home, especially monitoring devices; electronic games; receiving news and information via teletext; robotics; and other aspects of an electronic age that may become so common as to change living patterns. An index is included, giving access to a clearly written, if often conjectural, text that reports on the current state of the art and makes moderate predictions about what's to come. The illustrations are of inferior photographic quality.

838   **Lyttle,** Richard B. *People of the Dawn;* illus. by Heidy Fogel. Atheneum, 1980. 79-22766. ISBN 0-689-30750-0. 181p. $10.95.

8–   Lyttle describes the work of archeologists at sites in South, Central, and North America, the interpretations of artifacts found there, and the knowledge posited on the basis of those interpretations plus information about climate, resources available, and so on. Although heavily laden with detailed descriptions and comparisons of such objects as points and blades, this gives a fascinating picture of what a trained observer can deduce about a culture, and Lyttle makes it clear that archeologists—distinguishing between conjecture and fact—seldom claim more than high probability for their findings. Perhaps of greatest appeal to lay readers will be the details about how a dig is run and the evidence of parallel cultural details that indicate relationships between cultures; for example, the similarity in pottery decoration of Japanese sherds of 3000 B.C. and those found in an Ecuadorian site at a 5000-year-old level. A bibliography and an extensive relative index are provided.

839   **Macaulay,** David. *Mill;* written and illus. by David Macaulay. Houghton, 1983. 83-10652. ISBN 0-395-34830-7. 128p. $14.95.

7–
*

The precise and carefully labelled drawings of the three Rhode Island textile mills that Macaulay describes extend and illustrate a text that is clearly written. Like other Macaulay books, this one gives excellent background material about the social, political, and industrial matrices for its subject; the text is enlivened by the inclusion of journal entries that contribute to the establishment of these matrices. The mills, each of greater size and complexity, were all built and operated in the nineteenth century; an epilogue describes the changes that occurred in the twentieth century, with the closing of the last mill in 1955. Macaulay makes the details of building construction, mill wheels, and power train (the system of gears, shafts, pulleys, and belts that transfer power from wheel or turbine to machinery) comprehensible enough for any reader. A glossary is included.

840   **Macaulay,** David. *Motel Of The Mysteries;* written and illus. by David Macaulay. Houghton, 1979. 79-14860. Hardcover ed. ISBN 0-395-28424-4; Paper ed. ISBN 0-395-28425-2. 96p. Hardcover ed. $8.95; Paper ed. $4.95.

6–
*

In a clever and diverting spoof, Macaulay pokes fun at some of the aspects of our society, at archeologists, and at sensational journalese. His drawings are as meticulously detailed, as deftly executed, and as handsomely composed as in all of his earlier books, but more expressive of Macaulay's pointed wit and sense of humor. This is a record of the discovery and interpretation of a vast, complex burial site (a motel) in the ancient country of Usa; Howard Carson, a diligent amateur archeologist of the year 4022 has fallen down a shaft and made his great find. There are separate burial chambers, one of which is intact and contains a skeleton on a Ceremonial Platform (bed) facing the Great Altar (television

set) and—in the Inner Chamber—another skeleton in a white sarcopha-
gus (bathtub) is surrounded by sacred objects like the Sacred Urn and
Sacred Parchment. The repeated allusions to Carter and his discovery of
Tut's tomb may escape some readers, but there's enough sophisticated
but obvious humor to entertain them anyway, and it's all given high
polish by the serious and reverent tone of the writing.

841   **Macaulay,** David. *Unbuilding;* written and illus. by David Macaulay.
Houghton, 1980. 80-15491. ISBN 0-395-29457-6. 80p. $9.95.

5–
*
"On April 1, 1989," Macaulay begins, "Prince Ali Smith . . . suggested
that GRIP (Greater Riyadh Institute of Petroleum) buy the Empire State
Building." Planning to re-erect it and set it up as GRIP's headquarters
in the Arabian Desert, the prince negotiates the sale, hiring Krunchit
and Sons to dismantle the building. Thus, step by intricate step, a land-
mark is unbuilt. In the course of the (as usual) ingenious book, Macaulay gives a wealth of information, in text and illustrations, about the
complex structure of a modern skyscraper; the pictures are remarkable
for their beauty as well as for their informative detail, and Macaulay
fans will enjoy looking for the one touch of incongruity that they know
will appear somewhere in the drawings. Save for the fact that one particularly stunning double-page spread is marred by tight binding, the
book is a joy: accurate, informative, handsome, and eminently readable.

842   **McCaffrey,** Anne. *Dragondrums.* Atheneum, 1979. 78-11318. 240p. $8.95.

6–9
*
The third book in a science fantasy series (written for young people) is
as deftly structured and as smoothly written as its predecessors; again
McCaffrey has produced strong characters, new and old, a wholly conceived fantasy world, and a nice balance between problems that are present in any civilized society and a sense of humor that lightens both
exposition and dialogue. The protagonist here is not the masterharper
journeyman Menolly, but her protege Piemur, whose life changes when
his voice changes; a soloist, Piemur despairs of ever being able to sing
again, but he's quick to learn both of his new assignments and enjoys
them. He becomes an apprentice message-drummer, and that role is
used to mask his more important job, acting as personal scout for the
distinguished Masterharper. Piemur has a series of exciting adventures,
not the least of which are riding a dragon (used for transport in
Piemur's world) and acquiring his very own fire lizard.

843   **MacClintock,** Dorcas. *African Images;* illus. by Ugo Mochi. Scribner,
1984. 84-10565. ISBN 0-684-18089-8. 158p. $14.95.

5–9
The stunning cut-paper illustrations, most of which are silhouette form,
are as accurate as they are beautiful. The text, which is divided by type
of habitat, describes the animals that inhabit each variety of terraine in a
vivid fashion, commenting on appearance, individual and group behavior, feeding habits, hunting strategies, etc. A handsome book, and an

informative one. A list of the animals mentioned, divided by scientific classification, is provided, as are a glossary, a bibliography, and an index.

844   MacClintock, Dorcas. *Horses As I See Them;* illus. by Ugo Mochi. Scribner, 1980. 78-31778. ISBN 0-684-16116-8. 88p. $9.95.

6–   Cut-paper silhouettes, amazingly vigorous and detailed, illustrate a text that tells everything, but everything, about horses: anatomical parts, gaits, breeds, and history—both as an animal useful to man and as an animal used in recreation. The small print is a drawback, but is alleviated by broad outer margins and spacious placement of the illustrations. A final section is devoted to breeds of ponies; the writing is direct, informed, and informal.

845   McClung, Robert M. *Green Darner; The Story of a Dragonfly;* rev. ed.; illus. by Carol Lerner. Morrow, 1980. 79-18922. Trade ed. ISBN 0-688-22216-1; Library ed. ISBN 0-688-32216-6. 30p. Trade ed. $6.95; Library ed. $6.67.

2–4   Simply and authoritatively written, this revision of a 1956 title is improved by the format and the new illustrations; Lerner's drawings are elegant and sophisticated in black and white, yet completely realistic in their details. McClung begins with the ecological system of the pond community in which his individual Green Darner lives; he continues with an anatomical description, discusses courting and mating, moves to the birth and youth of an offspring and to some of its adventures. In the course of this account (narrative but not anthropomorphic) McClung provides additional facts about growth stages and anatomy, and about feeding habits, predators, and locomotion.

846   McCord, David Thompson Watson. *Speak Up; More Rhymes of the Never Was and Always Is;* illus. by Marc Simont. Little, 1980. 80-15260. ISBN 0-316-55517-7. 69p. $7.95.

4–7   Forty new poems from a major children's poet are included in a collection illustrated by deft, small drawings that are nicely matched to, and sometimes extend, the poems. This is the usual appetizing McCord smorgasbord: some word-play poems, many humorous selections, some (fewer) that are serious. Like all of McCord's poetry, these poems have a deceptive simplicity; they are light but they are also polished, often surprisingly informative, and frequently restrainedly lyrical.

847   MacCracken, Mary. *City Kid.* Little, 1981. 80-26547. ISBN 0-316-541869. 280p. $12.95.

7–   Luke is the city kid, seven years old, with an already-long record of theft, truancy, and arson, and he was chosen as MacCracken's charge in a program of a therapeutic tutoring. The book focuses on the relationship between teacher and child, and on the ways that were devised to help Luke with his personal and academic problems. Written with warmth and humor, the author's account is without educational jargon or sentimentality, and it's given balance by anecdotes about her classes (and very funny they are, often acidly so) since at the time the tutoring program was set up MacCracken had gone back to college for certification, although she had for many years been teaching disturbed children with success and sympathy. This has moments of poignancy or drama, wit, a yeasty writing style, and strong portrayal of characters; above all, it is a trenchant testimonial to the redemptive power of a program of intelligent and empathetic individualized teaching.

848   **McCullough,** Frances Monson, ed. *Love Is Like the Lion's Tooth.* Harper, 1984. 77-25659. Library ed. ISBN 0-06-024139-X; Trade ed. ISBN 0-06-024138-1. 96p. Library ed. $11.89; Trade ed. $11.95.

8–
*   Passion, not romance, is the theme of this fine small anthology. The poems, many in translation, from a great variety of times and places, express the intensity of love's various moods and stages, physical and spiritual; from the ecstasy of "The Song of Solomon" and E. E. Cummings to the obsessive pain of " 'Don't Touch Me!' I Scream at Passersby," by the Russian poet, Natalya Gorbanyevskaya; from the blunt tenderness of W. H. Auden and the self-assertion of Denise Levertov to the Turkish poet, Nazim Hikmet's, world-encompassing "Things I Didn't Know I Loved." A most welcome balance to the surfeit of formula romance.

849   **McGovern,** Ann. *Night Dive;* illus. with photographs by Martin Scheiner and James B. Scheiner. Macmillan, 1984. 84-7163. ISBN 0-02-765710-8. 56p. $12.95.

5–8   Having the story of experiencing night-diving told by a fictional girl of twelve gives this exciting book an appealing informality and immediacy; the subject may draw an even broader audience than that indicated. Beautiful color photographs show some of the creatures visible at night in the warm Caribbean waters; the narrator, who has had scuba lessons and whose mother, a marine biologist, is one of the diving party, is candid about her fears, ebullient when she gets over them, and sensible about safety precautions. McGovern uses no more fictionalization than is necessary to make the framework of the text convincing.

850   **McGowen,** Tom. *Encyclopedia of Legendary Creatures;* illus. by Victor G. Ambrus. Rand McNally, 1981. 81-10529. Trade ed. ISBN 0-528-82402-3; Library ed. ISBN 0-528-80074-4. 64p. Trade ed. $8.95; Library ed. $8.97.

4–6   Brief descriptions, written in a casual conversational style that often includes humor, are arranged alphabetically in an oversize book that is handsomely and lavishly illustrated by beautifully detailed, colorful, and imaginative paintings. The compilation includes many terms and represents the imaginary creatures of many cultures, and if it omits an occasional favorite (the spriggans, tomtens) that's understandable. A minor weakness is the index, which does not always have an entry for material contained in the book; there is none for "ghosts," for example, although a full column (two columns per page) is devoted to that subject.

851   **MacGregor,** Anne. *Domes: A Project Book;* written and illus. by Anne and Scott MacGregor. Lothrop, 1982. 81-11782. Paper ed. ISBN 0-688-00870-4; Library ed. ISBN 0-688-00869-0. 56p. Paper ed. $6.50; Library ed. $9.55.

5–   Meticulously detailed drawings (some using the cutaway technique) and diagrams illustrate an excellent text, first published in Great Britain, that shows the engineering and architectural advances that have been made over the centuries. Some of the simplest domes are still in use today (African huts, Central Asian yurts, Eskimo igloos) and some of the early discoveries of Roman builders are still incorporated into contemporary domed structures. The book, written in lucid, direct style, concludes with a description of the geodesic dome. The authors carefully explain the principles on which architectural variations are based; they include clear instructions for making models of two kinds of domes out of simple materials that are easily available. It is unfortunate that the tight binding obscures important details on some pages.

852   **MacGregor,** Anne. *Skyscrapers: A Project Book;* written and illus. by Anne and Scott MacGregor. Lothrop, 1981. 81-342. Paper ed. ISBN 0-688-00365-6; Library ed. ISBN 0-688-00368-00. 56p. Paper ed. $5.95; Library ed. $9.55.

5–9   Precise architectural drawings illustrate a description of early skyscrapers, various improved methods of construction, principles that have dictated construction methods, changing materials and styles, and the emergence of precast parts and standardized sizes. The illustrations usually are placed so that textual links are clear; occasionally the lack of labels or captions may evoke confusion. The writing is clear, the coverage good; the book also contains step-by-step (albeit separated within the volume) instructions for making a replica of a skyscraper.

853   **McHugh,** Elisabet. *Karen and Vicki.* Greenwillow, 1984. 83-14156. ISBN 0-688-02543-9. 150p. $9.50.

4–6   In a sequel to *Raising a Mother Isn't Easy* and *Karen's Sister,* the narrator is Karen, the twelve-year-old Korean adoptee whose veterinarian mother has married a man with three children. This story focuses on the conflict between Karen and her older stepsister Vicki; their differences are exacerbated by the fact that they have to share a room when the new baby comes; they've already argued because one is messy, the other neat, and Karen's special project for school (a time efficiency study) seems to Vicki an imposition. For various reasons the two girls adjust and achieve a modus vivendi, and the book ends with Karen suppressing her study results rather than embarass her sister. Like the first books, this is sunny in its relationships, giving as warm and positive a picture of a merged family as has been presented in the literature. The adopted children (Karen's little sister had also been a Korean orphan) feel loved and wanted, both sides of the family accept both parents, both grandmothers are accepted as everybody's grandmother. Nicely told, convincingly the work of a young adolescent.

854   McHugh, Elisabet. *Karen's Sister.* Greenwillow, 1983. 83-1741. ISBN 0-688-02472-6. 149p. $9.50.

4–6   In *Raising a Mother Isn't Easy* Karen, who is Korean-born and adopted by a single woman, gives up her efforts to find a husband for her mother and looks forward to the adoption of a little sister. This sequel begins with Karen's eager anticipation of the arrival of another Korean orphan—and Tae Ja, renamed Meghan, proves to be a five-year-old with a mind of her own. The story, told by Karen, is light and amusing, more appealing because of the warm relationship between Karen and her mother and grandmother than because of the plot, although Karen does adjust to the news that her mother, a veterinarian, is going to marry a widower with three children.

855   McHugh, Elisabet. *Raising a Mother Isn't Easy.* Greenwillow, 1983. 82-11714. ISBN 0-688-01827-0. 160p. $9.00.

5–7   The narrator, Karen, is almost eleven, a steady and reliable adopted child whose veterinarian mother is loving and disorganized, so that Karen worries about what Mom will do when she's left on her own when Karen leaves home. Now is the time, Karen decides, to scout around for the best husband for Mom. He must, of course, love animals; there are several other requirements on Karen's list. Unfortunately, the very nice man who's Karen's choice isn't her mother's, and Karen finally realizes that Mom is quite capable of managing her life. Karen is thrilled when, at the close of the story, Mom announces she's adopted another Korean girl; clearly the new sister is going to fill a niche in both their lives. A smoothly casual treatment of adoption and of cultural assimilation, this is written in a lively, informal style that has good dialogue, humor, and warmth.

856   Mack, Gail. *Yesterday's Snowman;* illus. by Erik Blegvad. Pantheon Books, 1979. 78-6090. Trade ed. ISBN 0-394-83662-0; Library ed. ISBN 0-394-93662-0. 22p. Trade ed. $6.95; Library ed. $6.99 net.

K–2   A child remembers the evening her mother stopped dinner preparations to take advantage of just the right kind of snow for packing, and suggested making a snowman. The girl, her brother, and her mother went outdoors and made a huge, wonderful snowman. It grew dark, people coming home from work stopped to look at the snowman, lights glowed on the snow, and they all went in and ate their meal. Cozy and warm, they listened to the rain. No more snowman, but a happy memory. The story is slight, but it's nicely told and nostalgically evocative; the delicacy of Blegvad's tones and of the tracery of black branches against the twilight sky, and the bright, small figures of mother and children echo and elaborate on the happy, tender mood.

857   **McKillip,** Patricia A. *Moon-Flash*. Atheneum, 1984. 84-2974. ISBN 0-689-31049-8. 150p. $10.95.

7–10   Kyreol, whose mother had disappeared from their primitive world when she was a baby, had become a woman and so her betrothal to Korre was formalized at the time of Moon-Flash, the peak of the year for their tribe. Kyreol is a dreamer, a questioner; although she knows (everyone in the tribe knows) where the world ends, she becomes curious and prevails on her childhood friend Terje to go along the river to the cliffs where the world ends—and that is where she learns that the world is huge and sophisticated, that her tribe is guarded from outside to preserve its simplicity, that the Moon-Flash is simply the flare of a moonship as it docks. This has a great deal of action and adventure, a gently developed love story, and a marvelously imaginative depiction of the complexity of technological adventure as seen through the eyes of a sensitive and intelligent woman from a primitive culture.

858   **McKinley,** Robin. *The Blue Sword*. Greenwillow, 1982. 82-2895. ISBN 0-688-00938-7. 272p. $11.50.

7–10
*   How often has a book started with a young woman coming out to a colonial outpost after being orphaned, with a promise of uniforms and romance looming? Harry (a nickname she prefers) is kindly taken in by the Resident, Sir Charles, as arranged by her soldier-brother; she promises herself that she'll be a proper young lady. This seems to be a formulaic romance, but McKinley rises far above this, for Harry is kidnapped by a local ruler, not for love but because his *kelar*, or psychic power, tells him he must. And indeed it is Harry, after intensive training, who saves his kingdom by going into battle with the fabled blue sword and her own psychic power. There is a love story, but it is a subordinate theme in a rich tapestry of fantasy and adventure, as the author creates a realm and a people with vivid clarity. Strong in structure and style, the book has characters who are depicted with depth and acuity, good pace, and a high sense of drama. This is the first book in a projected trilogy.

859   **McKinley,** Robin. *The Hero and the Crown*. Greenwillow, 1984. 84-4074. ISBN 0-688-02593-5. 288p. $11.50.

7–10
*   In a second story about the mythic land of Damar (the first of a projected trilogy was *The Blue Sword*) McKinley creates another dauntless and engaging hero-figure in Aerin, the king's daughter who knows that

the populace and court look down on her because her mother was a commoner and a witch-woman. It is not until after Aerin has won acclaim for slaying dragons that she meets the immortal Luthe and learns her true history and her full powers. With the magical blue sword, Aerin kills the arch-wizard who has ravaged Damar and whose imposed conflict has brought about the death of the king. Aerin weds the new king, becoming queen in her people's hearts as well as in name. Set in an earlier time, this has the same kind of sweep and color as did the first book; although related, it stands completely on its own. It is just as strong in characterization, perhaps a bit slower, in parts, in pace.

860   **MacLachlan,** Patricia. *Arthur, for the Very First Time.* Harper, 1980. 79-2007. Trade ed. ISBN 0-06-024045-8; Library ed. ISBN 0-06-024047-4. 128p. Trade ed. $8.95; Library ed. $8.79.

4-6   Arthur is ten. A quiet, literal child, he is unhappy because his parents
  *   squabble; he is unhappy because he has guessed his mother is pregnant; he is not totally enthralled at being taken to stay with Great-Aunt Elda and Great-Uncle Wrisby for the summer. He meets a lively girl his own age, Moira, who calls him "Mouse" rather than Arthur, and advises him to think less and do more; it is because Arthur changes and makes his mark that Moira, at the end of the story, calls him Arthur for the very first time. By then Arthur has learned a great deal about himself, has learned to care more for other people, and has gained self-confidence. Other people he cares about (Moira, her grandfather, his aunt and uncle, some animals) are well worth loving; MacLachlan has created a wonderfully original and lovable group of people. The story has a deep tenderness, a gentle humor, and a beautifully honed writing style.

861   **MacLachlan,** Patricia. *Cassie Binegar.* Harper, 1982. 81-48641. Trade ed. ISBN 0-06-024033-4; Library ed. ISBN 0-06-024034-2. 120p. Trade ed. $8.95; Library ed. $8.89.

4-6   It is not the plot (there really isn't one) that makes this so readable and distinctive a novel, but the flow of the writing, the easy mingling of exposition and dialogue, the polished merging of colorful characters and shifting relationships, and Cassie's continuing and believable growth in understanding herself and others. Cassie's embarrassed by her odd relatives and by the exuberance and vitality of her immediate family; she envies the prim and decorous life and home of her friend Margaret Mary, and is surprised that Margaret Mary loves Cassie's family and the sometimes slap-dash way they live. Cassie gets over a crush on a writer (she herself writes poetry) and adjusts to her grandfather's death and to change. Still waters run deep and clear here.

862   **MacLachlan,** Patricia. *Mama One, Mama Two;* illus. by Ruth Lercher Bornstein. Harper, 1982. 81-47795. Trade ed. ISBN 0-06-024081-4; Library ed. ISBN 0-06-024082-2. 27p. Trade ed. $9.50; Library ed. $8.89.

1–3   Softly-crayoned pastel pictures, simply and tenderly composed and nicely fitting the mood of the story, show the love that is the mortar of the text. In the quiet night dialogue between Katherine and small Maudie, as together they feed and comfort the baby, Maudie's story emerges. Her mother, increasingly disturbed, had needed to go away for therapy, and Maudie was taken to a second (foster) mother, Mama Two. The author does a good job, within the story, of having a social worker explain to a child, in very simple terms, why her mother has become unstable and what will happen. The tone is candid, the approach positive. It is not until the end of the story that the reader knows that the loving, gentle Katherine is Mama Two; the book ends with her telling Maudie, who has asked, "When is spring?" that "Whenever Mama One comes home will be spring." There have been other books in which foster parents were sympathetically portrayed; this is the nicest yet for the primary grades reader.

863   **MacLachlan,** Patricia. *Seven Kisses in a Row;* illus. by Maria Pia Marrella. Harper, 1983. 82-47718. Trade ed. ISBN 0-06-024083-0; Library ed. ISBN 0-06-024084-9. 56p. Trade ed. $8.95; Library ed. $8.89.

2–4   While their parents are away at a conference, Emma and her older brother Zachary are being taken care of by Uncle Elliot and Aunt Evelyn, who know absolutely nothing about children. They are fast learners, however, and affectionate people, and by the time it's their last day, Emma is so upset at their imminent departure that she feigns illness— which they don't fall for, because Elliot and Evelyn have learned a lot in a short time: like giving seven kisses as a morning greeting, and how to take care of an infant (Emma kindly teaches her pregnant aunt) and how to bend a rule. Funny, deft, and touching, a blandly written story about an engaging child of seven.

864   **MacLachlan,** Patricia. *Through Grandpa's Eyes;* illus. by Deborah Ray. Harper, 1980. 79-2019. Trade ed. ISBN 0-06-024044-X; Library ed. ISBN 0-06-024043-1. 40p. Trade ed. $8.95; Library ed. $8.79 net.

K–3   John describes a day spent with Nana and Grandpa, who is blind. He's impressed by how much sharper Grandpa's other senses are: he can tell the direction of the wind, identify the flowers on the breakfast table, correct John's notes when they are playing cello duets. The illustrations are all soft line and soft color, appropriate for the gentle quality of the story, in which the author makes it clear that Grandpa leads a full, active, and happy life. Grandma sculpts, by the way. No stereotypes here, just a warm, special relationship between a child and his grandparents, both busy and creative.

865   **MacLachlan,** Patricia. *Unclaimed Treasures.* Harper, 1984. 83-47714. Library ed. ISBN 0-06-024094-6; Trade ed. ISBN 0-06-024093-8. 128p. Library ed. $10.89; Trade ed. $10.95.

5–7   Willa, almost twelve, is an imaginative and sensitive girl who yearns to
        be interesting, to do something extraordinary. She thinks she's in love
        with the man next door, an artist for whom she poses while his wife is
        away; when she finally sees that the model in the white dress has his
        wife's face, Willa leaves a note that brings the estranged pair together.
        That's one of the ways Willa learns about love, in a tender and subtle
        book that has strong characters, a flowing style, and a perceptive depic-
        tion of familial problems and loyalties.

866   **MacLeod,** Charlotte. *Cirak's Daughter.* Atheneum, 1982. 82-1727. ISBN
        0-689-30930-9. 192p. $10.95.

8–   Jenny, nineteen, inherits a house and a fortune from the father she's
        never known, since Jason Cirak had deserted his weepy, ineffectual
        wife and their infant daughter. Coming to the small town where Jason
        had made his home, Jenny discovers that he'd been living under an as-
        sumed name; she also adopts an alias. When a stranger, an elegant
        older woman named Harriet Compton, appears at her door with a
        bloodstained jacket, Jenny realizes for the first time that her father had
        probably been murdered. MacLeod is adept at providing intriguing
        clues while maintaining suspense, and she creates strong characters
        who react and develop logically in a satisfying mystery story with a
        smooth style and convincing dialogue.

867   **McLoughlin,** John C. *The Tree of Animal Life: A Tale of Changing Forms
        and Fortunes;* written and illus. by John C. McLoughlin. Dodd, 1981.
        80-2789. ISBN 0-396-07939-3. 160p. $14.95.

7–   An oversize format affords the author, a science illustrator and a zoolo-
*   gist, splendid space for his meticulous drawings of life forms and for
        the many charts that show adaptive development of species; one set of
        these is cumulative, changing in scale as the book progresses. The lack
        of indication of comparative size is the one weakness of the book, but it
        is not pervasive. McLoughlin writes with lucid zest and occasionally
        with humor, clarifying the sorts of influences of the ecological environ-
        ment that induced adaptation, as well as those changes occurring by
        mutation. Comprehensive, informative, carefully organized and written
        with authority and vitality, this is an excellent history of the animal
        kingdom. A glossary and an index are provided.

868   **McMillan,** Bruce. *Here A Chick, There A Chick;* written and with photo-
        graphs by Bruce McMillan. Lothrop, 1983. 82-20348. Trade ed. ISBN
        0-688-02000-3; Library ed. ISBN 0-688-02001-1. 24p. Trade ed. $10.50;
        Library ed. $10.18.

2–5   Color photographs on facing pages are used to present contrasting con-
yrs.   cepts (stand/sit, asleep/awake, straight/crooked, etc) and the characters
        are fluffy, appealing chicks. The pictures begin with a cracking egg (in-
        side) and a bedraggled chick emerging (outside) and are usually good

illustrations of the concepts of opposites, save for a few double-page spreads like the one for here/there, where the chick is facing one way and looking at the eggshell, and then is moving away from it and facing the other way, or round/around, in which the chick appears to be doing exactly the same thing in both pictures, walking on a circular path of spilled seed. Nevertheless, useful—and certainly engaging.

869   **McNaughton, Colin.** *At Home;* written and illus. by Colin McNaughton. Philomel, 1982. 81-85295. ISBN 0-399-20878-X. 14p. $3.95.

2–4 years   One of a set of five books that cite opposite terms, with the meanings clarified by illustrations, this is small and square, with board pages that bear no text save for the terms. The illustrations make meanings quite clear, they're funny, and they are child-oriented; for example "wet" shows a child happily, messily splashing bath water, and "dry" shows him just as happily beaming from the enveloping folds of an enormous towel, while "full" shows the boy carrying a basket of eggs and in "empty" all the eggs are broken and the boy's leaning on the empty basket. The other four books in the series, which achieves its goal of conveying concepts of opposites effectively, are set at playschool, at a party, at the park, and at stores. There's no background clutter to distract the eye from the indefatigable plump boy who appears on every page.

870   **McNaughton, Colin.** *Autumn;* written and illus. by Colin McNaughton. Dial, 1983. 83-45235. ISBN 0-8037-0043-1. 10p. $4.95.
Spring; written and illus. by Colin McNaughton. Dial, 1983. 83-45233. ISBN 0-8037-0044-X. 10p. $4.95.
Summer; written and illus. by Colin McNaughton. Dial, 1983. 83-45234. ISBN 0-8037-0042-3. 10p. $4.95.
Winter; written and illus. by Colin McNaughton. Dial, 1983. 83-45236. ISBN 0-8037-0040-7. 10p. $4.95.

3–5 yrs.   Four hardbound books introduce the year's seasons to young children. This sprightly quartet focuses on activities appropriate to the season rather than on the season itself, so that the pages for *Autumn,* for example, show blowing leaves, bonfire meals, harvest time, and falling apples. The captions are just that simple: "Fallen apples," "Fallen leaves," and the colorful pictures fill but do not strain the page space with their action and humor.

871   **Madaras, Lynda.** *The What's Happening to My Body Book for Boys: A Growing Up Guide for Parents and Sons;* written by Lynda Madaras with Dane Saavedra; illus. by Jackie Aher. Newmarket Press, 1984. 84-16667. Trade ed. ISBN 0-937858-39-0; Paper ed. ISBN 0-937858-40-4. 217p. Trade ed. $14.95; Paper ed. $8.95.

6–9   A teacher of sex education courses writes with candor and objectivity about the physical and emotional changes that take place in human beings as they move into adolescence. The book is intended for boys and for their parents (to use separately or together, whichever is the most comfortable) and it is both reassuring and informative. While Madaras and her adolescent co-author deal in facts (also giving some about girls) they respond to the worries and fears that have been expressed to them by many boys. The diagrams are explicit and carefully labelled. An index and an annotated bibliography are provided.

872   **Maestro,** Betsy. *Traffic: A Book of Opposites;* illus. by Giulio Maestro. Crown, 1981. 80-29641. ISBN 0-517-54427-X. 29p. $8.95.

1–2   Brightly colored pages, with vehicles and background stripped of details, so that the solid masses of color have a poster-like simplicity, are almost distractingly vivid. Each page has one brief sentence, and the facing pages are paired to give contrast: "That house is *far* away," "This house is *near*," and "Take a *left* turn," "Take a *right* turn." (The book uses boldface rather than italics.) Eye-catching rather than appealing, the book can be used for reading aloud as well as for independent reading by beginners; although it comprises opposites of different kinds (size, position, direction, etc.) it can encourage observation and comparison, and vehicles usually appeal to children.

873   **Magorian,** Michelle. *Good Night, Mr. Tom.* Harper, 1982. 80-8444. Trade ed. ISBN 0-06-024078-4; Library ed. ISBN 0-06-024079-2. 304p. Trade ed. $11.50; Library ed. $10.89.

6–9   Although the protagonist of the story, set during World War II and first published in England, is a small boy, the book should appeal to readers old enough to appreciate the nuances and difficulties of the writing style and the implications of the situation. Willie, pale and frightened, is one of many London children sent to a small village for safety. He is deposited on old Tom's doorstep; a crusty loner, Tom really doesn't want this burden. He silently notes the boy's bruises and gradually learns that his emotions have been equally abused by a termagant mother who is a religious fanatic. Just as Willie is beginning to feel secure and make friends, a telegram comes from London, saying his mother is ill and wants him back. By this time the old man and the boy love and need each other, and when he doesn't hear from Willie, Tom goes to London. The ending is tense, dramatic, believable, and satisfying, a happy ending to a touching story of love. Magorian uses dialogue and dialect well, giving local color as well as using them to establish character. Save for the reflection of the current interest in the problems of child abuse, this is an old-fashioned story with timeless appeal.

874   **Mahy,** Margaret. *The Changeover.* Atheneum, 1984. 83-83446. ISBN 0-689-50303-2. 214p. $11.95.

6–9   A powerful fantasy from the noted New Zealand author whose *The Haunting* won the 1982 Carnegie Medal, this is imaginative, fresh in concept, and unusual in the depth of its character development and the subtlety of the love interest. The protagonist is Laura, who cannot convince her mother that her little brother is dying because an evil wizard has taken possession of his body. As a last, desperate measure Laura agrees to a changeover: her friend Sorenson, his mother, and his grandmother are all witches and they induct her into their occult world so that she will have the power to take possession of the wizard and save her brother. The fantasy is firmly rooted in realism and deftly structured.

875   **Mahy,** Margaret. *The Haunting.* Atheneum, 1982. 82-3983. ISBN 0-689-50243-5. 144p. $8.95.

5–7
*   This fantasy by an eminent New Zealand author is both a family story and a deft tale of inherited extra-sensory perception, the two elements beautifully merged. Barney, eight, is terrified by the repetition of images and messages that proclaim "Barney is dead," but through a gradual but well-paced development he discovers that he had had a great-uncle who had been a "magician," not only having ESP but able to evoke illusions. This was Cole, who had had a beloved brother, another Barney. Presumed dead for many years, Cole suddenly appears and there is an interfamilial confrontation. The ending is unexpected but logical, dramatic and satisfying. The style, the characterization, the consistency of the fantastic within the real, are all distinctive.

876   **Maiorano,** Robert. *A Little Interlude;* illus. by Rachel Isadora. Coward, 1980. 79-21521. ISBN 0-698-20496-4. 32p. $5.95.

K–2   Isadora's black and white pictures have the crystalline look of window frost, yet the figures of a small boy and a man show up strongly against the multilinear background of this small book. Arriving early at the theater for a performance of "The Nutcracker," Bobby, who is white, is enthralled by the playing of a black man, seated alone in the dark theater and improvising at the piano. They offer to teach each other, but Bobby can't really play and Jiminy Cricket (he says that's his name) can't dance; still, it's a happy time of sharing. A slight but pleasant fragment, pleasant because of the sharing, the warmth, and the atmosphere of the darkened, empty theater that is vividly evoked by the text and the pictures together.

877   **Major,** Kevin. *Hold Fast.* Delacorte, 1980. 79-17544. ISBN 0-440-03506-6. 170p. $8.95.

7–9   Michael is fourteen, his brother seven; when their parents are killed in an accident, adult relatives decide that the younger child stay with Grandfather in their Newfoundland village, while Michael is to go to a small city and live with Aunt Flo and Uncle Ted, who have two children. One of the children is Curtis, a quiet boy who is Michael's age; Michael finds it hard to understand why Curtis accepts his domineering father's harshness. He also finds it hard to accept the change from country to city life, and he misses the grandfather he loves. When Uncle Ted bullies him, Michael decides to run away; to his surprise, Curtis elects to go with him. Their tenacity in coping with solitude on their hiking-and-camping retreat is symbolized in the title; the story ends with the boys back in the village, where Grandfather is on his deathbed. Winner of the Canadian award for the best children's book of the year, *Hold Fast* is strong in characterization and in the perceptive depiction of Michael's adjustment to his parents' death and of his efforts to adapt to a new environment. It is Michael who tells the story, so that it has a consistency of viewpoint, and the one weakness of the story is that the use of local idiom or phonetic spelling in exposition ("I would a been just as well off" or "You wasn't so good to say anything flick about me . . .") is obtrusive, while in dialogue (where it is even more heavily used) it seems acceptable.

878   **Mangurian,** David. *Children of the Incas;* written and illus. with photography by David Mangurian. Four Winds, 1979. 79-12186. ISBN 0-590-07500-4. 73p. $8.95.

4–6   In the photodocumentary style for which the Gidal books were a prototype, Mangurian uses one member of the family he visited, an extended family in the Peruvian highlands, as the speaker. Framed by the author's notes and background information gleaned on two visits, the text is based on tapes made by Modesto, the oldest child in the family. Neither in the text nor in the photographs is there an attempt to evade or embellish: Modesto's town is drab, he finds the people dull and longs to live in the city, he comments almost contemptuously on the local officials. He is candid, as are the pictures; it is clear that life is a continuum of hard work that has not led the family much above the poverty level.

879   **Manniche,** Lise, ad. *The Prince Who Knew His Fate;* tr. from hieroglyphs and illus. by Lise Manniche. Metropolitan Museum of Art/Philomel, 1981. 81-10740. Metropolitan Museum of Art ed. ISBN 0-87099-278-3; Philomel ed. ISBN 0-399-20850-X. 39p. $10.95.

2–5   Manniche, a noted Danish Egyptologist, has illustrated an ancient story in a dramatic and colorful style, using the stiff posture of ancient Egyptian friezes. The hieroglyphic writing forms a running foot across the pages, and an afterword provides facts about both the story and the illustrations. The story, taken from a papyrus fragment in the British museum, is about a prince at whose birth seven goddesses proclaim that the child is destined to be killed by a dog, snake, or crocodile. The king puts the boy into a stone house where he will be safe, but relents when his son begs to go free and take his chances, after he has become a young man. He passes a test to gain the hand of a princess. It is she who collects the pieces of his body when a dog has savaged him, enabling the prince to live again—a resurrection theme used in the religious lore of ancient Egypt.

880   **Mark,** Jan. *Aquarius.* Atheneum, 1984. 84-6176. ISBN 0-689-31051-X. 224p. $12.95.

6–9   Driven out of his water-sodden village because he is a dowser, Viner (diviner) is captured and taken prisoner in a drought-ridden land after a tedious journey. In his new home, his talents are appreciated; in fact, he is chosen to be the new king, for here the king must dance for rain. Viner feels that the old king, Morning Light, is his friend and he doesn't want to replace him; an opportunist, the dowser uses his friend to gain his own ends. He makes Morning Light his prisoner and takes him back to the village, where his dancing brings the hot sun and makes him and Viner men of status. Mark is a deft word-spinner; her narrative flows along, colorful and compelling, with strong characters and natural dialogue.

881   **Mark,** Jan. *Thunder and Lightnings.* T. Y. Crowell, 1979. 78-4778. 181p. Trade ed. $7.95; Library ed. $7.89 net.

6–9   Winner of the 1976 Carnegie Medal, this is the story of a friendship be-
*   tween Andrew, who has just moved to Norfolk, and Victor, who has always lived there. The setting is important, both because of the richness of the local dialect and because Norfolk is known as "the world's largest aircraft carrier." For aircraft are Victor's passion; a poor student and a loner, Victor seems almost doltish until Andrew learns how knowledgeable he is about anything to do with airplanes. Victor's home is rigid and sterile, and he blossoms in the casual, untidy atmosphere of Andrew's home. And Andrew? For the sake of friendship, he gives up his own hobbies to share Victor's, to help his friend feel self-confidence. There's warmth in the depiction of Andrew's family, humor in the dialogue, and a distinctive individuality of writing style. The book has that rare quality of almost seeming to evolve its own story, as though the author were only a channel; Mark never comes between book and reader.

882   **Mark,** Jan. *Under the Autumn Garden;* illus. by Judith Gwyn Brown. T. Y. Crowell, 1979. 78-4779. Trade ed. ISBN 0-690-03903-4; Library ed. ISBN 0-690-03904-2. 211p. Trade ed. $8.95; Library ed. $8.79 net.

5–6   Matthew is a quiet, imaginative child of ten whose curiosity is stimu-
*   lated by his history class assignment, finding out something about the history of his Norfolk village. He begins an excavation, hoping to find remnants of an old priory, but his slow method and the interference of two other, older boys keep him from completing his project. Disgraced at school, he stumbles on an ancient ring. Too late for the assignment, but Matthew treasures his find nevertheless. This is the mild story line of a book that is rich in characterization, sensitive to relationships

among children, lightened by the humor of the dialogue and colored by local idiom. A gentle and perceptive story is distinctively English in flavor but its differences should present no barrier to enjoyment by children elsewhere.

883   **Mark,** Michael. *Toba;* illus. by Neil Waldman. Bradbury, 1984. 83-15679. ISBN 0-02-762300-9. 105p. $10.95.

4–6   Set in Poland in 1913, this is a series of vignettes about a naive and sensitive Jewish child of a blind tailor, whom she adores. Each of the stories is modest: Toba goes to the dentist, she finds a robin's egg, takes a train trip with her family, goes shopping with her mother. This is the first part, the jacket states, of a longer work based on the life of the author's grandmother. This is an impressive first book, graceful in style and tender in mood.

884   **Marshall,** Edward. *Three by the Sea;* illus. by James Marshall. Dial, 1981. 80-26097. Library ed. ISBN 0-8037-8671-9; Paper ed. ISBN 0-8037-8687-5. 48p. Library ed. $5.99; Paper ed. $2.50.

1–2   What fun, within an easy reader, to find a story that pokes fun at easy readers. Three friends, lolling about after a picnic lunch, tell each other stories. Sam and Spider say the story from Lolly's reader is dull (they're right) and volunteer to do better. Sam tells a story, then Spider tells a scary story that incorporates the characters from Sam's story and that really holds Sam's and Lolly's attention. The mild lunacy of the illustrations (an almost vertical hill, a neatly striped cat) with their ungainly, comical figures is nicely matched with the bland directness of the writing. This is good-humored and amusing, good practice for the beginning reader, and unusual in its presentation of storytelling within the story.   .

885   **Marshall,** James. *George and Martha Back in Town;* written and illus. by James Marshall. Houghton, 1984. 83-22842. ISBN 0-395-35386-6. 47p. $9.95.

K–2   The buck-toothed hippos who've pranced their way through earlier George and Martha books are seen here in five very brief vignettes about the vicissitudes and nuances of a peer relationship. Typical of the brevity, wit, and pithiness of all the stories is the first one: Martha finds a box marked "Do Not Open," and is taken aback when she opens it and then has to pick up George's entire collection of Mexican jumping beans. "You seem out of breath," George comments. "You don't think I opened that little box, do you?" asks Martha, giving herself away with an innocence most of the lap audience will recognize ruefully. Again, beguiling.

886   **Martin,** Ann M. *Stage Fright;* illus. by Blanche Sims. Holiday House, 1984. 84-47834. ISBN 0-8234-0541-9. 125p. $10.95.

3–5   Sara, the narrator, is very shy and self-conscious, and she is miserable when her fourth-grade teacher decides to put on a play in which every member of the class has a part. To make matters worse, Sara's mother can't understand how deep Sara's aversion to making a public appearance is: she insists that Sara try to enjoy it, and argues with her husband, who sympathizes with Sara. The dreaded evening comes, Sara gets through it, does not do very well, does not enjoy it—but concedes that Mom is right; she can do it if she has to. The sub-plot has to do with whether or not Sara's best friend will move or stay in town. That has a happy outcome, so the story ends on a positive note at a realistic level. Perceptive, restrained, at times quietly funny.

887   **Martin,** Eva, ed. *Canadian Fairy Tales;* illus. by Laszlo Gal. Douglas & McIntyre, 1984. ISBN 0-88899-030-8. 124p. $15.95.

4–6   Soft, romantic paintings by a distinguished Canadian illustrator precede each of the twelve tales that, springing from diverse European roots, have been changed over the years to take on a distinctively Canadian flavor. Themes and motifs pop up agreeably in unexpected places ("Fee, fi, fo, fum, I smell the blood of an Englishman" is in "The Three Golden Hairs," and in "Beauty and the Beast" Beauty is a male) and the three Ti-Jean stories are a staple of national legendry. Martin, a librarian and storyteller, provides adaptations that are smooth in style and lively in pace.

888   **Maruki,** Toshi. *Hiroshima No Pika;* written and illus. by Toshi Maruki. Lothrop, 1982. 82-1536. ISBN 0-688-01297-3. 48p. $12.50.

2–4   First published in Japan, this is the story of one family who was in Hiroshima the day the atom bomb was dropped. Seven-year-old Mii and her parents are eating breakfast when the terrible flash comes, and Mother puts her unconscious husband over her shoulder and runs with her child to the river. They are surrounded by the wounded and the dead, and Maruki's vivid paintings shows the tragedy of bare burnt figures everywhere and the heaps of rubble in a burning city. This is based on the experiences of a real family; Mii's father died of radiation burns, and Mii herself was permanently retarded, a seven-year-old as long as she lived. Maruki is an eminent artist and an active pacifist. This is a picture book with a message, and she has used both text and pictures to convey that message effectively: never again should there be a Hiroshima. The text points out that many who thought their lives were spared later died of radiation sickness, and that almost forty years later many are still hospitalized. "It can't happen again," says Mii's mother, "if no one drops the bomb."

889   **Marzollo,** Jean. *Amy Goes Fishing;* illus. by Ann Schweninger. Dial, 1980. 80-11598. Library ed. ISBN 0-8037-019-8; Paper ed. ISBN 0-8037-0011-X. 56p. Library ed. $5.89; Paper ed. $2.25.

1–2   Small, neatly framed pictures in cool colors illustrate a pleasant story for beginning independent readers, low-keyed but satisfying. On a Saturday when the other members of the family are busy. Amy and her father go fishing. At first Amy finds it as boring as her older siblings have said, but the companionship with her father, the delicious lunch, and the triumph of her first catch change her opinion. Fishing isn't boring at all, she concludes. "Never said it was," her father replies, as the story ends. Large, well-spaced print and a simple albeit not circumscribed vocabularly facilitate reading ease, and the story has the double appeals of success at a new skill and the amicable father-daughter relationship.

890   **Marzollo,** Jean. *Ruthie's Rude Friends;* by Jean and Claudio Marzollo; illus. by Susan Meddaugh. Dial, 1984. 84-1707. Library ed. ISBN 0-8037-0016-0; Trade ed. ISBN 0-8037-0015-2. 48p. Library ed. $8.89; Trade ed. $8.95.

1–3   Like children of other space scientists from many planets, Ruthie has come to Planet X10 while her parents do research. She meets two odd creatures, a flutter-fish and a child-pig; they are rude to her and she is rude to them. Annoyed, she disobeys a parental injunction and goes over the settlement wall, only to encounter a ferocious three-headed monster. Fish and Pig, who've followed to taunt her, try to save her but it is Ruthie's strength and ingenuity that defeat the monster and excite the admiration of Fish and Pig. There are apologies all around and Ruthie is much happier now that she's made friends on Planet X10. The plot is adequately structured if short on substance; the appeal of the book (in addition to the outer space setting, the odd creatures, and the theme of friendship) are the satisfaction of accomplishment and the light, humorous style. This should provide enjoyment as well as experience to the beginning independent reader.

891   **Mayne,** William. *The Blue Book of Hob Stories;* illus. by Patrick Benson. Philomel, 1984. 84-4231. ISBN 0-399-21037-7. *The Yellow Book of Hob Stories;* illus. by Patrick Benson. Philomel, 1984. 84-4230. ISBN 0-399-21050-4. Both books have 24 pages and are $7.95.

K–3   Like the *Green Book of Hob Stories* these two little books are fanciful in concept but matter-of-fact in tone, episodic diversions that are just right for reading aloud. Hob is a tiny goblin, plump and visible only to children, who busily keeps things running smoothly in a British home. He fixes clocks, sets the table, soothes the fretful baby, conducts negotiations with the tooth fairy, and copes with the many destructive or mischievous spirits that plague the household. The writing style has vitality and a distinctive flavor; the illustrations, hatched and softly colored and imaginatively comic, are a perfect foil for the text.

892   **Mayne,** William. *The Green Book of Hob Stories;* illus. by Patrick Benson. Philomel, 1984. 83-17317. ISBN 0-399-21039-3. 24p. $7.95.

K–3   A whimsical fantasy, this episodic tale about a small, corpulent, self-satisfied household spirit is illustrated with dark/bright drawings that use hatching to good effect. The adults in a British household cannot see the tiny Hob but children and animals can, and speak of him; Hob speaks of himself in third person much of the time, a device that may have to be explained to the audience or controlled by voice changes. Hob ousts a changeling and gets Baby back into his cradle; he gets rid of Mumps, all ready to attack Baby; he gets rid of Temper, lost by someone and left lying on the floor. All of this happens unbeknowst to the family, but Hob is happy to be busy and useful. A pleasant conceit, told in distinctive style; there is a companion volume, *The Red Book of Hob Stories.*

893   **Mayne,** William. *The Mouldy;* illus. by Nicola Bayley. Knopf, 1983. 83-6163. Trade ed. ISBN 0-394-86211-2; Library ed. ISBN 0-394-96211-7. 30p. Trade ed. $9.95; Library ed. $9.99.

2–4   "In the great garden of the world," Mayne begins, "there was peace before Mouldy came." Mouldy is a mole, and his tunneling disrupts the creatures of the garden, shaking the king's crystal palace, warping the walks, trampling the roots of the fruit trees. When the efforts of the Soldiers of the Thistle fail, the king's daughter Talitha (a winged daffodil) goes underground to do combat; Mouldy is so pleased by her attack (a punch on the nose feels good to him, the jab of her tiny knitting needle is a comforting back-scratch) that he asks her to marry him. "I'm not losing a daughter," says the king, "but gaining a Mouldy." Fortunately, the mole is fickle, and when a hedgehog scratches him, he decides she'd make a better bride. Thus a happy ending for all concludes a gentle fairy tale, simply and gracefully told and illustrated with delicately framed pictures that are richly colored, beautifully and intricately detailed, and striking in the conveyance of textures.

894   **Mazer,** Harry. *I Love You, Stupid!* T. Y. Crowell, 1981. 81-43033. Trade ed. ISBN 0-690-04120-9. Lib. ed. ISBN 0-670-04121-7. 185p. Trade ed. $10.50; Library ed. $9.89.

7–10   Seventeen and ever-ardent, Marcus wouldn't want anyone (especially his sophisticated friend Alec) to know he was a virgin, and he didn't himself understand why he couldn't get a girl. There was one person he could tell: Wendy, a childhood friend who'd moved back to town; she had a crush on Alec, and Marcus had a blazing crush on the young divorcee for whom he babysat. Finally, Marcus and Wendy decided they'd have sex together, just to find out what it was all about; once having had the experience, Marcus wanted more. And more. Not until after they'd fought about it and split up did Marcus realize that he'd fallen in love with Wendy. Despite the contemporary approach, this has old-fashioned, course-of-true-love appeal. The writing style has vitality, the characters and relationships have depth, and the dialogue has hu-

mor; this is written with a fond perception of the adolescent's needs
and pressures.

895   **Mazer,** Harry. *The Island Keeper.* Delacorte, 1981. 80-68735. ISBN 0-440-
03976-2. 192p. $8.95.

7–9   Sixteen, fat, and unhappy, motherless Cleo loved only one person, her
younger sister; with her sister's death, the story begins. Cleo cannot
face yet again the loneliness of being the outsider at a summer camp.
She runs away, stopping for camping gear before she reaches the Canadian island her father owns but never uses. The rest of the story is a
Robinson Crusoe saga, and very well done, a record both believable
and suspense-filled, and—when Cleo finds her canoe smashed and
faces being on the island for the winter—exciting. She gets away by
crossing the frozen lake, and she finds that her father and grandmother
are no more understanding than they were before the long period in
which they didn't even know if Cleo was alive. It may be realistic, but
it's a rather sad ending: Cleo simply decides to go back to boarding
school. She has the thought of the island to sustain her, but otherwise
her life hasn't changed. The author maintains interest with skill; like
O'Dell's Karana, Cleo has to learn wilderness living, and the details of
her coping are all believable and nicely paced.

896   **Mazer,** Norma Fox. *Downtown.* Morrow, 1984. 84-1137. ISBN 0-688-
03859-X. 216p. $9.50.

7–10   Pete has been living with his uncle Gene for eight years, since he was
seven, and for eight years he has been wondering where his parents
are, whether he will ever see them again, and if he is being followed by
the FBI. Pete's not his real name, and he has been living in fear and in
hiding because his parents, ardent political activists, had blown up a
college laboratory as an antiwar protest. Two people had been killed
and Pete's parents had been sought by the FBI ever since. At the close
of the book, Pete's mother, tired of being a fugitive, gives herself up
and goes to jail; Pete then has to decide if he will accept her suggestion
to stay with her friends who are near the jail so that she can see him.
This last problem—giving up his friends, disrupting his school, leaving
the uncle who has been his only guardian for so many years—is typical
of the burden foisted by a parent who has abandoned a child to pro-
mulgate a cause. Pete's whole life has been shaped and confined by his
burden. The story has some light and tender moments, but for the most
part it is a serious and sensitive consideration of a stress situation.

897   **Mazer,** Norma Fox. *Someone to Love.* Delacorte, 1983. 82-72755. ISBN
0-440-08311-7. 244p. $13.95.

9–   Shy and lonely, Nina finds college life overwhelming compared to her
small town; just as lonely, Mitch is a college drop-out because—although he had no academic problems—he had felt out of place. They

fall ecstatically in love and decide to live together; Nina hates lying to her mother, but she wants to be with Mitch all the time. When the relationship begins to fray, both are restless, both afraid to lose the security of their mutual commitment. Each is unfaithful, they quarrel repeatedly, and it is Nina who finally decides to break it off. Written with perception and sympathy, this speaks eloquently of the young adult's conflicting needs and emotions as he or she strives for security and stability and independence; Mazer sees keenly the ambivalence of older adolescents as they grope painfully toward maturity.

898   **Mazer,** Norma Fox. *Taking Terri Mueller.* Morrow, 1983. 82-18849. ISBN 0-688-01732-0. 212p. $9.00.

7–9   Terri had been told that her mother had been killed in an accident when she was four, and she had adjusted happily to being with her father, although she sometimes wished that they didn't keep moving from one place to another. It wasn't until she was thirteen and found a paper in a locked box that Terri realized her mother was still alive. Angry at her father, Terri locates and visits her mother; although she now knows that her father had taken her away and lied about her mother, when she has to make the decision about which parent she'll live with, Terri decides that it's Daddy who needs her most. This has good style and pace, an element of mystery and plenty of suspense to appeal to readers, and a convincing depiction of the intricacies of Terri's attitudes and relationships.

899   **Meltzer,** Milton. *All Times, All Peoples: A World History of Slavery;* illus. by Leonard Everett Fisher. Harper, 1980. 79-2810. Trade ed. ISBN 0-06-0241861-1; Library ed. ISBN 0-06-024187-X. 65p. Trade ed. $8.95; Library ed. $8.79.

5–7   The stark, dramatic scratchboard illustrations, softened by the beige background of the pages, are well suited to the serious prose, dry but inherently dramatic, of Meltzer's text. Although Meltzer makes an occasional broad statement ("It was Christopher Columbus who started the American slave trade") that may seem inadequately clarified, he writes for the most part with scrupulous attention to facts, his attitude as objective as it is possible to be when describing the bondage of human beings. He discusses slavery in all times, in all countries, putting some emphasis on black slavery in America, and concludes with a brief commentary on slavery today and what can be done to eradicate it. A bibliography and an index are provided.

900   **Meltzer,** Milton, ed. *The Black Americans: A History in their Own Words, 1619-1983.* Crowell, 1984. 83-46160. Library ed. ISBN 0-690-04418-6; Trade ed. ISBN 0-690-04419-4. 306p. illus. with photographs. Library ed. $12.89; Trade ed. $13.50.

7–10   Adding some new materials and deleting some from his three-volume *In Their Own Words,* Meltzer has produced a single volume that covers three and a half centuries of black life in the United States. The book consists of source materials: letters, speeches, newspaper articles, records of legal testimony, and excerpts from books; each is prefaced by editorial comment that gives background and context. From this collage a vivid picture emerges of the power, passion, and pride of black life. Sources are cited, and the index is full and carefully compiled.

901   **Meltzer,** Milton, ed. *The Jewish Americans: A History In Their Own Words 1650-1950.* Crowell, 1982. 81-43886. Trade ed. ISBN 0-690-04227-2; Library ed. ISBN 0-690-04228-0. 174p. illus. with photographs. Trade ed. $10.50; Library ed. $10.89.

7–   As he has so effectively done in earlier books, Meltzer uses primary source materials to record the attitudes and reactions of a people in a new land. Vivid and varied, the letters, diaries, and speeches give a colorful picture of Jewish life in the United States over three centuries. The author's helpful notes precede each selection; a carefully compiled index gives good access to the contents.

902   **Meltzer,** Milton. *The Terrorists.* Harper, 1983. 82-48858. Trade ed. ISBN 0-06-024193-4; Library ed. ISBN 0-06-024194-2. 192p. Trade ed. $10.95; Library ed. $10.89.

8–   Always rational and objective in tone, Meltzer begins his study with an examination of the history of terrorism, from the assassins of ancient times onward. The book focuses on the western world but is not restricted to it; in covering the various terrorist movements of the past and present, it gives balanced coverage and adheres cohesively to the proposition that terrorism is a policy of intimidation, a policy usually used for political struggle, in which the advancing technology of the centuries has created new methods of violence rather than new concepts. The final chapter is on the moral issues involved in the use of force and violence in a thoughtful discussion of whether or not the end does justify the means. A serious book, carefully researched, organized, and written, this is more up-to-date than Robert Liston's *Terrorism* and better written and balanced in treatment than the Harris book written on the same subject. A lengthy bibliography and an index are included.

903   **Meltzer,** Milton. *The Truth about the Ku Klux Klan.* Watts, 1982. 82-8532. ISBN 0-531-04498-X. 120p. illus. with photographs. $8.90.

7–   For over a century, the Ku Klux Klan has been perpetrating acts of violence and terrorism, primarily against Blacks, Catholics, and Jews, in its program of making the United States a country ruled by—and preferably restricted to—a white, Protestant, Nordic society. Begun as a social group after the Civil War, the Klan was used to maintain white supremacy in the South and spread into other regions, often condoned or even joined by ministers who were approached by Kleagles (recruiters) for support. KKK power ebbed in the late 1920's; in the last quarter century there has been a resurgence of Klan violence; although the KKK today is a smaller group, it is active, persecuting other minority groups as well as the three who have so long been targets for their hate. Meltzer, in his usual style of careful documentation and serious analysis, has written a sobering report that concludes with an itemized listing of KKK attacks and atrocities in the last few years; he concludes with two chapters that discuss what sorts of people join the organization and why, and the intensive recruiting amongst young people, and a final chapter: "What To Do?" The bibliography and index have been carefully compiled.

904   **Merriam,** Eve. *If Only I Could Tell You;* illus. by Donna Diamond. Knopf, 1983. 83-4377. Library ed. ISBN 0-394-96043-2; Paper ed. ISBN 0-394-86043-8. 81p. Library ed. $8.99; Paper ed. $2.95.

8–10   In a collection of short, tender poems, Merriam captures the delight and wonder of young love, the feeling that the love is unique, the absorption in self and the loved one, the desolation when separation comes. The poetry is deceptively simple, controlled in style and deep in its empathy and insight. A few of the selections are on other themes, other kinds of love, but most have to do with the aching romantic love of adolescence.

905   **Merriam,** Eve. *A Word or Two with You: New Rhymes for Young Readers;* illus. by John Nez. Atheneum. 1981. 81-1282. ISBN 0-689-30862-0. 32p. $8.95.

3–5   There is a pervasive simplicity and candor in this new collection by one of today's major poets for children; although not every selection is Merriam at her best, there are many particularly deft poems. Some of the poems are about words (particularly about rhyming words) and some have a sense of fun, although these are not really humorous poems. Some have the lilt of jump-rope verses, and all are appropriately directed, by subject interest and level of complexity, to a young audience; most of the poems could be enjoyed by very young children if they were read aloud.

906   **Merrill,** Margaret W. *Skeletons That Fit;* illus. by Pamela Carroll. Coward, 1979. 77-24155. 63p. $5.29.

4–6   Although Merrill covers material that has been the subject of other books for the middle grades, it is a solid piece of work that she offers, describing and classifing the vertebrates and emphasizing the fact that skeletal structure has, like other anatomical features, served to help each animal adapt to, and survive in, its environment. There is some discussion of evolution of species and some comparison of vertebrate structure, and the book is greatly extended by the illustrations, precise in detail, with a softness achieved by almost-pointillist technique—some of the best anatomical drawing since Ravielli. A vertebrate chronology, a glossary, a bibliography, and an index are appended.

907   **Metter,** Bert. *Bar Mitzvah, Bat Mitzvah: How Jewish Boys & Girls Come of Age;* illus. by Marvin Friedman. Houghton/Clarion, 1984. 83-23230. Library ed. ISBN 0-89919-149-5; Paper ed. ISBN 0-89919-292-0. 55p. Library ed. $10.95; Paper ed. $3.95.

5-7   In his first book, written in an informal style, staccato and often conversational in tone, the author gives the historical background for the celebration of induction into the adult religious community in the Jewish religion. He describes the preparation of boys (bar mitzvah) and girls (bat mitzvah) for the event, the ceremonies (with some variations in different countries) and the meaning of the occasion for the celebrant. A bit repetitive, but clear and informative. An index is provided.

908   **Meyer,** Carolyn. *The Center; From a Troubled Past to a New Life.* Atheneum, 1979. 79-12509. ISBN 0-689-50143-9. 193p. $8.95.

8-10   A moving and candid story about a rehabilitation center for disturbed adolescents, this is both intense and ordered, a detailed narrative about the staff and residents of an institution (The Center) that focuses on the long and hard struggle for David's security and self-confidence. Meyer makes the program of the Center vivid and memorable: the initial anger, the dynamics of group therapy, the intricate bonds between staff members and residents and among the residents themselves. And, in the background, the families: embarrassed, often hostile, more often lacking in understanding. David graduates, and by that time the reader feels a strong involvement and empathy. The book is based on the author's experiences as an observer in such a program, and the evidence of her acuity and honesty permeates the story.

909   **Meyer,** Carolyn. *The Luck of Texas McCoy.* Atheneum, 1984. 84-3061. ISBN 0-689-50312-1. 183p. $11.95.

6-9   Knowing that Texas was the only member of the family who wanted to keep his beloved ranch intact and keep on training horses, her grandfather left it to her in his will. Her mother and grandmother were angry when Texas refused to sell; they left her to move into town and it was left to the sixteen-year-old to make a go of it by herself. Texas is a strong character: independent, honest, dedicated, industrious. She falls in love with the movie star she's been hired to train for a Western; he becomes her friend but—realistically—no more, and by the end of the story it seems clear that Texas will respond to a lad from a neighboring ranch. The book has the appeal of making-it-alone, and the characterization and writing style are far superior to those in most western-setting horse stories.

910   **Meyer,** Kathleen Allan. *Ishi.* Dillion, 1980. 79-25574. ISBN 0-87518-093-0. 70p. illus. with photographs. $5.95.

5–7   Meyer gives some background material about the Yana Indians and
their four tribal groups (Ishi's was the Yahi) and about the persecution
they suffered when white settlers came to California. Most of the biography focuses on the way Ishi lived, following the Yahi cultural patterns; since he lived for many years in complete isolation, there is little
personal material. This changed when (in 1911) Ishi appeared in a white
town, a ragged and hungry man of middle-age; subsequently he was
taken to San Francisco, where anthropologists became his friends and
protectors, studying through Ishi's memories the Yahi life and language. This is adequately written and researched, although by no
means as well written or as extensive as Theodora Kroeber's *Ishi, Last of
His Tribe,* which is for slightly older readers.

911   **Meyers,** Susan. *Pearson; A Harbor Seal Pup;* illus with photographs by
Ilka Hartmann. Dutton, 1981. 80-13041. ISBN 0-525-36845-0. 58p. $9.95.

3–6   A crisp, straightforward text describes the rescue and rehabilitation of
an orphaned harbor seal. Taken to the California Marine Mammal Center, the two-week-old pup was named Pearson and became a special pet
of the staff. Good quality photographs of the round-eyed seal pup show
some of the equipment used to care for animals and to train them for
an independent life in their natural environments; the book ends with a
description of the return of a healthy, carefully trained Pearson to the
sea. Implicit in the well-spaced, continuous text is the loving concern of
those who work for and with animals, who are more interested in preparing young creatures for independence than in gaining their affection.

912   **Michel,** Anna. *The Story of Nim: The Chimp Who Learned Language;* illus.
with photographs by Susan Kuklin and Herbert S. Terrace. Knopf, 1980.
79-17501. Trade ed. ISBN 0-394-84444-0; Library ed. ISBN 0-394-94444-5.
59p. Trade ed. $6.95; Library ed. $6.99.

4–6   In an oversize book with many photographs and large, clear print, one
of the staff that worked with Nim, a baby chimpanzee, describes his
training. The text is preceded by an explanation of the project, teaching
an infant chimpanzee to communicate by using American Sign Language, and it concludes with a list of the words Nim learned. The book is
informative both as a documentary record and as an example of the scientific approach, but undoubtedly its appeal to readers will lie primarily
in the engaging Nim himself and in his achievements as pictured in the
text and the photographs.

913   **Miklowitz,** Gloria D. *Did You Hear What Happened to Andrea?* Delacorte,
1979. 78-72972. ISBN 0-440-01923-0. 149p. $7.95.

7–9   It happened when Andrea and Dave hitched a ride back from a long
day at the beach; the driver was letting them out of the car near David's
house, and then offered to take Andrea the extra mile to her house.
What he did was take her into the hills and rape her. The story, told by

Andrea, focuses on the emotional impact on the rape victim, both on her continuing fear of her assailant and her fear of ever being able to respond sexually, and on the dismay she feels at the reactions of her family and friends: her mother is too embarrassed to be candid, the girls at school show excited curiosity rather than sympathy, and her older sister thinks Andrea's "playing for sympathy." The book concludes with the rapist convicted and Andrea slowly recovering with the help of a therapist. Miklowitz gives a convincing and balanced picture (including a sympathetic and helpful police officer) and is forthright without being over-dramatic; the writing style and characterization are competently strong.

914   **Mikolaycak,** Charles, ad. *Babushka;* retold and illus. by Charles Miko-laycak. Holiday House, 1984. 84-500. ISBN 0-8234-0520-6. 26p. $14.95.

K–3   Like the Italian folklore figure, Befana, the Russian Babushka has become a beloved Christmas legend about the woman who, busy with her sweeping and cleaning, refused to accompany the three kings as they followed a star—and later repented and roamed the world trying to find the child who was a King. Children enjoy the legend because Babushka is said to leave small gifts for children wherever she goes. Mikolaycak has retold the story adequately, in a straightforward style; it is his stunning paintings that give the book impact, with strong Slavic notes in architectural and costume details, effective composition and use of color, and—a particularly moving touch—the gradual aging of Babushka from a fresh-faced young woman to a stooped and weary old woman.

915   **Milbauer,** Barbara. *Suppose You Were a Netsilik: Teenagers in Other Societies.* Messner, 1981. 81-2428. ISBN 0-671-32891-2. 157p. $8.79.

7–10   An interesting study in comparative anthropology contrasts the patterns of middle class, suburban adolescents (particularly in white families) in the United States with the cultural patterns in Netsilik, Ibo, Hutterite and Cheyenne families; for these societies the author describes the "uncontaminated state," i.e., the traditional mores and folkways, although she acknowledges frequently the changes that have taken place. Much of the book is devoted to general discussion of familial patterns, kindred groups, and various societal influences. Nothing startling here, and nothing new antropologically, but the book is adequately organized and written, save for occasional errors ("The moral and religious structure supply a rigid code of ethics . . ."), and it serves to stimulate consideration of the factors that influence cultural similarities and differences. A brief bibliography and a relative index are appended.

916   **Miles,** Betty. *Maudie and Me and the Dirty Book.* Knopf, 1980. 79-19783. Trade ed. ISBN 0-394-84343-6; Library ed. ISBN 0-394-94343-0. 144p. Trade ed. $6.95; Library ed. $6.99 net.

6–8   As part of a middle-school class project, Kate (who tells the story) and Maudie are asked to help first-grade children with their reading, in part by reading aloud to them. The girls are both delighted with how well their efforts are received, although Kate is a bit flustered by the way her story, *The Birthday Dog*, precipitates a frank, eager discussion by the younger children about reproduction. She is more than flustered when this sets off a storm of controversy, and really upset at the angry accusations by some adults. In the public meeting held at the high school, Kate's irritated when one of the parents of a first grade child shows one page of the book ("She should have read the whole book or not shown any of it"), and she makes a brief but pointed speech. The school board votes to continue the project. Democracy is exhausting, she decides, but she's exhilarated. Miles doesn't foist the issue of the freedom to read onto a plot, but makes it the crux of a lively, often funny, story that is well balanced by Kate's relationship with her warm, supportive parents, her rapport with a teacher, and her friendships, particularly her friendship with Maudie.

917   **Miller,** Frances A. *Aren't You the One Who . . .?* Atheneum, 1983. 82-13798. ISBN 0-689-30961-9. 209p. $11.95.

7–10   Although he had been cleared of the charge of killing his little sister and had been taken in by Ryder (the police officer in charge of the case) and his wife, Matt was always aware that the people he met at his new school might recognize the name, might be prejudiced. To orphaned Matt, the Ryders were his family, and their children a beloved brother and sister. Most people don't know, and some don't care, like the Schuyler children who become close friends. Matt's only problem is the track coach, who is openly hostile and makes participation a hardship; Matt is determined to run, however, as he had in the past. When a crisis situation arises, Matt almost runs away—but one of the Schuylers talks to Mrs. Ryder, and the love that she and her husband have for their foster son is so explicitly expressed that Matt kowns he really has a family and the security of their love. Well-defined characters and strong familial and friendship values give conviction and warmth; while the book lacks a strong story line, it gives, in good writing style, a believable picture of adolescents (Matt, Meg Schuyler, and the slow, kind orphan Don) who respond with courage and resilience to stress situations.

918   **Milne,** Lorus J. *The Mystery of the Bog Forest*; by Lorus J. Milne and Margery Milne; illus. with photographs by the authors and by Fred Bavendam. Dodd, 1984. 83-25495. ISBN 0-396-08318-8. 127p. $9.95.

5–9   A catchy title, but there's no "mystery" about the bog forest; the authors explain exactly how it forms, what stages it goes through as it matures, what plants and animals are the inhabitants. The text is lucid and comprehensive—in fact, its minor weakness is that it goes into so much detail about individual examples of flora and fauna that it becomes almost tedious. The many photographs are of varying quality but are adequately placed and captioned. There are occasional lapses of style or syntax, but for the most part the writing is as capable as it is authoritative. Separate lists of some of the plants and animals of American peat bogs precede the index.

919   **Milton,** Joyce. *A Friend of China;* illus. with photographs. Hastings House, 1980. 80-19545. ISBN 0-8038-2388-6. 126p. $8.95.

7–10   Admiring but not adulatory, this serious biography of Agnes Smedley— journalist, author, activist, feminist—covers the other parts of her life but focuses on her years in China where she marched and camped with the Communist guerrillas. The title is taken from the inscription "Agnes Smedley, a friend of China" engraved on her tombstone in a Peking graveyard for national heroes. Smedley had come to China as a journalist for a German newspaper; she stayed to work in medical service, to advocate feminine liberation, and above all to see and report on the guerrillas, the war with Japan, and the internecine battle between Chiang Kai-shek and the Communists. Ill and weary, she returned to the United States to be accused of being a Soviet spy, an accusation hastily retracted by the U.S. Army in 1949. In 1950, she died. Milton gives a trenchant picture of Smedley, but she also provides a great deal of information about China, based in large part on Smedley's own books and articles; the latter are included in a divided bibliography which is followed by a relative index.

920   **Milton,** Joyce. *Secrets of the Mummies;* illus. with drawings by Dolores R. Santoliquido and with photographs. Random House, 1984. 84-1963, Library ed. ISBN 0-394-96769-0; Trade ed. ISBN 0-394-86769-6. 69p. Library ed. $5.99; Trade ed. $4.95.

2–4   Simply if at times choppily written, this is a mixture of facts about ancient Egypt, mummies, and the process of mummification. There are also chapters on related topics, such as tomb robberies or the craze, during the Middle Ages, for taking medicine made of ground mummies. In a chapter on the discovery of Tutankhamen's tomb, Milton gives a hint of the careful way in which archeologists work. Pedestrian but often informative drawings are provided in addition to photographs of mummies and artifacts. This is not coverage in depth, but it's an adequate introduction that may stimulate further investigation by young readers.

921   **Minard,** Rosemary. *Long Meg;* illus. by Philip Smith. Pantheon, 1982. 81-11103. Trade ed. ISBN 0-394-84888-8; Library ed. ISBN 0-394-94888-2. 58p. Trade ed. $8.95; Library ed. $8.99.

4–6   There are many stories about the legendary Meg, and although it is accepted by many scholars that she did indeed live, there is no verification of the reality of the deeds for which she was famous. Here Minard spins a brisk tale of Long Meg's heroism when she posed as a man to join the army of Henry VIII when he invaded France. Sixteen, tall and strong, Meg was wounded in the battle for Boulogne; she led the laundresses of that city in an ingenious plan to save it from the besieging French army, and won the honor of a visit from the king. Lots of action here, in a story that has little characterization in depth but has historical use and is written in a direct, simple style.

922   **Mitchell,** Barbara. *Tomahawks and Trombones;* illus. by George Overlie. Carolrhoda, 1982. 81-21661. ISBN 0-87614-191-2. 56p. $5.95.

2–3   In a fictionalized account based on a true incident, Mitchell describes the way in which—warned by a friendly Delaware Indian—the residents of a small town averted an attack by hostile Iroquois. The setting is the Moravian village of Bethlehem, Pennsylvania, the year 1755. The residents had sent for some trombones so that they could celebrate Christmas as they had in the old country, called to church by a set of trombones. The peaceful town was feeling the results of the French and Indian War, although they had always lived in harmony with their Delaware neighbors. Warned of the attack, they sounded their trombones, and the attackers fled. Some of the detail is actual, based on diaries, and some is conjectural. The story is written in a direct and simple style, printed in large and well-spaced type. Useful for primary grades readers, this is both a Christmas story and a historical story that's just the right level of complexity.

923   **Mitchell,** Joyce Slayton. *See Me More Clearly; Career and Life Planning for Teens with Physical Disabilities.* Harcourt, 1980. 79-3768. ISBN 0-15-272460-5. 284p. $8.95.

7–12   In a serious, matter-of-fact approach to the problems of adolescents with physical handicaps, Mitchell encourages them to face the physical limitations of their condition, assess their abilities and potential, fight the stereotyped attitudes they encounter, and plan for the careers they choose. The special problems or limitations of particular kinds of handicaps are discussed in separate chapters; the author is especially encouraging and candid in stressing—in other chapters—those needs and interests that are common to all teenagers, disabled or not. Practical advice on coping with fearful or overprotective parents, with peers, prospective employers, etc. is included. A special section on vocational guidance, a list of sources for further information and help (by disability), of facts on getting about (by state), and a divided bibliography are included, as is an index.

924   **Modell,** Frank. *Goodbye Old Year, Hello New Year;* written and illus. by Frank Modell. Greenwillów, 1984. 84-4020. Library ed. ISBN 0-688-03939-1; Trade ed. ISBN 0-688-03938-3. 28p. Library ed. $9.55; Trade ed. $11.25.

K–3   Firm flyaway lines and solid, clear colors are used in cheerful line-and-wash drawings to illustrate a fourth engaging book about those enterprising boys, Marvin and Milton. This time they assemble noisemakers and paper hats to celebrate the coming of the New Year; knowing they won't be allowed to stay up until midnight, they each go to sleep and set an alarm clock. Marvin's doesn't go off; Milton sleeps through the noise; when they wake in the wee hours they celebrate anyway, at least until the neighbors' protests send them back indoors to indulge in cake and milk. Light, cheerful, with no trace of message, ethical concept, didacticism, or usefulness.

925   **Moeri,** Louise. *First the Egg.* Dutton, 1982. 82-5145. ISBN 0-525-44006-2. 99p. $10.95.

7–10   Sarah, in her senior year of high school, is baffled by the assignment in her Marriage and Family class: pairs of students are told to care for an egg for a week, keeping it intact and filling in a "baby book" record of their "child." The project is the catalyst for several dramatic changes and for a sharpened sensitivity that leads Sarah to new knowledge about her family and herself. She learns that her younger sister's birth had been resented by their father; her brother decides to leave home; her mother takes a first job; and Sarah becomes involved with her "parenting partner," David, who had always been withdrawn and caustic. This is a remarkably discerning story, smoothly written and with substantial characterization and dialogue, although the turmoil and emotion caused by the egg seem at times excessive, and the rapidity of reaction and change compressed into a very full week.

926   **Moeri,** Louise. *Save Queen of Sheba.* Dutton, 1981. 80-23019, ISBN 0-525-33202-2. 116p. $9.25.

4–6   At first the boy, King David, thought he was the only survivor of the Sioux attack. Weak from an attempted scalping, horrified by the sight of all the corpses in the wagon party, King David was overjoyed to discover his six-year-old sister, Queen of Sheba, alive. Determined to get both of them to the advance party that included their parents, King David faced a battery of obstacles, not the least of which was that the fretful, pampered Queen of Sheba was recalcitrant. She wanted cooked food. She wanted Ma. She wanted her own way. And the tired, hungry, wounded boy was patient and protective, not just because she was his sister but because he would have to face Ma and Pa. Although the story sags a bit here and there, it is on the whole a deft sustaining of suspense and mood, impressive in a book that has so stark a setting and so sparse a cast. Only once is there an encounter, almost in pantomime, between the two children and Indians. King David's realization of what it meant to native Americans to have white interlopers crossing their land, killing the buffalo for just their hides, and grazing their horses on the Indian pastures serves as a foil for the implicit depiction of the attack as a massacre of innocents.

927   **Mohr,** Joseph. *Silent Night;* illus. by Susan Jeffers. Dutton, 1984. 84-8113. ISBN 0-525-44144-1. 24p. $12.95.

All
ages

In an oversize book, Jeffers uses the space to full advantage for striking paintings of the town, the manger, the Holy Family, and the worshippers at the Nativity scene. The text consists of the words of the familiar carol, for which musical notation is appended. The first scenes: Mary and Joseph travelling through the starry night, and the silent streets of Bethlehem, are particularly effective in cool blues and greens, but the composition and use of color are almost as dramatic in the interior scenes, in which the tender faces and the play of light and shadow are outstanding.

928   **Moore,** Clement Clarke. *The Night Before Christmas;* illus. by Anita Lobel. Knopf, 1984. 84-4342. Library ed. ISBN 0-394-96863-8; Trade ed. ISBN 0-394-86863-3. 22p. Library ed. $10.99; Trade ed. $9.95.

K–2

Lobel's speaker, in her illustrations for the beloved poem by Moore, is the father of a Victorian family; the interpretations of the scenes are cozy, appropriately ornate (both the architecture in the exterior scenes and the furnishings in the interiors) in a fashion that manages to be traditional without being stodgy and that has an old-New-York charm.

929   **Moore,** Emily. *Just My Luck.* Dutton, 1983. 82-4582. ISBN 0-525-44009-7. 103p. $10.95.

4–6

Olivia, the narrator, is almost ten and unhappily convinced that she's less important than her parents (mother's just had a promotion, Daddy's just finished a novel) or her sister, a stellar achiever. Olivia yearns for a dog, but Daddy says that since he's not earning money, they can't afford one. Nevertheless, she puts her savings into a deposit on an expensive puppy; the only way she can earn enough for the balance is to get the reward for solving the mystery of a dognapping. When she does, the culprit proves to be an elderly friend—and Olivia has to choose between reporting him or pretending that the dog came back to its owner by itself—thereby losing the award and her last chance of getting the puppy. The plot is nicely balanced by warm relationships in a black family, by involvement with neighbors, and by Olivia's friendship with Jeffrey, a classmate. The characters are well-rounded, the pace brisk, and the writing impressive for its natural flow and percipience.

930   **Moore,** Janet Gaylord. *The Eastern Gate: An Invitation to the Arts of China and Japan.* Collins, 1979. 78-59816. ISBN 0-529-05434-5. 296p. illus. $24.95.

7–
*

An art educator, a seasoned writer who has lived in the far East, and herself an artist, Moore provides more than facts about Chinese and Japanese art history or even about the many art forms she discusses: she relates individual works, trends, and styles to cultural, philosophic, and artistic traditions of China and Japan. The book is profusely and beautifully illustrated with photographs of paintings, ceramics, gardens, architecture, sculpture, prints, furniture, and photography, and the author also provides pictures of the work of western artists to illustrate influences, differences, and similarities. The material on Chinese art and on Japanese art is divided by a section on the literature of the two countries. Moore's writing is serious but not dry, expert but not incomprehensible to the uninitiate, and remarkable for its equal success in giving small details or broad viewpoints. Notes, a glossary, a guide to pronunciation, an index, and an extensive divided bibliography are appended to a book that is as informative as it is handsome.

931   **Moore,** Lillian. *Something New Begins;* illus. by Mary Jane Dunton. Atheneum, 1982. 82-1723. ISBN 0-689-30818-3. 114p. $9.95.

3–   Decorated rather than Ilustrated, this collection comprises selections from earlier books and fifteen new poems that are beautifully carved, cameo-clear and delicate, small lyrics of the natural world. Although most of the material in the collection, which is divided by the titles of books from which the poems came, is easily available, it's pleasant to have them gathered in this book, and the new poems are of the fine quality that Moore's fans have come to expect.

932   **Morgan,** Alison. *Paul's Kite.* Atheneum, 1982. 82-3957. ISBN 0-689-50245-1. 113p. $8.95.

5–7   Paul, the eleven-year-old protagonist of *All Kinds of Prickles* had not been happy living with his cousin Joanna, Aunt Jean, and Uncle William, particularly because of the latter's unfriendly manner. Now he has come to London to live with the mother who'd deserted him (as his father had) so many years ago. A fading model, his mother is preoccupied with her own life and doesn't want it known that she has an adolescent son. Self-sufficient but lonely, Paul prowls curiously about London and is delighted when he can show Joanna around on her first visit. Joanna, unused to traffic, is hit by a car and when her parents come to London to see her, Paul really gets to know Uncle William for the first time. Telling Paul that he is about to serve a prison sentence for embezzlement, Uncle William (who had always seemed a model of priggish rectitude) urges Paul to come back and live with his family. So a lonely child rejected by his self-centered mother finds, for the first time since the death of his grandparents, that there is a place he's wanted and people who care for him. Morgan neither condemns nor sentimentalizes; she comes between readers and characters as little as it is possible for an author to do, and her well-paced story smoothly fuses the sharply-etched characters, the London setting, and the evolution of a solution to the problems of a resourceful and solitary child.

933   **Morris,** Terry Neil, illus. *Lucky Puppy! Lucky Boy!* Knopf, 1980. 79-27024. Trade ed. ISBN 0-394-84220-0; Library ed. ISBN 0-394-94220-5. 26p. Trade ed. $1.95; Library ed. $4.99.

3–6
yrs.

Like *Good Night, Dear Monster!* this is a small, sturdily bound wordless book, but it seems more likely to appeal to children, partly because of the familiarity of the boy-dog situation, partly because the pages tell the story clearly. The illustrations in both books are in cartoon style, not particularly adroit or polished, but uncluttered and simply drawn. A boy sees a puppy in a pet shop window, but has no money (he pulls out empty pockets to indicate this) and is so disconsolate he fails to notice a frisky dog that keeps running ahead of him to get his attention (at one point the desperate puppy stands on his hind legs and sings) until the very last moment. The boy whistles, the pup jumps into his arms.

934   **Morrison,** Dorothy Nafus. *Chief Sarah; Sarah Winnemucca's Fight for Indian Rights;* illus. with prints, photographs, and maps. Atheneum, 1980. 79-22545. ISBN 0-689-30752-7. 170p. $9.95.

7–10

Based on Sarah Winnemucca Hopkin's autobiography, on newspaper accounts, and on official documents, this biography of the Paiute leader is well-researched, serious but not dry in tone, neither laudatory nor unduly fictionalized, containing little dialogue. The text makes clear the bitter and repeated record of promises and treaties broken, and it lets Sarah's achievements speak for themselves. Uneducated, but dedicated and intelligent, she became an advocate for Indian rights in her writings and lectures, gained national renown, and was the first Native American to write a book (her autobiography, published in 1883) that was published in English. A strong figure, strongly depicted. An extensive bibliography of sources and an index are included, as are many reproductions of prints and photographs.

935   **Morrison,** Velma Ford. *Going On a Dig;* illus. with photographs. Dodd, 1981. 80-2776. ISBN 0-396-07915-6. 128p. $7.95.

5–7

After a discussion of what the science of archeology is and why it is important, Morrison describes the ways in which evidence is buried and ways in which it is discovered and identified. The text then focuses on an archeological site at which junior and senior high school students participate in the work after brief training programs; it concludes with descriptions of some of the sites, and the knowledge gained from them, in America, where—among other sites in various parts of the United States—there were settled communities thousands of years before the pyramids were constructed in Egypt. The writing style is occasionally awkward ("Archeology can be a fun science . . .") but the text is on the whole adequately written and organized. The index is preceded by information on the archeological programs for junior high, senior high, and adult groups—the Kampsville Field Schools mentioned above.

936   **Mother Goose.** *If Wishes Were Horses And Other Rhymes;* illus. by Susan Jeffers. Dutton, 1979. 79-9986. ISBN 0-525-32531-X; 31p. $9.95.

3–5
yrs.
Jeffers has chosen nursery rhymes about horses to illustrate with softly colored but strongly composed pictures in mixed media: line drawings in ink, colored by ink and pastel pencils. The result is effective, combining black and white people, slightly comic, with nicely textured and modeled animals.

937   **Murphy,** Jim. *Two Hundred Years of Bicycles.* Lippincott, 1983. 81-48608. Trade ed. ISBN 0-397-32007-8; Library ed. ISBN 0-398-32008-6. 60p. Trade ed. $9.95; Library ed. $9.89.

4–6
Photographs and drawings illustrate the history of bicycles, from the drawings of Leonardo da Vinci to the celerifere (which the rider used by running) to the Michaux "boneshaker" which was the first machine to include foot pedals, through many variants and improvements to the sleek and powerful machines of today. The text is well-organized, crisply written, and carefully indexed. A one-page bibliography and a photograph of a contemporary bicycle, with parts labelled, are appended.

938   **Murphy,** Shirley Rousseau. *Mrs. Tortino's Return to the Sun:* by Shirley and Pat Murphy; illus. by Susan Russo. Lothrop, 1980. 79-20694. Trade ed. ISBN 0-688-41921-6; Library ed. ISBN 0-688-51921-0. 32p. Trade ed. $7.95; Library ed. $7.63 net.

K–3
Mrs. Tortino, whose Victorian house had been surrounded by tall buildings that shut off light and fresh air, was determined not to move out of the house that had belonged to her family for generations. Then she had an offer she couldn't refuse, and—floor by floor—her house was hoisted up as a skyscraper grew on her land. Now her house is on top of a thirty-floor building; it's quiet, the garden is verdant, Mrs. Tortino's cat no longer wheezes, and all the construction workers who became friends while the building was going up have a party once a year. Not probable, but a satisfying story with a problem solved, and a wish granted. Mrs. Tortino is represented as a staunch, self-reliant woman who repairs the plumbing and replaces rusty pipes, and who—as the building is going up—becomes nonchalant about walking the beams and riding the construction elevator.

939   **Myers,** Walter Dean. *Hoops.* Delacorte, 1981. 81-65497. ISBN 0-440-03707-7. 183p. $10.95.

7–10
Seventeen-year-old Lonnie, the narrator, is a good basketball player and he knows it—but is he good enough to be spotted in a city championship? Good enough to get out of the ghetto and become a pro? He has faith in his coach, but both are under pressure to throw the final game, losing to suit financial sharks. Myers does a good job of building tension, and just as good a job of building the relationship between Lonnie and his coach, a bond of trust that develops slowly. At the end of the story the coach is stabbed and dies, so the winning of the crucial game

is not a formula-device; it is a lesson to Lonnie: there are rough people in the business of basketball, and if he wants to get out of Harlem and become a pro, he'll have to cope with them.

940   **Myers,** Walter Dean. *The Nicholas Factor.* Viking, 1983. 82-60083. ISBN 0-670-51055-6. 173p. $11.50.

7–10   A mystery and adventure story is artfully structured, with good pace and suspense, and is developed with both logic and drama. The protagonist is Gerald, a college student who has been convinced by a federal agent to join a conservative group called the Crusade Society, since there is reason to believe that the society is being used to gain power. The title refers to a child leader in the medieval Children's Crusade, and to the power of the dedicated young in any movement. Sent on a mission described as a simple social experiment, Gerald and other members of the society become suspicious about what is going on and for what reasons. Their prying unmasked, Gerald and a friend decamp and are pursued, narrowly escaping the vengeance of those Society leaders who are criminals; their curiosity and courage lead to the capture of the culprits who have caused many deaths amongst the Peruvian Indians with their experiment, and also the death of one of the young members.

941   **Myers,** Walter Dean. *The Young Landlords.* Viking, 1979. 79-13264. ISBN 0-670-79454-6. 192p. $8.95.

6–9   It's the same sort of group of adolescents who romped through *Mojo and the Russians,* with the addition of Paul, who tells the story and who is in love with Kitty. This time the gang acquires a slum building by chance, and most of the story is about their efforts to improve the property and to put it on a sound financial basis. While Myers inserts a few chapters that do nothing to further the story, they are just as funny as the rest of the book; like *Mojo,* the story has lots of action, good characterization and dialogue, and a casual but warm relationship among the members of the gang. The book gives an attractive picture of a black urban neighborhood, and while it has its yeasty share of zany characters, it is given depth by the tenderness of the shy romance between Paul and Kitty, and by the deepening understanding between Paul and the stern father from whom he had at first felt alienated.

942   **Namioka,** Lensey. *Valley of the Broken Cherry Trees.* Delacorte, 1980. 79-53605. ISBN 0-440-09325-2. 218p. $8.95.

7–10   Another adventure story (like *The Samurai and the Long-Nosed Devils*) set in 16th-century Japan, where Zenta and Matsuzo, two unemployed samurai warriors, come to a valley famous for the beauty of its cherry trees. They are horrified as everyone else to find that some of the trees have been mutilated, but not quite as baffled; they are not, however, fully prepared for the intricate political situation or the danger they must face when they begin an investigation of the malicious damage. Namioka evokes the place and period vividly, in a smoothly written and fast-paced story with unexpected twists in its development; the dialogue and characterization are most ably handled.

943   **Namioka,** Lensey. *Village of the Vampire Cat.* Delacorte, 1981. 80-68737. ISBN 0-440-09377-5. 200p. $9.55.

7–10   Like the three earlier books about the two young samurai, Zenta and Matsuzo, this story of medieval Japan has deft construction, well-paced action, and suspense. This time the two have returned to the village where Zenta's old teacher, Ikken, lives; they find the wise and gentle old man as terrified of the creature (human or beast) that has killed four young women as are the other and more credulous members of the small community. Warriors with a Robin Hood approach, Zenta and Matsuzo are determined to find the reputed "Vampire Cat" which scratches its victims, and capture or kill it. There's mystery and intricacy in Namioka's plot, strong delineation of characters, and a dramatic conclusion, yet always—here as in the earlier books—there is a substantive amount of historical research, effortlessly incorporated, so that the period details, the mores, and the customs are smoothly integrated.

944   **Nance,** John. *Lobo of the Tasaday;* written and illus. with photographs by John Nance. Pantheon, 1982. 81-14113. Trade ed. ISBN 0-394-85007-7; Library ed. ISBN 0-394-95007-1. 53p. $9.95.

4–6   Black and white photographs illustrate a book about the Tasaday, a tribe numbering twenty-six at the time (early in the 1970's) a group of journalists visited them on their island in the Philippines. "Tasaday" means "people of the home place," and the isolated Tasadays thought, until recently, that they and their friends were the only people on earth. Lobo, ten at the time of the visit, is used as an example of a boy's role in the primitive society, but this is more about the tribe than about Lobo, and it gives a full picture of the communal life, the respect for nature, the belief in an omnipotent being (the Owner of all things) and the ways in which the Tasaday live and work, dress, gather food, and play. A large part of the text, written in a direct style, dignified but not formal, describes the way in which a hunter, Defal, who had encountered the Tasaday and their Stone Age way of life, convinces them to trek to the edge of their rain forest and the way in which they react to the appearance and appurtenances of a government official who had flown in to help the tribe become prepared for contact with modern life, since it was anticipated that there would be an industrially motivated incursion into the Tasaday's remote rain forest. Fascinating.

945   **Nash,** Ogden. *Custard and Company; Poems by Ogden Nash;* comp. and illus. by Quentin Blake. Little, 1980. 79-25742. ISBN 0-316-59834-8. 128p. $7.95.

3–   The inspired lunacy of Nash's poems is wonderfully echoed by the
scratchy, flyaway line drawings that Blake has paired with selections he
has chosen for this collection. Children and adults enjoy the wit and
word play of the Nash-eye-view of the world, with his incisive comments sheathed in humor and with the nonsense of such poems as
"The Canary": "The song of canaries/ Never varies/ And when they're
molting/ They're pretty revolting," or, "I kind of like the playful por-
poise/ A healthy mind in a healthy corpus/ He and his cousin, the playful dolphin/ Why they like swimmin like I like golphin," in "The Por-
poise." Children enjoy Nash's invented words, a trick he doesn't abuse,
and the occasional elaborate departure from scansion, and if this makes
them more conscious of poetic form and the use of language, it's a peripheral bonus; the primary bonus is laughter.

946   **Navarra,** John Gabriel. *Earthquake;* illus. with photographs. Doubleday,
1980. 79-8938. Trade ed. ISBN 0-385-15080-6; Library ed. ISBN 0-385-
15081-4. 95p. Trade ed. $7.95; Library ed. $8.90.

5–8   A professor of geoscience, Navarra is both authoritative in his field and
practiced as a science writer; his text is logically arranged and his subject handled with clarity and range. He discusses the causes of earthquakes, the ways in which they can be measured and predicted, and
the various degrees of seismic activity, including tsunamis. The book
concludes with a discussion of coping with earthquakes, and with an
index. Unfortunately, several illustrations have been badly placed by
the publishers; for example, "The photo opposite was taken a few days
later . . ." is stated on a page discussing an earthquake in Pakistan; on
the opposite page are two drawings of the Nazca and South American
plates, while an unlabelled picture, two pages later, appears to be the
photograph to which the text refers.

947   **Naylor,** Phyllis Reynolds. *How Lazy Can You Get?* illus. by Alan Daniel.
Atheneum, 1979. 79-10444. ISBN 0-689-30721-7. 50p. $7.95.

2–4   When their parents go off for a week and hire a Professional Caretaker,
Miss Brasscoat, to stay with Timothy, Amy, and Douglas John, the
three children do not anticipate a jolly time. They are cooperative,
pleasant children but they aren't used to a martinet; they are also literal,
and when Miss Brasscoat grimly says "How lazy can you get?" or "Just
how messy can you get?" they show her. Tired of no smiles, strict cur-
fews, endless chores, and disagreeably wholesome foods, they are
amazed when, on the last morning of the week, there's a contretemps
(a pet crab gets into the food on the table) that actually makes their Professional Caretaker smile. They're even more amazed—and delighted—
when she laughs and says "How silly can I get?" and then shows them
by imitating a parrot. So Father and Mother come home to a scene of
rapport, and the children bid Miss Brasscoat an almost affectionate farewell. This doesn't have a strong story line, but it has a brisk, light writing style and plenty of action and humor to appeal to readers.

948   **Naylor,** Phyllis Reynolds. *A String of Chances.* Atheneum, 1982. 82-1790. ISBN 0-689-30935-X. 244p. $10.95.

7–9   Sixteen-year-old Evie's father is minister of the Faith Gospel church in a small Maryland town; Evie's used to the fact that her parents have taken in needy people (a retarded man, a stroke victim, a senile woman) but she's irritated when they invite her childhood enemy, Matt, to stay in her room while she's away for the summer. Evie is spending her vacation with a cousin who expects a baby, and she enjoys the peaceful, affectionate atmosphere of Tom and Donna Jean's home. When the baby comes, Evie adores him. It is almost as tragic to her as to Tom and Donna Jean when little Josh suffers crib death. Already questioning the faith in which she has heretofore stood firm, Evie angrily confronts her father, whom she adores, and her doubts are not solved despite her father's tenacious faith and patience. The story ends with a rapprochement with Matt, and it has a deft fusion of major plot threads (the relationships with Matt and another boy, Evie's love for the baby and grief at his death, and her despair and anger as she begins to examine her doubts about the tenets of her faith) and minor ones. Characterization and dialogue are handled with smoothness and depth, as Evie moves toward tolerance of others and understanding of herself.

949   **Neimark,** Anne E. *A Deaf Child Listened: Thomas Gallaudet, Pioneer in American Education.* Morrow, 1983. 82-23942. ISBN 0-688-01719-3. 116p. $8.50.

6–9   It was in 1814 that the young, frail minister, Thomas Gallaudet, met a deaf child of nine, Alice Cogswell, whose plight made him wonder if there were not some way to teach deaf children to communicate, to compensate for their sensory deprivation, and to equip them for fuller participation as adults. After a tour of European institutions for the deaf, he came back to the United States to plead for—and eventually establish—the first school for the deaf in the country. This biography is both a record of Gallaudet's life and his battles on behalf of deaf children, and a record of the status of treatment and education of the deaf as they changed over the centuries. Adequately written, believably fictionalized, and informative, the book is based on Gallaudet's letters and diaries; it tells a touching story of an admirable and devoted man. A bibliography, an index, and a list of national service organizations and centers for the deaf are provided.

950   **Newton,** James R. *A Forest is Reborn;* illus. by Susan Bonners. Crowell, 1982. 81-43882. Trade ed. ISBN 0-690-04231-0; Library ed. ISBN 0-690-04232-9. 28p. Trade ed. $8.25; Library ed. $8.89.

2–4   Black and white pencil drawings of plants and animals, softly shaded, beautifully detailed and textured, illustrate a clearly written continuous text, informative and straightforward in style. As a concluding note explains, the author has used flora and fauna of the Northwest to illustrate what the progression of change is after a forest fire, but the cycle is the same in all forests. The text begins with the fire that leaves only burned tree trunks standing, and explains how—from seeds deep underground, brought in by animals, or carried by the wind—a progression of plant life begins and changes until there is again a climax forest. A fine science book.

951   **Newton,** Suzanne. *An End to Perfect.* Viking/Kestrel, 1984. 84-7307. ISBN 0-670-29487-X. 212p. $11.95.

5–7   All's well in Arden's world, she likes the small town in which she lives, she has no problems at school, she loves her best friend Dorjo, and she is on very good terms with her parents and her older brother. The end to this happy state comes when brother Hill, bored by the small town school (which baffles Arden) ask if he can move to a larger town and live with his grandparents so that he can go to school there. Then there's Dorjo. Her vagrant mother, selfish and demanding, has again appeared to disrupt the life Dorjo and her older sister have made for themselves; Dorjo runs away, is taken in by Arden's family, and is ambivalent about returning home. Arden wants her friend to stay but realizes that Dorjo must learn to cope with her mother and that she can't keep her friend by her side forever, that there's an end to perfect. This isn't as strong a story as the author's *I Will Call It Georgie's Blues*, but it is just as acute in its perception of the complexity of familial problems, and it is just as polished and profound in its style and its depth of characterization.

952   **Newton,** Suzanne. *I Will Call It Georgie's Blues.* Viking, 1983. 83-5849. ISBN-0-670-39131-X. 204p. $10.95.

7–10   Neal, the narrator, is fifteen; his sister Aileen is several years older, his brother Georgie is seven; all three are heavily, nervously conscious not only of having to present a good public image as a Baptist minister's children but also of having to cope with their rigidly authoritarian, bullying father and with a tight-lipped mother who supports all of her husband's rigid strictures. Neal, himself having trouble in establishing independence and in hiding the fact that he's been secretly taking lessons in jazz, becomes even more worried about little Georgie, who has terror-born fantasies about his inadequacies. Their father's treatment of Georgie results in the child's retreat into a catatonic state; with this crisis, the family tensions are finally fully unmasked. Dad realizes for the first time how he has affected his children, Georgie gets treatment, and—although the situation is left with an implication of improvement rather than a sunny resolution—Neal defiantly plays his beloved jazz music in front of others, determined that he will no longer mask his real interest and his real self. This is a powerful, taut story of a troubled family; it is written with perception and polish, and it is moving in its sensitivity and honesty.

953   **Nigg,** Joe. *A Guide to the Imaginary Birds of the World;* illus. with woodcuts by David Frampton. Apple-wood Books, 1984. ISBN 0-918222-55-9.
160p. $24.95.

5–   An oversize book, spacious in format and handsomely printed, is devoted to the fictional and legendary birds or bird-like creatures of the
world. A page of description (other names, general characteristics, distribution, etc.) is followed by a one-page tale or myth, and then by a
pictorial page, with an impressive woodcut portrait of each of the thirty
birds shown. This will have some appeal as a browsing book or a curiosity, but it should also be useful to students of folklore.

954   **Nikly,** Michelle. *The Princess on the Nut: Or the Curious Courtship of the
Son of the Princess on the Pea;* illus. by Jean Claverie; tr. by Lucy Meredith. Faber, 1981. ISBN 0-571-11846-1. 22p. $9.95.

K–3   The pages of an oversize book are used to good advantage for paintings
that have a touch of Boutet de Monvel's romantic look, a resemblance
to Brinton Turkle's painting in the use of light and color, and a humor
that is Claverie's own. The text, light and fresh in style and treatment,
has been ably translated; it follows the search of Prince Caspar (whose
mother had passed the acid test of a sleepless night because one pea lay
under the stack of mattresses on her bed) for a bride, and it focuses on
the fact that perfection (like that of his dear mama) can be boring and
that a one-track personality can be irritating. What Caspar finally finds
is a princess who, while he was away, had visited his parents and had
had a nut put under her mattresses, and had slept very soundly indeed. The story ends with Caspar riding madly off so that he can catch
up with this admirable creature. And he does.

955   **Nixon,** Joan Lowery. *Bigfoot Makes A Movie;* illus. by Syd Hoff. Putnam,
1979. 78-31106. ISBN 0-399-20684-1. 48p. $7.95.

K–2   Well, assume there IS a creature called Bigfoot. How would it act if it
were young, friendly, and had a confrontation with people? In this unlikely but entertaining tale, a young Bigfoot sees another like himself
and reaches out for an amicable hug. The other creature slides out of its
skin and emerges as one of those human beings Bigfoot's parents have
told him to avoid. Then a girl comes along and talks to him; he doesn't
understand that there's a filming going on and that he is supposed to
chase her, but he does run after her to save her from danger. And
that's how Bigfoot gets into a movie, makeup and all. Everyone thinks
he's the actor in a Bigfoot skin; at least they think so until the actor
shows up, costume over his arm. Then they all run. Young Bigfoot is
disappointed, but he has a good story for his parents. Monster stories
are seldom as cheery as this, and Hoff's cartoon style fits nicely.

956   **Nixon,** Joan Lowery. *The Specter.* Delacorte, 1982. 82-70322. ISBN 0-440-
08063-0. 160p. $10.95.

7–10   Dina, seventeen, is the narrator; she is a cancer patient in hospital and is in a period of remission when nine-year-old Julie is brought in as a roommate. Julie's parents have been killed in a car accident, and Julie seems terrified of a man she thinks wants to kill her; his name is Bill Sikes and she is convinced he killed her father. She won't tell Dina all about it—but she wont't tell anything to the detective who's investigating the accident. Julie clings to Dina, so it is arranged that they both go as foster children to live with a nurse's aid, Mrs. Cardenas, who's retiring. There are two themes here, and they are deftly meshed: one is the mystery of Julie's background and her fierce jealousy of Dina (which almost culminates in tragedy) and the other is Dina's conviction that she cannot have even a limited future despite medical assurance that she may live for many years with treatment. The story has a firm structure, discerning characterization and relationships, suspense and good pace, and a story line that builds to a dramatic conclusion.

957   **Noble,** Iris. *Contemporary Women Scientists of America;* illus. with photographs. Messner, 1979. 78-21292. ISBN 0-671-32920-0. 158p. $6.97.

7–10   Noble begins with a chapter that reviews the careers of seven pioneers of the 20th century, describing their work and their problems in either getting an education or a position (or both) and citing their evidences of recognition for achievements. In the biographical sketches that follow, few names will be as familiar as that of Margaret Mead; the areas of specialization are anthropology crystallography, genetics, endocrinology, solid state physics, nuclear physics, marine biology, microbiology, and meteorology. The tone is admiring but not adulatory, the writing is straightforward, and the material emphasizes each subject's training and career without neglecting her personal life. A substantial relative index is appended.

958   **Norton,** Mary. *The Borrowers Avenged;* illus. by Beth and Joe Krush. Harcourt, 1982. 82-47937. ISBN 0-15-210530-1. 304p. $12.95.

4–6   Although this sequel to earlier stories about the borrowers gets off to a bit of a slow start (the first three chapters are about human beings, full size) it is just as clever and intriguing as the first books about the miniature people who live in buildings, unseen by most humans. Here Arrietty and her parents, Pod and Homily, have escaped from the Platters, the cruel couple who want to keep them captive and make a fortune by exhibiting them. The borrowers escape, find a new home, and have a reunion with their kin, but they know they are being hunted and they fear the Platters will call in Lady Mullings, who has extrasensory ability and a fine record as a finder of lost objects. Arrietty is really worried when she realizes that the Platters know that her little cousin Timmus is trapped in the church. The Platters break into the church that night but are caught when Mrs. Platter, seeing a small borrower climbing the bell rope, grabs for the rope and rings the church bell. The Platters leave the

country, and the borrowers are safe at last. The concept of the miniature people and their way of life is appealing, and it's given depth by
the adroit handling of dialogue and characterization; the writing is sophisticated and humorous.

959   **Nöstlinger,** Christine. *Luke and Angela;* tr. by Anthea Bell. Harcourt,
      1981. 80-8804. ISBN 0-15-249902-4. $8.95.

6–9   It's Angela who's the narrator in this touching and trenchant story by a
      major Austrian writer, convincingly told and smoothly translated. An-
      gela and Luke have always been best friends, she the leader and he the
      quiet follower. Then Luke comes back from a summer in England, and
      he's no longer the dependable, inconspicuous pal Angela's known: he
      dresses flamboyantly, he speaks out in class (to the point of infuriating
      one teacher) and he wants to kiss Angela. He does kiss Anglea, and she
      worries about whether she's normal, because she doesn't really enjoy it.
      However, when Luke becomes popular she's jealous; when he is taken
      up by an older woman (she's about 22) she's desolate; still, when the
      other woman jilts Luke and he is in despair it is Angela who comforts
      him, her love stronger than her jealousy. A touching story, lightened
      with affectionate humor and strengthened by its universal appeal, is
      effectively constructed and written with polish and perception.

960   **Noyes,** Alfred. *The Highwayman;* illus. by Charles Mikolaycak. Lothrop,
      1983. 83-725. Trade ed. ISBN 0-688-02117-4; Library ed. ISBN 0-688-
      02118-2. 40p. Trade ed. $9.50; Library ed. $8.59.

5–   The dramatic narrative poem may be familiar to many children, but for
      those to whom it is not known, this should be an excellent introduc-
      tion. Mikolaycak's paintings are effectively framed by ample white
      space, black and greys, with effective touches of pinkish red in strong,
      stark pictures of the beautiful girl who took her own life to warn her
      robber-lover by the sound of a shot that soldiers were at their trysting
      place.

961   **Numeroff,** Laura Joffe. *Beatrice Doesn't Want To;* written and illus. by
      Laura Joffe Numeroff. Watts, 1981. 81-447. Trade ed. ISBN 0-531-
      03537-9; Library ed. ISBN 0-531-04299-5. 28p. (Easy-Read Book) Trade
      ed. $3.95; Library ed. $7.40.

2–3   Beatrice doesn't like books, she doesn't like libraries, and she's a little
      nuisance to her older brother, who has to take her with him for three
      succeeding days while he works on a report. Beatrice won't look at
      books, she wants a drink, she fusses, and she certaintly doesn't want to
      participate in story hour; her brother, tired of "I don't want to," insists.
      A reluctant listener at first, Beatrice becomes captivated by the story
      and asks to see the book when story hour is over. When her brother
      comes to collect her, Beatrice seems mesmerized by the book. "We have
      to go home now," he says. No response. "Come on, Bea." "I don't

want to," says the new book-lover. The illustrations are a bit harsh in two-color illustrations, but they have humor, and the story is also amusing, simply written and printed in large type that's appropriate for the beginning independent reader.

962   **Oakley,** Graham. *The Church Mice at Christmas;* written and illus. by Graham Oakley. Atheneum, 1980. 80-14518. ISBN 0-689-30797-7. 33p. $10.95.

K–3   Like previous books about the mice and their friend the cat, who live in the church of an English town, this is merry and witty, with both text and pictures replete with action and humor. Here the two mouse buddies, Arthur and Humphrey, decide that they would like to have a Christmas party with all the traditional games and foods. To earn money for the party, they coax the cat, Sampson, into being raffled off; unfortunately, Sampson hates the couple who get him and slinks back, so the mice have to make a refund. After being chased by a policeman when they try caroling, the mice meet an evil-looking Father Christmas (Santa Claus) who is caught (he's a burglar) by the police; a sergeant dons the Father Christmas costume and—because the mice have been instrumental in the burglar's arrest—brings the church mice a huge hamper of goodies. It isn't the electric guitar, cuckoo clock, or pocket calculator Arthur and Humphrey had asked for, but it does provide party fare. In other words, the usual Oakley romp.

963   **Oakley,** Graham. *The Church Mice in Action;* written and illus. by Graham Oakley. Atheneum, 1983. 82-11394. ISBN 0-689-30949-X. 33p. $11.95.

K–3   Another amusing story for readers and listeners who have become addicted to the adventures of the church cat, Samson, and the enterprising mice with whom he lives in amity. Here the catalyst is the parson's sister, who grooms and perfumes the long-suffering Samson, giving the mice the idea of entering their cat in a show, which they plan to win (and do) by climbing on the judge and making all the other entrants misbehave. Then Samson is kidnapped by two men who have the erroneous idea that the contest winnings amount to a great deal of money. The way the mice rescue the cat is hilarious, a chase scene that's blandly told but frenetically pictured. Oakley is, as always, inventive in the pictorial expression of dastardly villains and ingenious mice.

964   **Oakley,** Graham, illus. *Magical Changes.* Atheneum, 1980. 79-2784. ISBN 0-689-30732-2. 32p. $10.95.

All   Using cut pages to make pictures that change, match, or mix is not a
Ages   new idea; what Oakley has done with it is to take the idea and play
*   with it brilliantly. He uses columnar connections for the halves of both pages, so that the narrow neck of a vase becomes a bedpost, a tree limb, a swan's neck, a factory chimney, a mushroom stem, et cetera.

There's a variety of mood and style (some combinations are romantic, some comic, some grotesque) but no variation in the imaginative quality of the concepts or the polished technique of his draughtsmanship and his painting.

965   **O'Dell,** Scott. *The Amethyst Ring.* Houghton, 1983. 82-23388. ISBN 0-395-33886-7. 214p. $12.95.

7–10   In a sequel to *The Captive* and *The Feathered Serpent,* O'Dell continues the stirring story of the young Spanish seminarian, Julian Escobar, who had been shipwrecked in the New World and become a god/ruler to the Mayan people. As this fine historical novel starts, Escobar has escaped from a vengeful Cortes after the death of Montezuma. Now he is back in his city, on the island he hopes to defend against the ruthless Cortes, and he finds his people have a hostage, a bishop who is wearing the amethyst ring that shows his status. Escobar lets his people kill the bishop and thereafter wears his ring, an error he regrets when he is later hounded by the Spanish explorers. In the end, after many adventures, Escobar returns to Spain, refuses the chance of being wealthy, and joins the Brothers of the Poor. This is both an exciting adventure story of a man corrupted by power, and a vivid account of the conquistadores who ravaged an ancient civilization, and it is notable for its structure and characterization as well as for the research that colors but does not clog the narrative.

966   **O'Dell,** Scott. *The Captive.* Houghton, 1979. 79-15809. ISBN 0-395-27811-2. 211p. $8.95.

7–9   The protagonist and narrator is a young, idealistic seminarian in sixteenth-century Spain, Julian, who is pressed into a voyage to the new world by his mentor, Don Luis. Julian, detesting the then-common practice of enslaving Indians, hopes that he can convert and save the natives he will meet. He is appalled by the rapacity of Don Luis, by his hunger for gold and his harsh treatment of the Indians; when the ship hastily sails away from their first island stop, laden with gold, it encounters a storm. Shipwrecked, Julian lives like Crusoe, helped by a Mayan girl who appears on what he had thought was a deserted island. The story, taut and dramatic, has a surprising ending, for Julian is himself the captive, enslaved by his own lust for power. The writing is fluid and trenchant, giving both a vivid picture of the Mayan culture and a moving picture of the fervent young man who is trapped by circumstance and his own unsuspected weakness.

967   **O'Dell,** Scott. *The Feathered Serpent.* Houghton, 1981. 81-7888. ISBN 0-395-30851-8. 211p. $10.95.

7–10   The young seminarian, Julian Escobar, who had come to the New World and been shipwrecked in *The Captive* is now acclaimed as the legendary god Kukulcán by the credulous citizens of the City of Seven Serpents. There are some who are not convinced, and one of them contributes to Julian's entrapment when he is on a visit to the Emperor Moctezuma in his splendid city, Tenochtitlán. Captured, Julian and his mentor—the dwarf Cantú—are pressed into menial service but escape and, as the story ends, Julian is homeward-bound, glad to be addressed again as the Lord Feathered Serpent, god Kukulcán. All of the action, color, and drama are set in the Mayan world around and against the fateful meeting of Moctezuma and Cortes, the beginning of the end of a fabulous era. It does not, however, seem remote, for O'Dell writes with a sense of high adventure and empathetic involvement; what makes this more than just an adventure story is the author's control of his medium.

968   **O'Dell,** Scott. *Sarah Bishop.* Houghton, 1980. 79-28394. ISBN 0-395-29185-2. 184p. $8.95.

6–9
*

Her brother had been taken prisoner by the British and died on a fetid prison ship, her father (unlike his son, a staunch Tory) had died after being tarred and feathered by local patriots, and Sarah was left alone in the world. Sarah tells her own story in this fine novel set in Long Island during the Revolutionary War. Grieving, fearful, and self-sufficient, Sarah wants nothing to do with either faction, although she has met some individuals on both sides who have shown her compassion. She heads for the wilderness, finds a cave that she makes her home, and fends for herself, helped on occasion by a young Indian couple. She goes to the village to attend a Quaker meeting in response to an invitation transmitted by her Indian friends, and finds that she is accused of witchcraft, held by the villagers to be responsible for the withering crops, a fire, a two-headed calf. Due to her one defender Sarah is exonerated, and she goes back to her cave, but she has realized her loneliness and promises her Quaker friend that she will come again. Despite a series of highly dramatic incidents, the story line is basically sharp and clear; O'Dell's messages about the bitterness and folly of war, the dangers of superstition, and the courage of the human spirit are smoothly woven into the story, as are the telling details of period and place. To many readers, the primary appeal of the book may be the way in which Sarah, like the heroine of *Island of the Blue Dolphins,* like Robinson Crusoe, makes a comfortable life in the isolation of the wilderness.

969   **Ofek,** Uriel. *Smoke Over Golan;* tr. by Israel I. Taslitt; illus. by Lloyd Bloom. Harper, 1979. 78-22488. Trade ed. ISBN 0-06-024613-8; Library ed. ISBN 0-06-024614-6. 184p. Trade ed. $7.95; Library ed. $7.89 net.

6–8

Eitan Avivi tells the story of his involvement in the battle on the Golan Heights. Eitan and his parents had moved to an isolated farm near a border army post, and his childhood had been a happy, busy one, with lessons from a teacher who came daily to a one-boy school, with the friendship of an Arab boy, and with visits to the friendly soldiers at the post. When hostilities began, Eitan's mother was away, and his father was ordered to rejoin his old military unit; Eitan was left behind to be picked up by a bus a few hours later. The bus never came. And that was how Eitan came to be involved in a dangerous and dramatic episode in which he and a wounded Israeli soldier captured an enemy officer and turned him over to the authorities along with a very useful set of maps. The translation from the original Hebrew is fairly smooth, although the dialogue occasionally has a stiff sound (an adult, speaking to six-year-old Eitan, dubs him "A right good fellow,") and the setting and pace add interest to a well-constructed story.

970   **O'Kelley,** Mattie Lou. *From the Hills of Georgia;* written and illus. by Mattie Lou O'Kelley. Atlantic/Little, 1983. 83-9414. ISBN 0-316-63800-5. 32p. $14.95.

2–4   Like Grandma Moses, Mattie Lou O'Kelley is self-taught, began painting in her later years, and is a noted American folk artist. Her naive pictures, wonderfully detailed, are used with a short paragraph on each page that describes the childhood episode or activity shown in the painting. Homespun-stylized, the paintings are fresh and distinctive in style; the minimal text is terse and direct, giving a picture of a rural childhood and the bustling life of a big farm family.

971   **Okimoto,** Jean Davies, *Norman Schnurman, Average Person.* Putnam, 1982. 82-9045. ISBN 0-399-20913-1. 125p. $9.95.

4–6   Norman, the sixth-grade son of a former football player, tells the story of his struggle to please his father by joining the Junior League Football Team even though he detests playing. Norman's passion is junk sales, and it is at a sale that he meets some new neighbors, Carrie Koski and her grandfather. Carrie's so pleasant and relaxed that Norman conquers his shyness and takes her on a date; Mr. Koski is so warm and understanding that Norman gains courage enough to tell his father he's quitting the team and even to feel comfortable about doing his own thing. No great events here, but the story's lightly humorous and the style is convincing as that of a child; relationships are perceptively drawn, and if the characterization isn't deep, it is believable and warm.

972   **Oleksy,** Walter G. *Paramedics;* illus. with photographs. Messner, 1983. 83-13388. ISBN 0-671-44274-0. 64p. $8.79.

5–7   Emergency medical care had long been available at several levels (ambulance crews, mobile heart units) but it was not until 1967 that the first paramedical unit was established. Special training for life-saving emergency procedures and the technology that makes direct communication with medical personnel at hospitals possible have enabled paramedics to save countless lives. Oleksy describes, in a brisk, straightforward style, the training of paramedics, the work they do, and the problems they have. A brief chapter discusses careers in paramedics; sources of information are cited, and a one-page bibliography and an index are provided. The material is inherently dramatic; the text is crisp and informative.

973   **Olney,** Ross Robert. *Farm Giants.* Atheneum, 1982. 82-1798. ISBN 0-689-30937-6. 44p. illus. with photographs. $10.95.

2–4   A clear, simply written text describes the large machines that are used on giant farms and ranches; photographs are carefully placed in relation to textual references. Olney explains how each machine works and for what special job it is used, expanding the informational value of the book by discussing the reason for the operation. For example, he explains that the disk plow chews up the stalks of harvested plants and makes it easier to fertilize the ground before planting a new crop. An index gives access to the contents.

974   **Olney,** Ross Robert. *Roller Skating;* by Ross R. Olney and Chan Bush; illus. with photographs. Lothrop, 1979. 78-27248. Trade ed. ISBN 0-688-41892-9; Library ed. ISBN 0-688-51892-3. 128p. Trade ed. $6.50; Library ed. $6.24.

6–   While this can't substitute for instruction or practice, it can help the beginner learn a good deal about roller skating, and it may provide some new information to the practiced skater. The authors are detailed and explicit in their descriptions of how to choose and care for skates, what sort of safety equipment to wear, and why, and how to learn the basic movements of roller skating. Other chapters in the book give the history of roller skating, evidence that attests to its increasing popularity, and facts about the kinds of specialized skating (roller derbies, bowl skating, dancing and disco dancing on skates, roller hockey, contests, etc.) that are gaining participants and fans, and facts about roller skating rinks. The writing gets a little gushy at times, especially in the captions for photographs, but on the whole the text is brisk and informative. A list of roller skating organizations, stores, and publications precedes the index.

975   **Olshan,** Neal H. *Depression.* Watts, 1982. 82-11004. ISBN 0-531-04496-3. 119p. $8.90.

7–   Olshan, a psychologist, begins with a general and fairly extensive discussion of what depression is, how severe or prolonged depression differs from the transitory if painful sadness individuals feel as a reaction to disruption in their lives, and how the diagnosis and treatment of depression have changed. He describes at length the most common causes of depression, the physical manifestations it can precipitate, the use of depression to get attention, and types of depression. Also discussed are suicide, symptoms and treatment, and the ways in which families and friends can help the depressed person. The writing style is rather dry, the type face making the pages look more difficult than they are to read;

the material is adequately organized, the tone authoritative, the information useful. A glossary, a bibliography, an index, and a list of sources from which help or information may be procured are provided.

976   Olson, Helen Kronberg. *The Strange Thing that Happened to Oliver Wendell Iscovitch;* illus. by Betsy Lewin. Dodd, 1983. 82-45990. ISBN 0-396-08147-9. 62p. $9.95.

K–3   One touch of fantasy is used in each episode of a very funny story about a small boy who discovers that if he puffs out his cheeks and holds his breath he can fly. Oliver Wendell uses this ability to good advantage after his first surprising experience (holding his breath to get his mother to buy a particular brand of cereal) to frighten burglars, save his baby brother from a bull, and "teach" some fledgling birds to fly. The family relationships are delightful (including a lively grandmother) and the writing style—particularly the dialogue—bright and breezy. The same qualities are in the brisk line drawings.

977   Oneal, Zibby. *A Formal Feeling.* Viking, 1982. 82-2018. ISBN 0-670-32488-4. 168p. $10.95.

7–10   The title is from an Emily Dickinson poem, "After great pain, a formal feeling comes—" and Anne's great pain has been the death of her mother, a woman who excelled at everything. Added to Anne's grief was her resentment at her father for his remarriage and at her stepmother, Dory, for being there at all; it didn't help that her older brother accepted Dory completely. Aloof and withdrawn, Anne in her "formal feeling" is surprised by the buried memories that return, and she's reluctant to admit to herself that she had angrily resisted her mother's high standards and her domineering ways. There is little action in this sensitive story, but there is growth and change, so that when it is time for Anne to go back to boarding school after her unhappy vacation, she can accept the status quo and can weep for the person her mother really was rather than the idealized woman she had been trying to remember. A candid story, this unfolds and grows smoothly, with a perceptive meshing of personalities and relationships that are strongly drawn.

978   Oneal, Zibby. *The Language of Goldfish.* Viking, 1980. 79-19167. ISBN 0-670-41785-8. 179p. $8.95.

7–9   "People in Northpoint did not have crazy children," and that's why Carrie, keeping an appointment with a psychiatrist as the story starts, is—according to her mother—"unwell." Carrie, thirteen, misses the days when she and her sister Moira pretended to talk to the fish; she sees Moira's growing sophistication and her interest in boys, and she doesn't want to leave childhood. Part of the story is told in flashbacks, so that the reader sees the physical effects of Carrie's deep dread: dizzy spells, shifting vision, trance-like moods in which the sense of time is lost. And one day Carrie wakes in the hospital after a suicide attempt; that's when she meets and decides to trust the psychiatrist. Even then, Carrie's mother insists on referring to Carrie's behavior as "an unfortunate incident" and to her daily visits to her therapist as "kind of like having checkups." One of Carrie's talents is art, and she cannot explain to Dr. Ross why she paints, over and over, the island in the fish pond; as time and her therapy sessions go by, Carrie slowly comes to understand that it represented a haven from growing up, from change. When the story ends, she is stable and mature enough to understand what her problem has been as well as to accept the changes that come with childhood's end. Adroitly structured and smoothly written, this has a fine narrative flow (and no trace, ever, of a case history of a nervous breakdown) and thoughtful, consistent characterization. Oneal writes with insight, compassion, and restraint.

979   **Oppenheim,** Joanne. *Mrs. Peloki's Class Play;* illus. by Joyce Audy dos Santos. Dodd, 1984. 83-25457. ISBN 0-396-08178-9. 28p. $10.95.

2–3   It is the star of the second-grade class production of "Cinderella," Stephie, who narrates the story of a disastrous dress rehearsal and a peril-fraught assembly hall production. This should evoke a recognition reflex from anyone who has ever been participant or spectator at a primary-grades school play; it's realistic, it's funny, it has a surprise ending that should appeal to younger children's sense of disaster-humor, and it's illustrated with softly colored drawings that have vitality if they lack grace.

980   **Oppenheimer,** Joan L. *Gardine vs. Hanover.* T. Y. Crowell, 1982. 81-43390. Trade ed. ISBN 0-690-04190-X; Library ed. ISBN 0-690-04191-8. 152p. Trade ed. $8.95; Library ed. $8.89.

6–9   Her ten-year-old sister Abby accepted a new stepfather and his two children (Drew was in Abby's age group, Caroline in Jill's) as she had accepted her parents' divorce, with cheerful equanimity. Jill, five years older, is shattered. She doesn't like her stepfather, and she detests her stepsister. Between them, Jill and Caroline make the household so miserable that their parents decide to separate—and nobody is any happier. When Jill and her mother both come down with flu, Abby telephones Caroline in desperation; they take turns nursing each other, since Abby and Caroline also succumb, and by the time everyone is well the breach has been healed and the Gardine and Hanover families reunited. Stories of adjustment in families grafted together have had similar themes, but they haven't always been this well handled. The story line moves on a continuum, but chapters are told alternately from Jill's and Caroline's viewpoints; in fact, until the last chapter, each begins with either Jill's or Caroline's name. There is a balance of other interests (school, friends) but the focus is on the two adolescents and the author perceptively explores their feelings toward their missing parents (Jill's father,

Caroline's mother) and their several insecurities that led to instant and sustained hostility.

981   Orgel, Doris. *Risking Love.* Dial, 1984. 84-5880. ISBN 0-8037-0131-4. 185p. $12.95.

6–9   Dinah, eighteen, tells her story almost entirely through the therapy sessions she's agreed to just to pacify her father, who worries about her decision to leave Barnard in order to be with Gary, the man she loves. Dinah feels that she's perfectly happy and knows her own mind, but as her sessions with Dr. Schneck go on, Dinah discovers her fears about losing love, fears engendered by her parents' divorce years ago. Orgel creates the atmosphere of the consulting room: the initial resentment, the growth of trust, the increasing ability to face oneself and maintain perspective. Characters and relationships are strong, and the story has good pace and momentum. Moving and positive, this is an impressive novel.

982   Orlev, Uri. *The Island on Bird Street;* tr. by Hillel Halkin. Houghton, 1984. 83-26524. ISBN 0-395-33887-5. 162p. $10.95.

5–7   In a fine Holocaust survival story, first published in Israel and based on the author's childhood experience hiding in the Warsaw Ghetto, eleven-year-old Alex builds himself an ingenious secret hideout in the ruins of a bombed building on the edge of an unspecified Polish ghetto. He lives there alone for five months, waiting for his father to come for him. Comparing himself to Robinson Crusoe on a desert island, he forages in the abandoned houses around him, with only his pet white mouse for company. Yet even as he hears the screams and shots of Jews being rounded up, he finds that a kind of normal life continues. He watches a girl in the streets outside the ghetto, and once he learns the secret passageways from the Polish Underground, he "crosses over" to the Polish section sometimes, and meets her, and plays with the kids in the park. The physical details are fascinating: what he eats, how he keeps warm, how he builds the hideout, the secret passageways that connect the lofts and cellars; all described in quiet, unemotional style. Self-pity is prevented by the very pressure of survival, and by Alex's knowledge of the fate of other Jewish children. But his control snaps after he has been forced to shoot a German soldier; and in the poignant scene of his father's return, Alex realizes how much he has suppressed, especially the terror that his father would not come.

983   Ormerod, Jan, illus. *Moonlight;* illus. by Jan Ormerod. Lothrop, 1982. 81-8290. Trade ed. ISBN 0-688-00846-1; Library ed. ISBN 0-688-00847-X. 26p. Trade ed. $9.50; Library ed. $8.59.

2–5
yrs.
*   In a book as charming as its companion volume, *Sunshine*, this wordless picture book, with soft, quiet line and wash illustrations, shows the amusingly protracted process of a child's bedtime. After she and her

parents finish their meal, the child makes a boat to float in her bath; the bath is followed by her father's reading of a story; this is followed by some comforting hugs when the child is frightened, then by parental acceptance of the fact that the child might as well stay up and look at a book. The story ends with sleepy parents putting the child to bed again, in a still, moonlit room. The pictures are distinctive for their composition and use of light and shadow; the story is distinctive for its clarity, its atmosphere of patient love, and its demonstration of parental sharing of chores and child care.

984   **Ormerod,** Jan. *101 Things to do With a Baby;* written and illus. by Jan Ormerod. Lothrop, 1984. 84-4401. Library ed. ISBN 0-688-03802-6; Trade ed. ISBN 0-688-03801-8. 28p. Library ed. $9.55; Trade ed. $10.25.

4–6 yrs.   A small girl (and her parents) play with and care for an infant brother or do the day's chores with the baby in the background. There is no story line, no dialogue, but there are—numbered—a hundred and one suggestions in the captions for pictures that have clean lines and clear colors and that are affectionate without being sentimentalized.

985   **Ormerod,** Jan, illus. *Sunshine;* illus. by Jan Ormerod. Lothrop, 1981. 80-84971. Trade ed. ISBN 0-688-00552-7; Library ed. ISBN 0-688-00553-5. 24p. Trade ed. $7.95; Library ed. $7.63.

2–5 yrs.
*   In a wordless picture book that has the appeal of familiar activities, a small girl—wakened by the sunshine on her face—climbs out of bed to rouse her father. Sleepily he stumbles into the kitchen to give the child food; together they take coffee to mother. Mother falls asleep again, father reads the paper, child goes off to dress and walks in with the clock. There's a flurry of activity as everyone gets ready to go off for the day. Couldn't be simpler or more clear, the acid test of the wordless book. And the illustrations are simply composed, with large but quiet areas of color and with realistic details; they are distinctive in the use of light and shadow, reminiscent of Brinton Turkle's work in the first pages particularly, as the sunlight creeps across the shadowed bedrooms.

986   **Osborn,** Lois. *My Dad Is Really Something;* illus. by Rodney Pate. Whitman, 1983. 83-1292. ISBN 0-8075-5329-8. 28p. $8.25.

1–3
*   Let's hear it for all the short, fat, kind, loving fathers who are slightly bald, wear glasses, and understand children. Harry George is beginning to get tired of the way his friend Ron boasts about his father; if Harry George brings a book his father's written to school, Ron says *his* father can tear phone books; if Harry George tells Ron about the model plane he and his father made, Ron says *his* father flies fighter jets. ("That figures," Dad mutters.) Then Harry George learns that Ron's father is dead; hurt because his friend has lied to him, he's mollified when Dad points out that Ron may have felt a need to invent a father, and maybe

they should take Ron fishing. So they become a threesome, and Harry George is a bit more understanding when he hears Ron boasting to classmates about how great Harry George's father is. And he's right. Warm, perceptive, funny, this is written in a simple but fluent style; the tinted line drawings echo the directness and realism of the story.

987   **Osborne,** Chester G. *The Memory String.* Atheneum, 1984. 83-15633. ISBN 0-689-31020-X. 154p. $11.95.

6–9   Set in prehistoric times in Siberia, this absorbing story has momentum and conviction as it explores two themes. One is the maturation of the protagonist, Darath, who yearns to be a great hunter like his father but also feels a responsibility to the tribe when his grandfather, its shaman, declares that Darath will succeed him. The other is the fate of the tribe: bitter weather and incursion by other tribes produce a scarcity of food that forces a decision to migrate to a better climate. The characters are firmly delineated and the writing style competent; the book gives a vivid picture of a primitive way of life.

988   **Otto S,** Svend. *The Giant Fish and Other Stories;* written and illus. by Svend Otto S; trans. by Joan Tate. Larousse, 1983. 82-81484. ISBN 0-8832-287-0. 75p. $10.95.

2–4   Three tales set in the Far North have good structure and pace, and give a vivid picture of the life-style and interests of children in each setting. The first story is about a small Eskimo boy who has an exciting and dangerous adventure while out with a dog-sledge in Greenland; the second tale is set in Iceland, where Jon is deemed old enough to go with the men and older boys to round up the sheep that have been summering on the mountain; in the third story, two boys in the Faroe Islands catch a huge halibut. The writing is brisk; the illustrations are handsome in line and composition, but particularly striking in the use of color: the cold blue-white of snow, the steely mountains, the clear, pale skies, and the glow of lighted windows in the blue-green twilight.

989   **Oxenbury,** Helen. *The Birthday Party;* written and illus. by Helen Oxenbury. Dial, 1983. 82-19792. ISBN 0-8037-0717-7. 16p. $5.95.
       The Dancing Class; written and illus. by Helen Oxenbury. Dial, 1983. 82-19791. ISBN 0-8037-1651-6. 16p. $5.95.
       Eating Out; written and illus. by Helen Oxenbury. Dial, 1983. 82-19802. ISBN 0-8037-2203-6. 16p. $5.95.

3–5   A new miniseries of books for the small child who's too sophisticated
yrs.   for Oxenbury's books for the very, very young like *Family* and *Dressing.*
  *   There are real plots here, but the same affectionate humor and the same clean, clear, bright illustration. In *Birthday Party,* a child chooses a present but hates to give it away, is miffed at the casual way the gift is received, has a splendidly messy time, and walks home triumphantly, enjoying the souvenir balloon all the more because it's clear that the

birthday child didn't want to give it up. In *Dancing Class,* there's a minor disaster when the pudgy, engaging dancers collide, but the enthusiastic neophyte enjoys it all, and insists on doing the gallop all the way home, clinging to the hand of a frazzled Mum. *Eating Out* also has the disaster humor small children enjoy, with an irritated waiter and spilled food leading to a hasty exit and a bowl of cereal at home. These are just right, in the tone, length, and simplicity of the stories, for the preschool child, and they should bring a recognition reflex from the audience and some smiles from those who read the books to them.

990   **Oxenbury,** Helen. *The Car Trip;* written and illus. by Helen Oxenbury. Dial, 1983. 83-5255. ISBN 0-8037-0009-1. 16p. $5.95.
The Checkup; written and illus. by Helen Oxenbury. Dial, 1983. 83-5346. ISBN 0-8037-0010-5. 16p. $5.95.
First Day of School; written and illus. by Helen Oxenbury. Dial, 1983. 83-7452. ISBN 0-8037-0012-1. 16p. $5.95.

3–5   In three very funny and all too realistic stories, each told in a bland,
yrs.   direct style by a young child, Oxenbury tells it like it is. The car trip is a
*   disaster, for example, with parents objecting to lion noises, child refusing to eat anything but candy and ice cream (and throwing up) and car breaking down. Verdict? "Today was the best car trip ever!" In *The Checkup*, the recalcitrant patient creates such havoc that the spent and injured doctor hopes he won't have to see the boy for another year. "I like the doctor. I think he's really nice." On the first day of nursery school, a wailing child is pried away from her mother, makes a friend, and has a fine time. The cleanly drawn, uncluttered pictures are small, bright, deft, and hilarious.

991   **Oxenbury,** Helen. *Dressing;* written and illus. by Helen Oxenbury. Wanderer/Simon & Schuster, 1981. 80-52220. ISBN 0-671-42113-1. 14p. $3.50.

1–2   Imported from England, a delightful book that meets a long-felt need
yrs.   for books for the infant bibliophile. The concepts are familiar, the heavy
*   board pages (nontoxic and easy to wipe clean) are sturdy and easy for a small child to handle, and the pictures are simply, skillfully drawn against a spacious white background. The pictures are paired: a shirt, labelled "Undershirt," is faced by a baby in diaper and undershirt; a picture of a sock, labelled, faces the baby looking with admiration at the bright sock after it's on. From diaper to hat, each stage of dressing is recorded—and—that's it: a record of familiar things.

992   **Oxenbury,** Helen. *Family;* written and illus. by Helen Oxenbury. Wanderer/Simon & Schuster, 1981. 80-52218. ISBN 0-671-42110-7. 14p. $3.50.

1–2   This has all the usefulness, the simplicity, and the appeal of *Dressing*
yrs.   and is in the same format, as are three additional books in the set:
*   *Friends, Playing,* and *Working,* the latter clearly based on the idea that playing, eating, and learning control of bodily functions are a baby's

work. In *Family*, the illustrations are paired by showing a mother, then a baby with the mother; a father, then the same round-faced baby with the father, and so on (sister, brother, grandmother, grandfather) and another roundfaced baby as companion to the first, who looks slightly baffled at having a companion who is a peer.

993   **Oxenbury,** Helen. *The Important Visitor;* written and illus. by Helen Oxenbury. Dial, 1984. 84-7112. ISBN 0-8037-0125-X. 16p. $5.95.

3–6   The very small girl who tells a brief but lively story is the unwitting cul-
yrs.   prit when her mother has an important visitor. Mr. Thorn came to talk about work, but what with his allergy to a hard-to-get-rid-of cat (who came back in when the child opened a window) and the impromptu dancing by the narrator, not much work was discussed. The illustrations are deft and comic, the story told with an ingenuous quality that never lapses into cuteness.

994   **Oxenbury,** Helen. *Shopping Trip;* illus. by Helen Oxenbury. Dial, 1982. 81-69274. ISBN 0-8037-7939-9. 14p. $3.50.

1–3   The first five books in this engaging set of board books for very young
yrs.   children showed an infant too young to be very mobile. In the next set
*   of five, of which this is one, the round-faced baby is not only capable of independent action, but manages to achieve a good bit of independent investigation and some damage, all of which leaves Mama limp by the ending of a shopping trip. A foray into a clothes rack, a broken packet of what looks like sugar, a raid on Mama's purse in a fitting booth followed by a sociable pulling back of its curtain, revealing Mama just emerging from the garment she's been trying on. Like the first books, this has no words and needs none; it is drawn with simplicity, humor, and flair. Other titles are *Beach Day; Good Night, Good Morning; Monkey See, Monkey Do;* and *Mother's Helper.* Fun, but more than that: these are geared to the toddler's interests and experiences.

995   **Oxford Scientific Films.** *Dragonflies;* illus. with photographs by George Bernard. Putnam, 1980. 79-25942. ISBN 0-399-20731-7. 27p. $7.95.

3–5   Enlarged photographs in full color show details of the anatomy and habitat of two varieties of dragonfly and one variety of damselfly. In the format usually followed in this excellent series, an unillustrated text gives information about appearance, habits and habitat, mating and birth, and—in this book—the changes and molts of the larval form, which is water-dwelling. The text is followed by captioned photographs, the captions picking up the salient facts of the text. A handsome book, and an informative one, this gives some understanding of the ecological setting and of the dragonfly's place in the food chain as well as of its own life cycle.

996   **Oxford Scientific Films.** *Jellyfish and Other Sea Creatures;* illus. with photographs by Peter Parks. Putnam, 1982. 81-10672. ISBN 0-399-20852-6. 30p. $8.95.

4-6   As are the other books in this excellent British series, this is profusely illustrated by first-rate photographs in full color. This follows the usual format of the series, with a few pages of fact-packed text that describes the species of coelenterata called jellyfish, explaining how they mate, reproduce, feed, function anatomically, defend themselves, and so on. The rest—and major part—of the book is given to photographs, fully captioned but not often giving an indication of scale. The book's use is undoubtedly wider than the middle grades range for which it is most suited, since the dignified text and handsome pictures should attract older readers as well, and the photographs alone can be appreciated by quite young children.

997   **Oxford Scientific Films.** *The Stickleback Cycle;* illus. with photographs by David Thompson. Putnam, 1979. 77-28754. 27p. $6.95.

3-5   Superb color photographs, life size or magnified, illustrate a text that is
 *   lucid and succinct, logically organized and written in a simple, direct style. The brief text describes the stickleback and focuses on the male, which assumes vivid coloration during the mating season; he courts the female, builds the tunnel-shaped nest, fertilizes and cares for the young. The photographic section that follows, which includes pictures of the embryo, has a running text at the foot, reiterating and expanding the facts given at the start of the book.

998   **Pace,** Mildred Mastin. *Pyramids: Tombs for Eternity;* illus. by Radu Vero and Mirela Zisu. McGraw-Hill, 1981. 79-11999. ISBN 0-07-048054-0. 192p. illus. with photographs. $8.95.

6-9   Well-researched and written with restrained enthusiasm, this is an interesting companion volume to the author's *Wrapped for Eternity: The Story of the Egyptian Mummy.* Pace describes in detail how the first pyramid was planned and constructed by Imhotep and how subsequent pyramids were built; she discusses the intricate ways in which the inner burial chambers were sealed to prevent the ravages of thieves, not always successfully, and the many incursions by thrill-seekers, archeologists, and believers in the cult of the pyramid form. There are also chapters on the pyramids of Central America; the text is informative, detailed, and logically organized. An index and a bibliography are appended.

999   **Paige,** David. *Behind the Scenes at the Aquarium;* illus. with photographs by Roger Ruhlin. Whitman, 1979. 77-24670. 48p. Trade ed. $6.95; Library ed. $5.21 net.

4-6   While Paige has used the Shedd Aquarium in Chicago as an example, he also describes other kinds of aquariums and much of the text applies to any aquarium. Profusely illustrated with photographs, many of which are in color, the book can give readers a fine introduction both to the beauty and interest of the exhibits and to the responsibilities of the administrators, collectors, exhibit designers, lecturers, guides, librarians, and other members of the support staff. The material is adequately organized: the writing style is straightforward. A glossary and index are included.

1000   **Parish,** Peggy. *No More Monsters For Me!* illus. by Marc Simont. Harper, 1981. 81-47111. Trade ed. ISBN 0-06-024657-X; Library ed. ISBN 0-06-024658-8. 64p. I-Can-Read Books. Trade ed. $7.25; Library ed. $7.89.

1–2   Simont never draws any more than is necessary, so the cheerful pink and green tints of his monster and his two human characters have only enough background detail to complement the story, simply told in first person by Minn (Minneapolis Simpkins). True, her mother had said no pets but she'd never specifically mentioned a monster, so Minn brought the unhappy little creature in out of the rain. That's how this juvenile version of a French farce starts, as Minn manages to get the monster out of sight whenever it appears—and whenever it appears, it's grown. Mom doesn't take Minn's reports on the monster literally but assumes her child is so anxious for a pet that she's invented a monster. So Minn takes the monster to its home, Mom promises a pet, and the story ends with absolutely everybody happy. Brisk, funny, easy to read, with the appeal of wish-fulfillment and the satisfaction of being able to identify with a child who knows something an adult doesn't.

1001   **Park,** Ruth. *Playing Beatie Bow.* Atheneum, 1982. 81-8097. ISBN 0-689-30889-2. 196p. $9.95.

5–8
*
    "Beatie Bow" is the name of a game that Abigail sees younger children playing, and she notices one waif-like girl who watches but never joins the play. Abigail's fourteen, resenting the fact that her mother is more than willing to take back the husband who'd deserted her for another woman, resenting even more her parents' decision to move from Sydney to Norway. That's the realistic setting out of which emerges a fantasy named the best Australian children's book of 1981. In this beautifully crafted time-slip story, the waif proves to be the Beatie Bow for whom the game was named—but she doesn't know why her name is known. Only when Abigail goes back to Beatie's time, a century ago, does a pattern emerge that answers both their questions. This lively story has action, suspense, strong characters, and an ingenuous knitting of past and present, so that each affects the other.

1002   **Parnall,** Peter. *The Daywatchers;* written and illus. by Peter Parnall. Macmillan, 1984. 84-5764. ISBN 0-02-770190-5. 127p. $16.95.

7–   Superbly detailed, elegant in line, bold in composition, Parnall's black and white drawings, spare in structure and artfully adapted to the layout of the oversize pages, are a striking accompaniment to his series of pieces on the various birds of prey he has observed. The writing style is dignified but not formal, a personal record of the author-artist's absorbed sessions of bird-watching. A series of appended notes gives information that fills in the facts noted in the text.

1003   **Patent,** Dorothy Hinshaw. *Bacteria; How They Affect Other Living Things.* Holiday House, 1980. 79-21567. ISBN 0-8234-0401-3. 128p. illus. with photographs. $8.95.

7–
*
High magnification pictures add interest to a text that, like earlier Patent books, is authoritative and carefully organized, accurate and explicit, written in a style that is serious but not heavy, and comprehensive in coverage. Patent begins by pointing out the fact that not all bacteria are harmful to living things, indeed that many are beneficial or necessary to certain natural processes; she discusses structure, variety, and ubiquity of this life form as a preface to chapters that deal with bacterial roles in digestion, with symbiotic relationships with other life forms, with luminescent bacteria, etc. Patent concludes with a discussion of some of the ways in which bacteria may prove useful in technological, agricultural, and medical research, or in applications of such research. A glossary, a bibliography, and an index are appended.

1004   **Patent,** Dorothy Hinshaw. *Butterflies and Moths: How They Function.* Holiday House, 1979. 78-20614. 160p. illus. $7.95.

7–
*
A zoologist who has already established herself as one of the major writers of science books for young people, Patent has again produced a text that is a model of clarity, accuracy, broad coverage, good organization of material, and an example of the scientific approach. Here she examines almost every aspect of lepidopterans: mating, reproduction, feeding, morphology, physiology, defenses against predators, life stages, coloration, and the ways in which moths and butterflies, in their various stages, are considered pests or benefactors by people. A glossary, a divided bibliography, and extensive relative index are appended.

1005   **Patent,** Dorothy Hinshaw. *Sizes and Shapes in Nature—What They Mean.* Holiday House, 1979. 78-12554. ISBN 0-8234-0340-8. 160p. illus. $7.95.

7–10   With her usual lucidity and authority, Patent discusses the complex subject of the relationship of the individual plant or animal to its environment, showing the meshing of the organism's response to such environmental factors as the medium (air, land, or water) in which it lives, the available food supply, the predators, etc. and how such factors influence the way species have adapted in their morphological development. The text discusses such adaptations with clarity, pointing out the ways in which skeletal structure, the digestive and circulatory systems, communication and courtship patterns, and changes during an individual life can depend on individual needs and environment. Carefully organized and fully indexed, the book also has a glossary and a divided bibliography.

1006   **Patent,** Dorothy Hinshaw. *Whales: Giants of the Deep.* Holiday House, 1984. 84-729. ISBN 0-8234-0530-3. 90p. illus. with photographs. $12.95.

5–   Illustrated with many photographs, this is a text with reference use, for Patent describes the behavior, anatomy, appearance, and habits of every species of whale, distinguishing between toothed and baleen whales. The book also contains information about whales in general (as mammals, as ocean dwellers, as social creatures) and discusses conservation, whale hunting and legislation pertinent to it, and the behavior (recorded or legendary) of whales in relation to human beings. Scientific and common names are provided in an appended list, as is an index.

1007   **Patent,** Dorothy Hinshaw. *Where the Bald Eagles Gather;* illus. with photographs by William Munoz. Houghton/Clarion, 1984. 83-20852. ISBN 0-89919-230-0. 56p. $11.95.

3–5   A fine introduction to the national bird, this focuses upon those bald eagles that gather each fall for the salmon spawning in Montana's Glacier National Park. Starting from this point, Patent describes the eagles' feeding activities, their subsequent southward migration, and eventual return to Alaska and the Northwest Territories for breeding. The text is straightforwardly factual, well-organized, and fluent. As fascinating as the topic itself is, equally interesting is Patent's parallel discussion of how scientists gather information about the eagles; and her discussion of visual and electronic tagging is comprehensive. Numerous large black and white photographs are well placed, and an index is appended.

1008   **Paterson,** Katherine. *Jacob Have I Loved.* T. Y. Crowell, 1980. 80-668. Trade ed. ISBN 0-690-04078-4; Library ed. ISBN 0-690-04079-2. 216p. Trade ed. $8.95; Library ed. $8.79.

6–9   ". . . Jacob have I loved, but Esau have I hated," was the quotation that her senile, spiteful grandmother had pointed out to Louise. That was at the time when Louise's twin, Caroline, was given money to leave the island and study, something Louise had dreamed of. Always, always, Caroline got what Louise wanted: beauty, a promising career, even the young man Louise loved. This theme of twin-envy is set on a small island in Chesapeake Bay, the setting made vivid and colored by local idiom. The story is told by Louise in retrospect, after she has broken away from the island and found her own career and her own family; it is brought full circle when she (now a nurse in a mountain community) delivers twins to a patient; the first is healthy, the second frail and needing attention, and Louise tells the newborn infants' grandmother to hold the first-born, "Hold him as much as you can." A strong novel, this, with depth in characterization and with vitality and freshness in the writing style.

1009   **Paterson,** Katherine. *Rebels of the Heavenly Kingdom.* Lodestar, 1983. 83-1529. ISBN 0-525-66911-6. 227p. $11.50.

7–9   Wang Lee, kidnapped by bandits and rescued by a woman posing as a man, is the adolescent protagonist of this historical novel set in China in the years 1850–1853. A simple peasant, Wang Lee does not understand the fervor that moves his rescuer, Mei Lin, and he feels only contempt for this bold creature with her big, unbound feet. Mei Lin is one of the many men and women who joined the Taiping Tienkuo, the Heavenly Kingdom of Great Peace; this is both a patriotic army dedicated to conquering the Manchu overlords, and a religious group influenced by Christianity and incorporating some of its tenets and practices. The historical and cultural details are vivid, the book giving a great deal of information about the country as well as about the Heavenly Kingdom and its warriors. It follows the lives of Wang Lee and Mei Lin as they participate (separately or together) in military marches, battles, and camp life, concluding with their union, at the close of the book, and their settlement into the ancestral hut of Wang Lee's family. This is a fascinating story, and well-told; if it does not have the emotional impact of Paterson's earlier historical fiction (*Of Nightingales That Weep, The Master Puppeteer*) it has pace and color, and it is particularly interesting in its reflection of cultural diffusion, as the militant leaders of the Taiping Rebellion fuse their interpretation of Christian doctrine with their own traditions.

1010   **Patrick,** Douglas. *The Stamp Bug: An Illustrated Introduction to Stamp Collecting;* by Douglas and Mary Patrick. McGraw-Hill, 1979. 95p. illus. $8.95.

6–   A sensible and well-organized text on stamp collecting for beginners stresses the fact that expensive equipment is not really needed, and advises against starting with an illustrated album. The Patricks give advice on buying stamps or removing them from envelopes, sorting and mounting stamps, and on stamps as an investment; they include a chapter for the advanced collector and an extensive, annotated glossary. The text, printed in double columns, is written in an informal, conversational style and lightened by some anecdotes.

1011   **Pearce,** Philippa. *The Battle of Bubble and Squeak;* illus. by Alan Baker. Deutsch/Dutton, 1979. 78-74460. ISBN 0-233-96986-1. 88p. $5.95.

4–6   Bubble and Squeak are the two gerbils that a boy who was moving away had given to Sid Sparrow. Sid's sisters adored them, his stepfather tried to be impartial but was anxious not to argue with his wife. And that was the trouble, the cause of the battle, for Sid's mother "didn't like animals, had never liked animals, and never would like animals." She surreptitiously threw the cage out, and when a conscientious dustman brought them to the house she had to cope with a hysterical small girl—and she promised her daughter she'd never again give or throw the animals away. That's the first round of the battle, and readers should be happy with the conclusion, but the question of whether the gerbils are kept or not is—while appealing in itself—not the core of the story. The core is really in the delicate balance of the parent-child relationship, and the facets here are explored with sympathy and percipience, especially in the characterization of the children's stepfather, who valiantly supports the children and sees their need for pets yet doesn't want to antagonize his wife and make it even harder for the children.

1012   **Pearce,** Philippa. *The Way to Sattin Shore;* illus. by Charlotte Voake. Greenwillow, 1983. 83-14152. ISBN 0-688-02319-3. 182p. $10.50.

5–7   In a carefully crafted story from a distinguished British writer, the reader is not presented with a full-blown mystery, but with a family story into which an element of mystery is introduced, grows, and unravels. Kate is curious about the letter her grandmother receives, especially when neither Gran nor Mother will talk about it. She knows it has something to do with the fact that her father's gravestone disappears; she wonders about the father who died by drowning on the very day she was born. The suspense is deftly maintained as Kate discovers more and more about that fatal drowning; the characters are strongly defined, the writing style fluent and polished.

1013   **Pearson,** Tracey Campbell, illus. *Old Macdonald Had a Farm.* Dial, 1984. 83-18815. Trade ed. ISBN 0-8037-0068-7; Library ed. ISBN 0-8037-0070-9. 23p. Library ed. $9.89; Trade ed. $9.95.

3–6 yrs.   As she did in the ebullient *We Wish You a Merry Christmas* Pearson uses only the words of the song as her text. Here the visual interpretation has less ingenuity, but it has no less charm, as the frolicsome animals cumulate. The drawings have wit, humor, and action; the text has the appeals of rhyme, rhythm, and cumulation. Music is provided at the back of the book.

1014   **Pearson,** Tracey Campbell. *We Wish You a Merry Christmas;* illus. by Tracey Campbell Pearson. Dial, 1983. 82-22224. Trade ed. ISBN 0-8037-9368-5; Library ed. ISBN 0-8037-9400-2. 22p. Trade ed. $8.95; Library ed. $8.89.

K–4   A group of young carollers, trudging about in the snow, is welcomed indoors by an elderly, hospitable couple. The children are as indefatigable in their eating as in their singing. When they get to "Now bring us some figgy pudding/And bring some out here," the hosts search their cupboards. No figgy pudding. The man departs, ultimately returns with a huge can of pudding, only to find the exhausted carol-singers sleeping. So, last page, the man and wife are gorging on figgy pudding, the pantry's in a mess, and the guests slumber on. The music for the familiar carol is appended, the concept's engaging, the pictures are cheerful and funny.

1015   **Peck,** Richard. *The Dreadful Future of Blossom Culp.* Delacorte, 1983. 83-5165. ISBN 0-385-29300-3. 183p. $13.95.

5–7   The humorous story of a girl with occult powers, *The Ghost Belonged to Me* introduced Blossom, in a fantasy set in 1913. In this sequel it is a year later, and the outspoken, pert protagonist is in disfavor at school ("There are better ways of getting attention than dabbling in the occult," her teacher says.) Working on a class project, a Halloween festival, Blossom is in a deserted house reputed to be haunted when she's catapulted seventy years into the future, into the room of a boy who at first thinks she's part of an Atari game. Readers should enjoy a Blossomeye view of our time, as she and Jeremy work out the problem of how she can get back to 1914. She does. Somehow Peck fuses the occult powers, the time-slip, and the 1914 milieu into a successful whole, and the cheerful candor and practicality of the main character make the story enjoyable.

1016   **Peet,** William Bartlett. *Cowardly Clyde;* written and illus. by Bill Peet. Houghton, 1979. 78-24343. 38p. $8.95.

K–2   Clyde is a huge but timid war-horse, and he lives in dread of an encounter with the ferocious dragon his owner, the bombastic Sir Galavant, yearns to meet. When the knight hears of an ogre that's devastating the countryside, he vows to track the monster down; Clyde, who quivers at a scarecrow, is terrified. They meet the ferocious creature, Clyde gallops off and throws his rider, and the ogre pursues cowardly Clyde out of the forest and catches him by the tail. But no ogre can bear bright sunlight, this one hastily retreats to the forest, and Sir Galavant, emerging, declares victory. Instant hero status for the knight; a facade of bravery for the horse. The tale is nonsensical, but the combination of swashbuckling knight and anti-hero Clyde, and the action that ends in victory, should appeal to the read-aloud audience. The writing is brisk and casual; the illustrations are colorful and vigorous.

1017   **Pelgrom,** Els. *The Winter When Time Was Frozen;* tr. from the Dutch by Maryka and Rafael Rudnik. Morrow, 1980. 80-21224. Trade ed. ISBN 0-688-22247-1; Library ed. 0-688-32247-6. 224p. Trade ed. $8.95; Library ed. $8.59.

4–6   A World War II story, first published in the Netherlands, is set on a farm near Amsterdam, where the compassionate Farmer Everingen and his wife, Janna, have taken in Noortje Vanderhook and her father as well as Theo, a consumptive refugee. The oldest Everingen child, Evert, is Noortje's friend and at times her confederate in spying on the Germans who have commandeered the barn and the parlor for living quarters. The family also takes in another family of four and the infant daughter of a Jewish couple that's been sheltering in a cave and disappears. It is a hard, bitterly cold winter; the Everingens share a meal with any refugee who comes to their door, even helping a young German deserter. There is no strong story line here, but the book is replete with action and drama, the characters are fully developed, the writing style smooth, and the translation fluent and colloquial.

1018 **Pellowski,** Anne. *The Nine Crying Dolls; A Story from Poland;* illus. by Charles Mikolaycak. Philomel, 1980. 79-25975. Trade ed. ISBN 0-399-20752-X; Library ed. ISBN 0-399-61162-2. 26p. Trade ed. $5.95; Library ed. $5.99.

K–3 Bright papercut collage pictures, busy with the print patterns of clothing, illustrate a traditional tale from Poland; the style of the retelling is brisk in tempo and smooth in style. Worried about Baby Antolek's crying, his mother goes to an old woman for advice, and is told to make nine rag dolls and throw them into the carts of passersby, so that when they are gone they will take Antolek's crying with them. It works like a charm. Unfortunately, each doll later causes the baby of the house to cry. At the ensuing discussion, nine mothers ask the same woman's advice, and are given the same remedy. Among the carts into which dolls are thrown is that of Antolek's parents, and he begins to cry again. This time the old woman gives a new suggestion: throw the nine dolls into the river. When his mother gets home, Antolek is jumping for joy, and "as far as I know, he is still laughing happily."

1019 **Perl,** Lila. *Don't Ask Miranda.* Seabury, 1979. 78-23835. ISBN 0-8164-3229-5. 164p. $7.50.

5–7 New in the neighborhood, ignored by her classmates, thirteen-year-old Miranda is thrilled when a boy in her class, Hal, comes into the bakery where she works part-time for "Aunt" Friedl. Even when she learns that Hal's friendliness is due to the fact that he wants her to help him win a school election, Miranda's pleased. Unhappy at home (father a boastful failure, mother a self-satisfied spendthrift), she turns eagerly to the new friends she makes at school, even when she realizes that they expect her to steal baked goods for them . . . and then insist she steal a purse. That's when Miranda balks. She also balks at moving again when her father announces he's had (again) a marvelous offer, and her parents agree to let her stay with Aunt Friedl and finish the year. Here, as in her other decision, Miranda shows her growing maturity, for she can now accept Aunt Friedl as imperfect, having learned that "Uncle" Heinrich was not Friedl's brother but her lover, and she can accept and love her parents. While the ending is not strong, the book has good characterization, convincing relationships, and natural dialogue, and it deals perceptively and candidly with the ethical conflicts that most children confront at some time.

1020 **Perl,** Lila. *Junk Food, Fast Food, Health Food; What America Eats and Why.* Houghton, 1980. 80-15928. ISBN 0-395-29108-9. 182p. Hardcover ed. $9.95; Paper ed. $4.95.

6–10   In a thoughtful and objective survey, Perl describes the impact made by big business processing and fast food chains on American eating habits, and discusses additives, facts and fallacies about health food, and the heavy consumption of junk foods, fat, and salty or too-sweet snacks. Based on careful research and written in a brisk, straightforward style, the book closes with a discussion of some of the ways in which consumer interests have changed the labelling of food and of some of the ways stores foster impulse buying. Included are a metric conversion table, a list of food additives, an index, a bibliography, and thirty-odd recipes using natural foods.

1021   **Perrin,** Linda. *Coming to America; Immigrants from the Far East.* Delacorte, 1980. 80-65840. ISBN 0-440-01072-1. 182p. $9.95.

7–10   One of a series of books on immigrants from large geographical areas, this covers the problems of Chinese, Japanese, Filipino, and Vietnamese in their adjustment to immigrant status in this country. In a text that is well-organized, clearly written, carefully documented, and objective in tone, Perrin covers the history of each group separately, describing the reasons they came, the difficulties they had in getting here, the financial, cultural, and personal problems they faced as newcomers, and the prejudice they have encountered, official and unofficial. Chapter notes, a divided bibliography, and a brief history of U.S. immigration laws are appended, useful adjuncts to a forthright text on the way in which the land of opportunity has treated Asian newcomers, and often their children and their children's children.

1022   **Pesek,** Ludek. *Trap for Perseus;* tr. from the German by Anthea Bell. Bradbury, 1980. 79-24862. ISBN 0-87888-160-3. 168p. $8.95.

8–12   The year is 2275, the setting a spaceship, and the theme is a society's control of the mind of an intelligent and resistant individual. Commander of the *Perseus III,* Steve Blair is separated from his crew when his ship is sent to investigate the disappearance of *Perseus I* and *II,* both lost. He finds that *Perseus II* is docked at an even older lost ship, the *Argo,* and that the community of *Argo* descendants is a tightly-organized society that has evolved a new ethical system, rigid and punitive. Pesek's pace is slow, but its very slowness makes what happens to Blair believable, as he succumbs to the philosophy of his Tutor; in an effective ending, he waits to receive and isolate the members of another ship, the *Perseus IV,* smiling ironically just as someone had smiled at him. There are many dramatic episodes that serve as foil for the slow process of Blair's conversion and that give validity and contrast to a science fiction story with unusual depth.

1023   **Petersen,** P. J. *The Boll Weevil Express.* Delacorte, 1983. 82-72816. ISBN 0-440-00856-5. 211p. $12.95.

7–10   Lars, fifteen, resents the fact that his domineering father feels that his son should stay at home and do his share of the farm work. Lars can't even get permission to go into town for an evening high school basket-ball game. Prodded by his new classmate Doug, who lives in a nearby home for juvenile delinquents, Lars agrees to run away. They plan to go to Idaho, where Doug thinks his father is and where he's sure they can get jobs. They don't plan on having Doug's younger sister insist on joining them, on not finding Doug's father or, when they go to San Francisco, finding that Doug's mother has moved and left no forward-ing address. Petersen doesn't preach, but the recital of the sordid, hopeless journey with its necessary evasions and hunger and anger speaks grimly of the lot of the drop-out vagabond. Lars is not a strong character, but Doug (a petty criminal, a liar, a boaster) is well-drawn, as is his more sensible and realistic sister. The story has good structure, adequate style, and a realistic ending: Doug agrees to go back to the juvenile home, and Lars, with some relief, goes home.

1024   **Pevsner,** Stella. *Cute Is a Four-Letter Word.* Houghton/Clarion, 1980. 79-23626. ISBN 0-395-29106-2. 190p. $7.95.

5–7   Clara has determined that it's going to be her big year, that while she's in eighth grade she's going to become popular, get on the cheerleading team, and maybe even catch Skip, the handsome captain of the basket-ball team. She definitely did not plan to have two friends training rats for a science fair in her basement, or have an uncongenial girl her own age (niece of her mother's college chum) living at their house and being hostile. All those things happen, as Clara tells her story, and they bring some surprising results, for Clara finds, after she's become Skip's girl, that he's shallow—and that her sense of values has changed—and that she'd rather have true friends than sycophantic ones. Not a new theme, the maturation of a young adolescent, but Pevsner treats it with sympa-thy and insight; the characters are rounded, the relationships change and develop naturally, and the humor of the dialogue and of Clara's convincing narration are skillfully blended with some of the nicely-meshed, more serious themes of friendship values, familial affection, and the achieving of self-confidence that accompanies a sense of per-spective about one's own worth.

1025   **Peyton,** K. M. *Flambards Divided.* Philomel, 1982. 81-15720. ISBN 0-399-20864-X. 272p. $10.95.

7–10   An addition to the *Flambards* trilogy should be welcomed by Peyton's fans, but even to those readers not familiar with the characters and the preceding events, this mature and discerning novel should appeal. Chris-tina, widow of a young World War I flyer, her cousin Will, has bought the Flambards estate from Will's brother Mark. She knows that Mark will disapprove, as do gentry and villagers, of her marriage to Dick, a former servant to the family. There is abrasion, not only because Chris-tina and Dick are uncomfortable with each other's friends and because Christina has given up a measure of independence because Dick is running the estate, but also because she has realized that she is deeply in love with Mark, who's always loved her. The story ends, after some unhappy adjustments, with a note of promise: the law that forbids a woman to marry her husband's brother is clearly going to be rescinded by Parliament. This gives a clear insight into the British class divisions in a rural society and it has good period flavor. The characters are drawn with depth and perception, and the writing style has a natural flow and momentum.

1026   **Peyton,** K. M. *Marion's Angels;* illus. by Robert Micklewright. Oxford, 1979. 79-40676. ISBN 0-19-271432-5. 152p. $9.95.

6–9   Everyone in the village thought Marion was a bit batty, a young girl like
*   that spending all her time and energy in caring for a deserted church. But her widowed father understood how much she loved St. Michael's and the beautiful carved angels below its roof. When the church is used for a concert, Marion is stunned by the playing of the pianist, Pat Pennington (hero of several earlier Peyton books) and becomes his friend; she and her father are equally impressed with Pat's wife Ruth. Marion, a believer in miracles, is sure that the famous American violinist who enthusiastically arranged a series of benefit concerts to save the church has come in answer to her prayers. She is torn with misgiving about his invitation to Pat to come to the States, torn because she feels on the one hand that it may mean the end of the marriage of Pat and Ruth, since the latter is already unhappy at how Pat's musical career has encroached on their time together, and on the other hand that it may bring happiness to her father, who has fallen in love with Ruth, whom she also loves. It's all settled, in a highly dramatic final sequence, by what Marion is convinced is another miracle. This is one of Peyton's best: perceptive, beautifully constructed, serious in its concerns but lightened by a gentle humor, and outstanding in characterization and dialogue.

1027   **Peyton,** K. M. *A Midsummer Night's Death.* Collins, 1979. 78-9822. ISBN 0-529-0543-1. 138p. $6.95.

7–10   The hero of a notable English author's *Prove Yourself a Hero,* Jonathan, is now a sixth-form prefect at a school he finds boring save for one master, Charles Hugo; Hugo is a mountain climber as well as a teacher, and to Jonathan he's the epitome of the just, intelligent, and brave man. All the more horrifying, then, when evidence points to the fact that Hugo has murdered another master, Robinson. There's no omniscience, melodrama, or last-minute disclosure here, but a well-crafted story line; the minor plot threads are supportive rather than distracting, and the characterization is strong and consistent. Peyton's writing is mature and polished, and the book gives a vivid and occasionally humorous picture of the vagaries and nuances of life at an English public school.

1028   **Peyton,** K. M. *Who Sir? Me Sir?* Oxford, 1983. ISBN 0-19-271470-8. 171p. $11.95.

6–8   Waiting for their teacher, who'd dropped into a pub after a ball game, four children from Hawkwood Comprehensive School are horrified when he comes out with a man from the exclusive Greycoats School and tells them a tetrathlon match has been arranged. Swimming, riding, target-shooting, and running. The Greycoats boys have tutors, their own horses, and swimming pools. The four Hawkwood boys have none of these, no experience, and little desire to be shoved into competition. After some preliminary training, the teacher gives up—but Nutty doesn't. Nutty's a girl, and her determination is fierce; she coerces, threatens, wheels and deals, and becomes one of a new team that trains on its own for several months, at the end of which the tetrathlon takes place, several adults having been coaxed into training the nervous quartet. This is a natural for film: the four Hawkwood contenders are tough, colorful characters (and their speech reflects this) and they all have hearts of steel and some soft spots; there's distinctive characterization, plenty of action, lots of humor, some moments of sentiment, and the story has an appealing plot and a breezy writing style.

1029 Pfeffer, Susan Beth. *A Matter of Principle*. Delacorte, 1982. 81-15288. ISBN 0-440-05612-8. 192p. $9.95.

7–10   Becca, the narrator, is seventeen. She's pretty, popular, a good student, and one of a small group who decide they will publish an underground newspaper when the school newspaper's advisor, Miss Holdstein, won't let them print an article that criticizes school policy. One of the group draws a suggestive cartoon of Miss Holdstein and the school principal, and the whole group is suspended—and told that an apology will end the suspension. The students sue instead, claiming violation of their constitutional rights. Eventually the case comes to trial and those students who hadn't already apologized are readmitted—but there's a long period before that in which, through Becky, Pfeffer explores the effects of pressure on individuals, the tension such pressures bring to families, the ambivalence the suspended students feel, the conflict between the issue of freedom of the individual or the press and the slander-by-innuendo of the cartoon. Pfeffer manages to present a complicated and clouded issue and keep the narrative moving with pace and vitality.

1030 Pfeffer, Susan Beth. *What Do Yo Do When Your Mouth Won't Open?* illus. by Lorna Tomei. Delacorte, 1981. 80-68731. Trade ed. ISBN 0-440-09471-2; Library ed. ISBN 0-440-09475-5. 128p. Trade ed. $7.95; Library ed. $7.45.

5–7   Reesa, twelve, has always had teachers who understood that she felt panic at the thought of reading aloud, and—since she's a good student— they've excused her. Now she has won a school essay contest and is horrified when she learns that she's supposed to read it aloud at the county level. Reesa tells the story believably, and her efforts to get over her phobia (with the help of a sympathetic psychologist) in two weeks are equally convincing. Her parents are proud, her best friend is supportive, and her biggest enemy is her jealous sister. When Reesa explodes and confronts her sister, the two girls talk about their relationship for the first time, Reesa accepts the fact that her phobia may in part be an attention-getting mechanism, and she is of course delighted to learn that her sister has been jealous. The story ends with Reesa's successful reading (no prize) after a deft build-up of suspense. Good pace, good style, and a perceptive handling of characters and relationships are the strong points of a story that may touch many readers who have shared Reesa's fears in varying degrees.

1031   **Phelan,** Mary Kay. *The Story of the Louisiana Purchase;* illus. by Frank Aloise. T. Y. Crowell, 1979. 78-22505. Trade ed. ISBN 0-690-03955-7; Library ed. ISBN 0-690-03956-5. 149p. Trade ed. $7.95; Library ed. $7.89 net.

5–8   No dry presentation, this; Phelan makes the intricate story of the purchase of the huge expanse of land known as the Louisiana province as exciting as a detective thriller. Using source materials (an extensive list provided at the back of the book) she unravels the ploys of international power politics as Jefferson worried, Napoleon wavered, and their several advisors and envoys used strategy and threat to achieve their goals. The reader gets a vivid picture of the manipulations of balance of power among France, Spain, England, Santo Domingo, and the United States as well as of the burgeoning city of New Orleans and what it meant to Americans as a port. Crisp and clear, with an extensive relative index to give access to the complexity of names and events.

1032   **Phipson,** Joan. *Fly Free.* Atheneum, 1979. 79-14661. ISBN 0-689-50149-8. 134p. $7.95.

7–9   The concern of a major Australian author for wild life is demonstrated again in a novel that is slow-moving but compassionate, sensitive, and gracefully written, the pace alleviated by natural dialogue and a dramatic final episode. Johnny, easy-going and often naive, earns money by trapping; he wants his classmate Wilfred (a serious, tense loner) to be able to join a school trip, and he offers to earn more money by extra trapping. Wilfred wants to help, but he's upset by killing animals; he's even more upset when some illegal bird trappers make a deal with Johnny to catch parrots for their pet shop. The boys quarrel, and Johnny slams a shed door on Wilfred although he knows his friend is terrified by enclosures; he goes off and is himself caught in an animal trap. So Johnny finds out what it's like to be trapped, and his pain and fear bring him to the decision that he'll give it up—if he lives. His father gets Wilfred's help in finding him, and there is a confrontation with the two men who've made the deal about bird-catching. There's enough tension to hold any reader, but nature lovers should enjoy the book particularly.

1033   **Pierce,** Tamora. *Alanna: The First Adventure*. Atheneum, 1983. 83-2595. ISBN 0-689-30994-5. 241p. $12.95.

5–8   Alanna, yearning to be a knight and have adventures, proposes to her twin brother that he go to the convent sorcery school she was supposed to attend and she go to the king's court and—pretending to be a boy— train as a page. This first of a projected series should win easy converts: it has the appeals of chivalric training, of Alanna's masquerade as "Alan," and of the high magic that Alanna and others learn and prac- tice. Alanna makes enemies, gains protectors and friends, succeeds re- markably at archery, swordplay, wrestling, etc. She saves the life of the prince, Jonathan, who becomes one of the few who know her secret (high probability of a future romance there) and knows that their shared first adventure will not be the last. Save for an occasional phrase that seems too contemporary for the setting ("Then try *this* on for size") the writing is smooth and spirited.

1034   **Pierce,** Tamora. *In the Hand of the Goddess*. Atheneum, 1984. 84-2946. ISBN 0-689-31054-4. 232p. $12.95.

7–10   A second story about Alanna, who has cut her hair and bound her breasts so that she can pass as a boy and train for knighthood. In this medieval fantasy, Alanna (Alan) grows up enough to fall in love, to ex- perience a sexual relationship, to pass the tests for knighthood, to par- ticipate in a war, and—above all—to expose and slay the wicked man who has designs on the throne and whose sorcery she must fight with her own magic. The fast-paced story ends with Alanna going off on her own to try for new adventures, and readers who have responded to the intriguing situation, the doughty heroine, and the easy flow of the story will doubtless look forward to reading about them.

1035   **Pinkwater,** Daniel Manus. *Alan Mendelsohn, The Boy From Mars*. Dutton, 1979. 78-12052. ISBN 0-525-25360-2. 248p. $8.95.

5–7   Leonard Neeble, boy outcast, tells the story of the adventures he and his friend Alan had; a newcomer, Alan was no more popular than Leonard in West Kangaroo Park or at Bat Masterson Junior High. In this exaggerated, tongue-in-cheek story of time-slips and thought control, Pinkwater lampoons con men and dupes, psychic powers, quack medi- cos, natural food faddists and assorted weird characters with great hu- mor if, occasionally, at great length. Leonard and Alan repeatedly fall for confidence tricks and repeatedly profit from them, as when they buy a Mind Control Omega Meter and find that, for them, it works. If noth- ing succeeds like excess, the author has achieved a triumph of improba- ble folderol.

1036   **Pinkwater,** Daniel Manus. *The Magic Moscow*; written and illus. by Dan- iel Pinkwater. Four Winds, 1980. 80-12785. ISBN 0-590-07583-7. 57p. $7.95.

4–6   Like Pinkwater's moose stories, this is an engagingly daft tale told in a bland, straightforward style, and the combination is highly amusing. Norman Bleistift, who tells the story, works for Steve, owner of a soft ice cream shop (the Magic Moscow); Steve is devoted to an old television program, Sergeant Schwartz of the Yukon, and buys a pup because it's a Malamute like Schwartz's dog. Pinkwater uses exaggeration (his dog wins every ribbon and cup at a dog show because he's the only dog left around after a wild chase scene) to good effect and his light, breezy style carries the improbable story along nicely.

1037   **Pitcher,** Diana, ad. *Tokoloshi: African Folk-Tales;* illus. by Meg Rutherford. Dawne-Leigh, 1981. 80-28470. ISBN 0-89742-049-7. 64p. $9.95.

4–6   First published in England, a selection of tales chosen by a teacher born in South Africa uses chiefly Bantu sources, although the adapter has given most of her characters only Zulu names. The tales are linked: "First Man and First Woman," a creation story, is followed by the title story (Tokoloshi is a magical being) in which the primal pair acquires their first animals, and in the third story, "The Calabash Child," First Man and First Woman acquire a son, etc. Each tale is brief, smoothly told, and dramatically structured; the book is an excellent source for storytelling or reading aloud as well as for independent reading. The illustrations are very handsome, black and white scratchboard drawings that have the soft precision of Peter Parnall's work and the drama of Leonard Everett Fisher's.

1038   **Platt,** Kin. *Brogg's Brain.* Lippincott, 1981. 79-9622. Trade ed. ISBN 0-397-31945-2; Library ed. ISBN 0-397-31946-0. 123p. Trade ed. $9.50; Library ed. $8.89.

7–10   Fifteen-year-old Monty is on the track team, but he has little ambition and little expectation of winning races. It's his father who keeps pushing Monty, who talks things over with the coach, who pushes so hard he almost makes the boy lose interest. One night he and Cindy (a mild but growing love interest) see a movie called "Brogg's Brain," and—as in the movie—a disembodied voice seems to spur Monty on to win a race. This is not, however, the formula last-minute victory: Monty's win brings him no new status, no kudos, just some personal satisfaction. Although this has less surface sophistication, it is in some ways more mature than other (not all) Platt novels, knitting the theme of the reluctant sportsman, the basic father-son relationship, the growing self-confidence, and the increasing relaxation in the boy-girl relationship into a sturdy and effective whole.

1039   **Plotz,** Helen, comp. *Eye's Delight: Poems of Art and Architecture.* Greenwillow, 1983. 83-5577. ISBN 0-688-02388-6. 107p. $10.50.

5–   From an anthologist as dependably discriminating as she is prolific, a new book is a welcome gift. Plotz has chosen from a wide time span, including fragments from ancient Greece and excerpts from the Bible, through centuries of poets, to many of today's best contemporary writers. The selections are logically grouped, varied in form and mood, and accessible through author, title, and first line indexes.

1040   **Plotz,** Helen, comp. *Gladly Learn and Gladly Teach: Poems of the School Experience.* Greenwillow, 1981. 81-2344. ISBN 0-688-00594-2. 144p. $8.95.

5–   A smorgasbord of academic and educational poetic commentaries, ranging from the substantial, sometimes wistful memories of reminiscence to the lighter, sometimes barbed, thrusts at educational institutions and their practitioners. Plotz, one of our best anthologists, has gathered a wide and nicely varied range of poems and grouped them under five headings. There are some poems from past generations or other language sources; most of the selections are contemporary, British or American.

1041   **Plotz,** Helen, comp. *This Powerful Rhyme; A Book of Sonnets.* Greenwillow, 1979. 79-14037. Trade ed. ISBN 0-668-80226-5; Library ed. ISBN 0-668-84226-7. 150p. Trade ed. $7.95; Library ed. $7.63 net.

7–   The compiler discourses briefly but knowledgeably on the sonnet form in her introduction, and uses sonnets about sonnets as the first section of this anthology; succeeding poems are grouped under the rubrics of daily life, politics and history, religion, love and friendship, and time. The selections range from sixteenth-century writing to the work of contemporary poets; Plotz has—as she states in the introduction—omitted some of the best-known sonnets of Keats, Shakespeare, Shelley, and Wordsworth in order to give space to lesser-known poems. Indexes give access to a collection notable for its broad range and its discriminating selectivity.

1042   **Pomerantz,** Charlotte. *If I Had a Paka: Poems in Eleven Languages;* illus. by Nancy Tafuri. Greenwillow, 1982. 81-6624. Trade ed. ISBN 0-688-00836-4; Library ed. ISBN 0-688-00837-2. 28p. Trade ed. $9.50; Library ed. $8.59.

K–3   The book's subtitle may be misleading; the poems are not in eleven languages, but the words from other languages are used in poems written in English and, in some cases, a poem is given in English as well as in another language. One poem, for example, consists only of the names of trees in Dutch, and it is followed by an English translation. The use of such languages as Indonesian, Spanish, Serbo-Croatian, and Native American is novel, appealing, and laudable; the paintings are spacious, bright, and clearly defined and composed; and the simply written, child-oriented poems are sturdy and easy to understand because of the care with which words from other languages are incorporated. The first poem, using Swahili words, is a good example; it begins, "If I had a paka/meow, meow/meow, meow/I would want a mm-bwa/ bow wow bow wow," and goes on to describe other wanted pets and then, "I'd want a rafeeki / good friend . . ."

1043   **Pomerantz,** Charlotte. *The Tamarindo Puppy; And Other Poems:* illus. by Byron Barton. Greenwillow, 1980. 79-16584. Trade ed. ISBN 0-688-80251-6; Library ed. ISBN 0-688-84251-8. 32p. Trade ed. $7.95; Library ed. $7.63.

K–3   Illustrated with colorful drawings that have an awkward naivete, this charming collection of poems plays with language, English and Spanish, in a variety of ways; meanings are made clear by context or repetition in many poems, while some are in English and use only Spanish names. This should please and be comprehensible to those small listeners to whom Spanish is a first language as well as to those whose first language is English. Samples: "Take your bottle / Little bottle / Take your little botellita / Little, little / Pequenita / Botellita . . ." or, "Nada is nothing / Nothing at all / Trip on a nada / You never will fall . . ." The poems are fresh and lilting, appealingly childlike in both subject matter and approach.

1044   **Poole,** Victoria. *Thursday's Child.* Little, 1980. 79-25767. ISBN 0-316-713341. 352p. illus. with photographs. $10.95.

8–   Like Doris Lund's *Eric,* this is a true, detailed, moving, and occasionally humorous account of a child's serious illness, the humor resting in some of the dialogue and in peripheral situations. Sam is seventeen, and has come home from boarding school for Christmas vacation when his parents decide he's had a bad cough for too long; what they discover is that he has a serious heart problem (cardiomyopathy) that is progressive, and that Sam's only hope for more than a few years of life is having a heart transplant. Sam's one of a big family, and there are innumerable financial and emotional problems involved for his parents, but they have marvelous support from family members and they have Sam's own courage to help them. Poole tells it all: the pain, the fear, the agonizing wait for a donor, the fear of failure through organ rejection, the lifetime of pills and possible infection ahead—all worth it because Sam lives. An absorbing book.

1045   **Porte,** Barbara Ann. *Harry's Visit;* illus. by Yossi Abolafia. Greenwillow, 1983. 81-20188. Trade ed. ISBN 0-688-01207-8; Library ed. ISBN 0-688-01208-6. 47p. Trade ed. $7.50; Library ed. $6.67.

1–3   Invited by a couple who are old friends of his father to spend a day with them and their three children, Harry (who's the narrator) is glum. He isn't prepared to enjoy himself, and for part of the day he is polite but cool. He isn't used to peanut butter on pumpernickel, he has it on white bread at home. There's no dessert. He has to spend time playing with Judy. He wishes he were home. But in the afternoon, Judy's brother takes him along to shoot baskets—and there's a low hoop, and he succeeds. Judy's brother buys him a snack! By the time his father appears, Harry is bubbling and loquacious, his chief concern being when he can visit again. The writing really sounds like the voice of a small, plaintive boy; the treatment is light but the emotions are deep and universal. Quietly funny, a small but memorable book.

1046   **Postma,** Lidia. *The Witch's Garden;* written and illus. by Lidia Postma. McGraw-Hill, 1979. 78-11414. ISBN 0-07-050535-7. 23p. $7.95.

K–3   First published in Holland, this story of seven small children who pay a
  *   visit to an old woman they've heard is a witch has a nicely fanciful twist; first the old woman proves to be a friendly soul who invites the group into her house for a snack, then she introduces the children to an elf. Only the youngest had believed her at first; now each wants to find his or her own house-elf. The story is, however, easily over-shadowed by the illustrations, paintings that are strong in composition and delicate in their intricate detail, varied in texture and mood, with some comic scenes of the children and several misty, romantic scenes of Little People. Postma uses color with restraint: one double-page spread of deep blue water, with soft green lily pads and reflections of black tree trunks has as contrast white water lilies and tiny, gossamer white figures of elfin creatures. Lovely.

1047   **Powers,** Bill. *Behind the Scenes of a Broadway Musical.* Crown, 1982. 82-2514. ISBN 0-517-54466-0. 83p. illus. with photographs. $13.95.

4–6   Although this may have a special appeal to readers who were Rosie (Maurice Sendak's *The Sign on Rosie's Door*) fans, it should interest any child who enjoys theater, and it may even attract older readers because of the details of the way in which a musical is put together. Powers does a good job, with clear and detailed explanations of casting, rehearsals, fittings, set design, and all the many technical arrangements such as lights, sets, and orchestration. The book is profusely illustrated with photographs of good quality, and the fact that the show, *Really Rosie*, has a cast of children adds to the book's appeal.

1048   **Powledge,** Fred. *So You're Adopted.* Scribner, 1982. 81-23278. ISBN 0-684-17347-6. 101p. $9.95.

6–8   The author was an adopted child and discusses his own attitudes and experiences in a candid and thoughtful book that considers the questions adopted children ask—or are afraid to ask—as well as their legal rights and their emotional conflicts. The text begins with a description of the legal protection offered adopted children over the centuries, societal changes in viewpoints about parental frankness, and the statistics on adoption. There is a chapter in which Powledge discusses searching for one's biological parents, and the slow changes in laws that have hitherto protected their privacy. A useful book, this concludes with an index and a divided list of publications and organizations that can give information about adoption.

1049   **Prelutsky, Jack.** *It's Snowing! It's Snowing!;* illus. by Jeanne Titherington. Greenwillow, 1984. 83-16583. Library ed. ISBN 0-688-01513-1; Trade ed. ISBN 0-688-01512-3. 47p. Library ed. $9.55; Trade ed. $10.50.

K–3   Whether the subject is the intricacy of one snowflake or a romp through a winter landscape where "the air is a silvery blur," these poems speak with immediacy and wit of the child's experience. Using colloquial language and rhythms, Prelutsky moves from concrete, everyday images ("I am shivering and shaking/like a pudding in a mold") to a wider world, and then back again; as in the wry, dreamy poem, "My sister would never throw snowballs at butterflies" ("she only throws them at me"); or in the dark humor of "The Snowman's Lament" ("For my ears are disappearing/and my eyes are coming loose") with its funny use of rhyme and assonance ("Now I'm thinner than a splinter"). Delicate pencil drawings in grey, white, and pale blue extend the humor and the range of mood.

1050   **Prelutsky, Jack,** comp. *The Random House Book of Poetry for Children;* illus. by Arnold Lobel. Random House, 1983. 83-2990. Trade ed. ISBN 0-394-85010-6; Library ed. ISBN 0-394-95010-0. 248p. Trade ed. $13.95; Library ed. $13.99.

3–7   The work of almost every major children's poet of past and present is
*   included in this anthology, as are some selections intended for adults but appropriate for children. Prelutsky (who has included many of his own poems) has designed the book for elementary school children, and many of the selections are also appropriate for reading aloud to younger children. The contents are arranged under such rubrics as "Nature Is . . . ," "The Four Seasons," "The Ways of Living Things," and "Nonsense ! Nonsense!" and the poems have been selected with loving and knowledgeable care. Every page has delicious illustrations by Lobel, some in color, and all beautifully incorporated into the page layout. Title, first line, author, and subject indexes give access to an impressive anthology.

1051   **Prelutsky, Jack.** *The Sheriff of Rottenshot: Poems by Jack Prelutsky;* illus. by Victoria Chess. Greenwillow, 1982. 81-6420. Trade ed. ISBN 0-688-00205-6; Library ed. ISBN 0-688-00198-X. 32p. Trade ed. $8.50; Library ed. $7.63

K–3   Macabre art with a silver lining, the often-gruesome Chess drawings have a robust humor of their own, for almost every lumpish human or lurking beast has either enough exaggeration or enough of a twinkle to be funny. Thus the illustrations are admirably suited to the often-ghoulish and very funny poems that Prelutsky writes with a strong use of meter and some entertaining word-play. The sheriff of the title is "short in the saddle and slow on the draw," and the ghostly grocer of Grumble Grove runs a non-existent shop with a great deal of spectral activity taking place; the catfish's one desire is to catch a mousefish, and the elegant centipede on her specially-built velocipede rates awards, "she merits medals / working all those centipedals."

1052   **Prince,** Alison. *Night Landings;* illus. by Ellen Thompson. Morrow, 1983. 83-19304. ISBN 0-688-02753-9. 144p. $10.50.

4–6   In a sequel to *The Sinister Airfield,* eleven-year-old Harriet and her friend Neil again become involved in a mystery; this time they are told by Rick, a boy who's hiding in a barn, that his mother has been coerced into cooperation by two vicious men engaged in a smuggling operation. Because he's heard the men refer obliquely to his mother's past involvement, Rick doesn't want the police to know there's going to be a drop at the airfield. This has just as much action as the first book, but is better structured; the characters are firmly drawn, the pace is brisk, and the dramatic ending doesn't depend solely on the children as the criminals are confronted and caught.

1053   **Pringle,** Laurence. *Feral: Tame Animals Gone Wild.* Macmillan, 1983. 82-60741. ISBN 0-02-775420-0. 110p. illus. with photographs. $9.95.

5–9   Pringle's text focuses, after an introductory chapter that discusses feral animals, on six animals; in separate chapters, he discusses birds, pigs, dogs, cats, burros, and horses, although the introduction notes that there are other feral creatures: goats and cattle, for example. Each chapter gives some historical background, describes the way they live and the dangers or potential dangers they pose to people, to other creatures and to the environment, and discusses the ways in which the feral animals are studied by scientists and the ways in which they are protected or pursued. Crisp, knowledgeable, and well-organized, the text presents this often-controversial subject with clarity and objectivity. A bibliography and an index are provided.

1054   **Pringle,** Laurence P. *Frost Hollows and Other Microclimates.* Morrow, 1981. 81-4066. Trade ed. ISBN 0-688-00714-7; Library ed. ISBN 0-688-00715-5. 62p. illus. with photographs. Trade ed. $6.95; Library ed. $6.67.

4–6   Direct and clear, Pringle's text describes the many factors that cause differences between microclimates and the larger ecological milieu within which they exist. He also points out how some of the plants and animals that are affected by the microclimate may, in turn, affect it; for example, ants in an anthill may vary their activities in relation to which side of their structure receives the most sunlight, but in the small scale of a microclimate, the structure itself may cut off wind or sun to influence what grows in the shadow of the anthill. The photographs are informative and are carefully placed in relation to the well-written and well-organized text; a glossary, a bibliography, and an index are provided.

1055   **Pringle,** Laurence P. *Lives at Stake; The Science and Politics of Environmental Health.* Macmillan, 1980. 80-14272. ISBN 0-02-775410-3. 154p. illus. with photographs. $8.95.

7–   In another thoughtful and thought-provoking book in his "Science for Survival" series, Pringle examines the known and suspected dangers in food, products, pollutants, job-related health hazards, and drugs that are a detrimental part of the total human environment. He describes testing materials, controls, controversy and testimony, and discusses the roles and responsibilities of citizens, governmental agencies, and industry. A well-written and well-organized text concludes with a list of some national groups working in the public interest, a glossary of terms, an extensive bibliography, and an index.

1056   **Pringle,** Laurence P. *What Shall We Do with the Land? Choices for America;* illus. with photographs. T. Y. Crowell, 1981. 81-43034. Trade ed. ISBN 0-690-04108-X; Library ed. ISBN 0-690-04109-8. 152p. Trade ed. $9.50; Library ed. $8.89.

7–10   Broad in coverage, precise in detail, objective and serious in tone, this
  *   excellent survey of the intricate problem of land use is written in a straightforward and authoritative style. Whether it is shoreline, forest, or the wilderness, rangeland or farmland, the decisions of today will affect the land and the people for generations to come. The hopes of conservationists, the needs for energy sources, the conflicting demands of individuals, agencies, business interests, and agricultural prerogatives all point to one multifaceted and crucial question: who has the right to decide? An index and a bibliography add to the usefulness of a timely and provocative book.

1057   **Prokofiev,** Sergei Sergeevich. *Peter and the Wolf;* translated by Maria Carlson; illus. by Charles Mikolaycak. Viking, 1982. 81-70402. ISBN 0-670-54919-3. 32p. $12.95.

K–3   Prokofiev's classic, designed to teach children the instruments of an orchestra, has been published in picture book form before, but never better illustrated. The translation is smooth, a bit more sophisticated than the 1960 edition published by Barnes and illustrated by Alan Howard; unlike the edition published in 1940 and illustrated by Warren Chappel, this does not include musical themes. The paintings are rich in color, dramatic in details of costume or architecture, strong in composition, with distinctive individuality in the faces of people and of the wolf.

1058   **Provensen,** Alice. *The Glorious Flight;* written and illus. by Alice and Martin Provensen. Viking, 1983. 82-7034. ISBN 0-670-34259-9. 39p. $13.95.

K–3   What more can one ask of a book than it be visually stunning, enter-
  *   tainingly written, and informative, and true? The restrained, dry humor of the simple but sophisticated text makes the story of Bleriot's long

struggle to build a machine that would fly a joy, and the paintings are striking in color and composition. Papa Bleriot and his family suffer patiently through eleven different models and innumerable assaults on Papa's body, until—in July of 1909—the indomitable aviator crosses the English Channel in thirty-seven minutes. How his family, which had seen him off, manages to be at the scene of his triumphant landing is a moot point, but it is probable that few readers will object. A smashing success for Papa and for the Provensens.

1059   **Provensen,** Alice. *Leonardo Da Vinci: The Artist, Inventor, Scientist in Three-Dimensional Movable Pictures;* written and illus. by Alice and Martin Provensen. Viking, 1984. 3-26005. ISBN 0-670-42384-X. 12p. $14.95.

4–8   Pull-tabs, pop-ups, and three-dimensional cut-outs are inlcuded in an
  *   oversize book in which these various forms of paper engineering are used to full and splendid advantage. The text describes the many investigations and accomplishments of the great artist and inventor, and the Provensens use rich color, wonderful marbled collage, and even a reproduction of the Mona Lisa as it stood on the easel, while Leonardo gravely faces the reader, brush in hand.

1060   **Provensen,** Alice. *Town & Country;* written and illus. by Alice and Martin Provensen. Crown, 1984. 84-12693. ISBN 0-517-55594-8. 29p. $9.95.

K–2   Oversize pages filled with colorful drawings, details that fill but do not seem to crowd the pages, interesting urban perspectives and rural landscapes are combined in a book that should make children feel that both city and country are nice places to live. The authors point out differences, but their accent is always positive. So much to do, so much to enjoy, wherever you live.

1061   **Purdy,** Susan. *Christmas Gifts Good Enough to Eat! A Holiday Cookbook;* written and illus. by Susan Purdy. Watts, 1981. 80-28510. Paper ed. ISBN 0-531-03542-5; Library ed. ISBN 0-531-04314-2. 95p. Paper ed. $2.95; Library ed. $8.90.

5–   An old hand at turning out better-than-average cookbooks for children, Purdy is careful about giving general instructions on terms, safety measures, measurements, and procedures. In this companion volume to her *Christmas Cookbook,* she also gives tips on wrapping, decorating, and mailing gifts of food. The recipes are clear and well-organized, listing equipment as well as ingredients. Step-by-step procedures are cited, illustrations are helpful and carefully placed, and red print is used to distinguish ingredients from implements and instruction. The recipes are grouped under the headings of cookies, candies, cakes and breads, savory snacks, and an omnibus category entitled "Sauces, Cheese, Condiments, etc." The index gives access to procedures as well as recipes.

1062   **Rau,** Margaret. *The Snow Monkey at Home;* illus. by Eva Hülsmann. Knopf, 1979. 78-31550. Trade ed. ISBN 0-394-83976-5; Library ed. ISBN 0-394-93976-X. 101p. Trade ed. $6.95; Library ed. $6.99 net.

6–9   Soft pencil drawings, realistically detailed and finely textured, illustrate a flowing and dignified text that goes through the life cycle of a male snow monkey, a Japanese macaque. Rau does not anthropomorphize, yet she establishes the monkey as a distinctive character while using his life to describe birth, child care, courtship and mating, communication, and the various and intricate patterns of individual relationships and group behavior within the monkey troop. An extensive divided bibliography is provided, as is an index.

1063   **Reading,** J. P. *Bouquets for Brimbal.* Harper, 1980. 79-2002. Trade ed. ISBN 0-06-024843-2; Library ed. ISBN 0-06-024844-0. 186p. Trade ed. $8.95; Library ed. $8.79.

8–10   Annie Brimbal is Macy's best friend and serious about acting, so Macy, who is the narrator of this sophisticated and sensitive novel, signs on for a job in summer stock just to be with Annie. But Annie is wrapped up in her career; Macy, doing odd jobs and feeling left out, falls in love with a man in the cast. It isn't until they become lovers that Macy begins to compare the way she feels about Don with the way Annie seems to feel about Lola, another member of the cast; then she realizes that what she had thought of as Annie's crush is Annie's love for Lola. Confused, bereft because she feels that a breach will mean the loss of the friend she loves, and ambivalent about her own feelings about homosexuality, Macy clears her confusion by a long talk with Annie. Smoothly written, the story is a perceptive exploration of patterns of sexual relationships and sex roles.

1064   **Rees,** David. *The Exeter Blitz.* Elsevier/Nelson, 1980. 80-13670. ISBN 0-525-66683-4. 128p. $7.95.

7–10   In his preface to the story, which won the Carnegie Award, Rees explains that he has made some changes for the purpose of his narrative but that the background details of one exceptionally devastating German air raid on the city of Exeter are substantially true. Rees focuses on the experiences of one family to show the drama and the devastation of the blitz; the youngest child, June, and her father are home when the siren sounds; the middle child and the book's protagonist, Colin, is thought to be with his mother at the shop where she works, and only his mother knows that he has left; the oldest daughter, Mary, is seeing a film with her friend Lars. All are trapped in one way or another; one of them is slightly wounded, and their home is partially destroyed. The blitz affects them—as it affects others in Exeter—in many ways beyond physical or material concerns; for Colin, it changes his attitude toward several people, especially toward a classmate who is a refugee from London. The viewpoint shifts, as the story moves from one family member's experiences to another, but it is the shift from one detail of a large canvas to another, not a disruptive process but a blending. The people are strongly defined, the story developed with pace and depth, and the details of the bombing raid dramatically vivid.

1065   **Rees,** David. *Quintin's Man.* Nelson, 1979. 78-26308. 128p. $6.95.

7–10   Luke, deeply in love with Cheryl, is delighted when her boy friend refuses to help her find a strayed horse; together they go to the hill called Quintin's Man (hence the title, for Cheryl later tells Luke that it was here she began to care for him) and share a first kiss. On their first date they become lovers; Luke's father, a widower, is well aware of this and speaks of it with open acceptance. Knowing how desolate his father has been since the death of his wife, Luke is determined that he will not commit himself to a permanent relationship; when his father dies (cardiac arrest) Luke is taken in by Cheryl's parents, who accept the fact that Luke and Cheryl are lovers although it disturbs them. The story line is not strong, but the author's compassion and perception give the book validity, and the consistency of characterization and nicely crafted writing style amply compensate for absence of a strong plot.

1066   **Rettich,** Margret. *The Tightwad's Curse and Other Pleasantly Chilling Stories;* tr. by Elizabeth D. Crawford; illus. by Rolf Rettich. Morrow, 1979. 79-17832. Trade ed. ISBN 0-688-22211-0; Library ed. ISBN 0-688-32211-5. 189p; Trade ed. $6.95.; Library ed. $6.67 net.

4–6   Smoothly translated from the original German, this collection of short stories consists of nicely varied, brief tales that have small mysteries with logical explanations; they are, as the subtitle indicates, "pleasantly chilling," rather than gruesome or melodramatic. For example, the ghost who haunts the house in the title story proves to be a man who, not knowing that the wife he'd left behind had moved away, has crept back into the house to effect a reconciliation. The stories are written in a lively and often humorous style and are deftly constructed, and the book should be useful for reading aloud as well was for independent reading.

1067   **Ricciuti,** Edward R. *They Work With Wildlife.* Harper, 1983. 80-7918. Trade ed. ISBN 0-06-025003-8; Library ed. ISBN 0-06-025004-6. 148p. Trade ed. $10.95; Library ed. $10.89.

7–10   In describing some of the kinds of jobs available to those who are interested in working with animals in the wild, Ricciuti stresses the need for early and proper education, is candid about the financial expectations and—in some jobs—the dangers, and gives ample information about agencies that can provide facts and institutions that offer training. Some of the material about specific jobs is anecdotal, giving a change of pace to a straightforward text; color is added through descriptions of the work of individuals, such as the studies of Cynthia Moss (East African elephants) in the chapter on field biology, or, in the chapter on wildlife law enforcement, the work of federal agents working undercover to track down smugglers of protected species. Some of the other careers discussed are wildlife management, nature writing, and serving as a game warden. Useful for vocational guidance, this should also appeal to the general reader; a list of informative organizations and an index are provided.

1068   Rice, Paul. *As Dead As a Dodo;* written by Paul Rice and Peter Mayle; illus. by Shawn Rice. Godine, 1981. 81-4062. ISBN 0-87923-401-6. 28p. $10.95.

4-6   First published in England, this is a catalogue of extinct creatures, primarily birds. Each recto page carries a framed painting, lavishly detailed in stylized and fanciful style, providing an ornate background for the creature on which it focuses. The colors are brilliantly jewel-toned, the drawing deliberately out of scale. The text on the verso pages that face each painting is written in an informal, almost jocose style. For example, "If you can imagine a zebra who has forgotten to put on the bottom half of his striped pajamas, you have an idea of how the Quagga used to look." Despite the levity, there is information to be gleaned, usually facts about how the animal got its name, what patterns of behavior are known, and how it became extinct.

1069   Riley, Jocelyn. *Crazy Quilt.* Morrow, 1984. 84-1017. ISBN 0-688-03873-5. 215p. $11.50.

6-9   In a sequel to *Only My Mouth is Smiling* it is again Merle, oldest of three children, who is the narrator. They live with their grandmother now; the disturbed mother who had taken them into isolation and poverty is in a hospital. Merle is torn between compassion for her mother, who wants desperately to come home, and the conviction that her mother is still very ill and needs institutional care. Fourteen, Merle is ambivalent about Grandma and her motivation, and equally ambivalent about some of her friends and classmates. She finally decides that each life is discrete and has its own pattern, just like the quilt that is a family heirloom. Serious, honest, touching, this is a perceptive book, with well-defined characters.

1070   Riley, Jocelyn. *Only My Mouth is Smiling.* Morrow, 1982. 81-18688. ISBN 0-688-01087-3. 222p. $9.50.

6-9   Merle is thirteen; Ron's eleven, Diane's nine, and they have all learned to recognize the symptoms that mean their mother is again losing touch with reality. Again, there are fights with Grandma—and this time, Mother herds them all on to a bus bound for the Wisconsin area where she owns an empty lot. Merle, who tells the story, describes the summer of living in a tent, starting school and moving into a rented house in the autumn, making friends, hoping that Mother's new job will help her stay sane, and worrying because Grandma keeps writing to the school authorities. As Mother's delusions of persecution return, Merle's fears lead her to call Grandma and start procedures for hospitalizing Mother. The story ends with the children ready to go home with Grandma, plans for family counseling, and Mother in hospital again. The situation in the book is serious but not macabre, handled with sympathy and insight, psychologically sound, and written with depth, candor, and skill.

1071   **Rinaldi,** Ann. *Term Paper.* Walker, 1980. 80-7686. ISBN 0-8027-6395-2. 220p. $8.95.

6–9   Nicki is a high school freshman who's dismayed, when her teacher is hospitalized, to find that her much-older brother Tony, also on the faculty, is taking over her English class. The story she writes is Tony's assignment: her term paper is to be an attempt to get Nicki to face her father's death, which she's refused to talk about. What emerges is not just Nicki's viewpoint of family affairs and relationships, but a tender story of the loving care and sacrifice that Tony, his wife, and another brother have made for the little sister they've raised (their mother died at Nicki's birth, their father took little responsibility) and of the way in which Nicki matures as she comes to understand the stresses on her family. The characterization and dialogue are strong, the writing style and plot development consistently structured and paced.

1072   **Rinard,** Judith E. *Zoos without Cages.* National Geographic Society, 1981. 79-3243. Trade ed. ISBN 0-87044-335-6; Library ed. ISBN 0-87044-340-2. 104p. illus. with photographs. Trade ed. $6.95; Library ed. $8.50.

5–9   Profusely illustrated with good quality photographs in full color, this is an excellent overview of the new kind of zoo first built in Hamburg in 1907, with open enclosures that simulate the native habitat of the animals within them. The text describes zoo procedures in caring for animals and discusses the preservation of species in captivity. There is also material about educational programs, field trips, volunteer activities, children's zoos and other aspects of zoo programs. The writing style is direct, the tone authoritative; an index and a brief list of books suggested for additional reading are included.

1073   **Rips,** Gladys Nadler. *Coming to America: Immigrants from Southern Europe.* Delacorte, 1981. 80-68742. ISBN 0-440-01340-2. 143p. illus. with photographs. $9.95.

7–10   Another well-written and well-researched volume in an excellent series (for example, Albert Robbins's book on immigrants from northern Europe) describes the newcomers from Italy, Greece, Portugal and Spain. Approximately half the book is devoted to the experiences of Italian immigrants; as in other books in the series, this discusses the reasons people decided to immigrate, the travel and entry conditions, the adjustment to a new country and usually to prejudiced treatment and poor working and housing conditions. The text frequently quotes from the immigrants' letters or their later accounts of their first years in the United States. Chapter notes, an index, a bibliography, and a brief history of U.S. immigration laws are appended.

1074   **Riskind,** Mary. *Apple Is My Sign,* Houghton, 1981. 80-39746. ISBN 0-395-30852-6. 146p. $7.95.

5–7   The daughter of deaf parents who used only sign language to converse with their children, Mary Riskind writes with both knowledge and understanding of a deaf child, his encounters with those who hear, and the range of attitudes deaf people may have about their handicap. The story is set in Pennsylvania at the time of the first horseless carriages (an invention that excites the protagonist and leads him into an adventure) in a school for the deaf. Ten-year-old Harry is at first homesick, but he soon makes friends, becomes excited about learning to draw and learning to talk. Aware that his father is ashamed of his own deafness (both parents are deaf) and that his mother is not, Harry learns to accept his situation as his mother has: a handicap rather than a stigma. The story has some strongly active episodes, a sensitive exploration of relationships, and an implicit but clear message that the interests, needs and fears of deaf children are the same as those of hearing children. The one artificiality of the book is in Riskind's efforts to evoke the style of sign language in dialogue ("Let-me carry to sleep-room?" "Yes. Go-on. Hurry," or "I here-soon four years. First not like. After-while you like.") but readers will undoubtedly adjust to this.

1075   **Ritter,** Lawrence S. *The Story of Baseball;* foreword by Ted Williams. Morrow, 1983. 82-20367. Trade ed. ISBN 0-688-01724-X; Paper ed. ISBN 0-688-02066-6. 148p. illus. with photographs. Trade ed. $12.50; Paper ed. $8.00.

5–9   It is the casual, flowing style and authoritative tone that make this historical overview of baseball better than most of the many books already available. Ritter describes the way baseball started (conceived not by Abner Doubleday, but by Alexander Cartwright) and the ways in which the game and equipment have changed, and the great stars of the past. This chronological survey is followed by separate chapters, in Part Two, on aspects of the game: batting, pitching, fielding, and game strategy. Ritter cites comments of players sparingly, writes with direct clarity, and communicates both his enjoyment of baseball and his understanding of the nuances of the game. An index is included; action photographs add to the book's nostalgic appeal to fans.

1076   **Roach,** Marilynne K. *Presto; or The Adventures of a Turnspit Dog;* written and illus. by Marilynne K. Roach. Houghton, 1979. 79-11746. ISBN 0-395-28269-1. 148p. $7.95.

5–7   Roach brings a few real characters from the 1760's (Samuel Johnson, Horace Walpole) to play bit parts in her story of the adventures of a small dog who runs away from the inn where his sole function is to turn the wheel that roasts meats. Presto, a travelling puppeteer had dubbed him, and that's the name he takes, for in this story the animals talk to each other and understand human speech. Presto finds the puppeteer in London and becomes part of his Punch and Judy show, but his life in the city is fraught with danger and adventure as he and his master meet the knaves and petty criminals (human and canine) who prey on others. Roach has put the story together smoothly, using just enough thieves' cant and eighteenth century idiom to give the tale color without drenching it.

1077   **Robbins,** Ken. *Building a House;* written and with photographs by Ken Robbins. Four Winds, 1984. 83-16513. ISBN 0-590-07887-9. 43p. $11.95.

3–6   Impeccably organized and lucidly written, this is one of the best books
  *   on construction that has appeared: the continuous text is broken into logical topics, the development is sequential, and the author has included all major facts without over-explaining any single procedure. The photographs are of good quality and are carefully integrated with the text, so that the reader can easily understand the steps, in order, by which an architect's plan produces a finished house.

1078   **Robinson,** Nancy K. *Veronica the Show-Off.* Four Winds, 1983. 82-18277. ISBN 0-590-07877-1. 119p. $7.95.

2–4   Veronica, who confesses at the end of *Just Plain Cat* that she hates her fancy school and her snobbish classmates, finally makes some friends in this companion volume. At first, trying to impress the other girls, she tells silly lies—like saying she has a horse because she knows that someone's interested in horses. It's a slow and sometimes painful process, but eventually, despite her showing off, Veronica makes two friends, and she tries very hard to change because she's learned that denigrating others can hurt their feelings. This has the same smooth narrative flow, the same perception as the story of Chris, and it has an even stronger characterization, one that evokes sympathetic understanding and shows a logical growth and change.

1079   **Rockwell,** Anne F. *Our Garage Sale;* illus. by Harlow Rockwell. Greenwillow, 1984. 80-16704. Library ed. ISBN 0-688-84278-X; Trade ed. ISBN 0-688-80278-8. 22p. Library ed. $9.55; Trade ed. $10.50.

3–6   In Rockwell's easily recognizable format (clean pictures, plenty of white
yrs.   space, large clear print) this gives a clear account of what a garage sale is and why people have them. The direct and simple text is in first person; the speaker is the younger child in a family that clears unwanted objects from attic, cellar, and garage to hold a sale in their driveway.

1080   **Rodgers,** Mary. *Summer Switch.* Harper, 1982. 79-2690; Trade ed. ISBN 0-06-025058-5. Library ed. ISBN 0-06-025059-3. 192p. Trade ed. $9.50; Library ed. $9.89.

5–7   And now, ten years later, a companion volume to *Freaky Friday*. Here the younger child, Ben, also known as "Ape Face," turns into his father and vice versa. This happens just as Ben is going off to camp and his father is going off to the West Coast to negotiate for a big part in the shake-up of the film company he represents in New York. The chapters are told alternately by Ben and his father, with contrasting type-faces used to help the reader distinguish between the two. It *does* get confusing, as each struggles to maintain his changed image; Ben is thunderstruck, for example, when the doorman at his Beverly Hills hotel gives him the keys to a car, since he's only twelve, and his father is equally frustrated when he has to make a telephone call to Ben and call him "Daddy" to give him advice on business matters while the camp director listens. Ben finds it hard to get used to having body hair and a deep voice; Daddy finds it hard to cope with a bully in his cabin. This is just as funny as *Freaky Friday*, it's told in a yeasty style, it takes some enjoyably acid pokes at the wonderful world of Hollywood, and it shows—in a light way that is not didactic—how much insight can be gained into personal relationships if one can really step into someone else's shoes. The transformation is reversed at the end of the story just in time to prevent a family explosion.

1081   **Rodowsky,** Colby F. *The Gathering Room*. Farrar, 1981. 81-5360. ISBN 0-374-32520-0. 186p. $9.95.

4–6   The story of a family that emerges painfully from self-imposed isolation is told effectively from the viewpoint of nine-year-old Mudge, who lives alone in a cemetery gatehouse with his parents. Not until an elderly great-aunt tracks them down does Mudge discover—half remembering—that his father had had a nervous breakdown after a friend was murdered. Mudge has been taught by his father, has never been to school, and has no friends save for the assortment of lively ghosts, a fantasy element introduced with no apparent purpose but, oddly, with success; despite the ghosts this is not a true fantasy but a realistic story with one fantasy element, rather pointless but quite diverting. It is Mudge who is most resistant to Aunt Ernestus and her insistence that the family must leave their solitude—but it is Mudge who finally, desperately, calls her to come and help when he sees that his parents cannot cope. There's a credibly happy ending to this well-crafted story, structured and peopled in an economical but forceful way.

1082   **Rodowsky,** Colby F. *H, My Name Is Henley*. Farrar, 1982. 82-12164. ISBN 0-374-32831-5. 184p. $10.95.

5–7
*   Henley tells the story of her peripatetic life with Patti, an irresponsible, self-indulgent mother who drags her child from city to city, walking out on jobs and imposing on friends until their money runs out and their friends can no longer put up with uninvited guests. They end at Aunt Mercy's (which seems to be on the Eastern Shore of Maryland) and that

is where Henley at last finds security and stability, refusing to go yet again with Patti when she quits a job and decides on another impulsive move. This is not a story in which plot is paramount, but it is a tremendously moving book, with the first-person viewpoint giving an immediacy and poignancy to Henley's dilemma as the daughter in a mother-daughter relationship in which the mother is less mature than her child. Fine characterization, fluid writing.

1083   Rogers, Jean. *Goodbye, My Island;* illus. by Rie Munoz. Greenwillow, 1983. 82-15816. Trade ed. ISBN 0-688-01964-1; Library ed. ISBN 0-688-01965-X. 83p. Trade ed. $9.00; Library ed. $8.59.

5–6   The story of some recent events in Alaskan history is told through the fictional account of twelve-year-old Esther Atoolik, who begins with the statement that she is the happiest girl in Alaska. She is happy because the summer in Nome is over and she is returning to her beloved tribal home, King Island, along with the other islanders. The book is set in 1964, when a government decision led to the closing of the school on the small, rocky island in the Bering Sea. Seen through Esther's eyes, it is a touching story of a people who must leave the homeland they love, and in the course of it the reader learns of the cultural patterns, the intricate communal relationships, the pride and love in an Eskimo family.

1084   Rosenberg, Maxine B. *Being Adopted;* illus. with photographs by George Ancona. Lothrop, 1984. 83-17522. Library ed. ISBN 0-688-02673-7; Trade ed. ISBN 0-688-02672-9. 43p. Library ed. $9.12; Trade ed. $10.00.

3–5   In a text illustrated with many photographs of good quality, the author stresses the problems adoptive children—especially those from other countries or those who look markedly different from other members of their families—have in adjusting to their new homes. The emphasis is positive here, assuring readers of the love and permanence of the adoptive relationship; the text is well organized and simply written; an appended note is addressed to adults, discussing contemporary adoption patterns.

1085   Rosenberg, Maxine B. *My Friend Leslie;* photographs by George Ancona. Lothrop, 1983. 82-12734. Trade ed. ISBN 0-688-01690-1; Library ed. ISBN 0-688-01691-X. 42p. Trade ed. $9.50; Library ed. $8.59.

K–2   In a photodocumentary about a child with multiple handicaps, the text is narrated by Leslie's best friend and kindergarten classmate Karin. Leslie is legally blind, has some hearing loss, a cleft palate, muscular disability, and ptosis of the eyelids. She's needed surgery several times, and she's a merry, friendly child whose classmates help her when help is needed, accept her as she is, and enjoy her company. The book should help children appreciate the fact that the differences between those who are handicapped and those who are not are superficial, and it's a testament to mainstreaming. Told in a direct, simple style that is convincing as the voice of a kindergartner, this has a good balance of information and casual prattle.

1086   **Rosenthal,** Gary. *Everybody's Soccer Book.* Scribner, 1981. 81-9230. ISBN 0-684-17295-X. 354p. illus. with photographs. $19.95.

6–   Written by a professor of physical education who is also a former soccer coach and sports writer, this is a book in which the beginner can find basic facts, the seasoned player can find excellent advice on both individual and team play, and the fan can wallow happily in soccer history. The history comes first and includes facts about the evolution of the sport and about some of soccer's dramatic moments, particularly in World Cup play. Rosenthal discusses tactics and systems of play, advocates soccer as a sport for women, describes common injuries and injury prevention as well as training exercises, and concludes with a detailed explanation of the rules, penalties and procedures of soccer. There's a mass of material here, and the print is small, but the full coverage, authoritative and lucid writing, and logical arrangement of subject matter amply compensate. Diagrams of official soccer signals, a glossary, a list of World Cup competitions, and an index are appended.

1087   **Ross,** Frank Xavier. *The Tin Lizzie; a Model-Making Book.* Lothrop, 1980. 80-14482. Trade ed. ISBN 0-688-41931-3; Library ed. ISBN 0-688-51931-8. 192p. illus. Trade ed. $8.95; Library ed. $8.59.

5–9   Although Ross provides basic information about materials and tools at the beginning of the text, this is not a book for beginning model buffs. The instructions are clear, but they are extensive, often procedurally complex, and the drawn-to-scale diagrams require careful interpretation; the step-by-step instructions in print are not matched by step-by-step diagrams. The models (1909 Touring Car, 1913 Pickup Truck, 1913 Runabout, and 1914 Speedster) are made of construction paper and rigid cardboard or matting board, with smaller parts made of matchsticks, toothpicks, woodstrips, and wire. Materials for decorating parts or holding them together are just as easily available as the basic materials.

1088   **Ross,** Pat. *Molly and the Slow Teeth;* illus. by Jerry Milord. Lothrop, 1980. 79-28644. Trade ed. ISBN 0-688-41962-3; Library ed. ISBN 0-688-51962-8. 42p. Trade ed. $6.95; Library ed. $6.67.

1–2   How frustrating, how demeaning! The only person in second grade who hadn't lost a tooth, Molly yearned to have her name on the Tooth Chart that showed how everyone in class had lost their teeth. She tried a little white stone under her pillow to fool the Tooth Fairy and found a dime and a note that told her good fakes earned a dime, but only for a real tooth would she get a quarter. She tied a string to a doorknob but decided not to try that method. One tooth wiggled but just wouldn't come out. Finally, her tooth stuck in an apple: joy! triumph! a quarter! And, at last, a spot on the Tooth Chart. Slightly scrawly line and wash drawings illustrate a modest, child-centered story that should provide, both because of the subject and the simple, direct writing, enjoyable fare for beginning independent readers.

1089   **Ross,** Pat. *Your First Airplane Trip;* by Pat and Joel Ross; illus. by Lynn Wheeling. Lothrop, 1981. 80-22642. Trade ed. ISBN 0-688-41989-5; Library ed. ISBN 0-688-51989-X. 34p. Trade ed. $7.95; Library ed. $7.63.

K–2   Although there are minor inaccuracies in the cartoon style drawings, they have a cheerful air that fits nicely with the restrained enthusiasm of the writing. The use of second person draws the audience into a participatory attitude, as the authors describe everything but everything, from boarding to reunion (with what appears to be grandparents) at the end of the journey. Two children travel alone here, and they learn all about the details of a flight.

1090   **Ross,** Tony. *I'm Coming to Get You!;* written and illus. by Tony Ross. Dial, 1984. 84-5831. ISBN 0-8037-01195-5. 26p. $10.95.

3–6 yrs.   Jagged lines, brilliant colors, and strange life forms appear in the illustrations for a story about a terrible hairy monster (sharp teeth, green horns, hairy body, i.e. all the usual accoutrements) who wreaks havoc on another planet and then decides to fly to Earth. There the monster finds Tommy Brown on its radar screen and roars the threat of the title. Tommy, meanwhile, peers anxiously about for monsters as he prepares for bed—and a surprise ending, visually specific, should assure members of the lap audience that it's all a joke and that there's really nothing to fear. Fresh, funny, dramatic, and appealing.

1091   **Rounds,** Glen. *Mr. Yowder and the Train Robbers;* written and illus. by Glen Rounds. Holiday, 1981. 81-2198. ISBN 0-8234-0394-7. 44p. $7.95.

3–5   "And here, for the first time, is the true and unadorned account," Rounds begins, and tells his version of the shoot-out in which our hero faced the desperados, including the part played by twenty-seven rattlesnakes. Thus begins another tall-tale Yowder romp during which he teaches a rattlesnake to tie itself into knots as shown in a Boy Scout Manual and uses his snake friends to help recover the loot (U.S. mail) that the four villains have stolen. To add to the joy of this breezy, funny story are the deft and comic line drawings and an engaging surprise ending.

1092   **Rounds,** Glen. *Mr. Yowder and the Windwagon;* written and illus. by Glen Rounds. Holiday House, 1983. 83-6183. ISBN 0-8234-0499-4. 43p. $8.95.

3–5   Another yeasty tall tale about the ingenious painter, inventor, and manipulator, Xenon Zebulon Yowder, again illustrated by the ebullient, scraggly sketches that are this author-illustrator's trademark, is just as funny as its predecessors. Here Mr. Yowder, while painting signs for a Missouri River steamboat, conceived the idea of putting sails on a wagon, since the westward-bound covered wagons moved so slowly. On his contraption's maiden voyage across the plains there were local dignitaries who, as the windwagon went faster and faster, howled their wish to be let off; but there was no way to stop and all aboard suffered with Mr. Yowder as the vehicle flew into soldiers, Indians, and a herd of stampeding buffalo. This ingenious extravaganza has action, humor, and a bland style that's in nice contrast to the nonsense of the plot.

1093   **Rounds,** Glen. *The Morning the Sun Refused to Rise;* written and illus. by Glen Rounds. Holiday House, 1984. 83-49033. ISBN 0-8234-0514-1. 43p. $9.95.

4–6   Rounds contributes another hilarious tall tale to the Paul Bunyan legend, a yeasty performance enhanced by comical and economical line drawings. When a great blizzard caused the axle of the North/South poles to freeze, the world stopped turning and the sun never rose. It was the King of Sweden who thought of calling in Paul Bunyan, whose cogitations finally produced an ingenious plan for dripping hot bear oil (from frozen polar bears) down the shaft of the axle and for using fermenting sourdough as rocket power to push off from the Rockies to the Appalachians (thus creating the Midwest) and start the world spinning again. The writing style is bland and witty, and the exaggeration and nonsense of the plot are in effective contrast to the style.

1094   **Roy,** Ron. *Awful Thursday;* illus. by Lillian Hoban. Pantheon, 1979. 78-14049. 41p. (I Am Reading Books) Trade ed. $3.95; Library ed. $4.99 net.

1–2   If beginning independent readers can ignore the probability that the protagonist couldn't tell, by the weight of the bag he was carrying, that his shopping bag held only an empty box, they should really enjoy the crisp, humorous dialogue and the familiar situation of trying to adjust to an Awful Truth. Jack, going home with his teacher's tape recorder in a bag, stops to retrieve a friend's ball; when he turns back, his bag is flattened and he's convinced a bus has run over it. The advice of friends and siblings doesn't help a bit; Jack broods and loses his appetite. And then his teacher calls—just what he'd been dreading—and apologizes for forgetting to put the tape recorder into the box she'd given him. O blessed reprieve! The Hoban illustrations add humor, and the nicely structured story is direct and simple.

1095   **Roy,** Ron. *Three Ducks Went Wandering;* illus. by Paul Galdone. Seabury, 1979. 78-12629. ISBN 0-8164-3231-7. 30p. $8.95.

3–6   Somewhat in the style of Pat Hutchins' *Rosie's Walk*, three ducklings
yrs.   scurry about, oblivious to what is happening behind them. In this case
 *   it's a series of predatory forays—and each time the bull—or fox, or snake—gets close, the ducklings blithely do just exactly the right thing, unaware of danger at their backs. There's a repeat pattern that encour-

ages listener-participation, as the ducks wander "right in front of . . ." the predator, and a nice ending, when they go back to the barnyard and are "right in front of (turn page) . . . THEIR MOTHER!" placidly she notes that they must need a nap and takes them under her wing. Action, fun, good pace, and the lively humorous pictures, featuring foxes with super-leers and the angriest bull for miles around, combine to create a totally engaging picture book.

1096   **Rubin,** Mark. *The Orchestra;* illus. by Alan Daniel. Douglas & McIntyre, 1984. ISBN 0-88899-009-X. 40p. $10.95.

2–4   After some introductory, slightly poetic, remarks about music ("All of these sounds are part of Nature's music," referring to wind, rain, and birdsong) the author gets down to business, describing the roles of conductor and composer, the makeup of the orchestra, and the several instruments in each "family" of musical instruments. There's a brief reference to a rehearsal, and then the theretofore rather scruffy-looking musicians appear, resplendent, in a final double-page spread, in performance. Both audience and performers are multi-ethnic in lively line and wash drawings, which have comic touches but are scrupulously realistic in the depiction of orchestral instruments.

1097   **Ruby,** Lois. *This Old Man.* Houghton, 1984. 84-14258. ISBN 0-395-36563-5. 195p. $11.95.

7–10   Greta herself doesn't understand why she is so strongly attracted to the hospital room of Old Man, as his family calls him. An imperious ninety, Old Man is the grandfather of Wing, a Chinese-American who becomes Greta's friend. Living in a home for girls because of her mother's situation, Greta receives support from other residents at the shelter as well as therapeutic counseling; her mother is a prostitute whose protector has plans for Greta, now that she's sixteen. Ruby handles this with dignity and perception, and she knits the facets of Greta's life with skill. The characterization is strong, the narrative flow steady, the style and structure by far the best of Ruby's novels to date.

1098   **Ruby,** Lois. *What Do You Do in Quicksand?* Viking, 1979. 79-14461. ISBN 0-670-75815-9. 199p. $9.95.

8–10   Far from a run-of-the-mill novel for young adults, this strong and moving story is told alternately by Matt and Leah; he's seventeen, an unwed father who has insisted on taking the baby girl whose mother was ready to give her up for adoption; she's fifteen and lives with an elderly, loving stepfather. Leah's mother is dead, her natural father has disappeared from her life, and she's buried her memories of an earlier stepfather who abused her sexually. All of Leah's love fastens on Matt's baby, Barbara, and she does her utmost to convince him that he should give her the baby. Matt doesn't like or trust Leah, but he finds it useful to let her give him help in caring for Barbara—until it becomes clear that Leah's obsessed, and indeed she takes the baby to her home, locks herself in a room she's stealthily equipped with gear for the child, and refuses to come out. Leah has a breakdown and is hospitalized, following which she has long-needed therapy and tells her doctor about the abusive stepfather, taking her first step toward stability, even accepting the fact that Matt is moving away and taking the baby out of her life. No sweetness and light here, but a trenchant picture of a disturbed adolescent that evolves believably as Leah's obsession grows and those around her realize that her tenacity is more than eccentric behavior. Well-structured and paced, with good characterization and dialogue and a candid exploration of human relationships.

1099   **Ruckman,** Ivy. *The Hunger Scream.* Walker, 1983. 83-6522. ISBN 0-8027-6514-9. 175p. $11.95.

7–10   In this novel about anorexia nervosa, Lily fits all the criteria for predisposition: middle-class affluence, conformity, achievement, good relations with her parents, adolescence. One other factor influences her: a desire to impress the boy next door, Daniel, when he comes home from college. Daniel's family is black, and although Lily's parents have always gotten along well with them, they don't approve of Lily's affection for Daniel, who loves Lily as a friend but is not in love with her. The writing isn't flawless, but Ruckman does a fine job of showing the progress of Lily's illness (and of her therapy and recovery) from the anorectic's viewpoint. More than most stories on this subject, this also shows the extent to which families must participate in the recovery program by being willing to discuss and accept changes in their own behavior and relationships.

1100   **Ruckman,** Ivy. *Night of the Twisters.* Crowell, 1984. 83-46168. Library ed. ISBN 0-690-04409-1; Trade ed. ISBN 0-690-04408-9. 153p. Library ed. $10.89; Trade ed. $11.50.

5–7   Both of his parents are out of the house when the tornado hits; Dan and his friend Arthur save their own lives and that of Dan's baby brother when the house crashes down over their heads. There is a long, tense series of encounters and disasters as Dan and Arthur try (successfully) to contact other members of their families, rescue an elderly neighbor, get news of friends and grandparents, and face—like others in their Nebraska town—the ravages wrought by the twisters that have hit it. Ruckman does a good job of creating and maintaining suspense, produces dialogue that sounds appropriate for a stress situation, and gives her characters some depth and differentiation.

1101   **Rudström,** Lennart. *A Family;* illus. by Carl Larsson. Putnam, 1980. 79-14291. ISBN 0-399-20700-7. 32p. $7.95.

5–
*   As in *A Home* and *A Farm,* the oversize pages are filled with the beautiful paintings of one of Sweden's most eminent artists. The text gives

information, on a facing page, about each picture and, in a set-off column in smaller type, small insets of sketches or etchings by Larsson, again with explanatory text; here the commentator often includes facts about the artist's technique. The full-page pictures, in soft color, are almost all of Larsson's wife and children, and they are delectable. The Victorian dress and architecture, the fidelity of detail, the humor and tenderness of mood, make the book a visual experience that is artistically instructive; at the same time, it has the warmth and intimacy of a family album.

1102   **Rylant,** Cynthia. *Waiting to Waltz: A Childhood;* illus. by Stephen Gammell. Bradbury, 1984. 84-11030. ISBN 0-02-778000-7. 47p. $10.95.

6–8   Soft, mysteriously misty pencil drawings illustrate a cycle of thirty poems that describe a girl's childhood in a small town. Most of the poems are about other people, animals, or the various problems and pleasures of growing up, establishing an identity and achieving status. Psychologically sound, perhaps more adult than childlike in its nostalgic appeal, the poetry (free-flowing and almost conversational) only occasionally rises to that high vision or felicitous phrasing that marks the best in poetic writing, but it is consistently of good quality.

1103   **Rylant,** Cynthia. *When I Was Young in the Mountains;* illus. by Diane Goode. Dutton, 1982. 81-5359. ISBN 0-525-42525-X. 26p. $9.95.

K–3   Based on the author's memories of an Appalachian childhood, this is a nostalgic piece as evocatively illustrated as it is told; the soft blues and greens and duns of the hills and trees merge and blur as background for the simple, sturdy figures. There is no story line, but a series of memories, each beginning, "When I was young in the mountains . . ." as the author reminisces about the busy, peaceful life of an extended family and their community. Quiet, almost static, this is given appeal by the warmth and contentment that emerge from an account of daily satisfaction and small, occasional joys, described with appropriate simplicity.

1104   **Sachs,** Marilyn. *Bus Ride;* illus. by Amy Rowen. Dutton, 1980. 79-23596. Trade ed. ISBN 0-525-27325-5; Paper ed. ISBN 0-525-45048-3. 107p. (Skinny Books) Trade ed. $7.95; Paper ed. $2.50.

6–9   All of the story is told in dialogue between Judy and Ernie as they ride a bus to or from school, and Sachs deftly develops characterization and story line through the conversations. Judy isn't popular; Ernie's never had a date, but he has a crush on Judy's friend Karen. He arranges a double date, and even has an evening alone with Karen, but by the time this happens, he and Judy have become close friends who confide in each other, and the discovery (his and the reader's) at the end that it's Judy he's really interested in makes a satisfying conclusion to a believable boy-meets-girl story. Sachs is most ingenious in her use of dialogue, and it is a real tour de force that such use accomplishes a double purpose, for the literary device also serves to make this very easy to read; this is one of the best books published yet as part of a high-interest/low-vocabulary series.

1105   **Sachs,** Marilyn. *The Fat Girl.* Dutton, 1983. 83-11697. ISBN 0-525-44076-3. 176p. $10.95.

7–10   Even though his beloved Norma chides him for his disparagement of
 *   the fat girl, Ellen, Jeff can't stop sneering at her. When Ellen overhears one cutting remark, Jeff is ashamed, tries to make amends, and spends a lot of time with Ellen after she threatens suicide. That's the end of Jeff's relationship with Norma and the beginning of Jeff's switch to the Pygmalion role, as he takes over an adoring Ellen's life. She obeys happily but she becomes more independent while Jeff falls deeply in love, needing to be needed, distraught when Ellen begins to make her own decisions. This would be outstanding as a novel even if it had no other psychological laminations, but it has. The intricacies of Jeff's relationships with his tense mother and his father (remarried) and the significance of the link between those relationships and Jeff's libidinal investment in Ellen are expressed with subtlety and insight, but they do not interfere with the narrative flow of a moving story with depth and insight.

1106   **Sachs,** Marilyn. *Fleet-footed Florence;* illus. by Charles Robinson. Doubleday, 1981. 76-56330. Trade ed. ISBN 0-385-12745-6; Library ed. ISBN 0-385-12746-4. 44p. Trade ed. $8.95; Library ed. $9.90.

K–2   She didn't excel at batting or throwing or catching, but Florence could run like a blue streak, and her magnificent tags brought her team, the North Dakota Beavers, into series contention the very first year she played for them. Her greatest rival was Fabulous Frankie, the catcher for the Yankees; she made him so angry when she caught every fly ball he hit the fans called him Frankie the Yankee Flipper. Then they ran into each other. Literally. It was instant love, and it led to marriage; Frankie joined the Beavers but was always over-shadowed by his wife, who set an all-time record for RCI's, Runs Carried In. ("Of course, she had to make sure that each player she carried in touched base before she did.") This bubbly spoof ends with a touch of magic and a dash of mystery, but it's the flagrant, tall-tale humor that is most appealing in a non-sexist baseball story that will appeal, no doubt, to many readers older than the read-aloud audience designated by the publisher. The blue-washed line drawings echo the ebullience and humor of the story.

1107   **Sachs,** Marilyn. *Hello . . . Wrong Number;* illus. by Pamela Johnson. Dutton, 1981. 81-3281. ISBN 0-525-31629-9. 106p. (Skinny Books). $9.75.

6–10   As she did in *Bus Ride,* Sachs tells her story just by the dialogue between two adolescents, an effective way to appeal to the target audience for this series, the slow or reluctant older reader. The subject is one with universal appeal, too: boy-girl relations, and it's handled with humor. Angie, nervously calling the popular boy on whom she has a crush, Jim, gets the wrong number but finds the party she's called (another Jim) friendly. They talk every evening, are convinced they are in love (sight unseen) and almost break up when Angie finds out that Jim's neglected to tell her that he has a very large nose about which he's been teased all his life—and that he's fibbed about a few other things. However, after a little plea bargaining, Angie says she still cares and they agree to meet at last. This is that rarity, a story written for a high-low series that has style and ingenuity enough to be a good read for all readers.

1108   **Sadler,** Catherine Edwards, ad. *Treasure Mountain: Folktales from Southern China*; illus. by Cheng Mung Yun. Atheneum, 1982. 82-1805. ISBN 0-689-30941-4. 66p. $11.95.

4–6   Six tales of the Chuang, Han, T'ung, and Yao tribes are retold in a smooth, flowing style and are handsomely illustrated with beautifully detailed pencil drawings, serenely composed. Several of the tales are long and incorporate several themes (filial piety, kindness to others, magical objects, greed punished, etc.) and some will surely be familiar to lovers of the genre, since they have appeared in picture book versions. Nice to read aloud or alone, and a good source for storytelling.

1109   **St. George,** Judith. *Mystery at St. Martin's.* Putnam, 1979. 79-17547. ISBN 0-399-20702-3. 151p. $7.95.

5–7   Ruth Saunders, twelve, is the narrator of a mystery novel that is well balanced by material about family and peers, but has suspense and (for once) a logical reason for the protagonist's investigating on her own. The mystery: why are counterfeit bills being traced back to St. Martin's, the church of which Ruth's father is rector? The logical reason for Ruth's exposing herself to danger: her father has told her not to meddle in church affairs. Ruth keeps meddling; she suspects almost every adult who is a major character and active in church affairs. St. George tosses in such issues as rehabilitation of criminals (her father hires one), women in the clergy (her father's parishioners object because he wants to hire a woman as his assistant) and how old one should be to have pierced ears. A well-paced story, with good dialogue and a concluding episode in which Ruth is trapped, alone in the church basement, with the counterfeiter.

1110   **Sallis,** Susan. *Secret Places of the Stairs.* Harper, 1984. 83-48442. Library ed. ISBN 0-06-025147-6; Trade ed. ISBN 0-06-025142-5. 160p. Library ed. $10.89; Trade ed. $10.95.

6–9   Cass is the narrator in a story in which she makes a series of discoveries about her family that affect her deeply. She's already dependent on her friends to help her weather the strain of living with a stepmother with whom she's uncomfortable and of visiting a mother who thinks Cass is trying to break up her new marriage. Cass learns that her mother had once been in a mental hospital, and that she herself has a sister hidden in a mental institution; she decides she will visit her sister and learns to love her. Because of Cass, both parents come to see her sister before she dies. The story is serious, at times depressing, but it has integrity and compassion to hold readers, and the complexity of the situation it presents is alleviated by the often-yeasty conversations between Cass and her lively best friend, Nadine.

1111   **Salvadori,** Mario George. *Building; The Fight Against Gravity;* illus. by Saralinda Hooker and Christopher Ragus. Atheneum, 1979. 79-14325. ISBN 0-689-50144-7. 152p. $10.95.

7–
*

Fine line drawings, not always labeled but carefully placed to best coordinate with the text, illustrate an excellent introduction to the basic principles and problems of the architect. Salvadori writes in a direct style, serious but not dry or heavy, and eschews technical jargon, although he uses correct technical terminology; the text is explicit and the material logically organized, describing the forces of tension and compression, the characteristics of natural and man-made building materials, and the ways in which architects and engineers overcome such natural forces as gravity and wind pressure. The author discusses not only general principles of building bridges and buildings but also the details: building foundations, the use of the arch, making floors smooth, stabilizing cables, the use of the truss, the construction of domes, pneumatic roofs. A relative index gives access to the interesting information that Salvadori has made easily comprehensible.

1112   **Sampson,** Fay. *The Watch on Patterick Fell.* Greenwillow, 1980. 79-20840. ISBN 0-688-80261-3. 106p. $7.95.

6–9

A suspense story, set in northwest England, that could be happening now or set in the future, combines a nicely-constructed, lively plot with some smoothly integrated discussions of the pros and cons of the operation of nuclear power plants and the problems of storing radioactive waste. Characterization is deft; the final episodes of the book are taut and dramatic, if not wholly credible, but the powered structure of Sampson's writing is such that one almost believes in the solution. Roger reveres his father, director of the Patterick Fell installation where nuclear waste is buried and where the staff is working toward safer means of disposal. He understands the importance of Dad's work (and that of their mother, who also works at the site) but his younger sister does not. Elspeth is thirteen, and angry about the dangers of the site; she joins a protesting mob. Still, when Dad sends his family away to live in the safety of false identities and thus escape the wrath of the evergrowing protest movement, it is Elspeth who runs away to return to Patterick Fell—and thus puts them all in danger.

1113   **Sancha,** Sheila. *The Luttrell Village: Country Life in the Middle Ages.* Crowell, 1983. 82-45588. Trade ed. ISBN 0-690-04323-6; Library ed. ISBN 0-690-04324-4. 64p. Trade ed. $12.95; Library ed. $12.89.

5–9   Profusely illustrated with black and white drawings, line and wash, this is a detailed description of life in an English village as it was in the year 1328, Irnham Village. At that time it was called Gerneham and was owned by Sir Geoffrey Luttrell; the book is based in large part on drawings made at the time and included in the Luttrell Psalter, a rare volume in the British Library. The text and pictures together give a comprehensive picture of the arduous life of the villagers, of the panoply of Sir Geoffrey's procession when he came to visit his village, of the seasonal tasks and the division of labor. There is a glossary but no index, which limits but does not preclude reference use; the book should appeal especially to readers who are interested in the historical period and to students who are investigating the feudal system.

1114   **Sandburg,** Carl. *Rainbows Are Made;* comp. by Lee Bennett Hopkins; illus. by Fritz Eichenberg. Harcourt, 1982. 82-47934. ISBN 0-15-265480-1. 82p. $12.95.

4–   Carefully selected, this assemblage of Sandburg poems includes many that are not often included in collections of his work intended for young readers. The poems have been grouped in six sections: poems about people, about the night, about the sea, about nature, about everyday objects, and about words and language. The quality of the writing is matched by the strong, dramatic wood engravings, one for each section, and is set off by the spacious format. Title and first line indexes are provided.

1115   **Sandin,** Joan. *The Long Way To A New Land;* written and illus. by Joan Sandin. Harper, 1981. 80-8942. Trade ed. ISBN 0-06-025193-X; Library ed. ISBN 0-06-025194-8. 64p. (I-Can-Read-Books). Trade ed. $7.25; Library ed. $7.89.

1–3   Tinted with reds and blues, the softly-executed line and wash drawings have a simplicity and neatness that fit the simple style and structure of the text. The story gives just enough details to help the primary grades reader understand some of the reasons immigrants had for leaving their homes and coming to American (in this case, a drought and a crop failure in Sweden) and some of the problems they had en route. The story focuses on Carl Erik, one of the children in the family that responds to a letter from relatives in the United States; Pappa sells the farm and uses the money to buy tickets to New York via Liverpool. It isn't always easy to make history comprehensible to younger children, and Sandin does a nice job of it.

1116   **Sandler,** Martin W. *The Story of American Photography.* Little, 1979. 78-24025. ISBN 0-316-77021-3. 318p. illus. $16.95.

7–   Daguerrotypes, stereographs, dry-plate, wet-plate, tintype . . . all of the old techniques of the early days are described and pictured in an interesting history that moves from stiffly posed groups and stern portraits to the documentary photography and the news pictures, the art photography and advertising photography of today. Not that the 19th century didn't have its landscape artists; early photographers were quick to realize the opportunity the camera afforded. While Sandler does not ignore inventions and improvements in film, cameras, and accessories, his emphasis is on the artists and either the techniques or the subjects (or both) that made their work distinctive. The writing is sequential, serious but not stolid, and very nicely integrated with the illustrations, which are profuse and superb. A substantial list of suggestions for further reading and an extensive index (in very small print) are appended.

1117   **Sargent,** Sarah. *Weird Henry Berg.* Crown, 1980. 80-13651. ISBN 0-517-54137-8. 113p. $7.95.

4–6   In a smooth meshing of fantasy and realism, an economically structured book strikes a new variation on an old theme: the existence of dragons in the contemporary world. Henry Berg doesn't know that the "lizard" he has is a baby dragon; all he knows is that his odd, endearing pet has hatched from an ancient egg that had belonged to his great-grandfather. Elderly Mille Levenson doesn't know Henry, but she gets in touch with him because she has had a visit from a dragon, a sophisticated creature sent over from Wales to find the baby that had been left behind a century ago. Henry wants to keep his pet; Millie, knowing that the dragon is in danger, wants to get him back to Wales. The conflict is resolved, the mission completed, and the story concluded with a logic that is right for the parameters of the fantasy. The writing has good pace and suspense, save for occasional daydreaming passages (Henry's) that slow the story a bit, but it's a fine and fresh adventure tale.

1118   **Sattler,** Helen Roney. *Dinosaurs of North America;* illus. by Anthony Rao. Lothrop, 1981. 80-27411. ISBN 0-688-51952-0. 151p. $10.95.

5–9   An oversize book gives intensive and extensive coverage to the topic, and is illustrated with carefully detailed drawings; comparative size is at times evident in the drawings but always available from the text. The author describes the three periods of the Mesozoic Era, with the topographical and climatic changes that affected the drifting continents and the life that existed on them. Each type of dinosaur is carefully described, with specific body measurements included, as well as facts about appearance and behavior; habitat is also discussed. A list of sites, by location, of North American dinosaur discoveries is provided, as are a reading list and a relative index. A comprehensive book, this, with reference use.

1119   **Say,** Allen. *The Ink-Keeper's Apprentice.* Harper, 1979. 78-20264. 185p. Trade ed. $7.95; Library ed. $7.79 net.

7–9   The setting is Tokyo, the time is five years after World War II, and thirteen-year-old Kiyoi tells the story. His parents are divorced, and the grandmother with whom he has lived has given him an allowance so that he can live alone, visiting her weekly. Kiyoi's ambition to be a cartoonist so impresses Noro Shinpei, Japan's greatest cartoonist, that he takes the boy on as apprentice. As Kiyoi describes the small events of the next few years, he gives a good picture of an adolescent growing toward maturity: gaining independence, gaining proficiency as an artist, adapting to changing circumstances, and making the decision to accept his father's offer to move (as Say did when he was sixteen) to the United States. This is Say's first book for older children, and although it lacks a strong story line it is full of incidents that give it vitality, it is smoothly written, and it has strong characterization.

1120   **Scarry,** Huck. *Balloon Trip: A Sketchbook.* Prentice-Hall, 1983. 82-23002. ISBN 0-13-055939-3. 68p. $10.95.

4–6   Profusely and effectively illustrated with black and white sketches, this oversize book describes in detail the author's journey with a Swiss balloonist, giving facts about how the balloon is constructed and flown. This is followed by a brief history of ballooning, and then by an account of a second flight, this time in a hot-air balloon (the first had been a hydrogen balloon) and then by a short bibliography and a list of ballooning organizations. The writing is informal, informative, and occasionally humorous, with a good sense of narrative.

1121   **Scheffer,** Victor B. *The Amazing Sea Otter;* illus. by Gretchen Daiber. Scribner, 1981. 81-4557. ISBN 0-684-16878-2. 144p. $11.95.

7–
 *   Black and white illustrations that have a textural quality and meticulous detail reminiscent of the animal portraits by John Schoenherr add minimally to the information given by the text but are extremely decorative. The text is impressive: authoritative, eminently readable, informative, and accurate. Scheffer, a specialist in marine mammalogy, has that rare combination of attributes for writing superb science books: an almost-lyric, controlled, flowing writing style, and a breadth of knowledge and experience. Here he describes the life of sea otters by taking a newborn animal and tracing its development in captivity and in the wild; the account is enlivened by conversations among the people who track, test, or trace the sea otter.

1122   **Schlee,** Ann. *Ask Me No Questions.* Holt, 1982. 81-6932. ISBN 0-03-061523-2. 228p. $14.50.

5–8   In a touching story, set in England during the Victorian Era, Schlee has so consistently kept the viewpoints and mores and language of the period that the book has no obtrusive or contemporary notes. It is based on a true institution, run by Mr. Drouet; Drouet in the story, as in life, is the master of a school for workhouse children, advertised as a place where the young will be well taken care of and will learn useful trades. In fact, as Laura, the protagonist of Schlee's story, learns, the children are barely fed and clothed while Drouet grows plump and prosperous. Laura and her brother have been sent out of London because of the cholera epidemic of 1847, and they stay—next door to Drouet's establishment—with their harsh, domineering aunt. Secretly, after they have met three of the starving children eating from Aunt Bolinger's pig trough at night, Laura brings food. She also secretly suffers, because to get the food she steals and lies. The book moves to a tragic conclusion, with cholera at Drouet's and the deaths of many of the children. The story is broadened by some sub-plots and deepened by the strong characterization. Drouet (again, as in life) is tried and found innocent.

1123   **Schlee,** Ann. *The Vandal.* Crown, 1981. 81-2859. ISBN 0-517-54424-5. 188p. $8.95.

7–10   In an intriguing novel set in a future England, the whole society is orga-
  *   nized on the principle that it is dangerous to the individual and to the society to remember the past. Each person has a memory machine that gives only enough information each day to enable one to function; all memories, even recognizing other people, are gone after three days. Paul is a maverick, starting a fire at one time, vandalizing property at another, but failing to recall what he has done or to understand the motivation for his rebellion. At the close of this memorable and deftly developed story, winner of the 1980 Guardian Award, he has found a friend who also is a misfit, a girl who remembers the past and therefore is an outcast, and there is an encouraging note as Paul and Sharon escape from the penal camps to which they have been sent.

1124   **Schlein,** Miriam. *Project Panda Watch;* illus. by Robert Shetterly and with photographs. Atheneum, 1984. 84-2914. ISBN 0-689-31071-4. 87p. $11.95.

4–6   Although this is primarily about the project set up in a mountainous Chinese nature preserve, and describes the ways in which pandas are caught for tagging (radio collars) and observed in the wild, it also gives a considerable amount of information that is more general. The text describes the panda's habitat and feeding habits, the inroads on panda population by destruction of bamboo forests, by natural causes or by people, and the many and often abortive attempts to raise and breed pandas in the world's zoos. A bibliography, glossary, and index add to the usefulness of an interesting book, well organized and well written.

1125   **Schuchman,** Joan. *Two Places to Sleep;* illus. by Jim LaMarche. Carolrhoda Books, 1979. 79-88201. ISBN 0-87614-108-4. 32p. $4.95.

K-2   So that seven-year-old David, who tells the story, could have the security of the same home and school, it had been decided, when his parents divorced, that he would stay with Dad, since Mom was moving to a city apartment to be near her job. Black and white softly shaded drawings (reminiscent of but not as skillful as Shimin's work) echo the emphasis of the story: both parents love David and want what's best for him. The text makes it clear that David is not unhappy with Dad, and that he likes their housekeeper; it's just that he misses Mom. She assures him that nothing he might do would bring about a reunion, that it's situation between the adults, and that she loves David just the way he is. A very supportive, rational treatment, nicely told at a comprehensible level, and making it clear that parental love—in this family—is rock-steady.

1126   **Schwartz,** Alvin, ad. *More Scary Stories to Tell in the Dark*; collected from folklore and retold by Alvin Schwartz; illus. by Stephen Gammell. Lippincott, 1984. 83-49494. Library ed. ISBN 0-397-32082-5; Trade ed. ISBN 0-397-32081-7. 100p. Library ed. $10.89; Trade ed. $11.50.

4–7   Like the first book, *Scary Stories to Tell in the Dark*, this is an excellent source of short stories for telling as well as for reading. Again, Gammell's black and white illustrations manage to be both graceful and ghostly; again, Schwartz has picked tales that are dramatically effective, at times chilling. Notes on sources are provided, as is a divided bibliography.

1127   **Schwartz,** Alvin, comp. *Scary Stories to Tell in the Dark*; illus. by Stephen Gammell. Lippincott, 1981. 80-8728. Trade ed. ISBN 0-397-31926-6, Library ed. ISBN 0-397-31927-4; Paper ed. ISBN 0-397-31970-3. 111p. Trade ed. $8.25; Library ed. $7.89; Paper ed. $4.95.

4–7   The dramatic black and white illustrations, misty and eerie, are just right for a ghostly anthology; many of the stories include suggestions to the storyteller ("Turn out any lights," or "Now scream") and this is indeed a good source for the storyteller as well as for reading aloud or for independent reading. Almost all the tales and poems are brief; some are humorous; all have been chosen with care for effectiveness and variety. Notes on sources are included, as is a divided bibliography.

1128   **Schwartz,** Alvin, ad. *There Is a Carrot in My Ear*; illus. by Karen Ann Weinhaus. Harper, 1982. 80-8442. Trade ed. ISBN 0-06-025233-2; Library ed. ISBN 0-06-025234-0. 64 p. (I Can Read Books). Trade ed. $7.95; Library ed. $7.89.

1–2   Although the six noodlehead stories that Schwartz has adapted from diverse sources are not as substantial in these versions for beginning independent readers, they have lost none of their humor. As reconstructed here, they are six episodes in the life of a silly family; they go to the pool and spend a happy day despite the fact that there's no water in the pool; Grandpa earnestly sits on a pumpkin as the grocer had suggested, waiting for it to turn into a horse; Sam and Jane are convinced, when they see fireflies, that the mosquitos have come after them with flashlights, and so on. Red and yellow are used in the uncluttered illustrations of a pointy-faced family. Pared-down prose, large print, and a direct style add to the appeals of a book that is appropriate in its brevity and humor for younger readers.

1129   **Schwartz,** Alvin, comp. *Unriddling: All Sorts of Riddles to Puzzle Your Guessery;* illus. by Sue Truesdell. Lippincott, 1983. 82-48778. Trade ed. ISBN 0-397-32029-9; Library ed. ISBN 0-397-32030-2. 118p. Library ed. $9.89; Trade ed. $9.95.

4—   Riddle collector par excellence, folklorist Schwartz has made this volume useful as well as entertaining by dividing his puzzles into categories, some of which depend on visual interpretation, many of which are based on traditional American humor. The quality is high, and the compiler provides answers to the riddle jokes, punctuation riddles, rebus riddles, letter riddles, etc., as well as information about sources, notes on the puzzles, and a fairly extensive divided bibliography. In sum, although this is primarily a collection to be enjoyed by children, it is also a useful book for the student of folklore.

1130   **Schwartz,** Amy. *Bea and Mr. Jones;* written and illus. by Amy Schwartz. Bradbury, 1982. 81-18031. ISBN 0-87888-202-2. 32p. $8.95.

K–2   Bea Jones announces that she's tired of kindergarten and beanbag games and sitting on that dumb green rug. Her father counters with, "Do you think I like my job? I'm tired of running for the 7:45!" What, suggests her father, if they trade places? So Bea catches the 7:45 and Mr. Jones appears in kindergarten with a note for the teacher, then performs so well that he becomes teacher's pet. Bea, too, does well, producing such a good new commercial for Crumbly Crackers that the boss gives her a promotion. And if readers think that each goes back to the old niches, they're wrong. Mr. Jones has found his true milieu, and so has Bea. So, the story ends, if you saw a very big kid getting into the movies for half price, or if you remember a very short executive having lunch with your father, you know who they were. A nice treatment of role reversal, this junior tall tale is told with simplicity and humor, and is illustrated with soft pencil drawings that have pudgy people, nice textural quality, and some funny details, such as Mr. Jones, lying on the floor and using blocks to spell out "antidisestablishmentarianism."

1131   **Schwartz,** Delmore. *"I Am Cherry Alive,"* the Little Girl Sang; illus. by Barbara Cooney. Harper, 1979. 76-58708. 28p. Trade ed. $7.95; Library ed. $7.79 net.

4–7   The poem " 'I Am Cherry Alive,' the Little Girl Sang," was first published in a collection by Schwartz, *Summer Knowledge; New and Selected*
yrs.   *Poems (1938–1958)* and it celebrates the joy of being alive, of being one-
  *   self, of being a child. "I am red/I am gold/I am green/I am blue/I will

always be me/I will always be new!" is the ending, and Barbara Cooney concludes with a series of seasonal tone poems to illustrate these lines. The delicacy of detail, the tracery of leaves against the sky, of the luminous sky itself, and the paintings of the child (singing for amused adults, marveling at a winter landscape, sitting quietly near a green, still pool in summer, her nudity reflected in the dim water) are a marvelous extension of the affirmation of the poetry.

1132   **Schwartz,** Howard, ad. *Elijah's Violin & Other Jewish Fairy Tales;* illus. by Linda Heller. Harper, 1983. 82-48133. ISBN 0-06-015108-0. 302p. $14.95.

6–   An impressive anthology for adults and young adults can be used as a source for storytelling, although many of the tales are long and complex enough to need simplification if they are to be told to younger children. The stories have been collected from diverse sources, cited in an appended section that precedes the glossary. The stories combine traditional fairy tale themes and motifs, blending them with the legends and folklore of Jewish oral tradition; they are also infused with Biblical characters and religious beliefs (several princesses convert to Judaism, for example) and they are competently retold.

1133   **Scioscia,** Mary. *Bicycle Rider;* illus. by Ed Young. Harper, 1983. 82-47702. Trade ed. ISBN 0-06-025222-7; Library ed. ISBN 0-06-025223-5. 48p. Trade ed. $9.95; Library ed. $9.89.

2—4   Soft, almost blurry black and white illustrations that have a dramatic quality illustrate a story that is told with quiet understatement and in a straightforward style. It is based on a real character, the great black bicycle racer Marshall Taylor, who won national and international championships when bicycle racing was a popular spectator sport at the turn of the century. Scioscia has made a pleasant family story of an incident in which the young Marshall, working as an errand boy at a bicycle store in an Indiana town, is encouraged by the owner to enter his first race—and Marshall wins the annual Indianapolis ten-mile bicycle race.

1134   **Scott,** Jack Denton. *Alligator;* illus. with photographs by Ozzie Sweet. Putnam, 1984. 84-9927. ISBN 0-399-21011-3. 64p. $11.95.

5—   Although Scott's text is continuous, it is so carefully organized that the material seems always sequential and comprehensible. The photographs are interesting but rather more repetitive than most of Sweet's work, and very occasionally not clear. The book describes the species, giving facts about habits, habitat, reproduction, appearance, and qualities that have made the alligator survive since the Mesozoic Era. Scott also discusses the successful efforts to build up the alligator population and the laws that protect this durable reptile. An index is provided.

1135   **Scott,** Jack Denton. *The Book of the Pig;* illus. with photographs by Ozzie Sweet. Putnam, 1981. 80-28386. ISBN 0-399-20718-X. 64p. $8.95.

3–5   With frequent kudos from uninformed pig-lovers as well as from more scientific observers who attest to the intelligence, amicability, and natural (if belied) cleanliness of the pig, this informative text just—but just— avoids being fulsome. It avoids the pitfall by providing facts in a straightforward style, giving details about popular breeds, behavior patterns, mating, care of young, and temperament. The text is continuous, the print large, the illustrations of good quality, well-placed but not captioned.

1136   **Scott,** Jack Denton. *The Fur Seals of Pribilof;* photographs by Ozzie Sweet. Putnam, 1983. 83-4599. ISBN 0-399-20779-1. 60p. $10.95.

5–9   Every summer over four million seals travel, some of them thousands of miles, to the Pribilof Islands to breed and mate, a migratory pattern believed by scientists to have begun about thirty million years ago. Scott describes the ways in which the bulls establish territorial rights, fighting each other for the females who arrive later; he discusses courtship, mating, care of the young, and other aspects of this huge colony of fur seals; he describes the careless slaughter—now stemmed—that once threatened extinction of the species. Save for some water pictures, the photographs are remarkable in their clarity; the text is outstanding for the vivid and authoritative picture it gives of the seals' life cycle and behavior patterns.

1137   **Scott,** Jack Denton. *Orphans from the Sea;* illus. with photographs by Ozzie Sweet. Putnam, 1982. 82-409. ISBN 0-399-208585. 68p. $10.95.

5–7   Profusely illustrated by photographs of excellent quality, this description of a wildlife haven, the Suncoast Seabird Sanctuary, is divided into sections that correspond to the organization's four purposes: rescue, repair, recuperation, and release. Some of the many varieties of birds (and an occasional snake or turtle) have been hurt by natural causes, some (often unintentionally) by people. The sanctuary's dedicated staff and successful program are described in a text that is lively, sympathetic, and informative, its message loud and clear.

1138   **Sebestyen,** Ouida. *Far from Home.* Atlantic-Little, Brown, 1980. 80-18328. ISBN 0-316-779326. 204p. $8.95.

6—8   Salty was thirteen. He had no idea who his father was; his mother (a
 *   mute woman) was dead, as were his grandparents; he lived alone with his great-grandmother and they were facing eviction. He took the note his mother had left, telling him to go into town to the home of Tom and Babe Buckley, where she had worked for many years. "GO TO TOM BUCKLEY HE TAKE YOU IN LOVE HIM," it said. The boy and the old woman are taken in on sufferance, Salty determined to earn his keep; the house is an almost-bankrupt boarding house; there are six adults and Salty. It will probably be clear to the reader before it is understood by Salty that Tom is his father and that the fact must be kept

from Babe, who has had many miscarriages and who is loved and protected by her husband. This is not a childlike story, but should have
some of the same kind of appeal that *To Kill a Mockingbird* has had to
many adolescent and pre-adolescent readers: a vividly created micro-
cosm of society, an abundance of sentiment without sentimentality, and
a protagonist who is drawn with compassionate percipience. All of the
characters are drawn in depth, in a moving story in which several of
them change believably in response to the others. For some it develops
that the boarding house can never be a home; for Salty, once he accepts
the limitations that Tom puts on their relationship, it becomes a home.
While Salty is the only child in the story, he is the focal point; in him
are the passion for justice, the need for love and security, and the need
to identify and belong that all children feel. A fine novel.

1139   **Sebestyen,** Ouida. *Words By Heart.* Atlantic-Little, Brown, 1979. 78-
27847. 160p. $7.95.

5–7   Set in the Reconstruction Era, this is an impressive first novel about
race relationships and nonviolence, written in an easy, vigorous style
and candid in its depiction of discrimination. To escape prejudice, Lena's father and stepmother had moved to Bethel Springs, an all-white
community; there had been no problems until Lena won the school
spelldown, when they had the first hint of trouble, arriving home to
find someone had been there and committed an act of malicious damage. The serious problem comes when a white woman hires Lena's father to do some work that a lazy white man, Haney, had neglected,
and Haney is openly vindictive. Papa goes off for a few days to mend
fences for someone, and when he doesn't come home, Lena goes off to
find him. Shot by Haney's son, Lena's dying father urges her to take no
revenge, but to save the boy if she can. Thus Lena learns, as she has
learned so much from her father, to forgive. A most moving story about
a black family strong in their love and pride.

1140   **Sefton,** Catherine. *The Emma Dilemma;* illus. by Jill Bennett. Faber, 1983.
ISBN 0-571-11841-0. 93p. $8.95.

3–5   First published in England, this is both a fantasy and an entertaining
family story in which Emma is catapulted in and out of an odd situation
by a blow on her head. What emerges in between is another, identical
Emma—only this one, who claims *she's* the real Emma, is transparent.
Nobody else can see her, although the family cat is aware that there's
an Emma who smells right but is invisible. The two Emmas squabble
much of the time, but the Other Emma proves to be very useful: she
plays pranks on the real Emma's least favorite people—and some of the
time that includes her siblings. Nobody can quite understand what's
going on (except the real Emma) and it is all very amusing (if one-track)
and filled with well-paced action. A nice blend of fantasy and realism,
in a story written with vitality.

1141   **Segovia,** Andres. *Segovia; My Book of the Guitar; Guidance for the Beginner;*
by Andres Segovia and George Mendoza; illus. with photographs by
Gerhard Gscheidle. Collins, 1979. 79-10277. ISBN 0-529-05539-2. 64p.
$9.95.

5–   Although Segovia's foreword states ". . . I offer here a few exercises
and observations for further technical development to the student with
no access to competent instruction," the book is really for beginners; it
gives such rudimentary information as staff, clef, types of notes and
rests, other musical marks; provides diagrams on reading diagrams,
shows hand and finger positions, provides lessons for practicing on
each string, etc. It concludes with a series of short musical studies arranged and fingered by Segovia, and with a glossary of musical terms.
While some of the color photographs are uninformative, most of them
augment the text; the material is logically arranged and the instructions
and explanations clear. The instructional material is prefaced by some
rather rambling but endearing comments by Segovia.

1142   **Seidler,** Tor. *Terpin.* Farrar, 1982. 82-11734. ISBN 0-374-37413-9. 90p.
$8.95.

6–   Now a member of the Supreme Court, Terpin Taft is on his way back to
his home town for a celebration in his honor. He hasn't been back for
thirty years, and has never heard from his father in all that time. For
Terpin had been a bitter disappointment to his family, his friends, and
his teachers. As an adolescent, he had felt such guilt and remorse about
a well-meant lie that he had taken to always telling the truth—and he
had alienated everyone. There is a mystic note in the story, a sober assessment of ethical concepts, a wry commentary on the superficiality of
human beings and their relationships, and a rejection of some of the
common standards and practices in our society. There are laminations
of meaning in this smoothly crafted story, nuances that may best be appreciated by the special reader.

1143   **Selden,** Bernice. *The Mill Girls.* Atheneum, 1983. 83-2672. ISBN 0-689-
31005-6. 180p. $10.95.

7–10   Illustrated with photographs and reproductions of old prints, this well-
researched triple biography gives not only capable sketches of the lives
of the three women who worked in the textile mills of Lowell in the
middle and late nineteenth century, but also a vivid picture of the industrial town and the developments in working conditions and labor
relations. Lucy Larcom and Harriet Robinson were concerned about
working conditions, but much of their time went to literary pursuits in
those years in which the young mill operators avidly attended lectures,
belonged to self-improvement groups, and contributed to women's
magazines; both produced a number of books. By the time Sarah Bagley
became involved in writing, the deterioration in working conditions led
her to focus her writing on labor unrest; eventually she became a mem-

ber of a commune, a reformer, and the first woman telegraph operator in the country. An extensive divided bibliography and an index give access to a text that gives a clear picture of some of the changes provoked by the Industrial Revolution and of the active women who were affected by, and in turn had an effect on, its progress.

1144   **Selden,** George. *Chester Cricket's New Home;* illus. by Garth Williams. Farrar, 1983. 82-24206. ISBN 0-374-31240-0. 144p. $10.95.

3–5   In a sequel to the stories about Chester that began in 1960 with *A Cricket in Times Square,* both author and illustrator adhere to the standards of excellence and the appealing qualities that attracted earlier readers. [Here Chester loses the stump in which he has been housed when a hefty person sits on it.] All his animal friends offer hospitality, but their homes are not right for Chester, and it is through the diligent efforts of Simon Turtle and Walter Water Snake that the cricket finds quarters he loves. It's the lively style, the strong characterization, and the humorous dialogue that give the book substance and sparkle.

1145   **Selsam,** Millicent Ellis, *Catnip;* photographs by Jerome Wexler. Morrow, 1983. 83-5416. Trade ed. ISBN 0-688-02462-9; Library ed. ISBN 0-688-02463-7. 47p. Trade ed. $9.50; Library ed. $8.59.

2–4   The large print, spacious page layout, and especially the clear simple writing make this carefully organized and handsomely illustrated book exemplary beginning science fare. Selsam gives some background information about the use of herbs in history, but focuses on the structure of the catnip plant, providing facts on its classification and on the research done on nepatalactone, the chemical it contains. She also includes instructions on how to store and dry it for use with cats. As always, one of the ways in which the author makes the book appropriate for its intended audience is to omit facts that are not important. An index gives access to the contents; the fine photographs, many magnified, are carefully placed and labelled.

1146   **Selsam,** Millicent Ellis. *Cotton;* illus. with photographs by Jerome Wexler. Morrow, 1982. 82-6496. Trade ed. ISBN 0-688-01499-2; Library ed. ISBN 0-688-01511-X. 48p. Trade ed. $9.50; Library ed. $8.59.

3–5   Prefaced by historical material about the evidence of cotton cloth in ancient civilizations and early manufacturing devlopments, Selsam gives her usual explicit and accurate explanation of botanical structure. Here, augmented by Wexler's handsome (often enlarged) photographs in color and in black and white, the text shows how the plants grow and flower, how the cotton boll grows and is structured, and how the cotton is processed from fiber to cloth. There are some photographic captions (in the first few pages) that are in the same type as the text and so placed that they may be confusing to readers, but for most of the book the placement is as careful and informative as the text itself.

1147   **Selsam,** Millicent Ellis. *Tree Flowers;* illus. by Carol Lerner. Morrow, 1984. 83-17353. Library ed. ISBN 0-688-02769-5; Trade ed. ISBN 0-688-02768-7. 32p. Library ed. $10.08; Trade ed. $11.00.

4–   Selsam has chosen twelve trees as examples of specimens bearing dif-
*   ferent kinds of flowers, so that the highly visible blossoms of the apple or magnolia are included, as well as the small flowers of the white oak or sugar maple. A page of concise, clear descriptive text faces each recto page that includes several detailed illustrations in scale, accurate, beautiful, and carefully labelled. This is easily assimilable botanical information, a felicitous union of talents.

1148   **Selsam,** Millicent Ellis. *Where Do They Go? Insects in Winter;* illus. by Arabelle Wheatley. Four Winds, 1982. 82-70976. ISBN 0-590-07862-3. 32p. $8.95.

2–4   There's a complementary precision in the text and illustrations here, the color illustrations (carefully placed and labeled) extending the succinct and accurate descriptions of a logically organized book. Each brief section ("Where are the beetles and bugs?" "Where are the bees and ants?" "What happens to grasshoppers, crickets, and katydids?") discusses the place and form (eggs or larvae, for example) or defensive measures used by insects to perpetuate life through the cold season. Useful for science units or for nature study, the book can also be read aloud to younger children.

1149   **Sendak,** Maurice. *Outside Over There;* written and illus. by Maurice Sendak. Harper, 1981. 79-2682. Trade ed. ISBN 0-06-205523-4; Library ed. ISBN 0-06-025524-2. 34p. Trade ed. $12.95; Library ed. $12.89.

K–3   A gentle yet powerful story in the romantic tradition, this long-awaited
*   successor to *Where the Wild Things Are* and *In the Night Kitchen* is illustrated with paintings that are with little question Sendak's most beautiful work yet. Soft in tones, rich in the use of light and color, with the grave dignity of the black and white art of *The Juniper Tree* softened here and given warmth, the pictures are particularly distinctive for the tenderness with which the children's faces are drawn, the classic handling of texture, the imaginative juxtaposition of infant faces and the baroque landscape details that might have come from Renaissance paintings. There is an occasional stylistic oddity in the writing ("The ice thing only dripped and stared, and Ida mad knew goblins had been there.") but it is not inappropriate in a text that often has a lyric quality, and that describes the magical rescue by Ida of her beloved baby sister, stolen by the goblins. Ida seeks the child outside over there, and finds her only because her sailor father's song reaches her and tells her how to outwit the goblins. (Mother, pining in solitude, takes no active role.) A love story, this should enchant all of Sendak's adult fans, who will also appreciate such details as Mozart in a little summerhouse, a background vignette that may be missed by younger readers and viewers. This is a beautiful book.

1150   **Severo,** Emöke de Papp, tr. *The Good-Hearted Youngest Brother: An Hungarian Folktale;* tr. from the Hungarian by Emöke de Papp Severo; illus. by Diane Goode. Bradbury, 1981. 80-28169. ISBN 0-87888-141-7. 27p. $10.95.

3–5   Many familiar folklore devices are used in this tale of three brothers who go out into the world to seek their fortunes: kindness rewarded, people turned to stone, bewitched princesses, and a three-part obstacle. To win the three beautiful princesses, the brothers must find three crowns, three pearls, and then guess which belongs to which enchanted flower; each time the youngest brother is helped to the solution by a creature to whom he had shown kindness. Of course, there's a triple wedding, with all the stone people brought back to life and rejoicing. Competently translated and told, the story is illustrated by full-page or double-page paintings, delicate in line and effective in composition, with dramatic use of color and with folk motifs in architectural and costume details.

1151   **Shachtman,** Tom. *Growing Up Masai;* illus. with photographs by Donn Renn. Macmillan, 1981, 80-25017. ISBN 0-02-782550-7, 42p. $8.95.

3–5   Known primarily for his television documentaries and nonfiction for adults, Shachtman writes in a clear, flowing style about the living patterns of the Masai herders, focusing on a brother and sister in one family. Describing the ways in which the children participate in tribal and family affairs, do their chores, and prepare for adult roles, the author gives a good picture of the strength and dignity of the culture; he concludes by commenting that, although some Masai have accepted roles in contemporary or urban life styles, most Masai prefer to live as their ancestors did, in the close-knit pattern of tribal communities. Some of the folklore of the Masai is incorporated into the text, and the photographs of the people, the landscape, and the animals of the region are handsome. Some Masai words are defined in a brief glossary.

1152   **Shapiro,** Irwin. *The Gift of Magic Sleep; Early Experiments in Anesthesia;* illus. by Pat Rotondo. Coward, 1979. 78-24 224. ISBN 0-698-30694-5. 64p. $5.49 net.

4–6   A well-researched account of the early uses of nitrous oxide and of ether is written with good pace and an instinct for the dramatic. Although the anesthetic effects of some drugs had been known for centuries, it was not until the mid-nineteenth century that it occurred to some medical and dental practitioners that the numbing effect, the "magic sleep" that had been useful in minor surgery, could be used for major surgery. The story is one of repeated efforts to have ether accepted as an anesthetic, of scoffing on the part of the medical establishment, and of the bitter competition among four men, each of whom felt he should be recognized as the discoverer of ether.

1153   **Sharmat,** Marjorie Weinman, *Gila Monsters Meet You at the Airport;* illus. by Byron Barton. Macmillan, 1980. 80-12264. ISBN 0-02-782450-0. 28p. $8.95.

K–3   If there's a lesson here, it's painless, as Sharmat at her best shows a Manhattan child (filled with dread at all the awful things he's heard about Arizona) meeting an east-bound boy (filled with dread about all the things he's heard about New York) at the airport. Our Hero quickly discovers that Gila monsters are not at the airport, that not everbody wears chaps and spurs. For goodness sakes, they even play *baseball!* The exaggeration is amusing, the style yeasty, with a nice final touch; the illustrations are comic and awkward, but add little that's not inherent in the story.

1154   **Sharmat,** Marjorie Weinman. *Mr. Jameson & Mr. Phillips;* illus. by Bruce Degen. Harper, 1979. 77-25665. 48p. Trade ed. $7.95; Library ed. $7.89 net.

K–3   Mr. Jameson and Mr. Phillips are animals, friends who decide that they must get away from the rush and slush of the city, and who sail off and find an isolated and beautiful tropical island. Settled at opposite ends of the island, they seldom communicate, writing and painting in amicable—if separate—content. A visitor comes, then other visitors, and before long their retreat is populated and filled with rushing and pushing. They find their old boat and sail off, but they can find no place that isn't crowded—and they finally have a Grand Idea. Happily, they settle down to live permanently on their boat, the *Home Sea Home.* The pictures are brisk, busy line drawings with green-gold-blue wash, and the chief asset of the story is the style: lightly humorous, bland, with vigorous dialogue and some nice snatches of silly rhymes by Mr. Jameson.

1155   **Sharmat,** Marjorie Weinman. *The Trolls of Twelfth Street;* illus. by Ben Shecter. Coward, 1979. 78-31788. ISBN 0-698-30716-X. 64p. Break-of-Day Books. $6.29.

1–3   Every hundred years or so, Eldred wondered what it was like at ground level in New York, and this time he coaxed his family into leaving their cave under the Brooklyn Bridge. Were there other creatures as stupid and ugly? ("I wish you wouldn't brag. . . ." Ma says.) "Pretty please with ointment on it," Eldred had begged, and Pa reluctantly agreed. "We can't stay more than a few hundred years." So they found a nice, dank basement and confronted human beings—and that's where the series of misunderstandings starts. Easy to read, very funny in just that nicely awful way small children enjoy, and illustrated with appropriately scruffy characters in the humorous pencil drawings.

1156   **Sharmat,** Marjorie Weinman. *What Are We Going to Do About Andrew?* illus. by Ray Cruz. Macmillan, 1980. 79-20535. ISBN 0-02-782440-3. 32p. $7.95.

K–3   A blithe fantasy is all the more engaging because of the calm, bland acceptance of Andrew's supernatural powers and because of Sharmat's understated humor. Andrew's parents try to be understanding and to encourage their children, but they find it a mild nuisance that Andrew is the only boy on the block who can fly. Or change himself into a hippopotamus, as he did in school. (His teacher gave him an "A.") Still, as Father explained, there were no hippos in the family lineage, and it was rather a family tradition not to fly, so perhaps Andrew could think about it? Andrew flew off and didn't come back for a week, during which time his parents could only think about what a dear and interesting boy he was. He returned with a daffodil and some cheesecake and the news that he'd missed his family. No moral is pointed; the silly, beguiling story ends with a dinner scene in which Andrew turns into a hippo, Father gives him three helpings of everything, and Mother is delighted that Andrew has such a good appetite. The illustrations, lightly tinted and hatched, have the same ebullience as the writing.

1157   **Sharp,** Margery. *Bernard into Battle: a Miss Bianca Story*; illus. by Leslie Morrill. Little, 1979. 78-11332. 87p. $7.95.

6–   Like earlier stories about Miss Bianca, the beautiful white mouse who led so many of the death-defying forays of the Mouse Prisoners' Aid Society, and her stalwart admirer Bernard, this has a deliberately nonsensical plot (rats invade the ambassadorial premises while the family and staff are on holiday, and it is the loyal mice who—with help—repel them) told in a wonderfully suave and witty style. As always, the derring-do could be appreciated by younger readers were they able to appreciate the light and polished style that mocks the romantic adventure tale; while it's lightweight, the story can be enjoyed for the mock raptures and heroics that make it as elegant a spoof as feathery fiction can be.

1158   **Showers,** Paul. *No Measles, No Mumps for Me*; illus. by Harriett Barton. T.Y. Crowell, 1980. 79-7106. Trade ed. ISBN 0-690-04017-2; Library ed. ISBN 0-690-04018-0. 33p. (Let's-Read-and-Find-Out-Books) Trade ed. $7.95; Library ed. $7.89.

1–3   As is usual in books in this excellent series, there is no extraneous material; Showers describes, in a direct and casual writing style, how preventive medicine can confer immunity against common childhood diseases. He discusses the way in which bacteria and viruses multiply, and how the leucocytes of the human body manufacture antibodies to attack the invaders when, in weakened form, they have been ingested by, or injected into, people. Sensible in approach, the book is in the first person; it is useful information that is nicely gauged for the beginning independent reader.

1159   **Showers,** Paul. *You Can't Make a Move Without Your Muscles*; illus. by Harriett Barton. Crowell, 1982. 81-43323. Trade ed. ISBN 0-690-04184-5;

Library ed. ISBN 0-690-04185-3. 34p. (Let's-Read-and-Find-Out Books). Trade ed. $9.50; Library ed. $9.89.

2–3   As with other books in this outstanding series, this has plenty of white space, large type and not too much of it per page, and a crisp, direct style. In other words, everything the very young reader needs to facilitate the reading experience. The pictures are equally comprehensible, modest drawings and diagrams carefully placed for good integration with the text. Showers describes how muscles work, occasionally suggesting to the reader that he or she try a simple home demonstration. The text explains the musculature of the human body with just enough detail to make the material clear but not so much that it will overwhelm the primary grades reader.

1160   **Shreve,** Susan. *The Flunking of Joshua T. Bates;* illus. by Diane de Groat. Knopf, 1984. 83-19636. Library ed. ISBN 0-394-96380-6; Trade ed. ISBN 0-394-86380-1. 82p. Library ed. $10.99; Trade ed. $10.95.

2–4
*
        Repeating third grade is a gloomy prospect for Joshua, not only because it's embarrassing, not only because it seems unfair (other kids were just as bad at reading), but also because the teacher, Mrs. Goodwin, looks like a tank. So much for appearances. Mrs. Goodwin proves to be helpful and understanding, coaching Joshua at her home every weekday, having him help other third graders with their arithmetic. It will surprise few readers that Joshua blossoms and is given early promotion. In addition to this warm depiction of a teacher-pupil relationship, the story has other relationships, astutely drawn: Joshua's parents, the former classmate who teases Joshua, the best friend who stoutly defends him. The dialogue is particularly good, often contributing to characterization, just as often crisply humorous.

1161   **Shreve,** Susan. *The Masquerade.* Knopf, 1980. 79-20073. Trade ed. ISBN 0-394-84142-5; Library ed. ISBN 0-394-94142-X. 184p. Trade ed. $7.95; Library ed. $7.99.

7–10   In a serious and touching novel about a family's response to social tragedy, Shreve examines the masks, the facades we all wear to protect ourselves from others, to lull ourselves into security. When her father is sent to prison for embezzlement, Rebecca, second oldest in a family of four children, shoulders the heaviest burden. Her mother is vague and charming, her youngest sister relies almost completely on Rebecca, her brother (a hypochondriac) and next oldest sister (wrapped in her own needs) find ways to escape. Their substantial home is sold, their furniture auctioned, and they move to a small apartment over a store. The others are bitter, sure their father is guilty, while Rebecca clings to a belief in his innocence, a belief not warranted by the evidence. Her father pleads guilty. Mother drifts out of touch with reality and is sent to an institution. Rebecca, heartsick, refuses to visit her father; she had always been the "good" girl, quiet and reliable, and she rebels and tries to change her pattern. Forced to reassess herself and her life, Rebecca removes the mask that both protected and blinded her, and accepts her father, finally, in realistic terms. This isn't a happy book, and it's marred by occasional errors (in one instance, the text states of the mother, "Alicia had met Edward Walker during her sophomore year at college," while sometime later it says, ". . . Alicia, who hadn't gone to college . . .") but it is written with great insight, it has strong and consistently drawn characters, and the narrative flow is smooth.

1162   **Shura,** Mary Francis. *Chester*; illus. by Susan Swan. Dodd, 1980. 79-6633. ISBN 0-369-07800-1. 92p. $6.95.

3-5   Jamie, who tells the story, is one of the five children on the block who find that Chester, the new boy, is a threat. Chester's amicable enough, but he unwittingly infringes on each of the other children's unique prerogative. He has more freckles than Jamie, he has more siblings than Amy, he runs faster than George, he has more pets than Zach, and he even outstrips Edie's claim to fame, a bald baby sister, by having twin baby brothers who are bald. Jealousy gives way to acceptance tinged with pride when Chester wreaks vengeance on the group's nemesis, an older boy who is a sadistic bully, and the five friends are soon boasting to others about the very things they'd resented earlier. A passionate pride in—for example—having a bald baby sister isn't quite convincing, but Shura carries it off with a light touch; the humor, especially in the dialogue, is the strength of the story.

1163   **Siberell,** Anne. *Whale in the Sky*; written and illus. by Anne Siberell. Dutton, 1982. 82-2483. ISBN 0-525-44021-6. 30p. $10.95.

K-3   Bold, stylized, effective in color and composition, the author-artist's block prints (and the story she tells) are based on the carvings of totem poles of the Northwest Coast Indians. Thunderbird is one of the animal folk heroes of Native American folklore, and in this simply told story Thunderbird punishes Whale because he is chasing salmon in the river, and elicits a promise that Whale will stay in the sea. The totem pole that shows the characters is shown at the end of this "why" story, and a page that describes the carver's tools and the ways in which colors for the painting of a totem pole were provided is appended.

1164   **Siegal,** Aranka. *Upon the Head of the Goat: A Childhood in Hungary 1939–1944*. Farrar, 1981. 81-12642. ISBN 0-374-38059-7. 214p. $9.95.

7-   Although Siegal's story is told by a fictional narrator, Piri, it is based on her own memories of the privation and persecution of Hungarian Jews under German occupation during World War II. Written in a vigorous conversational flow, the story is dramatic and moving, ending with stunning impact as Piri's family—or what is left of it—boards a train for a work camp at a place nobody's ever heard of, Auschwitz. This is a touching addition, effective and affective, to the growing body of books about the Holocaust.

1165   **Silsbee,** Peter. *The Big Way Out.* Bradbury. 1984. 83-15680. ISBN 0-02-782670-8. 180p. $11.95.

8–10   In a remarkably effective first novel, Silsbee depicts, from the viewpoint of the afflicted man's younger son, the despair, the fear, and the anger aroused by exposure to the irrationality and violence of a psychotic parent. Paul, fourteen, has come east with his mother to stay with her family, leaving an older brother to cope with Dad. It is clear that the latter needs to return to the mental hospital for further therapy; it becomes even more clear when Dad shows up and acts as though they were all one happy family. For Paul, who has had bitter thoughts of taking violent action (he throws the gun away), the conclusion brings a realization that he loves his father. The book is serious, dramatic, and convincing, although it is most convincing when it is least dramatic. Particularly sharp: the depiction of Paul's maternal grandmother, a hostile, nagging, petty tyrant, and the descriptions of extended family scenes in which everybody is being very, very careful about what they say and what they avoid saying.

1166   **Silverstein,** Alvin. *Aging;* by Alvin Silverstein, Virginia Silverstein, and Glenn Silverstein. Watts, 1979. 79-11890. ISBN 0-531-02863-1. 86p. illus. with photographs. $6.90.

6–   Since factors in our society have tended to increase the life spans of human beings, the old are an increasing part of the world's population. The Silversteins discuss the various changes that take place in old age, and what causes them; they point out the fact that senility has many causes and that some individuals remain alert and productive into very old age; in a separate chapter, they discuss scientists' theories on what causes aging and how influential environmental and genetic factors are. The text includes discussions of early efforts to counteract the aging process and of contemporary research in the field; it concludes with a survey of the roles of old people in our society (family patterns, mandatory retirement, and the problems of the aged). The writing is sober in tone, the material logically organized, and the text enlivened somewhat by anecdotes about, or comments on, some of the old people in our society who have made or are making major contributions. A bibliography and an index are provided.

1167   **Silverstein,** Alvin. *Runaway Sugar; All About Diabetes;* written by Alvin and Virginia B. Silverstein; illus. by Harriett Barton. Lippincott, 1981. 80-8727. Trade ed. ISBN 0-397-31928-2; Library ed. ISBN 0-397-31929-0. 31p. Trade ed. $9.50; Library ed. $8.89.

3–4   In simple terminology but without writing down to their readers, the Silversteins discuss (as they did for older readers in *The Sugar Disease; Diabetes)* diabetes, how it affects individuals, what medication can do (including what it can do if one reacts with either insulin shock or diabetic coma) and how one can adjust to a diabetic condition. The text also explains, accurately and clearly, the several ways in which too much sugar in the blood, the cause of diabetes, can be caused. A useful text, well-organized, concludes with a discussion of some of the research frontiers today, and a glossary.

1168   **Silverstein, **Alvin. *The World of Bionics;* by Alvin Silverstein and Virginia Silverstein. Methuen, 1980. 79-19024. ISBN 0-416-30221-1. 116p. illus. with photographs. $7.95.

6–8   Although this covers much of the same material as do *The Bionic People Are Here,* by Arthur Freese and *Bionic Parts for People,* by Gloria Skurzynski, it has a rather different focus, approaching the subject from the viewpoint of basic research on the animal world, and the application of that research (focused on each of the senses) to supplying the bionic knowledge. It includes, as do the other books, information on the prosthetic devices or machines that help human beings. The material is logically organized, the coverage is broad, the writing competent and authoritative. An index is appended.

1169   **Silverstein, **Shel. *A Light in the Attic;* written and illus. by Shel Silverstein. Harper, 1981. 80-8453. Trade ed. ISBN 0-06-025673-7; Library ed. ISBN 0-06-025674-5. 173p. Trade ed. $10.95; Library ed. $10.89.

4–6   Scratchy line drawings, occasionally macabre and usually humorous, illustrate a robust collection of entertaining poetry. Little of this is sensitive, and some of it is more slapstick than subtle, but there's a sense of fun and nonsense that should appeal to most children. Many of the selections have a memorable lilt, some almost like jump-rope rhymes. For example, "Hammock." "Grandma sent the hammock/The good Lord sent the breeze/I'm here to do the swinging/Now, who's gonna move the trees?" Not great poetry, but likely to be popular.

1170   **Simon, **Hilda. *The Magic of Color;* written and illus. by Hilda Simon. Lothrop, 1981. 81-5044. Trade ed. ISBN 0-688-00619-1; Library ed. ISBN 0-688-00620-5. 55p. Trade ed. $8.95; Library ed. $8.59.

4–7   Almost all books on color that have been designed for children focus
  *   on the colors in paint, so that blue and yellow always make green. Simon, skilled as an illustrator as well as a science writer, takes a broader approach and shows not only some of the effects and relationships of paint colors, but also those of the colors of light. She gives, in a smoothly combined use of text and picture, a great deal of information about color and color vision, demonstrates some of the ways in which combinations of colors may be manipulated to achieve specific effects, and shows how printing techniques make it possible to produce many colors from a few basic ones. Lucid, informative, and handsome.

1171   **Simon, **Norma. *We Remember Philip;* illus. by Ruth Sanderson. Whitman, 1979. 78-11691. 28p. Trade ed. $5.25; Library ed. $3.94 net.

2–4   There have been many good books that interpret a child's adjustment to death, most frequently the death of a pet, a friend, or a member of the family. Here the focus is on children's sympathy for one who is bereaved, as Sam and his classmates mourn the death of their teacher's son, a young man they've never met; the class members are fond of Mr. Hall, shocked when they learn that his son has died while mountain-climbing, and not quite comfortable when Mr. Hall returns to school. He's not the same, and it takes time before he laughs with them, or before he can mention the name of his son Philip. But one day he does—and when Sam asks if he might see a picture of Philip, it leads to a showing of slides in class: Philip from babyhood on. One of the girls suggests that the class plant a tree in memory of Philip, and when that has taken place, Mr. Hall tells the children how much their concern has helped, helped ease his grief and helped him have the courage to remember. The pictures are softly drawn and realistic, appropriate for the quiet and warmth of the story, which makes a clear but not didactic statement about sharing grief.

1172   **Simon,** Seymour. *Computer Sense, Computer Nonsense;* illus. by Steven Lindblom. Lippincott, 1984. 83-49492. Library ed. ISBN 0-397-32086-8; Trade ed. ISBN 0-397-32085-X. 56p. Library ed. $9.89; Trade ed. $10.50.

3–6   In his usual brisk and authoritative fashion, Simon poses a series of statements that reflect popular beliefs about computers, labels each "Sense" or "Nonsense" and explains why. This not only debunks fallacies but gives a considerable amount of information about computers lucidly. It gives facts about function and use and limitations, and even provides some information about programming.

1173   **Simon,** Seymour. *Danger From Below; Earthquakes: Past, Present, and Future.* Four Winds, 1979. 78-22283. 86p. illus $7.95.

5–7   A practiced science writer, Simon is lucid, accurate, and objective in describing theories, causes, effects, and measurement of earthquakes. Maps and diagrams are useful in supplementing the explanations of where quakes occur, and why, and of the newest devices and methods for predicting quakes and making it possible to minimize damages. The material is dramatic, especially in descriptions of some of the terrible quakes of the past, but the tone is calm, and the book concludes with advice on what to do if a quake hits and some discussion of future earthquakes. A list of U.S. earthquakes of 1976 (in more than half the states) and an index are appended.

1174   **Simon,** Seymour. *The Dinosaur Is the Biggest Animal That Ever Lived: And Other Wrong Ideas You Thought Were True;* illus. by Giulio Maestro. Lippincott, 1984. 83-48960. Library ed. ISBN 0-397-32076-0; Trade ed. ISBN 0-397-32075-2. 64p. Library ed. $10.89; Trade ed. $10.95.

3–5   Two pages are devoted to each popular fallacy, in a book that is admirably suited—by subjects, by level of reading difficulty, and by the type size and spacing—to the middle grades audience. Simon, an authoritative science writer, gives careful explanations of why it's not true that quicksand drags you down, or that lightning never strikes twice. Informative, intriguing.

1175   **Simon,** Seymour. *Hidden Worlds.* Morrow, 1983. 83-5407. Trade ed. ISBN 0-688-02464-5; Library ed. ISBN 0-688-02465-3. 47p. illus. with photographs. Trade ed. $10.50; Library ed. $9.55.

4–   A photographic essay, with text and pictures (some in color, some in black and white) is carefully organized so that descriptive commentary is contiguous to the related illustration. Simon, a polished science writer, explains clearly how the pictures were taken and what they show, so that readers can understand not only the wonders of human physiology or objects in space or other natural phenomena, but also the diverse and intricate machines that make magnification possible: fiber-optic tubes, field ion microscopes, orbiting satellites, strobe machines that can take six thousand photographs per second, CAT scans and other marvels of technology.

1176   **Simon,** Seymour. *Little Giants;* illus. by Pamela Carroll. Morrow, 1983. 82-14139. Trade ed. ISBN 0-688-01727-4; Library ed. ISBN 0-688-01731-2. 47p. Trade ed. $10.50; Library ed. $9.55.

3–6   Fine black and white drawings with stippled detail show each of the creatures that is a giant of its own species. Although the text that faces each full-page illustration gives measurements, the pictures in themselves give no indication of comparative size save for occasional background details. The book provides less than a page of text for each "little giant," and the creatures range from insects that are larger than most of their kind to such animals as the ostrich or beluga sturgeon. The material is accurate and interesting, but the fact that the arrangement seems haphazard and that the book has neither an index nor a table of contents limits access and indicates that the primary use will be for browsing.

1177   **Singer,** Isaac Bashevis. *The Golem;* illus. by Uri Shulevitz. Farrar, 1982. ISBN 0-374-32741-6. 96p. $9.95.

6–   A masterful retelling of the legend of the golem, the huge clay man created by a rabbi of Prague to help one of his people unjustly accused of a crime. Singer invests the dramatic story with color and compassion, vividly relating the story of the good and pious man, Reb Eliezer, who was accused of killing the daughter of a vindictive gambler and who was saved when the golem brought the child to his trial. Ordered by the Emperor to kill the golem, the rabbi who created him found that the monster he had created was no longer obedient, was growing destructive, and wanted to be a human being. He was killed at last when the rabbi erased from his clay forehead the name of God that had brought him to life. The grave, dramatic Shulevitz pictures, soft in execution and strong in composition, are admirably suited to the stark strength of the legend so vividly retold by the author.

1178   **Singer,** Isaac Bashevis. *The Power of Light*; illus. by Irene Lieblich. Farrar, 1980. 80-20263. ISBN 0-374-36099-5. 87p. $10.95.

4–6   Ingenuously awkward in composition, paintings in dark, bright colors illustrate the eight stories by a master-storyteller, one story for each night of the holiday. The binding theme, as the title indicates, is the light; even in the story of two blind children who love each other, it is by sitting near the warmth and comfort of the Hanukkah lamp that they find peace. Some of the stories are set in the time of World War II, some in the Warsaw ghetto, one in Brooklyn; the stories vary from realism to incorporation of the miraculous (the appearance of Elijah) but are united in their strong piety as they are in the polished craftsmanship and warmth with which they are written.

1179   **Singer,** Isaac Bashevis. *Stories for Children*. Farrar, 1984. 84-13612. ISBN 374-37266-7. 338p. $13.95.

4–   Most of the selections and excerpts included in this collection will be familiar to Singer fans, but some have not previously been published in book form. All the stories are told with flow and spontaneity, most of them will appeal because of their wit and humor, and it is a pleasure to have in one volume so much richness of oral tradition and individual creativity. Because of the title, adolescents may scorn the book (their loss) but many adults will enjoy it.

1180   **Singer,** Marilyn *The Course of True Love Never Did Run Smooth*. Harper, 1983. 82-48630. Trade ed. ISBN 0-06-021253-5; Library ed. ISBN 0-06-021254-4. 256p. Trade ed. $10.50; Library ed. $10.89.

7–10   This isn't the first book in which a boy and girl who've been childhood friends fall in love, nor is it the first in which the characters are involved in putting on a high school play—but it's better than most. Becky and Nemi are infatuated with the handsome brother and sister Blake and Leila; Becky suggests that Nemi, who's a film buff, create a movie so that he can give Blake and Leila parts. It works, but familiarity breeds awareness if not contempt: both protagonists find that physical attraction is not, after all, as strong as love. Not an unusual plot, but unusual treatment makes this a strong novel; the minor characters are sharply defined, the familial relationships are strongly drawn, with perceptive treatment of the dynamics of the acting group and especially of its gay members; the writing style has a smooth flow, natural dialogue, and good pace.

1181   **Singh,** Jacquelin. *Fat Gopal*; illus. by Demi. Harcourt, 1984. 82-21258. ISBN 0-15-227372-7. 34p. $12.95.

K–3   Although less formal (occasionally comic, in fact) than the Persian miniature painting on which they seem modelled, Demi's paintings (alternating with black and white drawings) are amusingly stylized. Fat Gopal is the Maharajah's jester, and he volunteers to solve the puzzle set the Maharajah (on pain of death) by his Nawab: measuring the earth from side to side and counting the stars in the sky and the rays of the sun. It would take a year, Fat Gopal says, and cost a million rupees. After wasting a great deal of time and squandering a great deal of money, the scamp finds a devious way out of his dilemma and even coaxes more money from the Nawab. Children should enjoy the excesses of a rogue in the folk-like tale as much as they enjoy the details of the colorful pictures.

1182   **Skolsky,** Mindy Warshaw. *Carnival and Kopeck and More About Hannah;* illus. by Karen Ann Weinhaus. Harper, 1979. 77-25643. Trade ed. ISBN 0-06-025686-9; Library ed. ISBN 0-06-025692-3. 74p. Trade ed. $7.95; Library ed. $7.89 net.

3–5   This is both a lively story, touching and funny, and a shrewdly affectionate exploration of the relationship between a child and her grandparent. Hannah loves being with her grandmother, who lives nearby, and she is delighted by Grandma's agreement that they'll go to the carnival; all does not go smoothly, however, for Hannah breaks a promise and Grandma hauls her home quickly. Then Hannah, staying overnight, remembers a story her grandmother had told about her own childhood and demands money; Grandma, irritated, takes her home in the middle of the night. The breach is healed, but Hannah's learned something about the give and take of human relations, and about the fact that you can get angry at someone you love. Some of the scenes in which Grandma indulgently plays school and then indignantly rebels against her teacher-grandchild are hilarious. Although the style of writing is different, Skolsky achieves some of the same earthy, warm realism that is in Beverly Cleary's writing, and both Hannah and Grandma emerge as real people, faulty and lovable.

1183   **Skurzynski,** Gloria. *Safeguarding the Land; Women at Work in Parks, Forests, and Rangelands.* Harcourt, 1981. 80-8805. Hardcover ed. ISBN 0-15-269956-2; Paper ed. ISBN 0-15-269957-0. 162p. Hardcover ed. $9.95.; Paper ed. $3.95.

6–9   The major part of this text consists of descriptions of the training and the careers of three women: a National Park Ranger, a Wildland Fire Specialist, and a Range Conservationist. This is not the usual quick scanning of a spectrum of jobs; Skurzynski follows the three subjects' careers closely and in detail, describing the problems they have had as women in traditionally male-dominated fields. The work itself, and the setting, are in each case dramatic enough to hold the interest of the general reader; to those interested in working in the wild as conservationists the book should be of even more interest. A range of useful lists is included: schools that offer degrees in park administration, forestry, or range management; pamphlets on careers in natural resources; and agencies like the Smithsonian Institution that furnish general information.

1184   **Skurzynski,** Gloria. *The Tempering.* Clarion, 1983. 82-9602. ISBN 0-89919-152-5. 178p. $10.95.

7–10   Set in 1912 in a Pennsylvania steel town, this is the story of Karl Kerner, not quite sixteen but anxious to do a "man job" as a steelworker rather than a "boy job." He gets a job but loses it the first day when his neighbor, Jame Culley, pulls a joke on the foreman and makes the man angry at both of them. Jame, eighteen, is courting Karl's sister despite the fact that there's a feud between the two families. In love with his teacher, Yulyona, Karl suspects that she is a wealthy man's mistress when he sees her in the man's house in a dishevelled state. He runs away with his friend Andy, but returns to learn that Yulyona is secretly married (keeping it secret so that she can keep her job) and to make a decision about his future. Yulyona wants him to stay in school and finish his education, while Karl feels he must become a worker. The author gives a vivid picture of the way in which poverty and life-style are shaped by the environment, in a story with a smooth style, excellent period details, strong characterization, and a deft meshing of minor plots.

1185   **Skurzynski,** Gloria. *What Happened in Hamelin.* Four Winds, 1979. 79-12814. ISBN 0-590-07625-6. 177p. $7.95.

5–7   An interesting contrast to Huddy's *Time Piper* in which a time machine explains what happened to the children of Hamelin, this offers an explanation in a historical fiction format. It's told by Geist, the poor orphan who works as a baker's boy, and who is at first dazzled by the cleverness and kindness of the itinerant stranger Gast. He even manages to get rid of the rats that plague the town, not by magic but by a ruse; he enchants all the children, not only by his piping, but by the sweets he distributes. What they don't know is that the sweets are drugged. The Pied Piper, Gast, does pipe the children out of town, and his motive—as in Browning's poem—is revenge, but they are not merrily skipping; the drugged children are plodding along to be sold into servitude. The author's appended note explains that, from the historical evidence on which Browning's poem was based, there was a tragedy involving the children in 1284 as shown in the town records of Hamelin, Germany, and that purple fungus ergot (which the piper feeds the children in this story) was known to cause epidemics of hallucination in medieval times. The story as told by Geist, one of the two survivors, is convincing; the material is inherently dramatic and smoothly written, and it builds nicely toward the tense final tragedy.

1186   Sleator, William. *Fingers.* Atheneum, 1983. 83-2662. ISBN 0-689-31000-5. 197p. $10.95.

7–10   The dilemma: Humphrey had been a child prodigy, a mechanically proficient but musically insensitive concert pianist; now that he was a very large adolescent, his wooden playing irritated audiences. His despairing parents decide to perpetrate a hoax: older brother Sam (the narrator, not a good performer but musically astute and knowledgeable) will write some music by the legendary "Laszlo Magyar," and Humphrey, drugged at dinner, will wake to be told that Magyar's ghost had dictated the new music. It makes a media splash—but odd things happen: Humphrey begins to believe in the spectral communication, an odd old man shows up at concerts in several cities, strange tales are linked to odd new developments. Not so strange is the fact that Sam, who gets no credit, becomes restive and eventually tells all to Humphrey. For most of the dramatic and often funny story, the strangeness is explained, but there are occult elements (precognition, for one) and there's some broad lampooning (the Russian music expert is named Alexandra Nitpikskaya) of types in the world of classical music. This has a lively pace, sharp characterization, good style, and often-acid humor.

1187   Sleator, William. *Interstellar Pig.* Dutton, 1984. 84-4132. ISBN 0-525-44098-4. 208p. $11.95.

7–10   Although it's hard to believe that Barney, the sixteen-year-old narrator, doesn't spot his three new neighbors as aliens ("You'll get the droop of it," "Well on twice thought," or "We're in fortune") the ingenuity, pace, and establishment of mood in this science fantasy triumph over that minor weakness. Drawn into their continuing game of "Interstellar Pig," Barney becomes aware that the game is part of life and that the three lavender-eyed aliens are a threat to his safety. The story grows in complexity, possibly to the point of confusion, and at one point Barney undergoes a metamorphosis, but the fantasy is consistent if not always coherent.

1188   Sleator, William. *Into The Dream;* illus. by Ruth Sanderson. Dutton, 1979. 78-11825. ISBN 0-525-32583-2. 137p. $7.50.

5–7   A compelling fantasy is written with increasing tempo and suspense, and is predicated on the supposition that extrasensory powers exist. It begins with Paul's recurring dream and his surprise when he finds that Francine, one of his classmates but not a friend, has been having the same dream. In their frightening dream, they are trying to reach a small child who is happily going toward a bright and curiously dangerous light. The two children discover that they can, to a limited extent, read each other's minds, and they agree that the child in their dream must also be telepathic; if they can find a common experience in their own lives, perhaps they can find who and where the child is. And that's the beginning of the final adventure, dangerous but successful. Nicely crafted, this will undoubtedly appeal to readers intrigued by the eerie and the occult.

1189   **Slepian,** Jan. *The Alfred Summer*. Macmillan, 1980. 79-24097. ISBN 0-02-782920-0. 119p. $7.95.

5–7   You'd think, perhaps, that a book about a handicapped child and another who is retarded and epileptic might be grim or sugary, but this isn't. Slepian has avoided the obvious pitfalls and has written a story that is touching without being sentimental, that smoothly moves back and forth between the narrator's viewpoint and that of Lester, the fourteen-year-old protagonist who has cerebral palsy, and that probes with sympathetic insight into the intricacies of pain and courage. Lester is overwhelmed by his overprotective mother, envious of the gentle love that supports Alfred, who is younger and retarded. Both handicapped children are enthralled when Myron, a neighbor, invites them to help him build a boat. Alfred, sunny and happy, does not see how Myron suffers in his family situation, but Lester does; he realizes for the first time that a "normal" peer has some of the same kinds of problems he himself has. The story line is not dramatic, but it's convincing, and it's buttressed by some exciting incidents, lightened by some moments of triumphant achievement for Lester, and mitigated in its seriousness by unexpected humor in the dialogue and in Lester's occasionally caustic comments.

1190   **Slepian,** Jan. *Lester's Turn*. Macmillan, 1981. 80-29467. ISBN 0-02-782940-5. 139p. $8.95.

5–7   In a sequel to the touching story *The Alfred Summer*, the gentle, retarded Alfred is in an institution and his friend Lester, an adolescent victim of cerebral palsy, is determined to get him out. Lester is convinced that Alfie would be better off if he were home with Lester; in fact, he tries to sneak Alfie out of the hospital and is caught. Lester, who tells the story, decides he'll get a job so that he can legally be responsible for Alfie. With the aid of some friends, Lester sets up a concert to raise money, and he's given permission to bring Alfie to the concert; Alfie becomes ill and dies of a ruptured appendix. Lester's despair and guilt are alleviated by a talk with the hospital director, a wise and compassionate woman who helps Lester understand that although he had some self-interest in making plans that involved Alfie, he was not in the wrong. "You can use and need and love at the same time," she says. This has the same wry wit, warmth, and sensitivity as the first book; it has depth and perception in the depiction of characters and relationships; it has a flowing style; and it is particularly adept in portraying Lester as an adolescent who has the same needs and problems as those peers who are not handicapped.

1191   **Slepian,** Jan. *The Night of the Bozos*. Dutton, 1983. 83-5564. ISBN 0-525-44070-4. 152p. $10.95.

6–9   Shy and reclusive, thirteen-year-old George is a musical prodigy who
  *   can play, repair, or build almost anything—but he can't make friends.
His one friend and his companion is his uncle, Hibbie, whose stuttering
has made him as isolated socially as George is. When they meet Lolly
(pretty, garrulous, unhappy) and go home with her to meet the carnival
folk of whom her family is a part, Hibbie is fascinated by the Bozo, the
man who—with face painted like a clown—taunts the carnival crowd
into throwing balls to see if they can tip him into the water. George is
aghast when Hibbie announces he is going to be the new Bozo, as fearful of losing Hibbie as he is apprehensive about Hibbie's ability to keep
up a rapid patter. Hibbie is a smashing success, and explains that all
the jeering and joking have always been in him, that only with the protection of a painted face can he feel free to talk without stuttering. This
major theme is balanced by other material about George and about Lolly, a touching trio that Slepian brings to vivid life in a story that, while
different from *The Alfred Summer*, shows the same perceptive understanding of those who are or feel set apart physically or emotionally
from others.

1192   **Slote,** Alfred. *C.O.L.A.R.: A Tale of Outer Space;* illus. by Anthony Kramer. Lippincott, 1981. 80-8723. Trade ed. ISBN 0-397-31936-3; Library
ed. ISBN 0-397-31937-1. 146p. Trade ed. $8.95; Library ed. $8.79.

3–5   In a sequel to *My Robot Buddy* Jack Jameson tells of an extraterrestrial
adventure when he, his robot twin Danny, and their parents land on an
uncharted planet. They have run out of fuel on their way back to earth,
and there's no way to let Space Patrol know where they are. Thus
trapped, they are attacked by hostile robots who prove to have run
away from their cruel masters and who try to brainwash Danny into
hating his human family. This is better constructed than the first book,
with more suspense and drama, and in addressing the prejudices of the
robot community it speaks to the bias within the human society.

1193   **Slote,** Alfred. *Love and Tennis.* Macmillan, 1979. 79-14914. ISBN 0-02-
785870-7. 163p. $7.95.

7–9   Both of Buddy's parents play tournament tennis, but his father is relaxed about Buddy's prowess, while his mother (divorced, and tense
about it) urges him to pull any trick he can, anything to win a match.
She even, to Buddy's dismay, arranges a three-week stint at a tennis
school, and he dislikes intensely the bitter rivalry, the whole milieu of
steely indifference to anything but the game. "Pity has no place in tennis," says the coach, "Love is only a score." Permeating the tough-
tennis theme is the problem Buddy has with his girl, who's just as avaricious as his mother, and the confusion he feels about his parents'
varying attitudes. Although his father predicts he'll be back, Buddy decides, at fifteen, that he'll quit tournament tennis. This is probably the
best of the few tennis stories that have been written; no formula plot

here, but a realistic and perceptive account of the pressures of the game and the conflicts they can cause. The characters are rounded, and there are logical connections between what they're like, what they do, and how they react to each other.

1194   **Smith,** Doris Buchanan. *The First Hard Times.* Viking, 1983. 82-60084. ISBN 0-670-31571-0. 123p. $9.95.

5–7   In a sequel to *Last Was Lloyd* Smith writes from the viewpoint of Ancil, Lloyd's one friend in Hanover, their small Georgia town. Ancil zealously nurses her dislike of the new stepfather, Harvey, who has brought the family to Hanover; she resents the fact that her sisters love him, is puzzled by the fact that even her paternal grandparents have accepted him, insists that her real father (missing in action ten years) is still alive, and particularly resents the fact that her mother and Harvey have insisted she take swimming lessons. It's a slow, painful, and reluctant process that brings a change in Ancil, and it's helped by learning that Lloyd, who had had two stepfathers and an overprotective mother, has had years of hard times, while this is her first. Smith is astute in her understanding and depiction of the intricacies of familial relationships and realistic in depicting the changes in Ancil. The characters are drawn with depth and conviction, and the style is fluent, marked by good pace and natural dialogue.

1195   **Smith,** Doris Buchanan. *Last Was Lloyd.* Viking, 1981. 80-29468. ISBN 0-670-41921-4. 124p. $8.95.

4–6   Lloyd, fat and lonely, was the butt of his sixth grade classmates' jeering, the one who was always chosen last in class ball games. He just stood there; never, never would he let them know how well he hit when he played with Mama's softball team. This poignant, trenchant story of an insecure, overprotected child moves briskly and is shaped by perception toward a positive ending as Lloyd begins to gain independence from his doting mother, to make new friends, and to learn new skills. He learns to ride a bicycle (Mama had been afraid he'd get hurt), he walks to the park alone (Mama had always insisted on driving him), and he cuts down on his compulsive eating (Mama had always loved seeing him eat a lot). The characterization and relationships (both those between Lloyd and his classmates, and those between him and the adults in the story) are solid and skillfully portrayed.

1196   **Smith,** Doris Buchanan. *Salted Lemons.* Four Winds, 1980. 80-66250. ISBN 0-590-07666-3. 233p. $9.95.

4–6   In a story set in Atlanta during World War II, ten-year-old Darby is the outsider, the newcomer. Having come from Washington, D.C. she's a Yankee, and the children in her neighborhood are slow to accept her, save for Yoko, who—although Atlanta-born—is an outsider in another way and whose family is, during the course of the story, sent to an internment camp. One of the few people who is kind to Yoko is the German storekeeper, Mr. Kaigler, himself the victim of suspicion and persecution. The sensitive treatment of ethical problems and human relationships is balanced by the continuing thread of plot about adaptability; for example, Darby braves a meeting with a reputed ghost on Hallowe'en night just to show the other children that she's not afraid, that she can be accepted. The structure of the book is diffuse, but the characters are strong, the issues are naturally incorporated and are sympathetically handled, and the characterization and writing style have depth and polish.

1197   **Smith,** Janice Lee. *The Kid Next Door and Other Headaches: Stories About Adam Joshua;* illus. by Dick Gackenbach. Harper, 1984. 83-47689. Library ed. ISBN 0-06-025793-8; Trade ed. ISBN 0-06-025792-X. 143p. Library ed. $9.89; Trade ed. $9.95.

2–4   Five more stories about Adam Joshua have the same endearing combination of exuberance, strong characterization and sensitivity as those in *The Monster in the Third Dresser Drawer.* Nelson, the kid next door, is scared of Adam Joshua's new puppy. Nelson likes things nice and neat, he likes to wear a tie, and is furious at the mess Adam Joshua makes in their tree-house. But after the friends unite against a bully and forget their differences, Nelson comes to spend the night, bringing two suitcases, a sleeping bag, his special pillow, "the one-eyed, one-armed, no legged teddy bear Adam Joshua had let him borrow again, and his tie." Children and the adults who read to them will respond with delighted recognition to Adam Joshua's problems ("What do you do if you're afraid to be brave?") and to Gackenbach's funny small drawings, which depict the vehemence of Adam Joshua's feelings and the details of his comfortable messy world.

1198   **Smith,** Janice Lee. *The Monster in the Third Dresser Drawer;* illus. by Dick Gackenbach. Harper, 1981. 81-47109. Trade ed. ISBN 0-06-025734-2; Library ed. ISBN 0-06-025739-3. 86p. Trade ed. $8.25; Library ed. $7.89.

2–4   In six stories about Adam Joshua, Smith establishes her protagonist as a boy whose small adventures and firm attitudes should evoke a recognition reflex on the part of most readers. He doesn't want to move. He is not enthralled when a baby sister arrives, less so when she's put in his room (just until her own is painted and ready) and substantially less so when she cries at night. Adam Joshua adjusts to the new home, the new baby, the new best friend, a strict babysitter, a loose tooth—all the important aspects of life. The small, realistic drawings have a humor that nicely echoes the humor of Smith's writing style, which cleverly incorporates repetition so that it becomes a stylistic asset: as a sample, "With Peter, Adam Joshua once collected ants from the back yard and put them in a shoe box to keep in the house. With Peter, Adam Joshua once collected ants from the house, where they got loose, and carried them out to the backyard again."

1199   **Smith,** Rukshana. *Sumitra's Story.* Coward, 1983. 82-19794. ISBN 0-698-20579-0. 168p. $9.95.

7–9   A first novel from England is based on the experiences of the author's young Asian friend and is a vivid account of the ambivalent feelings of a child transplanted to an alien culture. Sent out of Uganda by Amin, many Asians went to England, as did Sumitra Patel's family, so that their children might receive a good education. Sumitra, oldest of four daughters of an Indian family, is baffled by the prejudice she encounters and is torn between loyalty to, and love for, the traditional ways of her family and a desire to share the freedom and independence given to most of her English classmates. When she leaves school, Sumitra must choose: if she leaves home to work and live independently, she will be ostracized by her family; if she stays, she must accept an arranged marriage and a subservient role as an Indian wife and mother. Through her protagonist, the author strives for objectivity and understanding, in a story that is candid and thought-provoking.

1200   **Smith,** William Jay, comp. *A Green Place: Modern Poems;* illus. by Jacques Hnizdovsky. Delacorte, 1982. 82-2363. ISBN 0-440-02920-1. 225p. $16.95.

5–   Smith presents a broad range of twentieth-century poets, both prominent writers and those of less reputation, in an anthology that is divided into many sections (sixteen) and that represents the work of poets in many countries, although most contributors are American or British. The calibre of the selections is generally good, and the material is in general not already heavily anthologized. The one weakness, perhaps, is in the assignment of some poems to a particular section: Michael Pettit's "A Capella," for example, a poem about an old piano, in the section of poems about poetry, or, in the same section, a poem about the dance, "Merce Cunningham and the Birds." The pages are spaciously set, with fine line drawings as decoration; author, title, and translator indexes are appended.

1201   **Snyder,** Zilpha Keatley. *The Birds of Summer.* Atheneum, 1983. 82-13756. ISBN 0-689-30967-8. 185p. $10.95.

7–10   Living in a trailer with her shiftless, extravagant, yet lovable mother, Oriole, Summer (and her sister Sparrow, both illegitimate, children of two of the many men in their mother's life) is working and saving, grimly determined to protect Sparrow and find a better life for both of them. Oriole is arrested along with the surly man she's picked up, jailed on several counts (the man and others have been growing pot and are accused also of attempted manslaughter and resisting arrest) and Summer makes arrangements for her small sister to be taken in by a wealthy couple who love her. There's much more here: Summer's feelings about her father, a growing affection for a boy, a warm relationship with a teacher and his wife. All of it is smoothly knit together in a flowing narrative that is strengthened by the depth of characterization and the perceptive depiction of the relationship among the characters.

1202   Snyder, Zilpha Keatley. *Blair's Nightmare.* Atheneum, 1984. 83-15677.
ISBN 0-689-31022-6. 204p. $11.95.

4–6   In a sequel to *The Headless Cupid* and *The Famous Stanley Kidnapping Case,*
*   Synder again displays the strong characterization and clever plotting
that distinguished the two earlier books. Blair, the youngest child in a
second-marriage family, is loved and protected by his siblings and his
stepsister when he insists that there is a huge dog he meets at night;
the others know that their parents are disturbed at what they consider
Blair's wild imagination. But there IS a dog, and one by one the other
children see it and help it and hide its existence from their parents. The
tale is spiced by the inclusion of two escaped convicts who are in the
neighborhood and who are convincingly implicated, but it is even more
enjoyable for the humor, the depth of characterization, and the believable intricacy of family relationships.

1203   Snyder, Zilpha Keatley. *A Fabulous Creature.* Atheneum, 1981. 80-18977.
ISBN 0-689-30829-9. 252p. $9.95.

6–9   Fifteen, the intellectual son of intellectual parents, James had been re-
*   luctant to spend a whole summer in a mountain cabin. Then he found,
on a solitary ramble, the beautiful stag, proudly antlered, that accepted
the food James brought him. He also found Diane, and was smitten by
her voluptuous charms, although he soon found out she was dishonest
and a tease. He also knew that she, like her father, was a crack shot
and avid animal hunter; having kept the stag a secret from everyone
but Griffin, a thirteen-year-old who so loved and understood animals
that she actually tamed the stag, James in the end told Diane his secret
as a last, desperate bid for her attention. The outcome seems inevitable,
once Diane and her father know about the magnificent creature that to
them would be a prize trophy; there's an unexpected development,
however, in which James tracks down a runaway Griffin, knowing that
she would do anything to protect the fabulous creature. Or is it, as
James at last becomes aware of Griffin's integrity and beauty, Griffin
herself who is a fabulous creature? This beautifully developed story has
a remarkable integration of theme and plot, it has memorable characters, and it's written in a polished style that comprises some acidly
sharp characterization, strong family relationships, an appreciation of
nature, and one of the funniest bittersweet depictions of unrequited
first love in fiction.

1204   Snyder, Zilpha Keatley. *The Famous Stanley Kidnapping Case.* Atheneum,
1979. 79-12308. ISBN 0-689-30728-4. $8.95.

4–7   In *The Headless Cupid,* Amanda reacted with vehemence when her
mother married a man with four children. Here Amanda, although less
hostile, is still causing trouble; it's her boasting about her rich father in
the U.S. that causes the kidnapping. The family is in Italy, where
Amanda's mother has inherited property she can have only if they live

there a year. What the kidnappers don't bargain for is holding five children captive, and Snyder makes the whole affair believable and very funny. The story would be enjoyable in any case for the action, the humor, and the colorful setting, but Snyder gives it substance by good dialogue and characterization, by a fluid narrative style, and by the perceptively seen intricacies of the relationships among the children and the changes in Amanda.

1205   **Sobol,** Donald J. *Encyclopedia Brown's Book of Wacky Sports;* illus. by Ted Enik. Morrow, 1984. 82-84250. ISBN 0-688-03884-0. 112p. $9.25.

3–6   Sports fans usually enjoy reading about odd mishaps, freakish plays, and unusual happenings, and this not only has them in profusion, but describes them in a jaunty, informal writing style. The book is divided into five sections: basketball, baseball, football, boxing, and other sports. Lightweight but amusing browsing fare.

1206   **Sobol,** Harriet Langsam. *We Don't Look Like Our Mom and Dad;* illus. with photographs by Patricia Agre. Coward-McCann, 1984. 83-24040. ISBN 0-698-20608-8. 32p. $9.95.

3–4   Sensitive and candid, this photo-essay about two Korean boys adopted by an American couple, the Levins, shows a loving family which directly confronts its special conflicts. Joshua, now eleven, was two when he came from Korea; Eric, now ten, was a few months old; they have different mothers. As well as the usual adoptees' concerns about their origins and why their mothers gave them up, the boys must cope with looking different from their parents; "Most of the time the boys don't think about being Korean." Photos, some of them stiffly posed, show Eric and Joshua busy and socialized. But, like the Levins themselves, the book is honest about the difficulties: the family's being stared at in public; Eric's yelling at Joshua in a quarrel, "You're not my brother;" Eric when he was younger working very hard "to try to keep his eyes opened when he smiled, but he just couldn't." What finally emerges is the boys' enrichment and pride in being both Korean and American, and the most memorable photographs show Eric and Joshua with their mother handling the tiny clothes they wore when they came to America, and the Levins cooking a Korean meal together in their kitchen.

1207   **Sorine,** Stephanie Riva. *Our Ballet Class;* illus. with photographs by Daniel S. Sorine. Knopf, 1981. 80-28927. Paper ed. ISBN 0-394-85041-6; Library ed. ISBN 0-394-94821-1. 41p. Paper ed. $4.95; Library ed. $8.99.

2–4   Photographs of a class of five little girls and their teacher have a self-conscious charm. Cordelia, one of the five, is the narrator, which gives the text an immediacy and simplicity that are appealing; unlike first ballet books for older readers, this does not go into details about steps and positions, but rambles through a casual discussion of what fun it is, what you do, why one member of the class is good (no jealousy, the other girls accept this) and what happens when you get silly and stop working. The message does come through; it's work, hard work, that's nevertheless fun.

1208   **Southall,** Ivan. *The Long Night Watch.* Farrar, 1984. 83-48702. ISBN 0-374-34644-5. 160p. $10.95.

9–   "I promise to stay awake." So sixteen-year-old Jon begins his part of Operation S.W.O.R.D.; standing guard on the cliff, waiting to signal "the coming of the heroes of light." It is 1941, S.W.O.R.D. is an Australian Moral ReArmament type of organization of 100 people who have sailed for forty days and nights to a remote Pacific island. There, the Brigadier has promised, God will come and lift them up, away from the fire soon to consume the world. When Jon breaks his promise and falls asleep, the lights do come, but it is the Japanese invading the island. When they land they find five surviving teenagers, including Jon. The other ninety-five have disappeared. Short chapters alternate between Jon's Job-like arguments with God, and the stories of the Brigadier and the other teenagers. Southall has created a contemporary miracle story, with echoes of Daniel, and without any explanation for the mysterious disappearance. While the telling is difficult, with much introspection, the questions (there are no answers) and enigmas will keep readers involved in this unsettling and provocative story.

1209   **Speare,** Elizabeth George. *The Sign of the Beaver.* Houghton, 1983. 83-118. ISBN 0-395-33890-5. 144p. $8.95.

6–9   Set in the Maine wilderness in the eighteenth century, this tightly con-
*   structed story begins with eleven-year-old Matt left alone in the cabin he and his father have built. Pa has gone back to Massachusetts to bring Ma and little Sarah, and expects to be back in six or seven weeks, but it's many months before he returns, and in that time Matt has come to know and respect his Indian neighbors, to understand their feelings about the land and the white intruders, to feel honored that his Indian friend Attean bids him farewell as "white brother" and even offers to take Matt with him when his people break camp to go north on a hunting trip. The story has flow and pace, good style, and that careful but unobtrusive research that marks the best historical fiction.

1210   **Spencer,** William. *Islamic States in Conflict.* Watts, 1983. 82-20125. ISBN 0-531-04544-7. 90p. $8.90.

7–   A retired professor of Middle East history who has worked with many government agencies, Spencer writes with authority and provides a comprehensive, objective survey of internal and external conflict in the Islamic world. The text, well-organized, serious, and written in a straightforward style, analyzes the cultural, political, and religious patterns of the past as a background for the contemporary schisms within the countries of the Middle East, the intricate relationships among those countries, and the factors that influence each country in its problems today in relationships with the western world and in its role in the movement for Arab nationalism. A bibliography and an index are appended.

1211   **Spier,** Peter. *The Legend of New Amsterdam;* written and illus. by Peter Spier. Doubleday, 1979. 78-6032. Trade ed. ISBN 0-385-13179-8; Library ed. ISBN 0-385-13180-1. 23p. $6.95.

2–4   Wonderfully detailed paintings of the buildings and the people of the bustling town of New Amsterdam have fine perspective, use of color, vitality, and humor. Most of Spier's text describes the town and the way its inhabitants lived, worked, studied, and played, but Spier gives a bit of narrative interest by focusing on Annetje Jans Bogardus, a woman who had been out of touch with reality since her husband's death (he'd been killed by the Indians; there is no other reference to the native population or Dutch treatment of them) and who was teased by the children. "Crazy Annie," they called her, because she kept staring upward and shouting "People and stone . . ." Specious it may be, but it enables the author-illustrator to end with a surprise on the last page, a picture of the stone towers that today buttress the tip of the island. A map of the town in 1600 and a list of the occupants of each house or business enterprise are appended to a book that has a palatable text that complements the visual and historical interest of the illustrations.

1212   **Springstubb,** Tricia. *Which Way to the Nearest Wilderness?* Little, 1984. 84-870. ISBN 0-316-80787-7. 166p. $12.95.

4–6   In a very funny novel, alive with the kind of wit and snappy dialogue in Lowry's Anastasia books, Springstubb poignantly depicts the groping, complicated quality of relationships. Tired of being perceived as the "sensible" middle child ("When the dam busted, Eunice's role was a sandbag"), eleven-year-old Eunice reads *Walden* and dreams of escape to "a sunlit one room cabin in the woods" where she can look out for number one and, above all, get away from her parents' rising discord. When her friend Joy fails to get a coveted solo and is resentful, both girls vent their separate angers in a poison pen letters business, selling cards to their schoolmates for "When You Care Enough to Send the Very Worst." As demand for the ugly cards grows, Eunice is more and more sickened, shocked to discover "the level of loathing loose in the world"—and in herself, and she breaks with Joy and the letters. Her plans for escape from home are foiled when her mother beats her to it, and Eunice must help the family cope. Her mother returns, but, though both parents try, the tensions do not disappear, and her mother could leave again. But Eunice knows that *she* will not leave, and that in "the family rubble of pettiness and pain," and in her renewed friendship with Joy, "We're all in this together."

1213   **Stadler,** John. *Hector, the Accordion-nosed Dog.* Bradbury, 1983. 81-7713. ISBN 0-02-786680-7. 27p. $10.95.

K–3   A modest and quiet mountain dog, Hector becomes famous after he leaves school because of his pointing ability; he then wins eleven medals in pointing events in the Olympic games and becomes famous and wealthy. Then he has an accident, and his peerless nose gets crumpled; however, it plays music by itself (at least there are no paws used in the illustrations) and Hector rises again from obscurity to fame, this time as a concert artist. He and a lovely opera singer (starring next door in "Die Zaubernüsse") fall in love at first sight. This time, instead of frittering away his wealth on bistros and discos, Hector takes his bride back to the mountains. The concept is engagingly silly, the story is adequately told, save for the abrupt ending; the illustrations, line and wash, are comic if not polished; all of the characters are animals, and only occasionally does Stadler introduce a feature (the opera singer's ample bosom) that is not animal-like, although the activities are usually those of people.

1214   **Starbird,** Kaye. *The Covered Bridge House;* illus. by Jim Arnosky. Four Winds, 1979. 79-11418. ISBN 0-590-07544-6. 53p. $6.95.

4–6   Deft little lozenge-framed black or silhouette pictures illustrate a collection of poems that, with few exceptions, fall into two categories; lyric poems, usually about some facet of natural beauty, and narrative poems, which tend to be long and very funny. The lyric poetry is often moving and evocative, the narrative poems occasionally seem self-consciously comic; it's a nice mix, however, and there's little question that the humor and action of the longer poems will appeal to children.

1215   **Stearns,** Pamela. *The Fool and the Dancing Bear;* illus. by Ann Strugnell. Atlantic-Little, Brown, 1979. 78-26965. ISBN 0-316-81171-8. 167p. $8.95.

5–7   The fine, often elaborate details of the illustrations add romantic and humorous notes to a fantasy adventure that has pace and depth. A jealous queen has put a curse on a young king who loves her younger sister, and the listless King Rolf—and his equally moribund kingdom—can only be revived by a dancing bear. But what dancing bear? The combination of a wise fool, an acidulous itinerant bear, and the king go on a quest to find the clairvoyant who can lift the spell. There is plenty of action, and the tale has good pace and suspense, but it is in the writing style and the dialogue that Stearns excels; both are polished and witty. Realistic details are artfully blended with fantasy for a cracking good tale.

1216   **Stearns,** Pamela. *The Mechanical Doll;* illus. by Trina Schart Hyman. Houghton, 1979. 78-23451. 45p. $6.95.

4–6   An original story in the fairytale tradition is lavishly illustrated with ornately detailed and appropriately romantic drawings in Hyman's elegant style (with a number of well-endowed maidens peeking out of ornamental embellishments of clothing) and is told in a grave style and tone reminiscent of the fairytales by Oscar Wilde. Here a king, delighted with the gift of a mechanical dancing doll, banishes a young musician who, jealous because the king ignores him for the new toy, breaks the doll's arm. After a time of wandering the kingdom and playing his flute to earn his keep, young Hulun finds the broken metal pieces that were once the doll; he sells his precious instrument to buy the scraps and laboriously puts the doll together. Now she is solemn-faced and awkward, save when Hulun plays his flute—then she dances with grace. The king's evil son steals the doll from Hulun and brings it to his father, but when the doll refuses to dance, the king suspects there is something wrong. He orders the musician brought to him, and days later Hulun's still form is carried in—and the doll waters the dead face with her tears—and Hulun lives again.

1217   **Steig,** William. *CDC?*; written and illus. by William Steig. Farrar, 1984. 84-48515. ISBN 374-31015-7. 57p. $6.95.

4–   Those Steig fans who remember *C D B!* with delight will welcome this companion volume, and it will probably win new readers who enjoy word games and puzzles. Steig uses digits and letters (occasionally an ampersand or cent symbol) to form captions for his cartoon drawings, delightful in themselves. For example, a ballerina whose costume is tattered explains, "D 2-2 S C-D," and a creature from outer space is scanning the earth with a machine while the caption reads "N-M-E L-E-N."

1218   **Steig,** William. *Doctor De Soto*; written and illus. by William Steig. Farrar, 1982. 82-15701. ISBN 0-374-31803-4. 28p. $11.95.

K–3   Dr. De Soto is a mouse, a dentist, and an inventive, canny creature. Although his sign says, "Cats & other dangerous animals not accepted for treatment," he is too kind to ignore the plea of a miserable fox. He does the extraction, but he finds a way to keep the fox from succumbing to the temptation of mouse for dinner. The bland style is a foil for the ridiculous situation, and the triumph of the smallest should appeal to children. Both in text and the clever illustrations, there's the added appeal of Steig's ingenious ideas for dealing with size differential, as Dr. De Soto and his wife (who is his assistant) climb ladders to get to the mouths of larger (but not predatory) patients, or even get there via pulley and hoist.

1219   **Steptoe,** John. *The Story of Jumping Mouse*; ad. and illus. by John Steptoe. Lothrop, 1984. 82-14848. Library ed. ISBN 0-688-01903-X; Trade ed. ISBN 0-688-01902-1. 40p. Library ed. $11.47; Trade ed. $12.50.

K–3   This is a free adaptation of a Native American "why" story that ex-
*   plains how the eagle came to be; the tribal source is not provided. On oversize pages, the artist has used black and white to good dramatic effect, with handsome (occasionally crowded) pictures that show a

world scaled to the size of a small mouse, with a surer touch in the draughtsmanship than is found in most of Steptoe's earlier work. The story has a deliberate pace as it tells of the small mouse who sets off on a long journey to see the far-off land on the other side of a great desert. Helped by Magic Frog, Jumping Mouse uses some of his magic to give eyes to a bison and a sense of smell to a wolf. Thus handicapped, he continues his journey, but through the intercession of Magic Frog, he does better than reach the far-off land, for he bounds into the sky and becomes an eagle who lives in that delectable country forever—a pleasing ending, rather abrupt but dramatic.

1220   **Stevens,** Bryna. *Ben Franklin's Glass Armonica;* illus. by Priscilla Kiedrowski. Carolrhoda, 1983. 82-9715. ISBN 0-87614-202-1. 47p. $6.95.

2–4   Illustrated with line drawings in black, red, and white, this is a lightly fictionalized story, simply told, about the instrument Franklin invented after he'd heard a concert played on glasses of water. His glass armonica had a series of bowls, arranged on a spindle that went through the hole in the bottom of each bowl. The instrument became popular, briefly; Franklin wrote music for it, as did Mozart; it fell into disrepute because it affected performers adversely. In 1956 a glass armonica was built to honor Franklin's 250th birthday; today glass armonica music is played on electronic instruments. An interesting addition to the better-known facts about Franklin's ingenuity.

1221   **Stevens,** Kathleen. *Molly, McCollough, and Tom the Rogue;* illus. by Margot Zemach. Crowell, 1983. 82-45584. Trade ed. ISBN 0-690-04295-7; Library ed. ISBN 0-690-04296-5. 30p. Trade ed. $10.95; Library ed. $10.89.

3–5   In a folk-like tale, Stevens catches the cadence of Irish speech and follows the traditional pattern of the rogue outwitted. This cheerful story's earthy quality is nicely echoed in Zemach's sturdy, deft watercolor pictures. An itinerant rogue, Tom makes his money by finding a farm belonging to a rich farmer, buying a bit of land, and managing to "lose" a treasure map (just drawn) that shows treasure on that spot. When the farmer wants to buy the land back, Tom asks for extra payment. He meets his match in Molly McCullough, whose irascible father falls for the trick just as the others have; Molly is just as clever as Tom, however, and she finds a way to outwit him and also to woo him. A bright, brisk tale is also nice to read aloud to younger children.

1222   **Stevenson,** James. *The Great Big Especially Beautiful Easter Egg;* written and illus. by James Stevenson. Greenwillow, 1983. 82-11731. Trade ed. ISBN 0-688-01789-4; Library ed. ISBN 0-688-01791-6. 32p. Trade ed. $10.00; Library ed. $9.55.

K–3   Grandpa outdoes his own stellar performances of the past, when Mary
*   Ann and Louie serve again as a happy captive audience for a tall and very funny tale. This time Grandpa spins a story about his boyhood

hunt for an extra-large Easter egg to please the girl who lived next door. A magical journey, an amiable bear, a blizzard, a gaggle of sea monsters, and still Grandpa got home safely with his enormous egg from the Frammistan Mountains. To the delight of Louie and Mary Ann, the great big Easter egg still exists, in a deft ending to a story told with wit, pace, imagination, and affection. The illustrations, pastel confections, are just as comic and inventive as the text.

1223   **Stevenson,** James. *Howard.* Greenwillow, 1980. 79-16562. Trade ed. ISBN 0-688-80255-9; Library ed. ISBN 0-688-84255-0. 30p. Trade ed. $7.95; Library ed. $7.63 net.

4–6
yrs.
*

Line and watercolor drawings, softly colored and filled with wonderfully detailed scenes of New York City, illustrate a story that is told with verve and humor, and that has a surprise ending the lap audience (and their readers-aloud) should enjoy. A duck, Howard, misses his group's take-off for the south and then loses his way when he tries to catch up. Landing on a New York rooftop in a snowstorm, he flies down to investigate and makes some new friends, a frog and three mice, with whom he has a series of winter adventures. And then comes spring, and Howard hears his group overhead and flies off to join them. Then, the surprise. The illustrations are Stevenson at his best, but it's in the bland humor of the dialogue that the book's chief charm lies; for example, when Howard discovers the other ducks have gone, he asks some rabbits where they went. "Up in the air." "I know that," says Howard. A rabbit points out, helpfully, "Then they turned left."

1224   **Stevenson,** James. *We Can't Sleep;* written and illus. by James Stevenson. Greenwillow, 1982. 81-20307. Trade ed. ISBN 0-688-01213-2; Library ed. ISBN 0-688-01214-0. 32p. Trade ed. $9.50; Library ed. $8.59.

K–3

Grandpa does it again, in another tall-tale within a picturebook tale illustrated with Stevenson's blithe, animated line and wash drawings, in which Grandpa's adventures are framed in contrast to the free-standing pictures of the background story. Mary Ann and Louie appear at Grandpa's elbow and announce they can't get to sleep. "Strange," says Grandpa, he once had the very same problem, and he launches into an improbable tale (pictured as a small, mustachioed boy) of swimming across the ocean, riding a shark's fin, jumping onto an iceberg . . . meeting a dragon . . . being in a hurricane, etc. etc. The recital is punctuated by the children's queries and comments (especially about wasn't he tired *yet*) and by the time Grandpa finishes, the two children are fast asleep. Great pace, great fun, in a book that has a wonderful integration of text and pictures.

1225   **Stevenson,** James. *What's Under My Bed?;* written and illus. by James Stevenson. Greenwillow, 1983. 83-1454. Trade ed. ISBN 0-688-02325-8; Library ed. ISBN 0-688-02327-4. 30p. Trade ed. $10.50; Library ed. $9.55.

K–2   In a book that deals with night fears in a way that is both sympathetic and humorous, Mary Ann and Louie's grandfather (artful teller of tall tales in the other Stevenson books) describes his experiences as a small, frightened boy after the two children come down in a self-induced terror. Each of Grandpa's remembered horrors is dealt with rationally by the children, and when he tells them how he ran downstairs and was comforted by a grandparental offering of ice cream, they all troop off to the kitchen to see if they can find some. Grandpa, in the raffish drawings of him as a small boy, sports the moustache that Mary Ann and Louie are used to, and Stevenson makes the most of the imagined creatures of the night in his cheerful drawings.

1226   **Stevenson,** James. *The Wish Card Ran Out!* written and illus. by James Stevenson. Greenwillow, 1981. 80-22139. Trade ed. ISBN 0-688-80305-9; Library ed. ISBN 0-688-84305-0. 27p. Trade ed. $7.95; Library ed. $7.63.

K–3   Fresh, funny, lively, and pithy—what more could the lap audience ask? Stevenson's lightly colored cartoon style drawings are just right for this fantasy spoof of credit cards, fairy godmothers, the computer society, and meaningless catch phrases. When Charlie gets a charge card from International Wish he doesn't expect his dog to talk or his younger brother to disappear; storming the headquarters of I.W. he finds serried banks of computers as obstacles to finding little Billy and getting back home, but an amicable giant cockroach and a cleaning woman (a retired fairy godmother) help achieve both goals. Replete with action, wit, and humor.

1227   **Stiller,** Richard. *Your Body Is Trying To Tell You Something.* Harcourt, 1979. 79-87529. ISBN 0-15-299894-2. 128p. $6.95.

7–12   Stiller gives sensible advice, his writing style is casual but never cute, and—although he does not go deeply into discussions of particular illnesses—he does distinguish between psychosomatic and physiological bases for most of the illnesses common to young adults, not ignoring those that are common at any age. The text is sensible because it is calm, objective, and informative, and because it dispels popular fallacies (sweets don't give you acne, and it isn't communicable; here's what can be done to alleviate acne, and here's what can't, etc.) and points out some of the signals that indicate medical help is needed, and some that indicate self-help, or time, as the answer. A candid and informative book concludes with a glossary, a list of suggestions for further reading, and an index.

1228   **Stolz,** Mary Slattery. *Cat Walk;* illus. by Erik Blegvad. Harper, 1983. 82-47576. Trade ed. ISBN 0-06-025974-4; Library ed. ISBN 0-06-025975-2. 120p. Trade ed. $8.95; Library ed. $8.89.

3–6   Although the animals in this totally beguiling story talk to each other,
  *   all of their actions are quite realistic. A barn kitten who's taken into the

house by a farmer's daughter runs away; he loves the little girl, but can't abide being left at home still dressed in the tight clothes in which she's just taken him for a walk. He moves, a forced itinerant, from one home to another, homeless in the times between, and eventually—after a long, long trek—finds his way back to the house where a pair of animal lovers take in strays and where he had made dear friends—a dog and a rabbit. This has fine style, a quiet humor, good animal characters, and a protective affection that never becomes maudlin. A credible journey.

1229   **Stolz,** Mary Slattery. *Go and Catch a Flying Fish.* Harper, 1979. 78-21785. 196p. Trade ed. $7.95; Library ed. $7.89 net.

6–8   Taylor is thirteen, Jem ten, and B.J. is four; their father is night chef in a Florida restaurant, their mother a free spirit, an extravagant and beautiful woman who hates housework and goes off for hours at a time. Sturdy, intelligent, and composed, Taylor and Jem have adjusted to making meals, caring for B.J., and ignoring the increasing tempo and rancor of their parents' quarrels. Indeed, comparing their life with the regimented pattern of that of their friends, they feel lucky. Their parents are loving, and they are given freedom and responsibility. They are not, however, prepared for the trauma and bewilderment that comes when their mother decamps, although it is clear that they will adjust. The rupturing of a family is an old theme in children's books, but Stolz gives this one vitality by the perceptive depiction of people and relationships, and by balancing the story line with vivid descriptions of Jem's and Taylor's interest in the wild life around them.

1230   **Stolz,** Mary Slattery. *What Time of Night Is It?* Harper, 1981. 80-7917. Trade ed. ISBN 0-06-026061-0; Library ed. ISBN 0-06-026062-9. 209p. Trade ed. $9.95; Library ed. $9.89.

6–8   In *Go and Catch a Flying Fish,* a story set on the Gulf Coast of Florida, Taylor's mother had walked out. Now Taylor feels that her father is even more unhappy than she and her brothers, and it is little relief when her grandmother arrives and seems determined to curtail Taylor's freedom and to improve her dress and manners. Grandmother is critical; when Taylor's mother suddenly appears, Grandmother is caustic, and it's a relief to both Taylor and her grandmother when the latter departs. The story is balanced by other facets in Taylor's life; it has some dramatic moments, but plot is less important than the skilled, perceptive, and compassionate depiction of the intricate fluctuations and conflicting loyalties of interpersonal relationships and adjustments.

1231   **Strasser,** Todd. *Angel Dust Blues.* Coward, 1979. 78-31735. ISBN 0-698-20485-9. 203p. $8.95.

7–   Phencyclidine, angel dust, is the drug that causes the violent climax of this trenchant and honest story. Its protagonist Alex is seventeen, handsome, the son of wealthy parents who spend most of their time wintering in Florida. Alone, Alex has been restless and dissatisfied; he joins his friend Michael in drug-dealing and eventually he is caught. Released on bail, Alex confronts his parents, whose solution is psychiatric counseling; he really gains more security, however, from the girl he loves, who stands by even when he tells her what he's done. Michael, by now a fugitive, takes refuge in Alex's garage and seeks his help; Alex, realizing that the once-tough Michael has been destroyed by angel dust and the other drugs he takes, calls the authorities, who find a sick and wasted man in a coma. This is rough and tough, both in subject and language, but it is not didactic although Alex learns something from his bitter experience, and it's not overdone; Strasser's writing has a depth and candor that put the book's focus on the intricate and at times compassionate development of the characters and their relationships.

1232   **Strasser,** Todd. *Workin' For Peanuts.* Delacorte, 1983. 82-14070. ISBN 0-440-0940-1. 196p. $10.95.

7–10   Jeff, the narrator, is a beer vendor at a baseball stadium; his father— surly, idle, and domineering—is out of work, his mother supports the family by driving a bus. When Jeff realizes that the attractive girl he's talked to at games is the daughter of the family that runs the concessions, he's taken aback, but by then he's dated Melissa, is in love with her, and has had to come to terms with the differences in their status. They drift apart after Melissa's home is robbed by some gang members Jeff knows and dislikes; while Melissa knows he is innocent, she cannot accept the fact that he comes from the same social stratum as the gang. This is an honest, vigorous, and perceptive story, convincingly told from Jeff's viewpoint; it has sharp characterization and vivid depictions of Jeff's work situation and his relationship with his father.

1233   **Sullivan,** George, *Sadat: The Man Who Changed Mid-East History,* Walker, 1981. 81-50739. Trade ed. ISBN 0-8027-6434-7; Library ed. ISBN 0-8027-6435-5. 124p. illus. with photographs. Trade ed. $8.95; Library ed. $9.85.

5–8   Published before the assassination, this biography is written by a competent and practiced writer of nonfiction for children; it is as up-to-date as a published book could be, given the circumstances, and it has, pasted on the jacket in response to the tragedy that occurred between the dates of binding and of release, a comment by Anwar el-Sadat, with his life dates: "I would like them to write on my tomb, 'He has lived for peace, and has died for principles.' " While the writing style is not outstanding, the book is valuable because of its subject and has good organization and balanced treatment; it is objective in tone, candid about Sadat's role as a revolutionary and his collaboration with the Germans during World War II and admiring but not laudatory as the older Sadat worked for peace in the Middle East where he had so often in his youth been at war.

1234   **Sullivan,** Mary Beth. *Feeling Free;* by Mary Beth Sullivan et al. Addison-Wesley, 1979. 79-4315. Hardbound ISBN 0-201-07479-6; Paperback ed. ISBN 0-201-07485-0. 192p. Hardbound $9.95; Paperback ed. $5.95.

4–8   Photographs and text are taken from the television series about handicapped children, "Feeling Free," created by The Workshop on Children's Awareness. There are some stories, some quizzes, some suggestions for home demonstrations, a brief play, etc. Most of the text consists of statements by children with disabilities, particularly the five regular participants of the television series; Laurie, who's blind; John, who has a learning diability; Ginny, a dwarf; Gordon, who's deaf; and Hollis, a victim of cerebral palsy. Their comments are candid and extensive, and the book certainly fulfills the function of informing other children what it's like to be handicapped, and certainly it has a high potential for awakening understanding rather than pity. Just as certainly, it may assuage the feelings of handicapped readers that their problems are unique.

1235   **Sutcliff,** Rosemary. *Bonnie Dundee,* Dutton, 1984. ISBN 0-525-44094-1. 205p. $12.50.

7–10   Rosemary Sutcliff at her best is spellbinding, and she is at her engross-
 *   ing best in this story of John Claverhouse (called "Bonnie Dundee" by his followers and diverse uncomplimentary epithets by his foes) a Scottish Royalist who fought the Covenanters and died fighting to keep the house of Stuart on the Scottish throne. The story is told compellingly by Hugh Herriot, who grows from being a very young admirer of Claverhouse to a soldier in his service; it is told in retrospect, written by Grandfather Hugh so that his children's children may know what sort of man Bonnie Dundee was. There's a smoothly incorporated love interest, some stirring military scenes, and—above all—a felicitous blend of fiction and fact, the local and period details (and the Scottish idiom) permeating the writing in that seemingly effortless style that is the mark of the best kind of historical fiction.

1236   **Sutcliff,** Rosemary. *Frontier Wolf.* Dutton, 1981. 80-39849. ISBN 0-525-30260-3. 196p. $11.50.

7–10   Another absorbing historical novel by one of the best writers in this genre is set in Britain in the fourth century. Alexios, a young Centurion, is punished for his poor judgment by being sent to take charge of a frontier outpost manned by the Frontier Wolves, a band of native Britons who are dubious about the ability of their new leader. In a deftly structured and smoothly written tale, Sutcliff incorporates unobtrusively a great deal of information about the events and mores of the period, and she also writes a cracking good adventure story.

1237   **Sutcliff,** Rosemary. *The Light Beyond the Forest; The Quest for the Holy Grail;* decorations by Shirley Felts. Dutton, 1980. 79-23396. ISBN 0-525-33665-6. 144p. $8.95.

5–7   Sutcliff moves from the adventures of one knight of King Arthur's court to another's, but the separate episodes are tied by threads of relationships and overlaps and they are united by their theme: the quest for the Holy Grail, the cup used at the Last Supper. Grave, romantic, fluent, and reverent, the writing is perfectly suited to the auras of high valor and fealty that distinguished the chivalric code. This is not the only fine retelling of an Arthurian legend, but it is a particularly distinguished and cohesive one; it is not easy to read, but it is well worth the reading.

1238   **Sutcliff,** Rosemary. *The Road to Camlann;* illus. by Shirley Felts. Dutton, 1982. 82-9481. ISBN 0-525-44018-6. 143p. $11.50.

6–10   Third in a trilogy of retellings of Arthurian legends (*The Light Beyond the*
  *   *Forest, The Sword and the Circle*) this focuses on the love between Sir Lancelot, King Arthur's dearest friend and noblest knight, and Guenever, Arthur's Queen, and on the scheming Mordred, the king's illegitimate son, who uses that love to bring tragedy to all three at the end of their lives. Sutcliff is, as always, superb in the fluency with which she recreates a period; her characters come alive in bittersweet characterization, and her style is intense and flowing in this grave and poignant conclusion.

1239   **Sutcliff,** Rosemary. *Song for a Dark Queen.* T. Y. Crowell, 1979. 78-19514. 176p. Trade ed. $7.95; Library ed. $7.89 net.

7–10   The dark queen is Boudicca (Boadicea) and her story is told by an old harpist, Cadwan, who reminisces about her life and the fate of her people, the Iceni, during the time of Roman occupation. Cadwan had been her father's harpist, and remembered the Lady Boudicca as an imperious little girl, motherless at the age of four, wed to a man she spurned, raging and vengeful when her father was killed in battle, learning late in marriage to love her husband. And, last, as she is remembered in history, as the warrior-queen. Sutcliff is superb, as always, at bringing historical details into the story so smoothly that they are an integral part of the narrative fabric; her characters are strongly drawn and consistent in their actions and their reactions to events. Cadwan's account ends with Boudicca's defeat and her chosen death: "A long while since, I heard the women keening. Not any more. Nothing any more."

1240   **Sutcliff,** Rosemary. *The Sword and the Circle: King Arthur and the Knights of the Round Table.* Dutton, 1981. 81-9759. ISBN 0-525-40585-2. 261p. $12.50.

6–10   Using Middle English poems and ballads, the Mabinogion, Geoffrey of
  *   Monmouth, and Godfrey of Strasburg for her source material in addition to the *Morte d' Arthur* by Thomas Malory, Sutcliff has put together

the parts of the Arthurian legend so smoothly that they form a glowing, brilliant whole—like a stained glass window in which the total effect is much greater than the impact of each jewel-rich part. The language is flowing and courtly without the use of obsolete words and phrases, the men and women of the court are drawn on a grand scale and yet made mortal and vulnerable, and the book is so imbued with high magic and chivalric code that the dear, familiar heroes and their old, familiar deeds have a fresh dramatic appeal.

1241   **Switzer,** Ellen Eichenwald. *Dancers!* illus. with photographs by Costas. Atheneum, 1982. 82-1701. ISBN 0-689-30943-0. 275p. $14.95.

7–   A dedicated and knowledgeable dance buff, Switzer writes with an easy flow and in an informal style, so the mass of material with which she so expertly deals is eminently readable. Her text begins with a brief background, chiefly of ballet, and proceeds to a history of dance in the United States. Chapters are devoted to such subjects as the training and life style of dancers, dance companies and their choreographers, some rising stars, some established stars, and dance in films and on Broadway. The book gives a cohesive and comprehensive picture, it has good photographs, and the index is preceded by a useful bibliography.

1242   **Szambelan-Strevinsky,** Christine. *Dark Hour of Noon.* Lippincott, 1982. 81-48601. Trade ed. ISBN 0-397-32013-2; Library ed. ISBN 0-397-32014-0. 215p. Trade ed. $10.50; Library ed. $10.89.

6–9   Trina's story began on the day when the Germans declared war against Poland in 1939. Seven years old, she was sent to an internment camp with her family, then to a farm, then to a town where she and her parents shared a three-room apartment with another family. It was there that she became secretly involved in the underground activities of a group of children, none older than fourteen, who formed an independent cell within the resistance movement; they killed a vicious Gestapo officer, blew up a supply train, and eventually worked with the underground in the planning of the Polish Rising of 1944. Dramatic and moving, this story of Nazi occupation and Polish courage is believable and compelling, a grim picture of war's effect on the young.

1243   **Tanaka,** Hideyuki. *The Happy Dog.* Atheneum, 1983. 82-72248. ISBN 0-689-50259-1. 24p. $6.95.

3–5 yrs.   A series of wordless short stories has sunny, comic illustrations with plenty of easy-to-follow action. There are three stories, and each is told via three or four framed pictures per page. The dog, who never walks on four legs and actually might as well be a child, gets into trouble in the first tale when he dirties a sheet drying in the sun and ends with the sheet over him as he tries to clean it. Next, he gets thoroughly, happily wet on a rainy day; last, he has a few problems with a red balloon.

1244   **Tate,** Eleanora E. *Just an Overnight Guest*. Dial, 1980. 80-12970. Trade ed. ISBN 0-8037-4225-8; Library ed. ISBN 0-8037-4223-1. 192p. Trade ed. $8.95; Library ed. $8.44.

4–5   The story is told by nine-year-old Margie, who is even more appalled than her older sister when Momma brings a hostile, obstreperous four-year-old to their home. Margie can't stand little Ethel, resents sharing her bed, resents even more sharing her mother's attention, and is sure that when Daddy (driver for a long-distance moving company) gets home, Ethel will be ousted. What she learns is that Ethel is the child of her uncle and a white woman; the latter has decamped. Margie knows that Ethel had no toys, was often locked into her mother's trailer alone for the night, and was physically abused; although she's disappointed when Daddy comes home and seems to share Momma's feeling of re-sponsibility for Ethel, she's learned enough about duty and kindness from her parents to accept the overnight guest who's come to stay. A promising first novel, this gives an effective picture of a loving black family, and it's convincingly and consistently told from Margie's point of view.

1245   **Tate,** Joan. *Luke's Garden and Gramp*. Harper, 1981. 80-8445. Trade ed. ISBN 0-06-026139-0; Library ed. ISBN 0-06-026144-7. 138p. Trade ed. $9.50; Library ed. $8.89.

6–8   In two stories, Tate writes with gentle tone and sharp insight about two boys who have loving hearts. In the first, longer story Luke is a gener-ous and gentle nonconformist, a city child who is fanatically devoted to his garden. Bullied and beaten by some toughs who cannot understand him, Luke is less careful than usual and, taking refuge in a deserted cottage, falls to his death. The second story, although it has a happy ending, is almost as poignant, picturing the unhappy withdrawal of an old man when his family moves to an apartment where he has no space for a workshop and therefore nothing to do. It is his grandson who un-derstands, persists in hunting for space (and finding it) and gives his dear Gramp a reason to live. Polished style, perceptive characterization, and believable situations make the two stories memorable, although they are so low-keyed and subtle they may appeal chiefly to readers who appreciate nuance.

1246   **Tax,** Meredith. *Families*; illus. by Marylin Hafner. Atlantic-Little, Brown, 1981. 80-21316. ISBN 0-316-83240-5. 32p. $7.95.

2–3   Six-year-old Angie, who lives with her mother and enjoys visiting her father and his new family, comments on the family situations of other children—and those of a few animals as well. The black and white drawings, lively in the use of line, and texturally varied, echo the in-genuous humor of the text. What Angie tells readers is that there is enormous variation in families but that love is the core, whether it's a two-parent, single-parent, multi-generation, childless, or adoptive fam-ily. Simple, casual in tone, and very effective in delivering its message.

1247   **Taylor,** G. Jeffrey. *Volcanoes in Our Solar System;* illus. with photographs and drawings. Dodd, 1983. 82-19819. ISBN 0-396-08118-5. 95p. $10.95.

7–   A research scientist at the University of New Mexico, Taylor writes lucidly and enthusiastically about volcanoes that have been discovered in other parts of the solar system as well as on Earth, knowledge gained primarily through the recording and photographing devices on space probes. The text begins with a description of the different kinds of volcanoes and of how they are formed and function, and proceeds, in separate chapters, to discuss the volcanic activity—past and present—on Earth, the Moon, Mercury, Venus, Mars, and Io, one of the moons of Jupiter. Another chapter is entitled "Asteroids and Meteorites: The Oldest Lava Flows," and explains how scientists are able to understand the origins of such bodies. A final chapter focuses on some of the additional questions asked by planetary scientists and the planetary missions they hope may bring some answers. A glossary and an index are provided.

1248   **Taylor,** Mildred D. *Let the Circle Be Unbroken.* Dial, 1981. 81-65854. ISBN 0-8037-4748-9. 394p. $11.95.

6–9   In a trenchant, dramatic sequel to *Roll of Thunder, Hear My Cry,* which won the 1977 Newbery Medal, Taylor continues the story of the Logan family. This is as well written but not as tightly constructed as the first book, covering a series of tangential events so that it is a family record, a picture of the depression years in rural Mississippi, and an indictment of black-white relations in the Deep South. A young friend is convicted of a murder of which he is innocent, a pretty cousin is insulted by some white boys and her father taunted because he had married a white woman, an elderly neighbor tries to vote, the government pays farmers to plow their crops under, etc. The story is told by Cassie, the only girl in a loving family, and is at its best when she is writing about her family and not about the period.

1249   **Taylor,** Theodore. *The Trouble with Tuck.* Doubleday, 1981. 81-43139. Trade ed. ISBN 0-385-17774-7; Library ed. ISBN 0-385-17775-5. 110p. Trade ed. $8.95; Library ed. $9.90.

5–8   Thirteen-year-old Helen is the narrator of a touching dog story, written with good flow, pace, and structure. Tuck (Friar Tuck Golden Boy) is a handsome golden Labrador, three years old, when Helen and her mother notice that he has trouble seeing; a veterinarian confirms their fear that Tuck is going blind and suggests that he be put down or used for research. Helen refuses; her hope that Companion Dogs for the Blind will give her a guide dog is crushed, but some time later a staff member calls and says that they are retiring a guide dog whose owner has died. Tuck, by now blind, resents the new dog, Lady Daisy, but Helen refuses to give up in her attempts to train Tuck to lean against the other dog and so follow her—and the book ends with a happy Helen triumphantly showing her family the successful results of her patient, secret training sessions.

1250   **Tchudi,** Susan. *The Young Writer's Handbook;* by Susan and Stephen Tchudi. Scribner, 1984. 84-5312. ISBN 0-684-18090-1. 156p. $12.95.

7–12   A very sensible and fairly comprehensive book of advice that should be useful both to those adolescents who want to write professionally or those who simply wish to improve their writing skills. Both of the authors teach English at the university level, and their text is lucid and explicit; they do not believe it is possible to teach others how to write, but that there are ways to help aspirants improve the kind of writing they've chosen to do. They give good general advice and make specific suggestions (poetry, fiction, letter-writing, school papers, etc.) and conclude with a chapter on publishing. The index is burdened by personal names (Woody Allen and Peter Gay, for example, whose comments are cited) that give no clue as to the nature of the entry, but it's a minor weakness in an otherwise substantial book.

1251   **Terkel,** Susan Neiburg. *Feeling Safe, Feeling Strong;* written by Susan Neiburg Terkel and Janice E. Rench. Lerner, 1984. 84-9664. ISBN 0-8225-0021-3. 68p. illus. $9.95.

5–7   The authors, a specialist in child development and the director of a rape crisis center, are explicit and forthright, describing various forms of sexual abuse or harassment in a way that will help children understand their rights, recognize danger signals, and take appropriate action. The tone of the writing is not frightening but it is serious. This useful book concludes with a chapter that reiterates advice given earlier about telling parents or other adults promptly when there has been abuse or attempted abuse, and it gives toll-free numbers for national sources of assistance.

1252   **Testa,** Fulvio. *Never Satisfied;* written and illus. by Fulvio Testa. Faber, 1982. ISBN 0-571-12513-1. 25p. $10.95.

K–3   "How boring it is here! Nothing exciting ever happens," says one morose boy to another, in a minimal text that consists of similar dialogue. Using a device like that of Ellen Raskin's in *Nothing Ever Happens on My Block*, the boys plod on, grumbling about their boredom, while behind them all sorts of strange things happen. At only one point do the dialogue and the pictures meet: the boys are wishing they could see a panther, one pops out from behind a tree and says, "But I'm a panther," and the retort is, "I said *wild* panthers," as the boys go obliviously on. The humor of the concept should appeal to the read-aloud audience, and the framed pictures, spacious in composition, softly colored, and wittily conceived, are so integrated with the text as to achieve the best counterpoint between the blandness of the words and the extravagance of the background events.

1253   **Thomas,** Dylan. *A Child's Christmas in Wales;* illus. by Edward Ardizzone. Godine, 1980. 80-66216. ISBN 0-87923-339-7. 45p. $10.95.

5–   Ardizzone's marvelously evocative drawings, superbly economic in their use of line (some in color, some in black and white) are on almost every page of a prose poem that has become a classic in its time. Like any poem, this has a cadence that is better heard than read; whether children can cope with the long sentences, the imagery, and the allusions, and whether American children of today can appreciate some of the references, is moot. For those who are not daunted, the vivid, lyric remembrances of the joys of Christmas in a Welsh coastal town, a narrative made even more vivid by the artist, should be a joy; for all readers, however, there is much that should be a comprehensible and often diverting experience.

1254   **Thrasher,** Crystal. *Between Dark and Daylight.* Atheneum, 1979. 79-12423. ISBN 0-689-50150-1. 251p. $8.95.

5–7   Again, as in *The Dark Didn't Catch Me,* it is Seely, now twelve, who is the narrator. Seely's family is again on the move, her father hunting the employment that was so hard to find in the 1930's. When their truck breaks down, they move into an abandoned house and are befriended by the Meaders family; Seely is drawn to Johnny Meaders, a few years her senior. She quickly learns to avoid two other boys, the malicious and slightly retarded Fender twins whose avowed hatred of Johnny spreads to her because she and Johnny are friends. The story has a tragic death, as did its predecessor, for the twins kill Johnny; they are taken away by the authorities, but that is little comfort to those who mourn. Although somber, the book is so rich in characterization and so vivid in depicting life in rural Indiana during the depression years, that it is absorbing reading. Thrasher doesn't stoop to the invention of quaint characters or dialogue; the people are seen with compassionate insight, and their speech is richly flavorful rather than designedly homespun.

1255   **Thrasher,** Crystal. *End of a Dark Road.* Atheneum, 1982. 82-3958. ISBN 0-689-50250-8. 228p. $10.95.

6–8   Seely is the protagonist and narrator in a third book (*The Dark Didn't Catch Me* and *Between Dark and Daylight*) about Seely and her family, set in a small town during the Depression Era. Seely is fifteen now, deeply involved with her friends in the sophomore class, concerned about her friend Russell, whose stepfather abuses him and shoots him (which Seely is convinced was deliberate) and protective toward Peedle, the retarded boy often taunted by others. After her father dies, Mr. Avery, the school bus driver who has helped her many times in many ways, and Mrs. Avery hire Seely to work in their store; her mother earns money by baking, and the family plans to move to town so that Seely and her brother can go to better schools. This doesn't have as strong a story line as the first two books, but it is equally perceptive in its characterization, smooth writing style, and vivid depiction of a period and a community.

1256   **Thrasher,** Crystal. *A Taste of Daylight.* Atheneum, 1984. 84-2967. ISBN
0-689-50313-X. 204p. $12.95.

6–9   Fifth and last in a series of books about an Indiana family's experiences
during the Depression Era (the series began in 1975 with *The Dark
Didn't Catch Me*) this is as strongly written as the best of its predecessors. Other members of the family have died or left home by the time
Seely's mother decides she will move into a rented city house with her
two children. Although there are plot developments (friendship with
neighboring children, Mom's decision to remarry, Seely's being sent to
stay with a beloved older sister) the focus is on life in the time of a severe depression rather than on events; Thrasher does an excellent job of
evoking the period, but does not sacrafice writing style or authorial insight to do so.

1257   **Timpanelli,** Gioia, ad. *Tales from the Roof of the World: Folktales of Tibet;*
illus. by Elizabeth Kelly Lockwood. Viking, 1984. 83-19826. ISBN 0-670-
71249-3. 53p. $11.95.

4–6   Four folktales, rather lengthy and sometimes rambling, are included in
a book handsomely illustrated with symbols "of Auspicious Coincidence." As in folklore of all countries, the tales stress such virtues as
kindness, modesty, and filial obligation; in the first story ("The Boy, His
Sisters, and the Magic Horse") in fact, the outcast lad who has become
wealthy takes his parents to live with him in a palace despite the fact
that his father had put him in a pit with a stone over the opening. One
of the stories, "The Unwilling Magician," is a variant on a familiar
theme: a man gains a reputation (and a princess) by solving a series of
lucky or coincidental clues. Adequately retold here, the tales should be
a useful addition to the literature for storytellers.

1258   **Titus,** Eve. *Anatole and the Pied Piper;* illus. by Paul Galdone. McGraw-
Hill, 1979. 78-23513. ISBN 0-07-064897-2. 32p. $7.95.

K–3   It would be hard to imagine an Anatole who wasn't parented by Galdone as well as Titus, for the artist captures all the brio and humor of
the author's writing. In this newest tale, the mouse-hero's wife takes an
active part, for it is she, Doucette, who thinks of the way to rescue two
dozen schoolmice who have been captured by Grissac. Grissac is a flute
player and composer; hoping to win a contest for the best music about
small animals, he has lured the young mice (Yes, just as the pied piper
did) so that he can judge his compositions by their reactions. With the
help of the pigeons of Paris, the members of the Mouse Singing Society
effect a daring rescue, and Anatole composes "The Ballet of the Pied
Piper" as a victory celebration, with Doucette as prima ballerina. Nice
nonsense, this is written with flair and pace, and it has just enough
French in just the right places to spice the tale without stumping the
audience.

1259   **Todd,** Leonard. *The Best Kept Secret of the War.* Knopf, 1984. 83-18756. Library ed. ISBN 0-394-96569-8; Trade ed. ISBN 0-394-86569-3. 165p. Library ed. $9.99; Trade ed. $9.95.

5–7   Cam, the narrator, is ten years old; the setting is rural North Carolina; the time is the period of World War II, and Cam has two abiding interests. One is his concern for his father, who is in service; the other is the protection of an elderly man, Jeddah, who has run away from a nursing home and is in hiding. Cam's best friend Tal is irritated by Cam's pride in his father; Tal's father (who runs the nursing home with an eye to profits) tries to get Jeddah back and also makes advances to Cam's pretty, lonely mother. Todd has knit the plot elements together nicely, and the resultant exposé is both logical and satisfying, although it's perhaps a bit too neat. The story is capably written, with good pace and well-drawn characters.

1260   **Tolan,** Stephanie S. *The Liberation of Tansy Warner.* Scribner, 1980. 79-2853. ISBN 0-684-16523-6. 192p. $7.95.

6–9   Ninth-grade Tansy is thrilled when she is cast as Anne Frank in a school play; she knows her icy, disapproving father will show little response, but she can't wait to get home and tell her mother. Mother has always been warm, supportive, helpful, and *there.* But Tansy comes home to find a note from Mom saying that she has left and won't be coming back, that she has to "have some value in the world." Dad at first assumes that it's a brief act of defiance, but when he realizes his wife has left forever, he retreats into silence and apathy. It's up to Tansy and her older brother and sister to run the household and take care of family finances, and Tansy finds it hard to continue rehearsals, but she can't give up the play she loves. She's also determined to find her mother, does so, and learns that the breach is irrevocable; despite her love for her children, Mom can't go back to being a housekeeper dominated by an overbearing husband. The plot threads (home and school play) merge smoothly, and the story is expanded by Tansy's relationships with her peers, and deepened by the perceptive delineation of relationships. As often happens, the most unpleasant character in the story, Dad, is the most powerfully drawn, and the depiction is consistent; even when Tansy's moving performance as Anne Frank brings kudos from everyone who knows her, Dad—who has come to the performance as a duty—makes no attempt to approach Tansy after the performance.

1261   **Topalian,** Elyse. *Margaret Sanger.* Watts, 1984. 83-26022. ISBN 0-531-04763-6. 122p. illus. with photographs. $8.90.

7–   A few photographs are used to illustrate a biography that is candid and informative, adequately written despite an occasional jarring note, such as conflicting statements about the ages of Sanger's children. A dedicated and indefatigable pioneer in the long battle to legalize the dissemination of birth control information and devices, Margaret Sanger was frequently in conflict with the established order. The book has a good balance of personal and professional material; a brief reading list and an index are included.

1262   **Towne,** Mary. *Paul's Game.* Delacorte, 1983. 82-72750. Trade ed. ISBN 0-440-07039-2; Paper ed. ISBN 0-440-96633-7. 180p. Trade ed. $13.95; Paper ed. $2.50.

7–10   It all started innocently enough, with Andrea (who tells the story) and Julie trying a mind-reading experiment to relieve the boredom of a rainy afternoon. They discover Julie scores amazingly high on receiving Andrea's messages and Andrea's taken aback when Julie mentions it at a party. Andrea doesn't like Paul, who immediately becomes interested in Julie, and she's further upset when Julie and Paul start dating. She's sure Paul's really only interested in Julie's psychic ability and that he's using her in some way. Suspicion leads to apprehension and then to terror as Andrea finds her worst fears realized and learns that Paul's game is to induce Julie, via telepathy, to commit a vicious crime. Andrea intervenes and Paul is caught and convicted in a story that has mounting tension and suspense, that is believable if readers accept the validity of psychic powers, and that has firm characterization.

1263   **Townsend,** John Rowe. *Cloudy-Bright.* Lippincott, 1984. Library ed. ISBN 0-397-32090-6; Trade ed. ISBN 0-397-32089-2. 224p. Library ed. $11.89; Trade ed. $12.50.

7–10   In separate (usually alternating) chapters, Jenny and Sam are the narrators of an English love story that has pace and nuance, strong local color, and engaging protagonists who are beset by many problems typical of late adolescence. Sam and Jenny meet when he sees her using an expensive camera; having just lost a similar one and needing it for a contest, Sam prevails on a stranger (Jenny) to let him use her Hasselblad. It's a convincing and often entertaining move from a common interest to a reciprocal affection, and it's made an even more entertaining passage because of Townsend's skillful depiction of the two very different households from which Sam and Jenny come.

1264   **Townsend,** John Rowe. *The Creatures.* Lippincott, 1980. 79-2405. Trade ed. ISBN 0-397-31864-2; Library ed. ISBN 0-397-31865-0. 256p. Trade ed. $8.95; Library ed. $8.79 net.

6–9   In an expertly crafted science fiction story, Townsend envisions a world of the future in which (after war has decimated the population of Earth) a small colony of superior beings lives under a protective dome. They are Persons, colonists from another planet; the natives are Creatures, uncouth menial workers controlled by the Guards. Two of the Persons, Harmony and Vector (all girls have musical names, all boys mathematical ones) fall in love, which simply isn't done, and they leave their com-

munity and escape to hide among the Creatures. In the uprising of the
Guards and the counter-revolution of the Creatures, the young lovers
are spared—but it isn't the plot that's important, although that is constructed with care and pace, but what the author has to say about an
oppressed people and the bias against them, a bias Harmony and Vector lose as they live among the Creatures and come to realize that they,
too, are human beings, only beings who haven't had the advantages of
the elite. Provocative as well as entertaining.

1265   **Townsend,** John Rowe. *Dan Alone.* Lippincott, 1983. 82-49051. Trade ed.
ISBN 0-397-32053-1; Library ed. ISBN 0-397-32054-X. 224p. Trade ed.
$9.95; Library ed. $9.89.

5–8   When his mother runs off with a married man, eleven-year-old Dan is
taken in by his grandfather; it is from Grandpa's strident new wife that
Dan learns that the man he's always called his father is not his real father. His legal father is a shiftless scamp, but he gives Dan information
about a place to hide, and it is here that Dan goes after his Grandpa
dies, for he fears he'll be sent to a notorious orphanage. In his retreat
he meets another waif, Olive, who is as tough and resilient as Dan is
shy and tender. Dan finally finds his father (the Jewish glazier who's
been the butt of prejudice and derision to most of the people Dan
knows) and the story ends with his finding, at last, a happy home with
his real father and mother, and Olive. Townsend's tongue is clearly in
cheek throughout this entertaining melodrama; he must have had a
wonderful time drawing parallels to characters in Dickensian novels, for
echoes of Fagin, the Cheerybles, and others float through the story.
There's no attempt to imitate the style of Dickens, for the story is written in a straightforward style, and when there is any exaggeration of
the strong characters, it is clearly deliberate. The writing has good color
and pace, and even if read wih matching tongue-in-cheek, the book is
satisfying.

1266   **Townsend,** John Rowe, *The Islanders.* Lippincott, 1981. 81-47105. Trade
ed. ISBN 0-397-31940-1; Library ed. ISBN 0-397-31941-X. 248p. Trade ed.
$9.95; Library ed. $9.89.

7–10   On an isolated, uncharted island the descendants of the Deliverer and
his shipmates have been living for several generations. A rigid society
that lives by the words of the Book they have inherited, a book of laws
promulgated by the Deliverer, the islanders are suspicious and hostile
when two castaways are stranded on their shore. The two are followed,
in time, by others of their race (Polynesian, or a similar origin) and the
conflict that follows leads eventually to the discovery that the Deliverer,
so long revered, and his Book, so long obeyed, have recorded the sins
of a violent man. This is only discovered when a man is found who can
read, a visitor to the island where all belief has been based on oral
transmission of mores. The protagonists are two of the island's chil-

dren, Molly and Tom, who have befriended the castaways and who become involved in the conflict that leads to the exposure. This is nicely conceived and structured, written with good pace and style, and with the depth that readers have come to expect from Townsend.

1267   **Townsend,** John Rowe. *Kate and the Revolution.* Lippincott, 1983. 81-48605. Trade ed. ISBN 0-397-32015-9. Library ed. ISBN 0-397-32016-7. 227p. Trade ed. $11.50; Library ed. $11.89.

7–9   Graustark lives! Townsend does a very neat spoof on the novel of romantic adventure by sending a bright, brisk contemporary teenager, Kate, to the mythical little country of Essenheim. Kate has met the Crown Prince, Rudi, in London, and when he invites her to visit his home, she goes both because she finds him attractive and because her father, a journalist, is interested in the political unrest of Essenheim. What Kate gets involved in is not a single revolution, but a series of comic opera coups, as various factions succeed each other and Kate finds that her Lothario is less attractive than the dependable British reporter who's been covering the story. The author lampoons a range of political types, the action is fast and funny, and the whole is a romp—with some social satire there for those who see it.

1268   **Townsend,** Sue. *The Secret Diary of Adrian Mole Aged 13¾.* Avon/Flare, 1984. ISBN 0-380-86876-8. 208p. $2.25.

6–   First published in England, this is a comic, candid, and sophisticated account of the tribulations of adolescence. Adrian's parents separate and his mother goes off with the man who'd lived next door (she comes back); his father loses his job; Adrian is bullied by a lout at school, falls deeply in love, makes friends with an aging pensioner, etc. Adrian's appealing because he's such a decent chap; he's funny because his intellectual pretensions are so ingenuous; he's believable enough to make readers laugh with him more than they laugh at him.

1269   **Toye,** William, ad. *The Fire Stealer;* illus. by Elizabeth Cleaver. Oxford, 1980. 79-67169. ISBN 0-19-540321-5. 24p. $6.95.

K–2   One of the tales of Nanabozho, hero of many Canadian Indian legends, is simply retold for younger children and is illustrated in handsome, bright collages by Cleaver, who has won the prestigious Howard-Gibbon Medal for an earlier book, *The Loon's Necklace.* In this story, Nanabozho uses his magic to change shape, and is thereby able to steal fire and bring it home to ease his grandmother's last years. Thus his people learn to use fire, yet be alert to its dangerous quality; too, the story explains the bright colors of fall foliage, for Nanabozho asked his people to remember him and how the torch he carried had lit the trees with red and gold. A good choice for reading aloud or telling to young children.

1270   **Travers,** Pamela L., ad. *Two Pairs of Shoes;* illus. by Leo and Diane Dillon. Viking, 1980. 78-3386. ISBN 0-670-73677-5. 35p. $10.95.

4–6   From Middle Eastern sources, Travers has chosen two stories for pol-
*   ished retelling; her prose has the cadence of the formal oral tradition of
        classical Middle Eastern folklore, with its ornate speech and courtly ele-
        gance. In *The Sandals of Azaz*, a courtier proves his devotion to his king
        and his humility in acknowledging his humble start in life; in *Abu Kas-
        sem's Slippers*, a humorous tale, a merchant keeps trying to get rid of an
        old pair of slippers and, with each attempt, gets into a situation where
        the slippers come back and he has to pay a fine. The stories would still
        be entertaining were they not illustrated, but the illustrations add im-
        measurably to the book: graceful, ornately detailed and handsome in
        composition, they have the rich formality of Persian miniatures. While
        the book can be used as a source for storytelling, it would be a pity to
        miss the beauty of the pictures, framed in elegant borders, that will be
        enjoyed by independent readers or those to whom the book may be
        read aloud, sharing the art.

1271   **Turkle,** Brinton. *Do Not Open;* written and illus. by Brinton Turkle. Dut-
        ton, 1981. 80-10289. ISBN 0-525-28785-X. 29p. $11.50.

K–2   The strong, simple composition that is typical of Turkle is especially
        well suited to the still isolation of deserted beaches, and the combina-
        tion of rich color used with restraint and the framed squares of clear
        print adds to the visual appeal of the pages. The story is a nice blend of
        realism and fantasy, its protagonist a chubby, cheerful woman who
        lives in a small house near the ocean and delights in beachcombing.
        She's taken aback when she opens a bottle (it says "DO NOT OPEN"
        but there's a child's crying coming from the bottle and she can't resist
        letting it out) and a dark cloud emerges and turns into a ferocious ge-
        nie. After the first surprise, Miss Moody is not afraid; she tricks the ge-
        nie into turning into a mouse, and it's eaten by her cat (found, long
        ago, on the beach) and she gets home to find her one wish is granted:
        the handsome clock she'd once salvaged, which has never run, is tick-
        ing cozily away.

1272   **Uchida,** Yoshiko. *The Best Bad Thing.* Atheneum, 1983. 83-2833. ISBN
        0-689-50290-7. 116p. $9.95.

4–6   In a sequel to *A Jar of Dreams* Rinko, now almost twelve, is again the
        narrator. The only girl in a Japanese-American family, Rinko is dis-
        mayed when Mama decides that a family friend, Mrs. Hata, who is re-
        cently widowed and is struggling (this is the Depression Era) with her
        cucumber farm, needs help. Rinko thinks of "Aunt" Hata as eccentric,
        doesn't want to leave her family, and fears two small boys who will
        surely be a nuisance—but she goes, and she learns to cope with the
        work, to admire Aunt Hata's courage, and to appreciate Mama's feeling
        that it is part of one's Christian duty to help those in need. The writing
        style and characterization have depth and polish, the narrative has an
        easy flow, and the story creates vividly the atmosphere of the period
        and the California setting.

1273   **Uchida,** Yoshiko. *A Jar of Dreams*. Atheneum, 1981. 81-3480. ISBN 0-689-50210-9. 131p. $8.95.

3–5   A story of the Depression Era is told by eleven-year-old Rinko, the only girl in a Japanese-American family living in Oakland and suffering under the double burden of financial pressure and the prejudice that had increased with the tension of economic competition. Into the household comes a visitor who is a catalyst for change, Aunt Waka, a younger sister of Rinko's mother, a self-confident woman who encourages her brother-in-law to defend himself against persecution, to start his own business. For her niece, suffering from the bias she's met at school, Aunt Waka's serenity sets an example: Rinko realizes that the name-calling may hurt but that it shouldn't make her value herself any less. In addition to the jar in which she's saving college money, Rinko plans a "jar of dreams," a fund that can be used to visit Japan, now that she is no longer too embarrassed to acknowledge her Japanese heritage. Smoothly written, smoothly structured, this gives a picture of a time, a culture, and a child that is moving and is realistic in the extent of the change and development in Rinko and her family.

1274   **Ure,** Jean. *See You Thursday*. Delacorte, 1983. 83-5217. ISBN 0-385-29303-8. 194p. $12.95.

7–12   There are many books about a shy, lonely adolescent who falls in love, but none quite like this. In a story from England, Marianne (sixteen, awkward, friendless) is at first resentful when her mother rents a room to a blind music teacher, Mr. Shonfeld. He proves to be young, attractive, and independent albeit grateful for help that is given when needed. When Marianne's mother realizes that the two are attracted to each other, she asks Shonfeld to leave; the story ends realistically, with a promise of later happy solution. A perceptive book, this explores interreligious understanding and the adolescent's need for independence; it has depth and sensitivity in its depiction of characters and relationships, and a fluent style; it deals with many of the problems common to young adults with conviction and compassion.

1275   **Ure,** Jean. *What If They Saw Me Now?* Delacorte, 1984. 83-14981. ISBN 0-385-29317-8. 150p. $13.95.

7–10   When athletic English high-schooler Jamie is trapped into replacing the injured male lead in a ballet show, his one terror is that his friends will find out. As rehearsals continue, he gets to like his partner, upper-class dance-fanatic Anita, and discovers that ballet is the one thing for which he has a natural talent; but he is also desperately trying for a place on the baseball team, and talking tough about sex and girls with his friend Doug. Much of the comedy comes from the transitions Jamie has to make between his macho culture (with its scorn for men "messing about in tights and ballet shoes") and the obsessive, rarefied atmosphere of the rehearsal room. The cover showing an embarrassed muscular young man holding an aloof ballerina may entice boys as well as girls into a funny and liberating novel.

1276   **Ure,** Jean. *You Two;* illus. by Ellen Eagle. Morrow, 1984. 84-8947. ISBN 0-688-03857-3. 184p. $9.25.

4–6   When her father lost his job and had to take another at a lower salary, Elizabeth's family moved to a smaller house and she was transferred from a private school to Gladeside Intermediate, a public school. Taken aback by the crowded classes, the rough behavior of some of the students, and being teased because she was proficient in French and had high standards in English lessons, Elizabeth was desperate until she found a friend. Once she had Paddy, it was "you two" people referred to—but her mother didn't like Paddy and discouraged the friendship. When she and Paddy had a fight, Elizabeth felt lonelier than ever. It took a minor crisis at school, a wise principal's advice to Elizabeth's mother, and a gesture of forgiveness to set things right. The setting is an English school, but the group dynamics and the individual relationships should have a universal appeal. Characters and writing style are equally strong, and the author is most perceptive in depicting the loneliness of a child who is rejected by her peers and the contrasting joy and security when she has a friend.

1277   **Van Allsburg,** Chris. *Ben's Dream;* written and illus. by Chris Van Allsburg. Houghton, 1982. 81-20029. ISBN 0-395-32084-4. 31p. $8.95.

2–4   Unlike Van Allsburg's first two books, this is presented not as outright fantasy, but as a child's dream. Ben, curled in an armchair and studying for a geography test on great landmarks of the world, falls asleep to the soporific sound of rain. In his dream, Ben sails in his house through a flooded world, seeing such landmarks as the leaning tower of Pisa or the Statue of Liberty half-submerged. But was it just a dream? Ben's friend Margaret reports the same experience. The solidity and the perspective of Van Allsburg's fine-lined drawings are impressive, the text a vehicle for an idea rather than a story. The question is, who is the audience for this? What text there is reads as though it were designed for a read-aloud audience, but appreciation and recognition of the landmarks may require older readers, especially in such drawings as the one of the Eiffel Tower, which shows the intricate structural supports at an unusual angle, rather than the whole structure.

1278   **Van Allsburg,** Chris. *The Garden of Abdul Gasazi;* written and illus. by Chris Van Allsburg. Houghton, 1979. 79-016844. ISBN 0-395-27804-X. 31p. $8.95.

K–3   Taking care of a neighbor's bad-tempered dog, Alan is dismayed when
  *   the dog runs into the garden of a retired magician, Abdul Gasazi, especially because Gasazi's sign states "Absolutely, Positively No Dogs Allowed in This Garden." Gasazi, when Alan sees him and apologizes,

says he's turned the dog into a duck—but when a disconsolate Alan gets back, the dog is there with his owner, who gently tells the boy that the magician had been fooling him, that nobody can turn a dog into a duck. The story is rather flimsy, but that's amply compensated for by the illustrations, pencil drawings that are stunning in texture, composition, and chiaroscuro virtuosity, with special artistry in the solidity of forms and in architectural details.

1279   **Van Allsburg,** Chris. *Jumanji;* written and illus. by Chris Van Allsburg. Houghton, 1981. 80-29632. ISBN 0-395-30448-2. 28p. $9.95.

2–4   Two children, alone at home while their parents are gone for the afternoon, play a game they have found lying under a tree. Judy reads the rules for the game, "Jumanji," and realizes that it must be played to the end; not until they begin play do she and Peter know why that's true. With each roll of the dice, there's a new hazard: a menacing lion, a troop of destructive monkeys, a torrential monsoon, a herd of rhinos, etc. As soon as they reach their game goal and Judy yells "Jumanji" the air is cleared, all signs of the havoc caused by the animals disappear, and by the time Mother and Father return the children have taken the game back to the tree. As the story ends, they watch two other children find and retrieve the game. Freshly imaginative, a nice odyssey—from boredom to wild excitement and back to placid, everyday life—is adequately told and brilliantly illustrated, the soft black and white pictures (Conté pencil and dust) almost velvety in their soft texture. As he did in *The Garden of Abdul Gasazi* Van Allsburg uses the contrast of light and shadow, and the solidity of forms with distinct mastery.

1280   **Van Allsburg,** Chris. *The Mysteries of Harris Burdick;* written and illus. by Chris Van Allsburg. Houghton, 1984. 84-9006. ISBN 0-395-35393-9. 17p. $14.95.

All   The cover story for this wordless book is set forth in a preface; suppos-
ages   edly the fourteen pictures were the illustrations for a children's book by the mythical Burdick. A table of contents has subtitles that give some clues, but essentially the book consists of a series of black and white pictures remarkable for their play of light and shadow, for the handling of mass, and for the elegant composition. Each picture has some fey quality (a mysterious light, a nun suspended in space in a cathedral, a bird flying out of wallpaper) to stimulate the viewer's curiosity and—according to the preface—"to find the true meaning of Burdick's provocative art." A bobby-dazzler.

1281   **Van Leeuwen,** Jean. *The Great Rescue Operation;* illus. by Margot Apple. Dial, 1982. 81-65851. Trade ed. ISBN 0-8037-3139-6; Library ed. ISBN 0-8037-3140-X. 167p. Trade ed. $9.95; Library ed. $9.89.

3–5   The three mice of *The Great Christmas Kidnapping Caper* are back again, with Marvin the Magnificent (a Runyonesque character, inspired by his sizeable ego to more bravado than sense) as the narrator. He and Raymond, the intellectual and practical member of the trio, are distraught when their companion Fats disappears. Since they all live in the toy department of Macy's, it is suspected that Fats was in a doll carriage when it was sold. The story of how Marvin and Raymond venture forth into Manhattan to track down and rescue Fats is hilarious, its yeasty ingenuity verging deftly on the improbable. The three mice are distinct—if exaggerated—personalities, the style is colorful and breezy, the plot—deliberately unrestrained—is nicely structured and paced.

1282   **Van Woerkom,** Dorothy O. *Hidden Messages;* illus. by Lynne Cherry. Crown, 1979. 78-10705. ISBN 0-517-53520-3. 32p. $6.95.

2–3   Written concisely and clearly, this fine introductory science book describes the ways in which scientists observe natural phenomena, form theories, and test them. It begins with an anecdote about Benjamin Franklin's observation of what seemed to him ant communication, goes on to cite an experiment with moths by Jean Henri Fabre, and concludes with a discussion of the social behavior of ants, the way they secrete glandular liquids to communicate, the fact that these scented liquids are called pheromones, and it concludes with a conjecture about whether or not human beings have pheromones—and the fact that, if we keep asking questions as Franklin and Fabre did, some day we may have answers. The illustrations are clean in composition, subdued in color, and nicely matched to textual references; although they don't give scale, they do show comparative sizes of ant species. The text gives the phonetic pronunciation of pheromones as "PER-ah-monz."

1283   **Vautier,** Ghislaine. *The Shining Stars: Greek Legends of the Zodiac;* ad. by Kenneth McLeish; illus by Jacqueline Bezencon. Cambridge University Press, 1981. ISBN 0-521-23886-2. 31p. $9.95.

3–5   Like Alison Lurie's *The Heavenly Zoo* this gives brief accounts of some of the Greek legends of the stars; first published in France under the title *Quand Brillent Les Etoiles,* this is not quite as well illustrated as the Lurie book. The retellings of legends are equally brief but are more simple and direct in style, making them more appropriate for slightly younger readers or for reading aloud to children too young to be independent readers. Star maps for each sign of the zodiac are included at the back of the book; each carries the picture (Aries, Taurus, Gemini, etc.) that is also used with the retelling of the appropriate legend.

1284   **Veglahn,** Nancy J. *Fellowship of the Seven Stars.* Abingdon, 1981. 81-1120. ISBN 0-687-12927-3. 175p. $7.95.

7–10   Mazie, who tells the story of her involvement with the Fellowship in retrospect, is an adolescent whose parents have always been appreciative of the fact that she has been helpful and cooperative, unlike her brother Rich. Always in trouble, amoral, a drifter, Rich gets all the attention. Perhaps this is why the group life of Messengers of God, as the Fellowship members call themselves, is so appealing. Perhaps it's because each new member is welcomed with love. Mazie joins—and then she sees the pressure to conform to the rules, the pressure to earn money (selling pencils on the street) for the group, the defensive propaganda, the strictures of the cult. It isn't easy to break away, but Mazie does. This is perhaps the best of the several novels for young people about the cult commune; the first-person approach enables the reader to see why such groups are attractive and why their propaganda is insidious. The characters are portrayed with strength and conviction albeit with varying depth; the writing style is smooth. This may be written as an exposé, and indeed it serves that purpose well, but it is also a well-structured story that is not obscured by the message.

1285   **Ventura,** Piero. *Great Painters;* written and illus. by Piero Ventura. Putnam, 1984. 84-3423. ISBN 0-399-21115-2. 160p. $15.95.

5–   In an oversize book that is profusely illustrated with both Ventura's
*   own paintings (beautifully detailed, small-scale, ingeniously laid out on the pages) and fine reproductions of great paintings, a stimulating introduction to the history of painting from the thirteenth century to the years of Picasso's dominance. Readers may find some favorites omitted, but most of the major figures are represented, their work and importance clearly described. Notes on styles and periods, biographical notes, and an index are provided.

1286   **Ventura,** Piero. *Man and the Horse;* written and illus. by Piero Ventura. Putnam, 1982. 82-386. ISBN 0-399-20842-9. 80p. $11.95.

4–   First published in Italy, this handsome book describes and pictures the ways in which human beings have used horses, from prehistoric times to today. This is not a continuous text, but a series of brief comments (usually a paragraph or two) on topics (The Splendor of Persia, Trade Between East and West, A Medieval Knight) each of which is on a double-page spread. The small-scale paintings have restrained composition and use of color, and a spacious feeling; they have, particularly in architectural details, a treatment very much like that of Mitsumasa Anno. Not comprehensive, but informative and interesting because Ventura relates the subject to broader events of a particular time in a particular culture.

1287   **Vigna,** Judith. *She's Not My Real Mother;* written and illus. by Judith Vigna. Whitman, 1980. 80-19073. ISBN 0-8075-7340-X. 30p. $6.50.

K–3   Miles likes spending weekends with Daddy, but only when they do things alone together. He does not like Daddy's new wife, and when asked if they can't be friends he says he doesn't want to be. She's sad, but Miles doesn't care, she's not his real mother. Then, due to the fact that Daddy has to work, Miles has to go to an ice show with his stepmother or choose to miss it. He goes, but he decides to frighten her at the intermission; he hides, and then realizes he's lost. Her warm welcome when he's found, and the fact that she doesn't tell Daddy persuade Miles to proffer friendship. "But Mommy doesn't have to worry," Miles' story ends, "she's my only REAL mother." Although lightly told, this is convincing as the narrative of a small child who realizes that a stepparent can be a caring adult and that it is possible to accept one without betraying a natural parent. The light quality of the illustrations, clean and simple line-and-wash, extend the book's quality of simple directness.

1288 **Vincent,** Gabrielle. *Ernest and Celestine;* written and illus. by Gabrielle Vincent. Greenwillow, 1982. 81-6392. Trade ed. ISBN 0-688-00855-0; Library ed. ISBN 0-688-00856-9. 24p. Trade ed. $9.50; Library ed. $8.59.
Bravo, Ernest and Celestine! written and illus. by Gabrielle Vincent. Greenwillow, 1982. 81-6423. Trade ed. ISBN 0-688-00857-7; Library ed. ISBN 0-688-00858-5. 24p. Trade ed. $9.50; Library ed. $8.59.

K–2 First published in Belgium under the titles *Ernest et Celestine Ont Perdu Siméon* and *Ernest et Celestine, Musiciens des Rues,* these are illustrated in pastel-tinted pictures that are reminiscent of the work of Ernest Shepard, with lively line and delicate but controlled composition. In the first story, Siméon's name has been changed to Gideon, a toy that is lost when the bear Ernest and the mouse Celestine go for a walk in the snow. Ernest buys an armful of toy animals, but Celestine mourns for her Gideon until Ernest makes her a replica of the original. This first book ends in a celebratory Christmas party in which other mice children are made happy by the toys Celestine has spurned. The relationship between Ernest and Celestine, apparently avuncular or surrogate-parental, is echoed when other bears (adult) deliver other mice (children) for the party. In the second book, the two are having a hard time financially until, on Celestine's initiative, they go out as street musicians. He plays violin, she sings, coins rain down, and they spend all their first profits on presents for each other. These books don't have strong plots, but they serve quite adequately since they have a problem/solution structure and since they are permeated with affection; they are brisk in pace and should have universal appeal, both for the texts and for the engaging illustrations.

1289 **Vincent,** Gabrielle. *Ernest and Celestine's Picnic;* written and illus. by Gabrielle Vincent. Greenwillow, 1982. 82-2909. Trade ed. ISBN 0-688-01250-7; Library ed. ISBN 0-688-01252-3. 26p. Trade ed. $9.50; Library ed. $8.59.
Smile, Ernest and Celestine; written and illus. by Gabrielle Vincent, Greenwillow, 1982. 82-1075. Trade ed. ISBN 0-688-01247-7; Library ed. ISBN 0-688-01249-3. 26p. Trade ed. $9.50; Library ed. $8.59.

K–2 Like the first books in this series, *Ernest and Celestine* and *Bravo, Ernest and Celestine!* these sequels are illustrated with delicately-tinted drawings that have the liveliness of line and the humor that make Ernest Shepard's work distinctive. The paintings are not imitative, however, and they capture to perfection a child's mobile face, for Ernestine is more a child than a mouse; in these books all children are mice, all adults bears. The relationship between the protagonists is never made clear, although Ernest's role is parental. In the first book, Ernestine sulks so much when a planned picnic day proves to be rainy that Ernest agrees to go out anyway. In the second book, Ernestine finds a photograph album that shows Ernest with many other children. When she complains to Ernest that there isn't one picture of her, he explains that the children in the pictures are campers; they put on their best clothes and immediately go to a photographer's studio. Celestine gets over her jealousy and poses indefatigably. The stories, first published in Belgium, have a nice balance of brisk and gentle humor in their minimal texts, and the illustrations are deft in draughtmanship and echo the affectionate tone of the writing.

1290   **Vincent,** Gabrielle. *Merry Christmas, Ernest and Celestine;* written and illus. by Gabrielle Vincent. Greenwillow, 1984. 83-14155. Library ed. 0-688-02606-0; Trade ed. ISBN 0-688-02605-2. 32p. Library ed. $11.04; Trade ed. $12.00.

K–2
*
One of the most engaging twosomes in the picture book world, the kindly bear Ernest and his tiny ward Celestine, a mouse, are—happily—with us again. They have no money, so Ernest balks about giving a Christmas party, but Celestine reminds him that he had promised— and he agrees, one must always keep a promise. The rest of the story is filled with details of the preparation and the celebration (including a delightful episode in which Celestine is upset because Ernest disappears just as Santa Claus enters) and the deft, graceful watercolor illustrations augment and extend the story in the nicest way. A holiday bonus.

1291   **Vinke,** Herman. *The Short Life of Sophie Scholl;* tr. by Hedwig Pachter. Harper, 1984. 82-47714. Library ed. ISBN 0-06-026303-2; Trade ed. ISBN 0-06-026302-4. 192p. illus. with photographs. Library ed. $10.89; Trade ed. $10.95.

8–
Sophie Scholl was twenty-one when she died by the guillotine, accused of treason and aiding the enemy. What she and those who died for the same cause had done was to urge Germans to repudiate Hitler, end the war sooner, strike a blow for freedom and against Nazi tyranny. This is both an affective account and, at times, an affected one because of the rather pompous style. However, the sad story is intrinsically dramatic, and the author uses source materials and interviews to give variety and to gain authenticity.

1292   **Viorst,** Judith. *If I Were in Charge of the World and Other Worries: Poems for Children and Their Parents;* illus. by Lynne Cherry. Atheneum, 1982. 81-2342. ISBN 0-689-30863-9. 56p. $9.95.

3–6   Although there are a few poems in this collection that seem more appropriate for adults than for children, most of the selections are written from the child's viewpoint and are discerning, breezy, and amusing. Some bemoan the fact that a child's lot is fraught with woes, like the start of "Short Love Poem," which ruefully states, "It's hard to love/The tallest girl/When you're the shortest guy . . ." or—from the title poem— "If I were in charge of the world/There'd be brighter night lights/Healthier hamsters, and/Basketball baskets forty-eight inches lower." The ornamental illustrations, small and often framed, are intricately detailed line drawings and always elegant.

1293   **Voigt,** Cynthia. *Building Blocks.* Atheneum, 1984. 83-15853. ISBN 0-689-31035-8. 128p. $10.95.

4–6   In an interesting time-travel story, Voigt posits a boy of twelve who, living in 1974, finds himself in the bedroom of another boy and realizes that this ten-year-old child of the depression is his father. Brann's means of entry is falling asleep within a big construction of blocks that have been handed down in the family. What is unusual here is not the encounter but the subtlety with which Voigt uses it to help Brann see why his father has turned out to be the quiet, self-effacing man he is, and how the man's strengths have been masked by his meek ways. An excellent story of a father-son relationship, this is a smooth blending of realism and fantasy.

1294   **Voigt,** Cynthia. *Dicey's Song.* Atheneum, 1982. 82-3882. ISBN 0-689-30944-9. 204p. $10.95.

5–8   The strong characterization of *Homecoming* to which this is a sequel is one of the most trenchant facets again, in this story of the four children who live with their grandmother on the Eastern Shore of Maryland. Dicey, oldest of the four, is the protagonist, a self-reliant and resourceful thirteen-year-old who had brought her siblings to the grandmother they'd never seen when their mother (now in a mental institution) had been unable to cope. This is the story of the children's adjustment to Gram (and hers to them) and to a new school and a new life—but with some of the old problems. Dicey, in particular, has a hard time since she must abandon her role of surrogate mother and share responsibility with Gram. This is much more cohesive than *Homecoming*, in part because the physical scope is narrower, in part because the author has so skillfully integrated the problems of the individual children in a story that is smoothly written. Dicey learns how to make friends, how to accept the fact that she is maturing physically, how to give and forgive, how to adjust—in a touching final episode—to the death of the mother whose recovery she had longed for. A rich and perceptive book.

1295   **Voigt,** Cynthia. *A Solitary Blue.* Atheneum, 1983. 83-6007. ISBN 0-689-31008-0. 189p. $10.95.

6–9   This is the most mature and sophisticated of Voigt's novels, a bitter-sweet story of a boy whose mother is more devoted to saving the world than saving her child from unhappiness. Melody is beautiful, selfish, dishonest, and grasping—but all that seven-year-old Jeff knows is that she is his mother, tender and loving, and that she has left him a note saying she's gone: "there are people everywhere who need me," she has written. Several years later, after no word, Jeff visits Melody in Charleston and is enchanted by the city, the family home, and his adorable mother. It isn't until a second (uninvited) visit that Jeff realizes that Melody doesn't really love him, and when he faces her with this, she becomes vindictive and insulting. Jeff is shattered; by now he is an adolescent, and his father (depicted as a remote professorial type) sees that Jeff is troubled. At this point the relationship begins to change, and Jeff begins to realize that his opinion of his father had been shaped by Melody's sneering comments; when Melody appears again, Jeff and his father have moved to a new home, built a new relationship, and learned to know and show their love. It is in this new home that Jeff meets and loves Dicey Tillerman, the protagonist of *Dicey's Song* and it is here that the title reference occurs; each of them reminds the other, in their awkward, self-contained dignity, of the solitary blue heron they observe. Beautifully knit, a compelling and intelligent novel.

1296   **Von Canon,** Claudia. *The Inheritance.* Houghton, 1983. 82-23418. ISBN 0-395-33891-3. 212p. $10.95.

7–10   Miguel de Roxas is nineteen, a medical student in Padua, when he is
  *   summoned home to Spain to take over his father's estate. The year is 1580, and his father had killed himself rather than be burned at the stake by the Holy Office. A devout son of the Catholic church, a loyal Spaniard, the young man is quickly disillusioned and decides to flee from Spain. Pursued, he takes refuge with a Swiss printer and falls in love with his daughter Veronica; eventually he returns to Padua, but the envoys of the Inquisition find and pursue him, and he returns to Basel to wed Veronica and start a practice. The story ends with Miguel called to treat a patient who proves to be an old enemy; the man dies of smallpox, and this proves to be Miguel's last inheritance. As she did in her first historical novel, Von Canon has done an excellent job of creating a smooth synthesis of personal narrative and historical background; the pace of the book slows a bit when Miguel and Veronica are reading the manuscript of his father's biography, but the material in the biography gives a strong foundation, the events of the early sixteenth century making more clear the events of Miguel's lifetime. The characterization is strong and deep, the fusion of real personages and events with the fictional deft. A compelling book.

1297   **Von Canon,** Claudia. *The Moonclock.* Houghton, 1979. 79-1076. ISBN 0-395-27810-4. 159p. illus. $6.95.

8–10   Because she uses letters to tell the story, Von Canon is able to incorporate more details about the Turkish siege of Vienna in 1683 than could burden dialogue or slow the pace of exposition. It is perfectly natural for the bride, Barbara Schretter, to write to her concerned mother and her old friend Thresl, just as natural for her husband Jacob to write to Barbara after he has sent her to Innsbruck for safety. Although she has become fond of her middle-aged husband, twenty-year-old Barbara cannot resist an Italian suitor, and she hastens back to Vienna to avoid temptation. The letters are lively and informative, only occasionally straying into contemporary speech patterns (". . . they had enjoyed the evening no end . . .") and giving a vivid picture not only of the siege but also of the period; the characters are drawn in convincing depth, often with humor. A glossary and a bibliography are provided.

1298   **Waber,** Bernard. *Bernard;* written and illus. by Bernard Waber. Houghton, 1982. 81-13193. ISBN 0-395-31865-3. 48p. $10.20.

K–2   Bernard, a thoughtful dog, is disturbed by the quarreling of his owners (a couple who are about to separate) about who gets custody. Bernard just can't choose, when invited to do so, and runs off. He has a series of encounters in which he tries to show that he is quiet (watching a parade), a good watchdog (catching a robber), and gentle with children—but, while he's appreciated, Bernard's never invited to go home with anyone. Caught in a torrential rain, Bernard is picked up by his worried owners; they take him home and agree that whatever is done will be for their dog's good. This leaves the custody question unanswered, but it satisfies Bernard. The line and wash drawings are bright and are replete with action and humor, and the story is told with a recurrent pattern that should appeal to the read-aloud audience, with a brisk pace and light style.

1299   **Waldron,** Ann. *The French Detection.* Dutton, 1979. 79-10233. ISBN 0-525-30190-9. 129p. $7.95.

5–7   Persuasive, articulate, and strong-willed, thirteen-year-old Bessie convinces her parents to let her go in response to an ad that says, "Spend 1 month in a French village for $300." While Bessie finds that her seventh-grade French has not prepared her for rapid conversation, she improves quickly (the author's handling of French phrases and words is superb) and is able to take an active role in helping the owners of the French farmhouse project defy the man who is trying to oust them. In so doing, Bessie and her friends discover that the man is running an art theft ring, so there's a bit of danger to spice the action of a lively story. Nicely structured and told with brisk humor. As Bessie says when she learns what it means, "Quelle histoire!"

1300   **Waldron,** Ann. *True or False? Amazing Art Forgeries;* illus. with prints and photographs. Hastings House, 1983. 82-15722. ISBN 0-8038-7220-8. 158p. $11.95.

6–   First discussing the crime of art forgery and the many ways in which
        experts can detect a forgery (paint, canvas, color, craquelure, errors
        seen by x-ray or infrared photography, dating of wood, etc.) Waldron
        describes in good narrative style some of the most spectacular of mod-
        ern forgeries. A glossary of art terms, a list of artists, a selected bibliog-
        raphy, and an index are appended.

1301   **Wallin,** Luke. *In the Shadow of the Wind.* Bradbury, 1984. 83-19758. ISBN
        0-02-792320-7. 203p. $11.95.

6–10   An impressive historical novel about the conflict between white settlers
        and Creek families in Alabama in 1835 focuses on two families. Caleb
        McElroy is a white adolescent who feels friendship for Brown Hawk's
        family (he has rescued the old man's nephew and in turn been helped
        by Brown Hawk's niece, Pine Basket) but is in the unhappy position of
        being forced by his employer, wealthy Judge Travis, and encouraged by
        his mother to help in a plan to raid the Creek slave camp. Caleb takes a
        chance and warns Brown Hawk that the slave raiders are, he's just
        learned, planning to attack the Creek settlement. Since this is the time
        that whites are forcing the Creek to abandon their lands and emigrate
        to Oklahoma, Brown Hawk asks Caleb to help them by taking over the
        deed to their land. The long, sad story of deceit and betrayal ends with
        Pine Basket and her mother rescued from captivity by her brother and
        Caleb, and there is a closing section that describes the remaining years
        of their lives after they are in Oklahoma Territory. Many Creek Indians
        fought with the Confederacy when the Civil War came, to protect their
        holdings in slaves; Caleb, long-married to Pine Basket, joined the Union
        Army. A moving if somber story is convincing and dramatic.

1302   **Wallin,** Luke. *The Redneck Poacher's Son.* Bradbury, 1981. 80-26782. ISBN
        0-87888-174-3. 245p. $8.95.

8–   Jesse is sixteen, younger than his two brothers who seem as hostile and
        prejudiced as their father, the poacher of the title. Jesse loves animals,
        hates his father's trapping in their Alabama swamp, hates the fact that
        his father sells rotten fish and adulterated moonshine, and begins to
        hate his father when he deduces that Paw had murdered Jesse's mother
        many years before. When Jesse moves into town to work, he discovers
        that his brothers are KKK members, and he is heartsick; he makes some
        new friends: the daughter of his boss, and a black fellow worker. Both
        know that Jesse's growing anger has made him decide to kill his father.
        He doesn't; the problem of Paw's drunken bullying is solved in another
        way, so that the story has a positive and logical ending. Save for the
        fact that a medium (through whom the dead speak, including Jesse's
        mother) is presented as realistic, this is a most effective story, with a
        vivid conveyance of the setting as well as of the slobbering, threatening
        Paw, who is the strongest if least appealing character in the story. Jesse
        is almost a Billy Budd: kind, trusting, loving, patient but not perfect,

and it is his imperfection, his anger, that makes it possible for the reader to empathize with him, an empathy that heightens the suspense of the last portion of the book.

1303   **Wallin,** Luke. *The Slavery Ghosts.* Bradbury, 1983. 83-2679. ISBN 0-02-792380-0. 121p. $9.95.

5-7   Jake and Livy, twelve and thirteen, find Granny's adherence to the prejudice and panoply of the Old South irritating; they want no part of her elaborate plans for the annual Old Confederacy Celebration. Grandma even hopes to see the vaunted plantation ghost, wife of Colonel Ruffin who had been a feared and cruel slaveholder. It's the children who see the ghost, however, and it isn't Mrs. Ruffin but one of the slaves, Sarantha, who begs the children to rescue her child and other slaves who are in a nether world where they are still Ruffin's captives. Jake and Livy find the time gate and enter the other world in which Ruffin is still a tyrant; they manage to save the ghosts, who can then live as free spirits like other ghosts. When they tell their family about their adventures, the children's parents believe them; in fact, it makes their father realize how biased Granny's viewpoint had been. While the double fantasy (time-slip and other world) is complex, the story is written with enough pace and suspense to compensate for this; the book has a message, but it does not obscure the action.

1304   **Walsh,** Gillian Paton. *Gaffer Samson's Luck;* illus. by Brock Cole. Farrar, 1984. 84-10180. ISBN 374-32798-0. 119p. $10.95.

4-6   Here is a dependably fine writer at her best. Jill Paton Walsh writes
*   with sentiment but without sentimentality, in a story with a vivid, evocative setting. Her characterization is rich and strong, with a seamless knitting of people and events, a touching story of friendship between a young boy and a very old man, Gaffer Samson. His "luck" is a lucky charm, long hidden, that young James hunts for, finds, and passes on to someone else. Among its other strengths, this is a trenchant story about a child's courage and adaptability, as James works to become accepted in the rigid clan structure of the children in the village, to which he has just moved, in the English Fens.

1305   **Walsh,** Gillian Paton. *The Green Book;* illus. by Lloyd Bloom. Farrar, 1982. 81-12620. ISBN 0-374-32778-5. 73p. $9.95.

4-6   It is one of three motherless children (although it's not clear until the end which one, since the narrator at times uses "we" and "us" and at other times uses third person for Joe, Sarah, and Pattie) who tells the story of their flight with their father to a new space settlement. This has a roundly-conceived new world, a writing style that is polished and deceptively simple, and sturdy structure and characters in a well-placed story that has a Crusoe appeal.

1306   **Walsh,** Gillian Paton. *A Parcel of Patterns.* Farrar, 1983. 83-048143. ISBN 0-374-35750-1. 137p. $10.95.

7–10   A novel that is moving as a personal document, this is also impressive
  *   because it serves to illustrate dramatically the complexity and interde-
          pendence of community life. The time is 1665, the place a small English
          village that is being decimated by the plague and that finally agrees
          with its neighbors to choose isolation. The story is told by Mall, who
          loses her loved ones but finds love again when the long ordeal is over.
          Major characters are fictional, but many of the skillfully-integrated his-
          torical details are based on town records. A strong, strong story.

1307   **Walter,** Mildred Pitts. *The Girl on the Outside.* Lothrop, 1982. 82-267.
          ISBN 0-688-01438-0. 160p. $9.50.

7–9   A story about school integration is based on an incident of 1957 in
          which a white woman shielded one of the black students who were at-
          tempting to integrate a high school in Little Rock, Arkansas. Walter has
          made her white character another high school student, Sophia, who is
          wealthy, popular, and prejudiced; the black girl, Eva, is bright and
          beautiful, and she's guided by the advice of a woman based on the ac-
          tual NAACP official in the case. The chapters more or less alternate, so
          that readers can see the attitudes of both girls: Sophia angry, fearful,
          but increasingly ashamed and eventually sympathetic; Eva fearful but
          courageous. In the aftermath of the final, shameful incident of mob ha-
          tred, it is Sophia who benefits most by the joint departure from the
          scene; Eva has simply gotten away from a hostile mob, but for Sophia,
          the book concludes, "What she had gained was the beginning to the
          end of her pain." A vivid story is written with insight and compassion,
          its characters fully developed, its converging lines nicely controlled.

1308   **Ward,** Brian R. *Body Maintenance.* Watts, 1983. 82-50056. ISBN 0-531-
          04457-2. 48p. $8.90.

5–8   An explanation of the systems, glands, and hormones that control body
          chemistry, this is divided into brief topics (the adrenal glands, sleep,
          how hormones work, immunity, urine production, etc.) each of which
          is covered in a double-page spread, often with about half the space
          given to large, colored, and labelled diagrams. The information is accu-
          rate, the text written in a direct style and with correct terminology; an
          index and a glossary extend the usefulness of the book as a minor refer-
          ence source. Although the topical arrangement and brief treatment
          make the book rather choppy as an introduction to homeostasis, it is
          still both clear and informative.

1309   **Watanabe,** Shigeo. *Get Set! Go!* illus. by Yasuo Ohtomo. Philomel, 1981.
          80-22373. Trade ed. ISBN 0-399-20780-5; Library ed. ISBN 0-399-61175-4.
          28p. Trade ed. $6.95; Library ed. $6.99.

3–5   Gymnastic equipment presents a series of obstacles for the engaging
yrs.   little bear of *How Do I Put It On?* For the small child, always mastering
          new skills, these books have a quick appeal; Bear struggles; but he does

manage to walk the balance beam (although he falls) and vault the horse (well, almost) and crawl under the net (slowed by getting tangled) and he emerges with "Over the finish line! Hurrah! Did I win?" The drawings are clean, bright, and simple against an uncluttered background. Another nicely gauged, funny, and appropriate book for the read-aloud audience.

1310   **Watanabe,** Shigeo. *How Do I Put It On?* illus. by Yasuo Ohtomo. Collins, 1979. 79-12714. Trade ed. ISBN 0-529-05555-4; Library ed. ISBN 0-529-05557-0. 28p. Trade ed. $6.95; Library ed. $6.91 net.

2–4
yrs.
The first book in a series called "I Can Do It All By Myself," this is very brief, very simple, and nicely gauged for the young child. Clean crayon and watercolor pictures of a small bear are based on the wrong way/right way approach: "This is my shirt. Do I put it on like this? No! I put my shirt over my head." There is one sentence per page, and the text doesn't get into problems of front vs. back or left shoe vs. right shoe, but relates each garment to its location. Shirt, pants, shoes, and cap on, the bear trots off saying, "I got dressed all by myself." The lap audience should enjoy the triumphant expressions on the bear's face, as each problem is solved, as much as they enjoy the exploration of one of the big problems—and accomplishments—in their lives.

1311   **Watanabe,** Shigeo. *I Can Take a Walk!;* illus. by Yasuo Ohtomo. Philomel, 1984. 83-17397. ISBN 0-399-21044-X. 24p. $7.95.

2–5
yrs.
Like earlier Watanabe books, this stresses the achievement of a new skill in a child's repertoire of accomplishments that lead to independence. Unlike the earlier books, this focuses less on a physical skill than on self-reliance, as a small bear goes for a daring walk in which he climbs mountains (a dirt pile) and fords a river (puddle) and meets his father just as he's found himself in a spot of trouble for the first time. The read-aloud audience can share the satisfaction of the bear's final comment, "What a good walk!" The simple drawings and clean, spacious pages add to the book's visual appeal.

1312   **Waterfield,** Giles. *Faces.* Atheneum, 1982. 82-3935. ISBN 0-689-50251-6. 47p. illus. (Looking at Art). $11.95.

6–8
*
In the same series as the Conner books on art topics, this is the most impressive of the three: it has the same discrimination in choice of material, the same broad range of painting styles, and gives the same sort of background information about the pictures (and, in this volume, masks) and analyzes technique in a direct, informal style. Perhaps because Waterfield is a teacher as well as a museum curator, his approach to the reader is more polished than that of the writer of the other two books in the series.

1313   **Watson,** Clyde. *Father Fox's Feast of Songs;* written and with music by Clyde Watson; illus. by Wendy Watson. Philomel, 1983. 83-2967. Trade ed. ISBN 0-399-20886-0; Paper ed. ISBN 0-399-20928-X. 26p. Trade ed. $10.95; Paper ed. $5.95.

2–5
yrs.
Busily detailed paintings, often in banner position, illustrate a compilation of original songs that have simple melodies and accompaniments; the verses are chosen from *Father Fox's Pennyrhymes* and *Catch Me & Kiss Me & Say It Again,* and their lilting rhythms and rhymes are as engaging as ever when set to music. Cozy, cheerful, affectionate.

1314   **Watson,** Clyde. *Midnight Moon;* illus. by Susanna Natti. Collins, 1979. 78-26376. Trade ed. ISBN 0-529-05526-0; Library ed. ISBN 0-529-05527-9. 24p. Trade ed. $6.95; Library ed. $6.91 net.

3–6
yrs.
A warm, imaginative text is illustrated by tidy, bright little pictures framed with bands of star-studded sky. "Hop into bed & snuggle down in / pull the covers up to your chin / & I'll tell you a secret about the night," the text begins, and it describes a visit to the gentle, cheery old man in the moon who offers you "cinnamon stars in a silver bowl" and plays "ripples & windsongs & waterfalls" on his flute. Then back you go to dream moon-secrets until morning. The stuff that dreams are made of, this is a beguiling little bedtime book.

1315   **Watts,** Marjorie-Ann. *Crocodile Plaster;* written and illus. by Marjorie-Ann Watts. Andre Deutsch, 1984. ISBN 0233-96962-4. 28p. $9.95.

K–2
This is fantasy, lightly told and humorous in tone, but it's also an excellent hospital story, calculated to sooth and encourage nervous patients-to-be and perhaps to entertain those children who are familiar with hospital routines. First published in England in 1978, this has a few terms that American children may not recognize (although the context makes them fairly clear) but the gist of the story has universal appeal: a nervous crocodile is comforted by a child patient, kindly treated by the doctor and the nursing staff, happy to enjoy the play and crafts program, and relieved when a painful kink in the tail is straightened and put in a cast.

1316   **Weaver,** John L. *Grizzly Bears;* illus. with photographs. Dodd, 1982. 82-45378. ISBN 0-396-08084-7. 41p. $7.95.

3–5
A biologist writes crisply and sympathetically about the grizzly, using the experiences (without anthropomorphism) of a mother bear and her three cubs to illustrate the ways in which the grizzly mates, trains the young, survives, sleeps through the winter, etc. Weaver discusses the fact that the grizzly is an endangered species, and pleads with restraint for the preservation of this species. The material is logically arranged, the tone authoritative, the style smooth. An index is included.

1317   **Webb,** Sheyann. *Selma, Lord, Selma;* by Sheyann Webb and Rachel West Nelson; ed. by Frank Sikora. University of Alabama Press, 1980. 79-19327. ISBN 0-8173-0031-7. 147p. illus. with photographs. $9.95.

7–   Not intended as a record of the civil rights battle, this book, based on Sikora's interviews with Webb and Nelson, is a moving account of what those days of tension meant to Sheyann and Rachel, who were eight and nine at the time. The two girls speak alternately; the book begins with Sheyann's reminiscence of wandering into a nearby church and missing part of a school day. Rachel, who attended a parochial school, speaks of seeing Sheyann standing near the church where the meeting was going on, and learning next day that her friend had not gone on to school. Interspersed among their accounts are Sikora's brief statements filling in gaps and giving background information; within their accounts, the two girls speak of marching, singing, demonstrating, being set upon by troopers, becoming ill from inhaling tear gas—and, over and over, going to meetings, talking about those who had been jailed or beaten or killed. And, joined by white and black people from all over the country, starting on the march to Montgomery, a march that Martin Luther King, who had come to know both girls well, said was too strenuous. "So he said that we had walked far enough for little girls," and sent them back to Selma, "and he touched us on the head and went on down the road." A moving book, this needs no encomia; it is a record, unembellished, that can make vividly clear to readers what the struggle meant to those who were there.

1318   **Weiss,** Ann E. *God and Government: The Separation of Church and State.* Houghton, 1982. 81-17861. ISBN 0-395-32085-2. 132p. $8.95.

6–9   Weiss begins with a general discussion of some of the current conflict about issues related to the separation of church and state, goes back for a look at the historical development of attitudes toward religion in the United States, and then proceeds to a broad scrutiny of practices, laws, arguments, examples, and issues of our society in relation to the topic. She describes the role of religion in schools (and the controversy about it) and the ways in which its inclusion gets political support, such related issues as abortion, homosexuality, cults, and the teaching of evolution. The text is objective, giving arguments on both sides of controversial issues; it is well-organized and written in a direct, sometimes conversational style; it is thoughtful and provocative. A brief bibliography and an extensive index are included.

1319   **Weiss,** Harvey. *Machines and How They Work;* written and illus. by Harvey Weiss. Crowell, 1983. 82-45925. Trade ed. ISBN 0-690-04299-X; Library ed. ISBN 0-690-04300-7. 80p. Library ed. $10.89; Trade ed. $10.95.

5–7   Clearly written, with line drawings that are carefully integrated with the text and expand its concepts, this is an excellent discussion of the six basic machines: the lever, inclined plane, screw, wedge, pulley, and wheel and axle. While there are many books on the subject, few are as explicit in showing how these six simple machines are incorporated into other, more complicated ones. Physical principles are stressed, so that the reader can always see why a machine—or a combination of machines—works to produce a desired effect. A final chapter describes simple machines the reader can build.

1320   **Weiss,** Malcolm E. *Toxic Waste: Clean Up or Cover Up.* Watts, 1984. 83-23391. ISBN 0-531-04755-5. 83p. illus. with photographs. $8.90.

7–10   A careful examination of the problems of hazardous waste and its disposal in our highly industrialized, densely-populated society, this focuses especially on dioxin, the waste-product so toxic that its maximum safe level is one part per billion. Starting with an unsentimental look at "the good old days," Weiss then discusses the organic chemistry of several current hazardous waste products, how they are formed, and their physiological effects on humans; he shows that some wastes (like lead, mercury, and radioactive waste) are indestructible, but that new (though often costly) technologies can render most wastes harmless. Although he makes clear that he is on the side of the environmentalists, he presents industry's arguments fairly and in detail; he also shows that scientists do not agree on how dangerous the poisons may be to human health. Using current examples, especially the disaster at Times Beach, Missouri, he charges industry and government with neglect, and urgently and convincingly calls for clean-up and control. A brief bibliography and an index are appended.

1321   **Wells,** Rosemary. *Max's First Word*; written and illus. by Rosemary Wells. Dial, 1979. 79-59745. ISBN 0-8037-6066-3. 12p. $2.95.

2–3
yrs.
*

In a very small book with heavy board pages, Wells has created an engaging character, a very young rabbit called Max, and has managed to make a brief but nicely structured story that is deft and humorous. It's the sort of book that very young children ask for repeatedly and are soon "reading" themselves. Big sister Ruby tries to teach Max words; she says "BROOM, Max, say BROOM." "Bang," says Max. "Say APPLE, Max. YUM YUM, Max. Say YUM YUM." Max takes a bite and says "DELICIOUS!" The other three books in the set, *Max's Toys, Max's Ride,* and *Max's New Suit* have the same brio, humor, and drawings of expressive faces.

1322   **Wells,** Rosemary. *Peabody*; written and illus. by Rosemary Wells. Dial, 1983. 83-7207. Trade ed. ISBN 0-8037-0004-0; Library ed. ISBN 0-8037-0005-9. 28p. Trade ed. $9.95; Library ed. $9.89.

3–6
yrs.

Wells uses the concepts of toys becoming real if they're loved, of feelings of dethronement, and of sibling jealousy in so deft and light a way that they never obtrude on the story. The illustrations, in which the animals have vitality while the children seem lifeless, are bright and lively, with a humor that is echoed by the story, and the humor is spiced by some touching moments when Peabody, a toy bear, is rejected in favor of a newer toy, a doll. Annie, Peabody's owner, repeatedly warns her little brother Robert away from her bear: "Peabody bites," she says. Robert is envious but docile; however, he does ruin the doll (who drinks, walks, and talks) by sharing his bath with her, so Annie reinstates Peabody as her favorite—and Robert happily sleeps with the doll.

1323   **Wells, Rosemary.** *Timothy Goes to School;* written and illus. by Rosemary Wells. Dial, 1981. 80-20785. Trade ed. ISBN 0-8037-8948-3; Library ed. ISBN 0-8037-8949-1. 28p. Trade ed. $7.50; Library ed. $7.28.

3–5 yrs.   Timothy and the other bouncy little animals are as engaging because of their wonderfully expressive faces in brisk, bright illustrations as because of their universally childlike qualities, in a brief story that is both touching and funny. Timothy's first few days at school are marred by the obnoxious and critical Claude; each day Timothy hopes some disaster will befall Claude, but to no avail. Then another classmate, Violet, complains about Grace. "I can't stand it anymore. She sings. She dances. She counts up to a thousand and she sits next to me!" Well, what greater bond is there than the pangs of frustrated envy? Timothy and Violet immediately form a bond, and the story ends with "Will you come home and have cookies with me after school?" It's clear that school is going to be a joy thenceforward.

1324   **Wells,** Rosemary. *When No One Was Looking.* Dial, 1980. 80-12964. ISBN 0-8037-9855-5. 218p. $8.95.

7–10   Kathy, at fourteen, had been pushed by her parents and her coach, Marty, to win tennis matches; her younger sister, Jody, was contemptuous about the attention Kathy received and the selfishness she showed. Her best friend Julia, on the other hand, was loyally supportive; Julia, beautiful and secure, even went to Florida with Kathy when she took part in the National Championships. In fact, Kathy's only problem was Ruth Gumm, a stolid girl who didn't look good on the court but always managed to beat her—and then Ruth was found drowned in the club pool, although she was a good swimmer. Ruth's parents insisted it couldn't have been an accident, and both Kathy and her coach were suspected. At this point the story, already strong in style and characterization, becomes taut with suspense as Kathy struggles to prove her innocence and then to adjust to a terrible knowledge that someone had killed on her behalf because an even more important tennis match was coming up. Soundly structured, the story is left at this high, dramatic point; what Kathy does about her knowledge is for the reader to judge.

1325   **Wersba,** Barbara. *The Carnival in My Mind.* Harper & Row, 1982. 81-48640. Trade ed. ISBN 0-06-026409-8; Library ed. ISBN 0-06-026410-1. 210p. Trade ed. $10.50; Library ed. $10.89.

7–9   "Perhaps the whole thing started because I was so short," fourteen-year-old Harvey begins, explaining that his schoolmates ignore or taunt him, his mother has filled their Manhattan apartment with Irish setters

to whom she gives all her love and attention, and his father has re-
treated (either from the dogs, his wife, or both) to their suburban home.
The only stability and affection Harvey gets are from the family servant,
Holmes. So when Harvey meets a dazzling young woman on a bus (she
has hiccups, Harvey stops them) who takes him off for an afternoon of
champagne cocktails and confidences, it's instant love. Chandler is tall,
young, beautiful, an unsuccessful actress, and a loving person. Who
else would Harvey go to when he runs away? Chan takes him in, and
even sleeps with him (there's only one bed, there is no sexual or romantic relationship) and mothers him; she confesses that her parents
are bringing up her illegitimate baby daughter, and it is clear that she
adores and longs for her child. Harvey, who has his own checking account, is baffled by Chan's finances: at times she takes his money, at
other times she seems affluent. He learns, heartsick, from another person that Chan is a call girl and an alcoholic, and when he talks to Chan,
she announces that she is going home, joining Alcoholics Anonymous,
and accepting the offer of marriage from a man in her home town so
that she can have her baby. At the end of the book, Chan takes Harvey
to a carnival (he's confessed that he has always wanted to join one and
dreams about it) before she goes. The one weak point of the story (although some readers may feel that Chan is an unsavory character) is in
the depiction of Harvey's mother, so bound up in her animal rescue
work that she doesn't even notice her son has moved out. Wersba
makes the eccentric Chan and the unhappy adolescent believable characters with a tender relationship, and the style of writing is fluent, believably that of a precocious adolescent.

1326   **Westall,** Robert. *Break of Dark.* Greenwillow, 1982. 81-7237, ISBN 0-688-
       00875-5. 244p. $9.50.

R   In five long stories, Westall explores the frontier between rational nor-
7–   mality and the fantastic or occult. In one tale, told in first person, a
young man meets a sort of bionic woman, perfectly beautiful and beautifully perfect, who frightens him; in another, a World War II airplane
seems to have a life of its own, and in a third a prank turns into ghostly
persecution; the young minister in "St. Austin Friars" cannot believe
that a man who looks fifty and says he's almost two hundred can
calmly arrange his own funeral, and in the final story a policeman
hunts doggedly for an explanation for objects that disappear. The stories have variety of style and concept, but they are alike in having
sharply etched characters, good dialogue, and strong plots. Westall is at
his best here, a craftsman who writes with polish and a strong narrative
sense that gives body to five deftly structured tales.

1327   **Westall,** Robert. *Futuretrack 5.* Greenwillow, 1984. 83-14183. ISBN 0-688-
       02598-6. 276p. $10.50.

7–   In a science fiction novel of Britain in the next century, the society is
rigidly regimented, manipulated, and policed. The castes are ruthlessly

separated, but young Henry Kitson escapes his high, scientific status to have a holiday in Futuretrack London, a slum where he meets and falls in love with Keri, who is beautiful and tough, condemned to die as a racing cyclist. Together they plot an escape that takes them first to Scotland and then to the Fen country. Learning that Londoners are to be killed off, that the Fen people are being used as an exhibit (they've been left as they were in the previous century) and as breeders to be sent north, Kitson decides he will destroy the computer that controls the whole country. The plot is ingenious and fast-paced, with increasing suspense to add momentum and excitement. Carefully crafted and smoothly written, the story has a compelling thrust and a stirring ending with a wry twist.

1328   **Westall,** Robert. *The Haunting of Charles McGill and Other Stories.* Greenwillow, 1983. 83-1654. ISBN 0-688-02393-2. 181p. $10.50.

7–   A superb craftsman, Westall presents in this collection of eerie tales a marvelous variety of style, mood and subject, from a hilarious story about a plaintive woman's passion for handsome Count Dracula to the sinister tale of a cat that assumes human qualities and precipitates a murder. In these and other stories the author shows his versatility by suiting style to mood and by creating memorable characters within the brevity of the short story form.

1329   **Westall,** Robert. *The Scarecrows.* Greenwillow, 1981. 81-2052. Trade ed. ISBN 0-688-00612-4; Library ed. ISBN 0-688-00613-2. 185p. Trade ed. $8.95; Library ed. $8.59.

6–9   Thirteen-year-old Simon, in this English story, is already deeply disturbed by his mother's second marriage: he detests the jovial, sloppy, obese artist, Joe, who is his new stepfather; he resents the way his small sister fawns on Joe; and he bitterly compares Joe to his own father, handsome and brave, dead but still adored by his son. It is near his stepfather's house that Simon sees the three scarecrows that terrify him, effigies dressed in the clothes of three people who had died in a bitter love triangle decades before. In his own tortured, secret way Simon—already at odds with his mother and stepfather because of his recalcitrant hostility—uses the scarecrows as symbols for his internal struggle to conquer his anger and jealousy. This is more intense than Westall's previous books, more vehement in the protagonist's relationships with others, more obscure in his battle against the scarecrows; it is written, however, with the same fluency and conviction that have distinguished the other books by Westall, a winner of the Carnegie Medal.

1330   **White,** Ellen Emerson. *The President's Daughter.* Avon, 1984. Paper. ISBN 0-380-88740-1. 247p. $2.95.

6–9   It would have been easy to make this, both theme and setting, superficial and sensational, but it's neither; it is, instead, a sympathetic study of the results within a family of gaining national prominence and adjusting to a new life style. White makes the campaign and the election of the first woman president believable, and the story, reflecting the viewpoint of sixteen-year-old Meg, has both pace and insight as it examines the changes for Meg and her family as well as those unchanging aspects of love and trust that exist in warm, secure parent-child relationships. An added appeal is that the dialogue is animated and intelligent, spiced by an affectionate teasing between Meg and her parents or Meg and her friends.

1331   **White,** Jack R. *The Invisible World of the Infrared;* illus. with photographs and drawings. Dodd, 1984. 83-25441. ISBN 0-396-08319-6. 124p. $9.95.

5–8   Although there are traces of writing-down-to-children, the text of this informative book is on the whole direct and, since it is the work of an electro-optical engineer, authoritative. White explains the spectrum, and the infrared range of light waves; probably the parts of the book that will most interest readers, however, are the descriptions of how infrared instruments are used in various fields for research, and for such widely diverse areas as crime prevention, laser surgery, energy conservation, and the gathering of environmental information. An index is provided.

1332   **Whitney,** Sharon. *The Equal Rights Amendment: The History and the Movement.* Watts, 1984. 84-11817. ISBN 0-531-04768-7. 102p. $9.90.

7–10   In describing the history of the long battle for women's rights, Whitney shows how the current struggle was preceded by decades of reform and protest movements in the United States. This is both a history of the movement, including a discussion of the legal battle that came to defeat in 1982, and a reasoned argument for the cause it describes. The text is specific in citing partisan groups and individuals on both sides of the issue. Reintroduced into Congress in 1983, the Equal Rights Amendment failed by six votes to achieve the needed two-thirds majority. The material is well-organized, the coverage broad, the writing style direct and unpretentious. A list of suggested readings and an index are appended.

1333   **Wilde,** Oscar. *The Selfish Giant;* illus. by Lisbeth Zwerger. Neugebauer Press, 1984. 83-24930. ISBN 0-907234-30-5. 22p. $11.95.

K–3   Delicate, spacious, full-page ink and wash drawings, understated yet
 *   dramatic, illustrate Oscar Wilde's story of the giant who drives the children out of his garden and drives out summer with them, until they creep back in and he is saved by his reaching out to one tiny child. Zwerger's focus is on the human: she depicts an Edwardian world with innocent playful children; the giant is not a monster but a tall, gaunt, alienated man whose "conversation was limited." The illustrations perfectly express the story's yearning mood as well as its tension, with

large areas of white and pale wash between the diagonally opposed figures; and, in the most dramatic picture, the giant looms from one corner, a girl flees from another, and the tiny child cries bitterly "in the
farthest corner of the garden." Zwerger is the Austrian nominee for the
1984 Hans Christian Andersen Award for illustration.

1334   **Wildsmith,** Brian. *Daisy;* written and illus. by Brian Wildsmith. Pantheon, 1984. 83-12150. Library ed. ISBN 0-394-95975-2; Trade ed. ISBN
0-394-85975-8. 45p. Library ed. $9.99; Trade ed. $9.95.

K–2   Brian Wildsmith uses his lush palette to full advantage in an oversize
book in which half-pages are used between full pages to add a fillip to
the story, in the format of so many books by John Goodall. The illustrations are perhaps the chief attraction of the book, handsome in composition and use of color, but the story should also appeal to the read-
aloud audience; it describes a cow, Daisy, who succeeds not only in her
desire to see the world but also becomes a famous movie star. Eventually Daisy becomes homesick and pines for her English meadow, so
there's one last Hollywood film, "Daisy Come Home," that records
Daisy's parachute ride to the ground and her reunion with Farmer
Brown. As placid and pleasant as chewing a cud.

1335   **Wildsmith,** Brian. *Pelican;* written and illus. by Brian Wildsmith. Pantheon, 1983. 82-12431. Trade ed. ISBN 0-394-85668-6; Library ed. ISBN
0-394-95668-0. 60p. Trade ed. $8.95; Library ed. $9.99.

K–2   Wildsmith uses half-pages, in the style of John Goodall, to show
changes of scene in this story of a boy who finds a large egg that
proves to be a pelican and who makes a pet of the bird although it creates problems. The pelican likes fish and snatches them from fishing
boats and frozen food counters—but is slow to learn how to catch fish
from the river. It is useful, however, bringing groceries home in its beak
and carrying lunch to the boy's father when he's working in the fields.
Eventually the bird flies off to live with other pelicans, the punch line of
the story being that it is disclosed that the bird, who's been referred to
as "he" throughout the story, is a female. The text is adequate in structure, and the style is unexceptionable; it is, as is usually true of Wildsmith's books, the lavish and striking use of color in handsomely composed paintings that is impressive: the frozen food counter glows with
magenta and royal blue, the landscape is effulgently vernal, the farmer's
clothes are dazzling: yellow shirt and boots, blue pants, red and green
jacket.

1336   **Wildsmith,** Brian. *Professor Noah's Spaceship;* written and illus. by Brian
Wildsmith. Oxford, 1980. 80-40984. ISBN 0-19-279-741-7. 29p. $9.95.

K–3   Pollution comes to the forest, fouling the air and spoiling the plants.
Owl reports to the assemblage of unhappy creatures that he has seen a
huge object being built, and that perhaps the clever builder can help

them. He is Professor Noah, and it seems that he has been building a spaceship just so that he can rescue the animals and take them to another planet. Robots help, food for forty days and forty nights is collected, and the spaceship takes off just as the forest is consumed by flames. A dove is sent out to bring a leaf back from a tree, and it proves to be a leaf from Earth; the spaceship has travelled backward through time, and the happy animals joyfully debark on a still-verdant earth. Last comment, "There seems to have been some flooding here." A nice twist to the story of Noah and the Flood; although the writing is not distinguished, the concept of the story and the cast of animals should appeal to children. The paintings combine the beautiful and dramatic animals that Wildsmith fans will recognize and the bold use of color in geometric forms, especially triangles, that are the artist's trademark.

1337   **Willard,** Barbara. *The Country Maid.* Greenwillow, 1980. 79-19002. ISBN 0-688-80256-7. 184p. $7.95.

7–10   Sixteen-year-old Cassie comes from the country to work for the Garside family; shy and ingenuous, she becomes fond of the family, especially the daughter, Jean, two years her senior. Although she acquires a swain and a friend, another maid, Cassie never stops missing her home and her grandmother, who'd raised Cassie and her brothers and sisters. Part of the story is told from Cassie's viewpoint, part from Jean's; both have difficulties with their suitors and form a bond that has more depth than display, for Cassie will not step out of her servant role and eat with Jean, or attend a film with her. In the end, Cassie, disturbed when Jean's boyfriend tries to kiss her while Jean is away, abruptly leaves for Gran and home. The plot isn't strong, but the author's sensitivity to nuances in relationships, her polished style, and her fine ear for dialogue and dialect combine to create a memorable story.

1338   **Willard,** Nancy. *A Visit to William Blake's Inn: Poems for Innocent and Experienced Travelers;* illus. by Alice and Martin Provensen. Harcourt, 1981. 80-27403. ISBN 0-15-293822-2. 45p. $10.95.

K–5
  *
A delight. The oversize pages, simulating the appearance of old, faded paper, are used to full advantage in balancing art, print, and space; the illustrations, imaginative in concept, bold in composition and design but subtle in details and tones, are admirably suited to the effectively combined vigor and nuance of the poetry. One small error is in the illustrations, which show a stamp and postmark dated 1793, forty-seven years before the first postage stamps were used. The poems are variably humorous, thoughtful, or playful, with laminations of meaning; together the poems and pictures depict the engaging creatures who staff or visit an imaginary inn run by the visionary painter-poet.

1339   **Willey,** Margaret. *The Bigger Book of Lydia.* Harper, 1983. 82-48842. Trade ed. ISBN 0-06-026485-3; Library ed. ISBN 0-06-026486-1. 256p. Trade ed. $11.95; Library ed. $11.89.

7–10   This is a multi-faceted story, but its strongest note is friendship and its strongest appeal to adolescent readers will probably be the expression of young people's need for both security and independence. The book of the title is Lydia's journal, begun when she is ten and her father dies; in it are all her fears about being small (like all the members of her family) and all her imaginative drawings that express a child's fears and longings. The journal is lost, retrieved years later when Lydia and Michelle are about to part, and Lydia gives her book (herself) to her friend. By this time Lydia is an adolescent; she's still small and shy, she has discovered that she isn't comfortable with most boys, that she wants to drop out of school. Michelle, a victim of anorexia, has come to stay at Lydia's home, sent there by an insensitive, domineering father after she has been unsuccessfully treated at several hospitals. The laissez-faire attitude of Lydia and her mother, coupled with their supportive affection, helps Michelle recover to the point where she can face going home to a stern father and unhappy mother, while Michelle's friendship helps Lydia accept the fact that she must have the courage to finish her high school education. This is a remarkably good first novel, written with intelligence, wit, and insight; the characterizations and relationships are strong, the development believable, and the writing style fluent.

1340   **Williams,** Barbara. *Breakthrough; Women in Politics.* Walker, 1979. 79-3985. ISBN. 0-8027-6366-9. 186p. illus. with photographs. $9.95.

8–   Following a first chapter in which Williams surveys the participation of women in legislative, appointive, and administrative offices in the history of the United States, there are seven profiles of women who have attained positions of political importance. They are Genevieve Atwood, a state representative in Utah; Yvonne Braithwaite Burke, former U.S. representative from California; Janet Gray Hayes, mayor of San Jose; Millicent Fenwick, U.S. representative from New Jersey; Dixy Lee Ray, governor of the state of Washington; Esther Peterson, special assistant to the President for consumer affairs; and Nancy Kassebaum, U.S. senator from Kansas. In each case, the description of the subject's political career is emphasized, although personal information is provided. Candid if not probing, the writing is brisk and informal; it gives the reader insight into the obstacles women candidates encounter in a field traditionally dominated by men as well as into the vagaries of our political system, and it quite sharply defines the personalities of the seven women who are described. An index is included.

1341   **Williams,** Jay. *One Big Wish;* illus. by John O'Brien. Macmillan, 1980. 79-20533. ISBN 0-02-793060-2. 32p. $7.95.

K–3   Two-color illustrations that have a bucolic quality and more vitality than finesse illustrate a nonsensical tall tale in the folk tradition. Rescuing an old woman from a bramble bush, farmer Fred is granted a wish. Cannily, he wishes that all his wishes would come true; his first wish is for a million dollars, his second for a wagon big enough to hold the money, his third for horses big enough to pull the wagon, and so on until (Fred having said in despair, "I wish there were six of me so I could get it done.") six giant Freds, six giant wagons, twelve giant horses, and six million dollars are piled together in confusion. When Fred next rescues the old woman from a bramble bush and is offered a wish, he cannily says, "I wish you a very good morning." It's the sort of disaster humor small children enjoy, in a nicely told story, and the let-not-your-reach-exceed-your-grasp message is given with a light touch.

1342   **Williams,** Jay. *The Surprising Things Maui Did;* illus. by Charles Miko-laycak. Four Winds, 1979. 79-5069. ISBN 0-590-07553-5. 38p. $8.95.

K–3   Maui, the Polynesian deity, is one of the most popular figures in Ha-waiian folklore, and Williams has incorporated many of his legendary deeds as episodes in this book. He uses the storyteller's device of a catch-phrase opening for each episode: "In those days, long ago, things were different . . ." after introducing Maui as the eleventh child whose poor mother had given him to the God of the Sea to raise, and who re-turned as a young man who was as lazy as he was powerful. Maui cre-ates the birds, lifts the sky, forces the sun to lengthen its day, and pulls up an island when, taunted by his brothers for laziness, he agrees to go fishing. The book is oversize, which affords Mikolaycak a splendid op-portunity to use the space for lavish, flowing, imaginative paintings in dark jewel-tone colors set off by white space and defined by strong lines amid the swirling of blue-green waves or riotous burning tones of tropi-cal flowers.

1343   **Williams,** Vera B. *A Chair for My Mother;* written and illus. by Vera B. Williams. Greenwillow, 1982. 81-7010. Trade ed. ISBN 0-688-00914-X; Library ed. ISBN 0-688-00915-8. 32p. Trade ed. $9.50; Library ed. $8.59.

4–8   Bright, busy (but not too busy) paintings with decorative frames illus-
yrs.   trate a quiet but sunny story told by a little girl. Living with the odds and ends contributed by friends and neighbors after their home has burned down, the child, her mother, and her grandmother dream of the day that their jar will be filled with coins. Then there will be enough money to buy a really comfortable armchair that mother can sit in when she comes wearily home from work. The jar is filled, the chair is purchased, and all three members of the family revel in its comfort. This hasn't a great deal of action, but it has the satisfactions of a wish granted and a joint project completed, and it is pervaded by a feeling of family unity.

1344   **Williams,** Vera B. *The Great Watermelon Birthday;* written and illus. by Vera B. Williams. Greenwillow, 1980. 79-17058. Trade ed. ISBN 0-688-

80257-5.; Library ed. ISBN 0-688-84257-7. 25p. Trade ed. $7.95; Library ed. $7.63 net.

K–2   There really isn't much to this, yet it generates such warm feelings of family participation and community enterprise, and such cheerfulness and simplicity in conception that it's engaging. An elderly couple, owners of a fruit market, are so delighted when their first great-grandchild is born that they announce they'll give a watermelon to any child in the community who has the same birthday. There are one hundred who do. They decide, while waiting in line, to pool their planned parties, set up a huge table in the park, and celebrate. Many bring instruments, everybody has a whopping good time, and the birthday boys and girls form a club, naming it in honor of their donors, who've also been their guests. Children should enjoy the listing of participants ("82 little brothers . . . 70 fathers, 22 stepfathers . . . 51 grandmothers . . . 133 friends and neighbors . . . 41 aunts . . . and 1 great-great-grandmother"). The small line drawings, black and white, have green and pink (whole and cut) watermelons and balloons in festive contrast.

1345   **Williams,** Vera B. *Music, Music for Everyone;* written and illus. by Vera B. Williams. Greenwillow, 1984. 83-14196. Library ed. ISBN 0-688-02604-4; Trade ed. ISBN 0-688-02603-6. 31p. Library ed. $10.51; Trade ed. $11.50.

K–3   Another warm and tender story about Rosa, her family and her friends. Here the big glass jar is empty, the same jar in which money slowly accumulated to buy the chair in *A Chair for My Mother.* It is empty because Grandma is ill, and any money the family can spare is needed for her care. Even in her illness, Grandma is responsive and responsible; she thinks Rosa's idea of playing (with three friends) to earn money is a fine one and fortunately she's there (her first day out of bed) to cheer Rosa and her friends on when they play music for profit, to an appreciative audience, at a friend's party for her grandparents. Softly-framed illustrations are colorful and have an ingenuous spontaneity. A gentle, appealing story.

1346   **Wilson,** Gina. *All Ends Up.* Faber, 1984. 83-25300. ISBN 0-571-13196-4. 159p. $13.95.

6–9   Claudia, the protagonist, is open and bitter about the fact that she is an illegitimate child, and she punishes her mother repeatedly for this. She's also rude to her mother's suitor, and her rancor spills over to include her only two friends, Sylvie and Anna. The refuge in her life is a great-aunt; Belle lives nearby at the seaside and repeatedly welcomes all three girls on extended visits. There are no large, dramatic events in the story, but there is fluctuation in the three-way relationship among the girls, development and change in that between Claudia and her new stepfather, and particularly a growth in understanding between Claudia and Belle, who is her emotional anchor and whose death is shattering.

This has strength and consistency in characterization, it is written smoothly and perceptively; although it is set in England, the problems and concerns that are involved are universal.

1347   **Wilson,** Jacqueline. *Nobody's Perfect*. Oxford/Merrimack, 1984. ISBN 0-19-271463-5. 104p. $10.95.

6–9   Sandra dislikes her stepfather and yearns to get in touch with her birth father, although she knows from her mother that he may not even know of the existence of this illegitimate child. Oddly, it is a younger boy who becomes her friend and helps Sandra gain the courage to trace and confront her father, who proves to be a disappointment. Michael, her new friend, is far from that: bright, discerning, and forthright, he is so pleasant a companion that Sandra, at first ashamed because he's so much younger than she, is proud to acknowledge his friendship. This is a story written with sensitive understanding; the characterization, plot, and pace all have impact, and the treatment of relationships is realistic and perceptive.

1348   **Windsor,** Merrill. *Baby Farm Animals*. National Geographic, 1984. 84-16668. Library ed. ISBN 0-87044-530-8; Trade ed. ISBN 0-87044-525-1. 32p. illus. with photographs. $12.50.

3–6   There are many books about baby farm animals for young children, and
yrs.   this one, like most of the others, gives a minimal amount of information. This gives, in addition to facts about the animals, some facts about farm life and the care of animal young. Perhaps its greatest appeal will be the color photographs that take up most of the space on the oversize pages, for they make a marvelous showcase for the fuzzy, round-eyed or sleepy-looking ducklings, kids, chicks, lambs, and other beguiling babies.

1349   **Winter,** Jeanette, illus. *Hush Little Baby*. Pantheon, 1984. 83-12182. Library ed. ISBN 0-394-96325-3; Trade ed. ISBN 0-394-86325-9. 34p. Library ed. $10.99; Trade ed. $10.95.

2–5   A familiar lullaby is illustrated with softly-drawn pictures that are
yrs.   paired: the promise in warm earth tones, the let-down in grays. Some of the objects are pictured as real (the goat, the dog named Rover) while others (the horse and cart) are pictured as toys. The layout is spacious, with the verso page carrying a prettily-bordered line of text and the recto page the illustration in a plain frame of the same size. Daddy is young and bearded and loving, the setting is modestly rural, and the notation for the melodic line is provided on the last page.

1350   **Winthrop,** Elizabeth. *Belinda's Hurricane*; illus. by Wendy Watson. Dutton, 1984. 84-8028. ISBN 0-525-44106-9. 54p. $9.95.

3–4   Belinda, who was always sad when the end of August came and with it the end of her yearly stay with Granny, was pleased when there was a hurricane forecast and she knew that boats wouldn't be leaving the island. This is the story of Belinda's experiences during the hurricane, and they are both nicely told and nicely scaled to the interests of middle-grades readers. The background is dramatic, and the incidents realistic, as Belinda shows more courage than she's known she had, rescuing a dog she's never liked just because its elderly owner is so unhappy—and thereby making a new friend.

1351   **Winthrop, Elizabeth.** *Journey to the Bright Kingdom;* illus. by Charles Mikolaycak. Holiday House, 1979. 78-23261. ISBN 0-8234-0357-2. 45p. $7.95.

3–5   An adaptation of the Japanese folktale "The Rolling Rice Cakes" is illustrated with soft black and white pictures that have remarkable fidelity to traditional Far Eastern brush painting. Here the wife of a ferryman, a woman widely known for her perceptive sketches, goes blind, and when she has a baby daughter, Kiyo, the young mother carefully tells her all about the beautiful world around them. It is the mother who suggests, when Kiyo is older, that perhaps her daughter can find out about the legendary muscine kingdom of Kakure-sato. Kiyo befriends some mice, tells them that her mother would rather die than not be able to see, and is granted a visit to Kakure-sato, where there is no deafness or blindness. So mother and daughter go below the earth, where they gaze at each other with love. They receive the traditional gift of a tiny bundle of rice, but it is a magical gift that replenishes itself. The greater gift, for Kiyo's mother, has been the sight of her daughter. "Now, when I hear your voice, I can see your face in front of me. As long as I can see you, I am not truly blind." And when they return home, the mother cheerfully becomes independent; even in her old age she can see, the story closes, "inside her dark world the bright kingdom of Kakure-sato." The adaptation is nicely told, but it lacks the directness of the folk tradition; it reads aloud well but the pace is slowed by embellishment.

1352   **Winthrop, Elizabeth.** *Katharine's Doll;* illus. by Marylin Hafner. Dutton, 1983. 83-1408. ISBN 0-525-44061-5. 29p. $9.95.

K–3   Molly and Katharine are close friends; they share things, they help and teach each other, they even share Katharine's beautiful new doll Charlotte. Well, almost. Molly doesn't feel that Katharine shares Charlotte enough. They squabble. "Who did you come here to play with? Me or Charlotte." "Charlotte," says honest Molly, and goes home. Alone, Katharine finds that a doll is no substitute for a playmate, and the two girls soon make up. The soft pencil drawings have an ingenuous simplicity that echoes the same quality in the story, told with an easy flow; while this isn't a new idea in children's books, it's impeccably executed.

1353   **Winthrop, Elizabeth.** *Marathon Miranda.* Holiday House, 1979. 78-20615. ISBN 0-8234-0349-1. 155p. $6.95.

4–6   Miranda's older brother thought her asthma was psychosomatic, that she used it to get out of things she didn't want to do. Miranda knew better, and she was hesitant about joining her new friend, Phoebe, a dedicated runner in training for the Central Park marathon. However, Miranda worked at it and, by the time of the marathon, had learned how to pace herself and, although she trailed in late, made it all the way. That's the major plot thread of a nicely balanced story; minor plots have to do with Phoebe's difficult adjustment to the discovery that she's an adopted child, Miranda's mild problem in getting along with her brother, and the problem Miranda's elderly friend Margaret has in accepting the fact that she's been jilted by a younger man. It's a smoothly integrated story line, given warmth and balance by the loving family relationships and by humor; the dialogue is sprightly and natural, and the characters are consistent and well-defined.

1354   **Wise,** William. *Monsters from Outer Space;* illus. by Richard Cuffari. Putnam, 1979. 77-16504. 47p. $5.29.

3–4   Striking black and white drawings illustrate a crisp, direct discussion of the many ways in which people are led to observe—or think they observe—unidentified flying objects: unfamiliar flying craft, illusions of light, astronomical bodies such as meteors or Venus when it is low on the horizon. There is much less sensationalism here than in most books on the subject; Wise points out that some of the observers seek publicity, that some are suffering from delusions, and that some who are quite honest have simply not been able to account for the objects they have seen or photographed. He leaves the door open, but doesn't ask readers to share credulity.

1355   **Wiseman,** Bernard. *Christmas With Morris and Boris;* written and illus. by Bernard Wiseman. Little, 1983. 83-11962. ISBN 0-316-94855-1. 40p. $10.95.

1–3   The creator of other stories about Morris, a naive and literal moose, and Boris, a patient (usually) bear, has concocted a tale that has the sort of humor that's just right for beginning independent readers, and that is so simply written as to be an encouraging experience. Christmas colors are used in the cartoon-style illustrations for the story, in which the two animals find out about some Christmas practices. Morris has four legs, he says, so why can't he have two stockings to hang on the mantelpiece? Most of the story is in dialogue, and much of the dialogue consists of Boris explaining why Santa Claus won't want to play, that the Christmas stockings are not hanging up to dry, etc.

1356   **Wiseman,** David. *Jeremy Visick.* Houghton, 1981. 80-28116. ISBN 0-395-30449-0. 170p. $7.95.

6–8   Matthew first sees the gravestone of the Visick family while doing a school history assignment, and he is curious about the youngest Visick,

Jeremy. The bodies of his father and brothers had been recovered from a mine disaster in 1852, but Jeremy, twelve, still lay in the mine. First, Matthew sees visions of the Visick family; then he moves back into their time, where he becomes Jeremy's friend. All this takes place in a series of midnight rambles that have Matthew's family deeply troubled, especially in the final episode, in which Matthew narrowly escapes death in the old mine shaft but finds Jeremy's skeleton and insists that it be buried with the rest of his family. Wiseman does a good job of blending the realistic and the fantistic elements of the story, which moves with good pace and suspense; he also uses a natural device to give information about the old coppermines of the Cornish setting by having Matthew gather facts to help solve the mystery that haunts him.

1357   **Wittman,** Sally. *The Wonderful Mrs. Trumbly;* illus. by Margot Apple. Harper, 1982. 81-47737. Trade ed. ISBN 0-06-026511-6; Library ed. ISBN 0-06-026512-4. 40p. Trade ed. $8.95; Library ed. $8.89.

2–3   Mrs. Trumbly, the new teacher in Martin's class, is elderly, affable, and friendly. Since it's on his way, Martin walks her to her bus stop every day and soon considers her his best friend. Trouble comes to Paradise in the form of Mr. Klein, whose increasing attention to Mrs. Trumbly blossoms into love and marriage. Sulking, Martin feels he's lost his best friend until the wedding, when the new Mrs. Klein shows she's as loving as ever; she even puts his present, a bride and groom statue, on top of the wedding cake. And the next year, when she's not even his teacher, she comes to his first music recital. No great drama here, but an unusually warm picture of a teacher-student friendship, with a message (not obtrusively presented) that life isn't over for the elderly. The story is told with direct simplicity from Martin's viewpoint, and is appropriate for reading aloud to younger children as well as for the primary grades independent reader.

1358   **Wolf,** Bernard. *Firehouse.* Morrow, 1983. 83-1174. Trade ed. ISBN 0-688-01734-7; Library ed. ISBN 0-688-01735-5. 80p. illus. with photographs. Library ed. $8.59; Trade ed. $9.50.

5–7   Illustrated with dramatic photographs, this describes the working life of the two companies (Engine, and Tower Ladder) in a firehouse on Manhattan's Lower East Side. Wolf writes primarily of how the men work in their dangerous job of fire fighting and of the equipment they use, but he also discusses the way of life in the station, thus bringing in a lighter note of bantering conversation among the firemen. The text gives a vivid picture of the stress and dedication of their lives, and it's candid about the lack of cooperation (from heckling crowds to arsonists) that increases their burden.

1359   **Wolfe,** Bob. *Emergency Room;* by Bob and Diane Wolfe. Carolrhoda, 1983. 82-19878. ISBN 0-87614-206-4. 35p. illus. with photographs. $7.95.

3–5   Profusely illustrated with photographs of good quality, this is a sensible and informative description of the way a hospital emergency room functions and is staffed, of the ways in which different kinds of emergencies are handled, and of the ways in which people are treated in critical situations (possible heart attack or stroke) before they get to the emergency room. The authors are candid about the fact that some procedures may be painful, but reassuring about the care that is provided; the writing is accurate, direct, and sequentially organized.

1360   **Wolfe,** Louis. *Disease Detectives;* illus. with photographs. Watts, 1979. 78-11097. ISBN 0-531-02921-2. 64p. $5.90.

4–6   A text that describes the work of the Center for Disease Control includes interesting, often dramatic, material and gives accurate information but is weakened by a dry and at times choppy writing style. Wolfe discusses the various bureaus that handle special problems, such as the Bureau of Laboratories or the Bureau of Tropical Disease, explains investigative and preventive medicine and control of standards in U.S. laboratories, and focuses on national health problems, working through and, if necessary, with state agencies and cooperating with doctors throughout the world. A list of books suggested for further reading and an index are appended.

1361   **Wolitzer,** Hilma. *Wish You Were Here.* Farrar, 1984. 84-10112. ISBN 374-38456-8. 180p. $9.95.

5–7   Bernie Segal, the thirteen-year-old narrator, has a problem, He cannot accept the idea of a stepfather, and he's determined that when his widowed mother marries the irritatingly cheerful Nat, he'll run away to Florida and live with his paternal grandfather. Much of the story is devoted to Bernie's efforts to amass enough money for air fare, and he finally does acquire a ticket—only to learn that the surprise Grandpa has written about was that he was coming north for the wedding. The main plot is balanced by deftly-incorporated sub-plots: Bernie's first romance, his squabbles with his sister, his antipathy toward Nat (he gets over it) and his interest in a play in which his sister has a lead part. The story ends on a positive note that nicely avoids being sugary. Characters are firmly drawn, the story has good balance and pace, and it is strong in its easy, deceptively casual writing style, particularly in dialogue.

1362   **Wolkoff,** Judie. *Happily Ever After . . . Almost.* Bradbury, 1982. 81-18028. ISBN 0-87888-199-9. 192p. $10.95.

4–6   Kitty, eleven, and her younger sister Sarah are delighted when their divorced mother decides to marry Seth, they like his son R. J., and they adore Seth's parents, who warmly welcome the girls into the family. They like their father's wife and are enthralled when she and Dad produce a baby brother. In fact, they have only two problems: adjusting to the move from a suburban house to a Soho loft that is being renovated (for months) and worrying about whether R. J.'s rather nasty mother will win custody of him. This is far from the usual story of adjustment to divorce; it's a happy mingling of families (one Jewish, one Lutheran) and, as told by Kitty, a lively account of the usually-smooth relationships within the extended family. There's a great deal of warmth and humor in the story, a brisk pace to its development, and a satisfying, believable happy ending.

1363   Wolkstein, Diane. *The Magic Wings: A Tale from China;* illus. by Robert Andrew Parker. Dutton, 1983. 83-1611. ISBN 0-525-44062-3. 26p. $10.95.

2–4   Colorful ink and wash pictures with fine details and an appealing freedom of line, illustrate a Chinese folktale that is excellent for reading aloud or for storytelling as well as for silent reading. A little goose girl, enthralled by the first flowers of spring, wishes she could fly, like her geese, and see all the flowers. She puts water on her shoulders, flaps her arms, and tells the grocer's daughter that she is learning to fly. The grocer's daughter tries, the princess imitates her, and eventually all the women and girls are trying to fly; it is the goose girl, however, who is chosen by the Spirit in Heaven Who Grows Wings, and the delighted child calls as she flies, " 'Hello! Hello! It's spring.' "

1364   Wolkstein, Diane. *White Wave: A Chinese Tale;* illus. by Ed Young. T. Y. Crowell, 1979. 78-4781. Trade ed. ISBN 0-690-03893-3. Library ed. ISBN 0-690-03894-1. 29p. Trade ed. $7.95; Library ed. $7.89 net.

3–6
*   Wolkstein retells a traditional Taoist tale with great skill and style, suiting the fluent, subdued telling to the grace and tenderness of a gentle story. The softest imaginable black and white drawings, spare and restrained, complement both the telling and the tale, which explains the mystery of a small stone shrine in the hills of southern China. A poor farm lad who found and cherished a moon snail returned home one day to stealthily peer through his own window so that he might discover by what magic his house was cleaned and his meals prepared. He saw a shining goddess, White Wave, emerge from the jar where he had placed the moon snail, but he had broken the magic, and White Wave had to leave, telling him to call her name if ever he needed her. He called her name only once, at a time when he was near starvation, and suddenly his pot was filled with rice. Later, he told his children about White Wave, and with him they went to the shrine he had built, but in time the shrine crumbled and the man grew old and died, and, the book ends, "All that remained was the story. But that is how it is with all of us: When we die, all that remains is the story." Lovely.

1365   Wood, Audrey. *The Napping House;* illus. by Don Wood. Harcourt, 1984. 83-13035. ISBN 0-15-256708-9. 32p. $11.95.

K–2   Cool, somnolent paintings that have a quiet humor illustrate an engaging cumulative tale about ". . .a slumbering mouse/on a snoozing cat/on a dozing dog/on a dreaming child/on a snoring granny/on a cozy bed/in a napping house/where everyone is sleeping." A wakeful flea bites the mouse, who startles the cat, who claws the dog, and so on. The cool blues and greens are superseded by warm colors and bursts of action as each sleeper wakes, ending in an eruption of color and energy as nap-time ends. A deft matching of text and pictures adds to the appeal of cumulation and to the silliness of the mound of sleepers—just the right kind of humor for the lap audience.

1366   **Wood,** Nancy. *War Cry on a Prayer Feather: Prose and Poetry of the Ute In-dians;* illus. with photographs. Doubleday, 1979. 77-76272. Trade ed. ISBN 0-385-12884-3; Library ed. ISBN 0-385-12885-1. 108p. Trade ed. $7.95; Library ed. $8.90 net.

7–   Compiled as a symphony libretto at the behest of the Colorado Centen-
*   nial Commission, this anthology is illustrated with photographs (most of them from the 1890's) and comprises some moving prose statements and even more poetry. The poems are strong expressions of traditional attitudes and beliefs, rarely contemporary or citing an author. Both in the prefatory historical material and in the discussion by Woods of the life styles and problems of the three Ute tribes today, the reader is pro-vided an excellent background for understanding the tragic changes that have come to a once-strong people.

1367   **Woodford,** Peggy. *The Girl with a Voice.* Bodley Head/Merrimack, 1984. ISBN 0-370-30423-3. 187p. Paper. $6.95.

8–12   Rod, who is rather quiet and shy, is immediately smitten by Claudia when he joins the staff of a summer program for boys in Yorkshire. He's almost as quickly aware that she affects others the same way. He is *not* aware (although the reader is) that Claudia is deeply in love with a much older man who, in the course of the story, gives Claudia as kindly a brush-off as he can. The crux of the story, which is told in a vigorous but smooth writing style, is that Rod is the only person to rec-ognize the fact that Claudia has a remarkable voice, to encourage her to get training and make it her career, and to appear in public doing a joint program with her—a performance that leads to exactly the sort of result Rod had envisioned, when a member of the audience arranges an audition. Strong in the characterization of major and minor figures, the book has a pleasant flow and a sensible, mature approach.

1368   **Woodford,** Peggy. *See You Tomorrow.* Bodley Head/Merrimack, 1984. ISBN 0-370-30204-4. 143p. $10.95.

7–10   Seventeen-year-old Julia and her siblings are always aware of their fa-ther's precarious emotional stability, know that he has refused help for several bouts of severe depression, and understand that their mother's role is that of protector and tranquilizer. They are shocked when their father attempts suicide, and almost as disturbed when their frantic mother goes off for a few days to gain peace through solitude. Julia, who is angry at her father and recognizes his selfishness, still loves him dearly and tries to help him, as she does the young man (who also had tried to kill himself) who is in the same ward as her father and becomes his friend. This is a serious story, acute in its depiction of the intricacies of familial relationships, sensitive in portraying the ambivalence of Julia, who is basically a shy and private person who must adjust to the demands made on her by others. In this novel from England, it is style, characterization, and nuance that will hold readers rather than plot development.

1369   **Worth,** Richard. *Israel and the Arab States*. Watts, 1983. 82-20315. ISBN 0-531-04545-5. 90p. $8.90.

8–   In a comprehensive, detailed, and objective account of the causes and events of the conflict between the Arab nations and Israel, Worth begins with a brief history of the Jews and the partition of Palestine called for by the United Nations in 1947. The text, serious in tone and carefully organized, follows the intricate and often bitter history of political and military confrontation between Israel and the Arab states, a history in which the United States and other major powers were intermittent participants. The body of the text concludes its detailed coverage with the Camp David accord, although a final section, "Will There Be Peace?" gives brief coverage of events that followed, concluding with the assassination of Bashir Gemayel in 1982, and the clear evidence that the issue of Israeli security versus Palestinian rights remains as a core problem in the Middle East. A bibliography and an index extend the usefulness of a book that clarifies the complexity of that problem.

1370   **Worth,** Valerie. *Curlicues; The Fortunes of Two Pug Dogs*; illus. by Natalie Babbitt. Farrar, 1980. 80-15594. ISBN 0-374-31664-3. 51p. $7.95.

4–6   Both the text and the prim, tidy drawings of this period piece have a nostalgic appeal; Worth captures (and Babbitt reflects) the stratification and the sentimentality of the Victorian era. Two gentlewomen who, unbeknownst to each other, buy pug dogs from the same pet shop, are very much in contrast: thin, grim Miss Thorne never pets her dog, scolds the housekeeper, Mrs. Hart, for feeding it anything but scraps, and wants it to be only a well-behaved watchdog. Plump, kindly Mrs. Downey dotes on her dog, and makes so much fuss over him that the surly cook becomes irritable. It may be pat, but it is most satisfying that, when Mrs. Hart is fired and takes the dog with her, she eventually gets taken on to replace Mrs. Downey's surly cook, and the two pug dogs live with mistress and servants in complete amity. A gentle, sweet story with no pretensions to be more than an engaging diversion.

1371   **Wright,** Lawrence. *City Children, Country Summer*. Scribner, 1979. 79-1348. ISBN 0-684-16144-3. 203p. $8.95.

8–   Wright's articulate and animated writing style gives this account of the
*   summer visit of a group of city children (under the auspices of the
Fresh Air Fund) to an Amish community the flow and color of a work
of fiction. Most of the visitors are from minority groups; some come to
the same family for their country fortnight for several years in a row
and establish deep bonds; others are resistant either because of cultural
conflict or because of inherent problems. The text threads back and
forth from one host-guest incident to another, giving background on
both the ways of life and the individuals, contrasting institutions, illuminating changes. The author does not sit in judgment, but he does
draw some pithy conclusions about the effects of the confrontation, especially on the ghetto children. His characters are not case studies, they
come alive, and they are capable of evoking a reader's sympathy,
amusement, and understanding.

1372   **Wrightson,** Patricia. *The Dark Bright Water.* Atheneum, 1979. 78-8793.
223p. $7.95.

7–9   In a sequel to *The Ice Is Coming* Wirrun, the young aborigine hero of the
first book, is called again to the Australian countryside, where strange
things are happening. Restless spirits are abroad, and Wirrun must
search for the cause, for those spirits whose homes are being invaded
are troubled. Wirrun finds the source, the restless and unhappy Yunggamurra, a water spirit, who has been swept from her home and is
vengeful in her anger. Wirrun loses his best friend and companion in
his long search, but he gains love when a ceremonial fire changes the
Yunggamurra into a woman, and he knows why he has responded all
along to the strange and haunting melody calling him to the bright water. As before, Wrightson constructs a compelling tale, meshing fantasy
and realism artfully, and making the world of Australia's mythical creatures real and potent. Fine writing.

1373   **Wrightson,** Patricia. *Journey Behind the Wind.* Atheneum, 1981. 80-25005.
ISBN 0-689-50198-6. 144p. $8.95.

6–9   Wirgun, the Aborigine hero of *The Ice Is Coming* and *The Dark Bright Water,* is appealed to a third time to avert a danger in the land, a mysterious alien thing with no body, a thing that brings death. In the pursuit
of the nameless thing, Wirgun loses his mercurial wife, Murra, who had
once been a water-spirit and who returns to her element. Wirgun learns
that he must confront the terrible Wulgaru, master of the thing and
stealer of men's spirits. Wirgun is turned to stone, but his spirit joins
Murra and together they wander through the land. Like the two earlier
books, this is beautifully developed and paced, with vivid characters
and with that smooth blending of realism and fantasy that marks the
best in fanciful writing.

1374   **Wrightson,** Patricia. *A Little Fear.* Atheneum, 1983. 83-2784. ISBN 0-689-
50291-5. 111p. $9.95.

5–7   Deftly blending realism and fantasy, as she did in her earlier books about the legendary creatures of Australia, Wrightson has created a strong protagonist and an equally convincing antagonist. An elderly woman living in a retirement home, Mrs. Tucker steals away to the isolated cottage she's inherited, planning to live a life of busy independence. Repeatedly thwarted by the machinations of the Njimbin (an ancient Gnome who considers the property his realm) she is almost relieved when she realizes that someone or something is responsible for such queer events as an invasion of frogs or the disappearance of her god; she has been afraid it was senility that made her imagine what was happening. A satisfying solution of her problems ensues, Mrs. Tucker blandly agreeing with her daughter that a little house in town would be better than the lonely cottage—anything but a return to the nursing home. This has a taut, economical structure, suspense in the conflict, good pace and atmosphere, and a polished narrative style.

1375   **Wuorio,** Eva-Lis. *Detour to Danger.* Delacorte, 1981. 81-65501. ISBN 0-440-01892-7. 186p. $9.95.

6–10   There are both suspense and plenty of well-modulated action in an exciting adventure story set in Spain and told by Fernando, Duke of Herrera. Nando is rangy, red-haired, sixteen, and quite uninterested in his Scottish aunt's insistence that he stop on his way home to look at her property in another region of Spain. He has no idea that he will pick up a wily, adoring orphaned gypsy boy, or that his girl (also at school in Great Britain, also coming home for vacation) will join his attempt to unravel the mystery of what seems to be a neo-Nazi assembly in the house next door to Aunt Jane's and in the caverns beneath her house. The story is carefully structured and deftly told, with colorful characters and some serious moments to relieve the light, breezy style.

1376   **Yabuuchi,** Masayuki. *Animals Sleeping;* written and illus. by Masayuki Yabuuchi. Philomel, 1983. 82-24620. ISBN 0-399-20983-2. 29p. $8.95.

3–5   First published in Japan, this has paintings of half a dozen animals,
yrs.   shown first when they are awake and then when they are asleep: a flamingo stands on one leg, an otter sleeps on its back, a tiger sleeps on a tree limb, etc. The choice seems arbitrary and the coverage is slight, but the book can give small children the idea of variation and may provoke curiosity about other animals' sleeping habits. Although brief, this is an attractive book; the text is minimal, the pages spacious, and the paintings carefully detailed, accurate, and richly textured.

1377   **Yagawa,** Sumiko. *The Crane Wife;* tr. from the Japanese by Katherine Paterson; illus. by Suekichi Akaba. Morrow, 1981. 80-29278. Trade ed. ISBN 0-688-00496-2; Library ed. ISBN 0-688-00497-0. 28p. $8.95.

3–5   The soft technique of ink painting and the cool colors used by Akaba, recent winner of the Andersen Medal for illustration, add a romantic quality to a smoothly translated version of a familiar folktale. Akaba's line and wash are traditional in mood, spare in composition, and appropriate for the plaintive, patterned story of the wife who was lost to her husband when he disobeyed her admonition that he never look at her while she was spinning. A familiar motif in folk literature is used in a handsome book; this is a good version for reading aloud or for storytelling as well as for independent reading.

1378   **Yep,** Laurence. *Dragon of the Lost Sea.* Harper, 1982. 81-48644. Trade ed. ISBN 0-06-026746; Library ed. ISBN 0-06-026747. 224p. Trade ed. $10.50; Library ed. $10.89.

6–9   Most of this fantasy-quest story is told by a dragon, centuries-old, who has magical powers; she first meets the boy, Thorn, when she's taken the shape of an old woman to whom he is kind, and their wary relationship grows into a loving friendship through the course of the story, some chapters of which are told by Thorn. He calls the dragon "Shimmer" and shares her valiant quest for the evil Civet who, years before, had stolen the waters in which Shimmer's people had lived. There are magical and dangerous adventures, many of the characters and events based on Chinese myths, and the book shows Yep's versatility; this has the same fluent style as his realistic fiction, but it is beautifully adapted to the grand scope of high fantasy, it is deftly structured, and it's lightened by wry humor.

1379   **Yep, Laurence.** *Sea Glass.* Harper, 1979. 78-22487. Trade ed. ISBN 0-06-026744-5; Library ed. ISBN 0-06-026745-3. 213p. Trade ed. $7.95; Library ed. $7.89 net.

6–8   The story is told by eighth-grader Craig, who has just moved from San Francisco's Chinatown to the small coastal town where his father grew up and was a basketball star. Plump, short, and awkward at sports, Craig is constantly urged by his father to achieve at games; he's also treated with contempt by the two cousins who are at the same junior high, both because he's awkward and because they feel Craig acts more Chinese than American. What that means is that they themselves cannot accept their heritage, but that doesn't make it any easier for Craig. What does help is that he makes two friends: a nonconformist girl who's in his class, and an elderly man who helps him understand that he must do what he really cares about, who even speaks to his father about choosing one's own way. Old "Uncle" also helps Craig understand that his father loves him, but sees the path by which he gained approbation as the only path. There's a strong bond between Craig and Uncle Quail in their interest in the wonders of marine life; the sea glass of the title is a piece of junk glass polished by waves and sand. "Just junk," says Craig's friend Kenyon, but Craig thinks that time has brought the glass brightness and clearness, just as it has him. Yep writes with pace and polish, his narrative evolving naturally from the characters and relationships as they adjust, change, and gain insight; the changes are believable, and the author uses both the narrator-protagonist and his dialogues with others with great skill to illuminate attitudes, explore reactions, and further the action.

1380   Yep, Laurence. *The Serpent's Children.* Harper, 1984. 82-48855. Trade ed. ISBN 0-06-026809-3; Library ed. ISBN 0-06-026812-3. 288p. Library ed. $12.89; Trade ed. $12.95.

5–8   In a first-person account of Chinese peasant life, Cassia begins her story by describing her father's decision to go off and fight with the Manchu against the foreign devils who have brought opium into the Middle Kingdom. Although he and Mother have been active in the Work (the expulsion of the Manchu oppressors) they feel that they must unite against a common enemy. Cassia's mother dies, and the young girl rebels against her relatives' decisions, taking refuge in her home with little brother Foxfire until their wounded father returns. The rest of the story focuses on the generation gap between Father, an embittered political activist, and Foxfire, the dreamy youth who decides to go to America so that he can send money home to his nearly-starving father and sister. It is Cassia who bridges the gap, loyal to her father but pleading always for a reconciliation with Foxfire, remembering that they were of the Young clan, children of the serpent who must not fight each other. This is a powerful and vivid novel despite the fact that there are points at which the story sags because of slowed pace. The characters are strongly drawn, and the picture of the Chinese rural community convincing.

1381   Yepsen, Roger. *Train Talk;* written and illus. by Roger Yepsen. Pantheon, 1983. 83-4062. Trade ed. ISBN 0-394-85750-X; Library ed. ISBN 0-394-95750-4. 85p. Library ed. $9.99; Trade ed. $9.95.

5–   Although the text has some repetition and occasionally talks down to the reader ("You can't just yell at a moving train and expect the engineer to understand you") it should be a delight for railroad buffs and may even create a few. It tells everything but everything about electric signals, signs, symbols, hand signals, lanterns, engine signals, flares . . . what they signify and how they're used. Whistles. Tickets and timetables and the names of trains and even the tell-tale signs of danger on tracks and ties. There's lots of colorful railroad terminology and lots of information here.

1382   Yolen, Jane H. *Children of the Wolf.* Viking, 1984. 83-16979. ISBN 0-670-21763-8. 136p. $11.95.

6–9   Mohandas, fourteen, tells the story, based on fact, of Amala and Kamala, two feral girls reared by wolves in 1920s India. Villagers believe the two are *manush-baghas*, ghosts, but Mr. Welles (who runs the orphanage where Mohandas lives) is determined to civilize the girls and bring them to Christianity. While the girls are feared and taunted by the other orphans, Mohandas feels a kinship with their alienation, and so they become his responsibility. "Tame them," says Mr. Welles. The story of these "wild children" has inherent interest, and Yolen brings a strong pathos and drama to the story. Kamala and Amala never adjust to human society, and Kamala, particularly, in her torn up dress, clutching her rag doll, mumbling her few words, is affecting.

1383   **Yolen,** Jane. *Dragon's Blood.* Delacorte, 1982. 81-69668. ISBN 0-440-02087-5. 243p. $11.95.

7–9   On the planet of Ausdar there is only one way to become free if you are a bond servant, and that is to buy freedom. Jakkin decides that he will earn money by training a fighting dragon, since the planet's gaming pits are a large part of the economy. He steals a hatchling, takes it to a hidden oasis, and there trains the rapidly growing dragon to be a superb fighter, in part by having him respond to telepathic commands. The story ends with a dramatic flourish, when Jakkin's dragon wins his first fight, and Jakkin learns that his master had known all along about the theft and the training but had felt the boy's prowess should be encouraged. He also learns that Akki, the girl he loves, is his master's illegitimate daughter. Akki leaves, telling Jakkin he is too young, an ending that seems to indicate the probability of a sequel. The genre and the subject indicate a strong potential for the popularity of this story and any that may follow; in some ways reminiscent of the series (*Dragonsong, Dragonsinger*) by Anne McCaffrey, this is not derivative; it is written with good structure and pace, has a wholly conceived fantasy world, and is much better in writing style than Yolen's earlier books for younger readers.

1384   **Yolen,** Jane H. *The Gift of Sarah Barker.* Viking, 1981. 80-26443. ISBN 0-670-64580-X. 155p. $9.95.

6–9   Set in the mid-nineteenth century, this tightly structured story vividly portrays the primness and the passion of the Shaker community in which two young people fall in love despite the rigorous separation practiced as part of the faith. Both Sister Sarah and Brother Abel try to resist their love and longing, but are finally so obvious that they are banned from the community and go off, not unhappily, to seek a life together and to find Sarah's father. Sarah's psychotic mother had told her daughter that her father was dead; it is, in fact, the drama and the tragedy of Sarah's mother that is the most affective aspect of a story with good period details, strong characterization, and a writing style that indicates depths Yolen seldom achieves in writing for younger children or in writing fantasy.

1385   **Yolen,** Jane H. *Heart's Blood.* Delacorte, 1984. 83-14978. ISBN 0-385-29316-X. 238p. $14.95.

7–9   In a sequel to *Dragon's Blood* this second volume in a planned trilogy describes the efforts of the former bondsman Jakkin to rescue the woman he loves from the toils of a dangerous group of rebels. This science fantasy is set on a distant world where much of the economy is based on the rearing of fighting dragons; Jakkin's dragon, Heart's Blood, with whom he has telepathic communication, is killed in defending him. A soundly-structured story has good pace, color, and suspense.

1386   **Yolen,** Jane H. *Sleeping Ugly;* illus. by Diane Stanley. Coward, 1981. 81-489. ISBN 0-698-30721-6. 64p. (Break-of-Day Books) $6.99.

2–4   Yolen pokes fun at the patterned sleeping-princess story in a tale that's written with brisk simplicity and humor; although the parody seems at times forced, it is amusing, it has plenty of action, and it's easy to read. Beautiful but nasty, Princess Miserella is lost in the wood, repeatedly insults a fairy who has taken her to the cottage of homely but kind Jane, and loses her chance of getting home when the fairy awards Jane three wishes. After the second wish, all three fall into the traditional century of sleep; the young man who comes across them is smitten at the sight of the beautiful princess, but decides he should practice his wake-up kisses on the fairy and Jane. Jane, waking, is in turn smitten and sighs that she wishes he loved her. This is, of course, wish number three. Love and marriage lead to almost all living happily ever after: they keep the princess asleep, using her as a conversation piece to entertain their friends—or sometimes prop her up in the hallway to hold extra coats. Two-color illustrations alternate with black and white drawings, their static quality relieved by humorous details.

1387   **Yorinks,** Arthur. *It Happened in Pinsk;* illus. by Richard Egielski. Farrar, 1983. 83-1727. ISBN 0-374-34658-5. 27p. $11.95.

2–4   Chelm had better look to its laurels, because Irv Irving and other citizens of Pinsk are champion noodleheads. A man in comfortable circumstances, Irv is always disgruntled; one morning he wakes without a head. "Oh, Irv!" says his wife, "Every day you lose something. Your keys. Your glasses. Now this." Wearing a paper bag with a face drawn on it, Irv goes out to look for his head (at times he is greeted with glad cries of "Uncle Eugene!" or "Leo Totski! It's you!") and he finds his head being used as a model in a hat shop, runs off with it, and is never dissatisfied again. The pictures are as bland and funny as the story, and just as deftly executed.

1388   **Young,** Ed, illus. *The Other Bone.* Harper, 1984. 83-47706. Library ed. ISBN 0-06-026871-9; Trade ed. ISBN 0-06-026870-0. 30p. Library ed. $9.89; Trade ed. $9.95.

4–6 yrs.   A companion to the author's wordless story about a cat, *Up a Tree*, this is the story of a dog and his bone: dog dreams of bone, smells bone, and finds bone only to lose it while looking at the "other bone" in a pool of water. Simple pencil drawings (nicely framed with thin green line) clearly tell the action-filled story with fluid grace. Emotional content is expressed through the dog's eyes: a cocky sideways glance after stealing the bone from a garbage can, "what's *this*?" to the reflected image in the pool, and a look of utter pathos, bewilderment, and desolation after losing the bone to the depths.

1389   **Young,** Helen. *What Difference Does It Make, Danny?* illus. by Quentin Blake. Deutsch, 1980. 80-65665. ISBN 0-233-97248-X. 93p. $7.95.

4–6   The author, an executive officer of the British Epilepsy Association, makes no bones about the purposive nature of the story; her message is that people who have epilepsy are normal in every way save for having epileptic seizures and that these can be controlled by medication. Danny is a bright, lively youngster, liked by his classmates and good at sports. He's even won a cup for swimming. A new teacher learns that Danny is "epileptic" (the book stresses the fact that this is erroneous usage) and forbids him to take an active role in sports events, even in gym classes. Danny becomes morose and hostile; one day he plays truant, saves the life of a small child who's fallen into a canal, and emerges a hero. The gym teacher admits he's been wrong. Save for the convenience of the last incident, this is—despite the purposiveness—an entertaining story, written in a light, humorous style and having especially good relationships between adults and children.

1390   **Yue,** Charlotte. *The Tipi: A Center of Native American Life;* illus. by David Yue. Knopf, 1984. 83-19529. Library ed. ISBN 0-394-96177-3; Trade ed. ISBN 0-394-86177-9. 77p. Library ed. $10.99; Trade ed. $10.95.

4–7   Although it focuses on the structure, uses, and furnishing of domestic and ceremonial tipis, this clear, forthright text also gives a great deal of information about the cultural patterns of the various peoples known as the Great Plains Indians. The black and white drawings are meticulously detailed, showing structural variations and decorative patterns. An index is provided.

1391   **Zalben,** Jane Breskin. *Here's Looking At You, Kid.* Farrar, 1984. 84-5997. ISBN 0-374-33055-7. 136p. $10.95.

7–10   "Most parents are uptight about drugs, sex, and violence," sixteen-year-old Eric begins, "My mother's major concern was that I was too straight." When Eric meets Enid and discovers they're both foreign film buffs, his emotional horizons widen—and they expand even more when he meets Enid's old friend Kimberly, a pretty and popular cheerleader. Enid resents Eric's interest in her sexy friend, including the fact that Eric tries to be a jock for Kimberly's sake. This does not have the expectable, formulaic ending; Eric and Enid renew their friendship, but it is just a friendship, and both stay on good terms with Kimberly. The story is strong in style and in development of a triangular relationship, and the characterization has depth and consistency. In the end, Eric realizes that it was too much to hope for someone with Enid's mind and Kimberly's body. Nobody's perfect, he concludes, "You gotta take the whole chicken."

1392   Zei, Alki. *The Sound of the Dragon's Feet;* tr. from the Greek by Edward Fenton. Dutton, 1979. 79-14917. ISBN 0-525-39712-4. 113p. $8.50.

4-6   First published in Greece under the title *Konda stis Raghes,* a story that is imbued with concern for social conditions and reform is told by ten-year-old Sasha. The setting is Russia in the pre-Revolutionary period, and it is through her father and her tutor that Sasha sees inequality in living standards, educational opportunities denied other children less fortunate than she, and persecution by the establishment of those who dare to protest. A tract? No. Zei is too skilled a storyteller to let her message overburden her medium. Skillfully translated, the book has a lively flow and balanced treatment, as the curious, sympathetic, and intelligent Sasha quizzes her father, pokes gentle fun at the household staff, enjoys the unorthodox and effective teaching methods of her tutor, and delights in the small pleasures of a ten-year-old's life.

1393   Zerman, Melvyn Bernard. *Beyond a Reasonable Doubt: Inside the American Jury System.* T. Y. Crowell, 1981. 80-2451. Trade ed. ISBN 0-690-04094-6; Library ed. ISBN 0-690-04095-4. 217p. illus. Trade ed. $9.95; Library ed. $9.89.

7-   In a book that is lucid, explicit, informative, and exciting, Zerman describes the way the jury system began in the fourth Century B.C. (in Greece) and how it evolved into its present form and function. He uses some actual cases to illustrate both the drama of the trial courtroom and the unpredictability of juries, and he discusses every aspect of the system that a prospective juror might find useful, from the way a jury is chosen to the pronouncement of sentence and the aftermath of a trial. In a final chapter, "Twelve People of Average Ignorance," some of the weaknesses of the jury system are considered: possible racial imbalance, possible inadequate representation of segments of the community, the delaying effect of challenging prospective jurors, the cost to the public of sequestering jurors, and other debatable aspects. A bibliography is included; an index gives access to the provocative and comprehensive text.

1394   Zim, Herbert Spencer. *Quartz;* illus. with photographs and diagrams. Morrow, 1981. 81-4018. Trade ed. ISBN 0-688-00588-8; Library ed. ISBN 0-688-00589-6. 64p. Trade ed. $8.95; Library ed. $8.59.

3-5   Zim, always a dependably thorough and explicit science writer, prefaces a discussion of the many ways in which quartz is used in contemporary life with descriptions of its chemical structure, the way it is formed and shaped, and its peculiar properties. Photographs (some in color) illustrate the textual description of the variety of gem stones of quartz, and diagrams show the special property it has: piezoelectricity. The text is continuous, the print large and well-shaped, and an index gives access to the contents.

1395   Zimelman, Nathan. *Mean Murgatroyd and the Ten Cats;* illus. by Tony Tuth. Dutton, 1984. 84-1635. ISBN 0-525-44116-6. 20p. $9.95.

4–6
yrs.

Lively, scribbly line drawings, filled with humorous details, illustrate a story in which a girl uses her wits to solve a problem and protect her pets. Every day when Arabella tried to take her ten cats for a walk, the barking of Mean Murgatroyd (the bulldog next door) brought other dogs running and Arabella-and-entourage fled back indoors. Her efforts to buy a lion (a quest described with bland nonchalance) fail, but Arabella thinks of a fine—and more realistic—substitute and turns the tables, routing the dogs. To readers, this should be a satisfactory ending to a funny story that's told in a direct style, has good problem/solution structure, and a nice sense of the ridiculous.

1396   Zimelman, Nathan. *Positively No Pets Allowed;* illus. by Pamela Johnson, Dutton, 1980. 80-377. ISBN 0-525-37560-0. 29p. $7.95.

K–3

When Seymour Goldberg tells his mother he wants a pet from Farber's pet store, Mr. Farber says, "A look wouldn't hurt." "With Seymour," his loving mother explains, "a look always hurts." Nevertheless, she agrees to buy a gorilla, although the rule of the building in which they live is "no pets." After a rather eventful walk home, they meet Mr. O'Brien, the owner of the building; O'Brien is myopic and refers to the gorilla as the Goldbergs' visitor; because the visitor has obligingly carried in a very large piece of ice, the landlord hopes he'll stay forever. So does Seymour. Arrant nonsense combines piquantly with a bland style; the dialogue has flavor, and the story is fresh and funny, with soft black and white illustrations that verge on the grotesque but don't quite get there.

1397   Zindel, Paul. *The Pigman's Legacy.* Harper, 1980. 79-2684. Trade ed. ISBN 0-06-026853-0; Library ed. ISBN 0-06-026854-9. 192p. Trade ed. $8.95; Library ed. $8.79.

7–9

Again, as in *The Pigman*, the story is told in alternate chapters by John and Lorraine, and again it works nicely, especially since the friendship turns into romance and the new emotions the two feel are confided to the reader. Still feeling guilty about their late friend Mr. Pignati, John and Lorraine determinedly befriend an old man they find camping out in Pignati's vacant house. They bring an elderly woman they like to help them care for old Colonel Glenville, and the four of them go on a gambling spree in Atlantic City, a junket on which the two older people fall in love. Later, when the Colonel is in the hospital and dying, he insists on marrying Dolly. In the end, John and Lorraine have atoned in some measure for their part in Pignati's death, and they realize that his legacy to them was love, a love they were able to give the Colonel. This isn't quite as forceful as *The Pigman*, but it's a warm and compassionate story that's written with skill and insight.

1398   **Zisfein,** Melvin B. *Flight: A Panorama Of Aviation;* illus. by Robert Andrew Parker. Pantheon, 1981. 79-9462. Paper ed. ISBN 0-394-85042-4; Library ed. ISBN 0-394-94272-8. 119p. Library ed. $17.99; Paper ed. $11.95.

5–   While airplane buffs may most enjoy the historical aspects of this oversize and profusely illustrated book, the general reader may be most interested in the very handsome paintings, accurate in detail and almost romantic in the mood evoked by the beauty of Parker's luminous skies. Basically the broad pages have a three-column format, but this is broken and varied in different ways so that some pages use only one columnar space for text or have one large picture spread across the bottom of a page. This gives variety to the pages, which only occasionally seem overcrowded. The text is comprehensive in scope, covering the subject of manned flight from balloons to supersonic transport; since more than half the book's page space is given over to illustrations, it cannot provide full coverage of any individual aspects of flight history, but the author—Deputy Director of the National Air and Space Museum—writes with crisp authority. A bibliography and an index are provided.

1399   **Zolotow,** Charlotte. *I Know a Lady;* illus. by James Stevenson. Greenwillow, 1984. 83-25361. Library ed. ISBN 0-688-03838-7; Trade ed. ISBN 0-688-03837-9. 21p. Library ed. $9.55; Trade ed. $10.25.

K–2   Most small children derive a special pleasure from the affection of adults whose feelings could not possibly be construed as dutiful, i.e. dependent on familial obligation. Zolotow expresses this pleasure very effectively by having the narrator describe an elderly neighbor who is generous and welcoming and even remembers the name of your dog as well as your name! To children, names and identities are very important, and they are aware of the fact that many adults think of them as just "little girl" or "my neighbor's little boy." Stevenson has accommodated his usually humorous style to focus here on cozy interior and verdant outdoor scenes, a complementary bouquet.

1400   **Zubrowski,** Bernie. *Messing Around with Water Pumps and Siphons: A Children's Museum Activity Book;* illus. by Steve Lindblom. Little, Brown, 1981. 80-29462. Trade ed. ISBN 0-316-98876-6; Paper ed. ISBN 0-316-98877-4. 64p. Trade ed. $8.95; Paper ed. $4.95.

3–6   Zubrowski uses a series of open-ended home experiments to ask and
*   answer questions about the varied devices that can move water in different ways and for different purposes. He is a staff member of the Bos-

ton Children's Museum, and this and his other books are evidence of the excellent results when subject knowledge is paired with experience in working with children who are doing experiments. The diagrams are clear and carefully placed, the text moves from the simple and familiar to the complicated and less familiar; it doesn't give all the answers, but it gives all the facts through which answers can be found. None of the materials required is expensive or difficult to procure; safety warnings are given when needed; the light, enthusiastic tone suggests that the experiments are fun rather than work. In discussing siphons, pumps of different kinds, and thermometers, Zubrowski explains physical principles.

Appendix

Addresses of Publishers of Listed Children's Books

Prices given in this book are those prevailing at the time of the original review.
For information on current prices and availability, write to the publisher or consult the latest edition of Books in Print.

Abingdon. Abingdon Pr., 201 Eighth Ave. S, Nashville, TN 37202
Addison. Addison-Wesley Pub. Co., Inc., Reading, MA 01867
Apple-wood. Apple-wood Books, Inc., Box 2870, Cambridge, MA 02139
Arco. Arco Pub., Inc., 215 Park Ave. S., New York, NY 10003
Ariel. Ariel Books. See Farrar
Atheneum. Atheneum Pubs., 597 Fifth Ave., New York, NY 10017
Atlantic. Atlantic Monthly Pr., 8 Arlington St., Boston, MA 02116
Atlantic/Little. Atlantic Monthly Pr. in association with Little, Brown & Co.
Avon. Avon Books, 1790 Broadway, New York, NY 10019
Bantam. Bantam Books, Inc., 666 Fifth Ave., New York, NY 10103
Berkshire. Berkshire Traveller Pr., Stockbridge, MA 01262
Bluejay. Bluejay Books, Inc., 130 W. 42 St., Suite 514, New York, NY 10036
Bodley Head. The Bodley Head, Ltd., c/o Merrimack Publishers' Circle, 47 Pelham Rd., Salem, NH 03079
Bradbury. Bradbury Pr., Inc., 2 Overhill Rd., Scarsdale, NY 10583
Cambridge Univ. Pr., 32 E. 57 St., New York, NY 10022
Cape. Jonathan Cape, Ltd., c/o Merrimack Publishers' Circle, 47 Pelham Rd., Salem, NH 03079
Carolrhoda. Carolrhoda Books, Inc., 241 First Ave. N., Minneapolis, MN 55401
CBS. CBS Educational and Professional Pub., 383 Madison Ave., New York, NY 10017
Collins. William Collins Pub., 200 Madison Ave., New York, NY 10016
Coward. Coward, McCann & Geoghegan, Inc., 200 Madison Ave., New York, NY 10016
T. Y. Crowell. Thomas Y. Crowell Co., 10 E. 53 St., New York, NY 10022
Crown. Crown Pubs., Inc., One Park Ave. S., New York, NY 10016
Dandelion. Dandelion Pr., 184 Fifth Ave., New York, NY 10010
David. David and Charles, Inc., North Pomfret, VT 05053
Delacorte. Delacorte Pr. See Dell
Dell. Dell Pub. Co., 1 Dag Hammarskjöld Plaza, New York, NY 10017
Deutsch. André Deutsch, Ltd., Box 57, North Pomfret, VT 05053
Deutsch/Dutton. André Deutsch, Ltd. in association with E. P. Dutton & Co., Inc.
Dial. The Dial Pr., Inc. See Dell
Dillon. Dillon Pr., Inc., 242 Portland Ave. S., Minneapolis, MN 55415

For the address of any publisher not listed here consult the latest *Literary Market Place* or Bowker's *Books in Print*.

Dodd. Dodd, Mead & Co., 79 Madison Ave., New York, NY 10016
Doubleday. Doubleday & Co., Inc., 245 Park Ave., New York, NY 10017
Douglas & McIntyre. See Berkshire
Dutton. E. P. Dutton & Co., Inc., 2 Park Ave. S., New York, NY 10016
Elsevier/Nelson. Elsevier/Nelson Books, 2 Park Ave., New York, NY 10016
Faber. Faber & Faber, Inc., 39 Thompson St., Winchester, MA 01890
Farrar. Farrar, Straus & Giroux, Inc., 19 Union Sq. W., New York, NY 10003
Flare. See Avon
Four Winds. Four Winds Pr. See Scholastic
Godine. David R. Godine, Pub., Inc., 306 Dartmouth St., Boston, MA 02166
Green Tiger. The Green Tiger Pr., 1061 India St., San Diego, CA 92101
Greenwillow. Greenwillow Books, 105 Madison Ave., New York, NY 10016
Hamish Hamilton. See David and Charles
Harcourt. Harcourt Brace Jovanovich, Inc., 1250 Sixth Ave., San Diego, CA
    92101
Harper. Harper & Row, Pubs., 10 E. 53 St., New York, NY 10022
Hastings. Hastings House Pubs., 10 E. 40 St., New York, NY 10016
Holiday. Holiday House, Inc., 18 E. 53 St., New York, NY 10022
Holt. Holt, Rinehart & Winston, Inc., 521 Fifth Ave., 6th fl., New York, NY
    10175
Houghton. Houghton Mifflin Co., 1 Beacon St., Boston, MA 02107
Houghton Mifflin/Clarion Books, 52 Vanderbilt Ave., New York, NY 10017
Knopf. Alfred A. Knopf, Inc., 201 E. 50 St., New York, NY 10022
Larousse. Larousse & Co., Inc., 572 Fifth Ave., New York, NY 10036
Lerner. Lerner Pub. Co., 241 First Ave. N., Minneapolis, MN 55401
Lippincott. J. P. Lippincott Co., E. Washington Sq., Philadelphia, PA 19105
Little. Little, Brown & Co., 34 Beacon St., Boston, MA 02106
Liveright. See Norton
Lodestar. Lodestar Books. See Dutton
Lothrop. Lothrop, Lee & Shepard Co., Inc., 105 Madison Ave., New York, NY
    10016
McGraw. McGraw-Hill Book Co., 1221 Ave. of the Americas, New York, NY
    10036
Macmillan. Macmillan Co., 866 Third Ave., New York, NY 10022
Messner. Julian Messner, Inc. See Simon & Schuster
Methuen. Methuen, Inc., 733 Third Ave., New York, NY 10017
Metropolitan Museum of Art, Fifth Ave. & 82 St., New York, NY 10028
Metropolitan Museum of Art/Thames and Hudson. Metropolitan Museum of Art
    in association with Thames & Hudson, Inc.
Morrow. William Morrow & Co., Inc., 105 Madison Ave., New York, NY 10016
National Geographic Society, 17 and "M" Streets N.W., Washington, DC 20036
Nelson. See Elsevier/Nelson
Newmarket Press. See Macmillan
New York Graphic Society Books. See Little
Norton. W. W. Norton & Co., Inc., 500 Fifth Ave., New York, NY 10110
Oriel. Oriel Pr. See Routledge
Oxford Univ. Pr., 200 Madison Ave., New York, NY 10016

Pantheon. Pantheon Books, 201 E. 50 St., New York, NY 10022
Parents' Magazine. Parents' Magazine Pr., 685 Third Ave., New York, NY 10017
Parnassus. See Houghton Mifflin
Phillips. S. G. Phillips, Inc., 305 W. 86 St., New York, NY 10024
Prentice. Prentice-Hall, Inc., Englewood Cliffs, NJ 07632
Putnam. G. P. Putnam's Sons, 200 Madison Ave., New York, NY 10016
Raintree. Raintree Pub., Inc., 330 E. Kilbourn Ave., Milwaukee, WI 53202
Rand. Rand McNally & Co., P. O. Box 7600, Chicago IL 60680
Random. Random House, Inc., 201 E. 50 St., New York, NY 10022
Routledge. Routledge & Kegan Paul, Inc., 9 Park St., Boston, MA 02108
Schocken. Schocken Books, Inc., 62 Cooper Square, New York, NY 10003
Scholastic. Scholastic, Inc., 730 Broadway, New York, NY 10003
Scribner's. Charles Scribner's Sons, 597 Fifth Ave., New York, NY 10017
Seabury. See CBS
Shambhala. Shambhala Pub., Inc., 1920 13 St., Boulder, CO 80302
Sierra Club. Sierra Club Books, 2034 Fillmore St., San Francisco, CA 94115
Simon. Simon & Schuster, Inc., The Simon & Schuster Bldg., 1230 Ave. of the
    Americas, New York, NY 10020
Smithsonian. Smithsonian Institution Pr., 955 L'Enfant Plaza, Rm. 2100, Wash-
    ington, DC 20560
Sterling. Sterling Pub. Co., 2 Park Ave. S., New York, NY 10016
Thames. Thames & Hudson, Inc., 500 Fifth Ave., New York, NY 10110
Tundra. Tundra Books of Northern New York, Box 1030, Plattsburgh, NY 12901
Univ. of Alabama Pr., Box 2877, University, AL 35486
Univ. of Hawaii Pr., 2840 Kolowalu St., Honolulu, HI 96822
Vanguard. Vanguard Pr., Inc., 424 Madison Ave., New York, NY 10017
Viking. Viking Pr., Inc., 40 W. 23 St., New York, NY 10010
Viking Kestrel. See Viking
Wanderer. See Simon & Schuster
Warwick. Warwick Pr. See Watts
Workman. Workman Pub. Co., Inc., 1 W. 39 St., New York, NY 10018
Walker. Walker & Co., 720 Fifth Ave., New York, NY 10017
Warne. Frederick Warne & Co., Inc., 40 W. 23 St., New York, NY 10010
Watts. Franklin Watts, Inc., 387 Park Ave. S., New York, NY 10016
Westminster. The Westminster Pr., 925 Chestnut St., Philadelphia, PA 19107
Whitman. Albert Whitman & Co., 5747 W. Howard St., Niles, IL 60648
World. World Book, Inc., 510 Merchandise Mart Plaza, Chicago, IL 60654

Title Index

Developmental Values Index

Curricular Use Index

Anthropology, 830
Archeology, 186 431 838
Architecture, 441 841 851 852 1077 1111
Art, study and teaching of, 60 62 63 93
    120 235 264 311 323 457 501 585 673 706
    841 930 964 1059 1101 1116 1285 1312
Assemblies, 652
Astronomy, 54 263 352 757 834

Biology, 94 265 359 382 476 713 1003 1005
    1168 1308
Botany, 776

Christmas, 142 149 192 228 529 581 586
    612 714 914 927 928 962 1014 1061 1253
    1290 1355
City life, 340 591
Communications, 392
Community life, 424 882 1306 1344 1358
Consumer education, 270

Dancing, study and teaching of, 1241

Economics, 9
English, study and teaching of, 645

Farm life, 341 505 970 973

Guidance, and personal adjustment, 225

Health and hygiene, 138 677 975 1020
    1055 1167 1227
History, 465 815 922
History, ancient, 576 728
History, Austria, 209
History, Blacks, 533 900
History, China, 919 1009 1380
History, Egypt, 1233
History, England, 36 190 510 702 921 1113
    1239
History, Europe, 3 232 1242 1296
History, France, 174 190

History, Germany, 1291
History, Greenland, 539
History, India, 242
History, Israel, 309
History, Middle East, 80 466 1210 1233
    1369
History, New York, 1211
History, Russia, 584
History, Scotland, 616 1235
History, United States, 81 95 128 283 289
    383 392 394 415 418 419 544 620 643 731
    752 766 767 814 839 900 910 1021 1031
    1083 1209 1301
Hobbies, 501 655 1010 1087
Holidays, 924

Industries, 48 71 651 837 839 1020 1047
    1143 1146

Language arts, 402 1250

Mathematics, 59 206
Music, study and teaching of, 146 208 370
    372 617 1096 1141

Nature study, 195 331 759 777 788 918
    1054 1147 1148

Physical education, 12 40 1086

Reading aloud, 1 2 77 102 118 132 133 162
    221 235 275 277 295 304 305 306 322 345
    347 378 380 389 398 448 489 491 492 569
    570 575 578 600 614 641 642 644 649 665
    711 803 806 834 846 960 1037 1040 1050
    1108 1126 1127 1132 1169 1214 1221 1240
    1253 1269 1270 1283 1292 1343 1363 1364
    1377
Reading, beginning, 8 14 34 133 169 180
    230 247 272 277 384 413 489 497 513 567
    626 691 692 807 862 872 884 889 890 1000
    1045 1088 1094 1115 1128 1155 1158 1355

Reading Level Index

Titles are arranged in order of increasing difficulty, with books for the preschool child and kindergartner first, followed by books for independent reading beginning with grade 1. The reading range is intended to be indicative rather than mandatory.

All ages, 60 62 63 65 145 235 311 803 805 927 964 1280
1–2 years, 991 992
1–3 years, 16 794 994
1–5 years, 455
2–3 years, 1321
2–4 years, 108 446 572 657 869 888 1310
2–5 years, 76 135 152 205 240 317 625 749 868 983 985 1311 1313 1349
2–7 years, 688
3–5 years, 32 79 101 153 206 234 328 385 386 573 575 608 609 795 870 936 989 990 1243 1309 1323 1376
3–6 years, 77 117 132 279 454 461 571 636 719 933 993 1013 1079 1090 1095 1314 1322 1348
4–6 years, 31 97 105 177 244 555 623 793 984 1223 1388 1395
4–7 years, 61 173 179 207 316 754 769 1131
4–8 years, 1343
Kindergarten-grade 2, 1 30 39 41 42 47 193 196 197 257 273 274 308 315 343 353 367 391 406 408 421 437 439 447 491 542 546 547 563 574 618 619 637 638 653 681 737 750 772 784 785 812 822 835 856 876 885 928 955 1016 1060 1085 1089 1106 1125 1130 1225 1269 1271 1288 1289 1290 1298 1315 1334 1335 1344 1365 1399
Kindergarten-grade 3, 1 37 102 134 142 144 158 168 181 199 217 241 256 295 342 345 356 390 412 414 416 420 436 438 450 469 492 493 502 505 530 558 562 635 641 642 649 675 680 734 736 763 774 808 811 816 864 891 892 914 924 938 954 962 963 976 1018 1042 1043 1046 1049 1051 1057 1058 1103 1149 1153 1154 1156 1163 1181 1213 1218 1219 1222 1224 1226 1252 1258 1278 1287 1333 1336 1341 1342 1345 1352 1396
Kindergarten-grade 4, 656 714 831 1014
Kindergarten-grade 5, 1338
Kindergarten-grade 6, 281
Grades 1–2, 8 34 133 180 230 272 384 413 567 626 691 692 807 809 872 884 889 1000 1088 1094 1128
Grades 1–3, 14 169 247 277 489 497 513 640 862 890 986 1045 1115 1155 1158 1355
Grades 2–3, 69 70 183 191 192 222 268 347 449 568 717 744 751 788 922 961 979 1112 1159 1246 1282 1357
Grades 2–4, 9 33 35 36 78 107 113 116 162 175 194 195 228 229 254 278 280 292 305 330 409 423 443 459 468 504 569 570 591 593 600 601 611 624 639 668 669 678 679 711 719 758 759 783 786 845 863 893 920 947 950 970 973 988 1078 1096 1133 1145 1148 1160 1171 1197 1198 1207 1211 1220 1277 1279 1363 1386 1387
Grades 2–5, 879
Grades 3–4, 104 149 379 410 494 1167 1206 1350 1354
Grades 3–5, 12 46 91 118 124 143 150 158 163 198 213 223 224 226 227 231 252 253 262 276 287 306 326 331 378 389 398 419 429 448 483 485 487 503 510 541 544 548 559 566 581 590 594 614 622 665 670 722 742 756 777 787 791 810 818 886 905 995 997 1007 1084 1091 1092 1135 1140 1144 1146 1150 1151 1162 1174 1182 1192 1221 1273 1281 1283 1316 1351 1359 1377 1394
Grades 3–6, 130 237 245 282 324 397 501 550 585 706 821 911 1077 1172 1176 1205 1228 1292 1364 1400
Grades 3–7, 1050
Grades 3 up, 264 931 945

Subject Index

Type of Literature Index